Developmental Disorders

A Neuropsychological Approach

To the women whose love I have enjoyed:
my mother, *Charlotte*, my wife, *Vivian Auerbach*, and my
daughters, *Priscila* and *Tatiene*

Developmental Disorders

A Neuropsychological Approach

David Freides

BLACKWELL
Publishers

Copyright © David Freides 2001

The right of David Freides to be identified as author of this work has been asserted in accordance with the Copyright, Designs and Patents Act 1988.

First published 2001

2 4 6 8 10 9 7 5 3 1

Blackwell Publishers Inc.
350 Main Street
Malden, Massachusetts 02148
USA

Blackwell Publishers Ltd
108 Cowley Road
Oxford OX4 1JF
UK

Library of Congress Cataloging-in-Publication Data

Freides, David.
  Developmental disorders: a neuropsychological approach / David Freides.
    p.   cm.
  Includes bibliographical references and index.
  ISBN 1–55786–579–5 (alk.paper)
  1. Pediatric neuropsychology.   2. Developmental disabilities.   I. Title.
  RJ486.5.F74   2000
  618.92′8 – dc21   00–025851

British Library Cataloguing in Publication Data

A CIP catalogue record for this book is available from the British Library.
Typeset in 10 on 12½ pt Galliard
by Best-set Typesetter Ltd., Hong Kong
Printed in Great Britain by TJ International Ltd., Padstow, Cornwall

This book is printed on acid-free paper

Contents

Figures

Tables

Preface

This book is intended as an introduction to the study of neuropsychology and developmental disorders. Prior knowledge of neuroscience is not a prerequisite. It is intended for advanced undergraduate courses in psychology and special education and/or beginning graduate courses in clinical psychology, special education, social work, physical therapy, occupational therapy, and other clinical fields. Professionals, nascent or well established, working in the area of developmental disabilities who have little background or understanding of brain function, may find this book particularly helpful. Undergraduate students in neuroscience have told me that the material has helped give them a broad scheme within which to integrate the detailed knowledge they were acquiring in neurophysiology, neuroanatomy, genetics, or molecular biology. Some parents have indicated that they were helped to understand the nature of their child's disabilities. My goal in writing the book was to convey a sense of the way the brain operates and how this is crucially important in understanding the often mysterious or vexing aspects of behavior found in those with disabilities.

Neuroscience is changing rapidly as scientific work proliferates. My hope is that the foundation provided here will be useful to those who go on to further study in the neurosciences. For those who do not, I hope it will provide a basis for keeping up with media reports of new discoveries and new understandings. This is not a conservative book. I have gone out on a limb about a number of issues and procedures that seem promising to me but have not been solidly validated. Critics might feel that there is no place for such material in an introductory text, but I hope readers will sharpen their thinking and enjoy the process of evaluating the soundness of the author's judgment. I have made a strong effort to identify very specifically the more speculative material.

Scholarship is a collective enterprise, and I am indebted to many scholars for what I know. In the tradition of scholarly writing, I have often cited sources for specific bits of information or reviews of information. However, at the beginning of the book, where elementary neuroanatomy is reviewed, citations are sparse. I am not a neuroanatomist or physiologist and the material was derived from series of secondary and tertiary sources (Beatty, 1995; Boddy, 1978; Carlson, 1998; Gaskill & Marlin, 1993; Kandel, Schwartz, & Jessell, 1991; Kolb & Whishaw, 1996; Lishman, 1998; Thompson, 1985).

Several people, including some I have never met, have been kind enough to provide me with the benefit of their critical reactions to parts of the book. Laura Flashman read the entire work and provided me with both encouragement (which is awfully nice to get from a former student) and excellent editorial advice. Angela Gedye and Jerry Vogel read two chapters and gave me detailed feedback. Single chapters were read helpfully and critically by Gary Taylor, Lisa Hinkle, Ron Boothe, Kathy Haaland, Ellen Bolte, Michael Gordon, Bonnie Klein, and Anne Nguyen. The book is much better for their efforts and its flaws remain all mine. I am also indebted to several administrators at Emory University and its Department of Psychology who accepted my application for leave from teaching duties to work on this book.

Textbook authors rarely solicit direct comments from their readers. I suppose the critical comments anticipated from formal reviews provide enough of a challenge to one's self-esteem to satisfy even inordinate needs to ask for trouble. But scholarship really is a social process for me, and I welcome comments from any reader moved to write. I, of course, do not know how many readers will choose to react or what my resources in time, energy, or ideas will be to support the generation of useful replies. In advance, therefore, I cannot promise to respond, but I do promise to try. My e-mail address is dfreide@emory.edu. My postal address is Emory University, Department of Psychology, Atlanta, GA 30322. To all of you about to start reading the book, Bon voyage! I hope you find it helpful.

David Freides
Atlanta, Georgia

Part I

*Orientation to the Way
the Brain Functions*

1

Introduction: Some General Principles

The Nature of this Book

General features

This book is about disabilities affecting children that are due to some malfunction in the brain or nervous system. Children with disabilities are often the source of much anguish, sorrow, and stress to their families. They are also the object of much love, humanitarian effort, and therapeutic creativity on the part of their families and the professionals devoted to their care, education, and treatment. The goal of this book is to help students beginning their study of these conditions to increase their understanding of these children and their handicaps, thereby providing a sound basis for educating, treating, and living with them.

Since the handicaps discussed in this book have occurred because of impairment in the nervous system, understanding the way the nervous system functions normally and abnormally helps us to understand the handicap, the child's response to the handicap, and the overall nature of the child's behavior. It also sets the stage for grasping why some treatments work and some fail, and why some are more effective than others. Such an approach draws on a relatively new field of scientific inquiry called developmental neuropsychology, the study of brain – behavior relations during the course of gestation and childhood. This field combines detailed study of human behavior including the development of language, cognition, emotion, and action, with the findings of neuroscience, the study of how the nervous system develops and operates.

Although the emphasis in this book is on understanding and diagnosis, neuropsychological analysis often generates suggestions about education and remediation and is presented when relevant. On the other hand, current legislation or regulations about the treatment and education of handicapped children are not considered here because these matters are extensively discussed elsewhere and because these issues reflect time-bound and place-bound standards of practice. Parents and professionals with a good grasp of basic principles can implement such regulations as effectively as possible, but also be able to spot flaws in current practice and recommend changes. On the other hand, someone whose education has concentrated on current regulations and practice is likely to think exclusively in those terms and be limited by their flaws.

Given that the focus of the book is on the relationship between brain and behavior, and on pathology, information will be drawn from several different fields of medicine, including neurology and psychiatry, and of psychology, including sensation and perception, cognition, personality, abnormal, and developmental psychology. In varying degrees, each of these fields has its own intellectual traditions, methodologies, and findings and their integration is not always easily accomplished. The task is made somewhat easier by the rise in recent years of the field of neuroscience where these and other disciplines come together in an effort to decipher the puzzle of brain function and behavior in its broadest sense. There will, however, still be many places in this book which reflect the diverse origins of knowledge in this field.

Plan of the book

The book is in four parts. Part I contains seven chapters and presents basic features of the nervous system and its mode of operation. The next three parts concern groups of handicapping conditions. Part II reviews disorders which involve the state of the brain. The three chapters concern disorders of sleep, attention, and epilepsy. Part III also contains three chapters, each dealing with a disorder that involves mostly one modality, motor disorders and cerebral palsy, visual disorders and blindness, and hearing and language disorders. Part IV, with four chapters, deals with disorders involving several modalities, learning disabilities, psychosis especially autism, frank brain damage such as a head injury, and mental retardation. The book is cumulative in its organization, the earlier chapters providing a basis for understanding what comes later.

Some Broad Principles: An Introduction to an Approach

In this section, some ways of thinking about children with handicaps are introduced. To start, imagine a classroom of ten children with differing disabilities who are taught by a very skillful teacher. You begin your unobtrusive observation just at the time when the teacher has had to leave the room in order to take care of a child who has had a seizure. Under the circumstances, no one was available to take over the class, and it took ten minutes before the teacher returns. When he reenters the room he finds most of the children going about their business without signs of stress. However, three boys, each about the age of seven, are roaming around the room looking very disturbed. They speak incoherently, their eyes have a glazed appearance, they move rapidly through the room touching objects and occasionally knocking them over, but their behavior seems to have no purpose. From time to time they stop and rock their head and torso rhythmically.

The teacher acts decisively and quickly. First, he walks up to Adam, positions himself so that he looms visibly in front of the boy and makes eye contact by grasping the boy's face with his hands. Then, taking care not to say a word, signals with his hands and arms the following message in American Sign Language: "I am back, everything is OK. Go back to your reading." Adam first looks surprised, then smiles and returns to his desk and to his assigned activity.

After glancing around the room, the teacher walks over to Bob, takes him firmly but gently by the hand, speaks to him softly saying, "Let's go to the quiet room for five minutes. You'll get control real soon." Bob struggles for about ten seconds in the teacher's grasp. He then walks with the teacher to a bare room that is furnished with gym mats hanging on the walls and lining the floor, and nothing else. The door to the room, which can be bolted from the outside, has a window so that the interior can be observed. Bob enters the room and immediately lies down. He is quiet and appears exhausted. The teacher bolts the door and looks around for Charles.

Charles is rocking at this point and appears totally oblivious to all events going on around him. The teacher approaches him directly and without saying a word, picks up the boy and heads for a play area just outside the door of the schoolroom where there is a swing. En route, the teacher moves the boy in a manner which approximates the rhythm of his rocking. The teacher however also insinuates rhythms and movements of his own into his wordless dialogue of touch and motion with the boy. At one point, he even holds him at arm's length high above his head. When they reach the chair swing, the teacher clasps Charles against his chest and shoulder, sits in the swing and kicks off in a vigorous arc. In about two minutes, he allows the arc to taper and begins talking gently to the boy, reassuring him that everything is alright. Within two more minutes, Charles is asked whether he feels ready to return to the classroom. The boy nods assent, and they get off the swing and walk together to the classroom. The teacher goes to the quiet room, unbolts the door and invites Bob to return.

In the chapters to follow, concepts are developed which allow understanding of why the teacher behaved so differently with each child even though the children themselves were behaving so much the same. At this point the reader can begin the development of this understanding by considering several general principles or ways of thinking about behavior from a neuropsychological perspective.

The same behaviors are not necessarily generated in the same way

This idea may seem quite obvious, but it is listed first because the way psychology is applied in practice has been much influenced by behaviorism and behavior modification. This approach is often the most successful intervention used to treat many of the conditions to be discussed here. Nonetheless, some behavioral approaches to education and treatment rest on the assumption that the only necessary or useful information that needs to be considered when dealing with behavior is the behavior itself and such a perspective under some circumstances is excessively narrow and misses the point. Think about the behavior of crying. Every reader is familiar with crying while cutting onions, while in physical pain (in childhood at least), and when experiencing sorrowful emotions, as when a loved one dies. Many other readers have experienced or observed crying at peak moments of happiness or excitement, and crying solely in order to elicit sympathy (crocodile tears). Clearly, all crying behaviors are not the same and if, for some reason, it was desirable to "treat" crying, differing interventions for the varying conditions would be needed for them to be effective in a meaningful way.

Extending the example to a cough, in good medical practice, the cough is viewed as a symptom. It may be a consequence of an acute bronchial infection, either viral or bacterial, a chronic lung infection such as tuberculosis, food lodged in the throat, a fungus, or many other causes. The symptom initiates the search for the causal agent or mechanism of impairment in order to prescribe the most precise and effective treatment.

The approach taken in this book is that a similar orientation is appropriate for the analysis of behavior. Behaviors such as poor comprehension of language, poor reading and writing, awkward motor or social behavior are all symptoms that are the starting point for an analysis which seeks understanding of the mechanism of impairment. This will also be the case for a number of behaviors, e.g. compulsions or social withdrawal, which in the fields of abnormal psychology and psychiatry often are endpoints of the diagnostic process. Here, even such behaviors are treated as symptoms, as starting points for investigating possible mechanisms of impairment.

The term "analysis" might convey to some an emphasis on psychodynamic or Freudian principles. These and similar approaches emphasize motivational concepts, and motivations and thoughts inaccessible to conscious awareness. Within the neuropsychological orientation of this book, there is ample room for motivational concepts, and they are presented when appropriate. Furthermore, it will be clear that much of the operation of the nervous system is inaccessible to consciousness anyway. Accordingly, it may well be that a neuropsychological approach is a modern-day descendant of the intellectual quest that Freud initiated, but there is little here that would generally be called Freudian.

There are many possible levels of analysis

If you accept the idea that analyzing overt behavior into its components or underlying factors can be useful, it remains necessary to choose the level at which the analysis should occur. In this book, the level is mostly just below that of overt behavior. The concern is with information processing and motor output mechanisms and the knowledge we have of the neural systems that make those possible.

There are good reasons to think that this level of analysis is very useful. It is however only one of a range of possibilities, and other levels of analysis can also be useful. The relationships among levels of analysis can be confusing. Parents learning that their child has been diagnosed as "autistic" or "psychotic," terms having to do with the behavioral level of analysis, might be confused to learn that abnormalities at the biochemical and electrophysiological levels of analysis present in their child are not necessarily present in other children with the same diagnoses. Thus data from different levels of analysis may or may not coincide in children with the same symptoms. Such inconsistencies reflect the limitations of our current state of knowledge. On the other hand, the possibility exists that fruitful reorganizations in our thinking may occur precisely as a result of taking disparities from different levels of analysis seriously.

The meaning of the phrase "emotional disorder" is often misunderstood

The behavior of each of the children described earlier would certainly qualify as being emotionally disturbed. In ordinary conversation, such terms are applied to behaviors that do not seem appropriate to the situation, or which appear to involve excessive or inadequate emotional expression. As descriptions, such terminology is not objectionable. Unfortunately, the phrase "emotional disorder" is often used to contrast with the phrase "organic disorder." In this usage, there is often an implicit (if not explicit) set of meanings conveyed which indicate that the "emotional disorder" is "caused" by environmental factors, particular experiences and/or relationships, whereas the "organic disorder" is due to some harm to, or limitation of, the physical being of the individual. These meanings are often so strong that the presence of "emotionally disturbed behaviors" leads many professionals and members of the general public to concentrate exclusively on environmental and experiential factors in trying to understand and treat these behaviors.

Such an emphasis is disproportionate and leads to error. Emotional disorders can result as a direct consequence of some physical impairments of the brain, and/or as a result of experiences and events in which no damage whatsoever has occurred. To complicate matters further, they can also occur as reactions of the personality to changes in brain function and capability. The presence of emotional symptoms tells us nothing of the cause or source of the problem. This is particularly true since some of the most common and prominent reactions that occur after brain injury are emotional in their form of expression.

Accordingly, it is appropriate to use the term "emotional disorder" to describe certain behaviors. It is inappropriate and erroneous to assume upon observing emotionally disordered behaviors that they are, or are not, determined or caused by either organic or environmental factors or both. The presence of an "emotional disorder" may indicate that something is wrong, but it does not indicate what is wrong. This point is consistent with one made earlier, namely that the same behaviors are not necessarily generated in the same way.

Nature and nurture, tissue and experience, interact to produce behavior

The "treatments" provided by the teacher in the examples that began this chapter were all environmental or experiential interventions. Drugs, surgery, or electroshock were not used, although the teacher had definite evidence (the sort of which shall be explained in the later chapters of this book) of brain impairment in each case. It will also be recalled that the teacher's interventions were different for each child.

There is a strong tendency in our culture to view nature or tissue and nurture or experience as separate. Matters of the flesh and matters of the mind are segregated into separate domains and considered to be governed by different principles and different standards. In the field of treating disorders of behavior, this dichotomy often leads those with a "nature" or organic perspective to rely exclusively on drugs and physical interventions as the means of treatment. In those with a "nurture" or environmental perspective, education, psychotherapy, or behavioral interventions may be used exclusively and, as indicated earlier, often with no other consideration than the behavior itself.

Although the teacher's interventions were environmental, they were each governed by an understanding of the constitutional characteristics of the children and their handicaps in processing information. If drugs or surgery were available to treat each condition rationally and effectively, they would have been greeted with enthusiasm by the teacher because they would make his job much easier. If the events described above had occurred on the day the teacher first met the children, and therefore knew little about them, the interventions and the outcome would have been quite different.

Again, the understanding that makes possible such adroit selection of environmental interventions for nervous system handicaps must await the exposition and study of the rest of this book. For the present, the important general principle is that constitution or tissue does not operate in a vacuum, but interacts continuously with the environment to produce an emergent organization which in many ways is unique. There is a corollary to this concept of interaction between organism and environment, namely that not only does brain structure and function influence behavior but that behavior and experience can influence brain structure and function. This corollary is still not widely accepted even though there is ample research evidence of its validity (cf. Rosenzweig, Bennett, & Diamond, 1972; Greenough & Chang, 1988). The way in which experience may shape the brain is detailed in many ways throughout the chapters to follow.

Stress and self-regulation

The sequence of events in the vignette suggests that a fairly trivial event, the teacher's absence from the classroom (and perhaps witnessing a seizure) was a source of stress for some of the children. Stress is a term which conveys the idea of environmental threat and endangerment but has imprecise boundaries because it refers to a subjective state generally determined by some combination of objective external events, such as earthquakes, fires, or assaults, and internal sensitivity which varies across individuals. The children's disturbed behaviors simultaneously reflected their extraordinary sensitivity to stress and very limited coping or self-regulatory skills, the ways in which they respond to provocations from the environment. Stress and self-regulation are different aspects of the systematic organizations of the nervous system and of behavior, a topic that will be considered in chapter 4. The study of self-regulation is increasingly taking a central position in understanding behavioral pathology (Schore, 1994). That is, rather than defining behavior pathology on the basis of type of symptom, more consideration is being given to the adequacies and inadequacies of the strategies individuals use to respond to stress. There will be more about this later.

Specific and non-specific interventions

The tuning of the environmental response to the particular characteristics of the individual has two components which may be termed specific and nonspecific. Specific interventions refer to those directed toward reducing or compensating for whatever mechanism or function is impaired or deficient. Recall that the teacher did not speak to Adam but communicated with him in sign language exclusively, and that this reaction occurred to him alone. Adam was not deaf, but this was a specific intervention based on the teachers's understanding of which channels of communication were open to Adam during states of high excitement. On the other hand, the teacher treated each child identically in a number of ways. These included touching each child firmly but gently, looking at each child intently but with a comfortable smile, and, with the children other than Adam, talking to them in a relaxed, reassuring, tone of voice. These latter interventions are nonspecific.

Nonspecific interventions are extremely helpful and often necessary prerequisites for specific interventions. Where gaps in knowledge exist, nonspecific interventions are often the only kind that can be devised. Such interventions are comparable to the instructions to rest, drink fluids, and take aspirin given to the patient suffering from a severe cold. This can be contrasted with the prescription for a particular antibiotic given when the patient suffers from bacterial pneumonia. The specific treatment, antibiotics, most likely will also be accompanied by nonspecific treatments, and a successful outcome may depend as much on one as on the other.

The treatment of behavioral disorders follows similar patterns. Kindness, empathy, support, meaningful structure, good relationships, and the like are helpful to most everybody under most circumstances, and they are most often prerequisites for any other intervention, although there are exceptions. Note for example that the teacher did not speak at all to Adam, although soothing speech helped the other two boys and would help most other individuals as well. One goal of the present book is to develop understanding adequate to permit the design of specific interventions. This emphasis should not be construed to mean that nonspecific factors are unimportant. On the contrary, they are crucial, but are familiar and have been addressed extensively elsewhere.

2

Neurons: Building Blocks of the Nervous System

In order to comprehend a neuropsychological approach to handicapping conditions, some basic understanding of the structure and functioning of the nervous system is required. It will be assumed that the reader has not had the opportunity to study neuroscience or other approaches to understanding the biological basis of behavior. The scope and purpose of this book is to introduce nonspecialists to basic neuroanatomy and physiology in a way which should facilitate understanding of what follows and whet the appetite for more intensive study. Accordingly, technical language will be kept to a minimum, English terminology will be used wherever feasible instead of those Latin and Greek terms that biologists favor, and the goal will be a general grasp of the architecture and mode of operation of the nervous system rather than its fine detail. Nevertheless, the challenge to the novice is considerable.

The cell is the building block or unit by which biological organisms are constructed. Nervous systems are constructed from a particular kind of cell called the neuron that is specialized to transmit information. In this chapter, the structure and mode of function of the neuron will be described. In the next chapter, the discussion will turn to aggregates of neurons and their specializations within the brain, which is basically a vast collection of neurons.

The brain is said to have over a 140 billion cells. When that number is written out it looks like this: 140,000,000,000, or 14×10^{11}. Each cell has its own integrity and its own "space", however small. Cell widths are between 5 and 100 microns, or millionths of a meter. Spaces (between cells) are measured in nanometers, millionths of a millimeter, or thousandths of a micron. (Try to imagine a million discrete units between the boundaries of a millimeter.) This space is occupied by a salty fluid much like sea water, which along with surrounding neurons constitutes the environment or milieu of the neuron. The cell itself is teeming with smaller structures measured in Ångstrom units, which are ten millionths of a millimeter! As will be discussed shortly, all that a single neuron can do is generate a nerve impulse, and yet, from the organized firing of those 140 billion neurons, behavior emerges whose complexity ranges from sleep, to the gyrations of a gymnast, to your act of reading these words. In effect, your brain is working right now at understanding itself.

The Structure of the Neuron

What sets apart one neuron from another is their separate structures. Just as one can distinguish each of a dozen eggs in a bowl because each has a shell that defines any particular egg, so too are neurons separated by membranes that define any particular cell. While the eggshell is fairly uniform and largely inert, the neuron membrane is permeable, marvelously complex and not at all inert. This membrane is in constant interaction with its milieu and thereby with other near and remote neurons, regulating the interchange of substances within and outside the cell. Those changes determine the activity of the neuron.

Neurons must perform different functions and, not surprisingly, they come to take different forms and shapes. In almost all neurons, however, it is possible to identify three different structural features. In one part of the neuron the membrane walls enclose a relatively wide space. This area is called the cell body. It contains the nucleus of the cell, the part with the genetic coding mechanism that most living cells have, as well as a number of different substructures. The substructures have different functions including metabolism and the production of energy for the work the cell must do, the creation of the biochemical substances that perform its special job, the removal of waste products, and other functions.

There is a fundamental point to be emphasized here: the neuron is a living, active entity. The neuron functions by doing. It requires fuel (glucose, a simple kind of sugar) and oxygen and emulates the larger organism of which it is a part in that it expends energy and excretes waste products. It survives only a short time without oxygen or glucose (and a later discussion will cover some of the consequences of such deprivations). Neurons are also responsible for producing inaction, rest, and quiescence; that inactivity is not generally caused by the cessation of function but by changes in patterns of activity within the cells. In the organism as a whole, behavioral inactivity is as much caused by the activity of neurons as is behavioral activity. Total inactivity in neurons means that death has occurred.

As already mentioned, the function of the neuron is to process information. More will be presented below about what constitutes the nature of information and information processing. Whatever that may be, the neuron must in some way be able to register or receive information and then pass it on. It must have receptor capabilities, meaning that it must be able to sense information, and then it must be capable of reacting or responding so as to transmit that information. This introduces a duality which is present at every level of analysis of nervous system function. It is the distinction between input, or sensory, and output, or response, processes. Synonymous terms are receptor and effector, afferent (toward the neuron) and efferent (away from the neuron). Later, when considering higher levels of function. input processes will be related to sensing, perceiving, understanding, and knowing, while output processes will be related to action and the motor system.

At the level of the neuron, the cell is structured differently in those of its parts designed to receive information and those designed to react. The receiving portions are called dendrites from the Greek word "dendron," which means tree.

(Anatomical names are often chosen because they symbolize or look like some aspect of what they designate. In this case, the key feature is "branching.") Dendrites are portions of the cell membrane narrowed to thin filaments that often branch extensively. Some neurons have many dendrites organized in separate filaments, with one or two branches each. Some are organized with so many branches as to give the appearance of a lacy filigree.

The "action" part of the neuron is called an axon. Neurons generally have only one axon, which is a narrow, liquid-filled tube that often divides at its ends where there are small swellings called terminal buttons. These terminals are of great importance in information transmission and will be described in more detail shortly. The interior of the axon teems with activity, as much, if not more so, than in the cell body. For one thing, there are simultaneous streams flowing within the axon both toward and away from the cell body. This activity is termed axoplasmic transport. These streams contain the materials for the maintenance of the cell membrane and for the operation of the information transmission mechanism. They also contain substances absorbed into the cell that leaked from other sources both near and far. Whereas the dimensions of neurons are of the minute magnitudes described above, the lengths of axons often have more familiar dimensions; there are many in the millimeter range and some that extend a meter or more. A nerve fiber of the sort you can see in a dissection is generally made up of a bundle of axons. Thus the flow of activity within the axon has an exceedingly long way to go, given the scale of events in the nervous system.

In addition to neurons, the brain contains other cells called glia, a word which means glue. The symbolism here lies in that, as glue holds separate parts together, the glia hold neurons together. The neuron is intimately associated with particular kinds of glial cells called oligodendroglia. These oligodendroglia wrap themselves around the axon one or more times. If the wrapping is several layers, a thick insulating myelin sheath is formed. The sheath is formed in segments of about one-half to two millimeters in length, and the nerve is bare between adjacent segments of the sheath. These spots are called nodes of Ranvier (after the name of their discoverer) and play an important role in speeding and controlling information transmission. Outside the brain, on neurons in the rest of the body, the same kind of wrapping and myelin forming process occurs on axons, but the cells responsible are called Schwann cells.

Humans are born with all the neurons they will ever have since, unlike skin cells for example, they cannot be regenerated should they die. On the other hand, the myelinization process is far from complete at birth and will actually continue through the course of development to adolescence and, some authorities believe, beyond. It is thus apparent that the changes which occur with maturation which, for example, take the child from crude wriggling during the first month to, say, playing tennis at the age of 18, are not due to any increase in the number of neurons available. Such development is associated with myelinization, and with growth and branching of the dendrites, the rate and extent of which is influenced by the subject's experience. Since the operations of the neuron depend on its links to other neurons and on the nature of the internal milieu, destruction or impairment of myelin, as in the demyelinating

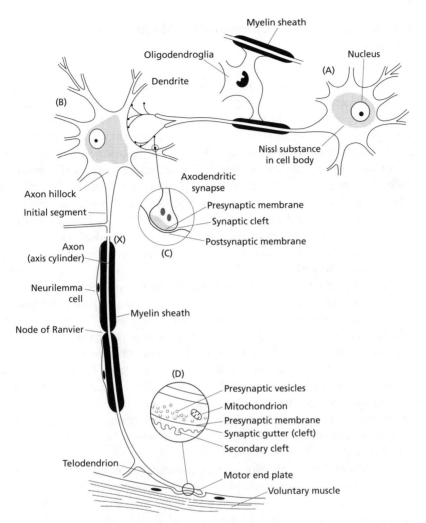

Figure 2.1 Schematic illustration of two types of neurons, the axodendritic synapse, oligo-dendroglia, the nodes of Ranvier, and the neuromuscular junction

diseases such as multiple sclerosis, results in impaired behavior even though the neuron may remain alive.

Figure 2.1 illustrates and summarizes the major structural features of the neuron. Several different types of dendrites and axons are illustrated. It should be noted that axons terminate either on other neurons where some aspect of information processing is performed, or on muscle fibers where they stimulate action. What this process is like, how the neuron transmits information or provokes action, is the subject matter of the next sections. First, there will be an introduction to what is meant by the term information, followed by a discussion of the way the neuron functions, both alone and in networks.

What Does the Term "Information" Mean, and How is it Coded?

There are two types of information and two ways of representing each kind. First consider the different types of information. Spatial information is determined by the organization of the features in the space being perceived. Thus, the appearance of one person's face is an organization of spatial characteristics which identifies them uniquely in comparison to another face. So too the features of a desert landscape differ from that of a mountain landscape. The differences are in the shape of the boundaries that mark the different features present and in such characteristics as texture, color, and orientation. (Orientation refers to position in space and is important: both a face and a landscape look quite different if turned upside down.) It is spatial information that enables us to differentiate the individual letters making up the alphabet. The reader who sees an "O" knows that it is different from the letters "C" and "Q" even though they are quite similar.

The other type of information is temporal. Such information depends on a succession of events over time. One example is a person's gait, or pattern of movement. Movement occurs from moment to moment through time and the information about the unique pattern depends on changes over time. One can often identify an individual merely by noting his or her gait. The most obvious and common types of temporally coded information are found in music and speech. A melody is intrinsically a pattern of change over time and depends on a sequence of sounds, and so too is speech. A single moment of a song or of speech is nothing but noise; that is, there is no information. The words "stop" and "pots," although containing roughly the same sounds, convey different information because the sequence of sounds is different.

Thus, spatially coded information can be grasped in a moment while temporally coded information depends on grasping the sequence of events over time in the correct order of succession. In some contexts, spatial information is termed simultaneous and temporal information is termed successive. The visual, particularly, and the tactile senses are very good at processing spatial information and only fair at dealing with temporally coded information. The auditory system is superb at processing temporal information and has only relatively crude spatial capabilities.

Human beings extended their information processing capability in the course of evolution by elaborating their temporal processing skills with a symbol system we call language. We have found a way to make distinct sound patterns symbolize classes of events and objects we can perceive, and we possess a highly complex wherewithal to communicate to others and be understood. The code of oral natural language depends on the auditory systems' special skill in temporal information processing, but we have gone further and found the means, apparently only 4,000 years or so ago, to symbolize this temporally coded information in sequential spatial symbols we call writing. These byproducts of human civilization probably represent the most complex information processing skills of which most brains are capable.

The distinction between temporal and spatial processing systems will loom large later in the book because there are persons who have limitations doing one type of processing but not the other. It can be said that the two types of processing are disassociable. (Disassociation is an important neuropsychological concept which means that two or more functions are independent because each is mediated by separate neural circuits. If one is injured or destroyed, the other may continue to function normally.) Nonetheless, when everything is normal there seems to be no great difficulty in translating information from one system to the other. This may be possible because spatial information, when analyzed carefully, is also temporal in nature. The moving pictures seen at the cinema actually occur because of the nervous system's integration of many, rapidly presented individual frames. Although looking at a painting in a museum leads to the subjective experience of perceiving it whole, one's eyes have actually moved three or more times a second, pausing briefly to capture first one part, then another of the totality. That a "simultaneous" image is put together from successive observations is not noticed. When moving objects are observed, the movement appears seamless, but this is because the brain puts together the static image from one moment and the static image of the next. However, since all that neurons can do is increase or decrease their rate of firing and the code used by the nervous system to register and store information is, like those used by computers, binary in nature (yes or no), all information processing is intrinsically successive. The essentially temporal nature of processing in the nervous system may provide the means by which translation between temporal and spatial domains is accomplished psychologically. Further consideration about spatial and temporal processing must await later chapters. Some details about how the neuron functions are discussed next.

How the Neuron Operates

There are four kinds of neurons: sensors, sensory and motor processors, motor effectors, and self-regulated pacemakers. They are classified according to the source of their input (to the dendrites), and the target of their output (of the axon). Sensors are the neurons in our sense organs which have the special capability of transforming physical stimulation from the outside world into patterns of neural firing. They are transducers, a term for any instrument that transforms one form of physical energy into another, e.g., a light bulb which changes electricity into light. The nervous system has neurons which are transducers for transforming light stimulation in the eye, sound stimulation in the ear, mechanical pressure in the skin, etc., into patterns of neuron firing. The sensory and motor processors make up the elaborate networks of neurons which receive their input from other neurons but send their information to muscle. To complete the picture, the self-regulated pacemakers are special groups of cells which transmit information to other neurons but appear to initiate much of their activity on their own with relatively little direct influence from other neural inputs. These types of cells are involved in such activity as the regulation of sleep–wake cycles or the maintenance of posture against the force of gravity.

There are no neurons that are both sensors and effectors. This means that there is no instance in which information passes directly from the external world to an action agent (muscle) without first being processed by other neurons. The following discussion of neuron function will focus on the most common kinds of neurons, the processors and the effectors, because more is known about their mode of function. Functions of several types of sensors will be described later when dealing with specific disorders.

The neuron carries out its function of transmitting information by having the property of irritability. The mechanism of this irritability has been shown to be due to specialized electrical and chemical characteristics of the cell, particularly of the highly complex and changeable features of the membrane of the cell wall.

The chemical reactions of which the cell is capable are governed by the electrical properties of particles of matter. Some atomic particles have positive electrical charges, while others are negatively charged. Their interactions (like charges repel and opposites attract) determine the outcome of chemical reactions. If, by using barriers, the electrical charges can be restrained from interacting, then a voltage builds up and the potentiality for electrical discharge is created. Physical devices that do this are called batteries.

The neuron at rest is in some ways like a miniature battery. Within its membrane, the electrical characteristics of the fluid are some 70 millivolts negative with respect to the fluid on the outside of the membrane. This is because the membrane of the cell has many working, energy-consuming, parts that actively pump certain ions (charged particles) into the cell and others out into the surrounding milieu. Free diffusion of the various ions is prevented by the membrane. By keeping them segregated, the electrical charge that gives the cell its battery-like capability is maintained. In that state, the neuron is said to be polarized.

When a neuron fires (what impels this will be discussed shortly), the membrane changes its physical characteristics mostly by opening pores that permit previously excluded ions to enter the interior of the cell. This process, called depolarization, involves a wave of electrical and chemical changes coursing down the neuron, from dendrite to cell body to axon. It is a wave because just as soon as the cell pores open and the ions are admitted at a particular point, they close and processes are set in motion to restore the prior electrochemical polarization. Some axons are insulated with the fatty material called myelin, produced by the oligodendroglia. This insulation permits particularly rapid transmission of impulses as the depolarization occurs from one unmyelinated axonal region (node of Ranvier, see figure 2.1) to the next.

When the wave gets to the end of the axon, a special set of events occur. Inside the button there are little containers filled with biochemically active substances. The containers are called presynaptic vesicles and the active substances are called neurotransmitters. The term "presynaptic" means before the synapse. The synapse is the space or cleft surrounding the terminal button, the gap across which the neural information must be carried. There are many different neurotransmitters and it is unlikely that all of them have yet been discovered. They vary in their chemical structure and because of this in their physical shape. It is their shape which determines their facility for transmitting information.

Information processing, which it will be recalled is ultimately the determination of whether a neuron will or will not fire, takes place at the synapse. The wave of electrochemical changes causes the synaptic vesicles to discharge their contents into the synaptic gap. When neurotransmitter is released into the synapse, some of its molecules find their way to the postsynaptic (beyond the synapse) membrane and to specific receptor sites on its surface. The match is by means of a lock-and-key mechanism, actually based on the three-dimensional shapes of the neurotransmitter molecule and the postsynaptic receptor site. The consequence of a fitted match between neurotransmitter and receptor is a change in the battery-like characteristics of the next neuron. Some neurotransmitters will open pores to permit positive ions to flow into the interior and depolarize it, while others will cause more positive ions to flow out of the cell and increase its polarization, or hyperpolarize it. Depolarization, we already know, is what happens when a cell fires. Hyperpolarization makes it harder for the cell to fire. Thus some postsynaptic potentials are excitatory (depolarizing and increasing the likelihood of firing) while others are inhibitory (hyperpolarizing and decreasing the likelihood of firing).

The presence of neurotransmitter in the synaptic cleft is of very brief duration because of two processes. The target surface of the next neuron releases an enzyme (a biochemical catalyst) which cleaves apart the molecules of the neurotransmitter and deactivates it. In addition, the terminal button which has just discharged proceeds to reabsorb neurotransmitter in a process called reuptake. So-called psychotropic (mind-influencing) drugs operate by selectively influencing these processes that occur at synapses, for example slowing or speeding reuptake or blocking the postsynaptic transmission sites. Neural poisons which can cause incapacitation and death also operate by influencing release, reuptake, and receptor availability at the synapse.

To understand more about how information is processed and transmitted between neurons, one must realize the variety of ways in which neurons may interconnect. As illustrated in figure 2.2, a neuron may have many axons (up to thousands) terminating on its dendrites, cell body, or even on its axon. Some of these connections will be excitatory while others will be inhibitory.

Part of the regulatory process is a simple algebraic summation of excitatory and inhibitory potentials. However, excitatory stimulation must exceed inhibitory stimulation by a given amount, called a threshold, for firing rates to increase. If excitation is below the critical threshold, the rates will not change. The concept of threshold will prove useful at many levels of analysis of nervous system function.

For neuronal firing to increase, the threshold of excitation must be exceeded during a brief period of time since subthreshold stimulation is dissipated and neutralized by processes very similar to the deactivation and reuptake already described in the synapse. Since a neuron may synapse with the terminal buttons of many axons, the neuron's reactivity will be determined by the rate of neurotransmission at each receptor site and by the particular spatial location of each site. Nearby sites have more potentiality for reinforcing each other, and all sites have the potentiality of cumulat-

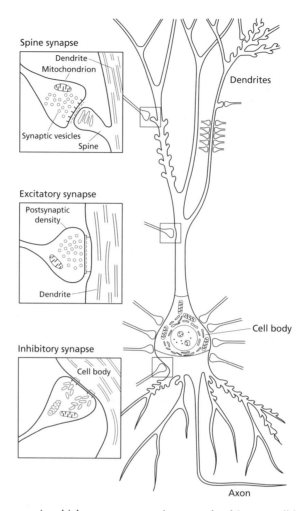

Figure 2.2   Some ways in which axons can terminate on dendrites or cell bodies

ing in their effect. This characteristic is called spatial summation. In addition, the rate at which the impinging axons fire also influences the likelihood of postsynaptic firing. If the time between successive firings is short enough, the neurotransmitter effects accumulate and the likelihood of exceeding the threshold for postsynaptic firing increases. This characteristic is called temporal summation.

One factor that complicates the summing mechanism is that some postsynaptic membranes also contain a mechanism that works much like an amplifier. For example, in much the same way a radio picks up very faint signals on an antenna and then amplifies those signals to a level where they can drive a loudspeaker so that sounds can be heard, so many neurons contain a mechanism (called cyclic AMP, the details of which are beyond the scope of this book) which performs in similar fashion. The evidence is that when neurotransmitters work directly, they transmit information rapidly. Those which require amplification operate more slowly. Receptors which receive direct transmission are called ionotropic, those which require amplification are called metabotropic.

The Neuron and the Way it Functions:
A Review and Summary

The unit of function within the nervous system is the neuron. Neurons have parts specialized for information input, the dendrites, and a part specialized for information output, the axon. The neuron exists in a milieu and functions by exchanging substances with the milieu through its cell membrane. The milieu therefore has a large influence on the functions of the neuron. The relationship between membrane and milieu is controlled by the glia, particularly the oligodendroglia, which produces an insulating myelin sheath around the axon.

The neuron functions by releasing neurotransmitter substances from the terminal buttons of the axon into the synaptic cleft. The effect of this release may be excitatory, in which case the neuron down the line is more likely to fire, or inhibitory, in which case it will be less likely to fire. Some neurons are transducers, some processors, and some effectors. Neurons are active agents and function by doing. Transducers and effectors are always excitatory. Processors are either excitatory or inhibitory. Neurons are arranged in complex networks and have multiple places of interaction. Information processing can be understood to involve complex interactions between excitatory and inhibitory responses summing spatially and temporally in networks of nerves. The fundamental principle is that the only action of which the neuron is capable is firing or not firing, and that the consequences down the line of this firing will be excitatory or inhibitory. If the nervous system is to be influenced or modified in some way, the intervention has to change some aspect of this process. Many poisons and drugs operate by selectively influencing some aspect of neurotransmission or reuptake.

The Neuron and the Way it Functions:
An Extension to Behavior

The details of neuronal transmission may seem far removed from an understanding of human behavior, but these differing levels of analysis can be linked. Behaviors such as habituation and sensitization are evident in the simplest of organisms as well as in man. Habituation is the tendency for behavioral reactions to diminish to repetitious stimulation. Repetition and familiarity elicit boredom whereas novelty attracts attention. This is true for mature adults, nonverbal children, and grasshoppers, and has been demonstrated in the laboratory in countless experiments. Behavioral reactions attenuate on repeated stimulation. This is not true of all stimulation, however. Habituation will occur only if the stimulation is of no significance to the organism.

Diminished responding to insignificant stimuli therefore permits useful allocation of resources to other matters.

How does this come about? It is easy to imagine, though inaccurate, as we shall see, that an adult judges the significance of some stimulation and then decides not to pay attention to it. But what about a baby, or a grasshopper? Clearly the mechanism would be different. Laboratory work on simple animals, later confirmed on mammals, indicates that repeated stimulation, followed by no other consequences, leads to decreased release of neurotransmitter at the terminal button. Such attenuation may last for days and appears to be a type of memory, since the nervous system must store what has been experienced before to "know" that what is occurring now is "boring" and of no significance.

Sensitization is similar but opposite in effect. Whereas habituation describes the reduction of reaction, sensitization involves an increase in response, particularly to stimuli that are noxious. Research has shown that sensitization is associated with an increase in the release of neurotransmitter into the synapse. However, control over this increase is not within the neuron itself but is a consequence of other neurons that impinge on and control the permeability of the membrane at the terminal button to substances that influence release.

It is too early to go into the ramifications of normal and abnormal habituation and sensitization. It should be clear, however, that a grasp of the neuropsychological mechanisms that underlie behavior permits an understanding of abnormality that sets the stage for devising effective strategies for treatment. Even at this point, it should be plausible that the balance of excitation and inhibition may be at the root of many disorders. Can the reader think of behaviors or disorders that appear to involve excess excitation or excess inhibition? The discussion will turn next to the development and structure of the brain.

3

The Development and Structure
of the Brain

Habituation and sensitization, it will be recalled, are ways in which behavior is influenced by experience, and occur in both humans and nonhumans. Of course, humans can do much more than habituate. Figure 3.1, which shows the relative brain size of several vertebrate species, suggests that the complexity and intricacy of behavior is related to the complexity and, to some extent, size of the brain. However, although simple and complex brains are very different, they share certain similarities of structure and organization. A grasp of the basic features of that structure will aid in understanding the immense complexities of the brain. This might be approached by comparing the brains of more primitive animals with that of man. Such comparative study has yielded much significant information. Here, however, understanding of the brain's structure will be approached from the point of view of the brain's gestation, the development that occurs between conception and birth.

Brain Development During Gestation

The process of development begins at the moment of conception, after sperm and egg have united. Cell division proceeds and the primitive precursors of later tissue are formed. In the outer layer of the developing embryo, in the part called the ectoderm, a portion of what will be the back of the baby thickens and forms a neural plate. This plate proceeds to grow up and around, and form a tube which extends through most of the length of the embryo. As the tube is formed, the upper end, slated to become the brain, widens a bit and takes on a somewhat different shape than the rest, which will become the spinal cord. This is illustrated in figure 3.2. Around 25 days after conception the front end begins to bend (see first two illustrations in figure 3.3). Since all this occurs within the first month of pregnancy, it takes place before the mother is likely to know that she is pregnant.

The brain is a complex three-dimensional structure which is difficult to visualize without direct anatomic study. It will be easier to grasp if what is kept in mind is that what is bending and folding is a tube. The crucial steps in the sequence are illustrated in the first four illustrations of figure 3.3. Note particularly the part labelled midbrain in the diagram. This is the place where there is a major bend in the devel-

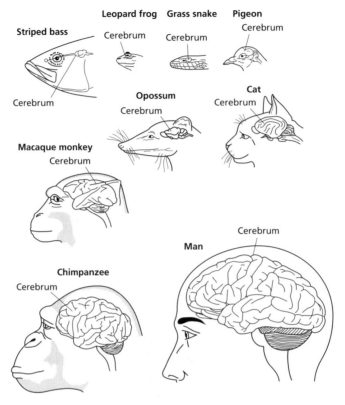

Figure 3.1   Relative brain size in several vertebrate species. Note changes in proportion of cortex to total brain size

oping fetal brain and it divides the primitive brain into its front and rear portions. The front portion is called the forebrain, the rear the hindbrain.

The midbrain does not undergo any further major division, but the forebrain and hindbrain do. Attending first to the front end, note the second through the fifth illustrations in figure 3.3. It can be seen that the frontmost area, the telencephalon, soon will bend back and grow over and then envelop the entire brain with a very elaborate mantle. The outer, visible part of the mantle, as seen in the diagrams, is called the cerebral cortex. Inside, not visible in the diagrams, are two other major structures called the basal ganglia and the limbic system. (These and other structures mentioned here for the first time will be described in more detail shortly.) Between the front end growing back and over and the midbrain is a connecting area called the diencephalon, from which two major structures develop: the thalamus and the hypothalamus.

Attending now to the area behind the midbrain, it would appear as though some force grabs the tube and shoves up another fold behind the bend that created the midbrain area. The major structures that emerge here are the pons at the bottom of

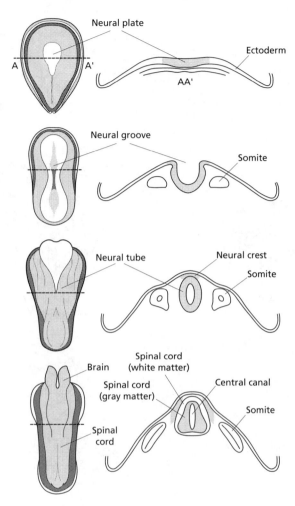

Figure 3.2   Early development of the nervous system

the curvature, the cerebellum at the top; the medulla is what remains after the shove. The medulla is continuous with the rest of the tube which bends no more and becomes the spinal cord. It can be seen in the sixth illustration in figure 3.3 that the basic structural differentiation of the brain is completed in about three months, or the first trimester of the nine months of pregnancy. There is much more growth and development needed before that brain can function very well, but the basic organization is already complete. As shall be discussed later, the first trimester, when the basic structure is being laid down, is the period of greatest vulnerability in the developing brain.

One complication probably needs mention at this point lest this discussion become unrealistically simple. The pattern of development of the neural tube is actually a

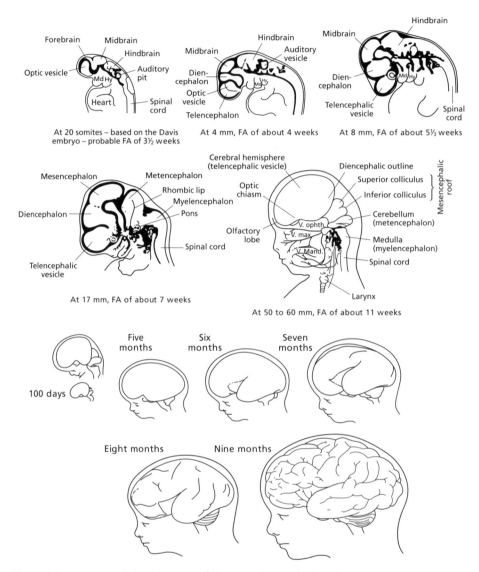

Figure 3.3   Gestational development of the brain (FA = fetal age)

matter of the right side and the left side each undergoing the bending, development, and growth described for the tube as a whole. The development on each side is in some degree independent, so that an additional burden on the gestational process is that it must be coordinated and end up coming together to create an intact organism. This is true throughout the body. Failure of coordination of the two sides can be seen in such visible anomalies as spina bifida or cleft palate. Such abnormalities can occur in the brain as well.

The outcome of all this development is the complicated structure present in the skull and spine of the newborn child. This structure is complete as to cell number but it has yet to undergo further development via the growth and proliferation of dendrites and increasing myelinization. There will also be times when many neurons will prove superfluous and will be sloughed. The next section will survey the mature brain and nervous system, and review its structure and organization in more detail. The discussion will proceed from the bottom up, peripheral nerves and spinal cord to cortex.

The Structure of the Nervous System

The spinal cord and peripheral nerves

The nervous system controls all of the functions going on in the body. It regulates the heartbeat, registers pain in the stomach or skin, keeps the body upright against the constant pressure of gravity, decides when the muscles are to move and the glands are to secrete, and does all this in an efficient and timely way. Some of the information it carries will be conscious and deliberate, as when a toe is stubbed or a decision is made to throw a ball, and much of it is processed without awareness. Awareness tends to be singular in nature, that is, only one thing at a time, perhaps a little bit more. On the other hand, a great many events are processed simultaneously without awareness.

Making all this possible are a series of complicated nerve networks that register internal and external events and control the actions of muscles, glands, and organs. All of the conscious activity, and a good deal of the unconscious as well, takes place via the spinal cord and the nerves which emerge from its bony structure. The body is arranged in a series of segments, and nerves from a particular segment of the spinal cord primarily enervate a particular segment of the body. It will also contribute to the enervation of adjacent segments but not to distant segments.

Segmentation is illustrated in figure 3.4. The various areas of the back are given separate names: cervical for the region of the neck, thoracic for the region of the chest, lumbar for the lower back and sacral for the small fused bones in our vestigial tail. The nerves for each area are separately numbered. Although the bony vertebrae continue all the way down the back, the spinal cord ends just about at the level of the bottom of the thoracic vertebrae. The spinal nerves for the lumbar and sacral regions emerge much like a horse's tail ("cauda equina") at that point (see figure 3.5). This makes possible the so-called "caudal (of the tail) block" type of anesthetic often used for women in childbirth since a single injection can affect the nerves that supply the entire bottom portion of the torso.

To obtain a greater appreciation of the organization and structure of spinal nerves, a closer examination of the spinal cord is in order. Figure 3.4 contains a diagram of the cord. For most vertebrates (animals with spinal cords), the back is the uppermost part of the body and the belly is at the bottom. The term dorsal means toward the top (keeping in mind the frame of reference of a four-footed animal) and the term

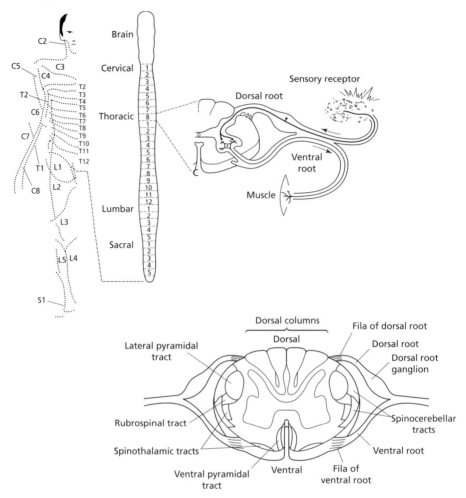

Figure 3.4   Segmentation of the control over the body in the spinal cord and cross-section of the cord

ventral means toward the belly. Inspection of figure 3.4 indicates that dorsal and ventral nerves emerge from the spinal cord which then combine to form a single nerve. The dorsal branch, or root, as it is called, contains axons from cell bodies packed into a thickening of the dorsal root called the dorsal root ganglion. A ganglion is a general term which refers to clumps of cell bodies. The dendrites for those cells are the sensory receptors (transducers) in the skin.

The axon terminals of the dorsal branch synapse with the dendrites and cell bodies of neurons inside the spinal cord. The neurons with cell bodies in the spinal cord have short dendrites. The axons of some of these neurons will also be short and synapse with other neurons in the spinal cord. These are the interneurons. Other

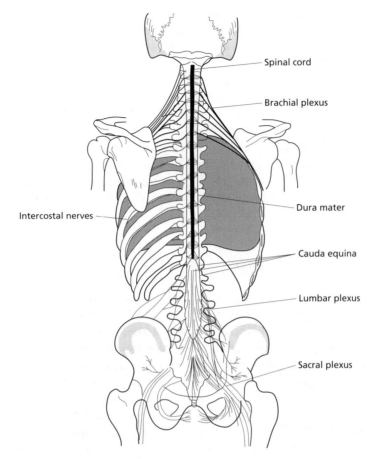

Figure 3.5　View of spinal nerves illustrating the way lumbar and sacral nerves emerge

neurons will have axons that head upward or downward toward the next segment, or they may even go all the way to the brain. Still other axons will leave the spinal cord via the ventral root and proceed to end upon a muscle. Those neurons whose axons enervate muscle are sometimes called lower motor neurons to distinguish them from neurons in the brain, which are also involved in motor control and which are called upper motor neurons. Lower motor neuron dendrites in the spinal cord synapse not only with axons from interneurons and dorsal sensory cells but also with axons coming down from upper motor neurons.

A grasp of this arrangement makes possible an understanding of a number of points regarding the way the nervous system is organized and operates. First, there is an orderly arrangement of input and output processes. There are neurons which have to do with sensing and there are neurons which have to do with action. This means that pathological processes may predominate in one and spare the other. Second, there are both peripheral and central influences on the excitation of muscle, since lower motor neurons synapse with both the axons from the receptor neurons in their own (and adjacent) segment(s) as well as with other axons coming down from the brain. Finally, there are cell bodies and many synapses in the spinal cord as well as myelinated axons coursing toward and away from the brain. A cross-section of the spinal cord has whiteish areas surrounding the relatively grayish butterfly shape within. The whiteish sections get their appearance from the myelin and contain the axonic pathways, while the gray matter contains cell bodies, dendrites, and synapses. Since gray matter is made up of neurons, much processing is going on in the spinal cord. White and gray matter will also appear in the brain. Remember that white matter is largely made up of nerve pathways, means of communicating between information processors, while gray matter is made up of neurons, the processors themselves.

The autonomic nervous system

A specialized part of the nervous system, the autonomic nervous system, provides the controlling circuitry for a large number of activities concerned with the regulation of energy use or metabolism. It has two divisions, one having to do with the creation and storage of energy reserves, or anabolism, the other with the expenditure of energy, or catabolism. A major anabolic activity is the digestion of food, which includes such components as salivation, the secretion of acids into the stomach, and the control of peristalsis, the wave of muscle contractions that moves food through the gut. Catabolic activity is mostly accomplished by changing the distribution of the supply of blood, moving it away from the gut and internal organs to the muscles that move the joints. Catabolic activity is involved in the so-called flight–fight reaction which occurs when the organism is threatened in some way or is under some other form of stress.

The anabolic aspects of the autonomic nervous system are under the control of the parasympathetic nervous system while the catabolic aspects are under the control of the sympathetic nervous system. The anatomy of these systems involves ganglia, clumps of neural cell body processors which lie outside the spinal cord. They also involve special spinal nuclei (clumps of cells serving as processors within the spinal cord) and pathways coming down the spinal cord from the brain, particularly from the part called the hypothalamus.

A view of the arrangement of the autonomic nervous system within the trunk is presented in figure 3.6. It will be noted that parasympathetic nerves emerge above and below the sympathetic, at the top, from the brain itself, and at the bottom from the lowest units of the spinal cord. The ganglia tend to be close to the organs which they enervate, implying a relatively selective or discrete pattern of control. By contrast the sympathetic nerves emerge through the ventral roots (along with the motor enervators) and proceed toward a chain of ganglia, called the sympathetic chain, which is situated outside but adjacent to the spinal cord. Some fibers synapse (undergo processing) in the chain while others pass through. The postsynaptic fibers

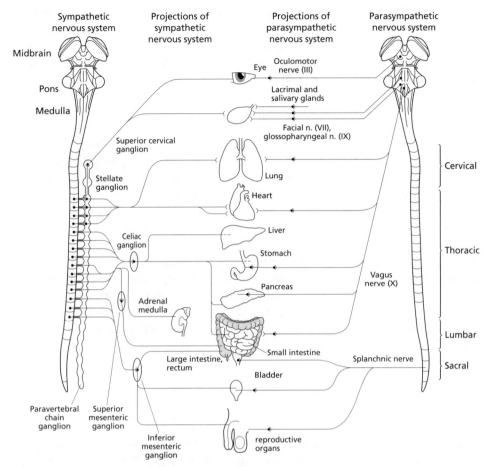

Figure 3.6 Diagram of the sympathetic and parasympathetic branches of the autonomic nervous system

and those passing through proceed to synapse with sympathetic ganglia which are often located at substantially greater distances from their target organs than is the case with the parasympathetic system. Also, in the sympathetic system, a single ganglion is likely to control several organs rather than only one. The consequence of this arrangement is a diffuse and general kind of control for the sympathetic branch. For stress situations, the system is arranged for all-out, indiscriminate mobilization. The two branches of the autonomic nervous system provide examples of diffuse and discrete control.

The autonomic nervous system is not only involved in building up resources and expending them under the stress of threatening situations but also is involved in reproduction through the control of sexual behavior. Interestingly, both the parasympathetic and the sympathetic branches are involved, the former in the earlier phases of sexual attraction and excitement, the latter in the orgasmic phase. Successful sexual activity is partially dependent on the timing of the shift from parasympathetic to sympathetic control.

Overall, the range of behaviors controlled by the autonomic system can be said to involve both the preservation of the self (flight–fight) and the preservation of the species (reproduction and maternal behavior). Such classes of activity, it can also be noted, are associated with powerful emotions such as fear, rage, anxiety, and lust. The hypothalamus and autonomic nervous system play a significant role in their elicitation and expression. Study of figure 3.6 shows that most organs are enervated by both sympathetic and parasympathetic fibers. The systems tend to be mutually inhibiting; that is, if the sympathetic system is active, the parasympathetic is inhibited, and vice-versa. The activity in either system can range in degree from minimal to extreme and the balance between them can be a matter of great delicacy, especially when no major environmental provocation is present for either kind of stimulation. To describe these relatively subtle qualities the term tone is used. For example, components of sympathetic tone are present when the organism is in a state of alert curiosity, while parasympathetic tone occurs in the late stages of learning and mastery. Thus, although the autonomic nervous system is involved in life-or-death (for individual or species) situations, it is also reactive in a subtle way during cognitive operations. These concomitant autonomic reactions have provided insights into thought processes and into cognitive handicaps.

The Brain

Discussion of the different portions of the brain will proceed from hindbrain to forebrain. Getting a sense of the architecture of the parts of the brain is difficult because most of its parts are concealed by the large cortical mantle, though remembering gestational development will help. To begin, contrast figure 3.7, a lateral (side) view of the brain from the outside, and figure 3.8, a view of what it looks like in a medial view, i.e. sliced down the middle (the knife blade passing through the nose and separating each nostril). In viewing figure 3.7, the only portions visible other than the cortex are the cerebellum, pons, and medulla, parts of the hindbrain. In the medial view, the relationships among these structures and between them and the rest of the brain are made more clear. Figure 3.9 shows the underside of the brain where there is a clear view of the lower surfaces of the cortex with medulla and pons cut away.

The medulla and pons

The medulla and pons are in many ways extensions of the spinal cord, with tracts carrying sensory messages to the higher centers of the brain and motor messages to the muscles down the spinal cord. Incoming information comes from several

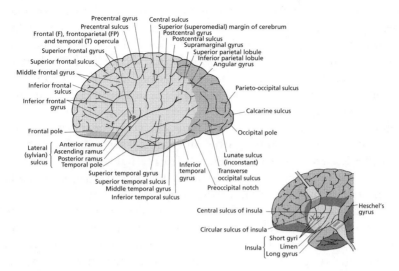

Figure 3.7   Lateral views of the left side of the brain

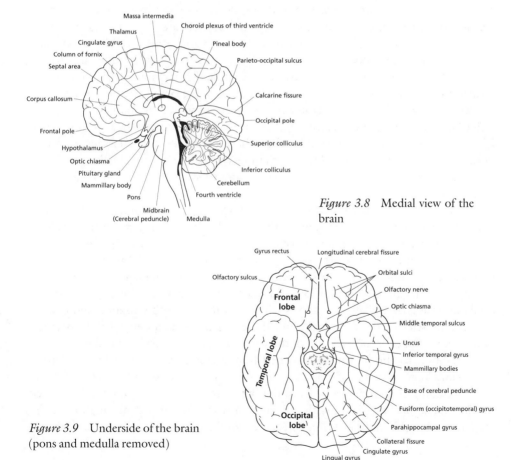

Figure 3.8   Medial view of the brain

Figure 3.9   Underside of the brain (pons and medulla removed)

sources. Part comes from the trunk and limbs and includes the sense of touch, body pain, heat and cold, and awareness of the position and movement of the limbs. Collectively, this information is called somatosensory (from soma, meaning body) sensation. Pathways for somatosensory information are joined by pathways bearing information from the ear, from the organ of balance located next to the ear called the vestibular system (to be discussed in detail in a later chapter), and from the taste buds on the tongue.

A noteworthy feature of the pathways of these tracts in the medulla is their decussation. Decussation means crossing over, and that is what happens. Pathways originating on the left cross over in the medulla to the right side and vice-versa. This occurs to both sensory and motor pathways. The upshot is that most events sensed on the right side of the body project (have pathways which go to) to the left side of the brain, and that the left side of the brain provides motor control for the right side of the body. It is said that enervation or motor control is contralateral, or from the opposite (contra) side (lateral). There are some pathways that are ipsilateral, controlled on the same (ipsi) side, but they are generally rather primitive, and their functioning is often observed only in pathological states.

Aside from carrying messages back and forth, the medulla and pons are the sites of a number of vital functions. In the dorsal portion of the medulla and coursing upward to higher centers, amidst the various tracts, there are fairly large areas of gray matter called the reticular formation. A reticulum is a net and the cells, axons, and dendrites of this area appear to form a kind of network. If a sleepy animal is stimulated in this area, it will become active and alert, and it is known that the reticular formation has much to do with the state of arousal of the organism. Not surprisingly, the reticular formation in the medulla has connections with every part of the nervous system. It reacts to external events, and can provoke other brain areas into states of reactivity. It is involved with what, at the behavior level, is called alertness or attention, and it is connected to centers in the pons which participate in the regulation of the sleep–wake cycle. Disorders of this system will be the subject of an entire chapter later.

Within the medulla and pons can be found nuclei which control many vital vegetative functions. These include centers for the control of breathing, heartbeat, and blood pressure. There is also a center for reversing peristalsis, causing vomiting. Most of these control mechanisms are found in pairs; one for excitation, the other for inhibition. The only nerves to emerge directly from the brain, the cranial nerves (see figure 3.10), have their nuclei in, and emerge primarily from, this area or from the midbrain just above. These are nerves which provide for both sensation and control over the muscles of the face, including those muscles which control the extremely precise movements of the eyes and of the voice box, where speech is produced.

In addition to the information carried by the cranial nerves and by the centers controlling vegetative functions, there are many other important processing functions going on in these lower areas of the brain. Two such functions will be singled out here. The first has to do with information from the ear. As information moves from the ear to the highest processing centers in the cortex, it may synapse with two

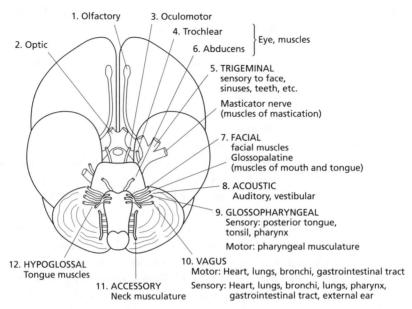

Figure 3.10 The cranial nerves

to four special nuclei in the medulla. When hearing is considered later, these centers will be of considerable significance in understanding certain disorders. The second has to do with the regulation of the fundamental way in which the body's movement is organized. As is discussed in more detail in the chapter on motor disorders, there are neural organizations, operative early in life, which control all of the muscles of the body simultaneously. These forms of control may persist pathologically in later life. Such primitive organizations are controlled by nuclei in the medulla. They draw on information from the position of the eyes; sensations from the skin, muscles, and joints; and from the vestibular system (described later), each of which has important nuclei in the medulla or pons.

The cerebellum

The cerebellum is the relatively large "little brain" (which is what the term means) sticking out from under the mantle of the cerebral cortex behind the medulla and pons. Although a great deal is known about the structure and function of the cerebellum, a great deal is also unknown. It is known to receive inputs from every sensory system, but especially from the vestibular system, from the muscles and joints, and from the eye muscles. The cerebellum is much involved with, and crucial for, the smooth integration of motor functions, of efficient and skillful behavior, and in making possible the brain's constant awareness of the body's position in space.

What is meant by "smooth integration" requires some additional explanation. Walking will be used as an example. If one observes the halting steps of a child learning how to walk, and compares those behaviors with the normal walk of a grown person, and then with the walk of a tottering drunk, an aged senile individual, and the Frankenstein monster-like walk of a robot, one can observe the consequences of normal and abnormal cerebellar function. The robot has no cerebellum, the child has not yet had adequate cerebellar myelination, the drunk has chemically cut off most cerebellar connections, and the aged person suffers from cerebellar deterioration. The "integration" that the cerebellum adds, has to do with the timing of the successive events required, the regulation of the intensities of each component reaction, and the provision of simultaneous control over the different parts.

With regard to timing, think of the number of muscles that have to be given excitatory messages for the body to walk, and think of the complexity of the sequencing that must be involved! Regarding intensity, some muscles must contract forcefully, while others just a little. For simultaneous control, think of walking normally and note that certain movements of one leg are accompanied by very different movements of the other, that both are accompanied by motions of the trunk and arms. Altogether this constitutes "gait." A smooth gait depends on the orchestration of countless discrete events.

If action is to occur, muscles must contract, and for that to happen excitatory messages must arrive at the muscles. Excitation alone impels action but provides little control over action. It is the equivalent of starting a car in gear that has no brakes. It will lurch forward rather than move smoothly. If it were possible to arrange for a slow controlled pattern of increasing excitation, perhaps the lurching could be minimized. However, real safety and true control depend on having intact brakes, some mechanism for inhibiting, and thus regulating the excitement. Analysis of cerebellar neuronal circuitry indicates that much of it is inhibitory. This is the area where excitatory events originating elsewhere are shaped, smoothed out, coordinated, and controlled.

A physician assesses cerebellar function by observing spontaneous gait, or gait while walking heel to toe, or requests the patient to touch his/her own nose and then the physician's finger as rapidly as possible. Normal cerebellar function is unobtrusive, and is another example of complex information processing that operates without awareness.

Recent research has added significantly to our understanding of the functions of the cerebellum. First, neuroscientists have been searching for the site where permanent changes occur after learning takes place. Thompson (1985, pp. 300–2) showed that the site for one type of learning, classical conditioning, is in the cerebellum, though these findings are still controversial. This kind of learning is present in both lower animals and man. The information registered has to do with the hedonic significance (degree of pleasure) of a particular pattern of stimulation; that is, for example, whether the sight of food will be followed by pleasurable (tasty) or unpleasurable (bitter) stimulation. Second, the cerebellum has been implicated in other aspects of cognition (Schmahmann, 1991; Courchesne et al., 1994). It appears to be particularly important for the rapid deployment and shifting of attention required in many situations and for higher cognitive functions. Further consideration of the role of the cerebellum in cognitive functions will await the discussion of motor functions and childhood psychosis.

The midbrain

On the upper surface of the midbrain, an area above the fourth ventricle (see below) known as the tectum (roof), there are two pairs of rounded bumps called the colliculi (see figure 3.8). The lower pair (toward the medulla), the inferior colliculi, are one of the complex relay stations between ear and cortex for auditory information. In lower animals the colliculi are the major centers for processing auditory information. The other pair of bumps, the superior colliculi, process visual information, and in lower animals are the major center for processing such information. It has been known for some time that the superior colliculi in humans control some automatic aspects of eye movement, particularly the tendency of the eye to move involuntarily toward any surprising or novel moving visual stimulus.

The lower portion of the midbrain is called the tegmentum (floor). This is an area containing the upper part of the reticular formation and axons that are connecting higher centers with the brainstem and spinal cord. It also is the site of a number of major nuclei, the periaqueductal gray matter, surrounding the aqueduct, a tube connecting the third and fourth ventricles (see below) whose cell bodies are involved in species-specific motor programs, such as mating behavior; the red nucleus, the source of the rubrospinal tract (see chapter on motor functions), which brings motor information from cortex (see below) and cerebellum to the spinal cord; and the substantia nigra (black substance), neurons rich in dopamine which project to the basal ganglia (all to be discussed shortly).

The ventricular system

Before continuing the discussion of different parts of the brain, consideration will now be given to a system of fluid circulation that is an important feature of its anatomy. The landmarks of the ventricular system will help the reader to visualize the brain's complex structure.

The brain is surrounded with liquid, the cerebrospinal fluid, which cushions it from physical shock. The fluid circulates though a space that entirely surrounds both the brain and spinal cord. In addition, this fluid circulates through cavities within the body of the brain; these cavities are called ventricles. The fluid not only serves as a physical cushion but also as a means for carrying nutritional substances and neurotransmitters to various cells and structures, and also for carrying away waste products and poisons.

The ventricles and the circulation of cerebrospinal fluid are illustrated in figure 3.11. Recall that, during gestation, a hollow tube is formed in the earliest stage of nervous system development. The ventricles are the descendants of the hollow space

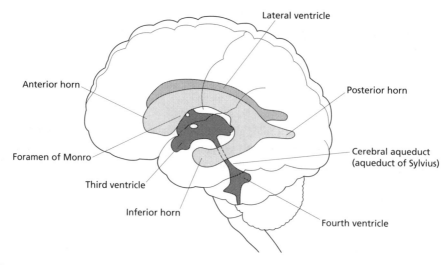

Figure 3.11   The ventricular system

in that tube in the brain: in the spinal cord, it is the central canal. Beginning with the central canal in the spinal cord, observe how, at the level of the medulla, cerebellum, and pons, the canal widens and projects forward to the pons and backwards to the cerebellum. This widening is called the fourth ventricle (for reasons to be described shortly). As the ventricular system is followed upward, it will be noted that it tapers into a narrow passageway (the aqueduct of Sylvius, the same aqueduct around which periaqueductal gray is found in midbrain) and then expands into a complex shape, something like a very irregular football with a hole at its upper third near the center but more toward the front. This is the third ventricle; it is situated in the midline and just above the midbrain. Finally, after a short communicating, bifurcating (splitting in two) passageway (the foramen of Monro), the ventricles blossom into two very large, curved horseshoe-shaped structures that penetrate the various parts of the left and right cortex. These are the lateral ventricles.

The names of the ventricles derive from their accessibility as one dissects from the outside, in. The first two encountered, the lateral ventricles, would be numbered one and two, but as it is not possible to decide whether to give precedence to the left or right side, they are simply called lateral ventricles. The other two are in the midline and pose no such problems, so they are called third and fourth, respectively.

The ventricular system has been presented at this point to facilitate understanding of the location of other structures. However, this is a suitable place to discuss some of the different problems that occur because of malfunctions in this system. Circulation can be impeded by some obstruction, by abnormal production of excess fluid, or by insufficient reabsorption. Each of these conditions will cause the fluid to cumulate excessively and produce an abnormal enlargement of the ventricles and an increase in pressure on adjacent and remote structures. This condition is known as hydrocephalus. In an infant whose bones are not yet fixed in position, the head itself will expand to an ungainly size. In an older child or adult, there is no place for the fluid to go, so it will compress and ultimately destroy adjacent tissues. In recent years a surgical procedure has been developed in which a shunt is placed in the ventricular system to drain off the excess cerebrospinal fluid into the blood stream and thus prevent the buildup of excess pressure. There will be more discussion about hydrocephalus in the chapter on brain damage.

The hypothalamus and limbic system

These structures are deep on the undersurface and at the base of the brain, quite literally, up and beyond the nose. As discussed later, if it is necessary to obtain recordings from this area of the brain, the electrodes often must be placed in the nasal passages or the throat, or on nearby bony structures such as the sphenoid. The location of the hypothalamus is fairly easy to specify. If the brain is viewed from the underside (figure 3.9), it is a group of nuclei that lie just above the area that begins with the X-shaped optic chiasm (where the visual system crosses over) and ends with the mammillary bodies (so named because their appearance is similar to the female breast). In a cross-sectional view of the brain (figure 3.8), it lies just above where the midbrain tapers after it has bent. Below the middle of the area, set deep in the bony structure of the skull, is the pituitary gland. Hypothalamic nuclei surround the lower and more forward portion of the third ventricle.

The relatively small area of the hypothalamus has powerful effects on the entire organism. The hypothalamus is involved in the regulation of a number of vegetative functions including body temperature, feeding, and drinking. In addition, as discussed earlier, the hypothalamus is crucially involved in the expression of emotion, including rage, fear, sexuality, and maternal behavior. The influence of the hypothalamus is, in part, mediated by the control its nuclei exercise over the autonomic nervous system.

Another way in which the hypothalamus exerts control is via its influence on the pituitary gland. This gland secretes hormones which circulate in the blood and other body fluids, and influence target organs via the same sort of lock-and-key mechanism described earlier regarding the fit between neurotransmitters and receptor sites. In other words, hormones circulate widely, and when they encounter a receptive target organ, they exert their influence there. Hormones, therefore, also convey information, but in a slower and somewhat less specific way than neurons do.

The front part of the pituitary gland secretes many different kinds of hormones. These include separate hormones that regulate growth; stimulate the thyroid gland, which in turn regulates the pace of energy consumption varying with the season and climate; regulate the amount of pigment in the skin; and control the menstrual cycle, the production of sex hormones, and the production of milk in nursing mothers. A pituitary hormone also regulates the output of the adrenal gland, whose products in turn are much involved in the response to stress of every type. The secretion of each of these hormones is under the immediate control of nuclei in the hypothalamus. In addition the hypothalamus is the site of the production of two other pituitary hormones which move down special channels and are secreted through the front part of the pituitary. One of these hormones is involved in the control of muscular contractions during birth, while the other influences the water balance of the body by controlling some of the functions of the kidney.

In contrast to the hypothalamus, the limbic system (see figure 3.12) is not as easily localized. It involves a number of nuclei and pathways that are nearby but not so neatly clumped together as the hypothalamus. They are grouped as a system because they are jointly involved in a number of related functions. One key portion of the limbic system is the structure made up of the fornix and hippocampus. Note one familiar landmark, the pair of mammillary bodies at the back of the hypothalamus which protrude visibly at the lower surface of the brain. The columns of the fornix rise from the mammillary bodies then arch backward and around until they merge with the complex structure known as the hippocampus (Greek for seahorse, because it seemed to an early anatomist to be similar in appearance). Near the termination of the hippocampus are a group of clustered nuclei called the amygdaloid complex. (It was originally called an amygdala, meaning almond, because it appeared to have that shape. The addition and modification implied by the word "complex" came with the understanding that it is not a singular structure.) The hippocampus is actually buried within the temporal lobe of the cortex, to be discussed shortly, an area close to where the hypothalamus is situated. If figure 3.9 of the underside of the brain is viewed, one can identify the structure labelled as the hippocampal gyrus, find the mammillary bodies, and imagine the arching connections in between. Note that each fornix straddles the midline of the brain.

Additional portions of the limbic system are intimately associated with the olfactory nerves (the nerves of smell coming from the nose) and their nuclei which are situated near to where the olfactory nerves enter the main body of the brain (see figure 3.12). Other areas include the septum, parts of the cortex, particularly the cingulate gyrus, the thalamus, the hypothalamus, and the mammillary bodies.

The limbic system and hypothalamus arouse and regulate much behavior. Whereas the reticular formation controls arousal and activation processes which differentiate sleep and waking states, these structures mediate the more selective kind of arousal and alerting that is associated with a particular kind of drive, motivation or emotion. They thus control several aspects of attention. The limbic system is also involved with orientation and habituation, and with many aspects of memory.

The thalamus

The thalamus is a somewhat egg-shaped group of nuclei straddling the third ventricle adjacent the midbrain area, above and somewhat back from the hypothalamus (see figure 3.13). The thalamus is known as a relay station in that information from each sensory modality synapses here (and hence is processed) before going on to the

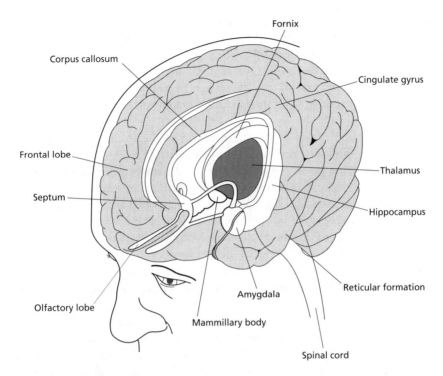

Figure 3.12 The limbic system

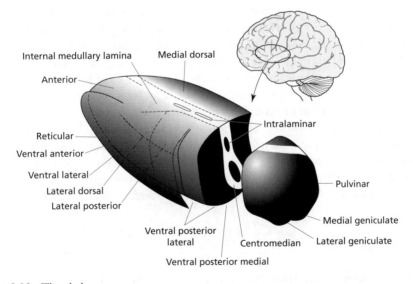

Figure 3.13 The thalamus

cortex and other areas. The nucleus for vision is called the lateral geniculate; that for audition, the medial geniculate; and that for somatosensory information, the ventral posterolateral nucleus (because within the thalamus, it is down below, at the side and toward the back of the thalamus). An adjacent nucleus, the ventral posteromedial nucleus (down below, toward the back but in the middle), is the site where somatosensory information from the face is integrated with information from the rest of the body.

Some of the complexities of the organization of the thalamus can be described with terminology similar to that used when discussing the discrete and diffuse patterns of enervation found in the sympathetic and parasympathetic branches of the autonomic nervous system. The nuclei of the thalamus are classified as to whether they are specific or nonspecific. The nuclei already described are specific nuclei, synaptic sites for the processing of information coming from individual sense modalities and projecting to areas of the cortex that process only information from those modalities. The other kinds of specific nuclei are not sensory, but they receive input from very specific sources and project to other very specific sources. For example, the ventral lateral nucleus receives input from the cerebellum and projects to a delimited area of the cortex.

By contrast, nonspecific nuclei obtain information from a variety of sources and project to a variety of sources. In the thalamus, the nonspecific nuclei receive information from many different areas of the brain including the reticular formation, the cerebellum, and the midbrain red nucleus and substantia nigra, and project to all areas of the brain. As one might expect, damage to specific nuclei has selective effects, while damage to nonspecific nuclei has broad effects.

The thalamus not only receives information from the periphery (via the sensory organs responding to the outside world) and sends it to higher processing centers including the cortex, it also receives information from higher centers and transmits it to the motor system. In addition, some of this information from above is employed to tune the state of excitability of the thalamus itself and other nuclei as well. Information is said to pass upward toward the highest centers of the brain, and pass downward toward lower centers or toward muscles. This two-way street, up and down, provides the means for informing different nuclei of the consequences of their activity or of their influence on the behavior of yet other nuclei. The circuitry permits feedback loops, the equivalent of an airline pilot repeating a message to the control tower so that the controller knows whether the message was properly received. This part of the architecture of the nervous system permits it to operate in a coordinated way. There will be more about this in the next chapter.

The basal ganglia

One of the limbic system structures, the amygdaloid complex is also part of another anatomic system, the basal ganglia. Like the hippocampus and fornix, the basal ganglia also loop from the amygdaloid complex in the cortex into the center of the

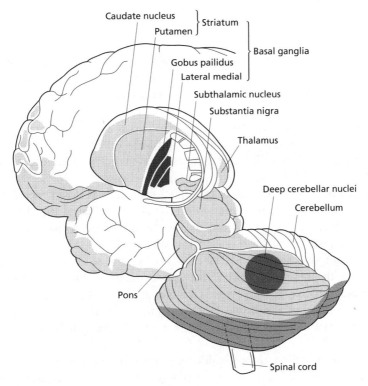

Figure 3.14   The basal ganglia and related structures

brain. The long looping structure is called the caudate (which means tail-like) nucleus, divided more or less arbitrarily into a tail section and a head section. Underneath and within the front part of the caudate are two relatively large, roundish on the outside but tapering toward the middle, nuclei called the putamen and the globus pallidus, which together are sometimes called the lenticular nucleus (see figure 3.14, the lenticular nucleus is not labelled). Recall that the hypothalamus and the thalamus straddle the third ventricle, the first below the second. The lenticular nucleus is lateral to (toward the outside of) those structures and the head of the caudate nucleus curves around the side of the thalamus as it arches en route to the amygdala. The thalamus and hypothalamus are medial to (toward the inside of) the basal ganglia.

The functions of the basal ganglia are only partially known. It is certain that they are involved in the control of movement, especially its more automatic aspects. One such function is the sheer initiation of movement. It may seem surprising that starting to move and moving are disassociable, but that appears to be the case. There are disorders in which the individual does not move but, if somehow primed to start, can go on with skill. There is some evidence for sensory and cognitive functions in the basal ganglia, particularly the caudate. There will be more information about the basal ganglia in the chapter on motor disorders.

The cortex

The largest and most obvious part of the brain is the cortex, the outer mantle that has grown back and over from the primitive forebrain. Cortex means bark, like the bark of a tree. In the course of its growth, the cortex folds and dips upon itself so that its overall area, if it were straightened out, would be substantially larger than what can be seen when the skull is opened. The result of this process produces grooves, called sulci (singular = sulcus), deep valleys called fissures, and the bulging parts of the convolutions called gyri (singular = gyrus). These features provide land-marks for naming and distinguishing parts of the cortex.

The most obvious fissure, the longitudinal fissure, goes down the center of the brain and divides it into nearly symmetrical left and right halves called hemispheres. Each hemisphere, when viewed from the side, can be seen to have a major sulcus or fissure (the terms used vary), called the lateral sulcus, which runs back and up from a point not very far from its front end. Below this sulcus lies one of the lobes of the cortex, the temporal lobe. If the lateral sulcus is spread apart as in figure 3.7 it can be seen that more cortex is visible, another lobe called the insula. Just beneath the surface of the insula lies the lenticular nucleus of the basal ganglia and then the thalamus above and to the rear and the hypothalamus below and to the front.

The other major landmark of the side view is the central sulcus. This sulcus is less easy to specify than the lateral sulcus. It is a vertical sulcus that begins slightly back from the midpoint of the top edge of the cortex and terminates near a point at about half the length of the lateral sulcus. The central sulcus separates the frontal lobe (in front) from the parietal lobe behind. The central sulcus has a descriptive character-istic that parallels the dorsal and ventral roots of the spinal cord, namely, separation of sensory and motor processing. Specifically, the gyrus immediately in front of the central sulcus (the precentral gyrus) is overwhelmingly involved with motor func-tions while that just behind (the postcentral gyrus) is involved with somatosensory information processing. If one goes further front or back the same principle gener-ally holds so that it can be said that the front of the brain is involved in the execu-tion of motor activity while the back is involved with information processing and storage.

There is one other lobe of the cortex, the occipital lobe. The occipital lobe's loca-tion at the back of the brain is easy to specify but its demarcation from the parietal and the temporal lobes is somewhat arbitrary. The occipital lobe extends from the rearmost portion of the brain to an arbitrary line drawn from the preoccipital notch at the bottom to the parieto-occipital sulcus at the top. The temporal and parietal lobes are separated by an arbitrary line which extends from where the lateral sulcus ends to the line that bounds the occipital lobe. See figure 3.7 for details.

Figure 3.8 presents a view of the inner surface of the cortex as seen from a cut through the longitudinal fissure. It will be noted that the gyri and sulci from the lateral surface extend over the top as they drop into the fissure. Below those exten-sions is a broad horizontally running gyrus called the cingulate gyrus which is one of the cortical components of the limbic system. Other cortical components of the limbic system can be seen in figure 3.9, which displays the underside of the cortex, with the cerebellum and the structures below the midbrain cut away. Here one can observe the parahippocampal gyrus in which the hippocampus and amygdala are buried, and the proximity of that deeply buried portion of the temporal lobe to the mammillary bodies and the hypothalamus.

Although the cortex looks uniform on the outside, its actual structure varies in different regions. The exposition of those differences is beyond the scope of this book, but the point is mentioned to emphasize that the functional differences about to be discussed are associated with anatomic and histologic (cellular organization) differences. Much has been learned about the functional organization of the cortex (cf. Calvin & Ojemann, 1994), and that will be considered next.

To begin this discussion, imagine being present when a neurosurgeon exposes the entire brain of a patient who requires neurosurgery, and then proceeds to stimulate different portions with an electrode that delivers a very small amount of current. The patient is awake and in communication with those working on him. Such procedures are possible because there are no pain receptors in the brain and those of the scalp and other tissues that have to be cut to get to the brain are numbed with local anesthetic. The only part of this scene that is unrealistic is the exposure of the entire brain. In an actual operation, a surgeon would expose only a portion large enough to perform the surgery required by the patient's condition. In other respects, this scene takes place often in hospitals all over the world.

Our surgeon begins by stimulating the left precentral gyrus about a third of the way from the top. The patient moves the fingers of the right hand. The surgeon goes somewhat lower, and the facial muscles twitch. The surgeon shifts to a corresponding point on the postcentral gyrus and applies the current and the patient does not move but reports some kind of sensation, tickling, pain or pressure, on the surface of the hand or face, depending on the location of the electrode. The surgeon moves the electrode to the calcarine fissure of the occipital lobe and stimulates the wall of that fissure in two different places on the left side. The patient reports flashes of light or color on the right side, one in the top half of what can be seen, the other toward the bottom. The surgeon then gently pulls aside the temporal lobe, as though to reveal the insula, and stimulates the now-revealed upper surface of the temporal lobe, on an area called Heschl's gyrus. When the outermost area is stimulated, the patient reports hearing low tones, but as the electrode is moved inward, higher and higher tones are reported. These findings occur when these and only these areas are stimulated.

As already noted there is separate representation in specific places on the cortex of the different sensory modalities and of motor functions. Motor functions are represented in the precentral gyrus of the frontal lobe, somatosensory sensation in the postcentral gyrus of the parietal lobe, auditory sensation in Heschl's gyrus of the temporal lobe, and visual sensation in the walls of calcarine fissure of the occipital lobe. Representation on the brain in these areas is quite specific. It is topographic in the motor, visual, and somatosensory systems in that specific areas of muscle, skin, or vision project to specific points on the brain. It is tonotopic in the auditory system in that specific tones are represented at specific places on the cortex in an orderly sequence. Areas with these characteristics are called the primary receptive and motor areas of the brain and are modality-specific.

The surgeon continues to explore with the electrode and stimulates the cortex in the areas adjacent to primary areas. The pattern of response changes. When the patient reports experiences after stimulation, they are mostly modality-specific, but now they are somewhat elaborated. Rather than the sounds, light flashes or colors, itches, and twitches that occurred when the primary areas were stimulated, there now might be rhythms or textures or part of an image or noise. The specifics of the response become less reproducible, and only on rare occasions does there seem to be a direct link between stimulation and report. Cortical areas with these characteristics are called secondary.

The reader might imagine that there are tertiary areas, and indeed there are. These are areas on the sensory side which lie between the primary receptive zones, especially around the area where the imaginary line marking the boundaries of the parietal, occipital, and temporal lobes intersect. Stimulation in these areas does not lead to any kind of consistent response. Indeed, for the most part no response is elicited, although there are rare instances when complex memories and dream-like sequences of complex scenes are reported. Such reports suggest that tertiary areas are multimodal, meaning that the experience elicited by the electrical stimulation combines information from all modalities into the rich brew that is similar to ordinary experience. The integrating characteristics of tertiary areas is the basis for also calling them association areas. When such terminology is used, primary areas are likely to be called sensory or motor cortex.

Since direct stimulation of tertiary areas yields little information, the surgeon explores in a different manner. He gets the patient to behave by asking him to perform such tasks as naming objects he is shown, remembering words or phrases, or making symbolic movements such as sticking out his tongue. From time to time, he stimulates an area of brain while the behavior is in progress without the patient knowing. The surgeon observes if the behavior is disrupted. If it is, then there is evidence that the area stimulated is involved in that behavior. If there is no disruption, the inference is that the particular area is not involved in that behavior. This is called brain mapping, and functional differences can be found at a distance of a centimeter or so.

The surgeon moves the electrode to the frontal lobe of the left hemisphere, to an area about a quarter to a third of the distance between the central sulcus and the front tip of the brain and about three quarters of the way down. The subject is asked to speak; for example, to recite a familiar nursery rhyme. While the recital is in progress the surgeon turns on the stimulation and notes that the coherent speech has turned to laborious utterances that make no sense. The surgeon moves the electrode to a comparable position on the right hemisphere, asks for the behavior again, and turns on the stimulation. No disruption occurs.

The surgeon next moves back to the left hemisphere and the region where the lateral sulcus is about to end, and places his probe on the first gyrus of the temporal lobe just below the sulcus. He asks a series of simple questions and listens carefully as the subject answers. At times he repeats the question just to make sure that the subject's responses are consistent. At times, again without the patient's knowledge, the surgeon applies the electrical current either during the time the question is asked or during the course of the answer. In the former case the subject acts as though no question were asked, or seems confused. In the latter, the subject sounds like he is giving answers but the words are nonsensical. When the surgeon repeats these procedures on the right hemisphere, the patient answers all questions just as he had when there was no stimulation.

The area stimulated in the left frontal lobe is called Broca's area. It was named after the neurologist who is credited with first describing this area as the locus of pathology of a disorder in which speech and language can be understood but cannot be expressed. The area stimulated at the back of the temporal lobe is called Wernicke's area, and it is named after the neurologist who is credited with first describing that area as the locus of a disorder in which speech and language are expressed fluently but are poorly understood, and where meanings are garbled. There are thus separate areas of cortex involved in understanding (sensory) and producing (motor) speech. The disassociation between the expressive aspects of speech from its reception and comprehension provides a clear example of how sensory and motor components are regulated in separate areas of brain. Also apparent is that speech could only be disrupted on the left side and not on the right. The specialization of the left hemisphere for speech and language demonstrates a special aspect of the organization of the human brain, namely that the two hemispheres, although similar in many ways, nonetheless serve different higher-level functions.

The distinctions between primary, secondary, and tertiary areas of cortex also distinguish between relatively simple sensations and more complex sensory and cognitive experience. It was once thought that the sequence of processing went from primary to secondary to tertiary. This is not the case. Upon stimulation, all three regions are roused to activity with near simultaneity, and the wiring diagram does not go linearly from one to the next. Instead, all three types of area are enervated from below. Primary areas are not much different on the left and right but there are major differences in tertiary functions in the two hemispheres. One generalization about this arrangement is that the left hemisphere is specialized for dealing with verbal functions and sequential processes and their memory while the right is specialized for visual spatial functions and simultaneous processes and their memory. Overall, then, the cortex has at least three functional axes. One might be called an up–down axis which is concerned with the relations between cortical and subcortical functions. A second refers to the dividing line of the central sulci and the relations between the sensory and knowing back of the brain and the action-oriented and planning front of the brain. The third has to do with the division created by the longitudinal fissure which divides the brain into verbal, sequential left and spatial, simultaneous right hemispheres.

Except for mentioning the motor cortex and Broca's area, no consideration has been given to the massive brain area in front of the central sulci, the frontal lobes.

This region of brain, despite its prominent size, has been the last to yield its secrets. For the primary area, the motor strip, the evidence is, as indicated, of direct connections to specific muscle groups. The secondary area in front of the motor strip, which includes Broca's area, is called the premotor cortex and is devoted to fairly direct elaboration and organization of different kinds of complex motor activity such as speaking and writing, and if one is a drummer, drumming. The tertiary area in front of the secondary areas and coming round the frontal poles (the front tips of the brain) to the underside is called the prefrontal cortex. Three regions of the prefrontal cortex have been distinguished. Dorsolateral areas in the upper half of the side of the frontal lobes (north of the outer corners of the eyes) have been implicated in what has been called working memory, the ability to hold in mind enough information from what has just transpired to be able to perform the next step, e.g. remembering that you just added eggs to the recipe so that you do not repeat that step again, a memory that will otherwise not be retained. Inferior, including orbital, prefrontal cortex is at the bottom of the side of the frontal lobes close to the temporal lobe and extending to the rounded surface at the poles. Medial prefrontal cortex is a further extension of the inferior and orbital segments and can be found on the under surface of the frontal lobes and seen in medial views. These portions of the prefrontal cortex are extensively connected to the limbic system and provide a link between motives and emotions and the organization of behaviors to deal with them. There will be more about the functions of the frontal lobes in subsequent chapters.

The corpus callosum and other commissures

As noted, the left and right hemispheres perform differently in regard to certain functions although they perform similarly in many other ways. The presence of two control systems requires mechanisms for their coordination or chaos will ensue. When both hemispheres function in similar fashion, it is necessary that they perform harmoniously and in coordination. When the hemispheres perform a distinctive function, one must be operatively dominant and be able to suppress interference from the other. This requires inhibition of neurons in an entire hemisphere that might otherwise be set to respond.

These functions, providing cross-communication and selective inhibition between the two sides, are made possible by commissures, bands of neurons that cross between the two sides. The most prominent commissure, and the one most likely to be involved in inhibition, is the corpus callosum, a massive band of fibers that can be readily seen in cross-sectional views of the brain (see figure 3.8). This structure interconnects corresponding points of the cortex on the two sides and many other points as well. There are other smaller connecting fiber bands. The anterior commissure connects portions of the front part of the temporal lobes and the amygdaloid complexes with each other. The hippocampal and thalamic commissures connect the right and left nuclei of these structures.

This completes the initial presentation of the structure and function of the brain and nervous system. More information will be added as it becomes relevant in each chapter about a particular kind of disorder. The next chapters, however, will further consider the way in which the brain functions.

4

Operational Characteristics of Neural Systems

In this chapter, a number of features of nervous system activity, some already introduced and some brand new, will be discussed and elaborated. Understanding these operational characteristics will make it easier to grasp the way in which the brain works. They will be repeatedly invoked as explanatory principles in the chapters on the various disorders.

Activity

Neurons are active, that is, they discharge periodically. For the most part, what determines whether the neuron is "at rest" or active is its rate of discharge. A neuron "doing something" discharges at a more rapid rate than one that is idling. When describing either single neurons or groups of neurons operating as part of a system (about which more will be presented shortly), the term tonic is used to refer to the condition of relative idling and the term phasic is used for relative activity.

The concepts of tonic and phasic activity can perhaps be most readily understood in the context of the motor system. If a person in a relaxed state bends an elbow, the neurons controlling the muscles that do the bending must go into phasic activity. Neural firing inciting the muscles to action emerges from that level of activity that preceded the elbow bend, the tonic level of activity. To bend an elbow, neurons do not change from inactivity to activity, but from one level of activity to another.

The most difficult aspect to understand is the relativity part. The tonic level of excitation in an olympic diver, five seconds before the plunge, is quite different from his tonic level a week before, just prior to reaching out to grasp a glass of water. In actuality, tonic levels of activity shift throughout the course of one's daily activities. There are periods of greater relaxation and periods of greater anticipatory tension, but the tempo of change, barring some emergency situation, is relatively slow, on the order of tens of seconds to minutes and even hours. Phasic activity is also relative, relative to the amount of work that must be done to perform the action intended. Phasic changes, however, are very rapid, on the order of milliseconds to tenths of a second.

One important reason for making the distinction between tonic and phasic, despite all this relativity, is that neural controls of tonic and phasic activity are partially independent, and hence may be separately impaired. For example, tonic activity is generally not under deliberate control while phasic activity often is. Thus there may be separate disorders of tonic and phasic activity, each of which may impede motor functions equally, though in different ways. These issues will be discussed in the chapter on motor disorders.

The terms tonic and phasic have their counterparts in sensory and perceptual activity. Just as specific acts emerge from the context of prior muscle tone, so too do perceptions of specific objects or events emerge from a broader context. The terms focal and ambient are the perceptual counterparts of phasic and tonic. For some purposes, the terms signal and noise are used. Both sets of terms draw attention to the context in which focal perceptual events take place. They are a significant component of important psychological theories such as Helson's adaptation-level theory (1964) or signal detection theory (Swets, 1964) where the influence of context on focal events is treated systematically. Such an approach is consistent with what is known about the way the nervous system works.

Only the briefest exposition of the ideas embedded in these theoretical approaches is possible here. On the sensory side, it appears that the brain registers all the stimulation impinging from the environment and from the musculature. At any point in time, of course, we are aware only of a tiny fraction of that stimulation, usually that portion which is of interest or which is focally attended. Thus the readers of these words are probably aware of these words and perhaps of the pages of the book, and maybe the comfort of the chair in which they are seated. They are probably not aware of the color of the walls of the room or of the way their clothing feels on their body or of the many sounds in their environment, yet their brain most likely has registered that information.

However, the ambient stimulation of which we are not aware affects what is perceived focally. Similarly, muscle tone will influence the execution of specific, phasic motor acts. The situation is further complicated because the brain not only pools the total of all current stimulation, but it also automatically takes into account the residue of prior experience stored in memory. Thus the tonic–phasic or focal–ambient distinction provides a specific example of unconscious processes influencing behavior.

Antagonism

General principles

Neurons are active, but there are two types of neuronal activity: excitation and inhibition. This information was presented earlier when the neuron was described. The discussion at this point will first be about the implications of having such an arrangement and particularly about the importance of inhibition. After all, all that is required for action to occur is that there be some form of excitation. Since there are significantly more inhibitory than excitatory neuron circuits, what purpose does inhibition serve? To begin with the conclusion, inhibition makes possible finely tuned control.

The point is actually quite obvious. Imagine an automobile without brakes on perfectly flat terrain with no other cars to dodge and no need for emergency braking. Figure the skill required to feed the engine just enough fuel (excitation) so that the car would run down and stop at the desired place. Such a skill could be learned, but it would take a long time and still be fraught with error. And of course it would be a skill useful in no real environment as we know it, where there are hills and stoplights and pedestrians and other traffic. Contrast this with the ease with which the car's position can be controlled if both inhibitory and excitatory capabilities are present, both gas pedal and brakes.

For ease of control, not only must excitation be tempered by inhibition, but both must be capable of graded release. Imagine what the ride would be like if the only alternatives were the full depression of the pedals controlling gas or brakes. The jolting, abrupt movements that would result would be extremely uncomfortable. So too in the nervous system. The fine control required for intricate behavior, e.g. sewing, handling a baby, or talking, is made possible by an exquisite balance between excitation and inhibition, where minute, highly controlled excitation can be released or suppressed as the demands of the situation require. The way in which this is accomplished by the nervous system is at least in part due to the complexities of neurotransmission, some details of which will be described next.

Neurotransmitters and neuromodulators

Before beginning it should be noted that a reasonably complete understanding of neurotransmission is not yet available. Knowledge increases exponentially year by year (e.g. see Cooper, Bloom, & Roth, 1996, the seventh edition in 26 years of a book that reviews detailed knowledge about neurotransmission). Furthermore, explanations of how the different components interact are revised frequently, in part because new components are still being discovered, and well-known components are found to function in different ways in different places. Originally, it was thought that there were only a few neurotransmitters and that a particular neuron operated via a single neurotransmitter. It is now known that there are upward of 100 transmitter substances, that a single neuron may release more than one transmitter substance, that the same transmitter may fit into different kinds of receptors on the postsynaptic neuron and that its effects will be determined by which receptor is activated.

For present purposes, some information will be presented about six of the best-known transmitter substances. They fall into two classes called neurotransmitters and neuromodulators. There is a third class called neurohormones and some understanding of what differentiates these classes will be useful. Oversimplifying, a neurotransmitter operates in a very brief time span (a millisecond or two, or less) at a particular synapse utilizing rapid and direct ionotropic transmission, and is either excitatory or inhibitory. Neuromodulators operate in fairly localized fashion but their distribution in the brain is not universal as is the case of the neurotransmitters. They appear in specific regions or in specific circuits and generally utilize metabotropic, second messenger system, transmission. Thus they operate somewhat more slowly and indirectly than neurotransmitters and, as their name implies, modulate, modify, or regulate neurotransmission possibly without actually providing the requisite primary excitation or inhibition. Nonetheless, it is known that they are important because specific neuromodulators appear to be malfunctioning in disorders such as schizophrenia and depression whose biology was a total enigma only a few decades ago. At the very least, drug treatments of these conditions based on hypotheses about transmitter functions have provided the greatest advances in the treatment of these conditions in recent years. The third category, neurohormones, released by neurons and by non-neuronal cells such as glands, exert their influence in the slowest manner of all. Whereas the site of action of transmitters and modulators is confined to the synapse into which they were released, hormones diffuse widely via blood or spinal fluid circulation, often at considerable distances from where they were released, and may influence many neurons.

The prime example of an excitatory neurotransmitter is the amino acid (a building block for proteins) glutamate and the prime example of an inhibitory transmitter is the amino acid gamma-aminobutyric acid generally known as GABA. These neurotransmitters are found all over the brain but there is very heavy representation of GABA neurons in the frontal lobe and cerebellum.

The first neurotransmitter to be discovered, acetylcholine, is the neurotransmitter at the neuromuscular junction, where it is the excitatory agent for muscle contraction. It is also an important transmitter in the chain of synapses regulating parasympathetic function in the autonomic nervous system. In the brain, however, it is mostly a neuromodulator and possibly even a neurohormone. This multiple manner of functioning for the same chemical substance is made possible by receptors for each type of operation. In the brain, it is important in circuits that regulate certain aspects of sleep, the perception of pain, and long-term memory. Depletion has been implicated in Alzheimer's disease, a degenerative disorder that produces mental impairment. A particularly rich source of cholinergic (acetylcholine-bearing) neurons is the nucleus basalis of Meynert, also known as the substantia innominata, located just above and slightly to the side of the optic chiasm in the general proximity of the hypothalamus.

The other neuromodulators to be mentioned here are part of a family of similar biochemicals called the monoamines. Two subgroups are distinguished: the catecholamines, which includes the neuromodulators noradrenaline and dopamine, and the indoleamines, with the neuromodulator serotonin. Important noradrenaline pathways are illustrated in figure 4.1. Note the location of the locus ceruleus, which is just under the upper part of the cerebellum, a particularly rich source of noradrenergic (noradrenaline-bearing) neurons, and note the widespread distribution of these pathways. Noradrenergic pathways have been implicated in such functions as short-term, phasic reactivity to novel stimuli and the orienting response, wakefullness, alertness, and attention to the external world. They are more heavily represented in the right as compared with the left hemisphere, and are also involved in the regulation of sleep. Excessive activity has been implicated in anxiety and panic disorders.

Dopamine pathways are illustrated in figure 4.2. Note that they do not project all over the brain but are confined to the brainstem, basal ganglia, limbic system and the prefrontal parts of the frontal lobes. An important source of dopamin-

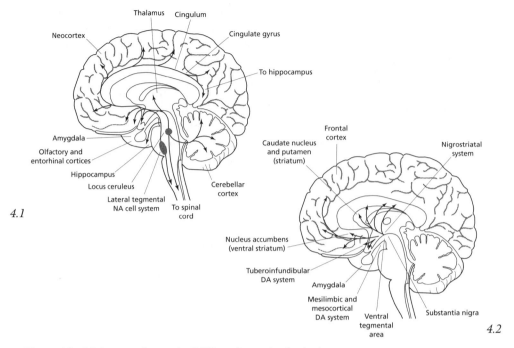

Figure 4.1   Major noradrenergic (NA) pathways in the brain
Figure 4.2   Major dopaminergic (DA) pathways in the brain

ergic neurons is the substantia nigra (black substance) which is a relatively thick layer of black-appearing neurons in the tegmentum of the midbrain beneath the superior colliculi (see figure 3.8). Dopaminergic circuits which are more strongly represented in the left as compared with the right hemisphere have been implicated in such functions as sustained attention and the maintenance of set controlled from within rather than by external events, control of emotion, feelings of optimism and pleasure, and the initiation and regulation of movement. Dopamine is known to be depleted in Parkinson's disease, a degenerative disease that first affects spontaneous movements and is thought to be excessive in the thinking disturbances found in schizophrenia.

Finally, serotonin pathways are illustrated in figure 4.3. Again, pathways extend all over the brain, but greater specificity is suggested by the presence of two types and many different receptors. A major source of serotonergic neurons are the string of raphe (meaning seam, the edge where two tissues are joined) nuclei which occur in or near the midline of the pons. Many of the cells in these nuclei fire spontaneously in pacemaker fashion. Much serotonergic activity is inhibitory but some is excitatory, depending on the type of neuron and receptor. Serotonin is associated with feelings of quiet alertness and well-being, and many drugs used to treat depression function by increasing available serotonin at the synapse.

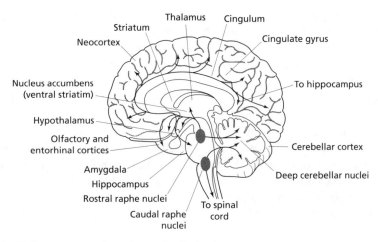

Figure 4.3   Major serotonergic pathways in the brain

Systematic Organization

The nervous system is a system. This obvious and redundant statement is a way of indicating that there are many separate components present, and that they are organized in their mode of operation. The form of the organization can be at least partially understood on the basis of certain principles which collectively are called systems theory (von Bertalanffy, 1968). The discussion of systems theory will begin with a consideration of relatively simpler closed systems which are present in many parts of the nervous system but can also be found in nonliving mechanical systems. Subsequently, open systems will be presented. This pertains to the nervous system in living organisms which, in some sense, organizes itself. This should become clearer as the discussion proceeds.

Closed systems

Comprehension of closed systems begins with the notion of a desirable set point, or norm, for the system. A simple example of a mechanism for creating a set point would be a thermostat in a home heating system with components such as a furnace, air blower, and ducts. The set point or norm refers to the desired temperature of the home, say 70 degrees Fahrenheit. The thermostat consists of a thermometer, moveable electronic contact points that can be set for the desired set point, and a system of wiring and switches that can ignite the furnace and initiate the fan or shut them both down.

   The common mercury thermometer provides analog information about the level of heat in the room. (Analog information makes use of observable events to provide information that is not readily observable. We could try to measure the heat in the room by asking people to rate how warm or how cold this is, but little agreement would be possible. Once it is known that a metal such as mercury expands as a function of its temperature, then thin columns encased in glass can be calibrated against known temperatures such as the boiling and freezing points of water. The expansion of the metal is then a precise analog of the temperature in the room. After calibration, the data can be reported in digital form, numbers.) If the day is cold the mercury will drop to a point where the contact will be made to the switch that turns the furnace and air blower on. Air will be warmed, blown through the ducts into the room, and gradually warm the room. Initially, the mercury will be below the set point, but as the room warms, the mercury in the thermometer will also warm and rise in its narrow column until it reaches the set point, whereupon the furnace and blower will shut off. With the passing of time, the temperature will then drop to a point below the set point, and the furnace will then come on again. All this is very familiar.

Feedback arrangements

What may not be familiar is that this arrangement involves negative feedback. Feedback is a term that refers to information about the state of a system which is in a form that the system can use. Negative feedback is information about deviation from the set point, so arranged (as in the thermostat) as to decrease, or negate (hence the term negative), the deviation from the set point. Negative feedback systems are designed for stability at the set point, arranged so that deviations from the set point will be brought back to that standard.

   Mechanical closed systems such as the thermostat and furnace demonstrate important properties of negative feedback systems that are of significance in understanding living systems and some of their pathologies. These properties are oscillation and phase lag, and both are inevitable in any negative feedback system. These properties are a consequence of the fact that feedback takes time to deliver, and that the mechanisms returning the system to stability take time to respond. Thus, when the set point temperature of 70 degrees is reached in the room, it may take a few minutes more before the mercury rises to the calibration for 70 degrees. The signal to shut down the furnace will actually be transmitted quite rapidly, but the air heated just before the furnace shuts down will continue to rise and thus tend to raise the temperature somewhat past the set point. Conversely, when the thermostat falls below the set point and the furnace is activated, it takes a few moments for the initial batch of air to heat up and start to rise, to warm the ducts, and to get into the room. In the interim, the temperature will fall lower before it starts to rise.

   Thus a set point does not represent utter stability but the point around which the function oscillates (goes back and forth). The actual temperature over the course of time shifts from being above to below the set point. Furthermore, the actual temperature in the room lags behind the mechanisms inducing change so that it takes a while after the furnace comes on before the room reaches the desired temperature. The magnitude of the oscillation and the duration of the lag determine just how stable the system actually is. A steam heat system, that may still be found in some older homes, may have more oscillation and a longer lag than a forced-air system.

The significance of this kind of analysis for understanding biological systems will be apparent to the reader if arms and fingers are held out in front, and an effort is made to keep them steady. In doing so, you are creating a motor set point. However, if observed very carefully, even the healthiest person will display some slight degree of tremor since all negative feedback systems oscillate in some degree. It will be noted that "stability" consists of rapid, tiny corrections of deviations from the set point. Difficulty in maintaining "stability" heightens oscillation due to inefficiency of the feedback loop. This could be because of slowness in registering the position of the limb, of transmitting the information, or of organizing and executing the corrective response. Disorders involving tremor or other types of oscillation can be considered as disorders of negative feedback.

Negative feedback operates to maintain a steady state; it generates stability. By contrast, positive feedback produces change. When positive feedback is operative, information about deviation from a set point is used to increase the deviation from the set point, hence the feedback is said to be positive. Intrinsically, a positive feedback condition is an unstable and dangerous state because, by itself, it leads to what is called a runaway. Since the feedback constantly increases the deviation from the set point, the system moves in one direction only.

Imagine the system controlling the beating of the heart operating on the basis of positive feedback alone during heart deceleration. If the set point were 70 beats per minute, and dropped to 66, the information about deviance would be used to amplify the deviation and the beat would then drop more. This process would continue until the heart stopped beating altogether. In the reverse case, acceleration, the rate of beating would speed up until it were going so fast that it would exceed its physiological capabilities. The whole system would crash.

One example of a positive feedback runaway in the physical world occurs when a public address system produces intensely discomfiting high-pitch screeches. What happens is that the sound being amplified out to the audience is picked up by the microphone and amplified again, and then this amplified sound is picked up and amplified again, and so on. All this takes place so rapidly that a sudden shriek is produced. The microphone and the loudspeaker have become linked in a positive feedback relationship in a state of runaway.

Something similar can occur biologically in the mechanisms controlling fear, if the person comes to fear the experience of fear itself. It would then happen that any experience that arouses fear would lead to more fear, and so on, until the person was in a state of helpless panic. Similarly, if the sensations of contracting muscles themselves become signals for further contraction, a runaway to muscle spasm occurs. The seizures of epilepsy can also be understood as a form of runaway. The concept is applicable to more complex behavior patterns. Runaway, e.g. in the form of excessive intake of alcohol, can be observed in some beginning college students who are living away from home for the first time and away from stabilizing negative feedback influences provided by parents.

Although positive feedback, by itself, is always dangerous because of the potentiality for runaway, it is absolutely necessary if the system is to be capable of changing its set points. Consider again the heart and its ability to control the flow of blood by fluctuating its rate of beating. If it were operative solely under negative feedback conditions, it would remain stable no matter what demands were being made on it. The heart beat would be the same while running a race, climbing stairs, or relaxing in bed. Clearly, in the real world, an organism must be able to invoke positive feedback mechanisms to respond to changes in circumstance. When the new set point is reached it must invoke negative feedback mechanisms to keep the new level stable as long as appropriate.

The meanings of the terms positive and negative feedback in systems theory, where they originated, have nothing to do with approval or disapproval or with good or bad. Such meanings are sometimes attributed to these terms. If it is said "A child needs positive feedback for their accomplishments in school," and what is meant is information about their success and rewarding praise as well, then such phraseology is a distortion of the meaning of the term in systems theory. It is probably impossible to eliminate this use of these terms, but the distinction in meanings should be clear, and the context should make it possible to avoid misunderstanding.

The term "feedback" implies that particular actions or phases of action are sensed and that they are regulated after the fact; that is, that the next action or next phase will be governed by how the prior event related to the set point and the positive or negative nature of the feedback. This implies that there must be sensing elements among response mechanisms. It turns out that this is true of the nervous system. Careful anatomical study has revealed that there are sensory afferents among motor efferent pathways. Consequently, a modification of the idea that sensory and motor functions are represented separately in the nervous system is required. The overall generalization still holds, but it must be understood in terms of predominance rather than absolutes. Design requirements for system control would preclude complete separation.

Feedback mechanisms control behavior if the behavior tempo is slow enough to allow time for the feedback mechanisms to operate. But what of the trill of the piano player, or for that matter, the speed with which a signature is written? And what about actions that willy-nilly have to be fast, like throwing a ball? It is not possible to throw a ball and also to slow the motion down enough to get any feedback and still propel the object.

It appears that, in addition to feedback mechanisms, the nervous system operates by means of feedforward mechanisms. These are mechanisms which anticipate, predict, and preset levels of reactivity for complex patterns of behavior and gauge effectiveness only after they have occurred. Feedback correction does not intervene during the behavioral sequence. Some of these feedforward mechanisms depend on experience and prior learning for their development. The examples of piano playing and handwriting are pertinent. The beginner operates slowly and laboriously, using negative feedback mechanisms to control behavior at every step. With repeated practice, skill and speed gradually increase. At some point control no longer depends on gauging some component action just accomplished and correcting whatever needs correcting, but on anticipation.

Other feedforward skills intrinsically do not allow a stage of learning based on negative feedback. This is true of throwing, for example. To be sure, the learning that takes place with feedforward mechanisms involves feedback after the act. The thrower observes the accuracy of the throw and decides whether they should throw harder, higher, or further next time. Such information comes, however, only after the act, and the feedback does not itself intervene during the course of the act of throwing. Special techniques such as filming an act and then showing it in slow motion are designed to introduce negative feedback into the sequence of activities, and this can be very helpful in speeding the development of complex feedforward skills. The fact remains, however, that superb levels of throwing and other feedforward skills appeared long before the invention of modern recording techniques. The reader will note that this description of feedforward mechanisms parallels the depiction in the previous chapter of some of the functions of the cerebellum.

Open systems

A heat-regulating system, which is a closed system, operates as designed. It has no way of renewing itself or adapting to changed circumstances such as infestation by fungal or bacterial agents and, of course, it does not design itself in the first place or grow itself to its adult stature. It also cannot learn as a result of its experience. Open systems engage in a constant interchange with the environment, an interchange which is not limited to information or energy but which includes an actual exchange of matter. Thus, for example, the proteins of the human body are turned over and exchanged about every 100 days (von Bertalanffy, 1968, p. 147).

The effect of the environment on the organism at a physical level can be seen in the way the height of individuals of Japanese descent has varied in recent decades. It is well known that height is determined by one's genetic inheritance. However, children of Japanese parents reared in North America have exceeded the height of their counterparts reared in Japan by two or more inches. Similarly, but at the level of mental processes, Cole et al. (1971) have shown the effect of schooling on the formal thinking qualities of illiterate African tribespeople. What appeared to be a constitutionally determined quality of thought turned out to be a consequence of a particular type of experience, lack of formal schooling.

The converse, in which comparable experiences nonetheless lead to different outcomes can be seen clearly in studies of the response to stress, where there are vast individual differences. For example, survival rates in elderly but healthy persons following attempts to move them from their residences because of urban renewal, is strongly related to whether they acquiesce or fight the dislocation, regardless of whether they move. The fighters survive the longest. Similarly, the effects of losing a loved one depend on the type and quality of the mourning response, just as the driving behaviors of one who has been in an automobile accident depend on how soon driving is resumed. These are examples of the consequences of coping technique, an aspect of executive functions and an issue that will be considered throughout the book.

The crucial difference between closed and open systems is that the former are arranged in a specific context while the latter arrange themselves as best they can in the context in which they find themselves; that is, they cope with their environment. This formulation draws attention to the active qualities of living systems and their interactive relationship with the environment. From the study of evolution, we learn that animal groups who adapt most successfully to their environments are the ones that survive. We also learn that, for most species, success in one environment means doom should the environment change. However, the course of evolution has been such that larger and larger areas of brain are dedicated to learning and thus to flexible adaptation in the face of environmental change. In humans this is evident in the vastly higher proportion of associative cortex as a percentage of total brain in comparison to that found in other animals. Such areas in humans in both the front and back of the brain consist of very large networks of cells with the potentiality for elaborate dendritic growth that occurs with experience. Such networks have been studied in computer simulations (Rumelhart & McClelland, 1986) and have the property of emergent organizations and of learning. Much of the organization of the brain networks responsible for coping and executive functions is developed by the third year of life (Elman et al., 1996, chapter 5).

A striking illustration of the possible impact of experience on the brain occurs in multiple personalities, a condition in which one person has a different personality at different times. Some scholars believe the condition does not exist because it is known to have been deliberately simulated for personal gain. There are, however, cases in which simulation does not appear to have occurred. Such persons have shown changes in aspects of function as their personality changed that, so far as is known, are not simulable. These have included the spectrum of sounds emitted in speech and brain wave patterns (Hughes et al., 1990). Such data imply different brain organizations for different personalities in the same brain. Available evidence indicates that multiple personality develops as a way of coping with very traumatic and difficult stresses such as sexual abuse in childhood. If continuing studies of such individuals verify that the same brain is capable of multiple organizations, then the range of coping possible in the human brain is impressive indeed.

Emphasis on open systems and coping contrasts with the view that our particular genetic makeup or one or another handicaps imposes constraints or limitations on possible adaptability. When such views are held by persons in power, whether in the role of parent, professional, educator, or government administrator, the potentiality for coping may be undermined, not by limits of brain adaptability, but by assumptions about limitations. A colleague of the writer, Dr Michael Zeiler, once toilet trained an entire ward of children with mental retardation in a few days, mostly by unlocking the door to the toilets. Someone had assumed that because the children were retarded they could never be toilet trained, so there was no point to allowing them access to the necessary facilities.

One final point about systems. The nature of a system has properties of its own beyond that of its individual components. Furthermore, because several components contribute to the operations of a system, it is often difficult knowing exactly how one system interacts with another. The kinds of linear analysis which prove so useful in mechanics, where for example one can calculate the effects of A (like an added weight) on B (the speed with which an object moves) may not apply. Thus for example, we know that drugs that increase the amount of serotonin in the synapse by blocking reuptake aid some people with depression. The idea that it is the amount of serotonin in the synapse that reflects the level of depression is almost assuredly not valid. The locus of the drug's efficacy for depression may be somewhere downstream or upstream in the system of which those particular synapses are a part.

Corollary Discharge

Although sensory and motor functions are largely represented separately in the brain – motor in the frontal lobes, and sensory in parietal, occipital, and temporal lobes – their separation, as previously mentioned, is not complete. Motor activity is tracked by information processing mechanisms for feedback purposes and muscles are used to orient the organism as a whole, and the sense organs in particular, to information of interest. For example, the eyes may move to a particular point in space in order to see what is there more clearly. Similarly, when action is taken, sensory information is produced which allows you to know that you have moved. A moving body or limb will generate somatosensory information in muscles, joints, and skin, but most of that information will be the same whether the arm has moved actively or been moved passively. The ability to discriminate whether you have initiated the movement or whether it was imposed on you is due to a corollary discharge, a signal which is part of the motor initiation process that informs the brain that the action is about to occur. Such signals are present in active movement and absent in passive movement.

The presence of this mechanism is very important. If you move your eyes voluntarily, the scene observed appears static and one has the sense of scanning what is out there, which, of course, is what has actually occurred. If your eye is moved by pushing the eyeball, the scene itself appears to move, which, of course, is not true. The explanation for the difference is that the pushed eye has not produced the corollary discharge which informs the brain of the intention to move, whereas such discharge has occurred when the eye is moved deliberately. Here then is another kind of feedforward mechanism which permits a person to differentiate what it is doing from what is being done to it. When the corollary discharge mechanism goes awry, one's own thoughts and fantasies (a type of action) may be attributed to others, which is a form of delusion (Frith & Done, 1988).

Hierarchical Organization

The similarities among, and the differences between, the brains of the various species and the human brain at various stages in the course of development have been discussed earlier. It is apparent that adult humans and animals and human babies share many similar capabilities, but it is also obvious that they differ in what they can do. As mentioned earlier, grasshoppers, human babies, and adults all habituate, but only humans past a certain age can read. These differences are encapsulated by the term hierarchy, which also implies an evolutionary perspective about the development of nervous system and behavioral capability. A hierarchical perspective views the accrual of capability, whether in the individual or across species, as having the form of supersession rather than elimination. That is to say, it appears that, as new skills are added, old patterns of behavior are integrated with the new, or are inhibited, but they are not lost from neurological representation. Some of the evidence for this perspective is that older or more primitive forms of behavior emerge when more recent or sophisticated capabilities are damaged or destroyed. For example, most of the symptoms of cerebral palsy will be explained in this way.

The hierarchical perspective suggests that, in the intact organism, both lower and higher capabilities are operative, for example habituation and reading, but that higher capabilities dominate. Some particular behaviors may be controlled either bottom-up or top-down hierarchically. Eye movements are such an example. If we are not looking for anything in particular, the eyes automatically respond to novel movements that appear on the visual scene. This is controlled bottom-up by rather primitive mechanisms, shared with animals throughout the phylogenetic scale, which keep track of possible dangers. On the other hand, eye movements may be governed top-down by high-level issues such as the search for a particular mushroom, or a face in a crowd, or for a contact lens.

Should damage occur which destroys higher capabilities, then lower patterns of function will emerge. When lower functions are impaired but higher functions are intact, the consequences which follow are less well understood. Since they are disassociable, it might seem that the higher would show no effects of the lower impairment. However it appears that this is not entirely the case. Higher functions suffer unpredictably when lower functions are impaired. This possibility will be relevant to an analysis of a number of conditions including some motor disorders and disorders of arousal and psychosis.

Hierarchical analysis is a very important tool in considering the neuropsychology of any behavioral condition, and a failure to understand hierarchical relationships can lead to serious errors of diagnosis and treatment. Only one example will be presented at this point as this issue will recur in later parts of this book. The example concerns common confusions between learning disability and attention disorders. Neuropsychologically, a learning disorder due, for example, to a language handicap which impairs the rate of learning to read, is hierarchically high, while an attention problem such as might be caused by impaired habituation, would be hierarchically low. Nevertheless, the two conditions can lead to very similar, if not identical, symptoms.

A child with a language handicap may easily become bored, frustrated, distractible, and inattentive in class. Since the language handicap may be relatively invisible and unappreciated, while the attention symptoms may be very conspicuous, the child may soon get diagnosed and treated for an attention disorder when it is a secondary complication and not the fundamental problem. By contrast, a child with an habituation problem may show no progress in learning to read because attention cannot be focussed on the learning materials, even though there is no difficulty in absorbing what there is to learn. If for some reason the learning difficulty was noticed first, the child might never receive treatment or understanding for what was really wrong, but instead might be subject to laborious and unnecessary special education procedures.

Understanding of hierarchical relationships has immense potential for the development of rational and effective treatment interventions. Note again a theme that has been presented before, namely that the symptoms or most conspicuous overt behaviors do not necessarily reveal the locus or the mechanism of the impairment causing the problem. The source of a problem may reside in hierarchically low, primitive functions which operate nondeliberately and are not accessible to consciousness or to subjective report. Hierarchical conceptions in neuropsychology provide a framework for understanding these complex and elusive operations.

Types of Impairment

Impairment of nervous system function occurs in two ways (Freides, 1976). The most commonly understood and universally recognized impairment condition is subtractive in nature and is often termed deficit. The word subtractive can be taken literally. It is meant to convey the idea that cells and tissues that should be present and functioning have been destroyed or rendered nonfunctional. Such would be the case if a missile penetrated the back of the skull and tore off much of the occipital lobe leaving the person cortically blind. It is the type of impairment found in most forms of mental retardation and cerebral palsy and some forms of learning disability. The other type of impairment condition, dyscontrol or disorganization, is well recognized in a disorder such as epilepsy, where competence is maintained despite episodic disruption, but may often be the mechanism of impairment in a wider range of disorders such as the psychoses. This will be elaborated as the book progresses. For the present, just imagine a condition that disrupts the functioning of the nervous system but may stop spontaneously or be arrested by treatment, leaving the organism intact and without impairment. When the mechanism of impairment is a deficit, the subject, by definition, is not intact. When the mechanism of impairment is dyscontrol, the behavior of the subject is deficient as long as the dyscontrol persists, but if the dyscontrol stops, the subject proves to be intact. It is often difficult to determine whether observable symptoms are due to one or the other type of impairment even though such knowledge may make possible more rational forms of treatment. Again, note that the concepts of deficit and dyscontrol presented here refer to mechanisms of impairment and not necessarily to overt behavior. Overt behavior may be equally and comparably impaired as a result of either underlying condition.

5

How the Brain Functions

Available knowledge as to how the brain functions is very incomplete. Although there are many known facts and observations, and much information about the details of brain function, understanding how brain activity gives rise to action, thought, feeling, creativity, and the like, is a long way off. A number of scientists scoff at the prospect of ever bridging the gap between mind and brain and thus perpetuate mind–body dualism and the schism between psychology and biology. The perspective taken here assumes that mind is a product of body, although it is clear that our understanding of mind far exceeds our understanding of how body generates mind. Such a statement does not devalue either the study of mind or of body in their own domains. But progress in one domain can inform inquiry in the other and useful hypotheses can be formulated that relate psychology to neuroscience. Indeed, such is the general underlying premise of the whole field of neuropsychology. Given such a fundamental assumption, one must still choose among several competing approaches to understanding such relationships. That is, an informed guess must be made as to which of the currently available theoretical orientations seem the most promising.

The history of the study of mind–body or brain–behavior relationships has polarized between those who have emphasized local functions and those who have emphasized the brain functioning as a whole. The former group views the brain as a network of different information processing organs, or in recently popular terminology, modules, each responsible for a relatively specific function. This view has been discredited in part because of its origins in phrenology, a scheme promulgated in the sixteenth and seventeenth centuries, in which bumps on the head were supposed to be indices of psychological capabilities. The opposing point of view, the so-called mass action hypothesis, emphasizes the functioning of the entire brain. It is based on data which indicate that impairment of function is more related to the overall proportion of abnormal to normal tissue than to the integrity of specific parts.

At present, this historical controversy is more apparent in textbooks than in either clinical practice or scientific research. Certainly, neuropsychologists spend a great deal of their time operating within a localist perspective; that is, they are very interested in the selective competencies associated with specific brain areas, and the consequences of localized lesions. The approach in this book, in which the consequences of more selective disorders such as cerebral palsy or blindness will be used to understand more complex disorders such as learning disabilities or psychosis, is within that tradition. Nonetheless, there are a number of brain systems whose effects occur widely, and mass action cannot be entirely disregarded.

The perspective on brain function taken in this book is strongly influenced by the work of the late Russian neuropsychologist, Aleksandr Romanovich Luria. Luria (1973) evolved his approach as a result of studying patients who sustained head wounds during World War II. His approach thus concerns the mature brain, and it will therefore be necessary to incorporate data and ideas from research on the immature and developing brain in order to deal with the subject matter of this book. The remainder of this section contains a scheme for thinking about brain functioning which is indebted to Luria, but which will be modified as necessary.

General Principles

A main contribution of Luria to theory about brain–behavior relations was the recognition that no psychological or behavioral function was localized in a particular area of brain. That is, a psychological function such as thought, or perception, or motor control was itself a highly complex organization of activities which relied on contributions from different areas of brain. The component processes themselves were relatively localized. In this manner, Luria provided a framework for integrating mass-action and localist orientations.

Luria also emphasized that each component process was organized hierarchically, thus further complicating the basic principles of analysis. Each component had a primary, secondary, and tertiary zone which represented separate and disassociable levels of complexity. These concepts will be explained more fully below.

One consequence of Luria's mode of analysis is to recognize that the same psychological impairment in different individuals may be due to rather different causes. Conversely, an impairment in a particular area of brain in different individuals may result in different symptoms depending on the overall organization of that brain. Despite the recognition of such complexity, Luria's scheme actually provides a simplified framework with which to approach any normal function or deficit in behavior. He suggested but three units of analysis and only one more is added here.

The Principal Functional Units

The unit for regulating tone and waking and mental states

Luria distinguished between three functional units. The term for the first is translated from the Russian as the unit for regulating tone and waking and mental states. It is a unit composed of those structures which are involved in both control of the sleep–wake cycle and of the variations in selective and general arousal that occur during waking states. Arousal refers to the readiness of a neural system for activity. The reticular formation in the lower portions of the brainstem and the nonspecific nuclei in the thalamus are the major structures involved, but they ramify and send processes to every part of the brain.

The different components regulating tone can be divided into those that follow their own rhythm or are involved in regulating internal states and those that are responsive to external events. Among those operating on internal states, the most general in its effect is that which controls sleep and awakening. More selective arousal occurs in conjunction with mechanisms that regulate biological needs such as food, water, and sex, the so-called drives or primary motives. These arousal mechanisms both follow their own rhythms and are reactive to external events. For example, interest in food fluctuates in a cycle that is related to the process of digestion, so that some time after the last meal one finds one's interest rekindled. Interest in food can also be stimulated by external events even if a person is relatively satiated, for example, when an individual walks past a bakery exuding the aroma of freshly baked bread or pastry.

Another reaction to external events which regulates tone is the orienting reaction, which has now been mentioned several times. It will be recalled that the orienting reaction is the response to novelty which leads to heightened interest in the environment and/or increased readiness to flee. If the environment proves to be noxious or threatening, self-preservative flight or fight (aggressive behavior) reactions will occur. Threats are not the only source of intense arousal. High-level mindsets about the environment's potentialities can also have strong arousing influences. There are people who are driven by their inner mental organizations, whether to plan a business, sell insurance or real estate, cure a patient, or resolve a scientific dilemma, who will be alert to events with any semblance of applicability to their preoccupations. Thus the insurance agent may try to make a sale at a party after hearing a chance remark, and an Isaac Newton can formulate a theory of gravity after being hit on the head by a falling apple while sitting under a tree in a revery.

It should be clear from the above discussion that Luria's unit for regulating tone and waking and mental states refers to mechanisms that control levels of consciousness and the deployment of attention. Recent research has illuminated the relationship between brain function and attention, and in doing so has helped resolve the mass action–specificity controversy. It appears that at times of new learning, when intense concentration and attention are required, almost the whole brain is involved no matter what the particular type of learning may be. As learning is mastered, and the skill or information processing becomes automatic, only more selected areas of brain are activated. At those times the brain is functioning more in accord with a localist hypothesis.

There is a limit as to how much information can be processed at a time. If this limit is exceeded, and an overload occurs, the system breaks down, and attentional mechanisms themselves are disrupted. The limits of processing capacity may be exceeded either because the information load is excessive or because there is a defect in processing capability. At present there is no way to measure processing capacity directly. What can be done is to study samples of normal individuals operating under specific information loads and establish norms with known levels of variability and fluctuation. This is the basic methodology of most psychological tests.

When evaluating disorders of attention, it is important to determine whether pro-cessing capacity is intact, whether attentional mechanisms are intact, or whether there is excessive overload of information and fatigue. When air-traffic controllers become inattentive and distractible, it is almost entirely certain that the problem is due to overload and fatigue since they were selected in advance with known processing capacity and attentional skill. In the case of inattentive school children, it is gener-ally not known which of the three possibilities is operative, but rational treatment will depend on an accurate analysis of the actual problem.

Hierarchical relationships in the unit for regulating tone are clearly present but their designation as primary, secondary, or tertiary (see chapter 3 discussion of cortex) is not as clear as such designations will be in Luria's other units. Arousal differenti-ating sleep and wake states is regulated in the brainstem reticular formation and must be considered primary. Arousal consequent to enduring high-level preoccupations, like thought and ideas, must be cortical in origin and tertiary in nature. This leaves as hierarchically intermediate both those systems responsive to internal regulations, the drive-related arousal mechanisms, such as sexual excitement, and those reactive to external novelty and threat, e.g. fear. Indeed, both involve anatomically interme-diate limbic and hypothalamic structures.

The unit for receiving, analyzing, and storing information

In the Luria scheme, the unit for regulating tone just discussed provides the energy and some direction for mental activity. The unit under discussion here is the actual operative mechanism for information processing. The general idea, found in Luria and throughout the scientific literature on brain function, is that the nervous system processes information by decomposing it into neuronally represented features, reg-isters and stores it sometimes for short and sometimes for long periods, and then reconstitutes it as needed to contribute to perception, thought, and action. All this is in the service of adaptation to a changing environment. Some of the material to follow has been encountered earlier, in chapter 3, but merits repetition in the present context.

The unit for receiving, analyzing, and storing information is divided into compo-nents whose demarcations are fairly clear. The scheme of classification begins with the separate sources of information, the sensory modalities. It will be recalled that each sensory modality projects specifically to an area of cortex; somatosensory to the front of the parietal lobe, auditory to the inner top surface of the temporal lobe, and visual to the rearmost portions of the occipital lobe. These are the primary zones of the unit. Most cells in each primary zone respond to information only in its own specific modality.

Some of the mechanisms by which the information contained in external stimu-lation is coded in the nervous system are known. It appears that there are cells within each zone which respond selectively to specific features in the information array. This has been worked out best in the visual system where evidence has been found that certain neurons and interlinked channels of neurons in the occipital lobe and elsewhere respond selectively to particular components of visual information, for example orientation and color. More detailed discussion of the operative mode of the visual system and comparable findings in other modalities will be found in later chapters.

A further idea of the nature of the information to be found in primary zones can be obtained by noting what is experienced when these zones are selectively stimulated during brain surgery or when such stimulation occurs spontaneously in partial epileptic seizures. The individual is likely to have modality-specific, simple sensory experiences such as flashes of light, particular sounds or noises, or a sensation of being touched or tickled, depending on what area of brain is being stimulated.

The secondary zones surround each of the primary zones. Whereas the cells of the primary zones tend not to send axons toward each other, the cells of the secondary zones are richly interconnected. Such interconnection permits greater complexity of information processing and greater potential for functional relevance or meaning. For example, a person might see a visual image rather than a flash of light, hear melodies or identifiable noises rather than meaningless sounds, or experience the texture, shape, and weight of a furry animal rather than just plain pressure or light touch.

Finally, the tertiary areas of the unit lie in the cortex between the primary and secondary areas. Here the modal specificity of the primary and secondary zones gives way to multi-modality. These zones are also association areas because specific modal information is combined, associated, and synthesized. Stimulation of these zones is associated with experiences which are much like ordinary experience. There are objects, locations, and events, and the various sensory modalities are experienced simultaneously, not separately.

It was initially thought that there were direct connections from primary to secondary to tertiary areas and that this chain of way-stations was the pathway through which information proceeded in the course of its processing. This notion is not in accord with the facts, the most noteworthy of which is that there are few if any direct connections between primary and secondary areas. Instead, available evidence indicates that cortical axons project downward to subcortical areas. Hence, information must flow downward before returning to other cortical areas. Furthermore, the primary, secondary, and tertiary areas are not activated in sequence, but essentially in parallel. That is, the differing areas appear to be activated simultaneously or nearly so. As indicated earlier the full picture of how this operates is by no means worked out.

On the other hand, we now know that the brain processes information about objects (shapes, configurations) separately from information about the location of objects. This disassociation is subjectively surprising to most people because it is difficult to comprehend how the two kinds of information can be separated. Nonetheless the evidence has become increasingly clear that such is the case. Part of the functional significance of the downward projection of cortically processed information may be to keep together these two aspects of information so that they are retained as event information and not as discrete objects or discrete locations.

Another aspect of this unit is lateral differentiation (Springer & Deutsch, 1985). In the human, the left and right hemispheres of the brain, while sharing many similarities, are not fully symmetric in structure and are often different in function. Considerable research effort has gone into understanding these differences because they seem related to the most complex information processing capabilities found in people. Much of the original understanding of these differences derived from observations that injury to the left hemisphere commonly results in disorders of language, while comparable injury to the right does not. From these and related data, the inference was drawn that the left hemisphere regulates and controls language. Furthermore, the left hemisphere also controls the right hand which is used preferentially for writing and other activities by most people so it came to be considered the dominant hemisphere. With little known about the functions of the right hemisphere, some authors actually thought it must be mostly useless. However, later work showed that the right hemisphere is specially proficient in visual spatial functions and that it also has a special role in the regulation of arousal. The right hemisphere then attained "equality" with the left and in some writings was considered to be dominant for non-verbal functions.

Later work gave rise to the idea that the left hemisphere is organized along modular lines while the right hemisphere is organized for mass action. Some of the evidence for this conclusion came from studies of soldiers who had endured penetrating wounds of the brain which often create fairly circumscribed lesions (Semmes et al., 1960). It was found that left hemisphere wounds led to impairments that depended on where in particular the wound happened to be, and that different places within the hemisphere led to different consequences. On the other hand, right hemisphere wounds had consequences which depended on the amount of tissue destroyed, irrespective, within limits, of where in the hemisphere the destruction had taken place. Such findings were also consistent with the idea that the right hemisphere has a special role in the regulation of basic arousal since a modular organization would not suit a general function such as arousal.

What are the psychological consequences of these different kinds of organization? There have been many attempts to formulate these differences in a way that is more general than the verbal–non-verbal distinction. One important concept is that the right brain operates in a holistic manner whereas the left functions analytically. The right captures overall patterns whereas the left breaks down complex patterns into their component parts. Confirmatory evidence was found when it was noted that patients who lose speech because of left hemisphere damage often can continue to sing whereas those who suffer right hemisphere damage continue to speak but lose their singing ability. It seems plausible that, for most people, singing and music generally involve getting the overall sense of the melody and the rhythm, a holistic type of information processing, while language is more precise and analytic. Confirmation of this idea came in a study (Bever & Chiarello, 1974) which verified that most people process music on the right, but also found that professional musicians do so on the left. When professionals listen to music, they can identify the key, the nature of the chord modulations, and how the music is put together. In other words, with professional training, music is analyzed, and that is accomplished in the left hemisphere.

This finding about a difference in brain organization between amateurs and professionals raises an interesting question. Since no one begins life as a professional, is training accompanied by a shift in dominance from right to left? The answer as we know it today is complex. For example, language appears to rely on inherited left hemisphere capabilities from the beginning. Nevertheless, Goldberg and Costa (1981) suggest that the right hemisphere is particularly adept at dealing with new information and is relied upon in the learning of any new task or knowledge, whereas the left makes use of old knowledge and previously developed skills. The right hemisphere is adapted to responding to previously unknown information and it responds by developing a neural model of what is being experienced. This idea is very much akin to Sokolov's notion of an orienting response to Piaget's idea about accommodation. Once the neural model is developed it is gradually transferred to the left hemisphere. The principle may not be applicable to learning the mechanics of language, but does appear relevant to the meanings and knowledge which language represents.

There is much more that can be presented about hemispheric differences, a complex and fascinating topic, and more is found in later chapters on pathology. At this point, Luria's second unit can be summarized by noting that it deals with back-of-the-brain sensory and perceptual functions and stored knowledge. Not only are there different sensory modalities through which information is obtained but also different types of information. Both hemispheres process all sensory modalities but the right hemisphere appears to be better able to process holistic, simultaneous, visual–spatial and new information whereas the left is superior in dealing with language, familiar routines, successive and analytic information. These ideas may not be separate and distinct. New information is necessarily holistic whereas analysis requires previous knowledge.

The unit for programming, regulation, and verification of activity

Whereas the second unit is located in the back of the cortex, the third is in the front. Its primary area is the motor cortex located in the precentral gyrus just in front of the central sulcus. It is the final pathway for the control of distinct muscle groups and possesses the same degree of specificity that the primary sensory zones have in representing particular areas and modalities of stimulation.

A muscle contraction is not by itself an adaptive pattern of action. It is the role of the secondary zone, in the premotor cortex, to organize these isolated muscle contractions into patterns of action useful in the real world. Luria uses the term kinetic (meaning movement) melody, to describe this quality of organization. Thus when one reaches for a door knob, one does not invoke actions from specific muscles, but rather an action pattern. To be sure, when a door knob is first encountered, some degree of specific muscle activation must occur as one learns what it takes to open the door. It is unlikely that most of us can remember our initial encounter with door knobs but we often can remember what it was like when learning to ride a bike or drive a car. We can also probably remember the change from deliberateness and awk-wardness to effortless, and almost unthinking (kinetically melodious) skill as learn-ing progressed.

The most advanced part of the third unit resides in the frontmost parts of the brain, the prefrontal cortex. Two major subdivisions of this area can be distinguished. The upper and lateral portions in the forward parts of the frontal cortex, portions that are visible in representations of the side view of the brain, are involved in higher-order control over kinetic patterns. An example of higher-order control can be found in the actions required to drive a car. There are separate kinetic melodies for turning on the ignition and pressing the accelerator, shifting gears, steering, and braking. In order to drive one has to execute these melodies in proper order, remembering what has already been accomplished and what has yet to be done. Earlier, this was described as working memory. Furthermore, one generally has to drive to a particular place, for some particular purpose. The overriding goal of getting some place and the series of steps that must be ordered in sequence to accomplish that goal are functions of these parts of the frontal cortex. Lesions here are associated with sequencing diffi-culties and with susceptibility to distractions which can interfere with the pursuit of any goal.

Sequencing a series of steps to attain a goal requires inhibition of the orienting reflex or else the sequence will be disrupted by orientation to the many interesting and distracting stimuli that exist in the environment. Consequently when the frontal lobes assume control of the direction of behavior, the orienting reflex is inhibited. Impaired frontal lobes allow disinhibition of orienting activity, and then sequential goal-directed behavior is easily disrupted.

This was demonstrated in early experiments on monkeys in a procedure called delayed reinforcement. One of several closed containers is openly baited in front of the subject and then a screen is lowered which delays access to the reward for a period of time. Normal monkeys, but not those with frontal lesions, were found to be able to remember which box was baited even after substantial delays. It was originally thought that the lesions produced a memory impairment, but then it was discovered that if the delay occurred in the dark, the lesioned monkeys did as well as the others. It became clear that the effect of the frontal lobe lesions was to make the subject vul-nerable to distraction. In the dark there was nothing much to be distracted by, so performance was not disrupted.

In general, frontal lobe impairments are associated with disinhibition of many sorts. Since the frontal parts of the cortex are myelinated only gradually through the course of childhood, babies and young children essentially lack functional frontal lobes. Sure enough, babies are generally not very goal-directed, are easily distracted, and generally uninhibited.

The other major subdivision of the prefrontal cortex is in the medial and basal portions of the lobe, those seen in medial views of the brain. These areas regulate and control what are probably the highest human capabilities, including many aspects of conscious activity, of planning and organization, of expectancy, and of judgment. They are particularly important for checking on one's responses, as to their adequacy, accuracy, appropriateness, and accord with the social and physical circumstances prevailing at the time. Such internalized feedback systems determine whether the person continues the behavior, searching for a more adequate solution or a more gratifying goal, or is content to turn off the sequence at any particular point. Inadequate behavior very often is a result of the failure to monitor behavior in accord with goal-determined standards and acceptable social restraints. Precisely such inadequacies characterize both individuals with certain frontal lobe deficits as well as those with mental retardation.

Putting it all Together

Any act or sequence of behavior depends on the integrity of each of the three functional units. Damage to any one will interfere with the adequacy of any behavior but in distinctive ways. The challenge to those working with persons with handicap is to be able to sort out and specify the locus and mechanism of impairment. To do so requires some way of signifying the individuality of the person, and to this end, a fourth unit is specified. No such unit appears in Luria's work.

This unit is called that which integrates the self in its environment. It is a unit which combines information about external space with that of body position so that persons may have a clear and comfortable sense of their own boundaries and of the boundaries of their environment. The major "organs" of this unit which are widely separated but closely interconnected in the brain are the vestibular system, oculomotor system, the cerebellum, and the somatosensory system, particularly its proprioceptive aspects. Whatever the locus of the corollary discharge (see chapter 5), those mechanisms which inform the brain as to whether it initiated its own activity, also belong here. These mechanisms probably originate in basal ganglia.

The vestibular system is a sense organ located near the inner ear, embedded in the temporal bone. It is a gyroscope-looking structure consisting of three semicircular canals and two spheroid-looking structures, the saccule and the utricle (see figure 5.1). Each of these structures is filled with fluid in which hair cells are suspended. As the head changes position because the body moves, or because it is tilted to one side or the other, the fluid inside the organ moves and, as it does, it causes the hair cells to bend. The positions of the different parts of the vestibular system register motion (strictly speaking the initiation or stopping, acceleration or deceleration) in any plane of movement. This sense organ provides a continuous stream of information to the brain about the motion of the body and the head, and provides data as to the locus of the body in space.

Further information about body position comes from the proprioceptors, a network of nerve endings present in the joints and muscle tendons which provide a continuous flow of information about the position of the trunk, neck, and limbs. Skin sensors sensitive to pressure and texture provide information about the immediate environment, i.e. what may be in contact with the skin.

Very similar and often redundant information is provided by the eyes via a system of sensors which register the position of the eyes as they move in response to changes in the real world. Eye movements (oculomotor) also register information about the

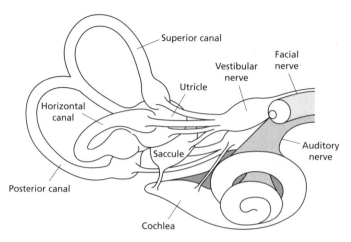

Figure 5.1   The vestibular system

body's position in space, and can serve to compensate for impairments of vestibular function. Discrepancies between vestibular and visual information about the position of the body in space, which occur when the eyes do not observe the events which alter the body's position – for example, if you are a child seated in the back seat of a car and too small to see out the window during a prolonged drive – can provoke nausea (Howard & Templeton, 1966). A rhythmic jerking of the eyes, called nystagmus, normally follows vestibular stimulation. Such jerking can be induced by rotating the body (postrotatory nystagmus), and it can also be induced when the body is static if the vestibular organ is artificially heated or cooled, for example, by pouring cold water into an ear. Vestibular and oculomotor mechanisms are so closely linked that eye movements can reveal the integrity of vestibular function.

The cerebellum is involved in the integration of complex motor movements. That is, the cerebellum is required for the execution of those kinetic melodies whose organization are part of our hereditary endowment. These would include such complex acts as the gaits of walking and running, reaching, and simple manipulation behaviors. Cerebellar participation also occurs in those learned kinetic melodies such as sewing or piano playing which involve the frontal lobes. Recently, evidence has accrued that the cerebellum is also involved in high-level cognitive functions so that its integrative role most likely extends beyond the organization of action patterns.

There is overlap between the fourth unit and all the others since, as just mentioned, both informational analysis and regulation of activity are involved. Regulation of arousal is also affected by this system. Instability of balance and insecurity about one's position in space are sources of intense, distressing anxiety and discomfort which preclude attention to outside events. On the other hand, vestibular stimulation – that is, the stimulation initiated consequent to either active or passive movement – has a quieting but alerting effect on nervous system tone. This effect is known to mothers of infants whose most effective means for calming them when crying is to pick them up and rock them (Korner & Thoman, 1972). It is also known to recreational dancers, gymnasts, and athletes of all kinds.

The term "self" is used in describing the present unit. This is a concept that has widespread utility in psychology, especially in the area of personality. Definitions of self often involve culturally (I am an American) and experientially (my family was very poor when I was growing up) determined contributions. The core of the self, however, has neuropsychological foundations which are found in all people as a consequence of the activity of the present unit. Specifically, self or personal identity has as its core the body image, a neural representation of the shape and functional characteristics of the body which is acquired as a result of the operations of this unit. The reality of such a neuropsychological entity is supported by data on individuals who, after enduring amputations, later experience sensations in locations which are no longer part of their bodies, so-called phantom limbs. Such localization of sensation is consistent with a prior intact body image.

The body image becomes a frame of reference for the integration of all experience. For example, space is not experienced in absolute terms of north, south, east, or west, but as a function of being above, below, to the right, or left of one's own body. In ways not entirely understood, the normal operation of the vestibular, cerebellar, somatosensory, and oculomotor systems, with their contribution to the construction of a body image, appears to play a crucial role in integrating information processing and learning of all kinds. Activation of this system may facilitate the operation of otherwise impaired systems. For example, a speech-impaired child may benefit more from a speech therapy session if it is preceded by movement and by vestibular stimulation or by massage, perhaps because attentional focussing is increased. On the other hand, impairment of this unit may be a general source of disturbance burdening other information processing systems. It is of interest that vestibular, somatosensory, and oculomotor impairments have repeatedly been found in schizophrenia (Freides, 1976).

The self is not only an emergent which derives from the activity of the units of which it is composed, but becomes an organizing force as well. Many persons search for and often find ways to deal with stress or maladaptive responses they are inclined to make. Psychotherapists regularly enlist the self of the client to help bring aberrant subsystems causing distress under control. Such behaviors are included in the category of self-regulation which may well be the hallmark of psychological normality. Almost inevitably, self-regulation includes the management of such mundane matters as diet, sleep, exercise, and some balance between work and recreation.

6

Constitutional Vulnerabilities during Development

This chapter will draw on the material already presented but focus on different stages of development. The important message is that events that affect the nervous system vary in their impact as a function of the stage of development in which they occur. They do so directly because the organism's level of development affects its vulnerability, and indirectly by interfering with development that would be taking place had the event not occurred.

Developmental Aspects of Constitutional Integrity

Terminology about nature and nurture

When discussing the meanings of the terms organic and emotional disorder in the first chapter, the concepts of nature and nurture were introduced. In this section, the meanings of terms used to designate various aspects of the nature side of things will be considered and put into developmental perspective, although it will prove impossible to disregard nurture. The next chapter will give more emphasis to nurture.

To begin, note that the terms organic and constitutional, and their related parts of speech, are largely interchangeable and synonymous, referring, in a general way, to the physical characteristics of the body. "Organic" perhaps has a slightly broader set of connotations since "constitution" more specifically refers to the architecture and physical structure of the tissues rather than to their physical mode of functioning. However, the nuance in meaning is ordinarily not very important.

What is important is the distinction between the term "genetic" and either the term "constitutional" or "organic," since many equate the latter with the former and this is not the case. Genetic characteristics are part of one's organic or constitutional makeup, but only part. Genetic makeup is determined at the moment of conception, and might best be thought of as a plan, in the same way that an engineering drawing is like a plan. The plan specifies the design of what is to be built and anticipates a good deal of the way it is to function. There are, of course, faulty plans and many disorders are due to genetic errors. However, there are many constitutional disorders that are not genetic. A plan, by itself, does not control the quality of construction.

For example, the design of an automobile may be superb, but the materials for the parts may be shoddy, the timing on the assembly line may be erratic, and the workmanship may be poor. The result may be a real "lemon" through no fault of the design. Flaws in construction may be fundamental to the ultimate quality of the vehicle, for example, if there is a poor weld in the frame or a hairline crack in the motor block. On the other hand, the problem may be relatively minor, like small leaks in the windshield mounting. Furthermore, the car may be "born" in fine shape but then receive poor maintenance or be in an accident, either of which will affect its constitution but not its original design. The constitution of the car is much influenced by its nurture at every stage of its existence.

The human situation is even more complex. The full development of the human occurs both in the womb and after birth and takes as long as 15 years. The genes specify the potential outcome and also organize the construction machinery that executes the design. Like the automobile, the constitution is influenced by the nurture it receives from the environment. Thus a child may have genes for fine teeth and good musical ability but if the diet lacks calcium, or the child has no access to musical instruments or training, it is unlikely that these potentialities will be realized. Actually, from the moment of conception until death, the organism is in constant interaction with its environment. The first environment is relatively static, the womb. After birth, it is the world as we know it, one that changes all the time.

The environment includes two types of features. One has to do with physical features, and includes such factors as climate, shelter, nutrition, space, comfort, and infectious and toxic agents. The other type of feature has to do with social factors, the patterns of communication and social relationships found in the child's family and wider society, and the child's particular place in that society. These two sets of features are not independent since social circumstances will exert a substantial, if not total, influence on the physical features of the child's environment. Some of the physical factors which influence constitution at each major stage of development will be reviewed next.

Genetic determination at conception

When sperm and egg unite to form the primordial new organism, the bearers of hereditary information, the 23 chromosomes from the mother and the same number from the father combine in pairs within the nucleus of that first cell. These 23 pairs of chromosomes will control the construction of the organism and be represented in every cell of the body. Represented on each chromosome are a great many genes, which singly and in combination control the timing and construction of the structure of the body, including the brain.

In the course of the process in which the sperm and egg have been formed, or in which the comparable chromosome strands come together when the egg is fertilized, genetic "errors" can occur. There are two kinds: chromosomal flaws or genic flaws. In chromosomal flaws, the large strands of chromosome material can be misrepresented (too many or too few show up in the new organism) or be misaligned. In genic flaws, particular genes on a chromosome may be missing or be ineffectual. Both types of flaws together are termed genetic flaws. If there is a chromosomal flaw, a major defect will be present in the resulting organism because many genes will be misaligned. If there is a genic flaw, the defect will be very selective, but its impact will depend on how crucial the missing or abnormal feature may happen to be. Is it a leak in the windshield or a flaw in the frame? Is it eye color, or the overproduction (when there are excessive chromosomes) of a neurotransmitter?

The consequence of most serious genetic errors is an organism that cannot live. The fetus will often die in the womb and be expelled in a spontaneous abortion (or miscarriage, as it is called) or will be born but live only a short time thereafter. There are, however, a number of genetic flaws which produce constitutions that are viable. The most commonly known of these conditions is Down syndrome, which produces individuals with similar appearance and mental retardation. This is a consequence of an error in the number of chromosomes, an error that may be present in every cell in the body.

A genic disorder may also produce mental retardation via a different route. In PKU (or phenylpyruvic ketonuria), for example, the child lacks a gene which controls the production of an enzyme, a biological catalyst necessary for the digestion of certain proteins common in food. The absence of this enzyme leads to an excess of these proteins in the blood stream and this high concentration, in turn, is poisonous to infantile brain tissue. As a result of this single missing gene, the child destroys many of its own brain cells and becomes retarded. This catastrophe can now be averted by changing the child's diet if detection is early enough.

Yet another type of genetic flaw affects the timing of events through the course of development. Some of these flaws occur during gestation, some early in infancy, and some have their effects in adulthood. For example, there is a type of genetically determined microcephaly (small brained) in which the openings in the skull are prematurely closed and hardened, having the effect of compressing the growing brain and producing retardation. In Huntington's chorea, a genetic flaw present from birth exerts its influence 35–45 years later by causing the early depletion of a crucial neurotransmitter. As a result, mental functioning in midlife deteriorates and this is soon followed by death.

Some of these conditions will be considered in more detail in chapters on mental retardation and motor dysfunction. For now, simply be aware of the different ways in which genetic errors can produce organic abnormalities.

Gestational factors in constitutional integrity

The sequence of gestation is under genetic control and, as mentioned earlier, is subject to errors in timing. Often, however, children born with evidence of errors in timing lack evidence of genetic defect. Often there is no explanation for the cause of such disorders, but research in teratology, the systematic study of abnormalities of gestation, has provided increasing evidence for the existence of whole classes of substances which are essentially poisons or disruptors of the gestational process. For example, mothers who took a tranquilizing drug called thalidomide during the first trimester of pregnancy gave birth to children with stunted arms and malformed hands.

There are many other more familiar causes of malformation in the fetus. Long known has been the increased risk for deafness, blindness, cerebral palsy, retardation, and epilepsy in children whose mothers contract rubella, a type of measles, during the first trimester of their pregnancy. Newer data have indicated that the consumption of alcohol and other drugs during pregnancy is associated with decreased mental competence and relatively subtle malformations of many body structures in the offspring. Most of these malformations are in the midline where the separately developing right and left halves have to merge.

The degree to which the appearance of the child is stigmatized provides a rough index as to when the impairing event took place. In general, those with gross deformities endured some pathological influence early in gestation, particularly the first trimester, while those with more subtle defects are likely to have suffered some aberration of the gestational process at a later stage. Thus spina bifida, a malformation of gestation due to the failure of the primordial neural tube to close completely, is a consequence of early disruption, whereas autism may be due to an error of later gestation.

Perinatal factors in constitutional integrity

"Para" or "peri" is a prefix meaning "around," and perinatal means around birth. The relatively short period of time from the very last stages of pregnancy, when the child's head moves toward positioning itself to enter the birth canal, to the time, three to five days after birth, when the child generally gives stable indications of being able to breathe, circulate blood, take food, and move in certain ways, is the perinatal period. The greatest and most rapid changes to which the organism will have to respond in the course of life will occur during this short time period, when many things can go wrong.

One of the major transitions that must occur at birth is the shift from obtaining oxygen passively from the mother's blood stream via the placenta to independent breathing. To accomplish this, there must occur a change in the way blood is circulated between heart and lungs. Since brain tissue begins to be damaged after only three or four minutes without oxygen, and sustains irreversibly severe damage in about ten minutes, onset of breathing is crucial to immediate life and the future capabilities of the child. Various conditions can produce anoxia, lack of oxygen.

The overriding importance of oxygen and breathing at birth is reflected in indices commonly used by medical personnel and others concerned with the newborn to quantify, however crudely, the general health of the newborn. The Apgar index is a rating from one (severely compromised poor health) to ten (thriving and healthy), with a rating of seven and lower considered to be "at risk." This index is based largely on the color and reactivity of the child. The Brazelton scale is a more elaborate assessment of the child's status at birth and for a few days thereafter, and generates a developmental quotient. Both indices have predictive value for the occurrence of later difficulty, be it obviously constitutional in nature, such as cerebral palsy, or a less obvious problem, such as hyperactivity or learning disability.

A source of difficulty during birth stems from the physical fact that a relatively large five- to ten-pound baby has to pass through a relatively narrow birth canal. Although there are mechanisms in the mother's body that dilate and enlarge the canal before initiating the contractions that expel the fetus, there is nevertheless a tight fit and ample opportunity for all kinds of squeezing and compressing of sensitive tissues, especially the brain. During the early stages of birth, the child's head moves to a position at the entrance to the birth canal. If the position attained is the normal one most advantageous for the birth process, the apex and rear of the skull will lead in pushing the child's body through. The bones of the skull of the normal infant are quite pliable and have space to move to absorb some of the shock. If, instead of the top of the skull, the child's buttocks or legs or face lead in the movement through the birth canal, a series of stresses will occur which the child's head does not absorb well. Such births are associated with a higher incidence of structural and behavioral impairments.

The real danger to health and life present during birth and immediately thereafter has led to the increasing "medicalization" of the birth process in Western society. Medicalization refers to the view by the medical profession and the public at large that pregnancy and birth are a kind of illness to be ministered by medical science, rather than a natural event, which, after all, each human being must experience. Consequences of this view have included obstetric practices which have ranged from using the hospital as the only "proper" site for birthing, to using heavy anesthesia for all births because of the pain that is often present. Some critics have suggested that this medical view has led to increased frequency of surgical birthing (Caesarian section), eliminating the arduous passage through the birth canal.

There have been strong reactions to some of these views and practices (see, for example, Arms, 1975). Some have focussed on the physical consequences of these practices for the vigor of the child. For example, anesthetic sufficient to deeply anesthetize the mother will also affect the baby and may interfere with initial breathing. The Caesarian section, aside from its own dangers to both mother and child as a surgical procedure, while precluding the stressful experience of ordinary birth, also precludes the early development of biological stress-coping mechanisms which occur during the process.

Critics have suggested that professional efforts in normal birth should be directed at helping the mother to cope with pain by teaching relaxation techniques and facilitating her active participation in the birth process. In this view, the standard reclining position with pelvis tilted upward which is convenient for attendants, but which make the mothers' work harder, should be changed. It is easier to give birth in some approximation of a squatting position where the birth is aided rather than opposed by gravity, and the final supply of blood in the umbilical cord goes to the child. According to this view, if a woman is actively participating in the birth of her child, it is less likely that it will be necessary to use mechanical aids such as forceps. These are a kind of tongs used to pull on the baby when spontaneous birthing is slow. Forceps may put pressure on the temporal lobes and can temporarily, if not permanently, deform the child's head.

The other major critique of the medicalization of obstetric practice stems from the view that human beings are social animals whose bonding to each other begins at birth. There is suggestive evidence that the moment of birth and the time shortly thereafter is especially propitious for the establishment of particularly enduring positive connections between mother (and father) and child. To foster this connection, parents must observe the birth and then be in physical contact with the child immediately after birth. The newborn child is often placed on the mother's belly, and the father is often able to hold the child for a period of time. A drugged mother and a drugged child are not able to experience those moments in such a way as to establish that strong bond. An absent father, of course, will not share in any of this experience either. This may not be of great significance to confident, mature, well-socialized parents who will probably relate to their children in a positive way no matter when they first encounter each other. But this moment of biological optimization for relationship formation may make a considerable difference to parents who are themselves emotionally deprived or insecure.

Constitutional vulnerability in infancy

Infancy is the period roughly from the end of the perinatal period when the child should be physiologically stable, approximately three to seven days after birth, to the onset of walking, approximately the first birthday. This is a period in life when the child is relatively helpless and very dependent on the care received from others. It is also, of course, the first period of independent life. Research indicates that infants are already showing their individuality.

Once the child leaves the womb, its nervous system becomes vulnerable to insult from four classes of variables. These variables are operative not only during infancy but during all subsequent periods of life as well. They are disease processes such as infections and malignancies, trauma (physical assault, whether through accident or attack), toxins (poisons), and allergic, autoimmune reactions. The first two are generally familiar dangers. Toxins are familiar in their dramatic form, as when a baby is given the wrong medication or ingests a poisonous substance. Less familiar are the relatively subtle consequences of toxic pollutants such as lead and mercury, which in small quantities may not cause acute symptoms but are associated with a variety of behavior disorders including learning disability and hyperactivity. The presence of autoimmune and allergic reactions in the nervous system is controversial and not well understood, but there is evidence which suggests that they may be underlying factors in a number of disorders.

Nutrition

Another class of variables, nutrition, also plays an important role in constitutional functions, one that may be of increasing significance as understanding of nutrition–brain relationships grows. Scholars of this subject have concluded that not only is protein intake related to the ultimate integrity and efficiency of nervous system function, but so also is intake of energy sources of carbohydrate and fat, and micronutrients, particularly the minerals iron, iodine, and zinc (Pollitt et al., 1996). The case of iron is particularly interesting. Inadequate intake of iron, a nutrient needed for healthy blood cells, is fairly common in many parts of the world in children 6 to 24 months of age. This deficiency occurs either because of generalized lack of food or cultural practices which keep foods rich in iron away from infants and young children. The condition is known as iron deficiency anemia and is temporary when it occurs because of cultural reasons, lasting from ages 6 to 18 months. The condition is not life-threatening and rates of growth remain normal, but the anemic child is often insecure, fearful, irritable, and difficult to manage during the period of deficiency. Lozoff et al. (1998) have shown that such children explore their environments less, elicit less interaction from both caretakers and friendly strangers, and in effect become more functionally isolated. Cognitive development also suffers. Subsequent remediation of the iron deficiency does not reverse this pattern of social interaction immediately and perhaps not in the long run either.

Another study relating early nutrition and development extends the list of important nutrients. McCullough et al. (1990) studied mother–infant interactions in an Egyptian village as a function of the mother's and child's intake of vitamin B6. The babies were all breast fed so the child's nutrition was almost entirely determined by the mother's nutrition. The availability of B6 could be determined by assaying the mother's milk. The findings were explicit. If the mother's milk fell below a specified value, typically because of limited protein in her diet, then there was a relationship between B6 milk levels and her infant's consolability when distressed, speed of build-up to a crying state, and irritability. In other words these children were difficult to care for and the more difficult ones had lower levels of B6. B6 was also associated with caretaker behavior since the ones with low levels were found to be less responsive to infant vocalizations, less effective in alleviating distress, and more likely to delegate child care to older siblings.

The reason why nutrition may play a particularly large role in early child development is that during the first three years there is a vast amount of dendritic growth and myelinization, much learning is taking place, and trajectories of development are being set for a wide array of cognitive and social functions whose realization will take many years. Iron, for example, is a component of hemoglobin in blood, which is the carrier of nutrients to all parts of the brain. Vitamin B6 is a crucial ingredient in the synthesis of GABA, the primary inhibitory neurotransmitter. If they are not adequately available, the child may lack the resources to respond even to a wholesome environment and may fuss instead. It is easy to imagine that such children will alienate those who care for them and may develop a reputation as being difficult. Their personalities may be considered inherited and relatively unmalleable when what is at work to begin with is a nutritional deficiency.

Temperament

Next to be considered are enduring characteristics, noticeable in infancy and continuing throughout life, which influence reactions to the environment. These

Table 6.1 Temperaments described by Chess and Thomas (1984)

Name of temperament	Explanation
1. Activity level	Readiness to engage in action.
2. Rhythmicity	Predictability of biologic regularity functions.
3. Approach or withdrawal	Tendency for initial response to novel situation to be positive or negative.
4. Adaptability	The ease with which initial reactions are modified in desirable directions.
5. Threshold of responsiveness	Intensity of stimulation required to elicit a reaction.
6. Intensity of reaction	The energy level of the response.
7. Quality of mood	Degree of pleasant, happy, as compared to sad, unpleasant behavior.
8. Distractibility	The effectiveness with which extraneous stimuli interfere with ongoing behavior.
9. Attention span	Length of time pursued in activity and tendency to continue in the face of obstacles or distraction.

Source: From Chess, S. & Thomas, A. (1984), *Origins and evolution of behavior disorders from infancy to early adult life*. New York: Bruner/Mazel, p. 42.

qualities are called temperaments and are constitutional in nature and are often genetically determined, though as has been noted above, may be influenced by nutrition and toxic substances.

Research on temperament in the United States was pioneered by Chess and Thomas and their associates (Thomas, Chess, & Birch, 1968; Thomas & Chess, 1977; Chess & Thomas, 1984) through a study which followed 133 children from 84 families from early infancy through adulthood. In this work, nine categories of temperament were described, which are listed in Table 6.1 (Chess & Thomas, 1984, p. 42).

A close reading of these dimensions indicates that three, 5, 8 and 9, are concerned with aspects of attention and sensory responses to the environment; two, 1 and 6, concern the quality of reactivity and motor responses; two, 3 and 7, concern the predominant pattern of basic emotional reactivity; and two, 2 and 4, concern control and self-regulation in the nervous system. In addition, number 4 appears related to ease of habituation while number 5 appears related to some features of the orienting reaction.

Thomas, Chess and Birch (1968) found that particular types of temperaments combined to form three temperamental constellations. The easy child was "characterized by regularity, positive approach responses to new stimuli, high adaptability to change, and mild or moderate mood intensity which is preponderantly positive." The difficult child was characterized by "irregularity in biological functions, negative withdrawal responses to new stimuli, non-adaptability or slow adaptability to change and intense mood expressions which are frequently negative. These children show irregular sleep and feeding schedules, slow acceptance of new foods, prolonged adjustment periods to new routines, people or situations and relatively frequent loud periods of crying. Laughter, also, is characteristically loud. Frustration typically produces a violent tantrum." The slow-to-warm-up child had "a combination of negative responses of mild intensity to new stimuli with slow adaptability after repeated contact, . . . mild intensity of reactions, whether positive or negative, and [mild] irregularity of biological function. . . . If given the opportunity to reexperience . . . new situations over time and without pressure, such a child gradually comes to show quiet and positive interest and involvement."

Each type of child would present quite different rearing problems to their families. It could be predicted that the difficult child born to parents possessing strong physical and psychological resources and much flexibility would have different experiences than if they had been born to families with limited resources and little flexibility. It could also be predicted that easy children might turn out rather well no matter what the family's resources. In general, such were the findings. Chess and Thomas (1984) report that to some extent one can predict adult outcome on the basis of the child's presenting temperament and the degree of conflict in the family. There were of course exceptions and complications and the reader might wish to consult original sources for a fuller description of that pioneering research.

Chess and Thomas (1984) implemented the general notion of constitutionally based behavior qualities (temperament) interacting with different family environments in what they called the goodness-of-fit model. Specifically, they hypothesized and confirmed that adjustment problems through the course of development may often be a consequence of a mismatch between the temperament and lifestyle of the parents and that of the child. A parent may easily perceive the impersistence, high activity level, or slow adaptability of certain children as negative, personally antagonistic behaviors. The resulting interaction with the child may lack empathy or understanding and often be marked by conflict and punishment. In many instances, Chess and Thomas report that active counseling which aids the parents in understanding their child's temperament and in finding positive ways of responding to those characteristics rapidly helps to resolve many family crises.

Research on temperament has improved methodologically, increased in amount, and has documented a number of the brain and autonomic nervous system mechanisms involved (Bates & Wachs, 1994). One salient body of work has been that of Kagan (1994) who has studied a group of children of normal birth who constitute about 20 percent of the population all over the world, who are intensely inhibited and shy. Such characteristics can be detected in infancy and persist into adulthood when they may be described as introverted. These persons are intensely reactive autonomically but generally inhibited behaviorally in their encounters both with the physical and social world. They contrast with the extroverted, those who are uninhibited behaviorally, outgoing socially, and minimally reactive internally and autonomically. Kagan found that caretakers of temperamentally shy children can help them to overcome isolation and learn how to initiate and respond to overtures for friendship, but that the emotional reaction pattern persists and must be managed throughout life.

Constitutional vulnerability during the preschool years

The preschool years last from the onset of walking to the onset of formal schooling, roughly from one through five years of age. It is a period during which children's constitutions are vulnerable to the same challenges as those described earlier. This is, however, the period which first reveals the integrity and relative strength of two major adaptive systems, motor functions and language, and also when the rudiments of higher cognitive functions and social relations begin to emerge. It is a period of development now subject to intensive study.

During the four preschool years, the child will progress from awkward toddling to a smooth repertoire of motor skills. These skills will simply emerge providing there is no undue restraint, space is available for movement, and objects and substances are available for manipulation. Specialized skills for athletic (throwing and kicking), academic (writing), recreational (knitting, guitar strumming), and ultimately vocational (typing, craftsmanship), purposes will begin their development during a later phase but the foundations are laid down during this early period. It is during the preschool years that signs of serious motor impairment are generally first clearly apparent.

At present, there is widespread consensus (although not complete agreement) that language capabilities are predifferentiated within the human brain but require a language community with its attendant stimulation to occasion its realization. Language emerges in the second through the fifth years with phenomenal rapidity since the child goes from no language at all to linguistic sophistication with a large vocabulary and complex, accurate grammar. Since the child gets a language in about four years, failure or limitations in constitutional determinants of language will become apparent during this phase.

Although motor functions and language "unfold," that is, are constitutionally based and emerge more or less in sequence without explicit instruction, the outcome is by no means free of influence from environmental factors. Parents who so fear germs and other dangers to the child's health that they will not allow interaction with other children, or opportunities for exploration or contact with any potentially "contaminated" materials, may find themselves with a child whose motor development is arrested. This will occur not on a constitutional basis but as a result of inexperience. In general, such motoric weaknesses are readily reversed as soon as the relevant experience is obtained.

Similar considerations apply to language behavior. The level of language mastery displayed by five-year-olds is not just a function of their constitutionally determined level of capability but also of the extent to which their environment has shaped and reinforced language behaviors. Research has implicated such variables as the degree to which the child's speech is listened to by others, is reinforced, or is corrected when in error, as influences on the ultimate level of skill attained. Compared to motor behaviors, it is not at all clear that environmental deficiencies in language stimulation and reinforcement during the first years can be readily overcome (Hart & Risley, 1995; Tomasello, 1995).

New cognitive functions and increasingly complex social behavior emerge during these years. An important focus of much research is the importance of the development of joint attention in the second year, shared attention directed at specific objects or events by child and caretaker which requires simultaneous focus on another person as well as an external event (Bakeman & Adamson, 1984). Evidence has accrued that this landmark interaction, which is social in nature, not only provides a basis for the further development of social behaviors including various types of play interaction, cooperation, and friendship, but also is an important component in early cognitive and language development (Tomasello & Farrar, 1986). Impediments to progress in these areas may come from limitations in the child, as occurs in autistic children, or from insensitive or inadequate caretaking behaviors (Landry et al., 1998). Overall, the evidence points to social factors as being of great import in most every aspect of human development.

Constitutional vulnerability during the elementary school years

This is the period when most children in Western society are involved in the basic phases of formal schooling. The period begins at about the age of six and continues to the onset of puberty, somewhere between the ages of 11 and 13 for most children. Between the ages of six and eight, a constitutionally based development occurs which is relevant to the higher levels of cognitive function. In the terminology of Piaget, this is the time at which concrete operations emerge. Whether one accepts a Piagetian view or not, there is ample evidence from many perspectives that substantial changes in the organization of cognitive function occur during this period. Perhaps the main proximal cause of this change is that a critical degree of myelinization of the corpus callosum is accomplished by the age of seven or so.

The term "concrete operations" refers to the ability to think logically on the basis of concrete premises and to organize one's thinking on the basis of categories rather then specific instances. Such capabilities are necessary in order to reason and to solve mental problems. About the end of the second grade and into the third, the curriculum in most schools begins to make demands on those skills. At that point some children begin to falter who up till then showed no sign of any deficiency. Most likely, failure at that time may be due to some constitutional limitation in the cognitive skill available at this high level of function. At present there is no way to verify the nature of the constitutional impairment. Nonetheless, careful study of these cases generally does not reveal any other explanation for their failure to keep up fully with their peers.

Constitutional factors in preadolescence and early adolescence

The changes of adolescence can be described as occurring in two phases. The first, called preadolescence, begins when the physiological transformations of puberty are initiated and ends with the advent of those overt signs which indicate that biological maturation has occurred. These are the onset of menstruation in females, ejaculation in males, and the development of secondary sex characteristics in each. The phase of early adolescence beginning after the overt onset of puberty and generally lasting about two years is usually completed by about the age of 16. This is a period in which the biological changes are assimilated into the child's personality. Afterwards, late adolescence is really the first epoch of adulthood, although many cultures do not always expect fully mature behavior from the individual as yet.

Preadolescence and early adolescence are epochs of great change with major hormonal transformations and growth in the size and shape of the individual's body. Aside from these obvious constitutional changes, with their significant social implications, another development is that the highest level of cognitive function also emerges about the time of puberty. This capability is called "formal operations" and refers to the ability to argue from arbitrary premises, that is, to engage in formal logic. The constitutional basis for the emergence of formal logic is not established and it is extremely difficult to separate the influence of experience from organic factors. Nevertheless, it appears that this capability is crucial for success in higher education and many other aspects of life. Two developments in the brain may be of considerable importance in the realization of these skills. One is the previously mentioned completion of myelinization. The second is of the completion of a process called developmental sloughing.

It will be recalled that all the entire supply of neurons one will ever possess is present at birth. In actuality, there is a considerable surplus. During the course of development, cells compete to establish interconnections; those which do not succeed in becoming parts of active circuits become superfluous. These cells serve no function, die and are removed, and the process is called sloughing. This process goes on throughout development, but there is a significant spurt of sloughing during adolescence. Failure of this sloughing to occur may leave a surplus of cells in the brain which may cause havoc by interfering with operational circuits.

Before completing this brief survey of constitutional and organic factors which influence the course of development, it is appropriate to refer back to the variables of trauma and toxicity. In Western society, there is a substantially increased risk of sustaining brain damage during adolescence via the use of drugs, the irresponsible use of automobiles, and as a result of physical assault, especially among socially disadvantaged males.

7

Psychopathology Inducing Experience and Handicap Dynamics

Context and Content of this Chapter

Although this book is written from a neuropsychological perspective, it cannot do justice to the operative mode of the nervous system if it neglects systematic consideration of the environment in which the nervous system functions. For humans, the most significant component of the environment is the person's society and culture. One need only note that one of the disorders considered in this book, learning disability, which often has a significant constitutional component, requires a literate culture for its very existence.

The specific sociocultural framework for this presentation will be late twentieth century Western society. Within the framework provided by present social circumstances, there are undoubtedly many ways of classifying the kinds of events and experiences which are associated with behavioral pathology. The brief classification scheme of environmental and experiential factors influencing pathology, which is presented next, is just one way of approaching so complex a set of variables.

The last section of this chapter will discuss some aspects of what can be called handicap dynamics. To be considered are the general psychological consequences of having a handicap to those who have them and those who live with or associate with persons who have them. From this perspective, a way of thinking about treatment interventions will be proposed.

Environmental and Experiential Events Associated with Pathology

Chronic understimulation and overstimulation

Although the nervous system is continuously active, its development and mode of operation depends on the intensity and patterning of the stimulation it receives from the environment. This generalization is bolstered by much evidence. Studies of the course of development by children reared in orphanages, where they had decent physical care but limited stimulation, revealed that their mental, social, and emotional development was grossly arrested in comparison to children reared at home or in more stimulating institutions. In studies on the effects of prolonged sensory monotony, normal adults became severely disorganized and unable to function. It is an obvious truism that if a child is not exposed to speech, language will not be learned. The same is true for riding a bike, reading books, or playing the violin.

As the tools and byproducts of cultural development have cumulated through history, more and more human capabilities have been revealed, some of which we now expect everyone to have. Everyone, more or less, is expected to master their native tongue, and to learn to read and write. The attainment of these skills depends on having the requisite neurological capabilities and the relevant training experiences. Exactly what the relevant stimulation is for proficient language is not fully known, but there is every reason to believe that it too exists on a continuum, probably several continua, because language is not a singular entity. It seems plausible that a child growing up in a language-rich environment, where language is used purposefully, with discrimination and subtlety, and where the child is listened to and encouraged to speak, is at an advantage over a child whose comparable experience is altogether less. The latter child may be said to have received chronic understimulation.

Understimulation can be quite gross in its impact, as in the case of the orphanage children, or quite selective, as when musical or athletic talent is not provided adequate training opportunity. It often occurs in the context of poverty where many human potentials often fail to be realized, but it can also occur in the midst of wealth and plenty, for example, when an oversheltered child is not allowed to play with other children, which limits the development of social and motor skills.

Chronic overstimulation refers both to excessive intensity of stimulation and a relative lack of patterning in the stimulation. Its impact is greatest during childhood but it can affect behavior at all stages of life. Chronic overstimulation can be said to occur in a home environment that is noisy, disorderly, excessively exciting, inconsistent, and chaotic. This may pertain to relationships or to the physical necessities of life such as eating and sleeping. The main psychological effect of this kind of environment is to influence the quality of ambient stimulation and hence the relationship between focal and ambient stimulation (see chapter 4). Under these conditions, nothing in particular is salient. Everything is either exciting or boring, and to be exciting, more and more intensity is required. The result burdens the perception and execution of the subtle aspects of behavior and coarsens the behavioral repertoire. Overstimulation may provoke the individual to develop special coping techniques in order to withdraw and escape, but it often leads to a chronic craving for excitement that leads to many problems in social adaptation.

Although chronic understimulation and overstimulation sound like opposites, they appear to have somewhat similar effects. Both are associated with less behavioral adequacy, but in different ways. The former can be thought of as leading to a kind of emptiness, the latter to cravings for so much excitement that it makes dealing with the mundane almost impossible.

Trauma and stress

Trauma can be defined as a time-limited, intense experience of stimulation which is beyond the range of intensities ordinarily experienced. Trauma may be circumscribed to a particular organ system, for example, a burn on the skin, or exposure of the ear to an extremely loud noise, or may involve the entire nervous system. The nature of the trauma may be entirely physical, as in the case of a burn, purely psychological, as when one experiences a profoundly humiliating social experience, or most commonly, some combination of the two, as when one is mugged or raped or in an automobile accident. Physical damage to the body generally, and to the brain in particular, may be irreversible. The term stress is difficult to define objectively but for present purposes will be considered to be the nervous system's reaction to trauma and to the anticipation of trauma. Given that the world can be a dangerous place, the stress reaction which mobilizes preparedness for fight or flight is an adaptive reaction. But the stress response appears to be designed biologically to deal with time-limited danger, and prolonged stress may mess up negative feedback reactions that would return the person to a non-stressed state when the stress was over.

The long-range consequences of brief trauma depend on a number of different factors. One group of issues concerns the locus, extent, reversibility, and type of damage to tissue and the developmental state of the organism. A small burn on the skin will soon heal in young and old but burns over a large area of body will subject the individual to a long and painful recovery requiring immobility and the endurance of much stress. The consequences of such experience will differ in an adult whose personality is formed and in a young child. The most significant damage to tissue in accidents and events involving assault may be brain injury. If the person is unconscious for a period of time, injury to the brain will generally be considered as a possible explanation for any ensuing symptoms, but even if the individual never loses consciousness, significant damage may still occur but may not be recognized.

Severe, if brief, trauma may provoke serious symptoms including emotional components of fear, anxiety, depression, and shame, and other symptoms such as disrupted sleep, that can persist for as much as a year or longer. The stress response may be associated to innocuous stimuli leading later to the development of irrational fears called phobias. The mode of coping makes a considerable difference in the ultimate outcome. If the driving-accident victim soon gets back to driving, phobic reactions are not likely to persist. If rape victims can communicate with their loved ones and are not ostracized or blamed for the traumatic experience, and particularly if new techniques of self-defense and empowerment are learned, then enduring negative effects, including phobias, are minimized.

Although trauma is generally not good for people, adequate coping will minimize, if not totally eliminate, the consequences of single, time-limited experiences. On the other hand, recurrent trauma, especially in situations where the person is helpless, appears to have enduring consequences no matter what coping techniques are attempted. Such circumstances include those of the chronically battered or sexually abused child, the tortured political or military prisoner, the concentration-camp inmate, or those in prolonged military combat. These individuals suffer from profound sleep disturbances, anxiety attacks, inexplicable kinds of tension, flashbacks (uncontrollable memories) of segments of their traumatic experience with replays of their emotional reactions as well, and recurrent experiences of guilt and shame. Such symptoms may be present chronically shortly after the trauma is over or may appear months or years later and may earn the diagnosis of post-traumatic stress disorder. Evidence has emerged that, in addition to whatever direct tissue damage may be sustained when persons are traumatized or subject to intense stress repeatedly over long periods of time, there appear to be long-standing changes in autonomic function, in tonic mechanisms that provide the background for focal experience, and for loss of tissue in the hippocampus, a structure in the temporal lobe that is part of the limbic system known to be involved with memory (Sapolsky, 1996). Prolonged trauma in adults burdens their personality heavily. Prolonged trauma in young children alters their personality.

Coping refers to responses made to stress situations and to their consequences. At the same level of stress, some will have adequate coping techniques while others will not. Furthermore, the same levels of stress measured objectively may have differing subjective impacts across individuals. Moving one's residence, for example, is a stress which most people endure successfully, but it can be the occasion of breakdown in a person who becomes severely mentally ill. The difference is attributed to vulnerabilities called diatheses that interact with stress in such a way as to lead to pathological outcomes. The concepts of stress-diathesis and coping provide a format for explaining the variability that can be found in reaction to stress. These concepts will be reencountered in later chapters. The model dictates that the coping techniques and/or the nature of the diathesis must be specified if the response to stress is to be understood. Avoidance of mourning, for example, is often seen as a maladaptive coping reaction, while inborn hypersensitivity may be implicated as a diathesis.

Loss and defeat

Loss can be defined as a failure of anticipated stimulation or reward, and is understood to refer primarily to social relationships. The most common causes of loss are the death of loved ones or the inevitable breakups in relationships which take place in the course of a lifetime. Loss also occurs when events detract from self-esteem. These events can be mostly or entirely symbolic in nature. For example, failure to receive an expected or hoped-for promotion or failure to pass an examination can have the same impact on certain individuals as the loss of a parent. Other losses of this type occur when a person prepares for a social role and then cannot realize, continue in, or move beyond it. Examples include the child rearer after the children are grown, the trained job seeker who cannot find work because of economic circumstances, the retiree who feels worthless, or the professional who cannot practice because of discrimination or social disruption. Loss is most profound if the person is helpless, and such is often the case when a loved one dies, but it can also occur in many other social circumstances.

Loss is also involved in two types of fairly common social stress: neglect and rejection. In both, anticipated stimulation is not received, in the first case, because the individual loses out to some source of competition, in the second, because of some form of negative, frustrational intent from the source. Neglect is exemplified by the loss of attention a healthy child may experience when a handicapped sibling receives most of the family's attention. Rejection would occur, for example, when a child receives less then he/she might otherwise get because a parent reacts negatively to a child's similarity in appearance to a disliked figure. Many loss experiences are abrupt and time-bound in nature. Others, including neglect and rejection, may occur over a long span of time in a chronic, recurrent fashion. Neglect is like understimulation, but in this case the stimulation is anticipated and that makes a big difference because strong elements of frustration and resentment become part of the picture.

The loss response is not some psychological quirk occurring in people who are very emotional, but is a response deeply rooted in biology and psychology worthy of scientific study (Harvey & Miller, 1998). The power of this reaction is testimony to the significance of the relationships and the strong bonds with others that humans form. The severance or frustration of those bonds is no casual matter. In its fullest form, the response to loss is called the grief reaction and involves intense feelings of depression, guilt, agitation, recurrent memories or thoughts about the missing person or event and much more. Intense grief is most commonly observed following the death of a loved one. However, consistent with a range of severity in the nature of losses, a continuum of grief reactions occurs which includes many of mild intensity.

The grief reaction, mild or severe, must be dealt with or else it will persist. Kübler-Ross (1969) and others have described the sequence of steps by which the grief reaction is resolved, a process termed mourning. Just as the enduring consequences of trauma depend on the way the individual copes with the experience, so too do the consequences of loss depend on the adequacy of the mourning reaction. When losses are singular and abrupt, as in the death of a loved one, the process, no matter how painful, is generally delimited in time. When the loss is chronic in nature, as when dealing with a handicapped child, the process is, in some sense, never-ending. The conceptualization and study of loss has received renewed attention.

Complex, chronic, family interactions

Systems theory, which plays so important a role in understanding the nervous system, also is helpful in understanding family behavior and the systematic way in which families determine the kind of stimulation each member experiences. Nervous systems are born immature and grow up, not in vacuums, but in families. It is the family that communicates the culture to the child, and each family does it in a unique and special way whose impact is a function of the temperamental and cognitive characteristics of each individual. The result may foster growth and the realization of potential or may reinforce pathological reactions. The way in which family systems actually contribute both to pathological reactions and healthy resilience has been a subject of study and a focus of professional intervention beginning in the last half of the twentieth century.

Newborn children are relatively powerless and entirely dependent on their care-takers. Although their power increases as they develop, it takes many years before it becomes significant. The uneven power relationships between parents and children constitute a fertile ground for pathological influence. Classic examples include family systems in which a child is tyrannized or is reinforced for failure or for antisocial activity or even is given premature responsibility or excessive sexual stimulation in order to satisfy parental needs. Freud vividly described such circumstances in one of his famous case studies although he chose to emphasize the child's (in this case, an adolescent) symptoms and to disregard the exploitative behaviors in the family. More examples can be found in the literature dealing with the analysis and treatment of such relationships, which includes many books and such journals as *Family Process, The American Journal of Family Therapy,* and *The Family Therapy Networker.*

When a child is handicapped in some way, and particularly when there is no basis for treatment, the family system is likely to be stressed in such a way as to amplify the flaws of its members. Interestingly, such difficulties are more likely to occur when a condition is relatively mild and less well defined than when it is extreme and there is not much room for controversy or doubt. In addition, there is often a strong tendency for well-intended caretakers to do more than is necessary for a handicapped individual and thus foster excessive dependency. The presence of a handicap, especially those that are not the most extreme, does not define the range of pathological behavior. It is always the interaction between the handicap and the family environment that determines the behavior. Because of this, there are times when treatment for organic conditions may be totally social and behavioral. For example, Madanes (1980) and Ferson (1970) have described how family relationships can profoundly influence the frequency of seizures.

Identity (self)-induced stress

This category of "environmental" stresses fits rather awkwardly into the list because identity resides within the person rather than in the environment. There are two ways to justify its inclusion. The first is that one's identity derives, at least in part, from prior experience and from the long-term impact of the environment on the person. The second is that the identity of the individual in some way creates its own environment. Sullen people provoke rejection whereas outgoing persons radiating warmth tend to find it reciprocated. Dependent individuals often find those who will care for them. In any event, the list of environmental determinants of pathology would be incomplete without taking into account how the identity itself, partially determined by the integrity of the nervous system, but as indicated, also determined by the particular experiences the person previously had, shapes its own subsequent experience.

A case in point can be seen when individuals with life-long intractable epilepsy find that they no longer have seizures because of successful treatment with surgery or drugs. Often, behavior patterns developed while coping with recurrent seizures, including dependency and passivity, will persist long after the seizures are gone. The explanation lies in that surgery or drugs for epilepsy are not likely to alter the personality. It must change independently, and it rarely does so spontaneously. Treatment for such individuals often must go beyond the purely medical in order to reap the benefits of successful medical intervention.

Handicap Dynamics

The presence of a handicapped child in a family almost inevitably involves some experience of loss. This sense of loss is likely to recur repeatedly, particularly at each milestone of development. Such repeated experience of loss may be more burdensome and emotionally taxing than a child's death. Awareness of such alternatives compounds the problem because it may increase feelings of guilt. A vivid description of what it is like to care for a severely handicapped child with a moving depiction of the ways in which families actually cope can be found in Helen Featherstone's (1980) *A difference in the family*. This is highly recommended background reading for the material covered in this book.

The problem of loss is not only one for parents and caretakers but also for the handicapped individuals themselves as they grow in awareness. Observations of the skills, accomplishments, and opportunities of others, which are precluded for them because of their handicap, leads to awareness of what might have been and to an ensuing experience of loss, even though the skill or capability was never present. Such feelings, if unmourned and unresolved, may actually interfere with efforts at training and rehabilitation so that the person is at risk for attaining a lesser level of skill than otherwise might have achieved.

Aspects of Coping with Handicap

Age of onset

Some conditions are present at birth, some develop gradually, and some occur suddenly, for example, as a result of illness or accident, at some point during the course of life. Timing of onset can make a big difference regarding the resources available to the person for habilitation. Thus blindness or deafness after a period of normal or even partial sensory function has different implications for education and habilitation than blindness or deafness from birth. On the other hand, a person sustaining an impairment later in life has to revise his/her identity in accord with the changes that the handicap imposes, and that may be a more difficult adjustment than the particulars of dealing with the handicap. For example, it is very hard for persons who have been managers to revise their self image after a head injury and accept positions as clerks, just as it is hard for honor students to find that they must struggle in order to learn. The earlier a deficit is sustained the easier it is to accomplish the transition.

Magnitude and overtness

Handicaps occur on a continuum of severity and of visibility or degree of stig-matization. Each condition has its range of expression from severe to mild and many conditions vary in the extent to which the handicap is immediately obvious. When the handicap is obvious it often has a powerful, negative emotional impact on any observer. The term stigma (plural: stigmata) which refers to obvious signs of difference and abnormality and has the connotation of something awful and unac-ceptable, may be used to describe the obvious abnormalities some people possess. The stigmata of handicap may include distorted physical features and uncontrollable behaviors including drooling, incontinence, excessive movement, awkward, near-incomprehensible speech, and seizures.

It would be nice to think that such manifestations are not troublesome to most people but this is not the case. Children are often notoriously cruel and rejecting when they observe such physical characteristics and behaviors, and adults generally experience strong aversive reactions which they must overcome if they are to relate to or care for individuals with such handicaps. Perhaps the reason underlying such negative reactions has to do with our own fear of how we ourselves would react if afflicted with a handicap, but aversive reactions appear to be the most common and frequent reaction. Sad to say, it is probably true that those who proffer friendship and care may have had to overcome aversion in order to do so rather than that they never experienced any negative reaction at all.

Labeling and diagnosis

Those with handicaps, whether mild or severe, without overt stigmatizing features – for example, some forms of learning disability or spatial impairment – have to face a different kind of social problem, namely a lack of understanding of what they are up against, of how their hidden handicap compromises their accomplishments. As a result they find themselves treated as individuals who do not have handicaps when they actually do. Since their achievements are likely to fall behind expectations, they are often, in an achievement-oriented society, accused of being lazy, irresponsible, or in some manner morally unfit. Thus it may often happen that those with stigmatiz-ing conditions find themselves expected to do less than they can achieve while those without overt stigmata are expected to do more.

This difficult state of affairs is associated with a common dilemma faced by fami-lies and caretakers of those with handicaps: whether to label and make known to the subjects and to others the nature of their handicap. The issue is most conspicuous when the handicap is not obvious. There are a number of conflicting aspects to the problem. One is that words or labels can create a stigma where none may otherwise exist. Labels can just as easily, if not more easily, be used as a basis for rejection than as a foundation for understanding. Another is that a label may convey the notion of finality and undermine the motivation to overcome or circumvent the handicap. A child might take the position, for example, that since he/she is learning-disabled, there is no point in studying.

Mainstreaming

Given that handicap often incurs rejection, and is often accompanied by segregation and discrimination, it has seemed to many that the remedy for such unfairness is to integrate the activities and education of those with handicaps into the mainstream. The rationale for this idea was that if people with handicaps were exposed to the stimulation that the non-handicapped receive, the latter would more readily overcome their aversive reactions and the former would benefit from "normal" stimulation.

There have been numerous attempts at mainstreaming and the experience has revealed both positive and negative consequences. Under some circumstances, individuals receive a richer brew of stimulation than they would have otherwise received and this results in accelerated achievement and greater feelings of accomplishment and self-satisfaction. In other instances, mainstreaming makes it difficult for people with handicaps to receive the special kinds of stimulation they might require or to go at the pace that is optimal for them. Of course the way in which a mainstreaming arrangement is implemented makes a large difference and such implementation depends on the training and understanding of those involved. As a result of these differing outcomes, parents of children with handicaps often are unclear as to which alternatives to support or pursue. In any specific case, the particular handicaps with their particular requirements and the actual skills of the personnel that would be involved might best guide the decision whether to mainstream. Emphasis on abstract principles such as "integration" may not lead to the best educational experiences available.

An Approach to Treatment, Education, and Habilitation of Handicap

Given the complexities associated with handicap, the following appears to be a sensible and rational approach to intervention:

(a)   **Awareness.**   Within the limits of the subject's capacity to understand, knowledge and awareness is preferable to ignorance. There is no way that people can mobilize their resources to overcome their problems unless they have some way of defining what their problems are. The message should always be that the definition of the handicap does not define the person but just defines the handicap. It specifies with what the person must cope. In doing so, the likelihood that insidious and corrosive attributions of laziness, craziness, and moral failure will occur and be incorporated into the personality is decreased. Labelling, diagnosis, and awareness does not mean walking around with a sign proclaiming one's disability. The knowledge is for those who need to know. Given continuing prejudice and discrimination against the handicapped, and given some of the untested assumptions that often accompany diagnosis (e.g. there is nothing that can be done for a child with Down syndrome or autism), considerable discretion in communicating such information may be in order. Such information is for those who can use it helpfully.

(b) **Loss and mourning.** The main reason why definition of the handicap may be actively avoided is that it confronts those involved with loss and the consequent emotional pain associated with loss. Part of dealing with handicap is dealing with loss and this means dealing with the anger, guilt, anguish, and pain of the mourning process. It also means dealing with it repeatedly since the handicap does not die. This is perhaps the hardest part of the educational process to endure and master.

(c) **Acceptance and incorporation into the self image.** If one is aware of one's handicap, is dealing with the loss and its emotional consequences, and knows where in the scheme of one's personhood the handicap fits, then one is in a position to make the best of things. Such inside emotional "work" sets the stage for the work of habilitation. The ordeals of training then have meaning because they represent an increased repertoire of behaviors and increased competence. As with everything else in life, if the persons close to the one with a handicap share and affirm this process, its accomplishment is much more likely. It is often difficult to work through such inner issues on one's own and a variety of individual, family, and group therapies are available to help out.

Self-acceptance and understanding of handicap has one additional important benefit. People with such understanding are in a better position to arrange their environments to accord with their own needs than are those not so equipped. Thus individuals with a hearing loss can ask people to speak louder and more slowly so that they can get the message, rather than settle for communications which they only poorly understand.

(d) **Effective treatment.** In some instances, a definitive treatment may exist. Thus a child with a reading disorder because of a subtle seizure problem, a rare disorder, might well respond to drugs which control seizures. The goal of much research on handicapping conditions is to find a way to treat the disorder definitively. Such interventions, when shown to be valid, return the subject to the mainstream and obviate the need for further special care if the identity can assimilate the change. Unfortunately, definitive effective treatments that constitute cures for handicapping conditions often cannot be found. This does not mean that nothing can be done.

(e) **Education, training and habilitation.** The lessons of the last 100 years are that, even though brain cells that die cannot be replaced, most every living organism can still learn and that therefore that something can be done. This means that with the right kind of stimulation and incentive some, and often much, progress is possible in all handicaps. Societal values have shifted so that any kind of progress is prized. Educational and habilitation research has as one of its goals the discovery of the most effective techniques that capitalize on this learning ability. Such learning is generally conceptualized as the mobilization of undamaged tissue or brain systems to compensate for the limitations created by damaged parts of the brain. It is the contention of this book that an understanding of the neuropsychological nature of the handicap will aid us in this process. The remainder of this book aims to increase understanding of particular disorders. Whenever feasible, the implications of this understanding for strategies of habilitation will be pointed out, but once again the reader is cautioned that this is not a "how-to" manual.

Part II

Disorders of State

8

Ictal Disorders: Epilepsy, Seizures, and Related Disorders

The three chapters in Part II concern conditions that affect the state of the person. "State" is a term, like tone, that refers to a general quality of responsiveness. This is perhaps most easily understood when considering the behavioral states of an infant which are largely limited to being asleep or being awake, the latter subdivided into being alert and responsive to the outside world or being distressed and crying. Transitions between these three states can also be noted. Specifications of state beyond infancy require more subtle distinctions and are presented in separate chapters which consider ictal states or seizures, sleep and its disorders, and attention and its disorders. Much as the behavioral repertoire of a crying baby will be dominated temporarily by its state, so too will sleep, seizure, and attentional factors influence functioning in any behavioral domain.

Why Use the Term "Ictus"?

The uncommon and probably unfamiliar word ictal was used in the title of this chapter in order to cue the reader that what is to come is probably new. When most people encounter the more familiar term, epilepsy, or related phrases such as epileptic seizure, they are likely to think of the very dramatic event in which an individual suddenly jerks uncontrollably, falls to the floor, and loses consciousness. Such an event is a major seizure but is just one type of expression of a disorder which can take many forms. The term "ictus" (adjective: "ictal") which is a synonym of seizure, is used in an attempt to break away from the singularity of that image and that meaning. In what is to follow, it will emerge that just about any form of behavior pathology may have ictus as its underlying cause. The chapter will begin with a description of the assessment technique which made possible modern understanding of seizure disorders and many other aspects of brain function as well, the electroencephalograph (EEG). The topic of ictus is then introduced with brief descriptions of a number of frequent and rare manifestations of these disorders in order to present some of the range of what can occur. Most of the rest of the chapter will be devoted to classifying and explaining these highly varied symptoms. Special attention will be given to seizures that appear primarily in infancy and early childhood.

The EEG – Technology, Output, and Concepts

Study of epilepsy and, as will be seen in the next chapter, of sleep, has been made possible by the development of techniques for registering the electrical activity of the nervous system. This is a field of study within the neurosciences called psychophysiology. It is defined by its methodology which measures detectable changes in physiological functions of different parts of the body. In humans these methods are almost always non-invasive, i.e. do not penetrate the skin and include, for example, heart rate or blood pressure. The psychological part of psychophysiology comes with comparisons of tonic states and phasic responses to changes in stimulation during measurement of normal and impaired individuals. For example, heart rate while resting and while watching a distressing photograph can be compared in persons who complain of excessive anxiety and those who do not. An important branch of psychophysiology is that which measures the electrical activity of the brain at the scalp, the EEG.

The procedure is attributed to a German psychiatrist named Hans Berger who in 1924 first discovered that brain waves could be successfully recorded, and that they had lawful and meaningful properties. An EEG is the product of an electronic device which permits the observation of events that are ordinarily difficult or impossible to perceive. Consider first a more familiar example, the stethoscope. As the reader knows, this is a device which enables the physician to hear the heart beat more accurately. The device placed on the chest registers the sound which is then mechanically (in older versions) or electronically (in newer models) amplified so that these sounds from deep within the chest can be heard easily. The part that registers the sound is called a transducer, that is, it registers the information in some manner. In the case of the stethoscope, some element in the device placed on the chest is changed by the vibrations emitted by the heart. The transducer for the EEG is an electrode, a small piece of metal that readily conducts electricity, which is attached to the scalp by various means (glue-like substances or tape) with an interface that assures good electronic contact. The electrode is attached to an insulated wire that goes to an amplifier.

Electrical activity at the scalp is a byproduct of neural activity from various sources including muscle and skin. Electrical activity coming from brain is not the most prominent. It is of small amplitude, on the order of microvolts (μV), millionths of a volt. The technical problem, originally solved by Berger, and vastly improved over the years, was to determine how to identify and amplify the brain waves and disregard the other electrical activity present.

This became possible as it came to be known that the different sources of electrical activity generated outputs in waveforms with different features of frequency and amplitude. Frequency refers to the number of cycles per second in which the waves of energy occur, while amplitude refers to the intensity of that energy transmission. It may help to grasp the meaning of the terms if it is realized that for sound, frequency determines pitch, and amplitude determines loudness. That being the case, different waveforms convey information. The problem then becomes deciphering the code by which this information is conveyed.

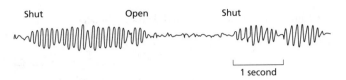

Shut   Open   Shut

1 second

Figure 8.1   Changes in brain activity as the eyes open and shut

Berger did not know in advance at what frequency and amplitude brain waves appeared. But with the crude amplifiers available to him at the time, he hit upon a number of discoveries which subsequently opened the way to the knowledge we have today. He found that a certain very regular wave whose frequency was about eight to ten cycles per second would often appear, especially at the back of the head, if his subject was awake, with eyes closed, and in a state of aimless revery or boredom. Since this was the first brain wave discovered, he called it alpha (α) after the first letter of the Greek alphabet. If eyes were opened and the subject began, for example, to think about next day's school work, the waves would change: they would decrease in amplitude and increase in frequency, to 14 cycles per second, or more. The waves would become shorter and faster. Berger called these waves beta (β). An illustration of this shift from the work of Lord Adrian (Adrian & Matthews, 1934), an early investigator who followed up Berger's work, can be found in figure 8.1. Today, frequency or cycles per second is specified by a term which honors the name of a pioneer in the study of electricity, Hertz. Henceforth, this convention will be used here. When you see "Hz," the abbreviation of Hertz, think cycles per second.

The shift from α to β waves was really quite remarkable since it made possible the observation of an objective change in brain activity that occurred at the same time as a subjective change in state and behavior. Understanding what determined the change in waves is fundamental to the comprehension of many ideas about brain function. Since an EEG electrode registers the summed activity of millions of cells, what must be grasped is first, what it means when so many cells generate large, relatively slow waves and then what it means when the same cells generate small, relatively fast waves.

To help understand this difference, imagine yourself walking across a rickety bridge at a river crossing. Every time your right foot takes a step, some energy, the result of your weight hitting the bridge, is transmitted to the bridge and sways it in one direction. When your left foot takes the next step, it would tend to sway the bridge in the opposite direction. The result might be that the bridge would sway a little with regular peaks and troughs. Now imagine being one of a large group of soldiers.

Each of the soldiers would produce their own little wave. If they are marching in lock step, then the peaks and troughs would coincide in time and the sway would be large. The energy from each individual would cumulate, so much so that the moorings of the weakened bridge might break up. To avoid such a catastrophe, those in charge would order the soldiers to break lock step and go across the bridge at their own pace. Under this condition, at any moment in time some soldiers' right feet might strike the pavement while others were stepping with their left. The forces

Table 8.1   EEG frequency bands and associated features (Brazier et al., 1961)

Name	Hz	Associated features
Δ	<4	Present in normal sleep, coma, mental retardation
θ	4–7	Present in the immature, associated with developmental disorders
α	8–12	Present during relaxed revery with eyes closed
β	>13	Present during information processing

would sum algebraically but the effect of one person would cancel rather than add to the effect of another. Overall, the amplitude of the sway would be small and the frequency would be fast.

The example teaches us that when energy from many units is produced simultaneously, or in synchrony, large-amplitude waves are generated. By contrast, when each unit is going at its own pace, or when there is desynchrony, only low-amplitude waves are generated because the energy from individual units tends to cancel out rather than cumulate with the energy of other units. Now recall that the psychological state associated with α, the more synchronized wave, was relaxed, perhaps bored, idling, while the brain producing β was working, i.e. actively thinking. This shift from idling to activity, from relative synchrony to relative desynchrony, provides one definition of a word that will be used often in the book, arousal.

Arousal is relative because waves slower than α were later discovered and, as technology improved and electronic means became available, higher frequencies that cannot be distinguished by the naked eye could be specified and measured. Brain waves whose frequencies were between 4 and 7 Hz were found in children and were named theta (θ), and even slower waves were found some time after a person fell asleep. These waves, between 1 and 3 Hz, were called delta (Δ). They were not seen in normal waking states. Higher-frequency waves have not been given Greek names but are characterized by numbered frequency bands, e.g. 40 Hz.

Although the definition of exactly which frequency should be included under each of the Greek labels varies somewhat from authority to authority, table 8.1 lists a commonly utilized specification for the wave bands regularly measured in the EEG (Brazier et al., 1961). Note that synchrony and arousal are relative and that, as you go down the list, the frequencies reflect more and more desynchrony. Also note that the order of the Greek labels derives from the history of their discovery and not the order of that alphabet.

Today, diagnostic EEGs are performed in many clinics and research laboratories all over the world. The method is basically the same as Berger's but electronic technology and standardization of procedures have vastly improved. Electrode placement (Jasper, 1958) is generally done in reference to standard locations (coded with numbers and letters – odd digits on the left, even on the right; codes ending in z are in the midline) determined by an international conference of EEG workers (Brazier et al., 1961). See figure 8.2 for an illustration of what it looks like to take an EEG and the 19 standard positions (17 on the scalp and one on each ear lobe) at which the electrodes are placed. The voltages generally measured are either the difference between each electrode and the average of that found in the two ear lobes (a referential montage) or the difference between several pairs of electrodes on the scalp (a bipolar montage). The brain waves are drawn on steadily moving paper on a machine whose generic name is polygraph (translation: many write) which has a pen for each electrode in a referential montage or for a pair of electrodes in a bipolar montage. The pen's deflections are a calibrated analog of the voltage at that site. (See figure 8.3 for a partial sample of an EEG of a normal individual who is awake.)

The clinical EEG is "read" and interpreted by a specially trained professional, generally a neurologist, who scans page after page of the EEG for evidence of the overall pattern of the EEG and for the specific incidence of normal or abnormal wave forms. In newer developments, data storage and analysis may be conducted by computer which samples and stores the voltages 100 or more times a second. When desired, the data can be presented for inspection on a computer screen and read like the paper record, but more importantly, when the data are in digital form, quantitative analyses of their features are made possible. There will be further information about this in a later chapter. The clinical EEG is largely a measure of tonic resting state. That is, subjects sit or recline in a relaxed posture and are not asked to do very much beyond opening or shutting their eyes. Certain activating procedures may also be used which will be discussed later in this chapter.

Ictus in Older Children and Adults

There are major differences in the quality of seizures that appear in infancy and early childhood and those that begin later in life, so they will be presented in separate sections, the latter group coming first. To begin, there are verbal sketches of some of the varied forms that seizures may take.

Some ictal symptoms

1. Jerky arms and hands.   A child of eight, eating cereal at breakfast, suddenly finds her right hand and arm, the one holding the spoon, jerking uncontrollably for about five seconds. The uncontrollable movements seem to begin at the elbows, which flail outwardly. Her spoon drops and milk is spilled. When this first happens, her parents think she is refusing to eat her cereal because she is angry at her brother.

2. Off in never-never land.   A little boy of six, sitting with a group of his peers listening to the teacher tell a story, is asked a simple question about what has just been said. The child has no answer and seems totally unresponsive for about ten seconds, his eyes apparently looking at a corner of the ceiling. The teacher calls his

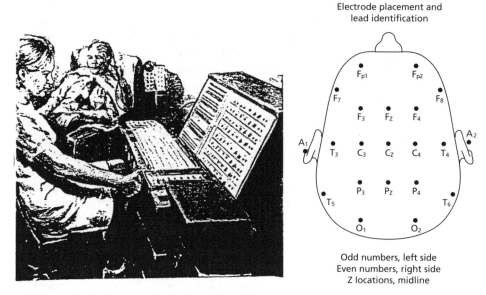

Electrode placement and
lead identification

Odd numbers, left side
Even numbers, right side
Z locations, midline

Figure 8.2 A polygraph and subject being given an EEG: standard position of electrode placements

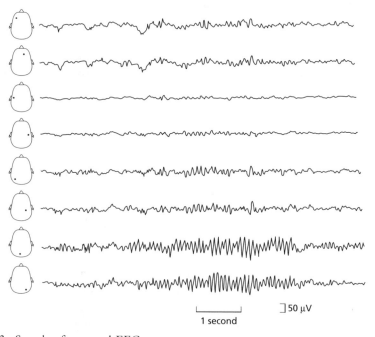

50 μV

1 second

Figure 8.3 Sample of a normal EEG

name again but just as she starts to utter the words, he smiles at her and says something with tangential relevance. The teacher is confused by the child's behavior, but other children begin to talk and she turns her attention to them.

3. Itching to fight. A boy of 13, who is quite bright and often does well in school, is shunned by most of his peers because he is often provoked to severe rage and fighting by events that others might barely notice. Thus he has gotten into fights when his name has been mispronounced, when another child has brushed past him accidentally in a crowded hall, and when he thought he observed his peers laughing and making fun of him even though they were not. Most of his fights are with males, but he has also struck females. As he gets into a fight he appears to be in an altered state, and when the fight is over and he has calmed down, he often cannot remember what provoked him. He has, at times, expressed the wish that his temper would be under better control, but he generally refuses to discuss his behavior.

4. Poor checker playing. A girl is prone to spells of staring, particularly while playing checkers or any game that required strategic, thinking. She was a poor player. (Siegel et al., 1992)

5. Language disintegration and recovery. A man goes through episodes lasting as long as several hours during which his language gradually deteriorates to a point that he can barely find words to utter. Later, language gradually returns to normal. (Lecours & Joanette, 1980)

6. Reading disruption. A teenager has episodes in which she would begin to read and then find her jaw jerking. If she stopped reading the jerking would cease. At times, if she continued reading, she would lose consciousness and her whole body would begin to jerk (Christie et al., 1988). Other children just show disruption of the reading process. (Oettinger, Nekonishi, & Gill, 1967)

7. Number disruption. Another person has episodes in which he becomes confused whenever doing math computations that are more complex than simple arithmetic. His work then shows many errors. This is especially likely if he is given verbal problems involving arithmetic. There are many times, however, when the work at this level is done successfully. This person never becomes confused while reading nonmathematical material while example 6 never becomes confused while doing arithmetic. (Anderson & Wallis, 1986)

8. Depression. A 15-year-old experiences unpredictable bouts of depression that begin and end suddenly and are very severe. The onset of depression, which might last from minutes to weeks, rarely has any relationship to events in his life. (Dreyfus, 1981)

9. Stomach aches. A ten-year-old is beset by stomach cramps that are unrelated to anything she eats. They occur at any time of day, but mostly in the morning.

Parents and teachers are convinced that she uses these pains as an excuse to stay away from school.

10.   Psychosis.   A 12-year-old reports vivid hallucinations that occur after experiencing flashes of light. The hallucinations always began in this way but their contents vary considerably. Sometimes they are scary and sometimes pleasant.   (Flor-Henry, 1969)

The phenomenon of ictus

If one thinks about the behaviors described above, it is apparent that for all their diversity they share a number of features. These include their variability, their unpredictability, their disruptive quality, and their compellingness. Prior to the invention of the EEG, enlightened thought saw those individuals with the more conspicuous of these symptoms as suffering from psychiatric disorders. Religious and popular opinion often interpreted such behaviors to indicate possession by the devil. It was only after the EEG had demonstrated that at least some of these symptoms were directly associated with abnormal brain electrical activity that such behaviors came to be widely accepted as symptoms of brain dysfunction. Since evidence for some of the behaviors described above is often not clearly associated with EEG abnormalities, their inclusion as types of epilepsy is controversial. These matters will be clarified as the chapter progresses.

One feature of ictus upon which there is agreement is that in some conditions the entire brain is affected while in others only a part. This contrast would be exemplified by the differences between a major seizure, where the person falls unconscious to the floor, and the situation where the child's arm jerks uncontrollably. In the former case, the whole of the person's behavior has been captured, in the latter only the movement of one arm.

This leads to another agreed-upon feature of epilepsy, which is its episodic character. This is a recurrent disorder that comes and goes. It is not like many other neurological disorders, e.g. a stroke, where large amounts of brain tissue die and those functions controlled by that tissue are subtracted from the repertoire of the brain's capability (although various kinds of compensation may later develop). Epilepsy's disruptive effects are present only during active episodes. There generally are no obvious signs that the disorder is present if the person is encountered between episodes. For some, the episodes appear to occur spontaneously, whereas for others, certain kinds of experiences appear to trigger the epileptic event. Although some ictal events are prolonged and can last for hours or even days, these are quite rare. Most are brief, lasting only from seconds to minutes.

These phenomena are puzzling and challenge understanding. Some concepts and ways of thinking can help explain why such disruptive events occur at some times and not at others. Some types of epilepsy that were studied first gave clues to at least some of the mechanisms of the disorder, and these will be described next.

Some principles determining ictal events and their ramifications: focal origins in epilepsy

1. Excitability. A normal neuron's functioning is dependent on its property of excitability, that is, its reactivity to inputs from other neurons or, if sensory neurons are involved, to changes in environmental stimulation.

2. Excitability in neural circuits spreads. This is another way of saying what was described as neurotransmission in the early chapters of this book. Excitability in one neuron can be transmitted from the axons of one neuron to the dendrites and cell bodies of others.

3. The spread of excitability must be patterned and channeled. Excitability must be regulated and inhibited or else it will spread uncontrollably and chaos will result. This is much like saying that wires carrying electricity must be insulated from each other or else they will short out, produce fires, blow fuses, and not do what they were designed to do. (For a review of recent knowledge about neural excitability see Knowles & Lūders, 1993.)

4. The control of the spread of excitability depends on the magnitude of the excitation, the properties of the neurons as well as the properties of the milieu. The term milieu here refers to the environment of neurons which largely consists of the fluids which bathe and nurture them and the cells which are adjacent. Some milieus appear to facilitate the spread of irritability while others resist such spread. Evidence supporting this principle comes from many sources including medical experience in treating certain forms of epilepsy. There are, for example, women whose seizures cluster during the latter part of their menstrual cycles. Such seizures may often decrease in frequency or disappear altogether if the patients are treated with diuretics, drugs which facilitate the excretion of liquid and affect the milieu but do not directly alter the neurons themselves.

5. Abnormal excitability of neurons is provoked by the disorganization of tissue. The best-known anatomic impairment that gives rise to seizures is the scar tissue that forms following a contusion. A contusion is a technical term for a sore or a cut, for example, of the knees or hands that just about everybody experiences at some time in life. Typically the skin will be torn and there may be bleeding. If the rent in the skin is large enough, there may be a scar afterward. The scar reflects the imperfect matching up of previously intact strands of tissue. If the skull is fractured and the bone is depressed into the brain substance, tissue layers in the brain are physically displaced and many cells die. If the depressed bone is removed and the person survives, natural processes gradually clean up the debris and the tissue reconnects, but a scar also forms. Scars in the brain are sites of excessive excitation and are found to be foci (singular: focus; adjective: focal) of seizure activity, places where at least some kinds of seizures originate. As might be expected, ictal activity is associated with lessened GABAergic activity and increased activity of excitatory neurotransmitters such as glutamate. (For a review see Schwartzkroin, 1993.)

6.   A seizure focus, often a scar, contains cells that fire at an abnormally high rate in a manner that is immune to input from other neurons.   It has efferent processes but lacks afferent input, or, in other words, it sends but does not receive. Surrounding the focus are more normal cells which do receive inputs and send outputs. These cells are susceptible to firing from the focus but they are also influenced by normal neuronal activity. If they are "captured" by the focus, a large enough mass of cells may be set to firing abnormally so that seizure activity will spread. If their excitability is inhibited by inputs from other sources then they can resist the spread of the seizure and dampen and insulate the output of the focus. (Schwartzkroin & Wyler, 1980)

From these principles, the following summary provides a basis for comprehending some forms of epilepsy. Normal neural activity goes awry at sites called foci where groups of neurons fire at abnormal rates and are immune to inhibitory activity. The focus may be a small area. For the process to affect behavior significantly, more brain must be involved, so the disturbance must spread. The amount of spread depends on the milieu which varies in facilitating spread and on the activity of adjacent neurons. Adjacent neurons may function to dampen and restrain further spread or may help it along. Their own state of excitability, which may depend on the current overall activity of the subject and on the way other populations of neurons are functioning at that moment, determines whether the entire brain will be captured, only a part, or essentially none. Neuron groups other than the focus thus serve as positive or negative feedback to the activity in the focus.

One set of events that exemplifies what was just described is called a Jacksonian march, named after a British neurologist, Hughlings Jackson, who was a pioneer student of this disorder. Consider the symptoms described in Symptom 1, above, labelled as "jerky hands." As it happens, this type of seizure has also been named after Jackson and is called a Jacksonian seizure, an uncontrollable movement of a muscle group, often in a limb. When there is a "march," the seizure process first may affect an arm, for example, but then captures the shoulders, the legs, and the head of the subject. At that point, jerking may give way to loss of consciousness and the person will fall. More will be presented later about the type of seizure that ended the sequence. For now, the important points to keep in mind are that the seizure begins at a particular place and then may proceed to capture the entire brain.

Given the behaviors observed, one might ask where in the brain does the seizure originate. Since it began with the arm jerking, it is plausible that it would be in the area of the motor strip involved in the control of the arm. Generally, such conjectures are verified by EEG data which indicate abnormality over the motor strip of the hemisphere contralateral to the jerking arm and normal activity elsewhere. As the Jacksonian march progresses, the EEG would show the spread of abnormalities to other areas and then to the other hemisphere. The kind of abnormalities on the EEG that suggest this kind of seizure activity are sharp waves or spikes because they are

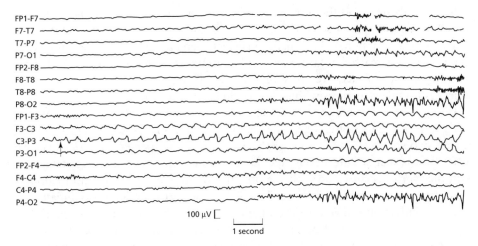

FP1-F7
F7-T7
T7-P7
P7-O1
FP2-F8
F8-T8
T8-P8
P8-O2
FP1-F3
F3-C3
C3-P3
P3-O1
FP2-F4
F4-C4
C4-P4
P4-O2

100 µV

1 second

Figure 8.4 EEG with spike activity first beginning in the left central region, then spreading to other regions in the left hemisphere

conspicuous in the ongoing EEG and look sharp or spiky. Spikes reflect sudden, massive, synchronous discharge of neurons. Figure 8.4 is an example of an EEG that begins in the motor area and spreads to other parts of the same hemisphere.

Ictal events reflect excessive synchrony. The seizure process, especially as it spreads, may be viewed as an example of a positive feedback runaway (chapter 4). The response to excessive synchrony in one place is to further increase synchrony elsewhere until the whole brain is captured. To stop a seizure process, some negative feedback must be introduced to the system to increase desynchrony. As will be discussed below, these principles have some use in helping people to cope with and arrest seizures.

If a focus can be anywhere in the brain, what happens if it is located in a sensory area? If a seizure is initiated there, no overt behavior will signal the ongoing ictus, as in the case of the Jacksonian seizure, because motor areas of the brain are unaffected. Although an observer will not be able to detect any changes, the person may have a variety of experiences depending on the location of the focus. Light flashes, tingly sensations, noises, or voices may be experienced. Note that unless the person is connected to an EEG machine and abnormal spikes are apparent in the appropriate areas – temporal lobe for auditory, parietal lobe for somatosensory, and occipital lobe for visual experiences – there is no evidence that corresponds to the person's experience. An individual reporting such events may easily be thought to be having hallucinations, perceptual experiences in the absence of objective events, and be suffering from a psychosis rather than a seizure disorder. A Jacksonian march can also occur with a sensory focus, i.e. the seizure activity can spread from sensory areas. If the initiating experience recurs regularly, it is called an aura and is experienced by the patient as a warning of the oncoming events produced by the march. An aura is the sensory equivalent of a Jacksonian (motor) seizure and provides valuable information about the location of the focus.

So far, only scars and the disruption of normal tissue organization have been presented as determiners of seizure foci. A number of others are known. One important type is a gestational abnormality in which benign tissue that does not belong there, called a hamartoma, grows into and infiltrates the temporal lobe. Another type is a consequence of excessive pressure, for example, from the growth of a tumor that squeezes normal structures within the confined space of the skull.

It might be noted here that a single seizure does not qualify for the diagnosis of epilepsy. Neurologists often make the diagnosis only after a person has suffered from at least two seizures. The reason for this is that up to 50 percent of individuals who suffer from a first seizure never experience another. However, the percentages vary with the type of seizure and with the presence or absence of EEG abnormalities, so the decision as to whether to wait and see if more seizures develop or to initiate treatment is a judgment call of physician, patient, and family (Aicardi, 1994, p. 279).

More consideration will be given later to what determines seizure disorders. At this point, there is some foundation for reviewing the way in which seizures are classified in older children and adults. It will then become apparent that the idea of a focus does not adequately account for the range of ictal events, and other mechanisms will be described.

Classification of seizure disorders

The International League Against Epilepsy authorized a group of experts to devise a classification scheme of the epilepsies. Their system was published (Commission on Classification and Terminology of the International League Against Epilepsy, 1981) and is widely used today. Table 8.2 contains a summary of the most salient aspects of that classification system. Although such classifications are subject to periodic revision, they are useful in becoming familiar with some of the disorder's complexity.

Examination of the table reveals that the classification is based on symptoms and on the distinction between partial and generalized seizures. Partial seizures capture only a part of the brain whereas generalized seizures involve the entire brain. In the former case one would see spikes only in a certain area, whereas in the latter they would be present all over the brain. Another issue in the classification system is the sequence of events. Does the partial seizure stay the way it began or does it "evolve" into some other type? In other words, is there some form of Jacksonian march? Finally, the scheme attends to whether consciousness is involved. Consciousness refers to the level of responsiveness of the individual. Its disturbances can range from a profound unconsciousness, in which an individual is unresponsive to all environmental events and loses control of posture, through varying degrees of awareness and haziness of control. The regulation of consciousness is in the deep structures of the brain, and disturbances of consciousness imply that the ictal process has spread to those centers.

The classification of seizure symptoms overlaps considerably with Luria's ideas about the primary, secondary, and tertiary association areas of the brain (chapter 5).

Table 8.2 The International Classification of Epileptic Seizures

---

I. **Partial (focal, local) seizures**
  (A) Simple partial seizures (consciousness not impaired)
    1. With motor symptoms
    2. With somatosensory or special sensory symptoms
    3. With autonomic symptoms
    4. With psychic symptoms
  (B) Complex partial seizures (with impairment of consciousness)
    1. Beginning as simple partial seizures and progressing to impairment of consciousness
      (a) With no other features
      (b) With features as in I.A.1–I.A.4
      (c) With automatisms
    2. With impairment of consciousness at onset
      (a) With no other features
      (b) With features as in I.A.1–I.A.4
      (c) With automatisms
  (C) Partial seizures evolving to secondarily generalized seizures.
    1. Simple partial seizures evolving to generalized seizures
    2. Complex partial seizures evolving to generalized seizures
    3. Simple partial seizures evolving to complex partial seizures to generalized seizures

II. **Generalized seizures (convulsive or nonconvulsive)**
  (A) Absence seizures
    1. Absence seizures
    2. Atypical absence seizures
  (B) Myoclonic seizures
  (C) Clonic seizures
  (D) Tonic seizures
  (E) Tonic–clonic seizures
  (F) Atonic seizures (astatic seizures)

III. **Unclassified epileptic seizures**
  Includes all seizures that cannot be classified because of inadequate or incomplete data and some that defy classification in hitherto-described categories. This includes some neonatal seizures, e.g. rhythmic eye movements, chewing, and swimming movements

---

The term "simple" is used to refer to manifestations of primary area activity while the term "complex" is used to refer to secondary and tertiary activity. Consider line IA of table 8.2, Simple partial seizures. Consciousness is not impaired so the brainstem is not involved and the unimodal (one sensory modality) symptoms are consistent with the activity of Luria's primary motor (twitching muscles, jerking limbs) or primary sensory (lights flashing, noises, itches) areas. The classification adds symptoms where the ictal event captures the vagus nerve and affects the autonomic nervous system. Here the focus most likely is in the hypothalamic and limbic area. The classification system also mentions "With psychic symptoms." Here the seizure focus extends into secondary and possibly tertiary cortical areas, producing more complex, multimodal (several sensory modalities), subjective experiences, perhaps hallucinations, or more complex behaviors such as buttoning and unbuttoning clothes, yet not spread beyond those areas.

Lines IB and IC of the classification scheme reflect the complexities of the way in which partial seizures may appear. In B, emphasis is given to whether disturbances of consciousness are present at the outset or appear in the course of the seizure. Whereas in category B the seizures remain partial, in C they progress to generalized seizures, to be discussed shortly. In practice, a diagnosis of Simple partial seizures is made when the symptoms are simple, unimodal, and non-progressive. Complex partial is diagnosed when the symptoms are complex, multimodal and/or affect consciousness in some degree. Secondarily generalized seizures are diagnosed when they progress to major seizures. The hallmark of partial seizures on the EEG is evidence of localization, a place where it starts. Complex partial seizures may be termed temporal lobe seizures if they are associated with foci in the temporal lobe, an area of the brain that appears to be particularly susceptible to ictal activity. They may also be associated with foci in the frontal lobe and, more rarely, elsewhere in the cortex. If complex behavior occurs, they may be called psychomotor seizures. Figure 8.5 shows an EEG with spikes to the front on the right side of the brain and no such activity on the left.

In classic neurology, psychomotor seizures have a stereotyped, rigid quality, which for some observers is their hallmark. A common symptom is a highly practiced, ritualized behavior, such as buttoning and unbuttoning clothes, or various grooming tasks. There is little question that these stereotyped sequences are the consequences of temporal lobe ictus. The attribution of ictal causation to less stereotyped, but episodic and disruptive subjective experiences and behaviors without other explanation, is far more controversial. This issue will be considered further later in the chapter.

Turning to line II, Generalized seizures, the classification scheme identifies those types of ictus in which the entire brain is captured instantly, where, so far as we know, there is no particular focus, at least in the cortex. The explanation of the curious parenthetical "convulsive or nonconvulsive" in the classification scheme will be considered below. Line IIE, tonic–clonic seizures, is considered first. This is the most familiar and common form of generalized seizure, and is convulsive. The term "tonic" refers to the presence of heightened, extreme, excitatory tone in muscles throughout the body. As a result the body goes stiff and falls. Stiffness alternates with the "clonic" aspect of the seizure in which the body jerks and convulses. During the tonic phase, breathing is arrested, and during the seizure, the individual is likely to be incontinent. The duration of each phase at the beginning may be four to eight seconds but then the stiffness decreases, the jerking becomes less extreme and the patient, breathing heavily, lapses into a quiet state of unconsciousness from which

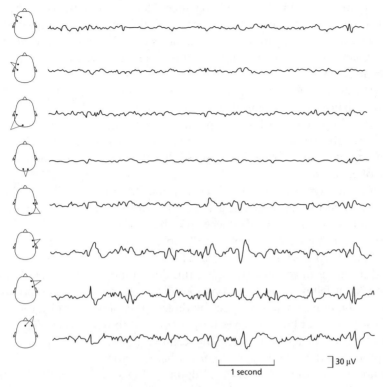

Figure 8.5 EEG in complex partial seizures. Note spikes on right but not on left side

he/she will gradually awaken in three to five minutes. For some time thereafter there is confusion and difficulty remembering. These conditions are called postictal amnesia and confusion.

This is a very dramatic and emotionally trying event to observe. It is often called a grand mal (big sick, in French) seizure. Although it can seem to last a lifetime, it is most often a self-limiting event that runs its course in four or five minutes. An observer might be tempted to try to stop or interfere with the seizure, but this can easily increase harm. What can be helpful is to cushion the fall, remove objects which flailing limbs might strike, and loosen clothing to aid breathing. These kinds of seizures have been known to occur in many talented individuals, the Roman general Julius Caesar and the Russian writer Fyodor Dostoyevsky to name two, and do not necessarily produce any changes in mental competence in the long run. Thus seizures are major manifestations of conditions of dyscontrol (see end of chapter 4). On rare occasions, a seizure does not come to a halt but persists for more than a few minutes. Such an occurrence, which is called status epilepticus, is a medical emergency which requires immediate attention.

Lines IIC, Clonic seizures, and IID, tonic seizures refer to conditions where only one of the two phases in tonic–clonic seizures is present. Such occurrences are quite rare. Also quite rare is line IIF, atonic seizures. Here we have the opposite, in some sense, of tonic seizures. Instead of going stiff, the body goes limp. The seizure process, instead of overexciting every muscle, suddenly cuts off excitation to the muscles. Again, the person will fall but, rather than keel over, is more likely to just sort of melt down.

Line IIB, myoclonic seizures, are characterized, by motor jerking. Unlike focal Jacksonian seizures, these occur all over the body, have sudden onset and are symmetrical when in pure form. The full appearance of the disorder is probably very rare in pure form although some of its components, known as myoclonic jerks, are quite common and often are normal in the sense that they occur when there is no other evidence of epilepsy.

The remaining type of generalized seizure, line IIA, absence seizures, also termed petit mal (French for "little sick"), is the source of the parenthetic statement, convulsive or nonconvulsive, for this is a seizure that is nonconvulsive. It is this type of seizure that has required a different sort of explanation than the focus–milieu–spread idea that appears to work so well for partial seizures. Absence seizures are described as short disruptions of consciousness, but this does not do justice to the fact that the subject does not fall or become unconscious. The disorder is most common in children and is sometimes hard to detect by direct observation because the child may only appear to stare or blink the eyes for perhaps two to ten seconds. The beginning and end of the seizure are abrupt, and the seizure is not followed by postictal amnesia or confusion. But the child is likely to miss what was going on while the seizure was present, not be able to respond if called upon to do so, and appear to be temporarily "out of it." There is a very specific "signature" or set of findings on the EEG for absence, three per second spike and wave, which will appear at all leads on the EEG. Figure 8.6 is an example of such an EEG.

Mirsky and Van Buren (1965) monitored and recorded the EEG while behavior was tested with a continuous performance test which requires continuing alertness and attention (see chapter 10) and other techniques in patients with absence. The impact of the seizure on attention and information processing could be observed directly. They determined that lapses of attention often preceded the appearance of the spike and wave on the EEG. They also learned that some information actually does get through during the course of the seizure. This led them to suggest that, subjectively, an absence seizure might be thought of as having the effect of a large sudden wave of noise. During its presence, most information is obliterated but some small proportion might be detectable. Such findings have been found by others and have been reviewed by Aicardi (1994, p. 102).

Because generalized seizures appear to begin simultaneously all over the brain, it had been assumed that there must be some sort of abnormal focus deep in the brainstem which sets off a seizure process that appears everywhere at the cortical surface all at once. The notion was a kind of upward Jacksonian climb rather than the lateral Jacksonian march. The term centrencephalic was used by Penfield and Jasper (1954) to convey this concept. The concept may or may not be valid for some convulsive seizures but a different kind of explanation of the seizure mechanism has arisen in the case of absence. This will be the subject of the next section.

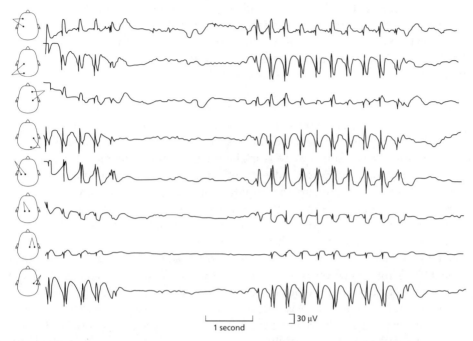

Figure 8.6 EEG of absence or petit mal seizure. Note 3-second spike and wave

Nonfocal, generalized seizure activity, especially absence

Absence seizures begin (and end) suddenly all over the brain and carry the remarkable three per second spike and wave signature, not the kind of data consistent with a focal site of origin from which excessive excitability spreads elsewhere. These phenomena have been the subject of study by many scholars who have tried to understand how this comes about. One researcher in this effort has been Gloor (1979, 1988), whose work exemplifies the search for a different kind of mechanism for generalized seizure production. His work takes account of the three per second spike and wave EEG pattern which has been a perplexing regularity in an area where most everything is irregular and unpredictable.

In experimental work with cats, spike and wave seizures can be induced temporarily by intramuscular injection of penicillin. In this context, penicillin is an epileptogenic (seizure-producing) agent. Studies of the details of seizure induction suggested that the effect of epileptogenic agents is to increase the excitability and, on balance, reduce the inhibitability, of cortical cells. Study of normal-functioning animals indicated that, when awake, the cortex was regularly bombarded with volleys of excitatory stimulation originating in the thalamus. This excitation is thought to be the final step in the chain of events known as reticular arousal. The excitation stems from nonspecific centers in the thalamus and below and affects the cortex as a whole. Normally, one can record these volleys of excitation in the thalamus and in the pathways from thalamus to cortex, but there is no evidence of them explicitly in the cortex. This changes when the epileptogenic substance is injected. Then, recordings at the surface show bursts of activity coincident with the bursts seen at the thalamus. It is inferred that in the normal cortex these bursts are inactivated by the inhibitory properties of the cortex, whereas when inhibition is reduced, the thalamic activity shows through at the surface.

The timing of these events is a crucial part of the evidence. Thalamic bursts which are ongoing in the waking animal, occur at the rate of about three per second. These bursts, when they do appear in cortex, take the form of spikes. The spikes at the cortex are each accompanied by waves. The spike and wave complex seen in experimentally induced epilepsy is similar or identical to that seen in human absence seizures. If the spike represents the breakthrough of thalamic excitation, what then does the wave represent? One explanation is that it reflects the inefficient, lagging inhibitory response of the cortical cells. In other words, three per second spike and wave represents a phase lag (see chapter 5), a failure of systemic timing of inhibitory functions. If the inhibition were more timely, the spike, and the wave, would not be evident. This interpretation of experimental research findings in animals was confirmed by depth electrode studies in humans with absence seizures.

The full story is more complex, but the upshot of this chain of evidence is to view absence seizures not as the consequence of an irritable focus that spreads, but of a cortex with weak or inefficient inhibitory capabilities that at times fails to inhibit normally occurring thalamic excitation efficiently. Such an explanation accounts for the generality of the seizure (it occurs everywhere on the cortex), its sudden onset and offset, its nonconvulsive character, the absence of postictal confusion or amnesia, and the continuing ability to process some information during the seizure. The explanation is also consistent with the evidence that many petit mal seizures tend to occur in childhood and disappear with maturation, a process which is generally associated with the development of greater inhibitory capabilities. That absence seizures may have different mechanisms of action than partial seizures is also supported by evidence that each type of disorder is benefited most by different medications.

There is another set of facts that Gloor's work helps to explain. Focal seizures appear to be fostered by conditions of relative synchrony, e.g. drowsiness and boredom, and occur less often in conditions of desynchrony as occurs with mental activity. When this writer took on the task of testing patients with focal epilepsy so uncontrolled that they were being considered for brain surgery, he expected to have to deal with any number of seizure events. I was amazed, however, that in the course of day-long testing of over 50 patients, no seizures ever occurred. A plausible explanation was that many of these persons led lives in which they experienced little mental stimulation, but while being tested the reverse was true and during that time seizures did not occur. By contrast, there are patients who are likely to have seizures when they are upset, overexcited, or overanxious, conditions that produce desynchrony. The question is why they are not immune to seizures under such conditions. Gloor's theory resolves this contradiction with evidence that some types of seizures are associated with excessive excitation. In these individuals, externally provoked excitement and desynchrony appear to overwhelm inhibitory capabilities.

The upshot of these considerations is that, as a general rule, seizure-prone patients are vulnerable to both extremes of too little and too much excitement. This is because many suffer from a combination of disorders, the subject of the next topic.

Clinical reality and treatment

The classification scheme in table 8.2 suggests relatively "pure" or "ideal" types. Such a scheme is useful in helping the observer to note the different ways in which seizures can present themselves. In reality, the actual experience of patients with epilepsy ranges from two episodes of one kind of seizure, through repeated experiences with the same kind of seizure at frequencies that can extend from once a decade to several times a day, to the experience of many different kinds of seizures, often with certain types dominating for years at a time and then giving way to other types. Many children with absence seizures are seizure-free in adolescence and adulthood but others go on to have tonic–clonic seizures. Often more than one seizure type is present in the same ictal event while in other cases any single ictal event may be of one type, but different ones will appear on different occasions. There is a condition known as absence status (like status epilepticus, but with petit mal rather than grand mal) in which a person continues to function despite ongoing and nonterminating absence (Myslobodsky, 1988). Andermann and Robb (1972) describe the subjective states of these individuals as ranging from prolonged subjective impairment ("bad" or "dull" days, when one feels very slow), through periods of obvious confusion, to periods of lethargy and stupor. Further consideration of these complexities is beyond the scope of this book but the reader who wishes further information might consult such papers as those of Rodin (1987) and Berkovic et al. (1987).

For some, seizures do not begin until adolescence or later. In general, if seizures first occur as late as middle adulthood or beyond, the more likely are they symptomatic of some other pathology, for example, a growing tumor or a metabolic disease. When there is no other pathology to which the seizure can be attributed, the condition is said to be idiopathic, a disorder with no known cause, and it is this situation that is classically known as epilepsy. However, just because seizures begin early in life does not necessarily make them truly idiopathic since some are associated with brain injury consequent to birth trauma.

There is strong evidence that many forms of idiopathic epilepsy are transmitted genetically, especially absence (Berkovic et al., 1987; Treiman & Treiman, 1993). The nature of the transmitted impairment is not known, though it is likely to vary for different types of seizures. It seems plausible to suggest that a milieu that is susceptible to seizure spread may be one type, and inadequate cortical inhibition may be another.

The most common treatment for seizures is medication. Although until recently there were only a relatively small number of anti-epileptic agents, they must be prescribed selectively since, as noted above, different agents appear to be more effective for different symptoms. The other problem is dose since an appropriate amount of the drug must be ingested regularly to maintain effective levels in the blood stream. This varies with the age, weight, sex, and unique characteristics of the individual, and must be titrated carefully by the physician, often on the basis of trial and error. Full knowledge of how anti-epileptic medications control seizure activity is not available but existing evidence suggests that some operate by blocking ion channels on the cell membrane that are needed for rapid firing and others enhance GABA activity (Ferrendelli & Mathews, 1993).

Drug treatment is effective in controlling seizures in a majority of cases. However, studies on the side effects of these drugs indicate the presence of both physical and cognitive changes. Generally, physicians are alert to such physical symptoms as eroded gums, changes in the skin, or liver disease, and switch medications or provide treatment for the side effects. They are generally less sensitive to frequently occurring cognitive changes such as difficulties in maintaining attention or processing information (Thompson & Trimble, 1982; Trimble, 1988). Such costs may well be worth the arrest or reduction of seizures, but many steps can be taken to reduce the medication required to control seizures and thus to minimize the side effects. However, when epilepsy is viewed as an affliction whose treatment is solely the responsibility of the doctor, and when the physician's concept is that the only meaningful treatment is medication, then these steps are all too often overlooked. These issues will be considered later in the chapter.

Despite the effectiveness of drugs, there are still many patients whose seizures are not well controlled. Physicians often would prescribe both increasing doses and more than one medication, particularly if more than one seizure type was present. Research on the efficacy of such polytherapy (multiple treatments) has clearly indicated that monotherapy (single treatment), is almost always as effective and with far fewer side effects. Monotherapy is the standard of practice in use today (Penry, 1986).

In cases of intractable (treatment-resistant) partial seizures, where a focus can be demonstrated, surgery aimed at removing the focus is available. The treatment was developed at the Montreal Neurological Institute (Penfield & Jasper, 1954) and is now performed in many centers throughout the world. It has contributed to much research on human brain functions (Novelly, 1992), since this operation, in particular, requires the exploration described at the end of chapter 3. Most such cases have foci in the temporal lobe and the surgeon wishes to remove the focus but spare enough tissue controlling memory and language so that he does not inadvertently do more harm than good. Since every brain is unique (Ojemann, 1979), not only must the location and extent of the focus be known (there is no point in removing a supposed focus only to find out it is not the true origin of the seizures), but also exactly where the centers for language and memory may be so they can be spared.

Surgery can be very successful and result in freedom from seizures, greatly reduced seizures, and/or decreased need for medication. The success of the operation has been found to vary with the age of the subjects (the best results before age 35) and especially with the discreteness and locale of the pathology. That is, patients with extensive pathology not confined to a cortical site are less likely to benefit (Crandall et al., 1990).

Another, more controversial, operation is available in a few surgical centers for patients with intractable epilepsy and extensive pathology: commissurotomy (cutting the commissures). In this procedure (Bogen & Vogel, 1962), the bands of tissue connecting the two hemispheres of the brain are cut, generally all or part of the corpus callosum, and sometimes the anterior or posterior commissure. The rationale of this surgery is that the development of a major tonic–clonic seizure depends on the capture of the entire brain by the seizure process. Research on animals had revealed that severing the commissures prevented the spread of seizure activity from one side of the brain to the other. Reports on a number of human cases so treated were quite positive although the outcome for others has been more dubious. Meanwhile, those individuals who have successfully survived such surgery have been the subjects for extensive studies about the differences between the hemispheres. Much of our knowledge about right and left hemisphere differences has stemmed from the study of just these people. Sperry (1982) won the Nobel prize for pioneering this work.

The most extreme surgical intervention is hemispherectomy (Crandall et al., 1990), where the cortex and underlying white matter are removed from an entire hemisphere, even at the anticipated cost of paralysis of the opposite side of the body. Again, this is done to stop the spread of ictal activity that leads to recurrent major seizures. If done early enough, the child may not only be seizure-free but may also improve in both cognitive and motor function. More information about the operation and its consequences is presented in the chapter on brain damage.

Ictus in Infants and Young Children

The general rule for seizures in infants and very young children who have relatively undifferentiated nervous systems is that they are more prone to seizures than adults and that they produce relatively gross, undifferentiated, and generally unlocalizable seizures. One might infer that they produce only generalized seizures, which in some sense is true, but these seizures are not associated with well-defined EEG patterns. All seizures in early infancy and some seizures in early childhood are different from those that appear later in the course of development (Freeman, 1995). The classification described above seems not to apply so they require separate consideration. Various classifications have been proposed but no consensus as to which is most suitable has been reached. For purposes of this chapter, several well-known seizure syndromes of early childhood will be described. It should be noted that these seizures often accompany gestational malformations and other pathological conditions so they might be considered symptomatic. However, in every instance a substantial proportion, if not a majority, appear to be idiopathic.

Seizure disorders unique to infancy and early childhood

Infantile spasms or West's syndrome

This condition occurs only early in life although there are rare reports of similar reactions in senility. Detailed descriptions can be found in Aicardi (1994, chapter 3),

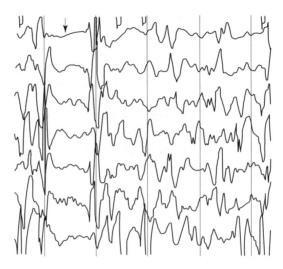

Figure 8.7   Hypsarrhythmic EEG pattern. Arrow points to voltage suppression which is when spasms occur

Dulac and Plouin (1993) and Freeman (1995). The seizures are spasms of the whole body, with bending at the waist, knees, and neck which are held for a second or two and then are repeated five or more times in a series. Such clusters of seizures may recur several times a day and also during sleep. Postictal signs are not common. These seizures will disappear altogether by the age of three or four or give way to other types of seizures. The EEG pattern associated with these spasms is called hypsarrhythmia, and contains high-voltage spikes all over the brain and an EEG activity suppression pattern that is associated with the spasms. A sample can be seen in figure 8.7, and has been described as electroencephalographic chaos.

The most commonly used treatments are steroids, drugs which stimulate the hypothalamic–pituitary–adrenal axis. Response to treatment is in part a function of whether other pathology is evident but children with infantile spasms face a high risk of mental retardation and a range of lesser consequences that can be found in many chapters of this book.

Pyridoxine (vitamin B6)-dependent seizures

The role of vitamin B6 deficiency in influencing temperament was discussed in chapter 6. It will be recalled that this vitamin plays a role in the synthesis of GABA. When, in the 1930s, a milk formula for feeding infants omitted B6, it was discovered that B6 was absolutely necessary for normal nervous system function. This was because, if the formula was the only food the infants consumed, intractable seizures soon appeared and persisted and then disappeared as soon as B6 was administered. Later it was discovered that some infants require inordinate amounts of B6 or else

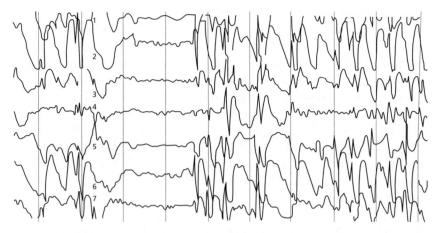

Figure 8.8 Slow polyspike waves with a background of slow disorganized activity seen in Lennox–Gastaut syndrome

they have seizures but that, again, these seizures disappear if adequate amounts, for them, are provided (Aicardi, 1994, p. 231; Scher, 1993, p. 642). It was also learned that excessive need diminished as they grow older so that the vitamin was a perfect anticonvulsant for this condition. Note that the symptomatic condition is named by its cure.

Lennox–Gastaut syndrome and myoclonic epilepsy

Seizure conditions in children with infantile spasms that do not respond to treatment, or subside spontaneously, often evolve into Lennox–Gastaut syndrome. For other children, this is the first manifestation of epilepsy. The condition is characterized by a combination of seizure types including generalized, tonic, tonic–clonic, myoclonic, atonic, and absence seizures. The most salient symptoms are unpredictable loss of muscle control leading to body-injuring falls so that often the child must constantly wear a protective helmet and be under constant observation by a caretaker. Often, the seizures accompany other neurological abnormalities and mental retardation is frequent (Freeman, 1995). The range of seizure types and symptoms leads to controversy about the limits of the diagnosis. For many experts, the presence of what are called slow polyspikes and waves such as are seen in figure 8.8 are diagnostic. The condition is resistive to known standard treatment and in only 20 percent are seizures arrested (Aicardi, 1993, p. 60).

Ketogenic diet-dependent seizures

The term heading this section is not found in the literature although it follows the model used in labelling seizures responsive to vitamin B6; i.e. the condition is named by its cure. There are a range of seizure types and associated conditions being cured including Lennox–Gastaut syndrome, but candidates for the treatment are described as suffering from severe, debilitating seizures which are unresponsive to available medications. The treatment, like that of vitamin B6 in B6-dependent seizures, is an ordinary nutrient, but unlike the B6 condition there is no explanation for its success. The treatment was initiated following the observation that seizures were arrested during starvation. Under such circumstances, the body digests its own fat as a source of energy and a metabolic process called ketosis ensues. Ketosis also occurs when there is little carbohydrate and much fat in the diet (DeVivo, Malas, & Leckie, 1975), and that is the treatment, although vitamin–mineral supplements and minimal amount of protein are also given (Barbosa, Freeman, & Elfert, 1984). This dietary treatment was discovered and used before anticonvulsant drugs were available and was an almost forgotten aspect of medical lore.

Interest has been renewed because a substantial percentage of children with a variety of otherwise intractable seizures have attained seizure control by this means after standard drug treatment failed (Schwartz et al., 1989). In one series of 150 diverse cases (Freeman et al., 1998), roughly a third of the children attained more than a 90 percent reduction in seizures and about 5 percent were seizure-free. The treatment is most effective when there is no other known accompanying pathology, and if the diet works, the children may gradually resume a normal diet without seizure recurrence. Although the reasons why the treatment is successful are unknown, Swink, Vining, and Freeman (1997), have pointed out that finding an explanation, which would have to link ordinary metabolic processes to seizure regulation, could alter the way in which seizures are conceptualized. Whereas the Johns Hopkins neurology department for a long time was about the only center in the United States to offer this treatment, it is currently utilized in many medical centers. Active research comparing the efficacy of variations in the diet and understanding the means by which seizure thresholds are raised now appears with some frequency in the research literature.

The Range of Ictal Phenomena and Some Extrapolations

The concepts of seizure threshold and kindling

To this point, seizures have been described as pathological conditions that occur to some people. In fact, seizures can occur to anyone under the appropriate conditions. For example, if an electric current of sufficient magnitude is applied to the scalp, a major convulsion will follow. This is actually the technique used in electroconvulsive therapy (ECT), a treatment used for certain forms of serious depression and, sometimes, for other severe psychiatric disorders. Another example occurs in diabetes, a disorder of the regulation of insulin, a substance which controls the metabolism of sugar. If there is excessive insulin, a person may go into seizures. Nondiabetics can be induced to seize by injecting them with excessive amounts of insulin. This was a method of seizure induction in early versions of convulsive therapy. Drugs such as megimide and others are also known to induce seizures in mammals.

Once it is known that seizures can be induced by certain procedures, the question naturally arises as to how much of the epileptogenic (epilepsy-causing) agent is needed to induce a convulsion. Studies on animals and on human volunteers (where the criterion was not actually having a seizure but showing spiking activity on the EEG) indicate that there is much variation. If, for example, the amount of current applied to the scalp is measured, it is found that some subjects require very little to show seizure activity while others require much more. The concept of a seizure threshold emerged from such data. In essence, this concept indicates that the process of generating a seizure is quantitative in nature, that in different individuals more or less epileptogenic provocation may be needed for an overt seizure to occur.

This concept, when applied to naturally occurring epilepsy, helps explain one of the most puzzling aspects of seizures – their episodic character. Why does the seizure occur sometimes and not others? The concept of threshold offers an approach to answering this question because it suggests the investigation of factors that might raise or lower the threshold. Some knowledge has been obtained about these issues, the most dramatic of which is a laboratory phenomenon termed kindling (Goddard, McIntyre, & Leech, 1969).

Kindling, in general parlance, refers to using easily ignited substances to start fires in more resistant fuels, e.g. hardwood logs. Kindling, in the epilepsy literature, refers to the cumulative effects of small doses of epileptogenic agents. Suppose that the smallest amount of electric current that will induce a particular strain of rats of a certain age to convulse is determined. The researcher then obtains a new sample of rats from the same strain and then waits till they are the appropriate age. The animals are then administered, say, one tenth of that current and, sure enough, they show no signs of convulsions. However, this subthreshold current is readministered every few days. In time, the previously innocuous shock becomes effective: the animals begin to seize with a dose one tenth of what is effective in a subject who has never been kindled. What changes occur in the animal at each stage of the kindling process and beyond has been the subject of extensive research, some of which will be considered shortly.

To start, however, kindling provides evidence that certain kinds of experience can sensitize the brain and lower the threshold for seizures. Now if this is the case, is it best to define a seizure disorder by the presence of overt seizures or by that process which raises or lowers the threshold for seizure activity? Not enough is known about the latter possibility to use it to define ictal disorders in humans, but a richer and potentially more useful understanding of this disorder is suggested. We are then led to consider, for example, what takes place when subthreshold seizure activity occurs. Although an overt seizure may not be present, subthreshold ictal activity might nonetheless affect such processes as attention, thought, and emotion. Some of our understanding about this issue comes from observations on interictal (between seizures) behavior of people known to suffer from epilepsy, especially complex partial seizures.

Interictal states

Effects on personality and emotion

From the analysis of focal seizures in sensory areas, it will be recalled that some forms of seizures produce purely subjective symptoms. In those cases, it can be assumed that seizure activity is confined to sensory areas. A person could experience light flashes or funny sensations on the skin but not be subject to any further subjective consequences of the ictal activity. Now consider the possibility that subthreshold ictal processes may affect other aspects of functioning, either episodically or chronically, and still not generate overt (motoric) seizures. This is likely to be the case when the prefrontal areas, temporal lobes, and the limbic system are involved.

Evidence for this comes from a number of sources, almost all of which are controversial in some degree. One such source is clinical data about the interictal behavior of patients with frank (overt) partial seizures of temporal lobe origin. Much clinical lore and prior research is captured in a study by Bear and Fedio (1977). Patients with diagnosed unilateral, epileptic foci and a group of raters who knew the subjects well (spouses, close friends, family members, or therapists) independently completed questionnaires about the personalities of each patient. If seizures did not affect the emotional life of a patient, people with epilepsy would be as diverse as the population at large. However, it was found that, as a group, the patients perceive themselves as humorless, dependent, and obsessive, and that the observers perceive them as angry, inclined toward intellectual–philosophical issues but circumstantial in their thinking. Right hemisphere temporal lobe foci patients tend to be more emotional while left hemisphere patients are more often preoccupied with ideas, and suspicious and mistrusting of others. These findings in some degree supported prior unsystematic, clinical observations that temporal lobe epileptics tend to show increased concern with philosophical and cosmic issues and tend to be deeply and mystically religious (hyperreligiosity), that they tend to be repetitive in speech and to be sticky (unable to come to a conclusion) and persistent in their mode of thought, that they often feel obliged to write endlessly about their thoughts and ideas (hypergraphia), and that their emotional experience appears to be particularly intense and changeable.

As indicated, these findings, which are interpreted to mean that the personality patterns are related to interictal subthreshold ictal activity, are controversial. Dodrill and Batzell (1986), in a thoughtful review, pointed out that subsequent objective evidence has indicated that some temporal lobe patients conspicuously show the traits described, but that they represent only a small portion of the patients with temporal lobe epilepsy. In addition they found evidence that, overall, type of seizure is not predictive of the presence of personality disorder, but that the number of seizures and magnitude of cognitive impairment is. Whitman and Hermann (1986) have provided a detailed discussion about social factors in personality disorders associated with epilepsy. The upshot of their argument is that social factors, including stigmatizing reactions to the term epilepsy and aversion to persons who get out of control or unconscious, play the largest role. This perspective suggests that personality consistencies among epilepsy sufferers are determined by ictal processes only indirectly. If society at large did not react to people with epilepsy the way it does, there would be much less uniformity in their personalities.

Effects on cognition

There are two components of the cognitive impairment in epileptics. First, given that the brain is abnormal at the site of a seizure focus, the functions controlled by those tissues are likely to be impaired. Second, the propagation of subthreshold seizure activity would be likely to disrupt whatever activity was going on wherever it spread, producing temporary disruption and, hence, at least temporary impairment. The former source of impairment would likely be permanent, but the second type might be reversible if something could be done to arrest the subconvulsive seizure activity. Evidence that this is the case comes from patients who have undergone successful surgery for temporal lobe seizures. They generally continue to perform poorly in those functions specifically controlled by the area of the seizure focus. Often, those functions may deteriorate further because what was previously not functioning well has been removed. However, significant improvement often occurs in other areas (Crandall et al., 1990).

There is much direct evidence that subconvulsive activity interferes with cognitive function. In one pioneer study, Grisell et al. (1964) studied the effect of interictal, subconvulsive epileptic discharges on mental processes in patients with seizures. While having their EEGs recorded, subjects were asked to depress a key for as long as they heard a tone which was presented at different durations with differing pauses between tones. Patients were given enough of a dose of an epileptogenic agent to assure that subconvulsive activity would occur while recording. Performance during subconvulsive activity and when the EEG was normal was then compared. Both reaction time and error rate went up significantly during the abnormal EEG activity even though no overt seizure took place at that time. Many other studies have similar findings (Woodruff, 1974).

Subictal states

Interictal states, described above, occur in persons known to have seizures. Subictal states, partial-seizure-like symptoms in individuals who have never experienced an overt seizure, will be described next. These include moments of inexplicable confusion, peculiar and unrealistic sensory experiences including both hallucinations and lack of sensation, temporary speech problems, rage episodes, etc.: in other words, a range of aberrant behaviors that may often be associated with ictal processes. Roberts et al. (1990) developed a questionnaire about such symptoms and determined the frequency at which such symptoms are self-reported in the general population. They found that almost all of the behaviors queried were reported by normals, but infrequently – any single subject acknowledging only a few symptoms and those less than once a month. In subjects at risk for cerebral dysfunction because they had been unconscious or had an illness with high fever, the incidence and frequency of reported symptoms increased significantly. When patients with verified brain damage were studied, the incidence went up dramatically even though none had ever had seizures.

In a later study, Verduyn et al. (1992) examined patients who had sustained only minor head injuries, a blow of some sort but no unconsciousness, but, as sometimes happens, subsequently developed a high incidence of the symptoms described in Roberts's questionnaire. Patients were treated with anticonvulsive drugs in an admittedly uncontrolled and non-blind study on the assumption that these were ictal phenomena. There was a high incidence of improvement. The authors discuss the controversial nature of their findings because their patients did not have the stereotyped behaviors which are generally agreed to be ictal in nature. They suggest that the phenomena they have observed, including the response to anticonvulsant drugs, could be attributed to partial kindling, where the seizure process has not captured the motor areas of the brain.

These ideas fit well with data and theory about kindling in animal research as reviewed by Adamec (1990). The effects of kindling which has stopped short of overt seizures are not found in spontaneous behaviors but in reactions to triggering environmental events. For example, a normal animal responds to the sight of its usual prey by attacking it, but one subjected to subseizure kindling may respond with fear and withdrawal. Thus, kindling, which superficially appears to have trivial effects until the seizure threshold is lowered enough to have a seizure, may actually have very profound effects on behavior.

An older literature has also implicated subictal mechanisms in behavioral and personality disorders. As examples, Monroe (1970) studied episodic instances of rage and aggression, Dreyfus (1981) reported on his own severe bouts of depression, and Jonas (1965) described a range of neuroses and personality impairments. Ictal involvement was suggested by the sudden onset or offset of the symptoms, their episodic and generally inexplicable occurrence, their ego-alien (this is not really me) nature, the occurrence of confusion and/or amnesia immediately following an episode, and a favorable response to anticonvulsant medication. More recently, Gedye (1989, 1991, 1992, 1998), studying episodes of uncontrolled behavior in mentally retarded individuals, has mustered evidence to suggest that many of these behaviors are ictal in nature and are partial seizures confined to the frontal lobes where seizure activity is known to be difficult to detect on the EEG.

This literature has not been widely accepted, mostly because the evidence cited has not been very convincing to many. One reason for the paucity of good evidence is that, for good reasons, it is hard to obtain. The only scientifically convincing evidence of seizure activity to date is a seizure pattern on the EEG. (Recall that, until the invention of the EEG, seizures were viewed as psychiatric aberrations or devilish possession.) This means that an episodic disorder, originating deep in the brain, must produce manifestations at the scalp at the time the person is hooked to an EEG machine. This is quite an order.

Consider the following scenario. A child suspected of an ictal disorder is given an EEG and the results are found to be normal. The procedure is repeated a second time and is again found to be normal, and then on the third try is found to be abnormal because spikes appear at the frontal and temporal leads. What is going on? One interpretation of these events would be that children are likely to be quite apprehensive the first times they enter an EEG lab. Such anxiety would situationally provoke heightened alertness resulting in a desynchronized EEG which would suppress ictal synchrony even if it were otherwise likely to occur. With repeated examinations, the situation becomes familiar, anxiety declines, and, if it is there, the ictal activity may become apparent. Under these conditions, the practicalities of life dictate that the evidence will probably never emerge. Few physicians would order two consecutive EEGs under these circumstances let alone three, and few insurance companies would pay the resulting fees.

In addition to situational factors such as anxiety, the diagnosis of subictal states is beset by the problem of how to capture an episodic event at the time that the person is attached to an EEG machine. This problem is present even when attempting to confirm that overt seizures are ictal and not imitations called pseudoseizures. What is needed is some technique that provokes existing ictal pathology to appear during the recording period without, of course, causing it to happen in the first place. Such techniques exist and they are termed activation procedures. The most commonly used are hyperventilation, intensified, voluntary, rapid breathing, which often provokes absence; photic driving, flashing a light at increasing frequencies into the eyes of the subject, which often provokes partial or tonic–clonic seizures; sleep, whose normal synchrony (see next chapter) is the occasion for seizure activity; or sleep deprivation, which is a general stressor of the nervous system. One might think that discussing emotionally loaded topics might activate focal limbic seizures, but such techniques could not easily be standardized and would have to be administered by a professional trained beyond EEG technology. When there is evidence that seizures are initiated by specific stimulation, then those stimuli may be presented during the EEG examination but the procedures are not standardized.

Other maneuvers have also been devised. If the episodic seizure will not appear during the duration of a particular recording, then, at great expense, the recordings can be made continuously. This can be done with telemetry, in which miniaturized equipment is mounted on the body and includes a radio transmitter which sends the information from the electrodes to recorders some distance away so that the person can move around freely, at least within the confines of a room or building. Another solution is to hospitalize patients, record continuously, and videotape their behavior simultaneously.

Finally, it is known that ictal activity not appearing at the scalp does appear in the brain. This has been well documented in research on animals. In humans, implanting electrodes directly into the brain is justified when surgery for major intractable seizures is being considered and the localization of the focus is a prime consideration. Implanted electrodes are often followed by continuous EEG and video monitoring. Implantation is a surgical procedure with relatively small risk, but penetrating

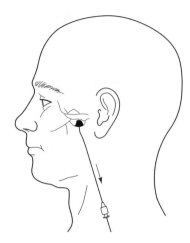

Figure 8.9   Placement of the EEG sphenoid lead

the skull is never a casual matter and would not be warranted if a subictal condition was being investigated. For now, knowledge that ictal activity can occur and be measured in brain tissue when no such evidence is available at the scalp provides a basis for continuing to seek objective evidence for an ictal disorder in many cases where such evidence has been hard to obtain.

Toward this end, a number of minimally invasive procedures have been devised. The goal is to place the recording electrode as near to the likely site of the ictal focus as possible, and the reader will recall that the likely focus will be in the limbic system, deep in midline structures and the inner medial surface of the temporal lobes. Put crudely, one can say that the focus is likely to be somewhere "up the nose." One such technique places the electrode in the naso-pharyngeal passage, very high in the throat. In another, a needle electrode penetrates the upper cheek and is made to rest adjacent to the sphenoid bone of the skull and face which is near the tip of the temporal lobe (see figure 8.9). Both procedures must be implemented by physicians rather than by the technicians who generally conduct EEG examinations. The latter procedure is favored because it produces more reliable results and picks up more abnormalities (Reilly, 1987) but both are still dependent on capturing episodic activity which may or may not occur during recording.

Thus, definitive diagnoses in subictal conditions are hard to obtain and the diagnosis is controversial. Nonetheless, the presence of ego-alien complaints, sudden onset and/or offset, amnesia or confusion, contextless behavior, sudden poor control whether provoked or not, might all raise the possibility of an ictal etiology. Some of these symptoms represent the mild end of a continuum of ictal pathology but can nonetheless have a large negative impact on a person's life. Other symptoms, such as uncontrollable rage, may seriously interfere with social behavior and lead to dire consequences, yet not be recognized as ictal in nature. Because ictus may occur in, and be limited to, any part of the brain, its consequences may mimic just about any psychopathological condition and erroneous diagnoses can easily be made. There is actually a large literature on psychoses that are really ictal conditions (e.g. Flor-Henry, 1969; Stevens, 1988; Lishman, 1998). It is almost assuredly erroneous to assume that all abnormal behavioral conditions are ictal in origin, but it may be equally erroneous not to consider that possibility in any particular case.

Behavioral Contributions to the Treatment of Ictal Conditions

As presented earlier, the primary treatment for epilepsy and related conditions is medication. Many patients respond very well and may never again suffer a seizure after being placed on medication. Others do not fare as well, and seizures recur despite differing medication regimes. The reasons for such variation are not fully understood. There is, however, both knowledge and clinical lore about some of the general factors which contribute to seizure activity. Such knowledge provides a basis for interventions which facilitate seizure control.

General health and activity, especially mental activity

Many patients with epilepsy report that they are more likely to have seizures if they are fatigued, emotionally distressed, consume alcoholic beverages, eat poorly, and, of course, neglect to take their medication on time. The author, early in his career, witnessed a Jacksonian seizure in an adolescent who came to a morning appointment without having had any breakfast but showed no such symptoms on other occasions when she had eaten appropriately. In other cases there appear to be no clues as to what behaviors might be associated with more frequent seizures. Indeed, such clues may not exist and the seizures are totally unpredictable. On the other hand, the clues may be there but are not noticed. On the whole, however, seizure frequency is related to general fitness and health. Control of seizures is generally a matter of facilitating neuronal inhibition and the regulation of excess excitation, and all factors contributing to that end should be helpful. Recently, for example, data have appeared about the importance of nutritional zinc in facilitating resistance to seizures (Sterman, Shouse, & Fairchild, 1988). Similar effects of exercise have been found by Eriksen et al. (1994). Sleep, exercise, nutrition, and management of stress are potentially accessible aspects of self-regulation that can make an enormous difference in the life of a person with a disorder of neuronal self-regulation such as epilepsy.

Patients with epilepsy are often stigmatized by others and this, in turn, leads to social withdrawal. This can lead to a situation where the individual spends much time alone, often with nothing much to do. There is probably no better set of conditions under which to foster seizures. Patients with seizures benefit from activity and social relationships that challenge their mental capabilities and require the learning of social skills. As suggested above, active thought appears to be a cheap, continuously available anticonvulsant. In the absence of an uncomprehending, generally indifferent, and often rejecting society, self-help associations for persons with epilepsy and their families often organize to provide activities that meet this need.

Responding to seizure-triggering stimuli and auras

Many seizures are preceded by specific sensory events or by responses such as auras in the subject. If such is the case, the individual may be able to learn how to avoid seizures by avoiding events in which the triggering stimuli will occur and/or by inhibiting the relevant responses. When an aura is present, it gives some conscious index to the subject that an ictal process is under way. Further spread of the seizure may be arrested if the subject learns to respond with some technique which will desynchronize brain activity. The reason this can work should be clear to the reader. Simply, if the brain can be made to desynchronize, then negative, stabilizing feedback is introduced which disrupts the positive feedback runaway and brings the ictal process to a halt. Some patients have learned on their own and others have been taught to "fight" seizures by responding to the aura with such activities as reviewing in one's mind and even reciting multiplication tables or quotations from Shakespeare or the Bible. The author is aware of a case in which the patient was not told for many years that she had epilepsy and whose seizures were under very poor control. When her condition was finally explained to her, she began to notice experiential clues about seizure onset and then began to find ways to arrest seizures once they began. Feldman and Paul (1976) found that awareness of the association between triggering events and subsequent seizures alone is helpful in controlling seizure frequency.

Dahl, Melin, and Leissner (1988) describe a series of explicit steps that can be taken to help arrest seizures. These are learning to discriminate relevant cues, e.g. sudden appearance of numbness in the left shoulder and drowsiness, and taking countermeasures, e.g. rubbing the numb spot vigorously with the right hand and otherwise engaging in stimulating behavior accompanied by appropriate and timely rewards. Dahl, Brorson, and Melin (1992) describe the positive effects of such intervention after eight years. Brown and Fenwick (1989) describe a combination of behavioral methods designed to prevent seizure spread beyond the focus by training the subject with techniques that increase inhibition and decrease neural excitation. Other methods are reviewed by Feldman, Ricks, and Orren (1983).

Specific treatment regimes – EEG biofeedback

I have saved, for the last part of this chapter, a description of a promising treatment for seizures and a number of other conditions as well. The story about the development of this procedure is an interesting example of scientific serendipity. The discoverer of the method, M. B. Sterman, is a biopsychologist who was engaged in basic research on EEG rhythms, sleep, and behavior when he noted a correlation between inhibitory behavior in his subjects, which were cats and monkeys, and the appearance over the sensory motor strip of a 12–14 Hz EEG rhythm (Sterman, 1986). Inhibitory behavior in laboratory animals is provoked by punishing the animals for engaging in behaviors they like to do. For example, a cat placed in a small confined chamber with an aperture into a large chamber containing interesting objects will readily enter the large chamber. If, however, such cats are punished for moving into the chamber, they will actively inhibit that tendency. During active inhibition, the EEG will show the 12–14 Hz rhythm which Sterman termed sensory-motor rhythm, or SMR, because of its locale. This rhythm incidentally is also found in sleep spindles and may there be a reflection of the motor inhibition associated with sleep.

For reasons that had to do with the research hypotheses he was working on at the time, Sterman decided to give these subjects biofeedback training to enhance SMR. Biofeedback is a term that refers to a class of procedures wherein information about processes which ordinarily produce no sensation, and hence convey no information, are transformed so that the subject can sense the process. To take a simple example, most of us ordinarily are not aware of our heart beat; but if we carried around a stethoscope, and used it to listen to our own heart beat, we would then have information we did not have before. If we wanted to change the rate at which our heart was beating for some reason, we would now have immediate information as to whether it was beating slower or faster as we tried different techniques to make it change. With that information, we would know which techniques worked and could concentrate on those.

Biofeedback can be arranged for just about any physiological process including skin temperature and muscle tension. Generally speaking the feedback is in the form of some analog of the process being fed back. To go back to the example of heart rate, the subject might not hear the actual heart beats but a sound that goes up in pitch as the heart rate goes up, and goes down in pitch as the heart rate goes down. Sterman provided such information about SMR amplitude to his cats and monkeys, and when the amplitude went up, he rewarded the animals immediately. Under these conditions, they learned to increase SMR.

The final part of this story is that he also determined the seizure threshold of each animal. It then turned out that the animals that had received SMR biofeedback training had higher seizure thresholds and were far more resistant to seizures than animals that had not received such training. Sterman then took a major intellectual leap and suggested SMR biofeedback training might help raise the seizure threshold in humans suffering from epilepsy provided that their seizures had a motor component. The initial report of the results of such a procedure appeared in Sterman and Friar (1972).

Since that time, the technique has been further studied by Sterman and his colleagues (e.g., Lantz & Sterman, 1988) and has been applied and elaborated by others. Many persons with epilepsy have improved so that they could get along on less medication or do without altogether. Although a number have not been helped, negative consequences or side effects have not been found (Feldman et al., 1983). Despite these successes, this type of treatment, as of this writing, has received relatively little attention. There are several possible reasons for this. The procedure is lengthy and expensive, requiring training sessions two or three times a week, over a period of many months. Research has yet to determine exactly which types of epilepsy are likely to benefit from such effort and expense. Its adoption implies an orientation which emphasizes learning and self-regulation on the part of the patient rather then healing on the part of the professional, and such changes do not occur readily. Finally, the equipment needed has been very expensive and required considerable technical expertise for its operation, so the work has been confined to a few research laboratories. Technological advances and reductions in cost in recent years make it likely that these techniques will receive more attention in the years to come.

Psychological intervention in the treatment of epilepsy – summary and food for thought

The discoveries of the EEG and of anticonvulsant medications have been major achievements in the history of neurology and of medicine. There are persons with epilepsy for whom a straightforward medical approach, diagnosis followed by pre-scription of medication, effectively deals with the problem. Unfortunately, this does not cover all, perhaps not even most, cases. Persons with seizures and with the range of subthreshold ictal conditions tend to have difficulties regulating many aspects of their lives besides the spread of seizure activity and the personal, "psychological" and the medical aspects of their lives are intertwined. An approach which considers behavior and experience as well as nervous system vulnerabilities offers the prospect of more effective and enduring treatment and a better quality of life for many epilepsy patients. For a recent review of some of these issues see Miller (1994).

This chapter on epilepsy concludes with the presentation of a report regarding the treatment of a seizure disorder which is entirely different from that which has come before. It is presented as a challenge to standard ways of thinking about the disorder. I leave it to the reader to consider to what extent it is believable and, if so, con-sistent or inconsistent with what has come before.

Madanes (1980), a family therapist, describes the case of a 15-year-old girl with recurrent, mostly nocturnal, seizures. During one hospitalization a grand mal seizure along with postictal confusion was witnessed by a physician so the diagnosis was not in doubt. The family therapist made the assumption that the girl's symptoms had some sort of protective function for the family, the nature of which was obscure, and that the illness may have given the family a certain kind of excitement. The family were all concerned about the girl's illness and they would awake to the sound of her moaning and gather around her and try to comfort her. If she had a seizure during the day, they were both sympathetic and terrified of the harm that might befall her. The family spoke at great length about her symptoms while the girl herself was rather taciturn and shy.

With all the family present, the therapist asked the patient to produce a seizure and the family to do what they usually do when she does. She tried but did not succeed, so the therapist asked them all to pretend that she was having a seizure and then to display their ways of helping her. Furthermore, they were asked to repeat this dramatization each evening at home on the rationale that this was designed to teach her to produce a seizure voluntarily because then she could choose voluntarily not to have seizures. The case took a number of twists and turns but the upshot was a disappearance of seizures and the appearance of rebellious behavior which gradually came under control.

9

Disorders of Sleep and Arousal

Overview of this Chapter

This chapter will consider Luria's functional unit that regulates tone and waking and mental states. It is convenient to distinguish two major subdivisions of the arousal system: one which controls sleep and the difference between being asleep and being awake, and one which regulates differences in arousal during the awake state. The latter refers, for example, to such differences in alertness and readiness for action which might be present if one were lying in a hammock on a lazy summer afternoon versus the way one would be if competing in a football game or taking an important final examination. This chapter is concerned with cycles of sleep and wakefulness and disorders to which they are related. The next will deal with attention during the waking state, and its disorders.

The discovery of the EEG played as important a role in understanding sleep as it did in understanding epilepsy. Just as there are standard ways of doing a waking EEG to aid in the diagnosis of seizure conditions, there are standard procedures and nomenclature for polysomnography, the polygraphic study of changes in EEG and other variables that occur in sleep (Rechtschaffen & Kales, 1968). Often only one electrode placement (either C_3, C_z or C_4, in the center or to the left or right, in figure 8.2) is used for this purpose. Other transducers register eye movements, respiration, and muscular activity for reasons that will become apparent as the chapter progresses. Persons arrive at the sleep laboratory near their usual sleep time, have the transducers attached, and sleep the night under the watchful eye of an attendant who notes both behavioral reactions and the responses on the polygraph. The report of this examination presents a quantitative description of the sleep pattern through the night, the dimensions of which will be described next. This quantitative depiction is sometimes described as one's sleep architecture.

EEG Characteristics of Sleep

Basic discoveries

When the EEG technique was still quite new, some scholars used it to study brain functions during sleep. Part of what they discovered was surprising and initiated modern understanding of sleep (Aserinsky & Kleitman, 1953; Dement & Kleitman, 1957). Given that the sleeper is inactive and resting, the first stages of sleep showed an expected pattern of increasing synchronization. However, after the first hour and a half, a remarkable change occurred. Although the person continued to be asleep, and was particularly inert with regard to body movement, the EEG waves desynchronized and looked much like they did when the person was awake. In addition, it was noted that beneath the closed eyelids of the sleeper, the eyes were moving in tandem, as though scanning an image. These facts were used to label this stage of sleep "rapid eye movement" or REM sleep. All other sleep stages could then be termed non-REM (NREM) sleep. After REM, the EEG reverted to slow Δ waves and, later still, the desynchrony and the eye movements reappeared. It was evident that the brain went through a series of cycles of relatively synchronized and desynchronized activity in the course of a night.

This is not the place to tell the story of how each piece of information about the nature of brain activity during sleep was uncovered. Instead, current knowledge about the nature of sleep will be summarized. Unless otherwise referenced, this material is indebted to reviews by Anch et al. (1988), Horne (1988), and Carlson (1998).

Sleep stages

It is now generally agreed that, in the course of a normal night's sleep, the brain goes through a series of stages which were defined by convention (Rechtschaffen & Kales, 1968). These stages, including the REM stage, are not unique to man, but are part of the biological heritage of the mammalian species. Figure 9.1 illustrates what will be described next.

In Stage 1 (which resembles REM except for the eye movements), there is some relative slowing of brain waves and increase in θ. If you try to rouse the person, it takes more stimulation, noise, or jostling to do so than if the person were awake. For an adult, about 5 percent of a night's sleep is spent in this stage. Stage 2 begins when wave forms unique to sleep, K complexes and sleep spindles, suddenly appear. Sleep spindles are so named because the amplitude of the 12–14 Hz waves, which last about a half-second, tapers at each end of the short burst, giving the wave the appearance of a spindle. These sleep spindles are related to brain mechanisms which control motor inhibition. The significance of K complexes, which involve singular high-amplitude waves vaguely reminiscent of the appearance of a written K, is less well understood. The presence of these wave forms leaves no doubt that the subject is asleep. Actually, the bulk of a night's sleep (45 percent) is spent in this stage. Stage

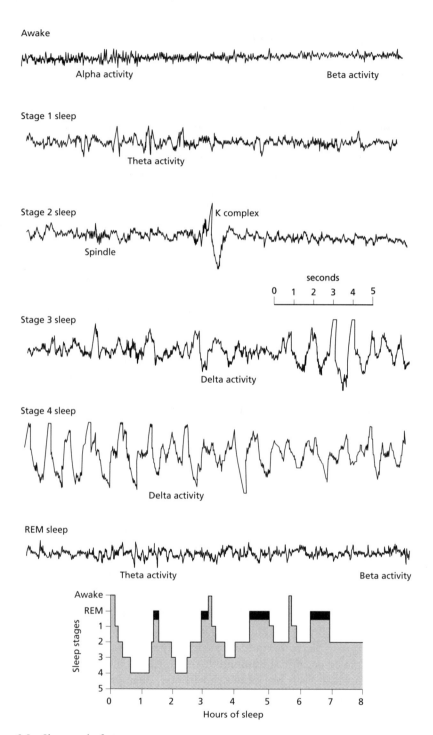

Figure 9.1 Sleep cycle features

3 is marked by the appearance of Δ waves, and Stage 4 by their predominance. This is a very deep stage of sleep from which it is difficult to rouse. Between 6 and 15 percent of a night's sleep is spent in this stage.

Stage REM generally begins about 90 minutes after sleep onset. (The time between sleep onset and REM onset is termed REM latency.) A series of changes occur: the EEG waves shift from the high-voltage slow waves of slow-wave sleep to low-voltage, hence rather flat, waves at mixed frequencies, with some β, but most at 2–7 Hz, rapid eye movements appear, the heart beats at a faster rate, and respiration increases. The physiological evidence is that the brain is being strongly aroused. However, at the same time, the voluntary muscles of the body are profoundly paralyzed. Only the involuntary muscles such as those of the heart continue to operate. The only other reactive parts of the body during REM sleep are the genitalia which regularly become engorged and excited. The average healthy young adult spends about 20 percent of the night in this stage of sleep.

A typical night of sleep will involve four to six cycles from Stage 1 through to Stage 4, and then Stage REM, and then back to Stage 1. The relative duration of each episode of REM increases through the night such that the longest normally occurs just before awakening. Growth hormone, which promotes anabolic activity (see chapter 3) is secreted maximally (80–90 percent of all that will be produced during a 24-hour period) during the first bout of Stage 4 sleep in normal children and adults. Secretion is linked to sleep mechanisms because a person who is deprived of sleep does not secrete growth hormone. Cortisol, which promotes catabolic activity, is almost totally absent early in the night. and does not reappear until some three to five hours after sleep onset. This synchronization of sleep and hormone activity tends to disappear in the elderly and in certain types of pathology. The point to note here is that mechanisms that regulate growth and maintenance of body structures are closely related to the integrity of the sleep cycle. Chronic disruption of sleep can interfere with growth in children, for example.

Developmental factors

During the course of development, important changes occur in the pattern of sleep. Newborns sleep 16 or more hours a day, about 50 percent of which is REM sleep. By six months of age, REM sleep is down to about 25–30 percent of sleep time. By three years, REM occupies about 20 percent of an average of 12 hours of sleep. By about 14 years, the adult pattern, eight hours of sleep with 20 percent REM, occurs. Aging and senility are associated with further gradual decreases of both total sleep and REM. Besides changes in percent of REM and NREM sleep during the first six months of life, maturational processes are also apparent in increasingly clear differentiation of the four stages of NREM sleep and in the gradual disappearance of breakthrough muscle twitches and body jerks into REM sleep muscle inhibition (Anders, Sadeh, & Appareddy, 1995).

REM sleep occurs maximally during brain development and after brain injury, so it appears to be involved in brain growth and repair. It increases after periods of intense learning (Smith & Lapp, 1991) and is relatively diminished in mentally retarded individuals. Delta sleep, on the other hand, is associated with repletion after vigorous physical activity and strain. It increases with exercise and starvation and varies directly with the level of a hormone secreted by the thyroid gland that regulates the basal rate of metabolism. Recent work (Horne, 1988) indicates that many of these findings depended on whether body temperature was elevated before going to sleep, which occurs, for example, with exercise. Temperature elevation, whether due to passive heating, prolonged exercise, or fever, leads to increases of slow-wave sleep.

Mental activity during sleep

If awakened during REM sleep and asked to report any mental activity, people will report dreams on the average of 83 percent of the time (Foulkes, 1966) with a fairly narrow range of variation (60–85 percent). These dreams tend to be narrative and sequential in nature, and they have vivid visual, and often emotional, qualities. By contrast, if a person is awakened from Δ sleep, the percentage of instances in which dreams will be reported is substantially less, and may be as small as zero but may go up to 70 percent, thus indicating considerable variation. The quality of dream reports is different. They tend to be more static and fragmented, less vivid and emotional, and more concerned with contemporary life experiences. All this is evidence of continuing mental activity through the course of sleep. It had appeared that the quality of dreaming varied with the stage of sleep. Antrobus (1983) and Foulkes and Schmidt (1983) found that if dream length is equated, these differences disappear. The main difference between REM dreams and slow wave sleep dreams is in their length.

Early hypotheses about cognitive activity during sleep were that it was always dominated by primitive emotion and that modes of thought present in dreams were also intrinsically primitive. It is now apparent that although strong emotions can show up in dreams, and may even disrupt sleep, most dreaming is fairly benign. There is continuity between the level of cognitive development shown in the waking state and the kinds of cognitive functioning that appear in dreams (Foulkes, 1982). Similarly, events experienced in the waking world may influence the contents of what we dream about, and dreams may often reflect current concerns and anticipated important events. On the other hand, sleep-thought contents may be quite remote from daytime thoughts and preoccupations. As will be noted when considering enuresis, below, wake and sleep cognitions can be, under some circumstances, directly related.

Neural Mechanisms of Sleep

Although it may appear that the progression from Stage 1 to Stage 4 sleep is simply a gradual decline in activity, in actuality, all stages of sleep are under active neural control and reflect the operation of different neural mechanisms. As everyone knows who has ever tried to force themselves to go to sleep, these mechanisms are not under voluntary control. Rather, sleep is regulated in humans much like it is in all mammalian species and is under the control of mechanisms in hierarchically older and more primitive parts of the brain. From what is currently understood, controls for slow wave and REM sleep are quite different.

Slow wave sleep

That Δ sleep is increased when temperature is elevated has been mentioned. It turns out that cells whose activity is associated with temperature regulation also regulate slow wave sleep. These cells are located at the base of the forebrain in front of the optic chiasm (see figure 3.9 for a general notion of the region) and near the front part of the hypothalamus. The region is sometimes given the acronym POAH, standing for preoptic–anterior hypothalamus. If stimulated electrically, or heated, firing of cells in this region increases the duration of slow wave sleep. If the cell bodies are destroyed, insomnia and death follow.

REM sleep

Although REM sleep is perhaps more complicated than Δ sleep, more detailed information appears to be available about its regulation. The sites of initiation are in two identified clumps of cells called nuclei that can be found in the upper part of the front end of the pons. These are the pedunculopontine (PPT) nucleus, and, somewhat to the front and above, the laterodorsal tegmental (LDT) nucleus. Both transmit cholinergically and send axons to the nearby reticular formation coursing through the pons, to nuclei in the thalamus, and to many regions of the frontal lobes, all of which produce cortical arousal. Increased firing in the PPT and LDT precedes the onset of REM and persists through the course of the episode. Also occurring are pontine, geniculate, occipital (PGO) spikes to the visual area of the brain, evident in the waking state when animals explore their environment and spontaneously during REM sleep (Horne, 1988, p. 287), which give rise to the imagery reported when awakened from REM. Axons from the PPT and LDT also link to the superior colliculi and can elicit eye movements. Finally, there are links to a nucleus just below the locus coeruleus which activates the magnocellular nucleus in the upper lateral portion of the medulla whose activity inhibits the motor neurons of the spinal cord and produces REM sleep paralysis. The entire system is contained in an area approximately 5 mm in diameter, has noncholinergic neurons in close proximity, and is closely linked to and modulated by both basal ganglia dopaminergic neurons and raphe nucleus serotonergic neurons (Rye, 1997). The complexity of REM regulation is such as to create many sites where things can go wrong and produce different kinds of pathology. Much has yet to be understood.

Some Disorders Associated with Sleep

General findings

Adults who sleep seven to eight hours a night have longer life spans than those who routinely sleep more or less (Hirshkowitz, Moore, & Minhoto, 1997), sleep is related to the functioning of the immune system (Everson, 1997) and to psychopathology (Ware & Morin, 1997). Furthermore, sleep is probably absolutely necessary for life (Rechtschaffen et al., 1983) but why this is so is still a great mystery (Horne, 1988). It is evident that impairments of sleep are associated with dysfunction in many aspects of behavior. In a number of instances, specific disorders of the sleep cycle are known, and several will be described next. Note that in these disorders, what is impaired or disturbed may be in the mechanisms controlling sleep stages. At times these are selectively impaired for unknown reasons. In other cases, the impairment may be due to physical trauma, such as a closed head injury. Throughout, note the role of environmental events and of coping techniques in shaping the nature of the disorder.

Functional insomnia

This is a fairly common condition whose main symptom is delayed sleep onset and increased sleep variability (i.e. less consistent sleep patterns) when no other type of disturbance such as those described below can be found. People with functional insomnia tend to exaggerate how long it takes them to get to sleep and how little they actually do sleep, but they do differ objectively in both respects from subjects without such complaints. These individuals tend to be more irritable, experience more stress, and have more symptoms of emotional distress and cognitive inefficiency than others. Given that everyone may experience stress and unhappiness at some points in their life, an interesting and unanswered question is the extent to which the sleep disturbance tends to increase the likelihood of further difficulty so that, in the long run, sleeplessness itself becomes an important cause of their emotional difficulty.

There are so many individuals beset by insomnia that they represent a lucrative market for those offering solutions. For many individuals the solution comes in the form of a sleeping pill, available over the counter or through prescription. Although medications may be helpful for a period of time, and some may be necessary during periods of crisis, no available drug is continually effective or provokes an entirely normal sleep pattern. Long-term reliance on drugs for the induction of sleep in people who are not otherwise ill tends, in the long run, to be detrimental to refreshing sleep and may have other undesirable consequences as well.

Approaches to treating insomnia in children

Babies begin life with alternating sleep–wake patterns that are unrelated to light–dark cycles of day and night. They gradually adjust their sleep–wake cycles so that by six months they can be expected to sleep the night with but one interruption for feeding and the rest of their sleep is obtained with a morning and afternoon nap. By two years, they mostly sleep through the night with no feedings and require only one afternoon nap (Anders, Sadeh, & Appareddy, 1995). Disruptions of this pattern may be due painful conditions such as colic or middle ear infections (see chapter 13) or may reflect modes of training and shaping the child's behavior in interaction with the child's temperament. Barring conditions of exhaustion, when fatigue may dominate all other considerations, sleep, ultimately, is a lonely event which requires separation from social interaction. How parents manage the intrinsic conflict between providing contact, nurturance, and support vs fostering individuation, self-regulation, and independence plays a large role in determining whether going to sleep is a generally pleasant transition or a burdensome time of conflict. Managing sleep issues is relatively easy with temperamentally easy children but requires inordinate skill and patience with "difficult" children (Ferber, 1995). Some aspects of this skill are easily observed. Does the caretaker implement the transition to sleep by winding down gradually, moving toward quieter, synchrony-producing activities or is the transition imposed abruptly? Is there a state of heightened excitability to wind down from, i.e. does the child experience interesting stimulation and manageable excitement during waking times? Is there consistency and patterning of events in the course of a day and night?

Approaches to dealing with insomnia in older children and adults

Understanding the nature of sleep permits a number of suggestions that can facilitate sleep for those with functional insomnia. Again, the approach is based on the notion that the early stages of sleep are marked by increased brain synchrony. Hence, behavior is organized to facilitate synchrony and inhibit desynchrony. Briefly, some or all of the following steps should be helpful:

(a)   A time period is allotted for nightly rest and is separated from other activity on a regular basis. The period should be consciously labelled and thought of as "rest" rather than sleep because rest can be voluntary, while sleep is not. This aids in preventing the word "sleep" itself from becoming a trigger for stress and desynchrony. This means that if one is obsessed with planning a party, or is raging over being jilted, or mourning a failed examination, one must set aside time to attend to those preoccupations so that they can be more readily excluded from thought during the nightly rest period. With children as with adults, sleep may be disrupted if issues that arise while awake are left unresolved or are not given some straightforward consideration.

(b)   Activities prior to rest-time are chosen that facilitate synchrony. As the time for the rest period approaches, exciting activities should be tapered, and the brain should be given time to prepare for the transition to sleep. If bathing is restful, bathing might help, as might listening to soft music, hearing a story told, reading an enjoyable novel, or drinking hot milk.

(c)   For older children and adults, a technique known as progressive relaxation (Jacobson, 1938, 1957) is easily learned and very useful. For youngsters, appropriate modifications can be improvised. Upon reclining, the muscles of the body, especially those of the jaw, neck, forehead, and shoulders, are deliberately relaxed. Such relaxation eliminates desynchronizing somatosensory messages which are produced by tense muscles, most often without awareness. In addition, deliberate deep breathing, which includes extending the diaphragm muscles (pushing out) while inhaling, contracting the diaphragm (pushing in) while exhaling, and holding the breath for several counts when the lungs are full, is a profoundly relaxing procedure and is useful for tension reduction at any time of day or night.

(d)   For older children and adults, the mind can be given synchronizing activity. The mental state which most allows sleep to occur is one in which there is no active ideation. It is, however, difficult to suppress all such activity. The solution is to give the mind a task, but the task itself should be intrinsically synchronizing. One such example is counting sheep jumping over a fence. Another derives from oriental meditation techniques and involves concentrating on the sensations of slow breathing including notation of the temperature changes that occur as air passes in both directions over the upper lip.

This last ingredient may seem far-fetched to those suffering from insomnia, but the activity makes sense and seems natural enough if it occurs following the preparation of the other steps. Overall, the prescription requires the individual to take personal responsibility for rest and for attention to the detail that makes sleep possible, much like one must take responsibility for one's diet or for one's hygiene (Jacobs, 1999). If a person with insomnia is not helped by these methods, more complex behavioral and psychological interventions are available through consultation with a competent professional.

Narcolepsy

This is a serious disturbance with a number of possible symptoms often beginning in adolescence (Bassetti & Aldrich, 1996). It is characterized by excessive daytime sleepiness and a major symptom of suddenly falling asleep. This is not the "snoozing off" of someone who is very tired or very bored who gradually drifts into sleep, but a precipitous shift from wakefulness to sleep which can occur, for example, while driving or crossing a busy street. If the person is standing and then falls, the fall is due to a sudden loss of muscle tone, called cataplexy. Such inability to move also may occur while trying to fall asleep or upon awakening and is called sleep paralysis. Another symptom is the experience of vivid, often nightmarish, visual hallucinations. Commonly, in narcolepsy, sleep in general is disrupted with disturbing dreams and excessive motor restlessness.

Narcolepsy is thought to be due to impaired timing of the various event sequences associated with REM sleep. Thus, sudden sleep is due to the onset of sleep without a REM delay. Cataplexy and sleep paralysis reflect the profound motor inhibition which ordinarily occurs only in the midst of REM sleep but now suddenly appears during wakefulness. The hallucinations appear to be carryovers into the waking state of the intense excitation that occurs in the visual system which ordinarily generated vivid dreams. There are a number of procedures used to establish the diagnosis including a sleep EEG. Perhaps the most telling is the Multiple Sleep Latency Test in which the subject is asked to sleep during the day at about two-hour intervals while the EEG is recorded. Rapid onset of sleep and short REM latencies under these conditions support the diagnosis of narcolepsy.

Narcolepsy is a difficult disorder to treat. The drugs which are most helpful are stimulants such as amphetamine, dexedrine, ritalin, and cylert, and are often used in treating the disorders described in this and the next chapter. Antidepressant medications are now also frequently used because of their long-term effects on noradrenergic and serotonergic arousing systems. The physician attempts to find a means of balancing the overactivity driving REM cholinergic mechanisms with monoamine activity regulating waking and arousal.

REM sleep behavior disorder

This disorder is the obverse of narcolepsy. Whereas in narcolepsy, the motor inhibition that occurs with REM sleep appears in undesirable and dangerous contexts rather than in the safety of one's bed, in REM sleep behavior disorder, REM motor inhibition is inadequate or non-existent (Schenck & Mahowald, 1996). As a result, the intense arousal of the brain and accompanying ideational and emotional activity leads to overt behavior while asleep that may be injurious to the dreamer and to nearby persons such as a sleep partner. The disorder appears most frequently in men past the age of 60, is often preceded by years of sleep talking, intense muscle twitching, and limb jerking, and has a significant association with neurodegenerative conditions such as Parkinson's disease and even with narcolepsy. The disorder also occurs in women and in younger individuals with no sign of degenerative disorder and, in these cases, appears to be somewhat predictive of the later onset of degenerative disorders. REM sleep behavior disorder symptoms appear to be quite responsive to an anticonvulsive medication, clonazepam, even though seizures do not occur.

Sleep apnea

In adults, this disorder is almost never identified by the patient. It is generally discovered by a bedmate and diagnosed during a sleep EEG. What the patient does complain of is sleepiness so this condition, like narcolepsy, is a type of excessive daytime sleepiness. The reason for the sleepiness in this case is that the person is being awakened as often as 100–300 times a night. The awakenings occur because breathing has stopped, sometimes for as long as two minutes, but more generally for about 10–45 seconds. The lack of oxygen (which is what apnea means) is a stress that prompts awakening, whereupon breathing resumes. The person most often falls back asleep almost immediately and continues to sleep until breathing stops again, whereupon the cycle is repeated. Such recurrent disruption plays havoc with sleep and leaves the person sleepy and fatigued, but without recollection of awakening.

Three types of sleep apnea have been described. Obstructive sleep apnea has as its hallmark loud snoring and is also associated with excessive weight. It tends to occur predominantly in men and individuals with narrow air pathways. As the name portrays, it is due to the closing off of the air pathway during sleep. Central sleep apnea is defined as an absence of respiratory effort, a decrease or absence of the automatic excitation of the respiratory muscles. As previously noted, motor inhibition is widespread throughout the nervous system during sleep, but here matters have gone too far. Mixed sleep apnea, the most common condition, combines the features of the other two types. Although apnea episodes may occur at any stage of sleep, they are particularly likely to occur during REM sleep when motor inhibition is most profound. There are a variety of treatment approaches, each dealing with the component symptoms. These include surgery, medication, weight loss, and muscle tone improvement. In general, the latter two have had the most success.

Sleep apneic conditions in children can be divided into the sudden infant death syndrome (SIDS), and the sleep apneas of childhood which are similar to those found in adults. SIDS is the leading cause of death during the first year of life in the United States. It peaks between two and four months, at a time when the overall organization of sleep, e.g. the percent time in REM and in slow wave sleep, is rapidly changing (see Glotzbach, Ariagno, & Harper, 1995, for a review). A full understanding of this condition has not been attained. It is known that the condition appears far more often under adverse socioeconomic circumstances and such related factors as inadequate prenatal medical care, maternal smoking, young maternal age, and low birth weight. It was originally thought that the proximal cause was an obstructive apneic episode, and related to this is evidence that the incidence of the condition is increased many times if the infant is put to sleep on its belly rather than nose up on its back. More recent evidence has implicated ineffectual mechanisms which rouse the infant when distressed. The picture is further complicated by news reports which suggest that some children who have died of SIDS have actually been suffocated in the course of child abuse.

Childhood sleep apnea is similar to the adult condition in that there is an increased incidence of snoring, signalling at least partial obstruction of the air passage, and some association with obesity. It is different in that the snoring in childhood is almost continuous whereas in adults there are pauses, there is little excessive daytime sleepiness and much daytime mouth breathing, the reverse of which is true in adults. Perhaps the main difference is that a surgically treatable, likely cause of obstruction is often evident in the children, enlarged tonsils and adenoid glands in the throat, and is generally not present in sleep apneic adults. This does not occur in all cases, however, and much remains to be understood about this condition (Carroll & Loughlin, 1995).

Enuresis

Somewhere past the age of three years, and certainly by the age of five, most children learn how to inhibit urination in sleep and to respond to urinary urgency by rousing from sleep and going to the toilet. Failure of this accomplishment is termed enuresis, obviously a developmental disorder. Another variety, sometimes called secondary enuresis, occurs when a child who has been dry resumes bedwetting. Most often, some psychologically significant stress is associated with such developmental regression. Since enuresis occurs during sleep, the sleep characteristics of bedwetters have been studied, and a number of interesting findings have emerged. Bedwetters tend to sleep very deeply (they are difficult to rouse), they tend to wet the bed during the first third of the night, and urination tends to occur during Δ sleep. Bedwetters tend not to have other sleep disturbances (Dollinger, 1982).

Approaches to treatment

If differing approaches to the treatment of enuresis are examined, some interesting relationships between mental activity during wakefulness and sleep, and excitatory and inhibitory relationships in the nervous system are apparent. Three approaches to the treatment of enuresis will be described next. There is considerable overlap among them although they focus on different aspects of bedwetting:

(a)   Enuresis is viewed as a symptom of biologic and/or sociocultural immaturity. During periods of military mobilization, authorities are often surprised by the high incidence of young men who are found to wet the bed. These individuals generally come from impoverished environments, are poorly educated, and are inexperienced and immature. Enuretic youngsters of school age also often appear to be relatively immature in social behavior, impulse control, and school learning skills. Accordingly, some experts view enuresis as just another aspect of lagging development. This perspective leads to an attitude that "it will cure itself in time." A related approach leads to a search for physical abnormalities in the urinary tract. In a small percentage of enuretics, urethral–bladder infections, structural malformations, or other abnormalities are found which, when corrected, are followed by the cessation of enuresis.

(b)   Enuresis is viewed as a failure to establish a classically conditioned response of waking up to the stimulus of bladder pressure. Urinary continence (the ability to inhibit excretion except as desired) is viewed as a product of the same type of learning demonstrated by Pavlov, whose dogs came to salivate at the sound of a bell. This approach gives rise to a treatment in which the child sleeps on a special pad, so constructed that wetting closes an electrical circuit which causes a loud bell to ring and which then rouses the child from sleep. This unpleasant experience comes to be anticipated when bladder pressure increases, and the child learns to avoid it by waking up. He can then go to the toilet and avoid wetting. This treatment has been quite successful in helping children to attain dryness, but many often regress afterwards. The treatment itself involves some expense, though not necessarily more than other forms of treatment, but does wrench the child from very deep sleep.

(c)   In this approach, enuresis is viewed as a form of symbolically (cognitively) mediated behavior. It is based on the observation that enuresis may be found in contexts in which the behavior itself, the wetting, appears to be meaningful. This is almost always the case in secondary enuresis. In some instances the meaning seems obvious, as when it occurs following the birth of a sibling or the death of a parent, or following sexual abuse. In other cases, the meaning is less obvious but discernible if family interaction is closely studied. For example, in a case from the author's experience, the enuretic symptom persisted until the child in question, a girl of nine, was told that she was to clean up herself when she wet, and that no other family members were to be awakened. It had emerged that enuresis represented a form of control she exercised over her mother who otherwise was dominant in every way. In another case, a boy of six, whose parents, beset by problems of their own and more brutal in their discipline than they probably wanted to be, had as his only form of assertion (and revenge), his nightly ritual in which he disrupted his parents' sleep.

The recognition that there are interpersonal, symbolic, and cognitive aspects to enuresis leads to a variety of daytime interventions, which are designed to influence aspects of behavior in sleep. Individual or family psychotherapy might search for stresses and relationships which affect the symptom. A frequent intervention, operant conditioning, focusses on the symptom alone, but nonetheless is cognitive in nature. The child is rewarded during the day (through charts with earned symbols which cumulate to obtain a desired incentive) for dryness at night. Such an intervention is often quite effective in helping the development of self-control during sleep. Whether it is the specific effect of the reward or nonspecific increased attention and positive support from parents that is crucial is not clear, but this is a simple, gentle method when it works.

Azrin and colleagues (1971, 1979) have pioneered efficient and very successful behavioral techniques which combine classically conditioned and operant procedures along with methods for training the child to discriminate cues for bladder urgency, increase bladder capacity, know what actions to take to effect dryness, and take responsibility for hygiene and cleanup when accidents occur. These methods were originally developed to train retarded individuals, many of whom were adults with long histories of incontinence. Formal descriptions of the method give little or no consideration to contextual factors that may have contributed to the development of the problem, but emphasize only the learning of an effective habit. Close attention to the details prescribed by Azrin, especially in his books for parents (e.g. Azrin & Besalel, 1979) suggests that he is much aware of the importance of sensitive, supportive parenting and hence what is needed when those circumstances are not present.

For clinicians who encounter less than supportive, and even exploitative, familial circumstances, a dilemma arises as to how to treat the enuretic symptom. There is so much to gain in the way of the child's self-control and confidence if methods such as Azrin's are implemented, and so much to lose if successful training is delayed, that it is tempting to proceed directly to training and avoid consideration of the contextual factors that may be giving rise to, or reinforcing, the symptom. On the other hand, the overtness and distress associated with the symptom provide an opportunity and some leverage to inquire into, and possibly alleviate, those circumstances which may be responsible.

One solution is to delay the initiation of habit training while data are gathered, an understanding of family dynamics is obtained, and remediation of exploitative issues is undertaken. Not infrequently, enuresis may be associated with some form of subtle or not so subtle abuse. Progress in dealing with those issues might signal that the time for intensive habit training was ripe. A skillful clinician might also find ways to weave interventions designed to increase habit mastery directly into the work with a family. Although enuresis can often be treated in isolation of the circumstances which may have given rise to the problem, successful treatment may, in the long run, do more harm than good. It depends on the underlying circumstances and meaning of the behavior.

Finally in considering enuresis and its treatment, a case report by a master therapist, Milton Erickson (1954), gives one much room for thought about mind–body relations and the power of suggestion. The case is of an attractive young couple, very much in love, who had both been enuretic all their lives and who both wet the bed each night of their nine-month marriage. Each thought him/or herself responsible, and each was extremely grateful to the other for not mentioning the morning dampness. They discovered the truth about each other when one commented that if they had a baby who slept with them, they could blame the baby for the wetness.

When they consulted Erickson for help with this humiliating problem, he prescribed, with appropriate preparation, the following: that for two weeks they were to drink freely before going to bed, and that they were to wet the bed, jointly and deliberately, before going to sleep. He also suggested that after two weeks, they could go to sleep in a dry bed, but that if they woke up and experienced wetness they would resume the ordeal for three more weeks! The couple did as they were told despite great difficulty in accomplishing the instructions. Two weeks later, on the first morning when they did not have to perform their ordeal, they found themselves dry, and without knowing why, remained dry thereafter. If the reader is puzzled about how this treatment worked, he/she might wish to consult the literature about therapeutic paradox and its effects, but the case further illustrates the linkage between experience while awake and events in sleep.

Sleep terrors

This is an extraordinary and dramatic event that most often begins with an intense and piercing cry followed by an apparent arousal from sleep which is only partial. The individual, heart pounding, breathing rapidly, and sweating, appears to be in a state of terror. and statements such as "it's going to get me" are common. The episode is generally short, lasting up to about four minutes. The person, most often a school-age child, may abruptly return to full sleep without having wakened, or may appear to be fully awake and much calmer in a short while and then return to sleep. There is no memory for sleep terror events the next morning.

These events are different from the more common experience of a nightmare, which is simply a bad dream. The latter are often remembered and generally occur during REM sleep whereas sleep terrors generally occur in Stage 3 or 4 NREM sleep. Interestingly, somnambulism, or sleep walking, which will not be further discussed here, also occurs in Stage 4 NREM sleep. The causes of sleep terrors are unknown but appear to be associated with emotional self-regulation, often in children whose daytime pattern of emotional expression is suppressed and overcontrolled (Rosen, Mahowald, & Ferber, 1995). Suggested treatments include anticonvulsant medication and a range of psychological interventions aimed at obtaining more optimal balance in emotional self-regulation. Often, such work also involves the child's family.

Depression and Mania

Some years back, and even today, consideration of depression and mania in a book with an emphasis on childhood disorders would have raised the objection that it was out of place, that depression was a disorder only of adulthood. In recent years that view has changed and there is a controversial but burgeoning clinical and scientific literature about these conditions in childhood (cf. Angold, 1988; Cantwell & Carlson, 1983; Kovacs, 1989; Rutter, Izard, & Read, 1986). If one grants that these disorders occur in childhood, the question still arises as to why they should be considered in a chapter on sleep and basic mechanisms of arousal. To answer this question, a discussion of the nature of depression and mania in both children and adults is in order.

Symptoms of depression and mania

Depression and mania are affective conditions, disorders of feeling, emotion, and, especially, mood. In depression, the person feels blue, low, sad, and unhappy. In mania, mood is euphoric, activity level and subjective confidence are high, and judgment is impaired. Both conditions have broad effects which influence many functions. Mania is much less common than depression, less is known about it, and it will be given less consideration here.

There is fair consensus about the main symptoms of depressive disorders (Cantwell, 1983; Hodges & Siegel, 1985; Carlson & Garber, 1986). In addition to mood changes, a number of other related symptoms are commonly described. These include anhedonia, an inability to experience pleasure; psychomotor retardation or agitation, slowing of motor activity and thought or, paradoxically, agitation marked by restlessness, pacing, hand rubbing or even shouting; and vegetative symptoms, such as decreased appetite and energy, constipation, and sleep disturbances, especially early morning waking. Depression often comes and goes, with durations ranging from weeks to months and sometimes even years, but can also be chronic. The incidence of suicide is high, not only in adults, but also in older children and especially adolescents.

Depressed people are likely to have and to express certain kinds of thoughts including ideas of worthlessness, pessimism about the future, and suicidal thoughts and plans. The quality of information processing declines when the tasks they are performing require initiative and organization, so memories for that kind of information are not retrieved very well (Weingartner et al., 1981). In children, there is commonly a change in attitude toward school and a decline in performance. In both children and adults, there is no decline in cognitive capability, although cognitive performance may decline when depression is severe and improve when it remits (gets better). However, since children are in the process of acquiring a repertoire of skills, depressions of very long duration in childhood can interfere with the development of social and cognitive competence (Kovacs, 1989). Manic persons, by contrast, are optimistic, and self-confident, though often their judgment is distorted and unrealistic.

Classification of depression and mania

Traditional approaches to classification

Among individuals with affective disorders, by far the greatest number experience only depressions, a very small number experience only mania and a somewhat larger number cycle between mania and depression. The cycling condition is called a bipolar disorder, while the others are called unipolar disorders. Unipolar depressions associated with environmental events have been termed exogenous or reactive and been thought to be relatively mild forms of the disorder, amenable to psychotherapy. Implicated environmental events may be remote, e.g. when someone who has experienced child abuse becomes depressed 20 or more years later, or recent, when someone loses a job and then becomes depressed. More severe manifestations of depression were called endogenous (meaning internally caused) and were thought to run in families, occur in older people, occur autonomously and not be reactive to environmental events, and not be amenable to psychotherapy but respond to a number of drugs and to shock therapy (a procedure in which seizures are induced with a jolt of electricity to the brain). Presumably, the exogenous type suffered from a functional disturbance whereas the endogenous type suffered from a more profound, organic impairment. Cortisol, a stress-related hormone, is hypersecreted in endogenously depressive adults and growth hormone is hyposecreted. The growth hormone findings in adults have been confirmed in 50 percent of diagnosed prepubertal children (Puig-Antich, 1983, 1986). Through the course of adolescence, the findings become increasingly similar to those of adults.

Recent revisions of the approach to classification and ongoing controversy

The validity of the exogenous–endogenous dichotomy was questioned when it was observed that some with typical symptoms of endogenous depression had sustained traumatic experiences in childhood or at onset of illness, and that in some persons with predominant exogenous symptoms, no precipitant could be found (Vogel et al., 1990). As a result, consideration of whether depressive symptoms were endogenous was often abandoned and the severity of the symptoms was gauged instead. Severe depression has come to be called major depression (American Psychiatric Association, 1994), and diagnosis, which is the basis for selecting subjects for research, often excludes consideration of the endogenous–exogenous factor.

Nonetheless, the exogenous–endogenous distinction has not died. A series of studies (e.g. Kiloh & Garside, 1963; Carney, Roth, & Garside, 1965; Rosenthal & Klerman, 1966; Grove et al., 1987) and comparative reviews (e.g. Mendels & Cochrane, 1968; Nelson & Charney, 1981; Leber, Beckham, & Danker-Brown, 1985; Push & Weissenburger, 1994; Brown, Harris, & Hepworth, 1994; Frank et al., 1994) all found evidence for the distinction. As a general rule, endogenous depression involved more profound anhedonia, decreased anger and hostility, and either psychomotor retardation or agitation. Making the distinction helped predict the course of the disorder and efficacy of treatment in groups of patients but was not always easy to make in the individual case. Differentiation rested on the depth of the anhedonia, the magnitude of motor slowing (whether or not agitation was present), the extent of vegetative symptoms, and the depth and pervasiveness of the depressed mood. Different authors emphasize one or another of the symptoms. Residual influence of the endogenous distinction can be found in current diagnostic procedures (American Psychiatric Association, 1994) in the qualifying term "melancholic features." Importantly, as depression recurs "nonendogenous depression may develop endogenous features . . . but endogenous depressions are likely to stay that way" (Rush & Weissenburger, 1994, p. 494).

In the classical view of endogenous depression just described, severity is a major attribute. The overall picture has been complicated immensely but creatively in work (Akiskal & Cassano, 1997) that has challenged this concept, suggesting that endogenous depression can occur on a continuum of severity, i.e. also be mild. Akiskal (1997, p. 14), reviewing data about mild depression wrote: "subtle 'endogenous features' are commonly observed: psychomotor inertia, lethargy and anhedonia, which are characteristically worse in the morning. Clinically, the striking features of dysthymia include habitual gloom, brooding, lack of joie de vivre, and preoccupation with inadequacy." Dysthymia is synonymous with persistent mildly depressed mood and Akiskal is presenting the case that endogenous characteristics can be found in some and be differentiable from nonendogenous depression. Along these lines, Roth & Mountjoy (1997), among others, agree that endogenous characteristics can be present in mild form and have presented a list of features that specify nonendogenous depression (p. 116). They also go on to argue that bipolar and endogenous depression are aspects of the same disorder, varying in the range within which the cycles swing and that both are different from exogenous depression. In effect, they suggest that endogenous vs nonendogenous is the crucial distinction in affective disorders and that severity of symptoms and even unipolar vs bipolar dimensions are not of importance with regard to the mechanism of impairment. This topic will be reconsidered below after considering research on causes of depression.

Causes of depression

One of the themes of this book is that particular symptoms may develop as a result of abnormalities of the nervous system, of experience in the environment, or of some interaction of the two, and that understanding the relative contribution of each is useful in devising rational treatment interventions. Depression is an outstanding example (Eisenberg, 1986).

Experiential factors in depression

It is common knowledge that when losses significant to the person occur (see chapter 7) or when things go wrong in the environment, symptoms of depression commonly occur. The experience of mourning a loved one, for example, almost always includes depressed mood. Systematic evidence supporting the idea that experience can provoke depression includes the large body of research on learned helplessness (Peterson & Seligman, 1985; Seligman & Peterson, 1986) which indicates that depressive symptoms increase after uncontrollable defeat (such as the loss of a job when a company fails, or suffering regular punishment without cause), and can be relieved both through changes in the meanings attributed to defeat and through corrective emotional experience, providing, of course, that the defeating experiences themselves actually come to an end. The corrective emotional experience might be appropriate mourning; the change in thinking might be a rational examination of what one's actual and realistic responsibilities have been.

Further evidence for environmental and experiential contributions to depression comes from an older literature on children who have been severely deprived of stimulation, care, and affection during early infancy, mostly because they are raised in institutions that cannot, or simply do not, provide even an approximation of the stimulation that family-reared children receive. These children develop a syndrome that has been termed "hospitalism" or anaclitic (meaning "leaning on" and referring to the utter dependency of an infant on others) depression (Spitz, 1945, 1946). The babies become dull, listless, and unresponsive and look and act very depressed. Fortunately, if the environment becomes more stimulating, the children respond well. Dependency has also been found to be an important factor in adult depression. Whereas complete dependency is simply an aspect of being an infant, some persons grow up with excessive dependence on, and strong need to obtain approval from, others. Such individuals are vulnerable to depression should they lose their sources of dependency gratification (Beck, 1967; Blatt, D'Affliti, & Quinlan, 1976; Zuroff et al., 1999).

By contrast, another kind of vulnerability to depression occurs in adolescent and adult personalities who are high achieving, excessively independent, and more specifically, have perfectionistic standards for themselves. They tend to define many situations as tests of their worth, and, if they experience non-success or failure, are vulnerable to profound depression (Beck, 1967; Blatt, D'Afflitti, & Quinlan, 1976; Frost et al., 1990; Hewit & Flett, 1991). Dependency-loss types of depressives may make suicidal gestures but rarely succeed: by contrast, failed-perfectionist depressives succeed all too often.

Perhaps the most frequently implicated environmental variable in adult depression is severe or prolonged abuse and stress, especially in childhood. Many persons presenting with depression have histories of childhood abuse (Nemiroff, 1995, 1996) and many individuals with post-traumatic stress disorders such as concentration-camp survivors or tortured political prisoners also suffer from depression (Yehuda, 1998). The study of these humans, and of animals that have been subjected to experimental stress (e.g. Weiss, 1991), has focussed on changes in the hypothalamic–pituitary–adrenal (HPA) axis, the endocrine system involved in the response to stress. Emerging work has implicated excessive production of corticotropin-releasing factor (CRF), a secretion of the hypothalamus, which regulates a range of modules activated under conditions of stress (Nemiroff, 1996). As mentioned in chapter 7, chronic stress and secretion of cortisol have been shown to lead to structural changes in brain, especially the hippocampus (Sapolsky, 1996).

Is there evidence in depression of constitutional changes other than those involving the HPA axis?

It was noted above that one line of research has implicated the HPA axis activated by chronic or intense stress as a mechanism for enduring depression. It is of interest that a test of HPA axis function studied intensively in depression, the dexamethasone suppression test (APA task force on laboratory tests in psychiatry, 1987), has been found to be abnormal in only about 50 percent of endogenously depressed individuals (Rush & Weissenburger, 1994), so by this criterion there is certainly room for other mechanisms of impairment. Evidence for three other brain mechanisms will be considered next.

REM sleep differences

It has often been found that the sleep of depressed persons is different from the norm. There are more awakenings through the night, reduced deep sleep (Stage 3 and 4), shorter REM latency, and increases in the number of eye movements during a REM period (REM density) (Rush & Weissenburger, 1994). REM episodes tend not to get longer through the night, but tend to decrease. The frequency of eye movements within desynchronized REM sleep epochs tends to be higher (Vogel et al., 1988). Developmentally, such findings have not been found in depressed prepubertal children; they emerge only in late adolescence (Puig-Antich, 1986). Vogel (1975, 1983) noted prior evidence that helpful treatments in endogenous depression, drugs and electroshock, both reduced REM sleep. He evaluated whether REM sleep deprivation was the mechanism of action of antidepressant treatments and the means by which the improvement in endogenous depression comes about by physically preventing REM from occurring by waking the person whenever a REM episode began. Doing this in the sleep laboratory to carefully selected endogenous and exogenous persons with active depression, Vogel et al. (1980) found that endogenous, but not exogenous, depressives improved following the same time course (approximately three weeks) taken by established treatments.

Vogel (Vogel et al., 1990) has gone on to develop a model of depression in rats. Animals are deprived of REM sleep during the third postnatal week by giving them daily doses of an antidepressant drug (which suppresses REM) and then, when they are mature, testing for depressive symptoms of anhedonia, reduced sexual and aggressive behavior, psychomotor changes, sleep patterns, and response to antidepressant drugs. The paradoxical finding that the drug that ameliorates depression in adulthood, and can cause it in adulthood if administered in infancy, in each instance by reducing REM sleep, has led him to grapple with the unsolved question of the function REM sleep. In this work (Vogel, Feng, & Kinney, in press) the suggestion is offered that the decrease in percent of REM sleep and the increasing REM delay that occurs in the first year of life is a normal maturational process that inhibits REM sleep, the accomplishment of which makes possible a normal repertoire of motivations and adaptive energy. Failure to inhibit REM sleep dissipates neural energy in sleep and leaves the individual depressed and anergic during the day. REM suppression in endogenously depressed persons also prevents the dissipation of neural energy and lifts depression. Whatever the validity of these ideas may prove to be, the approach is meritorious in that it opens up developmental processes in the study of adult depression and grapples with the salient and most devastating anergic symptoms of melancholic depression.

Differences in hemispheric activation

The two hemispheres appear to regulate and express different emotions. This has been observed in different contexts, two of which will be described here. Persons who have endured frontal one-sided strokes, conditions in which the blood supply is cut off to a part of the brain, or other subtractive lesions tend to respond emotionally in different ways depending on which hemisphere is involved. Persons with right hemisphere pathology tend to be cheerful and sometimes euphoric but also indifferent to what has occurred to them. They display mostly positive emotions. Persons with comparable left-sided pathology are likely to display agitation, worry about the changes that have happened, and display depression. They display mostly negative emotions. By contrast, if a patient sustains an irritative lesion of the sort that can give rise to seizures, excessive crying is associated with right-sided pathology, and excessive laughter with left-sided pathology. These generalizations are oversimplified because the exact position in the hemisphere and the sex of the subject may change the probabilities, but are supported by much diverse evidence (Silberman & Weingartner, 1986; Liotti & Tucker, 1995). Close reading of the above sentences may have suggested a contradiction since lesions in either hemisphere were associated with opposite kinds of emotion, but there is no contradiction. Irritative lesions provoke more of what the tissue is capable of, while subtractive lesions in one hemisphere make it hard for that side to compete with the other, so the other wins out. Thus laughter and euphoria are associated with left irritative lesions and right subtractions while depression and worry are associated with right irritative lesions and left subtractions. Activity in the right frontal hemisphere is associated with regulating and expressing negative emotions such as depression, fear, and anxiety while activity in the left frontal hemisphere is associated with expressing and regulating happy emotions.

Davidson (1988) has been in the forefront of studying relative activity in the two hemispheres in noninjured persons by means of quantitative EEG, a technique which was mentioned in the previous chapter and will be described in more detail in the next. He has mustered evidence in a series of studies with different kinds of depressives that depression is associated with more alpha activity, which, it will be recalled from the discussion in the previous chapter, indicates relative idling, in the left frontal lobe compared to the right. From these data, the inference is made that the right hemisphere is more active than the left in depression. In one study with such findings (Henriques & Davidson, 1991), the authors note that the pattern described appears to be related to vulnerability to depression in that it tends to occur in non-depressed relatives of depressed persons and does not vary with the magnitude or intensity of the depression. Right brain pathology has also been implicated in theories of depression by others (e.g. Flor-Henry, 1979).

Another proponent of right hemisphere pathology in depression is Brumback (1988), who has suggested that endogenous depression, rather than being rare in children, is quite common. The most salient symptoms may be quite varied and include both learning disorders and attentional problems, but if looked for, the core symptoms of depression can be found. Brumback musters evidence for a reversible (hence ictal-like) impairment of the right hemisphere. Depressed children are described as showing subtle motor symptoms on the left side of their bodies, mental impairments in functions that are controlled by the right side of the brain, and arousal deficits. These impairments and whatever symptoms may be evident (e.g. learning disability, hyperactivity, delinquency) and depression are all said to be relieved by anti-depressant medications.

Brumback is optimistic about treatment with medication. His position, after some years, has not received much research attention although evidence will be noted in the next chapter that some children with attentional symptoms respond well to anti-depressant medications. Initial efforts attempting to verify his hypotheses failed (e.g. Mokros, Poznanski, & Merrick, 1989). As these latter authors point out, there is often evidence of problems such as learning difficulty or hyperactivity prior to the onset of depression. The depression may well represent a reaction to life failures the child has experienced. It may then follow that serious failure, loss, or lack of support in childhood may lead to endogenous depression. Or it may be that Brumback is proposing to use endogenous treatments for conditions which are not endogenous. Evidence that childhood depression merits the endogenous classification is controversial.

Seasonal affective disorder (SAD)

Seasonal affective disorder, or SAD (Rosenthal & Blehar, 1989) is a recently redis-covered depressive syndrome whose defining characteristic is that it occurs season-ally. The best understood are those that occur as winter approaches and days become shorter. The condition is more common in regions of the world that have long winters. The brain mechanisms involved are those that respond to seasonal cycles and day–night changes, one component of which is the secretion of a substance called melatonin. Sufferers of SAD who become depressed as the bright light of summer wanes are treated by being exposed to bright light, and research indicates considerable improvement. There have been some studies of sleep architecture and the dexamethasone suppression test in SAD. In sleep there are some similarities to the findings in endogenous depression, especially greater REM density. The dexamethasone suppression test tends to be normal (Skwerer et al., 1989).

The report of a number of patients that they had been suffering from SAD since childhood led to a successful search for children with this condition (Sonis, 1989). Comparison of the symptoms in children and adults indicates that some differences from endogenous depression are present besides the seasonal recurrence that defines the condition. For one thing, adult SADs often eat and sleep excessively. Children more often report decreased sleep, increased irritability, but no change in eating. Although these youngsters are thus somewhat more similar to the endogenously depressed than adult SAD patients, they appear to respond as well as adults to treatment with light.

Issues in the diagnosis of depression

We have seen that a number of environmental and constitutional factors are associated with depression and that chronic environmental factors can alter aspects of brain structure as well as their mode of operation. As research progresses, our ideas about these disorders may be in for considerable revision. For example, there is evidence that treatment with light not only helps SAD patients but also helps individuals who show seasonal behavioral changes but who have never complained of depression, and also those with depression with no obvious seasonal component (Kasper et al., 1989; Kripke et al., 1989). Much of the controversy in the field is associated with the question of the existence of the endogenous condition. Stress system (HPA) abnormalities may be crucial to certain kinds of serious depression, but they are not consistent with the phenomenology of endogenous depression. An overactive HPA axis would be expected to induce anxiety and chronic overactivation which could lead to a depression-like exhaustion state. But in many endogenous–melancholic depressions there is no history of stress and no evidence of anxiety. These persons show decreases in reactivity and excitability, anhedonia, profoundly low mood, and vegetative symptoms. They are alive, but there is no liveliness, at least as indicated by motivated behavior. They are not particularly afraid although anxiety can also be present.

Such presentations may be clearly identifiable in some cases but not in others. Yehuda (1998), reviewing the neuroendocrine evidence differentiating major depression and post-traumatic stress disorder, which clearly originates in experience, found the changes of the HPA axis in the two conditions to be different. The details go beyond the scope of this text. Meanwhile systematic investigation of all the variables that have been implicated in depression are rarely examined in the same cases. Depression is largely a medical–psychiatric diagnosis, a perspective that tends to view a behavior disturbance as a pathological feature within the person, not a response to environmental events. (See for example the review by Angold, 1988, where environmental etiologies are not given any systemic consideration.)

The issue is important because if the environment provokes the reaction, then treatment might focus on the environment, or ways of coping with it, rather than on the depressive symptoms themselves. Psychiatric diagnosis may neglect environmental factors and focus entirely on the symptoms. Although this is easy to understand in the case of adults where, for example, childhood abuse may have occurred long before the onset of depression or appearance in the doctor's office, it is harder to understand in the case of children. Examples of how experience is neglected in favor of just examining the symptoms can be found in the cases described by Carlson and Cantwell (1983, p. 39) in their presentation of examples of childhood depression. Their first case, summarized below, is typical.

The child was a 9½-year-old boy who was brought to clinical attention for riding his skateboard at a dangerous intersection, hoping to be killed. This view of his behavior was not just an inference since he specifically asked his doctor to hospitalize him before he did kill himself. He also displayed sadness, self-loathing and anhedonia, all clearly symptoms of depression. The boy's history, however, included ample reasons why he might feel depressed, including parents who turned him over to relatives to raise with instructions that he be told they were dead, who retrieved him suddenly when he was 6½, disrupting a successful parenting relationship, and who then raised him with rigid discipline, physical punishment that "bordered on the abusive," and guilt-inducing messages that his behavior was responsible for his parents' serious illnesses.

A report from the group that studied temperament (see chapter 6) longitudinally (Chess, Thomas, & Hassibi, 1983) contributes to an understanding of how complicated sorting out environmental and endogenous factors may be. These researchers followed their subjects from infancy and knew a great deal about them before any developed serious depressions. Of the six who did, the symptoms were largely similar. In two cases depression occurred in the absence of environmental stress and in the context of family histories of depression, suggesting a strong genetic predisposition. (There is ample evidence of genetic factors in many cases of depression, e.g. Mendlewicz, 1985.) In the rest, there was evidence of parental inadequacy in dealing with their difficult, temperamental characteristics. The authors could infer significant environmental influence in these cases because other children in their sample with equally difficult temperamental problems had more effective parenting and escaped serious pathology. In evaluating most persons presenting with the symptoms of depression, the kind of information Chess et al. had available (difficult childhood temperament and inadequate care) ordinarily is not. Their report stands as a challenge to look beyond the severity of symptoms in determining endogenous status, a point that coincides with the views found in Akiskal (1997), already discussed. Further complications come from recent studies on the offspring of depressed parents which provide evidence that their environment is far from optimal so that the transmission of depression across generations may not necessarily be genetically determined (Gotlib & Goodman, 1999).

What can be learned about depression from efforts at treatment?

As described above when introducing the differences between exogenous and endogenous depression, it is commonly held that drugs and shock therapy are helpful in endogenous, but not exogenous, depression, and psychotherapy is helpful in exogenous, but not endogenous, depression. Data verifying such differences would strongly support the validity of the exogenous–endogenous distinction. One partial nonverification came from a study (Frank et al., 1991) which showed that psychotherapy during periods of remission (spontaneous improvement) could delay recurrence of a major disorder. A review of comparative efficacy of biological and psychological treatments of mild depression in adults found that each was effective, that the latter was somewhat superior to the former alone, but that the most effective effect was obtained with both treatments combined (Free & Oei, 1989).

Stronger disconfirmation came from a paper by Antonuccio, Danton, and DeNelsky (1995). They reviewed many reviews of many studies comparing the efficacy of drugs and psychotherapy in unipolar depression and concluded that the evidence does not support the distinction. It should be noted that physicians often prescribe antidepressant drugs for mild forms of depression, and reported improvement is roughly the same as it is in major depression though not necessarily better than response to a placebo, an inert pill that serves as a control for the suggestive effects of being treated. When efficacy of drug treatment is compared with different types of psychotherapy, insight-oriented interventions based on psychoanalytic concepts fare poorly, but several cognitive–behavioral and interpersonal psychotherapies have been found to be helpful, as good as, or better than, medications. No evidence of drug efficacy in children was found, which stands in stark contrast to prior reports of their usefulness. The positive effects of psychotherapy were more enduring than those of medications, which tend to be effective only while the drugs are being taken.

These conclusions applied equally to major as well as less severe depression, and psychotherapy was found to alleviate vegetative as well as other symptoms. The drugs involved were from the first generation of antidepressants and more recently formulated medications had not yet been subjected to comparative efficacy research. But in a later paper, Antonuccio, Thomas, and Danton (1997) present evidence that behaviorally oriented individual psychotherapy not only was at least as effective as one of the newer antidepressant drugs, Prozac, but was more cost-effective by 33 percent over a two year period.

(The scope of this book does not include detailed examination of different types of psychotherapy but a brief review might enable better understanding of the previous paragraph. Behaviorally oriented therapies approach the symptoms of a disorder directly and are aimed at fostering effective coping techniques. The therapist aligns himself with the patient in a problem-solving mode to rectify sources of distress. Thus anhedonia, rather than being viewed as a biological aberration, is seen as a consequence of not engaging in behaviors which produce positive reinforcement. Therapy involves learning techniques for obtaining such reinforcement. Depressed people interpret their experiences negatively and such thoughts lower mood. The therapist helps the patient to learn how to appraise defeats and limitations realistically and prevent the cascading cycle into depression. Depressed people often are socially maladept, which makes it hard for them to obtain support, so the therapist teaches them social skills which enable them to obtain gratifications they otherwise must forgo. Psychoanalytic and psychodynamic therapies view depression as resulting from powerful emotions that operate outside awareness so that the person is not able to control them. In depression, the emotion is often rage turned inward and directed against the self. Treatment is aimed at discovering the true nature of the motives that are present; therefore the term insight-oriented.)

Antonuccio and colleagues' work calls into question much conventional thinking about depression. Surely, proponents of the exogenous–endogenous distinction would argue that, despite the large number of studies reviewed and the range of severity considered, the distinction was rarely examined in a systematic way. Those who have had the experience of working with severe endogenous depressions often note the essential inaccessibility to interpersonal communication that these persons display, and without such communication there is no psychotherapy of any kind. In no study do improvement percentages approach 100 percent and these cases, they would argue, are probably mostly endogenous. Profoundly endogenous cases may represent only a small proportion of those diagnosed with depression. Those not wedded to the distinction would note that a number of the studies reviewed were of hospitalized patients, which should include a fair proportion of endogenous cases, and that vegetative symptoms, one of the hallmarks of endogenous depression, were at least as amenable to psychotherapy treatment as to drug interventions. Advocates of drug treatment would doubt that adequate drug efficacy studies were reviewed. The debate rages and must bewilder a beginning student.

Summary of the State of Knowledge about Depression and Some Speculations

1.   Depressive symptoms and conditions exist but whether this is essentially one condition which varies on a continuum of severity or two or more conditions with different, if sometimes overlapping, mechanisms of impairment, is controversial. Recent proposals that endogenous symptoms may appear in mild form mean that both endogenous and exogenous types may occur at all degrees of severity. There are no agreed-upon characteristics, either symptoms observed or self-reported, or biological or psychological test findings that unequivocally define either the exogenous or endogenous condition. At best, groupings of symptoms may have a high probability of making some degree of discrimination, but what evidence is there is not widely accepted.

2.   Some depressions commonly occur in families and they are assumed to have a genetic basis, but little is yet known about the specific genes involved, how they express themselves, and whether there may be different genetic types of depression.

3.   Some kinds of depression are associated with relative activation of the right over the left hemisphere. Data are needed about where this fits in with other data about depression such as patterns of sleep, neuroendocrine functions of the stress system, and details about the symptoms. That relative hemispheric activation runs in families of depressed individuals suggests that it may be a marker for genetic mechanisms that make one vulnerable to depression.

4.   Although depression sometimes appears in chronic and persisting forms, it often waxes and wanes. There are no explanations available as to what produces these fluctuations when they occur autonomously.

5.   One candidate theory for the genesis of depression, particularly of the exogenous type, involves stress and hyperactivity of the hypothalamic–pituitary–adrenal axis and excessive secretion of the corticotropin-releasing factor. Much work needs to be done on the relationship between the age of the subject at the time of stress, the duration and magnitude of stress, and the appearance of symptoms. When the stress occurs in early childhood, there may be a long period before symptoms appear, and how that can be is not known. Alternatively, differences may be present continuously once the stress has occurred but may not be easily discerned in childhood. This theory is important because it requires consideration of the subject's experience and precludes simply considering the depressive symptoms in isolation.

6.   A candidate theory for understanding endogenous depression may lie in an explanation of the functions of REM sleep. This line of investigation has the potential of explaining the availability of energy and motivation in the mammalian nervous system and then of the unavailability of energy in the depressed state. This theory seems well suited to fit with genetic findings once they are discovered. There may also be environmental events that influence the maturation of REM sleep mechanisms early in life and resulting REM regulation. At this time, this hypothesis has not been widely studied, however.

7.   If HPA axis changes (and apparently there are at least two types: that associated with post-traumatic stress disorder and that associated with major depression) are assumed to be one type of pathogenic mechanism and REM sleep disinhibition another, then the presence of some combination of these conditions in the same people does not invalidate the distinction. In order to validate the distinction, it is necessary only that some individuals be found who have only one of each of the pathogenic conditions. It would then follow that there would be at least three types of depression: stress-related, anergic, and a combined form, all three of which could vary in degree of intensity.

10

Attention and its Disorders

In this chapter, variations in arousal within the waking state are examined. It will be recalled (chapter 5) that arousal refers to the degree of readiness of a neural system for action. Differences in such readiness are obvious when one contrasts being asleep and awake. It is also not difficult to appreciate how different one's readiness for action is, for example, while sunbathing as compared to how one feels just before the start of an examination. The term attention is used to refer to a variety of preparatory activities which normally facilitate information processing. Subjectively, one can refer to how alert or interested or "turned on" a person is.

Humans may focus their attention on information external to themselves or on events going on internally, their bodily sensations and private thoughts. Shifts in this dimension of attention vary with environmental circumstance and the characteristics of the individual. One is more likely to turn inward when the environment is dull or unstimulating, but people vary as to how readily they turn inwardly. Introverts are persons who will pay relatively more attention to their inner reveries or anxieties even when exciting events are occurring outside, while extroverts will be oriented externally even in the face of monotonous and unstimulating circumstances (Strelau & Eysenck, 1987). The brain requires external stimulation for normal functioning. Under conditions of sensory deprivation, e.g. immersion in liquid in a dark and soundless environment, most people shortly experience extreme stress and reactions which range from mild anxiety to mental breakdown or psychosis (Solomon, Kubzansky, & Leiderman, 1962).

There is a large body of Eastern cultural lore concerning styles of living and techniques for maintaining emotional self-regulation, in which individuals are taught to focus attention inwardly, but in a controlled manner. These techniques include meditation, autogenic training, hatha yoga, and bioenergetics, and involve altered states of consciousness (cf. Ornstein, 1974; Appelbaum, 1979). There will not be much consideration given to these techniques in this book but they merit further study. Most of the rest of this chapter deals with the deployment of attention in the external world. There are many neural components required for arousal and attention, and there are a number of different types. Before considering disorders of attention, the nature of attentional processes will be reviewed.

The Nature of External Attention

Living organisms operate in environments that are constantly changing, affording opportunities for gratification of needs and of curiosity and also posing threats of danger. The organism's needs are in flux, changing over the short run with cycles of want and gratification and over the long run with maturation. Under these conditions, it is something of a miracle that orderly and patterned behavior can occur. There must exist mechanisms within the brain and nervous system which select, process, and stay with what information is relevant until an adaptive behavioral sequence is completed before shifting focus to something else. These mechanisms must be able to operate both bottom-up and top-down, i.e. allow hierarchically primitive responses, like flight, to command attention when life is threatened, and high-level controls to supersede other candidates for attention, for example, when studying for an exam instead of partying.

As suggested by Pribram and McGuinness (1975), McGuinness and Pribram (1980), Heilman (e.g. Verfaellie, Bowers, & Heilman, 1988) and Mirsky (1989), the term attention will be used to refer to different processes that make possible such selection and generate the subjective experience of awareness. Awareness generally follows attention: one becomes aware of selected aspects of the information present in the environment and largely (though not entirely) unaware of the rest. Once the relevant information has been isolated, some type of response must be selected. The response process itself is quite complicated given that there are many muscle groups from which to choose to produce action, that different actions may accomplish the same goal, and that lack of action, inhibition, may be the response chosen. Controlled action does not emerge without effective preparation. The term intention will be used to refer to preparation for action (Verfaellie, Bowers, & Heilman, 1988) and activation for the initiation of action.

Types of attention

General alertness, resistance to fatigue, and wakefulness

Given a restful night's sleep, there nevertheless will be considerable variation in level of alertness through the course of a day. There is strong evidence of daily rhythmic cycles of change in the level of activity of many physiological systems and of behavior (Moore-Ede, Sulzman, & Fuller, 1982). Many people, for example, experience a decrease in general alertness after lunch and for several hours through the middle of the afternoon, and in many cultures this is a time utilized for napping. In addition, people differ in their overall energy level, level of activity, and resistance to fatigue. There are some who show great endurance and consistently high levels of energy, those who show the reverse pattern and those who fluctuate, some predictably and some unpredictably. The biology regulating this kind of fluctuation in alertness is probably the same as that which regulates the sleep–wake cycle. In some manner not yet understood, the activity of the reticular activating system is changed over the course of the day.

Selective attention to novelty: orientation and habituation

In Pavlov's (the Russian physiologist who discovered classical conditioning) laboratory, it was noted that a well-trained animal who was salivating to the sound of a bell after it had been paired with food powder many times would change its behavior radically if someone new happened to come into the room. The dog would turn and look at the stranger, and the conditioned behavior would be disrupted even though the animal was restrained in a harness. If the stranger approached the dog, it would sniff at him or her and not pay attention to either the bell or the food powder. After a while, particularly if the stranger behaved calmly, the dog's behavior would revert to the previous pattern.

These events impressed Pavlov and particularly his student, Sokalov (1963), who proceeded to study them systematically. From these beginnings, a body of knowledge was produced about the behavior that occurs when novel events are experienced (cf. Graham, 1973). The general findings are that animals, even very primitive ones, register and store prior experience. When something novel occurs – that is, when there has been no prior experience – the organism responds by investigating the nature of the event. This involves receptor orienting activity, which is a class of behaviors that move the sensory organs to maximize the information they receive. Thus, the eyes turn to the object or event in question. The hands reach out to touch. The ears perk up and the head may cock in a particular direction to maximize auditory sensitivity. A dog will sniff and lick while a baby will touch, grasp, and often put objects in its mouth.

Receptor orienting activity is accompanied by many internal changes in the brain and peripheral nervous system. Overall, there is a mild increase in activity of the sympathetic branch of the autonomic nervous system, the EEG desynchronizes, sweat gland activity increases on the skin, and heart rate accelerates. It will be recalled (chapter 3) that sympathetic activity facilitates fight or flight reactions in the face of danger. Novelty, by definition, is an unknown, and hence potentially dangerous. Thus, the reaction to novelty has many components of the reaction to danger.

The reaction, both internal and overt, to novel events is termed the orienting reaction, or orientation. The reactions decrease, or attenuate, and finally disappear if the event proves to be benign and harmless. The process of attenuation is called habituation. The term habituation was encountered previously at the cellular level (chapter 2) when discussing how repetition of stimulation that has no consequence leads to decreased release of neurotransmitter at the terminal button. The habituation described here reflects comparable changes at a higher level within the nervous system. It is a type of learning, because novelty becomes familiar. As a result of the investigatory activity, a model of the novel event is thought to be constructed in the brain, constituting a form of memory. Benign familiar circumstances do not require investigation so the orienting response is inhibited. For noxious or dangerous events, the model leads to early anticipation of the flight-fight reaction.

One frequently used technique for studying orientation and habituation allows for the observation of both the strong initial reaction of the orienting response and its decline through the process of habituation. Sweat gland activity associated with sympathetic arousal is measured by placing electrodes on the hand and connecting them to electronic amplifying devices. A low-level, undetectable, electric current is passed between them, and its ease of passage can be measured as skin conductance (in units called mhos, ohms spelled backwards), which will vary with the degree of wetness at the surface of the skin. With appropriate connections from the amplifiers, the level in skin conductance can be displayed. The skin conductance of a subject comfortably seated in a quiet darkened room who suddenly hears a loud tone will, at that point, rise sharply (the orienting response). As the tones repeat every 30 or 40 seconds, the response decreases (habituation) and by the fifth tone usually disappears.

What has all this got to do with attention? The discovery of the orienting–habituation mechanism reveals that novel and dangerous stimuli automatically, compellingly, and selectively capture the organism's attention. Now, what might happen to attention if the habituation process did not occur? The organism would be living in a world where everything was always new and nothing was ever familiar. So, to take just one example, the awareness of our clothing which we notice briefly when wearing a garment for the first time or for the first few seconds after it is put on, generally commands no attention because it has habituated. If habituation did not occur, it might be very difficult to focus on anything else given that clothes can command attention. People wearing wool who are sensitive to wool will understand what this sentence means.

Where in the brain are the mechanisms that control orientation and habituation? Some evidence about the locus of these events was provided by studies of anencephalic children. These children are born without a cerebral cortex and can live for a few months at most. Brackbill (1971) found that they could orient, but not habituate. Other work (Pribram & McGuinness, 1975) has suggested that the control of orientation resides in the temporal lobe, possibly its most primitive medial structures, but that the cortex is required for habituation. The mechanisms of habituation and other aspects of memory are closely intertwined. Despite the contributions from the cortex, orientation and habituation can be considered relatively primitive, hierarchically low mechanisms serving memory.

Selective attention to emotionally salient events – limbic factors

As noted, habituation does not occur to events that are associated with danger. It is also not likely to occur to events which are exciting, pleasurable, and emotionally enjoyable. Thus even a thoroughly satiated person may show great interest in the products of a bakery, particularly if the person likes the odors of fresh-baked breads and pastries. Stimuli with emotional significance, including all those associated with the major biological drives involving personal or species survival, e.g. food, sex, fear, aggression, and social relations, are very resistant to habituation. If one wants to assure interest in events to which habituation and boredom may occur, the introduction of non-habituating limbic arousing stimuli, like food for an animal or money for a person, works well. Substances or events which are limbic-arousing and non-habituating are called rewards. It is well known that rewards influence and facilitate many types of learning, and their effects are manipulated by teachers, employers, advertisers, and governments in order to facilitate learning, work, sales, and compliance with the law. Rewards are a fundamental component of behavior modification techniques often used to treat behavioral symptoms. The brain mechanisms involved in reward-controlled attention, like the orientation–novelty type of attention, are hierarchically relatively low.

Unusual, perhaps abnormal, constitutional factors and aberrant early experience can change the attentional value of stimuli. Aggressive behavior appears to be a normal response to threat in that there are built-in biological mechanisms facilitating the fight for survival. However, some individuals can be supersensitive to stimuli provoking aggression and can experience provocation when most others do not. Such individually determined salience may be inborn but may also result from an unfortunate experience such as aggressive modeling, frequent abuse, or excessive punishment early in life. Sensitization can occur to any type of stimulus. Thus, given certain experiences, a particular individual may find certain foods to be irresistible or ordinary objects to elicit sexual interest and excitement.

Effortful selective attention and self-regulation: executive functions

The mechanisms of attention described above provide for the attentional needs of a large portion of the animal kingdom and are also present in humans. In a literate, technologically complex society where success requires complex information processing and rewards are often long delayed and symbolic, such attentional mechanisms are not enough. Suppose that on a beautiful spring day, when friends invite you to picnic and party, you have to study for an important exam in a subject you do not find interesting. Or suppose that you are an air traffic controller who has been watching a radar screen for six hours of routine take-offs and landings. Or suppose you are a second-grader who cannot join friends in play until a spelling assignment is correctly completed. In each case, effortful, voluntary attention will be required. Effortful attention is hierarchically high and depends on the integrity of the cortex, particularly the frontal lobes. Effortful attention is part of a group of mental operations often called executive functions. For these functions to occur, hierarchically lower attentional mechanisms often must be inhibited.

Barkley (1997) has aptly summarized current knowledge about major aspects of executive functions. The key neuropsychological concept is that of inhibition: effortful selective attention requires that many prepotent responses such as might be elicited by novelty or by limbic-arousing stimuli must be inhibited long enough to allow thought, consideration of consequences, and selection among alternative responses, planning, to take place. He specifies four major groups of functions that must develop to make this possible. These are working memory, the availability in mind of detailed recent nonverbal information necessary for problem solution; internalization of speech, the wherewithal to stop the stream of action and take the time talk to oneself internally and think through possible solutions and consequences; self-regulation of affect/arousal, inhibition of the immediate expression of emotion, especially negative and aggressive emotion, which generally produces a variety of negative consequences in the future; and reconstitution, problem-solving skills that can be utilized once inhibition of immediate responding has been accomplished and involves breaking behavioral sequences down into component parts (analysis) and selection, sequencing and recombination (synthesis) to effect a better response to accomplish one's goals.

Neuropsychological theories of attention

The title of this section is perhaps a misnomer because there are no comprehensive neuropsychological theories of attention. There are a number of attempts to link specific areas of brain to specific components of attention. One widely accepted generalization is that attentional processes call on contributions from all over the brain. Attention is not a function of a single area but the integrated outcome of the collaborative operation of many modules. The list of types of attention just described provides a ready basis for such a conclusion. To begin, attention depends on being awake and alert, so aspects of brainstem reticular formation must be involved. One attends to events which are registered by the sensory systems so areas of the brain devoted to sensory systems and to receptor orienting activity (e.g. eye movements) must be involved. The events must be understood, processed, or recognized in some way, thus involving brain areas devoted to perception, memory, and comprehension. Action must be planned so basal ganglia and frontal motor areas will be involved. Finally, higher-level regulation, planning, and organization of sequences of behavior will reflect the contribution of the frontal lobes.

Mirsky's elements of attention

One proposal about the components of attention (Mirsky, 1989; Mirsky et al., 1991) was based on data from neuropsychological tests obtained primarily from studying persons with absence epilepsy and persons with schizophrenia. Five components were isolated and linked to different areas of brain. These were: (1) Focus – the ability to zero in and beam one's attention at a specific aspect of the environment. (2) Execute – the motor activity that gives evidence that the attentional task was performed. (3) Sustain – the ability to respond to sequentially presented target stimuli and avoid responding to interspersed non-target stimuli over a long period of time and in the face of boredom. (4) Encode – the ability to process information, e.g. solve arithmetic problems or repeat the letters of the alphabet backwards. (5) Shift – to change previously successful problem-solving strategies or solutions when they cease to be effective.

The reader will note that components 1, 3, and 5 refer directly to aspects of attention and especially those that are aspects of executive functions. When attentional components are impaired, the processing of information or the execution of activity of which the person may otherwise be capable may be hampered or disrupted. On the other hand, components 2 and 4 in Mirsky's scheme refer to motor ability and information-processing skill. Attention disturbances appear in circumstances when the tasks given exceed capability. This point will recur below under the heading of overload.

The source of data for Mirsky's third component is a commonly used technique for assessing attention, the Continuous Performance Task (CPT) (Gordon & Mettleman, 1988; Rosvold et al., 1956), the original version of which Mirsky helped design. Although details about testing procedures are beyond the scope of this book, a brief description may convey how psychologists go about measuring attention by this means. The general rule in the design of tests of attention is to present tasks with minimal informational complexity so that the processing component is not difficult and only attention is required. Imagine a display on a computer screen or other device in which a symbol appears every second or so. The symbols may be letters, numbers, or abstract configurations, or may be something simple like a square that could appear in the top or bottom half of the display. The subject is provided with a button and is instructed to press it when a symbol designated in the instructions as the target appears, and to refrain from responding to all other symbols, the nontargets. Stimuli are presented in sequence for up to 30 or 40 minutes. The number of targets missed (omissions – inattention) and the number of nontargets to which a response occurred (commission errors – impulsivity) can be counted and compared to norms.

The sensory modality and the proportion of targets and nontargets can be varied, and the task can be made more difficult by instructing the subject to respond to a target only when it is preceded by another specified symbol, or only when the target repeats twice in succession. Incentives can be added and performance with or without concrete rewards can be assessed. Different types of CPTs have been used in research and are available for use in clinical assessment, and they vary as a function of what their designers believe to be the crucial issue that requires assessment. Each different design requires its own set of norms.

Posner's covert orienting of visual attention

Posner and colleagues have provided a more detailed analysis of one part of the range of attentional activity. Posner had long been studying cognitive functions by means of a general technique called mental chronometry (Posner, 1985). The basic method measures the time it takes to perform various mental tasks. In its simplest form, for example, persons are asked to make a response such as pressing a button when they perceive the onset of a signal, e.g. the sound of a tone. The time between the onset of the tone and the completion of the response, reaction time, is recorded. Subjects are then given a slightly more complex task. Two clearly different tones are presented and subjects are asked to respond only to the one with a higher pitch. Deciding which of the two tones had been presented (discrimination reaction time) takes more time than noting whether a tone has started (simple reaction time) and the duration of that difference can be studied for its relationship to talent, motivation, distractibility, the influence of incentives, or many other variables.

Cue given	Target on cued side	Target on uncued side

Figure 10.1 The Posner covert attention experiment in which eyes are kept focussed on a central cross. One of the squares on each side then brightens and the target (an asterisk) appears in that square or the other

In his pursuit of ways to study the timing of mental operations, Posner devised a technique for studying visual attention (Posner & Raichle, 1994). He hypothesized that visual selective attention would occur in the brain before the eyes would move to focus on the stimulus of interest. That is the brain decides what is of interest and then the sensory system gets this information. He devised a procedure to test this idea, which he called covert attention. On a screen, a subject sees a small cross in the center and two squares, one on the right and one on the left of center. While looking at the cross, a target, an asterisk, would appear inside one of the squares and a key was to be pressed as soon as the asterisk was detected. Subjects were forewarned that on 80 percent of the trials the correct square would be brightened just before the target would appear, but on 20 percent of the trials, the information would be erroneous and the target would appear on the opposite side. The amount of time between the warning and the onset of the target was varied. On half the trials it was 0.1 sec whereas it 0.8 sec on the rest. Both timing conditions are very fast but the 0.1 sec condition was too fast for eye movements to occur while they could occur during the longer interval. Posner reasoned that correct warnings should facilitate reaction time and incorrect warnings slow it down relative to another condition where no warnings are given at all. Verification of this pattern with a 0.1 sec forewarning interval where eye movements could not play a role would verify and provide a means of measuring covert attention. Figure 10.1 illustrates the procedure.

In many experiments, this finding was verified and Posner set out to learn exactly which portions of the brain were activated when a subject's attention was drawn to a particular location in space. He collaborated with Raichle and others by testing attentional behavior while simultaneously using brain imaging procedures which provide evidence about activity in different areas of brain. In a long series of studies summarized in Posner and Raichle (1994) they found at least three different psychological processes to occur, and the areas of brain that were activated in association with each process. By then studying persons with damage to implicated brain areas, they were able to verify the brain behavior relationship that had been uncovered. The first process was labelled disengage and referred to the release of attention from wherever it might have been focussed so that it was free to deploy elsewhere.

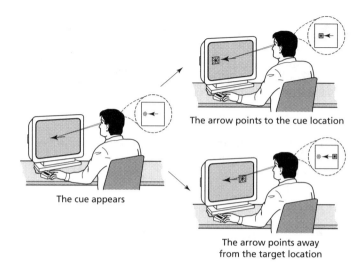

The arrow points to the cue location

The cue appears

The arrow points away
from the target location

Figure 10.2   The endogenous stimulation task used by Posner to study executive functions

Activation of the posterior parietal lobe (figure 3.7) was crucial for this function, and when this area of brain was impaired, subjects had difficulty disengaging. The second process was labelled move and referred to the actual shift of the attentional spotlight. Activation of the superior colliculus (figure 3.8) was implicated in this process. The third process was labelled enhance and referred to an enhancement of attention to the target once it was detected. Activation of the pulvinar (figure 3.13), a part of the thalamus that modulates increases of cell firing in the visual system, was implicated in this process. In the normal brain, this sequence proceeds quickly and unobtrusively. In the abnormal brain, the process breaks down at one of the stages depending on where the damage exists.

The behavioral test devised by Posner provokes attention mechanisms responsive to environmental changes and so provides a means of assessing the integrity of orienting responses to novelty and to limbic factors, but does not provide an assay of executive functions. He found that by changing one aspect of the procedure, he could at least begin to evaluate what he called the executive attention network. This change was to do away with the brightening of the area where the target would appear (exogenous stimulation) and provide an arrow in the center which might point either to the right or left. The arrow by itself does not attract attention to the right or left. The brain must first interpret the meaning of the arrow's direction and then attention is deployed because of centrally guided intent (endogenous stimulation). Figure 10.2 illustrates this change in procedure. With just this small change in procedure, the cingulate gyrus appears to play a central role. Finally, in yet other experiments which require sustained attention, an aspect of executive functions often called vigilance, areas in the upper, lateral parietal, and frontal lobes in the right hemisphere appear to be specially activated.

Clearly, attention is a very complex function mediated by many areas of brain, and where there appears to be some specialization of function in the right hemisphere. This complexity should be kept in mind as the discussion turns to disorders of attention.

Disorders of Attention

The symptoms and natural history of disorders of attention

Clinical examples

The following are examples of behaviors that can be described as inattentive. The reader, for the moment, should suspend any tendency to generalize or derive principles, and just think of the facts and their diversity.

Child A, 5 years old, accompanies his mother to the supermarket. Upon entry, he breaks away from her and races down the isles. When she finally catches up with him and secures him in the shopping cart, he maintains a constant barrage of behavior, reaching out for packages as the cart passes them by, requesting the purchase of first this and then that, and picking up and often dropping on the floor objects his mother has placed in the cart. His mother issues a series of instructions but compliance does not occur. This has been going on since he learned to walk. He kicked a lot during her pregnancy too.

Child B, 7 years old, during a quiet reading period in school gets up from his seat and wanders about the room, in the course of which he talks to several other boys, pokes one boy and one girl, and knocks a pen onto the floor. When the teacher asks him to sit down, he seems not to hear.

Child C, 10 years old, forgets to bring home assignments from school and complete homework on time, has great trouble deciding which clothes to wear, may often ask a question about which she is genuinely curious but pays no attention to the response so that the question gets repeated five minutes later. She can sit quietly and watch television for hours and is not restless or fidgety. Her behavior improves when the environment is structured and she receives rewards for fulfilling her responsibilities.

Child D, 18 years old, awakens from a coma following an accident in which the bicycle she was riding collided with a truck and, within a day or two, becomes so violent and uncontrolled that she must be restrained. This gradually gets better but a year later she is very "jumpy," irritable, overactive, and unable to concentrate.

Adult E, 32 years old, completed college in five years with low grades and has obtained and lost five jobs in the subsequent ten years. He was in sales and could attract customers but often lost business because he neglected to follow up necessary paper work and other details. He was married and had two children but would regularly forget such events as his wedding anniversary or his children's birthdays and often did not follow through on promises made to his wife and children. His wife was contemplating divorce.

Child F, 12 years old, while involved in playing a game, accidentally gets jostled by another boy. He immediately takes offense and begins a fight. This happens so often that he is soon shunned by most of his peers and excluded from their activities.

Child G, 14 years old, moves into a new home in July. In November, her school work begins to deteriorate and she behaves in a "spacey" manner, unable to concentrate or accomplish her work. Previously, she had been a popular honor student who participated in many extracurricular activities. She is aware of the changes and complains about them. She receives a number of different psychiatric diagnoses since repeated medical investigations are inconclusive. Finally, it is accidentally discovered that she was being poisoned by carbon monoxide from a faulty furnace in her new house ever since the heating season began.

Adult H, 58 years old, a competent engineer, finds himself unable to think clearly at times and somewhat forgetful of facts. While trying to work, he finds himself distracted with memories of previous successes and when he notices how far he has strayed from his task, he still finds it hard to get back on track. Within a year he is diagnosed with a brain tumor.

Child I, nine years old, is caught throwing erasers at another student when the principal walks unexpectedly into a noisy classroom. This child had been a good student previously and had not been described as having any problematic behavior. On the day in question, an inexperienced substitute who was ill-prepared to teach was in charge of the class.

Symptoms

Disorders of attention are defined by three major symptoms: inattention, impulsivity, and overactivity (Barkley, 1990). Inattention is nonresponsiveness to task demands, impulsivity is failure to inhibit behavior in accord with conditions and demand (waiting one's turn), and hyperactivity is movement greater than required for accomplishing task demands. One point of the examples is that everybody at some time is, in some sense, distractable, inattentive, and hyperactive. Fatigue, ill-health, or stress may all disrupt the control of attention. Another point is that when the brain is diseased, damaged, or poisoned the earliest and sometimes the only symptoms may be in the domain of attention and distractibility (Cohen, 1993; van Zomeren & Brouwer, 1994). Another point is that symptoms of inattention can vary with structure of the psychological environment. What then is a disorder of attention? This turns out to be a matter of some controversy.

It is not difficult to describe inattentive or hyperactive behaviors and to get agreement about their presence although the "eye of the beholder" may make a difference. What may be hyperactive to one observer can be just zestful or vigorous behavior to another. The goal here, to the extent possible, is to search for and understand the mechanism of impairment. Thus, it may be agreed that the individuals described have attentionally disrupted behaviors and/or are hyperactive, but it makes no sense to consider them as suffering from the same disorder unless it can be demonstrated that the mechanisms producing their disorders are the same and that the same treatment works as effectively in each case. The rest of this chapter examines this issue in one way or another. The discussion will not further consider those conditions in which the attentional disorder is secondary to some other well-known pathology. As shall be apparent this is not always so easy to determine.

Natural history of the disorder

The following is a composite life history of persons with primary disorders of attention. *In utero*, mother notices more kicking and movement than with her other children. As infants, they wriggle and move a lot and spend relatively little time inspecting their world. Once they begin to walk, they have to be watched constantly because they will go anywhere and everywhere. They show little anxiety and never really show fear of strangers, a development commonly occurring as early as nine months. During their preschool years, they might often wander off, they are often injured and their record of emergency visits to the doctor is higher than most, and in cold climates they lose more mittens than other children. In stimulating environments like a supermarket, they are especially difficult to control (see Child A, above).

Prior to school, the children play only briefly with particular toys or games and their social behavior is very limited. After entry into school, they are often ostracized from social group activity either because their distractibility keeps them from staying on target during games or conversations, or because they become aggressive and impulsive when having to wait their turn or experience other frustrations. Classroom activity is often a disaster because they do not sit still for very long and do not concentrate or pursue any line of activity for more than a few minutes. They often disrupt the behavior of others. Their grades are poor even though they often give evidence of being bright intellectually. Often they are very unhappy and lonely children who feel rejected by others and who have a negative self-image, but they rarely show their sadness overtly.

In adolescence, some changes occur: in particular, the constant overactivity and restlessness decreases, and it appears as though the problem has been outgrown. Careful investigation, however, indicates that for many, inattention and concentration problems persist so that it is hard for them to study or engage in organized behavior such as holding down a job. Their negative self-image makes them vulnerable to involvement in antisocial behavior, including delinquency and illicit drugs. Of those who make it to adulthood without becoming involved with the law, their ultimate social adjustment as measured by achievement, income, marital status, or subjective satisfaction with life is considerably less than that of people with comparable backgrounds such as their nonhyperactive siblings (Borland & Heckman, 1976; Lambert, 1988; Weiss & Hechtman, 1993). This life course indicates that hyperactivity is not a trivial problem but a tragedy of unrealized potentialities.

Some aspects of the history of the study of attention disorders

Early beginnings

A detailed history of how attention disorders were identified and of the ideas used to explain the observations made is beyond the scope of this volume. The reader is referred to Kessler (1980), Schachar (1986), and Barkley (1990, chapter 1) for detailed reviews. However, it is impossible to grasp current thinking without some historical perspective, and the crucial parts of the story will be presented next.

One key element in thinking about attentional disorders is the association between brain damage and the triad of symptoms described above: inattention, impulsivity, and overactivity. Although it had generally been known that such an association existed, the point was made vivid to the clinical community in the aftermath of an encephalitis epidemic of 1917–18. Encephalitis is an infection of the brain that can lead to death. Survivors often sustain substantial destruction of brain tissue and many children and adults demonstrated striking declines in behavior after they recovered. After head injury similar consequences, termed postconcussion syndrome, were observed (Benton, 1989). These observations provided a firm link between the symptoms of overactivity and inattention and brain damage.

The second key element in the story has to do with pharmacology or the study of the effects of drugs. In the history of medicine, each new drug is often tried out on any number of conditions beyond those for which it was originally deemed appropriate. It is also used in subjects who have more than one condition and sometimes the drug given for one condition appears to aid the other. In the late 1930s, a report appeared which indicated that benzedrine, at the time a new nervous-system stimulant which had been given as a weight reducer, significantly improved attention, behavioral control, and intellectual functions in hospitalized, behaviorally disturbed children (Bradley, 1937). After World War II, this work was picked up by others (e.g. Laufer & Denhoff, 1957).

Looking closely at the clinical histories of the subjects in the pioneer studies revealed that many of these children had histories of encephalitis, brain injury, or some other type of brain disease. The drug was reported to be effective in only a percentage of cases, but the outcome was not linked to a specific etiology: rather, it was linked to the symptoms they shared, hyperactivity. The important point is that a high proportion of the children initially found to respond well to stimulant medication had known brain abnormalities.

What then followed was a process with a logic of a certain kind. It was thought that if brain damage and associated hyperactivity improves with stimulant medication, then any child who is inattentive and hyperactive is likely to be brain-damaged (the children were often diagnosed as minimally brain-damaged), whether there was historical or objective evidence for this or not (the evidence often cited was circular; hyperactivity or impulsivity). Such a child, it was thought, should improve with the same medications as those that help the frankly brain-damaged. Based on this kind of logic, many children with inattention, impulsivity, and/or overactivity were placed on stimulant medications. The result of many research studies and clinical experience is that in 70–80 percent of children with hyperactivity it works (Barkley, 1990, p. 590), as we shall see, in some sense.

Awareness of the persistence of inattention after the decline of hyperactivity in adolescence meant that inattention and hyperactivity were not necessarily linked and raised the possibility that there were children with attention problems who were not hyperactive. Search for such children was successful (Lahey & Carlson, 1991). Thus there are children and adolescents who have persistent problems with attention but who have never been hyperactive, and another group who have been both hyperactive and inattentive, who, in adolescence, are only inattentive. An acronym terminology was devised to reflect this complexity. Because the attentional problem was thought to be primary (e.g. Douglas, 1972), the term Attention Deficit Disorder (ADD) was given first position and was then followed by a designation as to whether hyperactivity is or is not present, e.g. ADD + H or ADD − H. Often the primacy issue was avoided by using the designation ADHD meaning attention-deficit-hyperactivity-disorder. This diagnostic scheme was based on the symptoms observed or reported at the time of diagnosis, not the mechanisms of disorder, since none have been widely accepted.

More history: stimulant medication, a paradox and its apparent
resolution – the underarousal hypothesis

When it was verified that children with ADHD improved with stimulant medication, the result was thought to be paradoxical. This was because the children's symptoms looked overactive and overexcited yet the drugs that helped were stimulants. Children who were already relatively disinhibited could be expected to go off the deep end when given stimulants. The paradox was that the stimulants had a calming effect.

This paradox appeared to be resolved by a series of studies (cf. Satterfield & Dawson, 1971; Satterfield et al., 1972; Cohen & Douglas, 1972) on the resting level and, more often, the orientation and habituation of the skin conductance response. The paradox appeared to be resolved because the hyperactive children were found to have lower resting (tonic) skin conductances or orientation (phasic) responses than normal children, and these data were interpreted to mean that the children had "low arousal and insufficient inhibitory control over motor outflow and sensory input" (Satterfield, Cantwell, & Satterfield, 1974, p. 842). Hyperactivity was viewed as a direct failure of the arousal of inhibitory control. The suggestion was also made (Satterfield & Dawson, 1971) that overactivity might be a form of compensation, a way that children with insufficient inner arousal could provide themselves with more activation. This latter hypothesis did not focus on limited inhibitory mechanisms but on inadequate excitatory mechanisms. Hyperactive children were viewed as reviving themselves up with overactive behavior, much like sleepy people who wanted to be awake might pinch themselves. Stimulant drugs were seen as a means of increasing both tonic and phasic arousal. In many of the same studies in which the deficit in arousal was found, stimulants were found to help these children to more normal patterns of phasic and tonic activity.

Some 20 years after the flurry of research finding underarousal in ADHD, Weinberg & Brumback (1990) described individuals suffering from what they called a primary disorder of vigilance. When they had to sustain attention over a period of time, e.g. while listening to a lecture or writing a paper, these persons were often sleepy and fidgety, often yawning and stretching. As children, they were easily bored and sought stimulating activities on the playground where they participated vigorously. "The affected adult commonly falls asleep ('catnaps') when still (such as while attending church, watching television or a ball game, riding in a car or reading) but the naps are not refreshing" (Weinberg & Brumback, 1990, p. 723). Those so affected are described as uniformly caring, kindly, and compassionate persons who are well liked by their peers. The disorder is described as lifelong and likely to be hereditary. Not surprisingly, these individuals responded very well to stimulant drugs. If they stopped taking them, the symptoms recurred. The very clear clinical description of this disorder appears to this writer to be an array of symptoms that would earn an ADHD – H diagnosis.

Yet more history: the decline of the underarousal hypothesis and its persistence

This resolution of the paradox did not receive much acceptance. Hastings and Barkley (1978) published an influential review on psychophysiological research with hyperkinetic children. Although they found much promising evidence indicating lower phasic arousal in inattentive and hyperactive children, and, in their final paragraph, suggest that this line of research holds "great promise in advancing our understanding of hyperactivity," research interest in these hypotheses diminished. Barkley's (1990) later discussion of his own review in a major book devoted to attention disorders gives little space to this hypothesis and emphasizes criticisms and limitations of psychophysiological research. Similarly, Ross and Ross (1982, p. 83) judge research support for the hypothesis to be inadequate.

The hypothesis however did not die. One study (Rapoport et al., 1978) greatly enhanced understanding of the entire area. Prior research on the effects of stimulant medications, with a few possible exceptions, had been done only on children with symptoms. The effects of stimulants on normal children had not been examined because of the ethics of administering drugs to children who had no reason to receive them. However, the drugs are effective only for a short time and had a good safety record when used under medical supervision, and the researchers saw fit to study their own normal children. The results provided evidence that normal children react to the medication in the same manner as hyperactive children. Their attention and concentration became more focussed and inhibitory control was greater. This and other work also indicated that overarousal and anxiety can occur with excessive dosages.

This finding explained much. Increased attention in response to stimulant drugs did not depend on being hyperactive or inattentive. Consequently, improvement on the drug was no proof that the drug was needed. Whereas the underaroused children might truly need the drug, many others who show improvement on it might not need it. With this line of reasoning, evidence for underarousal becomes important.

Further evidence for the underarousal hypothesis has come with the development of techniques which measure of metabolic activity in different regions of the brain (the same type of procedure used by Posner). Zametkin et al. (1990) studied carefully selected adults who had been hyperactive as children, who were the parents of diagnosed hyperactive children, and who still complained of symptoms of inattentiveness. Adult subjects were studied, in part, because they could give informed consent for the invasive procedures used in the research. They were injected with a radioactive form of glucose, a type of sugar used for energy in the brain, so that its rate of consumption and hence level of metabolic activity could be measured. This was done while they were in an active state of information processing, in this case while responding to an auditory continuous performance test (CPT). This CPT required that they respond selectively to the least audible of three tones presented every two seconds over a period of more than a half-hour. Thus, the task was simple, but required continuing effortful attention.

Although there were no differences in the number of correct responses and errors, there were significant differences between the hyperactive and normal subjects in the level of metabolic activity at 30 of 60 different sites, the hyperactive subjects always being lower. Although brain areas where differences occurred were widespread, there was much involvement of the frontal lobes. The authors related these findings to previous research that had implicated the frontal lobes in disorders of attention.

Lou et al. (1989) studied resting levels of regional cerebral blood flow in groups of hyperactive and control children. Blood flow is related to metabolic activity; the more activity, the more blood is required. Findings were that the hyperactive children had less activity in portions of the basal ganglia and more activity in sensory regions. When administered stimulant drugs, activity in the basal ganglia increased and in the sensory areas decreased somewhat. The results indicated that the basal ganglia (which are intimately connected with the frontal lobes) provide the inhibitory control needed for the regulation of behavior. When there is inadequate basal ganglia activity, the subject's sensory system is overactive, responding to every input. Stimulants increase basal ganglia activity and thereby facilitate inhibitory control.

The study of Lou et al. (1989) had flaws. The subjects had a variety of problems other than attentional difficulty, and only tonic, not phasic, activity was studied. But an important contribution was the depiction of the relationship between two areas of brain and the implication of inadequate inhibitory control in the frontal lobes, an idea that will loom large in material to be covered shortly. More specifically, it suggested the basal ganglia as a source of underarousal in the frontal lobes and that such underarousal may actually be accompanied by overarousal elsewhere. These are data about a pattern of response in a complex system which have properties one might expect from an organ such as the brain.

Lou et al.'s (1989) biological data are consistent with ideas based on psychological data reported by Douglas (1984, p. 150) who suggested that the problem is "an impaired ability to modulate arousal or alertness to meet situational demands." Douglas's idea was designed to account for observations indicating that hyperactive children are often inattentive to only some aspects of a task but actually may be overattentive to others, for example, any rewards that might be present. Children with ADHD symptoms are often attentive to television, video games and rewards such as food or money but have much difficulty doing tasks such as homework or household chores. In older individuals, attention may be very intense while making a sale, but fall apart when doing the paperwork afterward. Since limbic arousal is often much in evidence, the problem does not appear to be the general kind of arousal regulated at the level of the brainstem reticular formation, which generally had been considered to be the source of the underarousal problem. Lou et al.'s ideas implicate the frontal lobes and perhaps the basal ganglia, a subcortical structure.

Considerable space has been devoted to the underarousal hypothesis because it has loomed large in thinking about the nature of the impairment and for a long time was the only hypothesis that was consistent with the evidence that stimulant medications were helpful. Underarousal has had at least two meanings. In one, it has been similar to sleepiness and implied inadequate general excitation such as is provided by the brainstem reticular activating system. In the other, what is thought to be inadequate is the arousal of inhibitory functions, particularly those in circuits involving the frontal lobe, which make possible the highest levels of executive function and behavioral control. Evidence for the latter hypothesis is considered in more detail next.

Executive function and frontal lobe disorder, overload, and adult ADHD

Executive function disorder

For many years, Russell Barkley has been in the forefront of scholars doing research on, and writing about, ADHD. In 1997 he published a book, *ADHD and the nature of self control*, which reflected the reordering of his thinking that had taken place over several years of frenzied thought about a massive amount of research and theory that had been accumulated about this condition. In this work, he focusses on that portion of the spectrum of the disorder that displays hyperactivity and impulsivity as major symptoms, views flaws or lags in the development of executive functions as the locus of the problem, and suggests that labeling the problem as one of attention is misleading. In emphasizing executive function disorders, Barkley acknowledges and cites many papers with this perspective that have been published throughout the twentieth century, and the reader curious about this history can find references from prior contributors there. Here, there is only space to summarize some of the main points Barkley makes about the role of executive functions in ADHD.

The first issue is which of two kinds of attention are being considered. One kind is externally presented and externally controlled by immediate reinforcements. It depends on sensory and perceptual registry of the relevant information and for the most part is a function of the back part of the brain. The second kind of attention is driven from within, requires inhibition of readily elicited and ongoing sequences of behavior, and is oriented to the gratification of long- rather than short-term goals. Required response inhibition is a function of the front part of the brain and an aspect of executive functions. Persons with ADHD + H show deficits of the second type whether or not they also show deficits of the first type, and it is the understanding of this relatively large and socially troublesome group that is addressed.

The key concept is response inhibition, and by this Barkley refers to the ability to inhibit a prepotent response from occurring (e.g. not blurting an answer but raising your hand and waiting to be called), to suppress an ongoing response (e.g. reaching to pull the fire alarm when there is no fire, but then stopping), and to inhibit irrelevant responses from intruding during delays accomplished by response inhibition.

Response inhibition is a primordial executive function, the first step that permits other executive functions to operate. Four groups of such functions are distinguished. The first is working memory, the ability to hold in mind all the components necessary for the solution of a problem. This capability has been studied in animals and does not depend on verbal skills. It is what is required if responding to a task in which two objects are presented on each trial and, after the first trial, one of the objects is from the pair presented in the prior trial, the other is new, and the novel object is the correct choice. To be successful, memory of the stimuli experienced previously must be available for comparison at the moment of choice. It is also what is involved when a soccer player, noting the speed and direction in which a teammate is running, keeps that information in mind (and other information such as the position and movements of opponent team members) when kicking a pass.

The second group of executive functions is internalization of speech. This is a uniquely human function that makes use of the symbolic powers of language. Behavioral inhibition gives people time to talk to themselves during which they can describe the situation with which they are coping, perhaps note less salient but significant facts, invoke relevant memories, reflect on possible solutions, and weigh long-term consequences. Language is potentially a powerful problem-solving tool, but people must give themselves time to think for it to occur.

The third group of executive functions is self-regulation of affect/motivation/arousal, which deals with the emotional components of experience. If these components are not well regulated, they can easily override the potentialities for control made possible by working memory and internalization of speech. Barkley has less to say about this dimension of executive functions and seems to view the emotions as just another aspect of life with which a person must contend. Weakness in establishing inhibitory control is another aspect of the weak inhibitory capabilities displayed in other areas. Such a view contrasts, for example, with the view of Schore (1994), who mustered evidence that learning to regulate affect is the key to learning self-regulation in other domains. He emphasizes that such learning is influenced by the way the environment meets the security needs of the child throughout the course of development. Related issues are the quality of relationships formed with caretakers and the overall balance between experienced emotional stress and emotional support.

The fourth group of executive functions is reconstitution, a somewhat awkward term that designates the creative problem-solving potentialities of the person. The idea again is that behavioral inhibition provides time to arrive at more effective solutions than those that might be prepotent in a situation. However, working memory, internalization of speech, and emotional control by themselves only offer the possibilities of finding previously tried and conventional solutions. Reconstitutive functions find novel and creative solutions.

Barkley (1997) reviews the evidence concerning the executive function impairments that can follow injury to the brain. Most children and adults with ADHD + H however have never had an injury, infection, or other pathogenic (pathology-inducing) event. He also reviews evidence from behavior–genetic studies about the relative role of heredity and environment in executive dysfunction. These studies utilize identical twins and persons with other degrees of hereditary relationship whose histories are free of pathogenic events. The evidence is consistent with very strong hereditary influence. In Barkley's view, such evidence helps explain the poor results obtained when attempts are made to train executive functions (e.g. Abikoff, 1991). Accordingly, he views ADHD + H as a lifelong chronic condition which must be coped with throughout life even though some may improve as a result of maturation. This is comparable to diabetics taking insulin and monitoring their diets throughout their lives. Since attentional problems are just one of several impairments secondary to impairments of behavioral inhibition, he has concluded that the term "attention disorder" is misleading and recommends that the condition be termed Behavioral Inhibition Disorder (Barkley, 1997, p. 313).

Overload

In depicting attention problems as secondary to executive function deficits, Barkley in essence is describing an overload condition. That is, those suffering from the condition lack the resources to meet the demands made of them. What is expected is beyond their capabilities, hence they are regularly overloaded. When such overload occurs they may be distracted, attend to irrelevant stimulation, become fidgety, tune out, or engage in inappropriate activity. Attentional disturbances may be apparent in any circumstance when the resources of the nervous system are unable to deal with the information-processing load. This occurs situationally in normals when short-term environmental demands for attention are massive, in youngsters when they are in an adult environment, in those who are retarded (chapter 17) when given information-processing loads of average complexity, and to the learning disabled (chapter 14) when the curriculum requires processing in areas where they are weak. There is a whole literature on the comorbidity of attention and learning disorders, and sometimes these disorders are even lumped together as one. To be sure a person might independently suffer from the two conditions, but more often one may be secondary to the other. The issue is important because treatment of the primary condition should take care of the secondary one, while treatment of a secondary condition may be a waste of effort and time.

Adult attention disorder

As noted earlier, following children with the diagnosis of ADHD to adulthood provided evidence that many of the impairments found in childhood did not disappear with maturation, although hyperactivity generally did decrease or even disappear. Symptoms such as restlessness, difficulty concentrating, excitability, impulsivity, and irritability often persisted into adulthood (e.g. Weiss & Hechtman, 1993). In the late 1980s and the 1990s, increasing clinical and scientific attention was paid to the problem of attention deficit disorder in adults (Nadeau, 1995), and the media disseminated the idea that the condition was not confined to children. Many persons who had never been diagnosed or treated began to request evaluations, often seeking an explanation for recurrent failures in their academic and work careers and in personal relationships. Study of these individuals generated the same sort of findings previously seen in children, the notable exception being obvious evidence of hyperactivity. Like the children, a large proportion of adults responded well to stimulant medications. Such findings were an important part of the basis of Barkley's conclusion that the condition was in many instances a chronic, lifelong problem.

Other variables implicated in attention disorders

ADHD or children with minds of their own? Not sick, just different

Earlier in the chapter, the phrase "eye of the beholder" was used to suggest that the symptoms of ADHD have to be observed and that what may be hyperactivity or inattention to one observer can be behavior that suggests playfulness, spontaneity, or independence of mind to others. This matter is not trivial. Since there is not yet a widely accepted objective measure for ADHD (although the potential for such development exists) selection of subjects for research is generally based on the responses of observers, generally teachers or parents, to questionnaires (e.g. Conners, 1973). These typically ask many questions as to whether or not the child has displayed a certain pattern of behavior over a specified time period. There has been a great deal of research on these questionnaires (see Barkley, 1990, appendix A, for a listing and review).

The results of this research (Barkley, 1990, p. 63) indicate that agreement may vary with the situation (e.g. playground, no; school room, yes), the observer (e.g. mother, yes; father, no), and the behavior (e.g. aggression, yes; attention, no). This led some authors (e.g. Schachar, Rutter, & Smith, 1981) to suggest that there might be pervasively (all or most circumstances) and situationally (certain circumstances only) hyperactive children. They and others (see Schachar, 1991) found ample evidence in support of such selective appearance of symptoms. Might such selection be due to a specific situation, e.g. a school room with an unliked teacher or, in accord with the overload hypothesis, subject matter that is impossibly difficult for the child?

Suppose children are described as overactive both at home and at school. Does that necessarily mean that their behavior is abnormal? One possibility that merits consideration is the mismatch hypothesis of Thomas and Chess (1977). In their observations of the temperamental characteristics of developing children, they noted that a number of active and exuberant children might run into difficulty if their parents happened to be particularly sedate and conservative, or if they went to a school that required a high degree of conformity and control. In neither case were the children or the adults "abnormal," but there was a clash of styles, hence the concept of mismatch. The treatment that resolved the difficulty was essentially a matter of explaining the nature of the temperamental discrepancies and the overall normality of everybody involved. In some cases, a change to a school with a different culture could make a diagnosis disappear.

Another view of the inconsistency comes from McGuinness (1985), a severe critic of the entire field of study. She is of the opinion (p. 177) that only a small proportion of the children designated as ADHD have etiologies involving disordered brain functioning. She reviewed research which suggested that children identified as hyperactive on questionnaires (the main technique for identifying such children) are most often boys. Indeed, a ratio of 3 to 6 boys to every girl is commonly found in studies of the prevalence of hyperactivity. Reviewing research on activity level differences between the sexes, she observes that boys normally time their actions more rapidly than girls (p. 192) and that it is the girls whose timing is most readily consistent with that of the classroom. Thus boys may be identified as hyperactive simply as a result of being boys. This perspective coincides with the mismatch idea discussed above.

The work of Zentall is related to this line of reasoning and will be represented here by summarizing one of her studies (Zentall & Meyer, 1987). The authors assumed that all persons have an optimal level of stimulation and that ADD + H children constitutionally require and hence seek a high level of stimulation. Thus ADD + H children were predicted to perform better on a dull task of attention if given additional stimulation. To test this hypothesis, ADD + H children were compared with matched controls on an auditory CPT under two conditions: CPT as the sole task and CPT combined with an opportunity to view slides with the subject in control of the slide advance button. With the CPT alone, the ADD + H children committed significantly more errors on the CPT than the normals whereas under high stimulating conditions they were no different from the controls. This may provide some sort of explanation for the behavior of some adolescents who insist on studying with the radio blasting.

Data which indicate that ADHD children require more stimulation for optimal performance are counterintuitive. Since the children look as though they cannot sort out what is relevant under conditions of ordinary stimulation, many educational programs have provided ADHD children with environments of decreased stimulation in the hope that they would then be able to attend to what was important. Zentall's findings suggest that this may be an error, that these children function best under conditions of high levels of stimulation.

Zentall's work puts at least some children described as having attention–hyperactivity disorders in a class with a particular normal personality type, the extroverted. There is a large body of evidence that extroverted personalities seek high levels of external stimulation and show little evidence of internal arousal such as might lead to the experience of anxiety (Strelau & Eysenck, 1987). It should be possible to sort out the extroverted from ADD + H by means of tests of executive function. There is nothing in the literature on extroversion that suggests that those individuals should have impaired executive functions.

Attention, aggression, and conduct disorder

Children with attentional problems often are impatient and impulsive, are prone to action, tend to experience little anxiety, and are often easily provoked to aggression. If these behaviors are present they often elicit rejection from their peers and are viewed as disobedient by adults. Diagnostically, more acronyms such as CD, Conduct

Disturbance, or ODD, Oppositional Defiant Disorder, have been added to ADD and ADD + H. There is considerable research on this coincidence of symptoms and some authors have actually suggested that hyperactivity may be an aspect of CD (e.g. Shapiro & Garfinkel, 1986). Others have thought that aggressive behavior was an outcome of hyperactivity (e.g. Wender & Klein, 1981). The link between attentional disorders and antisocial behavior presents a puzzle in sorting out etiology. Barkley (1990, chapter 5) points out that in children with both ADHD and CD or ODD, there is strong evidence of environmental familial pathology as evidenced either by poor child management methods, parental psychopathology (particularly maternal depression), or marital discord. Lillienfeld and Waldman (1990) come to similar conclusions. Barkley posits an interaction between a constitutionally based tendency in the child toward inattentiveness and overactivity and a family environment that reinforces or provokes aggressive or oppositional behavior. He does not particularly stress, although evidence will be presented later to this effect, that the hyperactivity itself can be induced by disturbed caregiving.

This then is a very different picture from the one pictured above as the natural history of the disorder. In that depiction, most of what appeared to be taking place stemmed from the characteristics of the child. Here, where aggressive and oppositional behaviors are conspicuous, there is evidence of a strong environmental component regardless of whether ADHD has any constitutional origins. One could guess that treating such children with stimulant medication alone might not be very effective. Satterfield, Satterfield, and Schell (1987), reviewing prior work, found that to be the case. They went on to compare the effects of drug treatment alone with what they term multimodal treatments, which also included psychotherapy with the child and the family, and found the latter to be far more effective in arresting delinquency than the former.

The author has had an experience which has served to make him very suspicious of much subject selection and diagnosis in research on ADHD. At a research presentation coming from a highly respected laboratory, he observed the videotaped behavior of a subject designated as ADHD. The child's social behavior before and after being placed on a stimulant drug was presented but none of the behaviors before or after appeared either inattentive or overactive. When a question was raised as to what qualified the subject to be diagnosed as ADHD, it was explained that he often bullied other boys and was very antisocial. It appears that many forms of behavioral dyscontrol may be given the ADHD diagnosis even though the regulation of attention is not a problem. For the most part the data are clear. Conduct disturbance and aggression are a problem, but they are not intrinsically a problem in the maintenance of attention.

Toxins

Among the case vignettes above, Case G was the story of a high-school student who suffered carbon monoxide poisoning and whose attentional skills, which had been superb, deteriorated dramatically. The case exemplifies the broader neuropsychological generalization that when the nervous system is insulted in some way, attentional skills are almost always affected. Recall that the early background for the development of ideas about ADHD included the consequences of the encephalitis epidemic and that many, if not all, of the subjects in early studies on the effects of stimulant medications had brain disorders.

Poisons can kill. The question is what effect do they have if the poisoning is subtle and prolonged, or if, after an acute poisoning, the person survives. Prolonged low-level poisoning due to absorption of heavy metals, particularly lead, has been implicated as a possible cause of ADHD. Lead enters the body of children as a result of being eaten, typically in chips of old peeling paint that contain lead, or through breathing air that contains large amounts of lead because of proximity to a lead smelter.

Although it seems plausible that absorption of a known poison to the nervous system should be associated with a sign of insult to the brain such as inattention, and there is evidence that intelligence is affected by even very low levels of lead (e.g. Bellinger et al., 1987; Hawk et al., 1986) the literature is actually controversial on the subject, with a number of studies finding no relation between lead levels in the body and indices of ADHD. The problem may stem from many sources including the difficulty of measuring lead levels in the nervous system, which is where it counts. Typically, the lead levels of more accessible tissues, e.g. hair, nails, baby teeth and even blood, are studied and they may or may not reflect what is going on in the nervous system. The position of Ross and Ross (1982, p. 89), who review the literature thoroughly, seems sensible, "undue lead absorption is implicated in childhood hyperactivity." There will be more detailed examination of the consequences of lead ingestion in chapter 16.

If the relation of heavy metals such as lead, a known poison, to ADHD is controversial, the suggestion that food additives, particularly salicylates, food dyes and preservatives, could cause ADHD, by Feingold (1975), was even more so. It should be noted that most of these substances are not natural foods but are manufactured from petroleum and coal tar derivatives. However they are in widespread use in the food industry and are often present in so-called junk foods. Feingold claimed that elimination of foods containing such substances could help children focus attention. A flurry of research followed and was thoroughly reviewed by Conners (1980), who found little evidence that ingestion of food dyes and additives led to ADHD in a large percentage of children. On the other hand, there was strong evidence that some parents, under double-blind conditions, could accurately gauge whether their children were consuming these substances. In earlier studies, objective verification of changes by means of "challenges" (administering the substance double-blind and testing for behavior differences when on and off) was almost never seen, but in later studies, when dosage was increased, such evidence was obtained.

Nevertheless, Conners (1980, p. 107) concluded that the answer to the question "Is there anything to Dr. Feingold's hypothesis?" might be "Yes, something – but not much and not consistently." This is a rather pale endorsement of an idea that may be relevant to some children. In the same paragraph, however, Conners expressed a more judicious view: "Most of the studies find a small number of children among those who showed improvement on Feingold's diet also react adversely when given a challenge of the colors in double-blind fashion. These findings suggest that a rather small number of children – perhaps less than 5% of these are genuinely hyperactive – have some specific sensitivity to the artificial colors." This writer views this work and this estimate as a significant contribution to understanding ADHD. The reader should be aware that this opinion is not widely shared. For example, Barkley (1990, p. 99) dismisses the hypothesis entirely. On the other hand, Graham (1989, pp. 181–90) also finds evidence that dietary changes are helpful in some hyperactive children.

Allergies

Feingold's medical specialty was allergy. His hypothesis about food dyes and additives was treated under the heading of toxins because these are not natural foods. Feingold also suggested that some children became hyperactive as a result of allergic reactions to perfectly ordinary foods such as milk, peanut butter, and wheat products such as bread or cereal. This hypothesis also has not received much support among professionals and researchers concerned with ADHD. However, evidence about the relationships between allergic reactions and ADHD has been reviewed by Marshall (1989), who finds much in the literature to justify a link between them.

The data surveyed by Marshall include the following findings. (a) Among many samples of ADHD children, the prevalence of allergy is greater than in the population at large. The alleviation of allergy symptoms can lead to the decrease or disappearance of ADHD symptoms. (b) Allergic reactions produce neurochemical changes in the autonomic nervous system that are comparable to changes found in ADHD, and may generate ADHD symptoms. The neurochemical response associated with allergy is similar, if not identical, to the underarousal pattern of response associated with ADHD. (c) It is not known whether allergic reactions can directly influence brain function but the possibility is there.

Marshall (1989) cannot determine from available data whether the behavioral symptoms of hyperactivity are direct consequences in the nervous system of the neurochemical changes that occur in allergy or are simply a result of having to endure the misery of allergies, especially if the person affected is a child with little understanding of what is taking place. A little-cited study by King (1981) found direct experimental evidence that double-blind exposure to allergens in known allergic patients produced adverse behavioral and psychological symptoms. This means that placebos, administered blindly, did not produce such symptoms. It is possible that the central nervous system is just as capable of reacting allergically as the linings of the nose or the skin, and that the major consequence of such allergic reactions are disruptions of behavior.

ADHD resulting from experience

In chapter 7, where experiential determinants of pathology were surveyed, one type was described as chronic overstimulation. Evidence for precisely such an etiology for ADHD was provided in a research report by Jakobvitz and Sroufe (1987). This work occurred in the context of a longitudinal study of child development that began with the birth of the children. Within the sample, some children met standard diagnostic criteria for ADHD by the time they were in kindergarten. The authors selected carefully matched children from the same study and searched for data earlier in development that might have explained the hyperactivity. One possibility was that the children were biologically or temperamentally different at birth or that they became so during their preschool years. Another was that they had been treated differently. The data available included biological characteristics at birth, aspects of temperament that most likely were constitutional in origin, and measures of parental caregiving style which were based on actual observations. What they found was that only one of 42 biological and temperamental measures differentiated the two groups (degree of immaturity at about the end of the first week of life), but two of three measures of observed caregiving were significantly different. The mothers of the hyperactive children had been observed to be more intrusive at six months and more overstimulating and seductive at 42 months.

Such data are not often available. They permit some sorting out of causal direction that is not possible in the usual situation when children and their parents are first observed only after symptoms have developed. When pathologic interactions between parent and child are observed later in life, it is impossible to determine how the pattern originated. In the Jacobvitz and Sroufe study, the children who were slated to become ADHD were no different from the others during the first years of their life, but their caregivers treated them differently. This then is evidence about environmental influence in some children with symptoms of ADHD. Barkley (1997) points out that parental behavior may be strongly influenced by parental genes so that it is an oversimplification to consider the influence purely of environmental origin. That argument has merit but if the behavior of the caretaker is the means by which the genes transmitting ADHD are expressed, there possibly may be an opportunity for intervention if caretaker behavior can be modified.

In any event, observation of hyperactivity and inattentiveness in a child who comes from a home that is chaotic or unpatterned, where overstimulation or inappropriate stimulation is frequent, should lead to attempts to stabilize and pattern the environment before relying on other forms of treatment. It may well be that successful interventions before adolescence can reverse the consequences of several years of chaos. There is some evidence to support this idea in the family therapy literature.

Effects of medication

Stimulants

The previous section reviews evidence which suggests that there are a number of conditions other than underarousal and executive dysfunction in which attentional disturbances may appear and which call for their own distinctive treatment. Nevertheless, if attention symptoms are present, they may be referred to clinicians, diagnosed, and treated with stimulant drugs. In what follows, the results of studies on the effectiveness of stimulant drugs will be examined relying primarily on reviews by Barkley

(1990), Jacobvitz et al. (1990), and Schachar (1991). As this material is considered, the reader should keep in mind the findings of Rapoport et al. (1978) about the attention-enhancing effects of stimulants on most everybody.

As noted earlier, there is strong evidence that stimulants are effective in changing behavior in 70–80 percent of children with diagnosed ADHD symptoms. Parents, teachers, and outside observers in both laboratory and natural settings note decreased task irrelevant and noncompliant behaviors. These findings are evident and repeatable only while taking medication, and medications are often stopped in adolescence. When long-term outcome is the issue (e.g. will diagnosed children treated with stimulants do better than those not so treated?) the results are less easy to interpret and are more controversial. These studies have evaluated such practical issues as social relationships, academic performance, and delinquency. Earlier studies were pessimistic regarding the efficacy of medication. Some recent studies are more promising in some respects.

Many possible explanations have been offered for this pattern of results which in their own way are paradoxical – short-term success and long-term ineffectuality. A few of these merit some consideration here. One concerns the problem of dosage and the possibility that many children receive the wrong amount. Sprague and Sleator (1977) provide evidence that the amount taken influences its effects. If the target symptoms are academic behaviors, less medication is needed than if the target behaviors are social skills. Unfortunately, if one goal is attained, the other is not, and might even be made worse. A flurry of research on dose occurred but the outcome is still not clear (Swanson et al., 1991), but it is evident that there are differences in the pattern of response to different doses. This implies that administering medication requires careful monitoring and assessment of its effects, a standard of practice that, unfortunately, is often not met.

Another issue is the timing of administration. Consider the commonly used stimulant, methylphenidate, or Ritalin, as it is known by its trade name. As drugs go, it is a relatively safe and fast-acting medication which is effective for three to five hours. Children are administered the drug in two or at most three divided doses, generally in the morning and at noon, and, if evening behavior is very disruptive, perhaps in the late afternoon. The drug should probably never be given within four to six hours of bedtime because its alerting properties will interfere with sleep, but some physicians have prescribed it in equally divided doses through the day. If the child's behavior is most problematic at school, some children only receive the medication on school days and not on weekends, holidays, or vacations. As noted, many stop taking the medications in adolescence. The long-term effects of these variations are not known.

Yet another issue is the psychological consequences on social status of taking medication. The society of children is notoriously cruel, and children who are different for any reason are often teased mercilessly by their peers. Such experiences undermine self-confidence and may negate some of the benefits of the medication. Furthermore children who have had academic and social problems because of ADHD, and who have been helped by stimulants, may still have impaired self-confidence because they view drugs as responsible for their improvement. The integration of the medication regime with the notion of a chronic handicap in executive functions, in those for whom this is appropriate, has, as of this writing, probably occurred only rarely. These influences on the social life and identity of the child have been studied by Whalen and Henker (1980) and have been termed emanative effects of drug treatment. Ross and Ross (1982, p. 196) take these issues so seriously that they recommend that no one other than pediatrician and parents be aware that the child is taking medicine. They indicate it is feasible to accomplish this feat and even keep the information from the child, but such secrecy and deception may cause more problems than those the secrecy is designed to avoid. However, both sets of authors also suggest effective ways of working with affected children openly to help them cope with these difficulties. Having a clear idea about the nature of the disorder present in a particular child should make it easier to deal with these issues.

Other medications used in attentional disorders

Medications developed for one purpose often are tried out on other conditions and unexpected efficacies sometimes appear when a drug is administered to deal with one condition but improves symptoms of another condition that happens also to be present. Recall that was how the efficacy of stimulants was discovered. Something of this sort appears to have occurred with regard to using anticonvulsant and antidepressive medications to treat attention and hyperactivity problems. There appears to be a considerable amount of such experimentation among clinicians seeking some way of assisting their patients with their attention problems but very little research. One intriguing report (Suffin & Emory, 1995) of a systematic clinical study involved 100 patients presenting with either attention disorders or depression. If displaying attention symptoms primarily, patients were treated first with stimulants. If not effective, they were then administered antidepressants, and if those were ineffective they were then given anticonvulsants. Those with primarily depressed symptoms followed a sequence of antidepressants, then anticonvulsants and finally stimulants. All participants were also subjected to a quantitative EEG (QEEG), about which more will be presented shortly. The data on medication efficacy was analyzed as a function of the QEEG findings. What emerged was that the EEG data predicted efficacy while diagnosis did not. Patients with excessive frontal alpha were responsive to antidepressants, those with excessive frontal theta were responsive to stimulants, and those with excessive frontal alpha and hypercoherence (to be explained later) were responsive to anticonvulsants. Such findings, if they can be verified, will require a different approach to diagnosis.

New Approaches to Diagnosis and Treatment

It will be recalled that Barkley (1997) put together the data in ADHD on the efficacy of stimulant medication and the failure of efforts to train cognitive and executive functions, and suggested that the condition was chronic and had to be dealt with chronically. In doing so he assumed that there was no way to change the inherent limitations of what was apparently a constitutional, often genetic, deficit in brain function. This position is sensible in the light of much about what is known concerning brain plasticity. There is, however, a minority view that is less pessimistic about altering brain function, one example of which, Sterman's biofeedback treatment of epilepsy, has already been mentioned. In this view, the brain is a learning machine and, if given the right information, can improve its functioning. A small but substantial body of research using EEG feedback techniques in the treatment of attention disorders has appeared, which will be reviewed next before this chapter is concluded. Before that can be presented, some explanation of QEEG is needed.

Quantitative electroencephalography

Fourier transform

As seen in chapter 8, the EEG at any electrode site emerges as a waveform analog of brain electrical activity whose amplitude increases and decreases at times with considerable regularity and at others irregularly. In analyzing the EEG, the clinician would note the appearance in some parts of the record of regular wave forms and the frequency at which they recurred, and this gave rise to the terminology already presented about alpha, beta, delta, and theta rhythms. In truth, such clear rhythmic regularity occurred only at times and had to be discerned amidst considerable activity that could not be specified as to frequency. With the advent of fast computers, wave forms could be digitized and subject to mathematical analysis. The analysis was based on a mathematical discovery by a French physicist, Baron Jean Fourier, in 1822 (Bracewell, 1989; DeValois & DeValois, 1990). which could specify how any complex wave form could be decomposed into simple waves at specific frequencies. Simple wave forms are called sine waves and this will be explained next.

Sine waves. If a waveform changes only gradually and regularly then the change can be seen as following the path of a circle, the bottom half moving forward instead of returning to its origins. See figure 10.3 for an illustration of this notion. The regularity of the change means that the height of the curve is at every point equidistant from the center of the imagined circle of which it is a part. Now look at the large circle in figure 10.3. Note that C is the point in the center of the circle and BC is a line that is the radius of the circle. BCD forms a right triangle and from trigonometry the sine of an angle is the ratio of the side opposite the angle over the hypotenuse. Since the hypotenuse (BC) is the radius, and is constant as long as the change continues to occur at the same rate, it follows that the height of any point on the curve (e.g. BD) is related to the sine of the angle formed with the center of the circle at that point. Recurrent curves reflecting continuously gradual change are, for this reason, called sine waves or sinusoids.

Sine waves can vary in three dimensions: frequency, amplitude, and phase. Frequency refers to how often, in space or time, the curve repeats its cycle. For EEG wave forms, frequency is measured in units of time, cycles per second, or Hz. Amplitude refers to the height of the waveform and generally reflects a dimension of intensity. In EEG, amplitude specifies intensity in microvolts; in vision, the brightness of

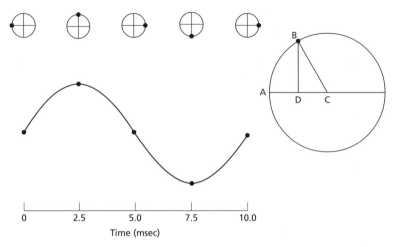

Figure 10.3 Regular curves as circle extensions. The height of a curve is a function of the sine of the angle it makes with the center of the circle

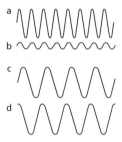

Figure 10.4 The waves *a* and *b* have twice the frequency of *c* and *d*. The amplitude of *a* is five times that of *b*. The frequency of *c* and *d* is equal but they differ 90° in phase

the light; and in audition, loudness of sound. Phase refers to the relative position of two oscillations. For example, the high point of one wave form may occur at the time of the low point of a second with the identical frequency. The second waveform is said to be 90° out of phase with the first. The stages of separation to that point would be between 1° and 90° and after, between 90° and 180°. Wave forms 360° out of phase are of course back in phase. Figure 10.4 illustrates what is meant by frequency, amplitude, and phase. A sine wave can also vary in orientation, whether it is horizontal, vertical, or somewhere in between with regard to some referent, but this dimension is not applicable to EEG wave forms.

Complex waves can be synthesized from and decomposed into aggregations of sine waves. Sine waves can be superimposed and combined by summing them algebraically, the result of which may have an appearance quite different from any of its components. The three curves of figure 10.5 represent two frequencies, one double

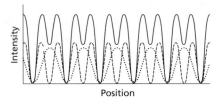

Figure 10.5   Two frequencies of same amplitude and phase and their algebraic summation

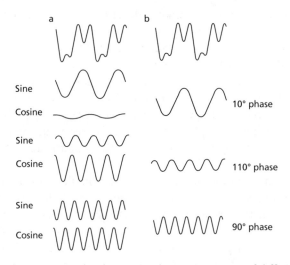

Figure 10.6   Complex waves can be decomposed into sine waves of differing amplitude, frequency, and phase

the other, but of the same amplitude and phase, and their point-for-point summation. Note how the summed wave's shape is dissimilar to that of its components though still regular. As more components are added, and particularly when they vary in all three dimensions, the shape of the resulting wave form can take on increasingly irregular characteristics. This is illustrated in figure 10.6, which also notes that Fourier's mathematics permits the process to go either way. Simple sine waves can be added to form a complex wave form, and a complex wave form can be decomposed into its sine wave components. In QEEG, the latter is what occurs. The wave form emerging at an electrode site is mathematically decomposed into its sine wave components. An example can be seen in figure 10.6.

A report of a QEEG consists of averaged amplitudes of each of the frequency bands (alpha, beta, etc.) at each electrode site and a calculation which conveys how much the amplitude is above or below the norm for the person's sex and age. Another measure, coherence, is a computation which reflects the extent to which activity at one site is similar to that at another. There are norms for coherence, and the presence of too much or too little coherence can be calculated between adjacent and long-distance sites in each hemisphere and for corresponding sites between the two hemispheres. There are a handful of normative data bases available that have emerged from the pioneering laboratories (Duffy, Burchfiel, & Lombroso, 1979; John et al., 1977; Thatcher et al., 1989) and a growing number of professionals using the technique. Duffy et al. (1994) report on the status and problems of the field as of 1994.

What is revealed in QEEG?

When the EEG is subjected to quantitative analysis, some amplitude for each of the frequency ranges, alpha, beta, etc., always emerges. Such data disconfirm existing concepts and require new ways of thinking about the EEG. For example, it was stated in chapter 8 that delta in the waking state is a sign of severe compromise of brain function unless the person is asleep. Since the QEEG reveals that all people have some delta buried in their EEGs in the waking state, that idea is no longer generally tenable, although it is still true if the delta activity is so strong that it "breaks out" and is visible in the raw EEG. With quantitative EEG, quantitative considerations must be taken into account. How much delta is there in comparison to other frequencies? Even more important, how much delta is present in comparison to norms? QEEG is of relatively little utility without normative data to which the individual case can be compared.

Another conceptual revision made necessary by the findings of QEEG is that the state of EEG is a function of the brain operating as a whole, i.e. mass action. Mass action was implicit in the presentation of ideas about synchrony and desynchrony and their relation to EEG frequency in the chapter on epilepsy. Going to sleep, for example, was viewed as a gradual process of synchronizing the brain from beta to delta. There may be some truth in this traditional view of the electrical activity of the brain, but a newer view, still being developed, is that the specific frequencies are a function of specific generators operating at different places in the brain (Steriade et al., 1990). For example, there is evidence that alpha originates with thalamic activity (Larson et al., 1998) and theta is thought to be associated with hippocampal activity (Steriade et al., 1990). The process of collecting relevant evidence and devising adequate theories for such data is under way at the time of this writing.

Contributions of QEEG to the study of attention disorders

Diagnosis.   Diagnostic studies with standard EEG have not contributed much to the understanding of attention disorders with the possible exception of ruling in or out the presence of an ictal condition. Although relatively few systematic studies utilizing quantitative EEG have appeared, they have shown promise both in providing objective indices that differentiate attentional problems from related conditions such as conduct disorder or learning disabilities and for differentiating different types of attentional disorder. For example, Mann et al. (1991) found ADD – H boys to show increased theta activity in frontal regions and decreased beta activity in posterior regions. These findings are consistent with both the underarousal and the executive dysfunction hypotheses in attention disorders. Chabot et al. (1996) reported QEEG findings on a large pool of subjects with learning problems, attention problems, or both, and showed how they could be used to differentiate the two conditions and even to specify which of two stimulant drugs would be best for particular subsets of those attention problems. The results are too complex to be presented in detail here, but it is encouraging that those with attention problems, but not the learning-disabled, showed excessive theta in frontal regions as was found in the Mann et al. study. Children with learning problems uniquely showed a number of coherence abnormalities. In another paper, Chabot and Serfontein (1996) were able to differentiate two kinds of attention problems based on QEEG. One was characterized as being similar to the ADD + H type and the other to the ADD – H type.

At the time of this writing, QEEG techniques have not been disseminated extensively, data bases have not been systematically compared, and details of technique have not been agreed upon, so it will take much work and probably a number of years before the full promise of QEEG can be realized. Lubar for example is in the process of creating a data base specifically for the diagnosis of ADHD.

Treatment – neurofeedback. The technique devised by Sterman to treat epilepsy, which utilized quantitatively analyzed EEG information as feedback, has come to be termed neurofeedback (Evans & Abarbarel, 1999). This differentiates it from other types of biofeedback which typically utilize information obtained from recording activity in the peripheral nervous system such as heart rate or skin conductance. It will be recalled that Sterman's procedure trained the person to enhance the sensory motor rhythm (12–14 Hz) over the motor strip. Lubar verified the brain underarousal hypothesis in attention disorders (Mann et al., 1992) finding excessive theta (relative synchrony) particularly at sites over the frontal lobes. He developed training protocols to augment beta while suppressing theta. In a study of 19 persons between eight and 19 years who were selected because they showed the EEG pattern found in Mann et al., Lubar et al. (1995) found that over 40 hour long treatment sessions, 12 participants (Group A) gradually reduced levels of theta while seven (Group B) did not. Group A showed significant improvement on a standardized CPT measure of attention and on objective measures of cognitive function in comparison to Group B. Although Group B did not give objective evidence of improvement, they were nonetheless rated by their parents as having improved as much as Group A. This research presents important evidence for correspondence between changes in the EEG and changes in target symptoms, thus suggesting that brain can be changed, while raising questions about the validity of rating scales, at least under some conditions.

There is no definitive evidence about the efficacy of neurofeedback yet, but such procedures are now being tried on increasing numbers of subjects and there are promising beginnings. It is an audacious project because it attempts to change the way the brain functions in a fairly direct manner, and contrasts with the still-legitimate pessimism expressed by Barkley about the amenability of ADHD persons to any treatment other than chronic drug treatment. The best evidence of efficacy comes from Lubar, and concerns what appear to be ADD – H persons. There have been claims that the whole spectrum of attention–hyperactivity disorders is equally amenable to neurofeedback, but such claims have not been accompanied by evidence that the training actually produces EEG changes. Much additional work is needed. Meanwhile the current state of the treatment art and its complexities are summarized in a comprehensive paper by Lubar and Lubar (1999). They disclaim cure of the condition as a target, but see evidence of improved function (p. 127), and devote considerable space to the complexities of treatment and the need for adjunctive work with other types of intervention in many cases. The efficacy of neurofeedback for at least some attention disorders seems promising but needs a great deal more research.

Summary Statement about Disorders of Attention

Available evidence suggests that there are primary disorders of attention which probably occur in two forms: one, a disorder of vigilance; the other, a disorder of executive functions. Perhaps the latter should be called not a disorder of attention but a disorder of response inhibition. The former is likely to be described as ADD – H and involve impairments of arousal in the back of the brain while the latter is likely to be described as ADD + H and involve impairments of frontal arousal. In a large proportion of cases, both conditions appear to be aided by stimulants which are generally effective while being administered. Improvements with drug treatments are not sustained after administration is terminated. Attentional symptoms may occur secondary to other conditions including toxicity, allergy, ictus, mania, depression, brain damage, and overloaded cognitive functions. Such secondary disorders may be hard to sort out from primary disorders of attention if the main pathology is subtle. Attentional symptoms may also occur in the context of chaotic patterning and chronic overstimulation during child rearing and/or ineffectual or aberrant efforts at socialization. Thus, sorting out what applies in the particular case requires careful study of both the neuropsychological status of the child and his or her family and social circumstances. Specification of primary and secondary types, a fairly recent development, should lead to more discriminating diagnostic procedures and to more efficacious and precise treatment interventions.

Part III

Disorders of Specific Modalities

11

Disorders of the Motor System

Although the terms "behavior" and "response" are used frequently in psychology, movement and its regulation is relatively neglected in the field as a whole. This is even true of behaviorists, psychologists influenced by the precepts of Skinner, whose main focus in psychology is observable, overt behavior. When their methods and ideas are examined, it is clear that the nature of the action is of little interest. Behavior is observed to provide an index about the information-processing mechanisms, motivations, and reward history of the organism. Such disregard of the motor system is changing as research on early cognitive development intensifies. In earlier phases of such research, motor development was viewed as a genetically determined, maturational process that provided the background for cognitive, language, and social behavior. More recently, motor functions have been linked systemically in development with perception and cognition so that it is not possible to relegate them to a background status. Rather, each of these components in a developing system is both cause and product in a cycle of systemic interaction. Much early learning involves doing, and what is done influences what is learned (Thelen, 1995).

In neuropsychology, it is impossible to disregard the intricacies of motor organization and control because many pathological conditions present primarily as impairments of motor function. Study of the mechanisms underlying movement is important for its own sake but also furthers knowledge about cognition, among others reasons, because sensory feedback accompanying overt activity (see chapter 5) is an important source of information and learning, especially early in life. This chapter begins with an analysis of the components of movement as found in the mature individual, goes on to consider the development of movement, reviews the highlights of what is known about the neuroanatomy and neurophysiology regulating movement, and concludes with descriptions and analyses of a number of motor disorders.

Components of Mature, Skilled Movement

Tonic background

Suppose that, while reading this text, you decide that a particular line merits special attention. Your arm and hand reaches for a pen resting nearby so that you can underline the crucial phrases. Terms such as "action" or "behavior" refer to the movement of the arm and the grasping behavior of the hand and fingers. Such movements are phasic events which emerge from a context which is termed the tonic background. Background includes such components as sitting or standing, and being stable and balanced because muscles in different parts of the body are active in opposing gravity and remaining upright. The "tonic" part in the phrase "tonic background" specifically refers to the "tone" of the muscles, their degree of stiffness and readiness for controlled action. Specific phasic actions such as grasping the pen include initiating activity when required with a quantity of effort just commensurate with the demands of the task. Too much tone or too little tone would burden or preclude execution of the task (Gordon & Ghez, 1991).

Phasic activity

Two types of phasic activity are generally distinguished: gross motor and fine motor. Gross motor roughly refers to movements of the entire trunk and the upper portions of the limbs. It includes rolling over, sitting, standing, locomotion, and reaching. There are three major fine motor systems. One involves precise movements of the hand and fingers and includes the so-called pincer grasp (seen at about the end of the first year that brings thumb and index finger together to pick up small objects) and such skills as managing knives and forks, sewing, writing, typing, etc. The other fine motor systems are the oculomotor system controlling the movements of the eyes (to be discussed in the next chapter), and the system controlling the muscles of the larynx (the voice box), throat, tongue, and mouth that produce speech (to be discussed in chapter 13). A number of aspects of phasic activity can be distinguished. These include latency or reaction time (the period between the onset of the occasion for action and the onset of behavior), speed, strength, direction, and efficiency.

Skill, memory, and praxis

Normally, tonic and phasic activity operate in a smoothly integrated fashion leading to the emergence of higher-level organizations called skills. Skills refer to specific domains of motor activity, e.g. sewing, writing, playing the piano, throwing a ball, or diving. Skills depend on practice and on some mechanism which stores the nature of earlier experience and makes it available when required in the present. What is stored is largely what is sensed by the tactual (touch), kinesthetic (movement), and proprioceptive (position of joints) receptors of the somatosensory nervous system and has been called motor memory (Baddeley, 1976, chapter 10). This type of memory has received relatively little attention even though it is an obvious reality to any individual who has learned to ride a bike and resumes this activity after many years. Motor memory is different from other types of memory such as that found in habituation, discussed earlier, or in recalling what you ate for breakfast this morning, which is called episodic memory. These different kinds of memory are described as independent because they are dissociable; any one may be impaired while the others are intact (Butters & Delis, 1995).

Considering motor activity alone, tonic and phasic activity are also disassociable. One can be intact and the other disordered. Some motor disorders are primarily impairments of tonic activity and others are impairments of phasic activity. Tonic disorders generally fall into two classes: either insufficient or excessive tone. Most phasic disorders reflect problems in regulating the onset, timing, sequencing, organization, or termination of behavior.

A term which designates overall facility, especially higher-level capability, for organizing and performing effective actions and action sequences is praxis. Disorders of such capabilities are termed dyspraxia or apraxia. (The reader will recall that the Greek prefix *dys* refers to impaired but not totally lost function, while the prefix *a* means without and implies total incapacity. Unfortunately, in common parlance the *a* prefix is often used when the *dys* prefix is actually intended.) The term which contrasts with praxis is gnosis. This term refers to overall facility in sensing, knowing, and understanding. Impairments are termed agnosia and dysgnosia. Gnostic functions and their impairments will be considered later in chapters on auditory and visual function. It is an oversimplification but nonetheless true that the front of the brain is the dominant location for praxis while the back is for gnosis. It is an oversimplification in that motor memory, a residue of action, is an important component of all information processing, especially early in development, while action is guided by stored sensory information of all sorts.

How does movement occur?

Although more will be devoted to this topic later, the basic elements will be presented here. In order to move, the bones of the body must have force exerted on them. The force that impels movement is muscle contraction. The only activity of which a muscle is capable is contraction. Muscles are arranged along the bones and they are connected via tendons from one bone to the next at the junction of the bones, places called joints. Consider for example the elbow joint which connects the upper and lower arm. To bend the elbow, muscles on the inner portion of the upper arm contract, pulling the lower arm toward the upper arm. For this to occur, the muscles on the outside must allow themselves to be stretched and must not contract at the same time, else the arm will be locked in a stiff position. To straighten the elbow, the reverse must occur, muscles on the outer part of the upper arm that are embedded in the lower arm must contract while those on the inner surface allow themselves to be stretched.

Thus instructions from the brain to the muscles are highly complex and must be coordinated and timed very carefully. It is crucial, if the bending is to occur, that messages to contract or to refrain from contracting be sent to the appropriate muscles at the right time or chaos will occur. Observe a baby trying to perform an action, to get an idea of how difficult even simple motor activity can be.

Terminology – descriptors of movement or action patterns

Before proceeding, a terminology for describing movement and action patterns is needed. This terminology arose in the fields of neurology, physical therapy, and reha-

Table 11.1   Descriptive terminology for movement

Term	Definition
Flexion	Bending a joint
Extension	Straightening or stretching a joint
Adduction	Moving a limb toward the center of the body
Abduction	Moving a limb away from the center of the body
Prone	On the under surface of the body: lying on the belly
Supine	On the upper surface of the body: lying on the back
Pronation	Move toward the belly or underside
Supination	Move toward the back or topside
Dorsiflexion	Move back: describes movements of neck or wrist
Ventroflexion	Move down: describes movements of neck or wrist

bilitation to provide a convenient way to communicate about movements and their impairments. The terminology distinguishes between whether the movement bends or straightens a joint, and often specifies a direction using the body as a frame of reference (see table 11.1).

This terminology is not entirely coherent and may be confusing to beginners. However, it quickly becomes familiar with use. Note that some of the terms are synonymous, for example, extension and dorsiflexion of the neck. A more profound idea is embedded in the terminology. The brain does not orchestrate the activity of single muscle fibers but works with groups of fibers called motor units. The muscle fibers of each motor unit serve the same function, for example flexion or extension. When the muscle activity is highly refined and very precise, as is true of eye movements, as few as four motor fibers may compose an entire motor unit, whereas when the activity is relatively crude, as many as 2,000 motor fibers may be in one motor unit (Rowland, 1991).

The development of movement

Readers may recall what it was like when they learned to do cartwheels or throw a ball accurately, and the endless practice and toleration of error that was required before mastery was achieved. Of course they know that they did not attempt such activity as infants but came to the task later, after a repertory of foundation skills had been developed. Children must practice and work at all of the skills that are to be acquired. But they must have some kind of rudimentary start. These beginnings are provided by reflexes which are genetically determined organizations of muscle tone and phasic movement elicited by particular sensory stimuli. Some reflexes have a specified developmental sequence of emergence. Such genetically organized foundations of movement are examined next, first for the tonic, then for the phasic aspects of movement.

Muscle tone organization

To begin, consider the following experiment by the English neurologist Sherrington (1923), which was a pioneering contribution to understanding the biology of tonal regulation. Sherrington was trying to understand where muscle control resides in the brain. He found that if he made a cut in the brain of an anesthetized animal above the pons (see figure 3.8), a very dramatic reaction occurred. The animal suddenly went into and then remained in total extension. Every muscle became rigid and the animal stretched itself out stiffly with neck arched backwards. When Sherrington then made a cut below the pons, quite the reverse occurred; every muscle became flaccid, and the animal went limp. In both cases, the animal could not move, first because there was too much tone, later because there was too little.

What was learned from this experiment was that there are centers in the pons which are responsible for continuously exciting the muscles of the body; that normally, this excitation is regulated by inhibition coming from above the pons. When the first cut was made, inhibitory stimulation to the pons was blocked so that unbridled excitation from the pons resulted in stiff overexcited muscles and a rigid animal. That the excitation stemmed from the pons was verified by the second cut which blocked that excitation from getting to the muscles so that they then went limp.

The Sherrington experiment revealed that there are active centers in the pons that continuously excite the muscles to produce tone, and that there are active centers above the pons, probably in the thalamus and cortex, that continuously inhibit and regulate that excitation. Knowledge about these patterns of muscle tone organization comes from the study of the development of movement in animals and in prematurely born children. Excitation and inhibition occur in patterns of organization called tonic reflexes, some of which will be described next.

Tonic reflexes

Tonic reflexes (Payton, Hirt, & Newton, 1977) are not easy to visualize or understand from reading about them. It might help to imagine each reflex as one of a series of different signals, each of which is connected to a series of switches producing different responses. An example might be an electronic console that controls the events on a theater stage. At certain signals, the curtain or a scenery backdrop may be raised or lowered, the lights dimmed or the colors changed. The reader then needs to learn what sensory information (which signal) elicits what pattern of response (change in what the audience sees).

Perhaps the most primitive tonic reflexes are the tonic labyrinthine prone and the tonic labyrinthine supine. The term "labyrinthine" is the adjectival form of "labyrinth," a synonym for the vestibular system, the source of information regarding the position of the head in space. The eliciting stimulus (the signal) is the position of the body, either on its belly or back. The response (what can be seen) is the posture of the child. If the child is prone, the body goes into total flexion, the so-called fetal position, with arms and legs bent under the trunk and the neck and head down. If the child is supine, the body goes into total extension, much like the animals in Sherrington's experiment. Note therefore how the tone of every muscle of the body is under the singular control of the vestibular system – on belly, flexion; on back, extension. Accordingly, a baby that changes position *in utero* is likely to give its mother quite a jolt!

Subsequently, developing reflexes provide increasingly differentiated control of muscle tone. The symmetric tonic neck reflex affects the top and bottom halves of the body (through an imaginary horizontal line at the navel) differently. The eliciting stimulus is the position of the neck. If the neck is dorsiflexed (the signal), the upper limbs (arms) extend and the lower limbs (legs) flex (the change that is apparent to the observer). If the neck is ventroflexed, the upper limbs flex and the lower limbs extend. The reflex following neck dorsiflexion can be remembered if one thinks of the position of a cat while begging for food – neck extended looking up, forelegs straight (extended) and hindlegs folded (flexed). The reflex following neck ventroflexion can be remembered by thinking of a cat eating, – head down, forelegs bent (flexed) and hindlegs straight (extended).

Another important early organization is the asymmetric tonic neck reflex which differentially affects the right and left halves of the body (through an imaginary vertical line running from nose to navel). Again the eliciting stimulus is the position of the neck, whether it is turned to the right or the left. The limbs on the side to which it is turned will extend and those on the other side will flex. The effect this has is reminiscent of a fencer's posture with the body and head turned sideways toward an opponent, the arm nearest the opponent is extended, holding the weapon, while the other arm is bent (flexed). With this reflex, the tone in the right side of the body will change from extension to flexion if the head turns from right to left. The reverse will occur on the other side.

The symmetric and asymmetric tonic neck reflexes have a kind of reversibility. That is, they are generally thought of as operating sequentially with neck position provoking or eliciting limb tone. But they can work the other way. A child with a disinhibited asymmetric tonic-neck reflex who for some reason voluntarily moves into a fencing position may find the head locked in a position either to the right or left depending on which arm is extended. It is unlikely that a child will voluntarily adopt a fencer's position but there are all kinds of reasons why he or she might extend both arms in front, and this could elicit a reverse symmetric tonic neck reflex.

A case in point occurred when a retarded child was trained with behavioral methods to tie his shoes. He accomplished the task successfully while working on a shoe set on a table in front of him, but continuously failed when the shoe was on his foot. Careful analysis of what transpired indicated that, as both arms were extended to reach the laces of the shoe on his foot, the symmetric tonic neck reflex was elicited which then led to neck dorsiflexion. He then lost eye contact with the laces and had subtle tone changes in his fingers so that the tying process failed. In this example, phasic fine motor learning was disrupted by a disinhibited tonic reflex. Mastery of the phasic task depended on learning how to inhibit that reflex.

The development of muscle tone

Tonic reflexes are normally inhibited and are not in evidence early in the course of development. They can often be observed in premature children and those with brain abnormality and, at times, appear spontaneously but transiently in normal children during the first year of life. Since the reflexes are inhibited and not just absent neurologically, it is possible with special techniques to find evidence for them even in normal adults. Tokizane et al. (1951–2), for example, studied changes in muscle tone on extensor and flexor muscle groups following prolonged neck turning with electromyographic (EMG) techniques. This is a procedure comparable to EEG except that the electrode is placed over a muscle. Muscle tension and muscle activity produce patterns of measurable electrical activity. They found evidence consistent with tonic neck reflex activity, with increases and decreases in limb flexor and extensor tone which varied with the position of the head. Berntson and Torello (1977) found comparable evidence with specialized behavioral techniques.

The changes observed on EMG by Tokizane et al. were not accompanied by overt movements of the limbs; nor were they detectable if the tone was tested by manipulation of the limbs, a common clinical procedure (Fiorentino, 1963). To detect flexor tone, for example, the observer grasps a relaxed limb and then gently extends and flexes it. If there is resistance to extension and facilitation of flexion, there is evidence for increased flexor tone even though the limb itself has not moved into an overtly flexed posture. Once beyond the first year of life, inhibition of tonic reflexes is normally so great that it can be detected only by refined electrical or very sensitive behavioral methods. If the tonic reflexes are only partially inhibited, they can be the basis of pathological motor behavior. There will be more about this later in the chapter. At this point it should be clear that, in normal development, inhibition of tonic reflexes is accomplished mostly during gestation with some further inhibition occurring during the first year or so of life.

The organization of mechanisms controlling balance

If you were to drop a puppy or kitten accidentally from a supine position, you will generally be relieved to note that it lands upright squarely on its feet and suffers no harm. Dogs and cats are born with special reflexes which accomplish these ends. Human beings are not so fully equipped at birth but take about five or six years to become fully mature in this respect. Two sets of reflexes are involved, the righting reactions and the equilibrium reflexes (Payton et al., 1977; Weisz, 1938), and they will be discussed next. Their emergence and efficacy depend on normal progress in inhibiting tonic reflexes.

Righting reflexes

These are a group of automatically evoked, patterned reactions stimulated by displacement of the body or some of its parts from a balanced position in space. They serve to keep the body aligned (rather than twisted) while prone or supine, or, if upright, with the head centered and aligned vertically with gravity. The sensors for these reflexes (the signals) are complex and include the vestibular system, proprioceptors, the eyes, and the oculomotor system (see chapter 5 and the discussion of the unit which integrates the self in the environment). Three different types of righting reaction will be described.

Neck righting is normally present at birth and is stimulated in a body that is prone or supine if the head is turned. The reflex reaction is for the rest of the body to rotate in the same direction so as to keep head and body aligned. The consequence is that the baby rolls over. This is the way babies begin to learn to roll over. Initially, the trunk follows the head and neck like a sack of potatoes. With later maturation and development, this involuntary gross action comes under voluntary control, and the body shifts position in a more segmented and controlled fashion. Evidence of such segmentation and control is generally observable by six months of age.

Optical righting reflexes are observed when a child is held by outstretched arms. If in a supine or prone position, the head moves upward, ventroflexing from the supine position and dorsiflexing from the prone position. If held upright at the waist but tilted to the right or left, the head automatically moves toward the midline. If the child is blindfolded, and put through the same procedures, these reactions are called labyrinthine righting reflexes because the main source of information about the position of the head comes from the vestibular system when vision is blocked. Both optical and labyrinthine righting reflexes appear during the first six months of life and persist at a reflex level for five or so years. Afterwards, they can be inhibited voluntarily. Thus normal eight- year-olds, if held and tilted to the right, may not straighten their heads to the upright simply because they can stop from doing so if they wish. However, they should be able to move their heads voluntarily to the upright position on request.

Equilibrium reflexes are the most complex of the body reflexes. They serve to return the body to stability when it is off balance. Beginning about six months of age, equilibrium reactions become increasingly complex as motor development progresses from rolling over, to sitting, crawling, walking, and running. For example, the earliest forms of equilibrium reaction can be seen if the mattress on which an infant is lying supine or prone is jostled. Both arms and legs will abduct reflexively to maintain symmetric balance. A mature form of an equilibrium reflex can be seen if the arm of a person is suddenly pulled to one side, threatening the person's stability. The other arm and the head will move in the opposite direction of the destabilizing pull, and a large number of comparable muscular adjustments will be made throughout the body, all quite automatically and involuntarily. Equilibrium reflexes obviously do not disappear, but remain throughout life.

The development of phasic reactions

Gross motor skills – reflex precursors

If a newborn is held at the waist and the soles of the feet are bounced on the surface of a mattress, the legs are likely to stiffen. This reflex is called the positive supporting reaction and the response is strong enough to support the baby's weight and permit a kind of rudimentary standing. If the feet are placed on a treadmill or the baby is propelled forward while the balls of the feet are in contact with the surface, the legs alternate in thrusting forward, like in walking. After a few months, these reactions will disappear while the child is upright but will reappear about the time walking begins, at about the age of one.

Gross motor skills – primitive directed movements

Observation of babies suggests the presence of two kinds of limb movement directed at objects in the environment. The first is a slow reaching movement with an imprecise trajectory. Such movements are termed slow writhing movements. A child reaching for an attractive object may follow a meandering course before attaining the goal. Alternatively, the child may suddenly flail into very rapid, jerky motions called ballistic movements. Both types of limb movement will come under increasing inhibitory control in the course of development, but the former will be regulated by negative feedback mechanisms, the latter by feedforward mechanisms (see chapter 4).

A more limited but immediately relevant-for-survival reflex is the rooting reaction. If the cheek is touched, the head turns toward the source of stimulation. This reaction facilitates the infant's location of the nipple and enables feeding.

Fine motor skills – specific discrete reflexes

As noted, the fine motor system has three major components: the hands and fingers, the movements of the eyes, and the control of speech. Obvious discrete reflexes are present at birth in each of these areas and are precursors for later developments. For hands and fingers, the grasp reflex is apparent. Any object coming in contact with the palm of the open hand elicits a simultaneous flexion of all the fingers which results in a simian (ape-like) grasp. A normal child can support almost its entire weight with the strength of this reaction. Of relevance to the muscles of the mouth is the sucking reflex. This organized pattern of local muscle activity makes possible the ingestion of food. The strength and efficiency of this reflex can strongly influence the child's early social relationships. If the reflex is weak and feeding is slow, the process can be laborious and frustrating to child and caretaker alike and burden their relationship.

Of relevance to the visual system is a reflex that is responsible for changing the focus of the lens of the eye to deal with near and far images so that they are seen clearly. This is accomplished by tiny muscles which change the shape of the lens and thus its focus. The process is called accommodation. By the end of the first year of life, lens accommodation will come to operate at nearly fully mature levels. At birth, however, the focus is under control of the optical placing reflex in which focus is relatively fixed at about 10–12 inches. This is about the distance between mother's face and child's eyes while a baby is nursing. Such an arrangement increases the likelihood that the first visual configuration that is seen clearly and often is the mother's face, and probably contributes to bonding between mother and child.

Gross motor development

Assuming that the inhibition of tonic reflexes and the development of righting and equilibrium reflexes is on schedule, children progress through a sequence of gross motor development (Gesell & Ilg, 1943; McGraw, 1969). These landmarks in motor development are listed next, along with the age at which they commonly appear. Some variation from these norms, even in the direction of lag, is of little importance. However, significant lags do often provide the earliest clues that something is not right.

(a) Head control: 4 months; (b) sitting: 5–6 months; (c) crawling: 6–8 months; (d) standing: 11 months; (e) walking: 12–14 months; (f) running (defined as forward movement during the course of which both feet leave the ground): 2–3 years.

Between the ages of five and eight, children should be able to master such complex forms of gross motor control as are involved in hopping separately on each foot, jumping jacks, and skipping. These routines can constitute a useful screening device that survey all major component gross motor skills expected in normal development. Note that hopping separately evaluates motor control of the right and left halves of the body, jumping jacks evaluate the integrity of motor functions in the upper and lower halves of the body, and skipping assesses the overall coordination of the two sides of the body.

Many individuals go on to develop athletic skills of various kinds. This is accomplished by means of practice, almost endless in duration and frequency, if high levels of skill are to be attained. When one observes the graceful and almost effortless manner in which teenagers may, for example, throw and catch a ball, one may forget the literally countless practice trials that precede such skill.

Fine motor development

The sequence of emergence of fine motor skills is not as sharply differentiated as gross motor skills. One major landmark is the appearance of thumb–finger opposition at about 11–12 months of age. This particular capability permits the manipulation of small objects and probably has made possible most of the artifacts of civilization in that it has allowed for the development of tools. Later, in the second, third and fourth years, children will learn to use food utensils, but full mastery may not occur before the ages of seven or eight, a long learning process indeed. As this develops, children come to learn the independent control of each finger. Possibly the last commonly shared fine motor skill is in the manipulation of writing instruments. A three-year-old will scribble with a crayon using a simian grasp while the six-year-old embarks on the arduous task of learning to write. This is a process that may take five or more years before fluent mastery is achieved.

Many people develop advanced fine motor skills which are marvelously complex. Typing, sewing, and playing the piano are examples. What they all share are the prerequisite hours, weeks, days, months, and years of practice required to achieve mastery. Fine motor skills are no different from gross motor skills in this regard. Further consideration of eye movements and speech, the other fine motor systems, will be found in later chapters.

Theoretical interpretations of motor development

In psychology, the traditional interpretation of the sequences in development just described has been that the actions involved are preprogrammed genetically for emergence in a particular sequence (cf. Gesell & Ilg, 1943; McGraw, 1969). Thus the stepping movements seen in the newborn were thought to reveal that the brain has an inherited plan for walking that is initially inhibited when it first appears because the child cannot utilize it, only to emerge later when the child is ready. Thelen (1995) describes research which showed that the stepping movements did not disappear. A baby in the supine position continues to display these same movements which, in this context, are described as kicking. The explanation for the cessation of the movements while upright turned on the rapid weight gain of the baby during this period, which consists mostly of fat rather than muscle. In the upright position, the baby's strength was not adequate to move the increased weight. The physics of managing the weight while supine was easier and so kicking could occur. Thelen argues that the organization of behavior is not preprogrammed genetically but emerges from the interaction of the bodily structure of the organism, the environment, and its constraints (e.g. gravity), and the organism's activity. Genetics play a crucial role in determining the structure of the organism, including those structures capable of storing and retrieving information, but programs for complex actions are gradually learned and are not written in final form by the genes. (There will be further consideration of genetic influence in subsequent chapters.)

Brain Mechanisms in Movement

Although a great deal is known about the relationship between component functions of movement and various aspects of neuroanatomy and neurophysiology, the fact is

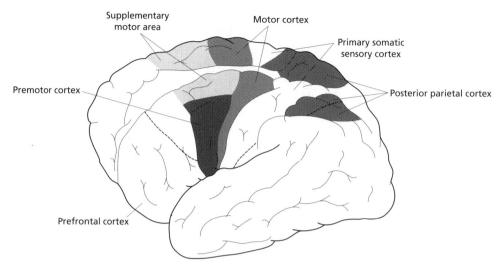

Figure 11.1   Areas involved in motor control, especially the supplementary motor area

that we do not know how the nervous system comes to control the wondrously complex movements of the body (see for example the issue of a journal called *Behavioral and Brain Sciences*, 15, no. 4, 1992). Here we will review some of the highlights of what we do know. I am indebted to detailed discussions in Boddy (1978), Kolb and Whishaw (1990), Kandel, Schwartz, and Jessell (1991), Beatty (1995), and Carlson (1998), for this presentation.

Four major arenas of activity have been described that are involved in the regulation of movement, two of which are in the brain. One of the brain arenas is divided into two parts: the pyramidal system which originates in the precentral gyrus (see chapter 3 where this and other areas of brain anatomy are described) and the extrapyramidal system, mostly the basal ganglia. The other brain arena might be termed a motor accessory system which involves diverse areas of brain including one at the top called the supplementary motor area (see figure 11.1), the premotor and prefrontal cortices, and the cerebellum. The third major arena is the spinal cord, and the last is the neuromuscular junction, the place where muscle contraction is actually provoked. Effective muscle control is impossible without sensory input that provides information about the contraction of muscles, the position of limbs, and the orientation of the body with regard to gravity.

Some of the ways in which this complex system operates will be discussed in more detail next. The reader should keep in mind that there are neural circuits that control both voluntary and automatic phasic responses, and others that control tone which are mostly involuntary. Pathology of movement can occur at any place along the chain between the brain and the neuromuscular junction and then into the muscle itself. The discussion begins at the level of muscle and the neuromuscular junction.

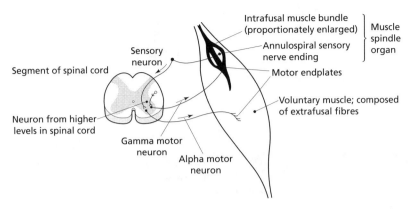

Figure 11.2 Part of the wiring diagram of muscle: alpha and gamma motor neurons and sensory feedback from intrafusal fibers

Coordinated muscle activity underlies movement

The structure of muscle and its enervation

Muscles contain two kinds of fibers. The predominant kind, called extrafusal fibers, do the work when a muscle contracts. The other kind, called intrafusal fibers (which are the type of muscle present in muscle spindles), do little muscle contraction but go along and stretch when the extrafusal fibers stretch. The extrafusal fibers are enervated by large axons from alpha motor neurons. These originate in the spinal cord and are efferent, i.e. they convey the imperative message to act. All messages to act coming from the brain have synapsed at least once with dendrites of the alpha motor neurons in the spinal cord. The intrafusal fibers are under the control of small-diameter axons of nerve fibers called gamma motor neurons. Although the muscle spindles cannot do heavy work, they are involved in setting the tone of the extrafusal fibers and anticipating their work load. The operation of this anticipatory system is often made evident if while walking down the stairs there turns out to be one step less than anticipated. The foot comes down quite hard, revealing this tone setting anticipatory process made possible by the gamma efferents.

Muscles are not only enervated, they are also equipped with sensors which provide feedback regarding their activity. Sensory nerves with receptors sensitive to stretch, called annulospiral endings, originate on the muscle spindle (these are sometimes called gamma afferents). They change their rate of firing as a function of the degree to which the muscle is stretched. See figure 11.2 for a sketch of this arrangement. Another source of sensory information about muscle activity comes from the Golgi tendon organ, which is embedded in the tendon which attaches muscle to bone (see figure 11.3). The sensors fire at a rate proportional to the intensity of muscle contraction and hence give information about the magnitude of work being done by the muscle.

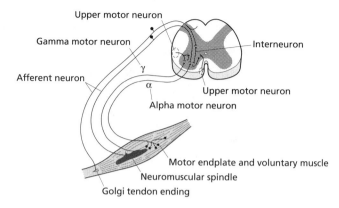

Figure 11.3   Position of Golgi tendon organs, tension and work monitors for muscle

A muscle contracts when action potentials arrive at the neuromuscular junction, the site where nerve and muscle synapse, and the neurotransmitter, acetylcholine, is released. On the muscle side of the synapse is a structure called the motor endplate. Excitation of muscle at the synapse is much like excitation at neuron–neuron synapses, all or none. Of course, the amount of work muscles have to perform varies. Gradations of muscle work are determined by the number of muscle fibers stimulated to react and the rapidity with which they are reactivated after they have just completed a contraction.

Local control of muscle contraction – stretch and spinal reflexes

All muscles can do is contract. If a muscle contracts, some other muscle on the other side of the limb is going to be stretched. Such stretching will also be registered by the sensory apparatus of that muscle and be transmitted to the spinal cord where it will synapse with the alpha motor neuron that will send back a message to that muscle to contract and thus eliminate the stretch. The stretch reflex is thus an automatic tendency of stretched muscles to contract, all regulated at a level no higher than the spinal cord and not involving neurons in the brain.

The most familiar example of stretch reflexes is the patellar (kneecap) reflex. If you are sitting high enough so that your legs are dangling without support, and you are struck sharply just below the knee, your leg is likely to kick up briskly. What has happened is that the sharp blow stimulated Golgi tendon endings and provided (false) information to the nervous system that the muscles of the leg had been flexed and that the extensors had been stretched. The involuntary response was to contract the extensors (see figure 11.4). If the leg extensors contract, the leg kicks so that the stretch is eliminated. The intensity with which the bottom of the kneecap is struck is much greater than the usual stimulation the receptors receive, which helps explain the intensity of the kicking reaction.

Sometimes, the kneecap stimulus is correctly administered to a normal nervous system, but the reaction does not occur. As a matter of fact, this failure can be made

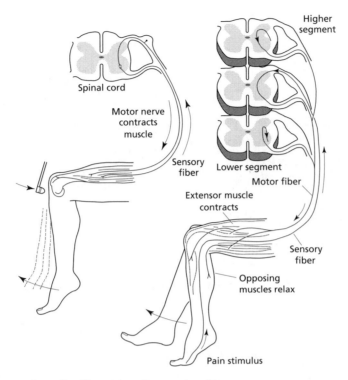

Figure 11.4 Patellar reflex illustrating the stretch reflex

to occur simply by making the subject aware of what is happening. Such awareness brings brain factors into play which can override the spinal mechanisms controlling the reflex. This occurs so commonly that physicians go to some effort to distract their patients when conducting this examination. The anatomical arrangements in the spinal cord that make possible "higher" brain influence on "lower" reflex mechanisms are that there are interneurons in the spinal gray matter called Renshaw cells that inhibit the stretch reflexes of antagonistic muscle groups opposing the intended action. For present purposes the important point to retain is that conscious and deliberate higher brain activity (e.g. thoughts) can alter the expression of relatively automatic activity.

During the course of a medical examination, the reader may have also experienced the procedure in which the physician taps the limbs with a small hammer near several joints of the body other than the knee. What is being examined is the reaction of the muscles, which will be rated on a scale of activity from nonreactive and hypoactive through normal to hyperactive. These are tests of the integrity of spinal reflexes. More importantly, they are tests of the resting tone of the muscles and their readiness to react. Low tone indicated by hypoactive reflexes and high tone indicated by hyperactive reflexes are both signs of pathology.

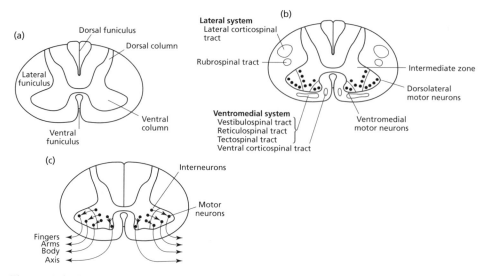

Figure 11.5   Organization of the pathways and processors in the spinal cord

The organization of muscle control of the body

Figure 3.4 illustrates a cross-section of the spinal cord and shows its organization. The reader will recall: (a) sensory and motor divisions in the form of dorsal and spinal roots, respectively; (b) division into myelinated tracts (long insulated pathways) called white matter because of appearance and gray matter (sort of butterfly-shaped in cross-section) which contains neuron processors; and (c) that any particular place in the spinal cord has primary connections to sensors and muscles enervated by that particular segment, but that there are connections with nearby segments and with the brain so that the functioning of each segment is subject to their influence as well. Figure 11.5 contains more detailed information that will enable greater understanding of the relationship between anatomy and function.

Spinal cord – long pathways

Note the areas in figure 11.5a labelled "funiculus" (Latin for cord, plural: "funiculi"). The dorsal funiculus transmits mostly afferent somatosensory information, that is, sensory information from skin, joints, and muscles involving touch and proprioception going to the brain. The lateral and ventral funiculi transmit efferent information, that is, commands to the muscles. These, in turn (see figure 11.5b) are subdivided into the lateral corticospinal and rubrospinal tracts in the lateral system and the vestibulospinal, reticulospinal, tectospinal, and ventral corticospinal tracts of the ventromedial system. Note the way the terms are formed, with an adjectival beginning referring to a part of the brain at the beginning and ending in "spinal." This designates from brain to spine, an efferent direction. There are many terms here.

It is important to try to visualize these structures so close study of the diagrams is highly recommended.

These efferent tracts in the white matter are positioned in a manner that aids in remembering the functions they transmit. The more medial or nearer to the center, the more involved in the regulation of the trunk. The more lateral or to the side, the more they involve the limbs and the digits, the fingers and toes.

Consider the ventromedial system first. The vestibulospinal tract originates in the vestibular system, the tectospinal tract in the superior colliculus (see chapter 3 discussion about the midbrain), and the reticulospinal tract in the reticular formation. The first brings information about the position of the body with regard to gravity. The second controls automatic orienting movements of the eyes to visual stimuli and contributes to attention. The third activates and regulates the arousal system relative to all forms of sensory stimulation. The axons of single fibers in these tracts do not project to single, or even just a few segments of the spinal cord, but project to many (see figure 3.4) and furthermore project bilaterally (the tectospinal tract is an exception here) so that a fiber coming down on the left side of the cord will synapse with gray matter neurons on both the right and left sides. These are not tracts for discrete movements of a few muscles but do control the overall organization of trunk movements.

The lateral system involves two major tracts: the lateral corticospinal and the rubrospinal. Both initiate in the cortex but the rubrospinal fibers have synapsed in the red nucleus, a group of red-appearing cells in the midbrain. Both of these tracts come from the opposite side of the brain, having crossed over at the bottom of the medulla where they formed a structure which struck some early anatomists as looking like pyramids and so gave rise to the terminology about the pyramidal system. The corticospinal system fibers synapse directly onto motor neurons controlling the digits, while the rubrospinal system fibers synapse with neurons in the spinal gray matter that in turn project to limited segments of the body and control movements of the shoulders, arms, and hands. Thus the lateral system provides for selective and specific movements of the limbs and especially the fingers.

Spinal cord – gray matter organization

The white matter fibers coming down from the brain will terminate on neurons in gray matter somewhere in the spinal cord. The positions of the motor neurons in the gray matter parallels that of the fiber tracts in that those that are most medial, the ventromedial neurons, control trunk movements and those positioned more laterally, the intermediate zone and dorsolateral motor neurons, control limb and digit movement (see figure 11.5c). Obviously, the number of motor neurons controlling the limbs and digits (those that synapse with the lateral system tracts) will be more numerous in those segments of the spinal cord where the nerves going to the limbs emerge. Within the clusters of gray matter neurons controlling limbs and digits (not illustrated), the more laterally positioned cells regulate extensor movements while the more medially located cells regulate flexor movements, thus providing an anatomic counterpart for the functional organization described earlier.

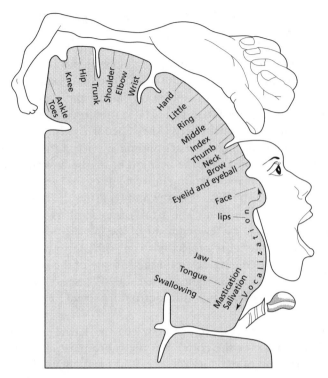

Figure 11.6   The motor strip homunculus

Cortex – the motor strip

Some of the earliest knowledge about the motor system came with the discovery of the representation of different body parts along the precentral gyrus, sometimes called the motor strip (figure 11.6). The so-called homunculus (little person) has very enlarged fingers, hands, and mouth area, reflecting the detailed and precise muscle control of which those parts are capable. The homunculus is also upside down in that the control of the upper portions of the body is at the bottom of the cortex while the control of the lower portions is at the top and actually overlaps into the medial portions in the longitudinal sulcus.

Given the functions of the tracts of the spinal cord, it will come as no surprise that the cells from the finger and arm areas of the motor strip are the origins of the lateral tracts and the cells from the trunk areas originate the ventromedial system. The main difference between the tracts for the fingers in comparison with the arms is that muscle control for the fingers is monosynaptic – that is, a single cortical neuron will synapse directly with a single motor neuron in the spinal cord – whereas for the arms, the brain neurons will synapse with other neurons within the spinal cord which project only to other neurons in the cord. These in turn will link the brain neurons with a group of motor effectors controlling the arm. The latter arrangement is found in the ventromedial system but the pool of interlinked neurons is even greater.

Synaptic organization that is singular permits precise independent control of the muscles. This is what is needed if, for example, you are to have the wherewithal to move your little finger up and down on a piano key. Pooled control making use of populations of cells would be needed to control movements that employ many joints. Of course, the opportunity for very discrete control of the digits does not mean that other types of control are not present. Before one can move the fingers individually, one has a simian grasp, so the organization for that kind of movement must be present as well. The pathways to the arms and fingers all decussate (cross over) in the medulla, so motor control of the limbs is contralateral. The pathways to the trunk only partially decussate so that its motor control is partially ipsilateral and partially contralateral. This means that injury to one side of the brain which might devastate limb functions on the other side may still allow fairly good bilateral motor control of the trunk.

The upshot of having somewhat independent systems for the control of digits, limbs, and trunk is that each may be separately impaired. This enables understanding of the different effects of different kinds of pathology in the brain and spinal cord. It also provides an anatomic basis for the distinction between fine and gross motor functions. What is missing in this account are the sources of tonic as compared with phasic enervation. Some relevant information can be found below.

Other major brain influences on motor function

Basal ganglia

The basal ganglia were introduced in chapter 3 and illustrated in figure 3.14. Another, more schematic, illustration of its dissected parts can be seen in figure 11.7. These subcortical nuclei are the major components of what has been called the extrapyramidal system. There are five major nuclei: the caudate nucleus, the putamen, the globus pallidus, the substantia nigra, and the subthalamic nucleus. The caudate and the putamen share cell types similar to that found in cortex and together are called the neostriatum. The globus pallidus derives from a phylogenetically older part of the brain and may be called the paleostriatum. These striatal nuclei surround the thalamus and lie just below the insula (see figure 3.7). The substantia nigra is in midbrain and has two zones: the pars reticulata and the pars compacta. The pars reticulata is histologically similar to the globus pallidus, and can be considered part of the same system or module. The pars compacta is a major source of the neurotransmitter dopamine. Although these structures influence motor functions profoundly they receive neither input from nor output to the spinal cord. Thus their role is that of a modulator, albeit a very important one.

There has been considerable progress in understanding the anatomy and physiology of the basal ganglia. They receive input from a wide variety of sources and, via the thalamus, project primarily to the frontal lobes. The circuitry appears to be discrete and there are at least four separate systems (Alexander, Crutcher, & DeLong, 1990; Mega & Cummings, 1994), a motor system which links to the motor strip

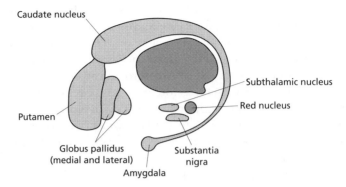

Figure 11.7 A schematic, dissected view of the basal ganglia and thalamus

adjacent to the central sulcus; an oculomotor system which links to the frontal eye fields, a region in the vicinity of Broca's area (see figure 11.8); a prefrontal system which links to dorsolateral and orbitofrontal cortex; and a limbic system which links to the anterior cingulate gyrus (just above the corpus callosum: see figure 3.8) and medial and ventral portions of the frontal lobes. These linkages imply basal ganglia involvement in voluntary action including its initiation; in eye movements and attention; in higher-level cognitive processes including planning, organization, and the monitoring of action; and in emotional regulation. Further detail is beyond the scope of this book, but an initial approach to understanding the way these circuits operate can be suggested. Fine regulation of any system occurs when there are many layers of control, thus permitting the balance between excitation and inhibition to be nuanced and responsive to meet changing demands. The problem is that the modulators which make possible smooth control may themselves be selectively impaired and consequently promote excessive excitation or inhibition in some or all of the circuits. The nature of the behavioral symptoms will depend on precisely which circuits are affected (because they are separate), the nature of their malfunction, and what effect the discrete malfunction has on the operation of the system as a whole. Basal ganglia abnormalities give evidence that they are modulator dysfunctions when they temporarily normalize under circumstances such as extreme stress. Such normalizations may lead observers to question the authenticity of the pathological condition.

Much information about the functions of the basal ganglia has come from advances in understanding Parkinson's disease, a disorder which is associated with a depletion of the neurotransmitter dopamine because of the death of cells in the substantia nigra. There is marked slowness of movement called bradykinesia, a decline in self-initiated movements, a stooped posture, a mask-like face, a rhythmical tremor at rest and cogwheel rigidity, in which a rigid limb, when passively moved, first resists, then gives way a little, then resists and so on. These changes are accompanied by a progressive decline in mental competence called dementia. That the disease, at least in its early and middle stages, is due to modulator abnormalities and not to primary deficits in

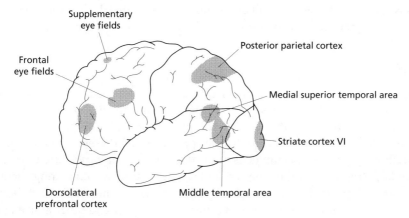

Figure 11.8 Cortical areas involved in the regulation of eye movements

motor activation is evident from observations (Behrman, Teitelbaum, & Cauraugh, 1998) that certain kinds of activating instructions can normalize, at least temporarily, the halting gait of the Parkinson patient. More dramatic evidence can be found in anecdotal reports of normal function under conditions of intense emotional arousal. Thus, a patient who may have sat passively for a number of years and hardly ever moved, may get up and call the fire department and rouse the neighbors after smelling smoke, but then revert to inactivity.

A precursor of dopamine, L-dopa, when administered orally, was found to replenish dopamine. When first tried, striking increases in the activity of Parkinson's patients occurred, and there was promise of cure. However, it has proved difficult to titrate the medication, and excessive uncontrollable movements often appeared, symptoms as debilitating as insufficient movement. Rapid, uncontrollable movements and subsequent dementia are the major symptoms of a hereditary disorder called Huntington's chorea which also is now known to involve neurotransmitter abnormalities in the basal ganglia. In this condition, the primary abnormalities appear to be in acetylcholine and GABA. Together, the two disorders and the data obtained following L-dopa treatment indicate that basal ganglia abnormalities produce disorders marked by excessive excitatory or inhibitory modulation.

Parkinson's disease is generally a disorder of middle to late maturity and will not be further considered in this book. It should be noted however that juvenile forms of the disorder have been reported although they are rare and the literature about the disorder is sparse (cf. Askenasy et al., 1990). The author visited such a case, a boy of about eight, at his own home. He was referred for possible autism, the subject of a later chapter. The young man was unbelievably inert in spontaneous movements and facial expression and tellingly displayed cogwheel rigidity when his limbs were moved. However, these symptoms were not in evidence when he was interviewed later in a physician's office. My interpretation of these contrasting findings was that this was another example of the phenomenon which occurred when the older chronic Parkinson's patient moved so adroitly on the occasion of a serious fire.

Cerebellum

The cerebellum is a major component of the fourth unit of the brain described in chapter 5, that which integrates the self in its environment. Its location and shape is illustrated in figure 3.14. Although the cerebellum occupies only about 10 percent of brain volume, it contains more than 50 percent of all the brain's neurons. Complete removal of the cerebellum does not lead to any loss of muscle strength or inadequacy of perception. Its functions are indirect, adjusting and correcting the output of the motor system to accord with feedforward goals and feedback information derived from somatosensory processing during movement and other available information such as that provided by vision (Ghez, 1991). It makes possible ballistic movements and, without a well-functioning cerebellum, Luria's kinetic melodies could not occur. When the cerebellum is compromised, ataxia results. These are symptoms in which the components of movement are present but their coordination is impaired. An example of ataxia is the so- called Frankenstein walk, in which each limb is propelled independently and the arms hover rather than swing.

The cerebellum has three functional divisions (Ghez, 1991) whose inputs and outputs are illustrated in figure 11.9. The vestibulocerebellum facilitates the control of balance and eye movements, the spinocerebellum adjusts ongoing movements for both the trunk and the limbs, and the cerebrocerebellum coordinates the planning of limb movements. Note that the structure of the cerebellum has similarities to that of the spinal cord in that the medial regions in the center regulate trunk movement, and the regions most to the side regulate the movement of the fingers and are involved in planning. A person with an impairment of the medial regions might walk awkwardly but be able to move arms and legs smoothly if lying supine. On the other hand, unlike the spinal cord, control is exercised only to the ipsilateral side. If the right side of the cerebellum were damaged and the left intact, both ballistic and slow following movements would be possible on the left side, but only slow following but not ballistic movements would be possible on the right.

The longstanding view of the functions of the cerebellum confined its influence purely to motor activity. Newer discoveries, particularly about the cerebrocerebellum and parts of the vermis (see figure 11.9) have extended these integrative functions to all aspects of information processing (e.g. Ivry & Keele, 1989; Schmahmann, 1991). The processing goes on elsewhere in the brain: the role of the cerebellum, as is the case for motor functions, is that of a modulator, a system that amplifies or inhibits neural function as demanded by the activity in which the organism is engaged. Thus the cerebellum may be a kind of volume control for sensation, may contribute to the suppression of attention to irrelevant or distracting information, and regulate the rapid switching on and off and shifting of attention that may be required in many situations. The areas most involved in these higher functions are those which evolved most recently. They are also the parts that decline first with age (Raz et al., 1992).

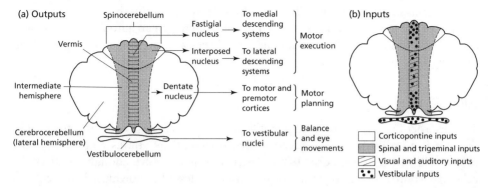

Figure 11.9 Schematic view of inputs and outputs of the cerebellum and its different functions

Supplemental motor area

This is an area of cortex at the top of the brain and in front of the motor strip (see figure 11.1). It is best known as an area involved in the control of eye movements but recent work has increasingly implicated it as contributing to bilateral motor coordination and motor planning. For example, activity in this area has been shown to precede voluntary self-initiated activity in the motor strip. There is thus another area that can be separately impaired to produce its own selective effects on motor function.

Disorders of the Motor System

With the background presented above, the nature of many of the pathologies of the motor system is more easily understood. The order of presentation will go from the periphery to the brain.

Disorders of muscle and the neuromuscular junction

Muscular dystrophy

Strictly speaking these are disorders of muscle and not of the nervous system. They are most often genetically transmitted and are disorders in which the mechanisms of muscle contraction are impaired.

Myasthenia gravis

The main symptoms are fatigue which ranges from drooping eyelids and decreased stamina to gross incapacitation. This is a disorder of neuromuscular transmission at the neuromuscular junction. The pathology is apparent in the muscle receptor portion of the junction and apparently is a consequence of an autoimmune reaction, a situation in which the body attacks its own tissues as though they were some kind of foreign invader.

Poliomyelitis

This disorder has also been called infantile paralysis because it frequently attacks children. It is a result of a virus infection that preferentially attacks and destroys the motor cells of the spinal cord. If the destruction is extensive enough to affect the cells that control breathing, then death ensues unless the individual is placed in a device that will artificially induce breathing. Often the virus attacks motor neurons controlling the lower portion of the body, leaving a flaccid paralysis of the legs that requires continuous wheelchair use.

Cerebral palsy

This is a nonprogressive disorder of posture (muscle tone) and movement (phasic muscle activity) beginning in early childhood (Taft, 1995). It has been associated with a variety of gestational and perinatal events including prematurity, prenatal and postnatal stroke (where the blood supply is cut off from part of the brain; see chapter 16), anoxia, traumatic birthing, and infection. Nonetheless, none of these conditions invariably results in cerebral palsy and only a small percentage of infants with these conditions will later have the disorder (Kuban & Leviton, 1994). Some who show signs of impairment early in life appear to "grow out of it." In one major study, one half the children with cerebral palsy diagnosed at the age of one year were normal by their seventh birthday. There are several different types and several common symptoms. It is useful to depict such distinctions for instructional purposes, but pure forms are rare. In addition, children with this motor disorder rarely are free of other symptoms of brain damage. For example, a large proportion of those with cerebral palsy have epileptic seizures and over 50 percent are retarded intellectually, the topic of a later chapter).

Cerebral palsy may be divided into kinetic and akinetic disorders. Akinetic disorders are characterized by insufficient movement while kinetic disorders have excessive movement. In akinetic disorders there is excessive tone in some or all muscles, a condition called spasticity (adjective, spastic). The resulting rigidity locks the subject into particular postures. Two types are observed. Unilateral spasticity or hemiplegia (hemiparesis is a milder version) affects one side of the body and is more likely to affect arms and the upper torso in comparison to the legs and lower torso. The disorder appears on a continuum of severity ranging from no obvious signs of paralysis but inability to hop on one foot, through spasticity of an arm (arm held stiffly and adducted) with the ability to walk, through inability to walk but with normal functions on one side. Bilateral spasticity, or diplegia, affects both sides of the body and is more likely to involve the legs and lower torso than the arms and upper torso. The continuum here would range from inability to perform jumping jacks, especially the

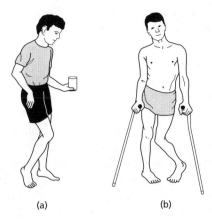

(a)   (b)

Figure 11.10 (a) Spastic right arm, leg involvement less, normal left side. (b) Spastic legs, normal arms

bottom half, while being able to walk, through being confined to a wheelchair but with normal use of the arms, to having all four limbs affected. The latter is termed quadriplegia. Mild forms of hemiplegia and diplegia are illustrated in figure 11.10.

Readers can test their growing knowledge of neuropsychology if they consider the following question. Which spastic condition, hemiplegia or diplegia, is more likely to follow a stroke and which might follow infections or anoxia? The answer is that stroke, by its nature, might occur in one part of the brain and thus produce a hemiplegia, but it is unlikely that viruses or bacteria would prefer neurons on the left side over the right or vice-versa. On the other hand the reader should be aware that if you receive a stroke on one side of the head, there is nothing to stop you from having another on the other side. The result might be a double hemiplegia which could look like a diplegia or a quadriplegia.

There are several different types of kinetic disorders. Athetosis (adjective athetotic) refers to uncontrolled, slow movements. The head and neck, the shoulders, or the arms and hands may spontaneously move in a continuous fashion. These may be thought of as disinhibited and unregulated slow writhing movements. Another type is chorea (adjective choreic). These are uncontrollable fast movements and can be thought of as disinhibited and unregulated ballistic movements. Fast and slow may combine in what are called choreoathetoid movements.

Cerebral palsy also includes rarer forms of kinetic disorder. The most common of these is ataxia (adjective ataxic). Here the problem is in coordination of ballistic and complex movements. Thus, for example, the subject may walk in a step-by-step fashion and always appear to be in danger of toppling over, or may not be able to smoothly execute any rapid movement. The problem is inadequate cerebellar modulation of complex movement, not the movement itself.

Finally, a variety of tremors may sometimes be seen in cerebral palsy. A tremor is an involuntary rhythmic movement of a body part. The description typically includes whether tremors are intentional or resting tremors, that is, whether they appear only when the subject is attempting an intentional movement or whether they occur only when the body parts involved are at rest. Another feature is whether they are symmetrical or asymmetrical, that is whether they proceed in one direction as much as the other or whether they extend more in one direction or phase than another. It will be recalled that tremor may be viewed as a consequence of excessive delay of negative feedback (chapter 4).

Cerebral palsy is traditionally treated by various forms of physical and occupational therapy, at times supplemented by drugs, surgery (to allow spastic joints to bend), and recently some forms of biofeedback. One classic physical therapy approach to treatment (Bobath & Bobath, 1964; Bobath, 1966) views spasticity as a condition in which tonic reflexes dominate motor control. The symptoms of spasticity often appear in the same divisions of the sides and parts of the body as are found in tonic reflexes. Treatment consists of inhibiting tonic reflexes, for example by placing the patient in a reflex inhibiting posture, so that normal or near-normal, developmentally sequenced, phasic movements and their accompanying sensations can be elicited. (An example of a reflex inhibiting posture would be to place the person with a disinhibited tonic labyrinthine supine reflex which ordinarily would provoke excessive extensor tone into a posture of total flexion.) The approach is called neurodevelopmental treatment. A review of this area of professional activity (Barry, 1996) identifies the limited but definite range of accomplishments of this approach. Part of the difficulty may be that, in many cases, motor neurons and phasic mechanisms are also involved in the production of spasticity (Adams and Victor, 1993). Some improvement is possible in all children but success varies with the magnitude of the damage the child has sustained and the deficits present in functions other than motor. Often relatively little can be accomplished with those who are severely impaired.

An interesting approach to ameliorating the symptoms of spasticity makes use of the botulinum toxin. It will be recalled that the active neurotransmitter at the neuromuscular junction is acetylcholine and the botulinum toxin is a poison which inhibits the release of acetylcholine. In attenuated form, a graded blockage of neurotransmitter release can be accomplished which can relieve the excessive activity of spastic muscles (Russman, Tilton, & Gormley, 1997). This is a treatment which does not deal with brain functions where the pathology resides, but with its peripheral consequences. It is used most frequently to prevent contractures in which, following prolonged spasticity, muscles stiffen and permanently resist stretching, immobilizing joints in maladaptive postures. The treatment requires local injection of the toxin into specific muscles and several may be treated at a time. The effects of each injection persist from three to eight months and then wear off, but can be repeated. The side effects are minimal even though the substance injected is a toxin.

The etiology of cerebral palsy is still obscure in most cases. Early systematic writings implicated perinatal events and birth injuries such as delivery with the rump coming first, or anoxia. To be sure, some cases can be traced to such events but they are in the minority. A relatively high incidence of cerebral palsy is associated with extreme prematurity where there is a susceptibility to hemorrhage in the area around the ventricles. This will be discussed in more detail in chapter 16. The majority of full-term babies who develop cerebral palsy apparently sustained damage a consider-able time before birth. Spasticity is associated with damage to the pyramidal system and kinetic disorders with damage to the basal ganglia (Filloux, 1996). The causes of this damage are unknown but some kind of blockage or insufficiency of blood supply is suspected. Recently an alternate hypothesis has emerged based on two sets of facts. The first is that should one of a pair of identical twins be stillborn, the sur-vivor is likely to develop cerebral palsy. The second is that with modern imaging pro-cedures used to visualize the developing fetus, generally a sonogram, twins may be noted to be present early in the pregnancy only to have one disappear by the time of birth. In this case it is thought that one fetus dies and disappears via some process such as reabsorption. Again the survivor is likely to develop cerebral palsy. Pharoah and Cooke (1997) have suggested that the dead twin is, in some way yet unknown, toxic to its sibling's brain and that this may be the source of the pathological process that leads to the majority of spastic cerebral palsy cases. At this writing the evidence is not in.

Tourette syndrome

This fairly rare and until recently rather obscure condition has become more famil-iar to the public as a result of its depiction in a number of books, television docu-mentaries, and dramas. Unquestionably, the condition challenges many of our assumptions about human behavior, voluntary control, normality, and pathology.

Scenario: A classroom of fifth-graders is going about its usual business. A child is, at the teacher's request, interpreting the meaning of a poem the students have just read when the class as a whole is distracted by a peculiar grunting sound emanating from one part of the room. This sound is repeated a number of times till the teacher identifies its source and asks the child who has made the sound if there is something he wanted to say. He says, "No, thank you" somewhat abruptly and the teacher turns back to the child reciting, when the young man in question moves his left hand with middle finger extended in a gesture that is unmistakably obscene and utters four epithets in succession that are not ordinarily expressed in polite language.

Such behavior would ordinarily be described as immature and childish, or rude and impolite, or aggressive and uncontrolled, or just plain bad, and, in most instances, would elicit some form of reprimand, exclusion from class, or punishment. It would ordinarily not be described as sick behavior or the symptoms of a brain disorder. Nonetheless such behavior may well be a consequence of a disorder of phasic inhi-bition and control called Tourette syndrome. The disorder is named after Gilles de la Tourette, who in 1885 published a case study of a prominent woman, the Mar-quise de Dampierre, who lived a long life beset by such symptoms (Bruun, 1988).

Tourette syndrome is one of a large number of conditions described in the medical literature called dyskinesias, that is, flawed or impaired movements (Fahn & Erenberg, 1988). It has a range of symptoms and there is some controversy about which specific cases qualify and which do not, a situation that is inevitable when the definition of a disorder is based on symptoms. However, there is fair consensus that four classes of symptoms, simple and complex motor activity and simple and complex phonic activity are at the heart of the disorder, and that individuals who have both motor and phonic symptoms clearly qualify for the diagnosis.

"Phonic" symptoms refer to sounds made by the voice and mouth and "motor" refers to overt actions. "Simple" designates a seemingly meaningless, relatively brief act like a grunt or flicker of the eyelids or a jerk of the shoulder. "Complex" designates behavior which in other contexts is seen as having intentional meaning and can include saying words, phrases, and sentences, or engaging in complex activity such as obscene gestures, touching other people in undesirable ways, or frank aggression. In all cases, the behavior has an uncontrollable quality. Such involuntary behavior is often termed a tic.

Tourette syndrome is a disorder that generally begins in childhood, sometimes as early as two years of age but more frequently in the middle childhood years of seven to nine (Bruun, 1988) and may last a lifetime. The specific tics emitted generally change over time but they tend to decrease somewhat with age or may even disappear entirely. Any particular disappearance may only be temporary, however, since the symptoms wax and wane, often appearing to fluctuate with stress of one sort or another. Many individuals come to be able to inhibit their symptoms voluntarily at least for a period of time. Thus many children learn to inhibit their tics while in school and then seek an opportunity to give them free reign in private where they will not suffer social embarrassment. This means that they may be able to suppress their symptoms while being examined by a researcher or clinician.

Tourette may be thought of as a motor disorder due to failure of some mechanism of motor inhibition. It should be noted, however, that many patients report that, preceding the action, they experience an intense urge to perform the act. They "experience an uncomfortable feeling or sensation that is relieved by carrying out the movement (the tic). When tics are suppressed, this sensation continues, and the urge to move increases in intensity. The subsequent movement provides relief and there may even be an increase of tic movements to obtain this relief if the tics have been suppressed for a considerable period of time" (Fahn & Erenberg, 1988, p. 44). This description makes the action voluntary and deliberate but the sensation involuntary. The condition is still abnormal because most people, after all, do not have irresistible urges to grunt or jerk their shoulders or engage in obscene gestures.

The intertwining of sensory and motor functions is characteristic of the way the basal ganglia modulate behavior, and it is these structures that have been implicated as the culprits in the genesis of the pathology. Current descriptions (Singer, 1997; Leckman & Cohen, 1999) emphasize abnormalities in the "motor" circuit between basal ganglia, thalamus, and frontal cortex. Since these circuits are known to contain topographically specific representations of different parts of the body, the potential exists for explaining why specific muscle groups are activated in particular tics. The "limbic" circuit is implicated in regard to the disinhibited emotional expression often found in complex phonic and motor tics.

Individuals with Tourette syndrome are helped by learning ways to avoid shame and explain one's condition to others, and by nonspecific interventions such as understanding and support. Some medications are utilized. Their rationale, generally, is precisely the reverse of that used in Parkinson's disease. It will be recalled that, in Parkinson's disease, decreased overt activity is thought to be related to the depletion of dopamine, hence treatment is aimed to increase this neurotransmitter. Tourette syndrome, by contrast, is a disorder of overactivity, and so drugs which decrease available dopamine are in order. Two such drugs are haloperidol and pimozide. Some years ago, a medication used for the treatment of high blood pressure, clonidine, which also has indirect effects on dopamine, was reported to be helpful (Cohen et al., 1979). More recent reviews (Carpenter et al., 1999) suggest that in some centers it is now the drug tried first in the treatment of Tourette disorder since it appears to aid about 25 percent of patients. This recent review also describes drugs that turn the rationale for treatment described above topsy turvy, but nonetheless are reported to be effective for some patients. Drugs such as pergolide are dopamine agonists, i.e. they increase the activity of dopamine, but nevertheless are found in some cases to be associated with a reduction in tics. Clearly, there is much to be learned about pharmaceutical interventions.

The effects of drug treatment are slow to emerge, drugs often have side effects, and when effective only diminish the intensity of the symptoms. There is consequently considerable controversy as to whether such treatment is really useful. When it does help, clonidine appears to alleviate complex tics rather than simple ones (Leckman, Walkup, & Cohen, 1988) which may be an important clue about both the nature of the disorder and the effects of the medication. That is, complex tics are influenced by a variety of factors, some of which are social in nature. Simple tics more frequently are a direct manifestation of aberrant brain modulation. A drug which aids complex tics more than simple ones may have its major effects on sites different from those that are responsible for involuntary motor jerking.

An alternative or a supplement to medication is intensive behavior modification (King Scahill, Findlly, & Cohen et al., 1999). Currently emphasized treatment procedures for tics include training in self-monitoring, relaxation, and habit reversal. These training techniques teach subjects to be specifically aware of the variety and frequency of their tics, to learn to relax, and yet to engage in behaviors that oppose and inhibit tic expression in a socially inconspicuous way. The treatment may be somewhat arduous and time-consuming and some parts require expert instruction, but Peterson and Azrin (1992) claim considerable success with these methods and none of the side effects that often accompany the use of medications.

Tourette syndrome is rarely found in pure form. Two other major symptom patterns often accompany this condition, attention-deficit–hyperactivity disorder (see chapter 10) and obsessive-compulsive disorder which will be discussed next. Basal ganglia pathology has been implicated in all three disorders.

Obsessive–compulsive disorder

The symptoms of this disorder have been described in most textbooks of abnormal psychology and until recently have been considered to be functional or neurotic disorders, i.e. reactions of a normal nervous system to some aberrant circumstance or condition of child rearing or the environment. Obsessions refer to repeated, uncontrollable thoughts, and compulsions refer to repeated uncontrollable actions. The two are often linked; the action as will be noted is often associated with the thought.

The symptoms themselves are relatively circumscribed and cluster into a number of groups. Rasmussen and Eisen (1991) have described these subtypes as: (a) contamination obsessions, a sense of being dirty, poisoned, or infected which often compulsively requires some form of cleansing, for example repeated hand washing; (b) somatic obsessions, repeated thoughts that the person is ill or becoming ill with some dread disease; (c) sexual and aggressive obsessions, recurrent thoughts that one has committed or will commit unacceptable, often horrible, sexual or aggressive acts; (d) need for symmetry and precision, extraordinary requirements for neatness, orderliness (books must be lined up on the bookshelf by size) and sometimes symmetry (one must walk through a doorway precisely in the center); (e) hoarding, literally an inability to discard possessions; (f) pathologic responsibility or doubt, despite repeated checking never being sure that the alarm is set, the door locked, etc.; and (g) religious obsessions, for example, whether a religious rite was performed as prescribed or whether one has committed one or another type of sin.

These clusters of symptoms often have characteristics of a particular time and place and thus reflect what is learned. Thus, for example, somatic obsessions are likely to focus these days on AIDS rather than on tuberculosis as in the past, and religious obsessions will vary with the community and the particular faith of the individual. Obsessive–compulsive symptoms have near-universal themes that show up across different cultures. This includes concern about health, grooming, and cleanliness; resources to aid survival; and the security of the boundaries of one's territory. The notion is that these basic preoccupations are universal, increase the likelihood of survival, and have come to be represented by action patterns that are programmed into the brain. The disorder is viewed as the release of these adaptive behavior patterns from inhibitory regulation and from feedback. For example, the person locks a door, checks the door knob, and observes that it is secure yet is immediately beset by doubt so the actions must be repeated several times.

That obsessive–compulsive disorder is associated with brain malfunction has been supported by research utilizing imaging techniques. Like any area of research, there have been problems in establishing reliable measurement techniques, but consensus is emerging as to some specific abnormalities (McGuire et al., 1994; Cottraux & Gérard, 1998, Saxena et al., 1998; Leckman & Cohen, 1999). Most studies and reviews find evidence of overactivity in orbitofrontal regions of brain, areas involved in limbic regulation and self-monitoring. The overactivity in the frontal cortex is thought to be related to overactivity found in such modulators as the caudate nucleus, the anterior cingulate gyrus (figure 3.8) and the thalamus. As more comes to be known regarding the complex, multilayered circuitry of the basal ganglia and their connections to the frontal lobes, greater understanding of the details of the disorder emerge and more specific strategies of treatment become possible.

Available treatments for obsessive–compulsive disorder include drugs, behavioral interventions, and in extreme cases neurosurgery. At the time of this writing, drugs that interfere with the transport of serotonin, including the currently popular serotonin reuptake inhibitors, drugs initially developed for the treatment of depression, are the mainstays of pharmacologic intervention (Pigott & Seay, 1998; Carpenter et al., 1999). These medications increase the availability of serotonin at the synapse. Placebo-controlled studies have provided evidence that their administration is associated with 20–40 percent symptom reduction. As in depression, it generally takes one to two months before positive effects take place, suggesting that the helpful action of the drug involves some kind of reorganization of brain circuitry. There are a number of side effects associated with these medications although the newer drugs have less. In severe cases that are nonresponsive to other treatments, relief may be sought by removing part of the anterior cingulate gyrus, one of the areas noted above to be overactive in brain imaging studies. Follow-up of 18 patients (Baer et al., 1995) who had received this treatment found improvement in less than half.

Most reviews now agree that an effective, currently the most effective, form of treatment is a type of behavior therapy called exposure and ritual prevention (ERP). In this procedure, individuals who engage in rituals are persuaded to situate themselves in the vicinity of the cues that elicit those behaviors and remain there without engaging in the behaviors despite feeling very anxious or uncomfortable (Marks, 1997). In learning theory terms, these are the conditions under which extinction takes place, and the extinction of the ritual is the target. These procedures have been studied for over 30 years and have led to increasing refinements based on systematic evidence of efficacy. In recent years, Marks reports that techniques have been developed to teach patients how to engineer their own exposure experiences so that, in effect they become their own therapists. The treatment is without side effects and, when effective, enduring. March and Mulle (1998), among others, have written a detailed manual on how to use these techniques with children.

Imaging studies comparing the brain before and after treatment have found activity reductions in previously overactive areas in those whose behavior has improved (Schwartz, 1998). This was true for both drug and behavior treatments. There perhaps is nothing special about a drug treatment changing brain function in the manner intended, but the evidence regarding the behavioral intervention has provided some of the most convincing evidence to date of the effects of behavior on brain. Schwartz, who has participated in the imaging studies, has also made use of these brain–behavior findings to modify the approach in behavioral treatment (Schwartz, 1996). He has devised a sequence of steps that accompany the ERP extinction procedures which make use of the highest cognitive skills available to the patient to deal with the disruptive and intrusive anxieties emanating from flawed subcortical functions. The four steps are: (a) relabel, in which patients learn about the research findings on brain overactivity and relabel the symptoms as a medical condition rather than a personal flaw; (b) reattribute, in which patients view the symptoms as mistakes and false messages coming from their overactive brains; (c) refocus, in which they learn how to decrease the salience of the symptoms and work around experiences which previously claimed their immediate attention; and (d) revalue, in which symptomatic urges and thoughts are gradually relegated to insignificance. Schwartz calls this a cognitive biobehavioral treatment. When the technique works, changes in attentional deployment become increasingly automatic. However, the technique does not work for everybody, and requires further research.

Dyspraxia

Apraxia was originally described in adults who had lost an ability they previously had as a result of some injury or impairment of brain. They no longer could organize and perform voluntary movements even though the required muscles were intact and functional. Examples of action patterns used to test apraxia in adults include waving goodbye, pantomiming the use of a hammer, blowing a kiss, and writing a letter, folding the paper, putting it in and sealing an envelope, and stamping it. Patients were requested to perform these acts verbally or they were asked to imitate the examiner's performance (visual copying). If feasible, they were observed to see if they could self-initiate such acts under appropriate circumstances. Their impairments varied from total inadequacy, suggesting degradation of stored motor programs, to difficulties in accessing such programs either via verbal instruction or imitation, to problems with organizing an effective sequence from a store of components. Apraxia was also diagnosed if, in performing a task such as pantomiming hammering, the limb and fist were used to represent the hammer itself when, normally, a grasp gesture would be made and it was the observer's task to imagine the shape of a hammer. Adult apraxia was found to be associated with damage to the left hemisphere or to white matter that connects to or from the left hemisphere. In most persons the left parietal lobe was found to be the repository of stored motor programs derived from previous experience, while the left supplementary motor area, among others, appeared to be the site where the enactment of a specific motor plan was organized (Heilman & Gonzalez-Rothi, 1993; Banich, 1997).

This type of apraxia referred to familiar, well-learned skills. But what if the task were novel? Constructional praxis refers to the skills needed to deal with tasks which require the active organization of structures in space for which old solutions are generally not available. Examples include copying and/or remembering complex abstract designs, assembling jigsaw puzzles, or practical challenges such as packing a filled suitcase or storing food in an overcrowded refrigerator. Deficiencies on these tasks are associated with damage to the right hemisphere, occur on a continuum, and tend to be termed dyspraxia (Kolb & Whishaw, 1996; Banich, 1997). A crucial aspect of all these tasks is one's sense of space, a topic which will be further considered in the next chapter.

Praxis is also invoked to describe the development of skilled organized movements in the maturing child. Cermak (1985) points out that there are wide differences in the way adult and developmental praxis impairments have been studied. In children, the issue generally is the acquisition of motor competency rather than its loss, the methods of testing praxis differ, and the pathology is frequently termed dyspraxia rather than apraxia. Conditions termed dyspraxic in children may actually consist of one or more of a variety of specific impairments (see the next section on the clumsy child) but one important finding that recurs is the frequency with which tactile–kinesthetic abilities are impaired when motor functions are inept or clumsy. Tactile refers to the sense of touch and kinesthetic is another term that refers to sensors in the muscles and tendons which provide information about the movement of joints. It is thought that the learning of skilled movement and related developments such as that of the body scheme is hampered because only degraded records of previous actions will be stored and will be available later when needed. It will be harder for a child with tactile–kinesthetic deficits to "know" what the "feel" of a more effective or less effective movement may be like and so it will be harder to learn the more effective movement.

Clumsiness and motor awkwardness

The author, observing a playground many years ago at a school that served children who were deaf and others who had learning impairments, noted the following. The deaf children, who were identified by wearing a special truss-like apparatus that carried large hearing aids and batteries, ran and played with perfectly normal agility while the learning-disabled, without such encumbrances, often appeared tentative, awkward, and clumsy. I was quite naive about these matters at the time, and reacted with surprise because I had assumed that deafness was the more severe handicap and thus was more likely to have other impairments present. What I have learned since is that deafness is likely to be a circumscribed condition while learning disabilities are a group of symptoms with diverse mechanisms of impairment often including motoric clumsiness (Morrison, 1985). These latter symptoms are of concern in this section. Further discussion of deafness and learning disability is found in later chapters.

Motor clumsiness (Gubbay, 1975) is a major component of what has been called "neurological soft signs" and/or "minimal cerebral dysfunction" (Touwen & Prechtl, 1970; Gardner, 1979). These symptoms represent the less severe end of a continuum of disability. Thus, for example, spasticity of the right side of the body that prevents walking is a hard sign while the inability to hop on the right foot would be a soft sign. Just about any of the conditions described in this chapter may appear in attenuated versions producing soft signs. This chapter closes with a description of the way these "soft" symptoms can appear, and thus to some degree provides a summary of its contents.

Children with chronically hypotonic reflexes will show a kind of slow, slouchy, relatively tentative set of action patterns, while those with hypertonic reflexes will show quick movements. Perhaps more dramatic might be the sudden disruption of limb control shown by a six- or seven-year-old with subtle disinhibition of tonic neck reflexes. Such symptoms might be especially difficult to discern because they would appear only when the child was ill or fatigued, for example at the end of a long school day. Such children might try to copy an assignment from the blackboard but would experience loss of control of the writing hand because, as they turned their heads to follow the teacher, the asymmetric tonic neck reflex would be partially disinhibited. Depending on the direction the head was turning, extensor or flexor tone would then dominate control of the limbs.

Children with sluggish righting and equilibrium reflexes will likely be insecure in their movements and have difficulty with the competitive games of childhood, since actions that compromise balance are often involved. Such children are doubly vulnerable to anxiety. On the one hand, their insecurity about balance continuously and directly provokes anxiety. Secondly, their ineptitude leaves them subject to social humiliation and ostracism which may further increase their anxiety. Without special support and training, they may not practice their motor skills and may fall further behind.

Children with mildly disinhibited slow writhing or ballistic movements generally do not show overt signs of such behavior else they would attract clinical attention. If they are asked to stand with their eyes closed and their arms extended in front of them, one of the tests used to uncover such a condition (Fiorentino, 1963), they may show choreoathetoid movements after 20 or 30 seconds. The significance of such findings is that a burden on the child's functioning is revealed. Under ordinary conditions, the child's movements look normal. But if excited, under stress, or attempting to learn some complex maneuver, such disinhibited components are likely to emerge and interfere with efficient action. What will be observable is clumsiness or failure to accomplish what they set out to do, but the culprit will be the disinhibited response.

The child with a subclinical Parkinsonian condition would also be sluggish in initiating movements but then be able to perform reasonably well. It might thus appear that this was a relatively unmotivated child rather than a child with an activation problem. By contrast, the mild Tourette syndrome child may initiate activities very frequently and may be diagnosed as hyperkinetic. This, indeed, may be the actual mechanism of impairment in some forms of hyperactivity.

The child with subclinical ataxia might have all the component movement skills present but be slow or deficient in attaining the smooth integration required at high levels of skill. Such a child may be agonizingly slow in learning to skip, ride a bicycle, or engage in cursive writing. Finally, as in the more severe conditions, the particular limitations found in a specific child are likely to appear not in pure form but in various combinations.

The relatively obscure nature of these kinds of deficits may evade identification and remediation. Children with such clumsiness may readily note their own inadequacy in comparison to their peers, and experience inferiority and poor self-esteem. Because of failure and discouragement, they are likely to withdraw from physical activity and thus not have the experiences out of which a well-defined body image emerges. This in turn further burdens their ability to regulate and deal with anxiety and, it will be recalled, they are likely to have to deal with more anxiety than most children because of vulnerability to imbalance.

This state of affairs is most unfortunate because most conditions of clumsiness can be improved with major benefits to self-confidence and self-esteem. A variety of interventions appear to be beneficial, many of which are generally not considered to be formal treatments. Formal treatment is sometimes called movement therapy and is administered by physical and occupational therapists. It involves diagnosis of the particular limitations of a child and an explicit program of remedial activities in the context of a one-on-one relationship or small group of children. Equally beneficial results, however, may come from training in karate and other movement regimes of oriental origin such as tai chi, swimming, exercise regimes that involve rhythmic movement, trampoline, and folk dance.

In general, these are activities that require the coordination of the two sides of the body, involve much vestibular stimulation, and allow for the slow development of mastery without undue pressure of competition. Enlightened school systems now include programs with such activity in their physical education curricula, so it may not be necessary to enroll in specific outside activity. By contrast, activities with strong performance pressure, such as competitive athletics or ballet lessons, do not appear to be useful in remediating mild motor deficits and should be avoided as an initial mode of intervention. They are optional after progress has occurred in overcoming clumsiness.

12

The Visual System and its Disorders

This chapter and the next concern the two major sensory systems from which information is obtained about the world: vision and audition. Vision is put first because the visual system of humans is not as unique from an evolutionary point of view as the auditory modality. There are many species that have sharper vision than humans and we learn a good deal about human vision by studying them. By contrast, although language capabilities have been discovered in some primate species, its extensive development is exclusively human and it is central to human social behavior and to the complexities of human technology and culture. Language ordinarily capitalizes on special auditory capabilities and that topic will be considered next. An invented language that depends on visual information processing, sign language, will also be considered in the next chapter when deafness is discussed.

The first parts of this chapter examine what there is to be seen and how information is conveyed in light. This is followed by an introduction to the structure and functioning of the visual system, the apparatus that registers that information. Throughout the presentation, selective defects of the system and their impact on behavior are described. In the final sections of the chapter, the nature and consequences of blindness and visual handicap are considered. There will also be some discussion of what vision selectively contributes to cognition.

The Nature of Visual Information in Light

Light

Light is defined by physicists both as a wave of energy of a certain frequency, i.e. a wave whose length is some fraction of a meter, and as a stream of tiny particles called photons (Bruce & Green, 1990). Explanations of this dual definition and associated controversy in physics are beyond the scope of this book. The photon concept is useful in understanding that one or more of those particles striking the visual transducer sets off the physiological processes that lead to visual experiences. The wave concept is useful in understanding the information about color and form conveyed by this process. There will be more about this later.

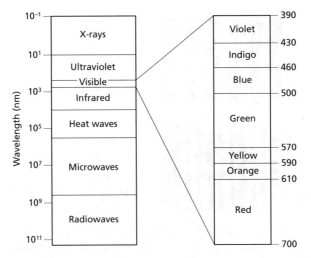

Figure 12.1   Electromagnetic radiations and visible light

Light, as we experience it, is the small visible portion of a range of electromagnetic radiation that extends from minuscule x-rays through radio waves that can be hundreds of meters long. The visible portion of this spectrum ranges from about 390 nanometers (abbreviated nm) to 700 nm. One nm is 10^{-9} meter or 0.000000001 meter. This information is presented in figure 12.1. It can also be seen that particular colors or hues are associated with particular wavelengths of the visible spectrum. When we see white, or colorless light, we are seeing all the frequencies mixed together. When we see a particular color, only a portion of the spectrum is striking the eye in that area. When a rainbow occurs, or when white light is passed through a prism, combined frequencies are sorted out into their components. The reader will note that this "sorting out into their components" is what is accomplished mathematically by a Fourier transform (discussed near the end of chapter 10 when presenting quantitative EEG).

What is visible in light?

A number of different features contained in the light are registered by the visual system. These include shape, color, orientation, position in space, perspective, and movement. Each of these features is a field of study in itself. Here, shape will be singled out for special consideration.

What conveys information about shape or form?

Shape is determined by edges, and visual information signifying an edge is essentially a matter of sharp contrast in the light. Consider a simple example of a square of yellow cloth placed in the middle of a larger square of blue cloth in the middle of a

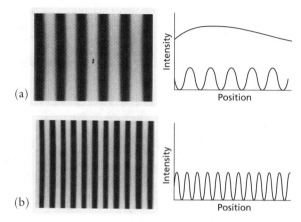

Figure 12.2   Gratings at two frequencies. (taken from T. N. Cornsweet, *Visual Perception*, New York: Academic Press, p. 314). The reader should imagine a gradual transition from the darker to the lighter regions of the grating and back; this applies also to figures 12.3 and 12.4(b).

square wooden table. The boundaries of the blue and yellow cloths are clearly demarcated by the change in color from the woodsy brown of the table, to the blue of the middle cloth, to the yellow of the top. If the yellow cloth were replaced by a blue cloth of the same size and was placed very carefully with no puckered edges casting shadows, then it might be very difficult to discern the shape of the top cloth.

There is a means of measuring and objectively specifying the edges present in the light that are perceived by the visual system. Such measurement rests on the concept of spatial frequency, a somewhat difficult concept to comprehend when first encountered. To do so requires consideration of some facts and ideas in physics and mathematics. As this material is presented, the reader should keep in mind that the goal is to comprehend the physical properties of the information that the visual system will process.

The determinants of shape – spatial frequency.   Imagine a space in which contrast (a change in the light) varies continuously, shifting gradually from darkest black to whitest white. This can be seen in a visual stimulus called a grating, two of which are illustrated in figure 12.2. These gratings change from darkness to lightness and back gradually. The graph to the right of each grating symbolizes the regularity of change, and one can note that the magnitude of intensity goes up and down across space. The gratings differ in how many changes in contrast occur over the same distance. There are two cycles from minimal to maximal and back in the second one for every one in the first. The second grating can be said to be twice the frequency of the first.

Now elaborate these examples in your mind in two ways. Imagine halving the frequency of the first grating in figure 12.2 over and over so that far more space than exists on the page is needed to see even two dark bands on the resulting low frequency grating. Conversely, imagine doubling and redoubling the frequency of the second grating so that the dark areas are packed into a dense high frequency grating.

The next step in the explanation will require you first to look up from your book and examine the walls of the room in which you find yourself, or the structure of

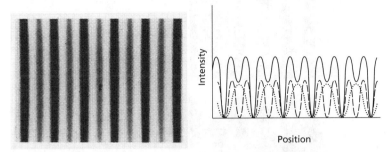

Figure 12.3 Algebraic summation of gratings in figure 12.2 (taken from T. N. Cornsweet, *Visual Perception* (New York: Academic Press, 1970), p. 314).

some nearby building if you are outdoors. If you attend to the corners of the room or the building, you will observe a vertical line of contrast going down from the corner (probably caused mostly by shadows unless the two walls coming together are of different colors). If the room is small enough, or the building far enough away, you may be able to see two corners simultaneously and perceive two parallel vertical lines (and, of course, horizontal lines as well) that provide you with a sense of the overall structure of the room or building. Those lines are far apart and, like the grating that was halved repeatedly, consist mostly of low frequency spatial information.

Next, observe a letter printed at the conclusion of this sentence.   H   The letter H also has two parallel vertical lines. These are close together and, like the grating that was doubled repeatedly, consists of information that does not contain any of the low frequency information such as that found in the example of the walls of a room, but only high frequency spatial information.

The upshot of the explanation so far is that the gross outline of the shapes we observe is conveyed by low spatial frequencies while fine detail is conveyed by high spatial frequencies. There is a problem at this point, however. Both the letter H and the lines created by the intersection of the walls of the room are quite sharp and not at all fuzzy, but the gratings which exemplify and define spatial frequency change gradually and there are no sharp edges.

How can spatial frequency explain the sharp edges which convey information about shape?   Something must be added in order to attain a sharp edge. In order to explain this, some further elaboration of figure 12.2 is necessary. First is the idea that spatial frequencies can be superimposed and combined by summing them algebraically, and that the result may have an appearance quite different from any of the components. This idea was previously presented and illustrated in figure 10.5. Here that figure is repeated in figure 12.3 along with the combination of gratings which it represents, the summation, point for point, of the frequencies in the two gratings of figure 12.2. Because they are being summed, you will note that there are places where figure 12.3 is higher than either of the graphs in figure 12.2.

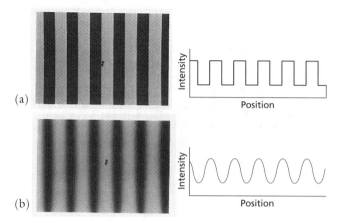

Figure 12.4   Illustration and representation of a square wave and sine wave of the same frequency (taken from T. N. Cornsweet, *Visual Perception* (New York: Academic Press, 1970), p. 313).

The second idea, that regular curves can be described mathematically as sine waves, was also presented in chapter 10 and illustrated in figure 10.3. Review of those materials at this point is a good idea. Imagine now a grating with abrupt contrasts, changing suddenly from darkest black to whitest white. Here there are sharp edges and the waveform is called a square wave. Figure 12.4 presents a square wave grating and a sine wave grating of the same frequency. To the right of each of the gratings is a wave form representing changes of intensity (in this case blackness) across space. The same frequency means that the distance between the center of the black and the center of the white of the square wave is equal to the distance between the peaks and troughs of the sine wave curve. This can be observed in figure 12.5 in the first figure on the right where the graphs are superimposed.

Figure 12.5 illustrates an interesting property of sine waves: how summing non-sharp edge sine waves can produce sharp edges. The first two figures on the left in figure 12.5 repeat the wave forms for a square wave and then a sine wave of equal spatial frequency. Below the sinusoid are the odd multiples (3×, 5×, 7×, 9×, etc.) of the sinusoid. On the right there are illustrations of what happens as these odd multiples are summed with the sine wave. With more and more high-frequency components added, the curve of the summed sine wave comes increasingly to approximate the square wave. The lesson to be learned from the physics of light is that sharp edges do not exist in light which is composed only of sine waves but emerge from superimposing and combining higher frequency with lower frequency sine waves. Extrapolating to brain it can be expected that the brain does register sine waves but not square waves. It creates sharp edges by combining information from both high frequency and low frequency sine waves.

To go back to our example, the lines formed where the walls of a room come together, low frequency spatial information, and the lines of a printed letter H, high frequency spatial information, will both be fuzzy unless they are accompanied by their own superimposed higher spatial frequencies. This may all seem very obscure but

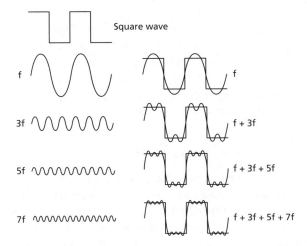

Figure 12.5   Sharp edges emerge as the odd multiples of a sine wave are added to the sine wave

Figure 12.6   An image of a famous person with high-frequency information removed

perhaps an intuitive grasp of what it takes for the light to convey sharp edges and fine detail, namely high frequency spatial information, can be seen in figure 12.6, a representation achieved by removing high frequency information from the illustration. It is an image of a famous figure from American history. One can make out the major features (low frequency information) but much detail (high frequency information) is missing. Comparable blurred images are presented on television when the details of controversial or endangered individuals are obscured by electronically removing high frequency information from the areas of the screen where their faces occur.

Summarizing, the shapes and forms that appear in space can be specified quantitatively by spatial frequency sine waves which gradually change from white to black

with intermediate shades of gray in between. The gross outlines of shape are specified by relatively low spatial frequencies, but the sharp edges and fine detail depend
on high frequency sine waves. Sine waves vary in frequency (recurrent change per
unit of distance), amplitude (intensity), phase (correspondence of starting points in
the cycle: see figure 10.4), and orientation (horizontal, vertical or somewhere in
between). According to the Fourier theorem, complex shapes can be built from sine
waves and also be decomposed into sine waves.

Other information conveyed in light besides shape

Besides the information about sharp edges, there is information in light about color
and brightness, location in space, and movement. The latter subject merits some
special discussion to prepare for what is to come. Recall that in chapter 2 two types
of information were described – spatial and temporal. So far emphasis has been given
to visual spatial information processing. Temporal information processing in the visual
system will be considered next.

Temporally coded information.   Temporal information is conveyed by changes over
time. One example of visual temporal information is semaphore code, the system
used to communicate visually by ships at sea which employs flashing lights in a kind
of visual Morse code. This is a good prototype of visual–temporal information, but
it is certainly not part of everyday experience. Actually, with one very important
exception, visual temporal information is not present much in the everyday world.
The exception is the information conveyed by movement.

We experience movement easily and automatically and generally do not get confused about what is moving in the world and what are our own movements, whether
they be of the eyes, the head, the limbs or the whole body. (See discussion of corollary discharge in chapter 5.) When we move through space, we are aware of our
changing position partly as a result of the changes in what we see. Change in visual
input as an observer moves in space is called optical flow, a concept developed by
Gibson (1966). "Flow" refers to the sense that, as we move forward, the world looks
like it is passing to each side of us. Another type of movement perception is when
we are not moving and an object or an animal does move. For much of the animal
kingdom, this is the only subject matter ever registered by the visual system since
non-moving objects are not seen at all (Kandel et al., 1991). In this kind of movement perception, shape contours successively change position in space over a short
period of time.

The key idea is that movement information requires some processor that is sensitive to high frequency temporal information or rapid changes in time. By contrast,
when events are static and not moving, or moving very slowly, low frequency temporal information is being conveyed. In the visual system, those processors that deal
with high frequency spatial information and low frequency temporal information (like
the print of this book) are separate from those that deal with high frequency temporal information and low frequency spatial information (like a lunging animal).
When scientists want to study spatial information processing they use gratings. When

studying temporal information processing, they utilize flicker, making some stimulus, often a grating, appear and disappear at some rate in time, or making the bars of the grating move across space at some rate.

Measurement of visual functions. In an earlier era of visual research, scientists utilized what intuitively appeared to be very simple stimuli as they studied the workings of the visual system. Such stimuli might be a spot of light or a simple shape such as a bar. In actuality, a spot of light includes all visible frequencies and a bar, which has sharp edges, is composed, as discussed above, of many spatial frequencies (DeValois & DeValois, 1990, pp. 9–11). Since that is the case, truly simple stimuli convey specific spatial and temporal frequencies, and such stimuli, flickering, moving or static gratings, are the stimuli used in modern vision research. These developments have not yet had much influence in clinical neuropsychology.

Anatomy and Functions of the Visual System

The visual system includes the eyes and the pathways to the lateral geniculate nuclei of the thalamus, the superior colliculi, and the occipital cortex at the back of the brain. The system also includes several pathways moving forward from the occipital lobes. These structures, their functions, and some of the things that can go wrong are described next.

The eye

Structures and functions of the eye up to the retina

The basic structure of the eye is familiar to most individuals from high school biology and will be reviewed only briefly here. Figure 12.7 shows the outer, transparent layer of the cornea; the circular muscle band called the iris that opens and closes, admitting more or less light into the eye; and the lens that bends and focusses admitted light onto the retina, the area where the light sensors and early processors are situated. Also of note are the sclera, the white cartilage-like case of the eyeball, the ciliary muscle which by tensing or relaxing restrains or allows the lens to bulge and thus controls its shape; the vitreous humor, the jelly-like liquid which fills the eyeball, and the choroid membrane, the dark membrane immediately behind the retina toward which the sensors point.

The eyes are situated in a bony orbit, within which they have a range of movement. Movement for each eye is controlled by three pairs of extraocular muscles which are illustrated in figure 12.8. The muscles are arranged in such a way that they can move up or down, to the left or right, and diagonally, to some extent like one moves a cursor on an Etch-a-sketch toy. Movements of the two eyes are coordinated and consist of two kinds: conjunctive movements and vergences. In conjunctive movements, the eyes move together in tandem. There are two kinds of conjunctive

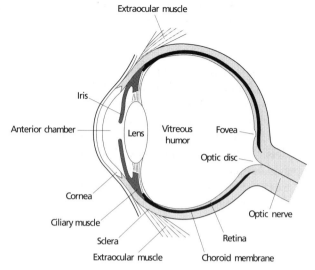

Figure 12.7 The structure of the eye

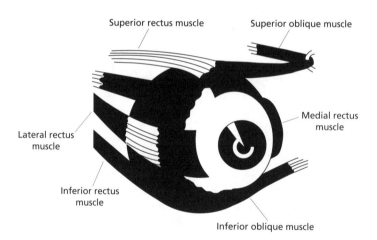

Figure 12.8 Muscles controlling eye movements

movements: slow following and ballistic. Slow following movements occur when your eyes monitor the course of someone walking across a room. Ballistic movements are rapid, the eyes jumping from wherever they happen to be to another point in space, for example, if you were watching an instructor and suddenly a door at the side of the classroom opened, someone entered, and your eyes were drawn to see who it was. A ballistic jump of the eyes is called a saccade; typically saccades are remarkably precise. Vergences occur when the eyes move inwardly toward the nose (convergence) or outwardly toward the ears (divergence) in order to deal with objects that are near or far away. If the eyes are moving inwardly to view something close up, the left eye moves to the right, and the right eye to the left so they are not in tandem. They should, however, move symmetrically, i.e. inward or outward to the same degree.

Much of the time, the visual system is reactive, responding automatically to events going on in the world. At other times, eye movements are deliberately controlled from within, for example, if one is searching for an object or a person. Sometimes, the material being viewed is static but complex. This occurs when reading, looking at pictures, or scanning the horizon. In these instances, the information to be extracted depends on how systematically the eyes scan what there is to be seen. Thus, eye movements are responsive both to events in the environment that elicit attention and to the internal motives and intentions within the person. This distinction was encountered previously in chapter 10 in the presentation of Posner's ideas about covert attention.

Some common pathologies of the parts of the eye (except for the retina)

The cornea helps bend the rays of light entering the eye so that they will focus on the retina. If there are imperfections and unevenness in its surface, a condition called astigmatism, rays of light may be redirected randomly and the resulting image will be blurred. Corrective lenses, especially contact lenses, may alleviate the problem.

The other part of the eye that bends light to permit sharp focus on the retina is the lens. The lens contributes to what are probably the most common visual impairments: nearsightedness (technically called myopia), and farsightedness (technically called hyperopia). In myopia, light from distant objects is focussed in front of the retina, and only nearby objects are seen sharply. In hyperopia, light from nearby objects is focussed behind the retina and only distant objects are seen clearly. Differences in the shape of the eyeball may be responsible for some of these impairments, but the accommodative ability of the lens also plays a role. Accommodation refers to the ciliary muscles' control over the shape of the lens. As the muscle changes tension on the lens, it can become rounder or flatter, thereby changing its focus. As people get older, this accommodative ability decreases and focussing on close objects becomes more difficult. The resulting farsightedness, when it comes with aging, is called presbyopia. Accommodative disorders are treated with corrective lenses. Incidentally, normally focussed vision is called emmetropia.

The other most common pathology of the lens is cataracts. These are cloudy opacities of varying degrees of severity in the lens that prevent the passage of light. Mostly, these develop late in life but they can also occur in the young, even in newborn infants. If the severity warrants, the opaque lens can be removed surgically and be replaced with an artificial lens.

The muscles controlling the position of the eyes produce the most precisely controlled movements in the entire body. Precision and coordination are necessary if each eye is to obtain an image that is similar enough to the other so that the two can be combined into a single image. Unfortunately, some are born with imbalances of muscle control so that the eyes do not operate in tandem and, while resting, do not line up symmetrically. This condition is commonly called "crossed-eyes" and, technically, strabismus. Under these circumstances the brain receives two images (called diplopia) which compete for attention.

Since the brain cannot deal with two disparate views of the world simultaneously, there will initially be some rivalry and alternation between the two images. Over time, images from one eye may win out, and the other will be suppressed permanently. The cells in the brain dealing with the image coming from the suppressed eye will atrophy from disuse. Depending on how long the process goes on, permanently decreased capacity for sharp vision and even blindness may follow. An abnormality stemming from disuse in the visual system is termed an amblyopia. When strabismus occurs, part of the treatment may include patching the good eye, thus forcing the child to use the eye whose image was not being used and thus saving it from complete atrophy. The strabismus itself may be treated with special exercise regimes and/or surgery.

Except when they move as part of the process of perceiving, the eyes appear stable. In truth, if the eyes were truly stable, images would fade and even disappear (Sekuler & Blake, 1994, p. 268). They do not fade because tiny eye movements called minisaccades, which are invisible to ordinary observation, occur normally all the time. On the other hand, spontaneous, visible, tremor-like oscillations are ordinarily not normal and require medical investigation. Such a condition is called nystagmus. Nystagmus, however, can be induced in normal persons by rotating (twirling) them and then stopping abruptly. The resulting involuntary tremor of the eyes is called post-rotatory nystagmus.

Structures and functions of the retina

The retina contains two kinds of transducer cells which react to light. They are named roughly on the basis of their shape: rods (relatively thin) and cones (somewhat more rounded before tapering) (see figure 12.9). Cones are found exclusively in a small area near the center called the fovea, predominantly in an area surrounding the fovea called the macula, and are sparsely represented in the rest of the retina, an area called the periphery. Rods predominate in the periphery, are sparsely present in the macula and do not occur in the fovea (see figure 12.10). Rods and cones face backward in the retina toward the choroid membrane so that light has to penetrate a mass of overlaying cells and axons before reaching the transducers.

There are a number of functional differences between rods and cones. Three different kinds of cones are selectively responsive to particular light frequencies within the visible spectrum and register color. This occurs only when the overall intensity of light is sufficiently bright, a condition called photopic vision. Although nothing can be seen in absolute darkness, there is a considerable range of dim illumination in which forms can be made out although color is absent. Vision in dim light, called scotopic vision, is mediated by the rods. Most everybody has had the experience of going from darkness to light and vice-versa and finding that it took up to a half minute or longer for the eyes to adjust so that one could see. What is happening is that the cells of the retina and the brain are shifting from one type of vision to the

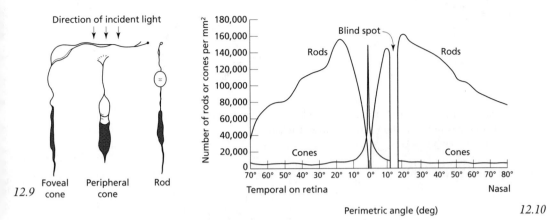

12.9

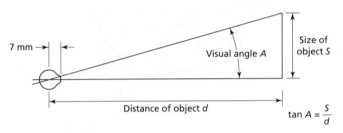

12.10

Figure 12.9 The appearance of rods and cones

Figure 12.10 The distribution of rods and cones in the retina

$$\tan A = \frac{S}{d}$$

Figure 12.11 Calculation of the visual angle

other and the process of dark or light adaptation takes time. Full adaptation (maximal adjustment) to a particular light level may take four or five minutes or even longer.

Visual angle – a measure of retinal image. To understand the organization of the retina and the way in which differing objects stimulate it, there has to be some way of describing relative size. It is obvious that any object takes up a greater proportion of what can be seen as it gets closer and closer to the eye. The image on the retina increases in size although the size of the object of course does not change. The size of the image on the retina is measured by visual angle.

Figure 12.11 contains a description of how the visual angle is calculated. Recall that, by convention, a circle is divided into 360 degrees (symbolized 360°), 360 equal segments around the perimeter, 180 for each half and 90 for each quarter. If lines are drawn from the exact center of a circle to any two places on the perimeter, the line will form an angle, which is measured in degrees, minutes, and seconds. A minute of angle (′) is a degree divided 60 times, and a second of visual angle (″) is a minute divided 60 times more. From high school trigonometry, recall that the tangent of an angle in a right triangle is the ratio of the side opposite to the side adjacent. For all

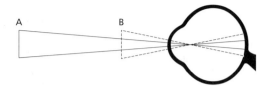

Figure 12.12   The closer the object the larger the visual angle. A and B are the same size but B stimulates more of the retina because it is closer

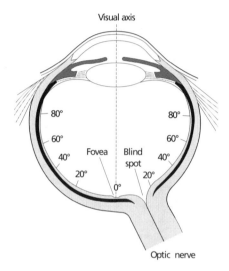

Figure 12.13   The range of visible angles, and the location of fovea and blind spot in the left eye

practical purposes, the 7 mm inside the eyeball can be ignored when evaluating the visual angle of an object several feet or meters away. It then follows that the ratio of the height of the object divided by the distance of the object from the eye is equal to the tangent of the angle. Knowing the tangent, the size of the angle can be looked up in a trigonometry table. Figure 12.12 is an illustration of how the nearer of two objects of the same size creates a larger visual angle. Some idea of relative size may be obtained with the following examples. A quarter at arms length (70 cm) produces a visual angle of 2°, the same quarter at 90 yards, 1′ and at 3 miles, 1″. A lower case pica type letter at 40 cm, which is normal reading distance, produces a visual angle of 13′ (Cornsweet, 1970, p. 445).

The fovea, which contains only cones, covers only 1° of visual angle, the surrounding macula only about 5°. The fovea, which is generally the target of central vision, thus covers only a very small percentage of what is visible. This is illustrated in figure 12.13 which shows the central axis of vision of the left eye, the range of angles extending on either side, and the presence of a blind spot, which is where the axons from the cells of the retina form the optic nerve.

Functions and pathology of rods and cones.   Rods and cones are susceptible to different pathologies. Since there are three different kinds of color-sensitive cones, one or more can be nonfunctional, producing different kinds of color blindness without changing scotopic vision. Cones can be destroyed selectively by some pathologic processes leaving only peripheral vision. In these cases, nothing is ever sharply seen. On the other hand, rods can also be destroyed selectively and this will lead to a kind of tunnel vision.

Normally, one must focus as sharply as possible in the fovea if one wishes to perceive fine detail. However, this strategy is not maximal if, for example, one is trying to insert a key into a lock in the dark since the cones are nonfunctional under scotopic conditions. A better strategy then is to try to look out of the corner of the eye to get whatever information is available under those conditions. But what of the children, often with pathologic conditions such as autism or mental retardation, who may stare fixedly out of the corner of the eye in photopic conditions? It seems plausible to raise the question of some type of pathology in foveal, cone-mediated, vision.

Visual fields – the definition of visual space.   Imagine a vertical line going right through the center of the fovea, macula, and periphery dividing each retina into two parts. The part on the side nearest the nose is called the nasal retina. The other part, that nearest the temples (the part of the head just in front of the ears), is called the temporal retina. Note in figure 12.13 that the blind spot is in the nasal retina.

The way the different parts of the outside world impinge on the eye is illustrated in figure 12.14. The diagram presumes the eyes are looking at something straight ahead, at the middle letter R in the word ARROW. The line connecting the center of the face and that letter divides what can be seen into a left and right visual field, abbreviated LVF and RVF. Light moves in straight lines and must pass through the narrow opening of the iris to penetrate to the retina. As a consequence, light coming from the LVF will reach the nasal retina of the left eye and the temporal retina of the right eye. Light coming from the RVF will reach the temporal retina of the left eye and the nasal retina of the right eye. This means that each visual field is represented in each eye, and that it is not true that the left eye deals with the LVF and the right eye with the RVF. Each reader should study the illustration and verify these relationships between what is "out there" and where the retina is stimulated when it is looking straight ahead.

Light on the retina – initiating images.   The structure of the retina, is illustrated schematically in figure 12.15. The starting point is to imagine rods and cones packed tightly together in the retina. Figure 12.10 informs us, for example, that over 140,000 cones occur per square millimeter in the fovea. As a first approximation, these transducer cells might be thought of as a grid of pixel sensors. A pixel on a television screen is the smallest unit that can emit some kind of light. If you look closely at a photograph printed in a newspaper you will come to perceive that the image is made up of tiny dots, also called pixels, which collectively form the shapes being illustrated. Now consider the light coming from an object when it gets to the

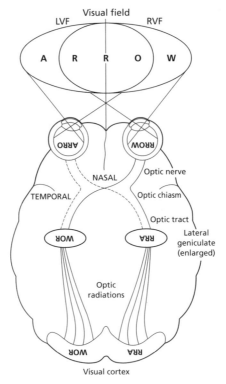

Figure 12.14 The right (RVF) and left (LVF) visual fields, the area stimulated on the retina, and projection to the lateral geniculate and the occipital cortex

retina, for example, a pencil in the middle of a piece of white paper. Some cells, depending on their spatial position in the retina, are going to be stimulated by the whiteness of the paper and some by the color of the pencil. A group of cells situated in a straight line register the light coming from the pencil, and the surrounding cells register the white. It is a useful oversimplification to imagine that each retinal cell might register and be responsible for one of the pixels that will make up the image of what is seen.

Visual sensation begins as some portion of the light falls on and stimulates particular transducer cells and other parts stimulate different cells. The spatial organization out in the world is represented, in some sense, in patterns of reaction in the mosaic of cells in the retina. One might think that a two-dimensional image of what is out there is registered on the retina but there is only limited truth in this idea. We do not "see" in the eye but in the brain, and much elaborate processing is necessary before the rich, colorful array of three-dimensional objects in spatial perspective is apparent to us. The process begins in the retina.

Retinal processing. As seen in figure 12.15, no transducer, rod or cone, projects back directly to brain. There are roughly at least three levels of cells and at least two

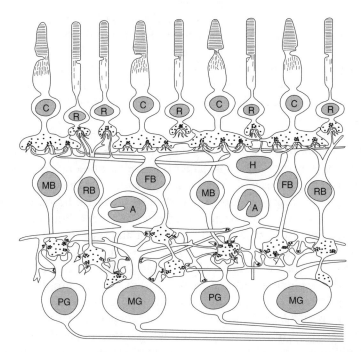

Figure 12.15 Schematic view of the structure of the retina. Notice roughly three layers: transducers, cones (C), and rods (R); collector cells, types of bipolar cells (MB, midget; RB, rod; and FB, flat), amacrine cells (A) and horizontal cells (H); parvocellular ganglion cells (PG) and magnocellular ganglion cells (MG)

sets of synaptic connections. The transducer cells, the first layer, synapse with collector cells which include the bipolar, horizontal, and amacrine cells, and these in turn synapse with ganglion cells. It is the axons of the ganglion cells that make up the optic nerve. Thus there is a good deal of processing (synaptic activity) in the retina.

Some sense of the nature of this processing can be obtained by understanding the different ways in which the layers of retinal cells are interconnected. Some populations of transducer cells appear to be broadly interconnected both within layers and between layers so that many transducer cells might ultimately synapse with a particular ganglion cell. With such an arrangement, any changes taking place anywhere among those cells will lead to a reaction from that particular population of cells.

Sharp distinctions of what is happening within the field being stimulated will not occur since information from many sources is being pooled via their interconnections and thus cannot be differentiated. That group of cells will, however, be very sensitive to anything stimulating any component part. This is the organization that is common for cells in the periphery. Other cell populations are interconnected such that only one or two transducer cells synapse with a ganglion cell. This is an organization that makes possible sharp discriminations between changes in the light. Under these conditions, some cells will be registering the color of the pencil, in our example, and some will be registering the whiteness of the surround (Bruce & Green, 1990, p. 38). This is the organization that is common in the macula and fovea.

It thus appears that there are at least two ways in which visual information is processed in the retina. One is very sensitive about the occurrence of events but not very good about the details, the other provides detailed information. A closer look at figure 12.15 shows that some of the ganglion cells are quite large relative to others. This characteristic provides one of the bases for labels applied to channels, separate streams of information and separate types of processing that arise in the retina and extend to cortex (Regan, 1982). The larger cells are part of a magnocellular channel while the smaller cells are part of a parvocellular channel. It is a general rule of neural tissue that larger cells respond more rapidly then smaller cells. Beyond this difference in speed of response, much has been learned in recent years about other differences between the channels so that they constitute what amounts to two visual systems.

Magno and parvo (as they are often abbreviated) cells respond in different ways to stimulation. Neurons in magnocellular channels show increased rates of firing (respond) at the beginning and end of stimulation while neurons in parvocellular channels show increased rates of firing over the course of stimulation. Magnocellular neurons are particularly responsive to low frequency spatial information (gross outlines) and are relatively nonreactive to high frequency spatial information (fine detail). In addition, they are very reactive to high frequency temporal information (moving objects) and are relatively insensitive to low frequency temporal information (static objects). Parvocellular channels show reverse sensitivities. Since the channels are separate yet must work together in order to see, they must be coordinated in some way. One aspect of this coordination is that activity in the faster magno channel will inhibit activity in the parvo channel. Processing of detail stops when things move.

The upshot of this arrangement is that the parvo channel is responsive to relatively static fine detail such as is found in print or in the details of a face, while the magno channel is reactive to movement and change. Magno's capacity to inhibit parvo activity has probably facilitated survival. Information about change and movement in the environment is given priority by the nervous system so that, for example, the moving image of a stalking animal supersedes an analysis of its beauty.

In earlier work, mostly on the visual system of the cat, comparable distinctions were made with a somewhat different terminology. These terms are still used in some areas of research which will be considered later in this book. Magnocellular systems were termed transient channels and parvocellular systems sustained channels. Although there is some question as to their exact correspondence in the research literature, the terms will be treated as synonyms here.

Neural pathways from retina to cortex.   Large groups of axons leave each eye in a bundle called the optic nerve. At a conspicuous place visible on the underside of the brain, called the optic chiasm (see figure 3.9), some of the axons split off and project to (go to) the other side. The fibers which have synapsed with transducers in both nasal retinas will cross over in the optic chiasm to the opposite hemisphere whereas those from the temporal retinas will remain on the same side. Thus, the nasal retinas project contralaterally; the temporal retinas, ipsilaterally. The upshot of this arrangement is that information from the LVF is transmitted to the right hemisphere and information from the RVF is transmitted to the left. This is illustrated in figure 12.14.

The fibers containing parvo and magno channels proceed through the optic chiasm and end up in a segregated and orderly way in a portion of the thalamus (recall from chapter 3 a centrally located nucleus that serves as a relay station between the senses and the cortex) called the lateral geniculate nucleus (see figure 12.14 and see also figure 3.13). However, only about 20 percent of the cells in the lateral geniculate are relay cells (Lehmkuhle, 1993). They convey the information to the primary visual areas of the occipital cortex at the back of the brain via pathways called the optic radiations. The presence in the geniculate of many cells other than relay cells suggests that much processing is going on there. Many of these details are known but are beyond the scope of this presentation. Of interest here, however, is that the spatial topography of the image is preserved and that some of the input to the geniculate is from the occipital cortex, thus indicating the presence of feedback loops and system control operations (not unlike the thermostat described in chapter 5).

One other pathway from the retina.   Beyond the optic chiasm, something less than 20 percent of the fibers coming from the retina branch off to an area of midbrain called the superior colliculus (Sekuler & Blake, 1994, p. 105). The superior colliculus is located in the roof (tectum) of the midbrain and its location is depicted in figure 3.8.

The superior colliculus is a phylogenetically "old" area that serves in fish and amphibians as the major visual processor. (Note: the adjacent inferior colliculus is involved in audition.) In humans, it is known that information about location in space needed for initiating and directing voluntary eye movements is processed there as well as in other areas including cortical regions. From chapter 10 it will be recalled that this was the area involved in the "move" function in Posner's analysis of covert attention (Posner & Raichle, 1994, p. 50). It is therefore evident that the superior colliculus is importantly involved when attentional focus is changed from one part of the visual field to another, whether or not the eyes also move.

Pathology in neural pathways.   Given the fairly complex connections and long distance from eye to occipital cortex, things can go wrong (tumors, strokes, infections) at varying points along the way. Since there is point-for-point representation of what is being seen, disruption of specific segments may lead to differing scotomas (blind spots).

Figure 12.16 illustrates the varying field defects (another term for scotomas) that can ensue from disruptions in specific places. Except for total blindness as seen in the cuts labelled A and G, the terminology describing the visual symptoms is in Latin. The places marked B, C, and D produce hemianopias, blindness in half the visual field. In C and D the scotoma is in the same half of the visual field in each eye, a

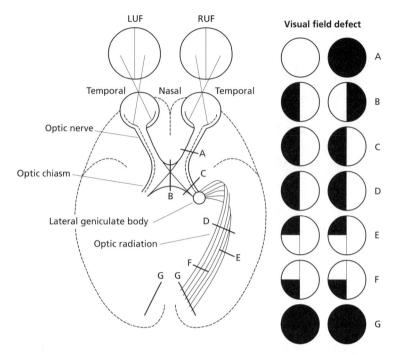

Figure 12.16 The field defects (scotomas) that result from lesions in particular portions of the visual pathway

condition called a homonymous hemianopia. This means that, given a right hemisphere lesion, the person looking straight ahead would not see anything on the left side of space. If the impairment were on the other side of the brain, then there would be no vision in the right side of space. When the chiasm is cut, as in the area marked B, the right eye cannot see to the right and the left cannot see to the left, a condition called a bitemporal hemianopia. Notice that, in this condition, the nasal pathways that cross over are disrupted. For the right eye, this means that information in the right side of space is lost and in the left eye, the left side of space is lost.

Continuing the examination of figure 12.16, it can be noted that homonymous quarters of the visual field can also be blinded. If the lower portions of the optic radiations which pass through the temporal lobes are disrupted, then the upper quarter of the opposite visual field is blinded (E), and if the upper portions which pass through the parietal lobes are affected, then the lower quarter of the opposite visual field is blinded (F). On the diagram, the label G is marked to indicate disruption in both hemispheres, a condition that will produce total blindness. This type of blindness would be called cortical blindness to differentiate it from impairments in the eye or the optic nerve (marked A).

Very often, scotomas, even substantial ones like the hemianopias, may go unnoticed by the person who has them, and they are documented only on formal examination. This is possible because gaps in visual continuity can be filled in by compensatory eye and head movements.

Information processing in occipital cortex

The optic radiations end in the occipital lobe synapsing with cells in what is called the primary visual area. This area is also called Area 17, the striate cortex, and more recently Area V1. The primary visual cortex is situated most toward the back of the brain, and, as processing progresses to secondary and tertiary levels, areas situated further forward in the brain are involved. The complexities of what transpires would take volumes to describe and only some highlights will be reviewed here.

To begin, it can be noted that there is considerable amplification of central vision in going from retinal transducer to cortex. About 25 percent of the cells of the striate cortex are devoted to processing the information transmitted from the central 2.5° of visual angle (DeValois & DeValois, 1990, p. 95) and 80 percent of the cortical cells deal with the central 10° of visual angle (Drasdo, as cited in Sekuler and Blake, 1994, p. 117). Following the distinctions noted earlier, this means that much of cortical processing is the processing of parvocellular channels which remain segregated from (though connected with) magnocellular channels. Recall that parvocellular channels remain closely linked to particular transducer cells in the retina which have reacted to a narrow segment of the visual field. It has also been discovered that particular cells react to events in their visual field in very selective ways during cortical processing. These discoveries were the work of many scientists including Hubel and Weisel, who won the Nobel prize for their contributions in 1981 (Hubel, 1988).

Early discoveries – visual feature analyzers

Understanding the early stages of information processing in the cortex is facilitated by having some idea of how such knowledge was obtained. Hubel and Weisel and others made use of techniques developed earlier for recording activity in single cells in the brain. This requires a technology that can make electrodes small enough to penetrate a single cell, electronic recording techniques that can pick up minuscule voltages, and prior knowledge indicating when the electrode was reporting activity inside or outside the cell. In the beginning, such work was done with animals, mostly cats. They were immobilized in such a way that neither the body, head, nor eyes could move, yet the animal was awake and could see straight ahead. In this way, the researchers could be specific about what was visible to the subject. Then stimuli would be introduced to specific places in the visual field and the researchers would observe whether there was a response in a particular cell and what that response might be. Recall that all a cell can do is raise or lower its rate of firing.

Using this method, it was discovered that specific cells were responsive to events going on only in specific parts of the visual field. Such data supported the idea that the topographic relationships found in the retina and in the lateral geniculate are preserved in the early stages of cortical processing. As the mapping of these areas progressed, the researchers had a pretty good idea of where to look for responsive cells, but during the early stages, the process was much like looking for a needle in a haystack.

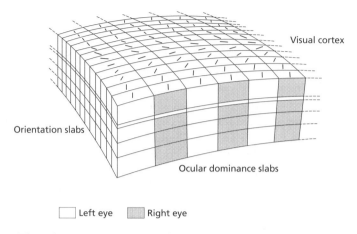

Left eye   Right eye

Figure 12.17   The columnar organization of the visual cortex

In Hubel and Weisel's pioneering work, they discovered that there were cortical cells that were most responsive when there were sharp changes in the light such as are produced by borders or edges, the determiners of shape. Given the presence of an edge in the visual field, they found that particular cells were most responsive to edges of a specific orientation while other nearby cells were just as selectively responsive to edges in another orientation. In further work, cells were found which were selective for other features that are present in vision such as color, direction of movement, and overall size (Sekuler & Blake, 1994). This gave rise to the general notion that, by having cells that were selectively responsive to particular features of the visual environment, the brain decomposed the complexity of the overall array into its components. Later research has revealed that the striate cortex has a very patterned organization in columns of cells which are perpendicular to the surface and which extend through all the layers of the cortex.

The cells in a particular column all respond to only a very specific orientation of the stimuli impinging on the retina, and are adjacent to and clustered with other columns of cells with regularly changing orientations such that all possible orientations (180°) are covered. A grouping of columns preferentially sensitive to a great many visual features impinging on a particular point on the retina of one eye is called a hypercolumn. Adjacent to each hypercolumn is another which deals preferentially with information from a comparable point in space impinging on the other eye. Thus hypercolumns alternate from the left and right eyes and a pair registering the same point in space may be called a visual module (see figure 12.17).

Thinking through what we already know, one or a few cones in the temporal macula of the right eye and one or a few cones in the nasal retina of the left eye, each responsive to a point in the left visual field not far from midline, will preferentially stimulate adjacent hypercolumns in right striate cortex. The adjacent right and left hypercolumns are part of the mechanism for binocular vision, the fact that we normally see with two eyes, each of which has a slightly different view. There will be more about binocularity shortly.

Slabs of columnar striate cortex map all areas of the retina with many more hyper-columns for the macula than for the larger periphery. Although much still remains to be learned about how these components are reassembled to produce the unified and complex imagery we experience normally, awareness of separate receptors for specific features helps account for a number of visual pathologies such as color blindness.

In discussing processing at the level of the retina, mention was made that specific features of visual experience were processed in specific channels. Up to some level in the occipital lobe, the cells responsive to specific features are linked synaptically with cells going back to the retina in highly segregated circuits. Further progress in under-standing the nature of feature detection in the visual system came with research that made use of gratings and took into account the magnocellular–parvocellular distinc-tion. These developments, which made possible research in humans as well as animals, are described next.

More recent developments in understanding occipital processing

Once it became known that the visual system does not see images, but constructs images from detectable features such as spatial and temporal frequencies, the question was raised as to how to measure the functioning of the different feature detectors. With regard to spatial and temporal frequencies, one major measuring technique, now used intensively for more than 30 years in visual research and coming into increasing clinical use, is the contrast sensitivity function. A description of the procedure and some of the data supporting its validity are described next.

Contrast sensitivity function (CSF).   Return to figure 12.2 which illustrates gratings of different spatial frequency. Recall that when spatial frequency is low, the regions where the dark and light are most extreme are spread apart, while when frequency is high, they are close together. Spatial frequency can be measured by the number of cycles per degree of visual angle. In human vision, low spatial frequencies range from about 0.1 of a cycle per degree to about 1 cycle per degree. Middle range spatial frequencies are roughly between 1 and 10 cycles per degree while the higher frequencies range from 10 to approximately 50–60 cycles per degree.

The visibility of a grating will also be affected by how dark and how light the grating gets. This is represented by the height and depth of the waveform and is termed contrast. The most highly contrasting gratings go from blackest black to whitest white. Contrast can be measured, for example, with a light-sensitive photo-cell that evaluates how much light comes from the lightest and darkest parts of the grating. A calculation is made, subtracting the measure of light from the darkest part from that from the lightest part yielding a difference. This number is then divided by the total, the sum of the measures coming from the lightest and darkest parts. Thus, contrast is a measure of percent difference.

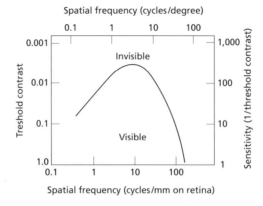

Figure 12.18   A normal adult contrast sensitivity function (CSF)

Now suppose you wished to determine whether a particular grating was visible, that is whether you could see its darker and lighter parts as opposed to some uniform shade of gray. It seems intuitively reasonable that the higher the contrast the more visible the grating. With suitable electronic equipment, the maximal intensity of the whites and blacks of the grating could be changed. Actually, such equipment is not unfamiliar to most people since television sets have a control that does just that – the one labelled "contrast." For a grating, turning the contrast up means that the blacks become blacker and the whites become whiter. Turning the contrast down means the whites and blacks both move toward the grays. If the contrast of gratings were turned down continuously, there would come a point at which stripes could not be seen and it would all look uniformly gray even though some contrast was still physically present. The amount of contrast just before everything looks uniformly gray is termed the detection threshold. That threshold is a measure of how sensitive the visual system is to contrast at that particular frequency.

The contrast sensitivity function displays contrast thresholds for a range of frequencies. The plot of threshold versus frequency for a normal human adult can be seen in figure 12.18. Look closely at this plot. The abscissa is labelled "Spatial frequency (cycles per degree)." Degree refers to visual angle. Note that the distance on the graph between 0.1 and 1 degree is equal to that between 1 and 10 degrees which in turn is equal to that between 10 and 100 degrees. This is a logarithmic scale, a way of compressing a very wide range into a compact space. This type of scale is commonly used in research on sensory systems.

The ordinate is labelled "threshold contrast" on the left and "sensitivity (1/threshold contrast)" on the right. These are two different ways of looking at the same data. Going from bottom to top, the numbers get smaller on the left which means that contrast gets less and less, whereas the numbers get larger on the right which means that sensitivity gets greater and greater. The ability to detect small contrasts is the equivalent of high sensitivity. The numbers on the left convey how sensitive the visual system can be. Suppose that the grating has 50 percent contrast which for example

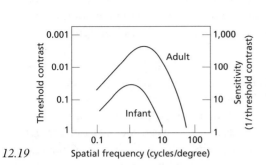

12.19

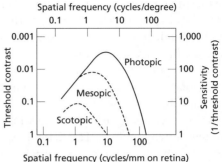

12.20

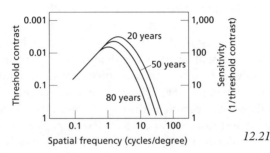

12.21

Figure 12.19   CSFs for adult and infant
Figure 12.20   Adult CSFs under three light conditions
Figure 12.21   Adult CSFs at different ages

would occur if the lightest portion had a light meter rating of 0.75 and the darkest 0.25. That would be read at 0.5 on the left and 2 ($1/0.5 = 2$) on the right. You can see, however, that at some frequencies, the visual system is sensitive to contrasts less than 0.01. This means that at those frequencies, a difference in contrasts between 0.505 and 0.495 or less can be detected. The curved line inside the graph demarks what is detectable by the visual system. Above the line, the eye cannot detect contrast; below, it can.

Now consider the meaning of the two curves in figure 12.19. Examine the curve for the adult. Note that there is a peak of sensitivity around 4–6 cycles per degree and that sensitivity falls off on either side. Now consider the curve for the infant. Note that it is similar to that of the adult but that peak sensitivity is at a lower frequency, and that sensitivity falls off more sharply in the higher frequencies. This implies that if you tried to teach an infant to read letters of the size of this text (recall that such stimuli are conveyed by high frequencies), you would fail for many reasons, including their not being able to see the letters.

Next examine figure 12.20. This presents contrast sensitivity functions for normal adult vision under three conditions of illumination: photopic (with adequate light; identical to the curves presented in figure 12.18), mesopic (at twilight), and scotopic (in darkness). It can be seen that peak sensitivity moves to lower frequencies and higher frequencies are cut off altogether. You can infer from these curves what you already know: it is difficult, at best, to read in dim light and impossible in the dark even though you may be able to make out large shapes. Finally look at figure 12.21. and see how age affects the CSF.

At this point it may appear that contrast sensitivity is much like acuity which most every one has had measured by reading a chart of letters or symbols of declining size at some distance. The most commonly used index of acuity, the familiar Snellen chart (named after the Dutch physician who devised the measure), yields a measure consisting of two numbers. The first refers to the distance between the eyes and a target stimulus. By convention, testing takes place with the subject 20 feet (or 6 meters) from the stimulus, so this term is 20 (or 6). The second number refers to a letter whose size at 20 feet subtends a visual angle of 5 minutes. Long ago Snellen found letters of this size to be discriminable by healthy young adults with no visual complaints. If subjects can see and identify such a letter, they are said to have 20/20 vision, which is considered normal. If they can only identify letters subtending larger visual angles at 20 feet, visual acuity is less than normal. The Snellen chart provides a series of increasingly large letters for inspection which are numbered in increasing increments to 200. Individuals with 20/200 visual acuity must be only 2 feet away in order to identify what a person with normal vision can identify at 20 feet. Put another way, that person can read at 20 feet what a person with normal vision can read at 200 feet (Sekuler & Blake, 1994, pp. 92–3). Acuity is measured in bright light and is a measure of how small a letter or other symbol on the chart can be seen. Small letters are essentially conveyed by high frequency information so sensitivity to the highest frequencies measured by the CSF and Snellen acuity are equivalent. The advantage of the CSF is that it measures functioning throughout the range of spatial frequencies. This proves to be important for a number of visual functions.

What is the relationship between the CSF and channel theory? Recall that animal research had given rise to the idea that particular channels in the visual system convey particular features inherent in visual information. Blakemore and Campbell (1969) conducted an illustrative experiment which was one of many which provides answers to the question posed in this section. They made use of the phenomenon of adaptation. This is a characteristic of the visual system in which persistent stimulation of any aspect of the visual field over a period of time – whether a particular location, color, orientation or shape – temporarily decreases the system's sensitivity to that feature. They asked subjects to look persistently at a grating of a particular spatial frequency and then determined contrast sensitivity for that and other frequencies. The CSF for subjects adapted to two different frequencies can be seen in figure 12.22. You will note the deflections from the regular pattern of the CSF seen in figure 12.18. Similar deflections can be seen in pathological conditions, for example certain strokes of the occipital lobe or disorders such as multiple sclerosis, a disorder in which the myelin covering the axons deteriorates and often involves the optic nerves. Such visual defects were not measurable until the CSF came into use.

Such findings provide evidence which suggests that the CSF is the overall outcome of a system of channels, each of which is tuned to a particular frequency. Tuning

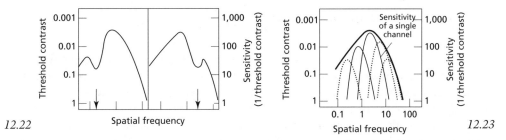

12.22   12.23

Figure 12.22 Changes in CSF resulting from adaptation at two frequencies
Figure 12.23 Hypothetical generation of the CSF from channels sensitive to narrow frequency bands

means that the cells in the channel are most responsive to a particular spatial frequency even though they also respond to a lesser degree to adjacent frequencies. Together, channels covering the range of visible frequencies generate the CSF. This is illustrated in figure 12.23. Magnocellular channel function is measured at the left side of the graph; parvocelluar, at the right. The actual number of channels that exist to deal with the range of spatial frequencies visible to humans is somewhat controversial with estimates ranging from five to ten. Although space does not permit a consideration of this issue here, there was a similar controversy about the channels for color vision, and it is now accepted that there are three color channels within the parvo system.

Recall that the channels sensitive to high spatial frequencies, the parvo, are also insensitive to high temporal frequencies. On the other hand, magno channels are sensitive to high temporal frequencies. Temporal frequencies can be studied by causing gratings to flicker. Flicker is a term used to describe fluctuations of a visual stimulus in time. The simplest change in a grating is to vary the blacks and whites over time. For simplicity, imagine a grating that contained just one dark and one light bar. A computer program could be arranged which transformed the dark part to light and the light part to dark at some rate, say 1 Hz (a reminder, 1/sec), and then repeated this on a continuing basis. Now imagine gratings of differing spatial frequencies and flickerings at faster and slower rates. For any particular spatial frequency, one could study contrast sensitivity thresholds to a range of flicker rates. When this is done, what is found normally is that contrast sensitivity at high spatial frequencies is not influenced by flicker rates but that fast flicker rates do flatten the drop-off in contrast sensitivity at low spatial frequencies.

Over all, the CSF provides an extremely valuable set of measures that can reflect the integrity of many important details of the operation of the visual system. Although this technique has been used in research for several decades, it has not had widespread use clinically as yet, and it has not been discussed in most books or manuals on neuropsychology or education. This is likely to change in view of important findings regarding visual dysfunctions in reading and other behaviors which will be discussed in a later chapter on learning disabilities.

Binocularity and its measurement

Earlier it was noted that information from comparable points in space impinging on each eye will stimulate adjacent hypercolumns in the cortex. This is part of the mechanism for binocularity, that we ordinarily see one image with two eyes that are set slightly apart. Binocularity and the disparity between the two eyes provides information about depth and contributes to seeing a three-dimensional rather than a flat world. This topic is treated extensively in most books about visual perception. Meriting consideration here are some of the consequences which follow when the two images do not fuse.

First, consider what happens when the eyes focus on a point in space. The total pattern of information received by each eye will be near identical at and near the point of fixation but there will be discrepancies elsewhere. Where you focus will determine what you see. If you select a small object or a mark three or four meters distant, say, on a wall a few steps away, and hold a finger up in the direction of the target, you will notice that when you focus on the target you will see two fingers and if you converge your eyes and focus on the fingers, you will see two targets. Yet ordinarily we do not notice such doublings, or as they are termed, diplopias.

The reason for this is that the brain fuses the two images in some manner. Part of what determines the way this is accomplished results from competition between the two eyes, called binocular rivalry. This can be clearly illustrated with an instrument known as a stereoscope, a device which holds two different visual stimuli and presents one to each eye. If the stimuli are, for example, photographs of the same scene but from slightly different perspectives, such as is seen by each eye, then the viewer will obtain a vivid impression of depth. If the scenes are entirely different, then the two images cannot be fused and instead what will be seen will be portions of one view as well as portions of the other. The images will not be stable but will shift from moment to moment (Sekuler & Blake, 1994, pp. 228–9). This shifting is the basis for the term rivalry, since it appears that the eyes, under these circumstances, compete, and sometimes one wins out, partially or entirely, and sometimes the other.

It was previously noted that, if eye muscles are not coordinated properly, the two eyes will not be able to focus in tandem and hence will continuously present discrepant, unfusible images to the brain. As mentioned, strabismus will lead to amblyopia in one of the eyes because the brain cannot tolerate continuing unresolved rivalry. It might be noted that some children with severe strabismus do avoid amblyopia because they find a way to observe with one eye closed, and favor a different eye on different occasions. Thus images from each eye are processed by the brain at some time and atrophy does not occur. Under these conditions, however, depth perception will suffer.

Even when the brain is presented with two similar views, as the eyes normally do, the fusion that does occur does not partake equally from each view. This can be illustrated by again looking at the target on the wall, but this time, quickly, but carefully, line up your index finger so that it is pointing toward the target. Now close one eye and then the other and note whether the image moves. Most individuals will note

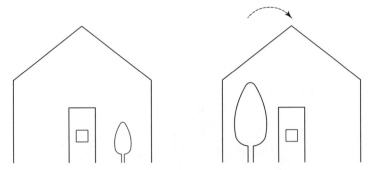

Figure 12.24 Example of stimuli used in the Dunlap test. When the stimuli diverge to where fusion breaks, one of the trees is observed to move toward the door

that, when shifting from binocular to monocular vision, the scene will not move when one eye is closed but shifts noticeably when the other is closed. The eye open when the scene does not shift is the sighting dominant eye (Coren, Porac, & Ward, 1979, p. 267). Thus it appears that one of the eyes is "more equal than the other" and that the fusion that occurs is not the fusion of equals.

Stein (1993) has used a procedure developed by Dunlap (cited in Stein, 1993) to study this type of eye dominance. The procedure involves an instrument called a synoptophore, a stereoscope with a device that enables one to diverge or converge the stimuli presented to each eye. If the stimuli have many correspondences, as is true of ordinary binocular vision, then the two images are fusible. If a fused image is increasingly diverged, there comes a point at which the two images separate. Stein makes use of stimuli such as those in figure 12.24. When viewed in a synoptophore with the stimuli fused, the sketch of the house with one door and two trees, one tall, one small, will be perceived. The tall tree will be registered by the right eye and the small tree by the left. As the images are diverged, there will come a point at which the fused image will break into the two contributing images. Just before this happens, one of the two trees will be seen to move while the other is stable. The subject reports which one moves. As the reader may infer, the eye actually observing the stable stimulus is the dominant eye on that trial.

If the Dunlap test is repeated say ten times, most adult subjects will report the same tree to move on each occasion. Such data are interpreted to mean that the individual has stable binocular control. Young children do not have such stable control but this develops over time. Stein (1993) reports that, by the age of five or six, only 52 percent have achieved stable binocular control; by age 11 the figure is 90 percent.

Further processing beyond the occipital lobe

Klüver and Bucy (1939) described a group of behavior changes that occurred in animals following bilateral removal of the anterior portion of the temporal lobes. Comparable symptoms have also been found in humans and the condition has been

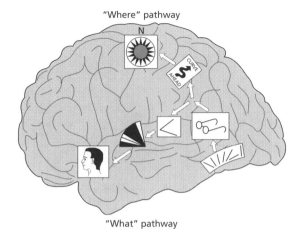

Figure 12.25 Schematic view of the temporal lobe (what?) route and the parietal lobe (where?) route of visual information processing

termed the Klüver–Bucy syndrome. Briefly, the syndrome involves changes of appetite and emotionality (indiscriminate eating, increased docility, and indiscriminate sexuality) and of visual behavior. The change in visual behavior involves the loss of the meaning and significance of what is seen. Thus Klüver and Bucy's animals would pick up and mouth objects that they previously would have rejected. The sight of a familiar nonfood or distasteful object no longer had the same significance once the temporal lobes were gone. For present purposes, the importance of the Klüver–Bucy syndrome is that it drew attention to advanced visual processes taking place in the temporal lobes. Much has been learned about these processes in the intervening years and some of this information will be summarized next.

Two visual systems

Recall our old friends, the parvo and magno channels. In calling them channels, emphasis was placed on their separate integrity. Nevertheless, these channels and their targets in the lateral geniculate and cortex are adjacent to each other and often intertwined. Once the processing in the occipital lobe has occurred, however, a rather large separation takes place. Parvocellular channels progress forward in the brain in what might be called a southerly route via dorsolateral and inferior temporal pathways while magnocellular channels progress forward in a northerly route via medial temporal, then superior temporal and medial superior temporal, and finally, the posterior parietal cortex (figure 12.25). The parvo-southerly route processes information about color and shape, answering the question "what?," while the magno-northerly route processes information about the location in space of objects, answering the question "where?" (Lehmkuhle, 1993; Mishkin, Ungerleider, &

Macko, 1983). It is inferred, though the details are largely unknown, that the northern and southern routes recombine in the anterior temporal, frontal, and limbic systems to make possible full visual experiences. The knowledge available about the differing pathways has made possible a better understanding of a number of very puzzling clinical conditions. Some of these will be considered next.

Impairments of the magnocellular, parietal (northerly) route. With lesions of the parietal lobe, recognition and discrimination of objects may occur, but localization in space may not. An animal may not be able to learn a spatial discrimination which involves, for example, learning whether a reward can be found on the left or the right arm of a maze. In humans with lesions of the parietal lobe, a condition known as neglect is often found. This is a deficit of attention to one side of space. Neglect, a term derived from clinical observations, refers to more than just the visual modality. The reader is referred to Heilman, Watson, and Valenstein (1993), to which the following material is indebted, for a comprehensive review.

Since each hemisphere responds to information in contralateral space, one might expect that parietal lesions disrupting magno pathways in either hemisphere would produce deficits in awareness and localization of information in contralateral space. This is not the case. The majority of obvious symptoms of neglect is to the left side of space and is associated with right hemisphere lesions.

The explanation of this condition involves several steps. First, normally each hemisphere is responsible for maintaining awareness on the opposite side of space. The two hemispheres are in balance so that there is an equal tendency to attend to each side. Second, when an impairment weakens one side, the balance shifts and the intact side dominates the impaired side. This means that if the left side is intact and the right impaired, the person will have a strong tendency to look toward the right because the weaker right side cannot successfully oppose the left's tendency to attend to the right. Generalizing, it is apparent that if there is a consistent tendency to turn to one side, the side to which one turns is the one that contains the impairment. This principle is applicable if the source of weakness is subtractive in nature. However, if there is an irritative condition such as a seizure focus that increases excitability, the opposite pattern of reaction may occur.

Third, the two hemispheres are ordinarily (the many exceptions are beyond the scope of this discussion) not equivalent with regard to their ability to monitor space. The left hemisphere monitors the right side of space while the right hemisphere is capable of monitoring both sides of space. This makes the right hemisphere rather special in comparison to the left with regard to the processing of spatial information, and has led to its being termed as "dominant" for spatial information. (In the next chapter, the left hemisphere will be described as "dominant" for verbal information.) Thus, left-sided lesions may not lead to obvious signs of neglect because the bilateral capability of the right hemisphere will compensate for any deficiency on the left side of the brain. By contrast, the left hemisphere cannot compensate for gross deficiencies on the right, so the left side of space is the most likely to be subject to neglect. Finally, relatively subtle impairments may elude the dominance principle and subtle signs of neglect may appear on the right. This may occur if, for example, subjects are asked to bisect lines; individuals who show no obvious signs of right neglect may mark the midline much to the left of where it actually is.

What is meant by mild versus severe neglect can be made more vivid by means of real examples. For severe neglect, consider that a patient may notice the food only on one side of the plate and disregard the rest until someone rotates the dish so that the neglected food is moved into the non-neglected visual field. Bisiach and Luzzatti (1978) had Milanese patients with right hemisphere lesions describe from memory the familiar buildings on the main plaza of Milan from two perspectives, standing at one side of the plaza and then on the opposite side. The patients in each instance neglected the left side of space although their performance summed over both perspectives clearly indicated that they were quite familiar with the entire square.

By contrast, relatively mild neglect may be the explanation when a child gets scraped and bruised on one side of the body and not the other. If such a bias is consistently present, it strongly suggests inattention. Voeller and Heilman (1988) have suggested that this type of neglect and right hemisphere impairments may underlie certain types of attention deficit disorder. This view adds yet another mechanism of impairment as a cause of attention dysfunction.

Impairments of the parvocellular, inferior temporal (southerly) route.   There is a condition called blindsight (a contradiction in terms) which occurs in some individuals who have been blinded as a result of cortical damage (Weiskrantz et al., 1974; Weiskrantz, 1986). These individuals cannot see in the sense that they report not being able to see and cannot identify objects visually. Nonetheless, if instructed to identify and locate pictures that will be flashed at the top, bottom, right, or left of a screen and to guess if not sure, they perform far above chance in locating the object even though they do not have a clue as to what it was (Riddoch, 1917; Weiskrantz, Warrington & Saunders, 1974). Clearly, what is happening here is a dissociation. The magnocellular, northerly pathways dealing with information about "where" are still intact, while the parvocellular southerly pathways conveying "what" information are impaired or destroyed (Cowey & Stoerig, 1991).

The same distinction was demonstrated in an experiment on normal subjects, by Graves and Jones (1992). Imagine that you are observing a blank round surface like a clock and that you are told that a small dot (high spatial frequency information) might appear during a short, specified, interval at any one of six positions, either 1, 3, 5, 7, 9, or 11 o'clock. You are to report whether you see the stimulus and where. If the stimulus is not seen, you are to guess where the stimulus might have been. The stimulus is presented some of the time so that it can readily be seen, but at other times it is presented so fast that it is not visible. Of course normal subjects do very well when the stimulus is presented at durations that are visible. When the duration is so brief that it is not visible, guessing as to its location can be quite accurate. The same disassociation described for blindsight is thus evident in normals.

Much like the term "blindsight" is a verbal contradiction, the idea that one can see and yet not be able to make out shapes seems equally contradictory. Nonetheless, patients have been observed who can detect light, depth, and movement and identify colors who nonetheless have great difficulty recognizing, matching, copying,

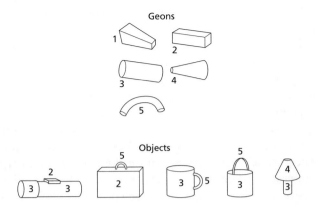

Figure 12.26   Some geon shapes and the way they can be combined to form objects

or discriminating simple visual forms. Impairments in identifying (knowing) what is being seen are called agnosias. Again, the topic of this clinically observed symptom is very complex and the present introductory discussion will be confined to its simpler elements. For a detailed review see Bauer (1993), to which this presentation is indebted.

In one type of agnosia, subjects have particular difficulty in recognizing the identity of the same object when seen from different perspectives. These types of symptoms have been grouped together as apperceptive visual agnosia, the term "apperceptive" referring to missing features of perception (shape) that permit discrimination and identification. Some remarkable work by Biederman (1987) and colleagues on normal object perception has provided potentially powerful theoretical and empirical tools to analyze apperceptive agnosia. Beginning with the observation that objects are easily identified and discriminated with great speed despite many transformations of perspective, he has proposed that there may exist a major intermediate step between the Fourier analysis of the spatial frequencies producing edges and the integrated perception of objects we all commonly experience. This intermediate step makes use of a hypothetical (at present) feature detector mechanism that extracts elementary components of three-dimensional shapes. Biederman terms these elementary components geons and they are illustrated in figure 12.26 along with illustrations of how geons are combined to produce the array of objects we can perceive in the real world. The theory postulates that: (1) there are a finite number of such features, perhaps two dozen or so; (2) there are a finite number of potential relations between geons, e.g. above, below, next to, etc.; and (3) separate neuronal networks, one for the shape and one for the relationship, combine to specify the shapes that we see (Biederman & Cooper, 1991a). Biederman and Cooper (1991b) have provided evidence that these capabilities are present in both hemispheres. Verification of the geon hypothesis would imply that the locus of damage that produces apperceptive agnosia is also the neuronal circuitry that makes possible geons. An updated review of research on object recognition can be found in Biederman (1995).

The geon hypothesis in the visual system parallels an older idea found in the study of language; namely, that language is composed of a finite number of elementary units, called phonemes, that can be combined in many ways to produce words. This will be considered further in the next chapter.

Another type of agnosia is prosopagnosia, where a face can be recognized as a face and the sex of the face can often be discriminated but visual identification of familiar faces, those of family members, friends, and even oneself is gone. This is not a global defect in memory or in verbalization, since persons can be readily identified on the basis of the sound of their voices or features detected by senses other than vision. There has been considerable interest in this highly specialized type of defect because the data suggest that faces have a special status (see Kolb & Whishaw, 1996, p. 260 for a discussion of this issue and Bruce & Humphreys, 1994, for a review). Closer examination of prosopagnosics has revealed other difficulties such as farmers not recognizing their cows, or lifelong bird-watchers losing their ability to identify specific species. Such deficits would suggest that we frequently use our ordinary perceptual skills recurrently in areas of special interest and that near everybody develops special interest in the faces of friends and family. This once again verifies the social–familial nature of our species, but it makes the neurology of face perception not very special.

Putting it back together: the composition of the visual world.   The exposition so far has taken the rich brew of our visual experience and decomposed it, separating it into major pathways dealing with "what" and "where" information, and further broken down the process such that just about every aspect of visual experience including shape, color, orientation, and movement, has separate cells mediating that specific component of the informational array. If such is the process, there must be some place where it comes together so that we can identify what we see. How and where does this occur? The answer to that question is that we do not really know, although there is a variety of information that provides strong clues.

One source of such information comes from another type of agnosia which is termed visual associative agnosia (Bauer, 1993). One characteristic of this disorder is that there is difficulty integrating the different components of what is seen and a failure of holistic perception. Recall that sharp foveal vision is only one degree of visual angle and that macular vision is only five degrees. Unless complex objects are seen at a considerable distance, the perception of the whole requires the integration of several views of the parts of the object and of its context. Thus, the view of a house constructed in a particular architectural style requires the integration of the component parts, the shape of the door and entryway, the presence of pillars, the number and shapes of the windows, the number of floors, the kind of roof, etc. When a house is seen, these separate features are generally brought together into an integrated image of that particular house. Persons with difficulties integrating components into a whole may be limited to a feature-by-feature view of the house and never sense its overall organization. If they tried to draw the house, they might portray first one feature then another, rather than provide an overall outline first and then fill in the details as most people would.

Biederman et al. (1997) provided evidence that object recognition, which requires the integration of geons and allows identification through a wide range of spatial perspectives, is intact in patients who have had much of the anterior portion of a temporal lobe removed. These data imply that this aspect of the answer to the what? question and to the construction of unified imagery is accomplished in the occipital lobes or at the very back of the temporal lobe.

In other types of visual association agnosia, visual stimuli can be copied or matched so that the analysis of shapes, including their holistic aspects, is preserved. Nonetheless, there may be difficulty identifying pictures and objects, and the behavior with regard to objects will take place in a manner reminiscent of animals with the Klüver–Bucy syndrome. Objects will be "seen" but their meaning, class, or significance will not be known (Bauer, 1993). Such conditions are associated with lesions which extend into the most anterior structures of the temporal and frontal lobes and the limbic system.

Summarizing, information in the light is decomposed by the brain into its components as it goes from retina to occipital cortex. There a process of construction begins as the information moves forward to the temporal, frontal, and limbic lobes where shape, color, movement, and location are imbued with significance derived from memory and emotion. These events are taking place in near simultaneity, most certainly in less than 0.1 of a second. It is highly unlikely that there is a single neurological locus where the image comes together in an integrated whole. Rather it appears that vision, as we experience it, emerges from the operation of networks of widely separated subsystems of neurons that extend over much of the brain. There is thus evidence of mass action (see chapter 5) and of modular local function as well. If vision is constructed, it would imply that an adult, seeing for the first time, would have to learn how to see. There are such cases and this implication has been verifed (Senden, cited in Hebb, 1949).

The Development of Visual Capability

The human child is not born with a fully mature visual system. Different components attain adult levels of function at different rates. This means that what is visible to the child will be different from what is visible to the adult. Boothe, Dobson, and Teller (1985) provided a comprehensive review of research findings on visual development which will be the source of the information presented in this section unless otherwise referenced.

Accommodation

Accommodative changes refer to alterations in the shape of the lens that allow the eyes to focus clearly on objects near or far. The newborn is reported to have a relatively fixed accommodation at about 19 cm, approximately $7\frac{1}{2}$ in. By three to four months of age, accommodation appears to be at least roughly appropriate to target distance.

Pupil size

Newborns, like adults, react to light by constricting their pupils, but the magnitude of the change is smaller and the overall size of the pupil opening remains smaller. The smaller the size of the aperture, the greater the depth of field; that is, the greater the range at which focus is sharp. Thus infants may experience less blur than adults and may need to accommodate less. If accommodation is at about 19 cm and depth of field is high, then the physical properties of the system are such that a nursing infant with eyes open will have the mother's face appear in sharp focus. The regularity of this visual experience may be such that the first object the child comes to recognize is the mother's face (or other primary caretaker if they hold the child while feeding), an experience that should facilitate early social bonding.

Eye movements

Newborns can respond to targets appearing in the visual field with ballistic saccades. They are not very accurate in attaining the target but appear to get there with a series of approximations. Initially, there are no slow following movements, just a series of catch-up ballistic saccades. Gradually, after about six to eight weeks, slow following movements become interspersed with ballistic movements. Initially, slow following movements will stop at the midline and the child will lose the target as it moves into the opposite visual field. By about six months of age, the arrest in following at midline becomes momentary and following continues to the other side with only what has been called a "midline hitch." This temporary disruption in smooth following does not disappear until the child is six or seven years old, sometimes later.

The explanation for the onset and disappearance of the midline hitch should be apparent to readers if they recall that responsibility for the control of perception of one side of space is in the opposite hemisphere. If one gets to midline and moves toward the other side, the brain must shift control from one hemisphere to the other. Smooth transfer of control from one hemisphere to the other takes a long time to develop.

If a newborn were to fixate on nearby objects, limited vergence capability would generate a double image but the newborn apparently does not react to such experiences. Vergences that enable the fusion of separated images in the two eyes are generally present by about four months of age.

Developmental changes in anatomy and physiology

Studies of changes at the level of neuron, synapse, and myelin reveal that considerable development takes place after birth. Some examples include: (a) changes in the length and density of the cones in the macula which do not reach adult status until about age four; (b) development of parvocellular cells in the lateral geniculate nucleus which reach adult size by the end of the first year; magnocellular development which takes twice as long; (c) large increases in myelination of the optic nerve during the first two years which continues thereafter at a slower rate; and (d) a pattern of increasing synaptic density in cortical areas occurring over the first eight months followed by a gradual decrease in the number of synapses to the adult level which is approximately 60 percent of the eight-month peak and which is not achieved until about the 11th year. The upshot of these and many more changes is that the immature system is greatly influenced by the nature of the visual experience obtained. Evidence about this comes from a number of areas of research and will be discussed next.

The role of experience in organizing visual functions (use it or lose it!)

In the early 1970s a series of scientific papers appeared which dramatically demonstrated the role of experience in actualizing the behavioral potentialities of the brain. Perhaps a fairer formulation is the converse; that without adequate stimulation, neural mechanisms may atrophy and constrain or limit behavioral capability. Perhaps one of the most compelling demonstrations came from Hirsch and Spinelli (1971), who controlled the visual experience of kittens in a special way. They were kept entirely in the dark except for two four-hour periods each day when they were fitted with a special mask containing lenses and stimuli on which the lenses were focussed. One eye always focussed on vertical lines and the other on horizontal lines. When the animals were between 10 and 12 weeks of age, the receptive fields in the optical columns of the cortex were studied with techniques similar to those used by Hubel and Weisel. They found that the experience had altered the responsivity of the orientation cells such that they no longer responded to the orientation which had not been stimulated.

Similarly, Blakemore and Cooper (1970) exposed kittens from two weeks to five months of age to a binocular visual environment consisting either of vertical or horizontal stripes. They found that animals not exposed to stimuli of a particular orientation lost the ability to respond to that orientation while they continued to respond normally to the stimuli with the orientation to which they had been exposed.

These experiments on animals involved a radical change of the visual environment. Their implications for human development may not be important since human babies are not usually subject to such distorted or selective stimulation. However, Freeman, Mitchell, and Millodot (1972), hypothesizing that stimulation is required to activate neural potentials, studied humans born with astigmatism. Astigmatic defects of the cornea have the effect of presenting distortions to the retina which make it impossible to resolve high spatial frequencies in different parts of the visual field. Since the defects in the cornea are permanent, the same areas of the retina, and hence the same cortical cells, suffer continuing distortion. The authors studied adult subjects whose astigmatism was later corrected optically so that they now might be thought to be free of distortion. They found, however, that the distortion was permanent. Since the stimulation of the retina with appropriate corrections was no longer distorted, there was evidence that the defect lay in the responsiveness of cortical cells. The years of distorted stimulation had led to a permanent decrease in acuity.

This work illustrates a principle of broad significance. The mechanisms in the brain that analyze the environment perceptually require exercise and practice as much as the muscles do in order to become skillful and strong. Early experience is crucial for initially organizing such potential and avoiding atrophy. Later experience will help determine the degree to which the behavioral potentials inherent in the tissue will be realized.

Some General Considerations about Visual Contributions to Cognitive Function

Before concluding this chapter with a section on blindness and its consequences, the particular contribution of vision to mental function will be considered. There are some cognitive theorists who take the position that information is information, and that the modality through which the information enters the nervous system is a relatively trivial issue. There may be some sense in which this is true, but the neuropsychological evidence suggests that modality is important, and that specific sensory modalities are particularly adept at dealing with specific kinds of information (Freides, 1974). What can be stated about vision is that it is adept at integrating information and that, in turn, this makes it a superb processor of spatial information.

First consider the notion of vision as an integrator. If several light sources each conveying a different color (recall, each is a different frequency) of the rainbow were made to converge through a small opening, and a person viewed the light as it emerged on the other side, what would be seen is a single color, most likely white or colorless light. By contrast, if several different piano keys are depressed at once, thereby producing tones at different frequencies, the ear will perceive each tone and the overall sensation will be that of a chord, a multiplicity of frequencies.

Next consider these facts about two-stimulus fusion, a procedure in which two brief stimuli are presented in succession with differing interstimulus intervals (ISIs), the time gap between the two stimuli. As the ISI is shortened, there comes a point that is so brief that the two stimuli, though still separated by a gap, can no longer be perceived as distinct and are experienced as one. That time-value can be called a two- stimulus threshold duration. The particular details of any procedure will influence the results but, as a rule of thumb, the auditory two-stimulus threshold is approximately 1–2 milliseconds (msec) while the visual two-stimulus threshold is 40–50 msec, 20–50 times longer. What this implies is that the auditory system is capable of differentiating stimuli at very brief intervals while the visual system integrates information at those intervals and does not differentiate them until they are much more widely separated in time. From this perspective, vision is relatively inefficient in processing the details of successive events.

What this makes possible, however, is the integration of diverse information from many points in space into some sort of unitary whole. Das, Kirby, and Jarman (1979) suggested that this feature of the visual system is central to an entire mode or type of information processing which they termed simultaneous processing, which contrasts with another type called successive processing. The former encompass skills that make use of imagery (not necessarily visual) and reflect relatively instantaneous understandings and conceptualizations about events and experiences. The terms intuitive and holistic are often used to describe such information processing. Successive processing is more deliberate and logical and requires a step-by-step sequence. The terms "logical" and "analytic" are often applied descriptively.

Both simultaneous and successive processing capabilities are present in most individuals and are utilized as demanded by circumstances. Thus, one does not ordinarily have the time to analyze a stranger's body posture, gestures, facial expression, and voice intonation in order to devise a strategy of interaction with that person. Rather one forms a quick impression (simultaneous processing) in a social situation and maintains it until further information is available. Later, one might mull over an interaction, weighing positive and negative experiences, sorting out the deceptive from the genuine (successive processing).

Individuals differ in their skills and preferences in utilizing these modes of information processing. There are some who for whatever reason prefer to rely on one mode of processing predominantly even though they may be capable of both. There are others who emphasize only one of these types of information processing because of a deficiency in the other. This may constitute quite a handicap. You have grasped much of the nature of these kinds of processing if you understand the following statement. Deficits in simultaneous processing are more likely to influence social skills while deficits in successive processing are more likely to interfere with academic skills.

As mentioned, among the simultaneous processing capabilities, spatial skills are of great importance. Kolb and Whishaw (1996, p. 439) point out that there are three different psychological subspaces, each of which may have a distinct neural representation. First there is body space, which largely depends on somatosensory information and the body image. This enables you to differentiate places on your body and to know where stimulation is occurring. Second, there is grasping space, that envelope surrounding the individual that is reachable by movement of the limbs. Finally, there is distal space, which is the space beyond one's reach. Although body space is largely based on somatosensory information, it can, in some respects, be enhanced by vision. Grasping space is largely visual-motor, a combination of somatosensory information derived from the acting limb and the visual information derived from looking at the action. Finally, knowledge of distal space is largely dependent on vision. To be sure, one can obtain distal spatial cues through hearing and from olfaction but these sources are relatively impoverished and slow in comparison to vision.

There are a number of talents built on these sensory and perceptual foundations that enable people to locate themselves in space. They can differentiate what is to the left and right, front and back, in egocentric space (space where the self is the reference point) and in allocentric space (space with objective external coordinates such as are found on maps). Spatial skills are needed for the comprehension of geometry, for judging distances in driving a car, for reading maps, and for developing subjective maps of where things are, for arranging items in a drawer, or for the construction of any kind of object. Spatial skills are also involved in generating images. Images may be spatial types of memory, reconstructing information previously observed, such as a friend's face, or may be novel constructions, something not previously experienced such as a new design for clothing or a building or any object. Individuals vary considerably in the ease and frequency with which they employ images.

Vision and imagery and spatial skills should not be equated, nor are they synonymous, though they do overlap. Imagery can be nonvisual, auditory, olfactory, or somatosensory, and spatial information does not have to be visual (you can close your eyes and know whether sounds are coming from the left or the right). Nonetheless, vision appears to be the most adept, efficient, and dominant spatial processor. Dominance, for example, can be observed if one watches a film whose audio output comes from a projector in the back of the room. The sound will be localized not at its actual source but at the screen, and visual spatial perception thus dominates auditory localization (Freides, 1974). When challenged with spatial issues, most individuals utilize visual processes, if they can, to deal with that information. When weakness in spatial processing is evident, deficits in the visual system are generally also present.

Blindness and Adjustment to Blindness

The nature of blindness

Most people would define the term "blindness" as meaning that you cannot see. Nonetheless, now that some of the complexities of the visual system have been presented, it should be apparent that blindness may be due to disruptions of the visual circuitry in many places, and that the functional outcome will depend on just where the disruption occurs. That there can be partial types of blindness, scotomas, has already been discussed. Not previously mentioned are disorders that produce severe impairments either only in central or in peripheral vision. In the former case, the person will be unable to see anything small sharply; in the latter case the person will have sharp "tunnel vision" but not be able to sense what is going on peripherally. In addition there are many individuals who cannot see any forms sharply but who do register differing degrees of light and thus may have some means of detecting looming objects. Finally, it is not known what proportion of individuals who report having no visual experience do have blindsight.

In order to study blindness, some definition is required. One commonly accepted measure of functional blindness combines two criteria: (a) vision that can be corrected in even one eye to no more than 20/200; and (b) a visual field that subtends an angle no greater than 20° (Jan, Freeman, & Scott, 1977). In most studies, subject selection may be further qualified on the basis of history, report of residual visual function, or other criteria. One type of residual function that is sometimes retained within the definition of blindness is light perception, the ability to distinguish shades of gray and nothing else.

Some persons are born blind, in which case they may never perceive color or form of any kind. For others, blindness can occur adventitiously, as a result of some pathological process or injury that occurs after birth. The age of subjects at the time they lose their vision, and its integrity prior to complete loss, will influence the manner in which the individual adjusts to blindness. One condition that for a time induced blindness in a large number of infants was retrolental fibroplasia. This occurred when premature babies were provided extra oxygen to make it easier for them to breathe, and it then emerged that too much oxygen destroyed the cells of the visual system. A child who was blinded under these circumstances would have had very little visual experience and development would be largely equivalent to that of the congenitally blind. On the other hand, a child blinded at age seven by trauma or disease would have already obtained much visual experience.

Problems of rearing the blind

It belabors the obvious to state that vision is an important sensory system and that its absence produces an enormous deficit. It is perhaps a little less trite to point out that blindness prevents children from becoming aware of the people and objects in their environment unless they can be reached by touch or make noise. Blind individuals are at a major disadvantage when it comes to examining the environment at a distance. Ordinarily, children learn about the world and themselves by acting on the affordances of objects they perceive. Affordance, a term coined by Gibson (1966), refers to information conveying the possibilities of action (like a small round object can be kicked or thrown, containers can be filled and emptied of their contents by pouring), and blindness cuts off this most available source of information about what might be done. As capacities for mobility develop, obstacles are not readily perceived and harm to self and objects may occur. Consequently, blind children are often hesitant and anxious and restrict their behavior, turning away from exploring the world. For example, after learning to stand independently and then walk, most children are observed to practice their newfound mobility eagerly. Blind children, on the other hand, often cling to familiar objects and are reluctant to move independently (Kasten, Spaulding, & Scharf, 1980).

Beginning in the second year of life and increasingly thereafter as language develops, communication via the auditory–verbal channel gradually allows the introduction of information about the unreachable, distant world that can compensate to a considerable extent for the absence of vision. Before that, the child is informationally impoverished and needs extra care and sensitive exposure to stimulation. Striking a balance between the extra protection the child requires, providing adequate stimulation, and fostering independent activity is the challenge posed to caretakers (Warren, 1994, p. 61).

Advice by experts on the rearing of blind children (Cratty, 1971; Fraiberg, 1977; Jan, Freeman, & Scott, 1977; Kasten, Spaulding, & Scharf, 1980) uniformly emphasizes the dangers both of overprotection and of understimulation. In chapter 9 there was a description of anaclitic depression found in normal children reared in institutions which provided good physical care but little in the way of stimulation. Blind children are deprived of visual stimulation and their environment may overprotectively limit their mobility and access to other stimulation. One consequence of such circumstances is that they may experience far less movement and associated vestibular stimulation than the sighted child. Thus even though there may be no impairment of the vestibular system, its function in integrating the self in its environment (see chapter 5) may lag significantly behind what would occur in normal development.

Limited vestibular and other types of stimulation appear to be the most plausible explanation for the observation that blind children frequently display "mannerisms" and "stereotyped behaviors" not unlike children with anaclitic depression or, as will be presented in a later chapter, those with autism. These behaviors include rocking, hand flapping, self-injurious behavior such as biting and head banging, and other stereotyped movements. There is also a class of movements fairly unique to the blind which involve pressing on the eyeballs and nearby bone structures to the point that the eye sockets can become abnormally depressed or sunken (Jan, Freeman, & Scott, 1977). Collectively, such behaviors are sometimes termed blindisms.

Spatial perception and cognition in the blind

Given that vision is the most adept spatial processor, the question arises as to what kinds of imagery and what kinds of spatial analysis occur in the blind. There is a large and diverse literature on this subject and only a few highlights will be reviewed here. It should be kept in mind that blind individuals are not uniform in the repertoire of their other cognitive skills. They will vary in general intelligence, hearing, somatosensory skills, and conceptual abilities and these skills in varying degrees will influence the quality of their cognitive functions.

Obstacle avoidance

Most people, at one time or another, have observed blind individuals walking while using a cane. In addition to such obvious functions as aiding in the detection of curbs, mud-puddles, buildings, fences, and the like, the cane also functions as a noise maker as the bearer taps with it repeatedly. Perhaps more rarely, a blind person may be observed to ambulate freely without the aid of a cane, yet not bump into either other pedestrians or stationary obstacles. What accounts for this capability? As suggested above, some of these skills may be attributable to residual visual function. Many legally blind individuals have light perception and can discriminate different shades of gray to some extent. Any object that looms close up will cast shadows and provide relevant information about proximity. People with this capability and some without light perception may possess blindsight localization skills.

Beyond these possibilities, research by Dallenbach and colleagues at midcentury (e.g. Supa, Cotzin, & Dallenbach, 1944) provided evidence that skill in obstacle avoidance is dependent on echolocation. In echolocation, the organism emits a sound (e.g. tapping a cane) which is reflected back to the ears when it hits an obstacle. The sound has localizing characteristics which depend on the distance, size, and other features of the obstacle. Blind persons can learn to respond to these features providing they can detect high pitched sounds. Sighted individuals can develop this capability, but such learning ordinarily does not occur because there is no need for it. Persons blinded relatively late in life who could benefit from it may not be able to learn the skill since high frequency auditory discrimination skills tend to deteriorate with age. Warren (1994), reviewing more recent research, notes that there has been relatively little activity in this area but that there is some evidence that increasing numbers of children born blind attain this skill as they get older. Some effects are not seen until the age of seven or later, and some blind children never become echolocators.

Braille reading

A system of symbols made up of raised dots which can be felt by the fingers provides a means of encoding language. Learning to decode these tactual symbols makes it possible for the blind to read. The system was invented by a French blind person, Louis Braille, who lived in the first half of the 19th century (Jan, Freeman & Scott, 1977). With as much practice as it takes to learn to read visually, the blind can become quite adept at extracting the information contained in the series of raised dots which constitutes the alphabet (see figure 12.27). However, Braille reading is three to four times slower than visual reading. When vision is not available, other modalities can be utilized. Haptic Braille reading and auditory echolocation can compensate for visual loss. The potentialities of the other modalities are never as fast or efficient as the most adept, but information processing potential is substantial. Special educators and therapists make use of this concept in working with handicapped persons.

Spatial concepts and related behaviors

A review by Warren (1994) finds that most blind children have essentially egocentric conceptions of space. This means that their sense of where things are positioned in the world is in reference to themselves – to their right, left, and so forth. As a rule, children blinded adventitiously after substantial visual experience do much better spatially than those blinded from birth, and may develop allocentric spatial concepts. In addition, notable exceptions of more sophisticated development in the born-blind have been reported, but Warren laments that we have little understanding of what experiences or talents made possible those achievements.

Verbalisms

It was mentioned earlier that language becomes a vehicle for overcoming some of the spatial limitations of the blind, especially those having to do with distal space. However, language and linguistic concepts do not just appear in a fully mature fashion. They develop as a result of experience. What then does it mean if a child learns words designating experiences they could not possibly have, an output sometimes called 'verbalisms'? Is not such speech just a kind of sham and should not such concepts be discouraged? Cutsforth (1932) raised such questions when he found that, when asked to describe objects, both congenitally and adventitiously blind chil-

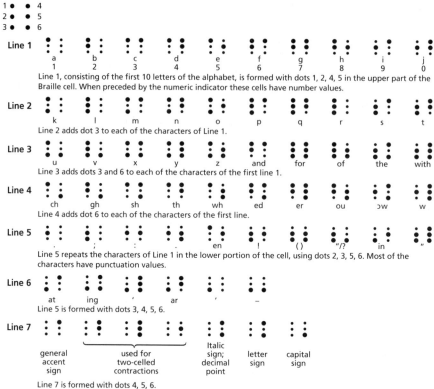

Figure 12.27   The Braille alphabet

dren gave a large percentage (near 50 percent or more) of visual qualities as their responses. Warren's (1994, p. 139) review of subsequent research found that there was considerable evidence that Cutsforth's estimate of the incidence of verbalisms in the speech of the blind was excessively high. Beyond that, there is evidence that the incidence of verbalisms declines with age and experience and is inversely related to intellectual competence. Such findings are interpreted to suggest that, even if the initial use of visual concepts may be a form of parroting, such language does facilitate social contact with the sighted and grows in meaningfulness as the terms are used in different contexts. Warren concludes that blind children should not be discouraged from using visual terminology and that every effort should be made to augment their experience so that they can enrich the meaning of the words they have.

Imagery

Consider the following experiment. A subject is asked to memorize a list of pairs of words. The list of pairs is presented for the first time and then the list is presented again. This time there is a pause after the first word in each pair, and the subject is asked to recall the second. This is repeated for a number of trials and the number of correct second words on the list is counted. Now suppose that two kinds of word-pair lists are created. One might be of words like "green" and "palace," the other of words like "thunder" and "crash." The first group are words conveying visual qualities; the second, auditory qualities. Rates of learning the lists were compared in groups of verbally bright, sighted and blind adolescents. The results of a number of such studies indicate that blind persons learn lists with auditory qualities faster than lists with visual qualities. The sighted subjects are not differentially affected by the two types of word lists (Warren, 1994, pp. 175–80).

The assumption behind such studies is that imagery facilitates memory and that it is harder for the blind to learn when the imagery is not available. In studies where subjects are given objects to feel and asked to report directly about the imagery elicited, born-blind tended to report tactual imagery whereas the later-blinded referred to visual imagery. Overall, this work suggests that being blind deprives the person not only of immediate visual experience but also of tools that may contribute to many cognitive processes. Apparently, even a few years of visual experience may make possible later use of visual imagery.

Lack of vision does not mean lack of spatial imagery. The congenitally blind are capable of developing complex spatial imagery skills despite the absence of visual experience. Kerr (1983), for example, asked college-educated adults to image various familiar scenes (e.g. a car parked in a driveway) and then to imagine locating within the scene familiar objects present under three different conditions: pictorial (e.g. on the car's roof, there was a soccer ball in a box); concealed (e.g. in the trunk there is a large soccer ball in a box); or separate (e.g. in a driveway two houses down, there was a soccer ball in a box). Both congenitally blind and sighted subjects were asked to tell the examiner when they were able to image what was described. Previous research had indicated that imaging the pictorial was fastest followed by the concealed and then the separate condition. The pattern of findings for the congenitally blind, providing they were familiar with objects specified, was identical to that of the sighted except that it took them longer to do each task. Such differences in time are consistent with the longer time it takes to determine the shape of an object if one is palpating it as compared to looking at it.

This chapter concludes by examining the nature of the imagery present in the dreams of the blind. To begin, it should be noted that the blind do dream, as often and in the same manner as do sighted individuals. Kerr, Foulkes, and Schmidt (1982), studying both congenitally and adventitiously blind college graduates, found them to have dreams whose structural complexity and imagery matched those of sighted control subjects. The congenitally blind had complex spatial concepts; however, they were not visual. Thus, one subject reported a dream in which a bank teller machine was situated in an oblong room, but close questioning revealed a sense of space, form, and spatial relationships without any specific visual content. By contrast, the adventitiously blinded who had lost their vision as teenagers, describing dreams occurring about ten years after they were totally blind, report vivid visual experiences. Such data are consistent with the idea that, once visual experiences have occurred, the components are available for constructive cognitive use as images.

13

Hearing, Language, and their Disorders

The topic of this chapter is hearing and language. As indicated earlier, language capabilities are uniquely human. Despite fascinating and important recent evidence that other advanced primates have language capabilities (Savage-Rumbaugh et al., 1993) and a few can even understand English, no animal other than ourselves uses language and oral communication in the ways, and to the degree, that we do. More than that, as tribal and social animals, much, if not all, of our social intercourse is conducted linguistically. That being the case, limitations or impairments of language capability strike at the very heart of our adjustment to life. Thus, although there are aspects of hearing which are important to many human activities ranging from awareness of threat (sirens or the sounds of an intruder) to pleasure (bird calls or music), only language skills will be emphasized.

The position taken here is that ordinary language rests on the integrity of the auditory system and that hearing and language development are closely intertwined. This means that if there are limitations in certain auditory skills, there will likely be problems with language development. This does not mean that audition and language are identical. There is much evidence for the special and independent nature of language. That language does not have to be auditory is obvious to anyone reading this. All written language is conveyed to the brain via the visual system, the deaf can learn sign language which is also read visually, and the blind obtain language information through touch by reading Braille. Nonetheless, the emphasis here is that ordinary language is rooted in hearing. If audition is impaired, persons have to find alternate means to process language information. That challenge has its own problems which will be considered as they arise in this and later chapters.

The chapter begins with a presentation about the nature of sound and about the way the ear and the peripheral hearing apparatus respond to sound. The anatomic pathways to the temporal cortex and beyond will then be presented with some consideration of the consequences for audition of lesions or impairments over that route. A major portion of the chapter then addresses the neuropsychology of language and the kinds of impairment that appear during the course of development. The final section concerns deafness, with major emphasis on what has been learned about language education for those with severe auditory impairment.

The Nature of Sound

Vibrations and the media through which they pass

Sound originates when some object or structure (e.g., a tuning fork, violin, or set of vocal cords) is made to vibrate. This can occur when it is struck, bowed, or air is passed over a taut but movable surface. It can also occur if a wet finger is rubbed along the rim of a glass partly filled with water. However the vibration is initiated, energy in the form of a travelling wave emanates from the source and moves out in all directions, dissipating with the distance from the source. The speed with which the energy moves is a function of the physical medium in which it occurs. If a three meter steel bar, suspended from the ceiling, is struck at the low end, the vibrations will reach the high end of the bar sooner than they will reach a point three meters away in the air from the steel bar. This is because sound travels at the rate of more than 5,000 meters per second in steel but only 340 meters per second in the air (Sekuler & Blake, 1994). If the steel bar were suspended in a pool of water, the speed of transmission through the water would be 1,500 meters per second, intermediate between air and steel. The relatively slow rate at which sound is transmitted through the air is the reason why thunder, which is caused by lightning, is often heard some time after the lightning flash is seen. (Light travels at the rate of approximately 3×10^8 meters per second.)

Frequency, pitch, and the complexity of sound

The energy initiated by vibration emerges in the form of waves fluctuating at specific frequencies measured in cycles per second, or as described earlier, Hertz (Hz). If a partially filled glass of water is rubbed with a wet finger, vibration at a single frequency may occur. The frequency of a vibration is experienced by a listener as a specific pitch and the single frequency emanating from the glass is experienced as a pure tone. Figure 13.1 illustrates the pressure waves that occur after a tuning fork is struck. Other waves may also be emitted by the tuning fork, but the strongest wave and the one which determines its pitch is called its fundamental frequency. If vibrations are initiated by a nearby explosion, a great many frequencies will be emitted simultaneously which will be experienced as a loud noise. If a large range of frequencies are generated simultaneously and continuously over a period of time, but at a comfortable level of intensity, the sound is experienced as a complex hiss. This sound is called white noise and is often used in experiments on hearing. The vibrations emanating from the vocal cords of a speaking person are also complex, though in a special way that will be presented later in the chapter. Indeed, there is considerable complexity in the frequencies emitted when a single key on a piano is struck or when a single note is played on the violin. Although each may be tuned to the same pitch, and thus emit the same frequency, each will also emit other frequencies simultaneously which will give each instrument its characteristic tonal quality or timbre.

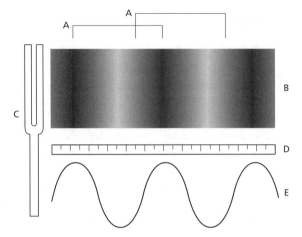

Figure 13.1 Pressure waves of sound. The tuning fork (C) sets up wave-like motion of the molecules in the air which produces pressure waves (B). Wavelength (A) may be measured (D) between any two comparable points on the wave. The pressure wave may also be represented as changes in time (E)

Thus, although the basic component, sound, is a wave emanating from a vibrating source at a specific frequency, the actual sounds encountered by the ear are only very rarely pure tones. Generally, the ear is stimulated by complex and changing sounds and needs special mechanisms to process the information conveyed by such complexity. The term modulation is often used to refer to changing sound characteristics and there are two kinds – frequency and amplitude modulation. In frequency modulation, pitches are being changed; in amplitude modulation, intensities are being changed.

Complex sound waves can be decomposed into their simple sine wave components by means of Fourier analysis in the same manner as described in chapter 12. Similarly, complex sounds can be synthesized by combining simple sine waves of differing frequency, amplitude, and phase.

Intensity and loudness of sound

The intensity of sound is conveyed by the amplitude (height and depth) of the sound waves. The energy of a vibration dissipates as it moves away from its source. As this occurs, the amplitude attenuates (becomes smaller), although the frequency remains the same. Sound intensity is measured in logarithmic units which, it will be recalled, represent widely dispersed quantities in a conveniently small number of units. The unit, named a decibel (a name honoring Alexander Graham Bell, a pioneer student of hearing as well as an inventor of the telephone) is abbreviated as dB. It is based on a ratio of the energy present in a particular sound to the minimal intensity audible to the ear. The number of decibels of intensity associated with a particular set of

Table 13.1 The decibel scale and the sound intensities that approximate particular levels

0	Threshold of hearing	
10	Normal breathing	
20	Leaves rustling in a breeze	
30	Empty movie house	
40	Residential neighborhood at night	
50	Quiet restaurant	
60	Two-person conversation	
70	Busy traffic	
80	Vacuum cleaner	
90	Water at foot of Niagara Falls	← Beginning of danger level
100	Subway train	
120	Propeller plane at takeoff	← Prolonged exposure can cause hearing loss
130	Machine-gun fire, close range	
140	Jet at takeoff	← Threshold of pain
160	Wind tunnel	

events is illustrated in table 13.1. Note that ordinary conversation is at the level of about 60 dB and that prolonged exposure to sounds above 100 dB is likely to produce damage to the hearing system. It can be noted that some types of music are often played at intensities higher than 100 dB.

The auditory system, which processes information conveyed by sound, has three anatomic loci: the peripheral apparatus consisting of the outer, middle and inner ears; the pathways from the inner ear to the cortex which contain six major relay stations; and the auditory processors in the auditory cortex of the temporal lobe and beyond. The anatomy of each of these areas and some of their pathologies will be presented next.

The Transduction of Sound: the Outer, Middle, and Inner Ear

An overall view of the peripheral hearing apparatus is presented in figure 13.2. The illustration provides some sense of the relative size of the different parts. As a point of reference, the visible outer ear measures 6 to 9 cm (2.5–3 inches) while the audi-

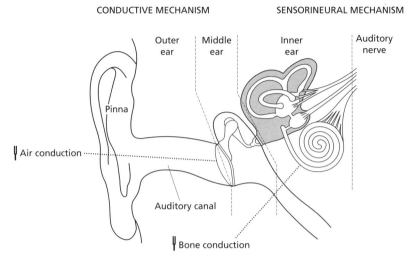

Figure 13.2   Overview of the outer, middle, and inner ears

tory canal is about 2.5 cm long (1 inch) and 7 mm in diameter ($\frac{1}{4}$–$\frac{3}{8}$ inches). The visible and accessible parts are larger than the structures of the middle and inner ears. The inner ear is the place where vibrations are transduced into nerve impulses so that the information can be conveyed to the brain. Each part is now considered in turn.

Anatomy and function of the outer ear

The outer ear consists of the somewhat ungainly structure visible on each side of the head which is commonly called the ear but is technically termed a pinna and a short, quite irregular tube called the auditory canal. It is hard to discern any aesthetic beauty in the pinna and one might wonder whether there is any function which such an ungainly structure might serve. It turns out that the irregular surface of the pinna alters incoming sound waves in such a manner as to aid the brain in deciding whether sound is coming from in front or behind, a discrimination that is particularly diffi-cult if the sound is coming from a source that is not at all to one side or the other. Similarly, the size and irregularity of the auditory canal maximizes the transmission of sounds between 2,000 and 5,000 Hz and somewhat dampens both higher and lower frequencies (Handel, 1989). As shall be presented later in the chapter, these frequencies are those uttered in speech.

Pathology of the outer ear

Not very much can go wrong in the outer ear. Rarely, individuals are born with a pinna missing or with a blocked auditory canal, but these can be reconstructed or

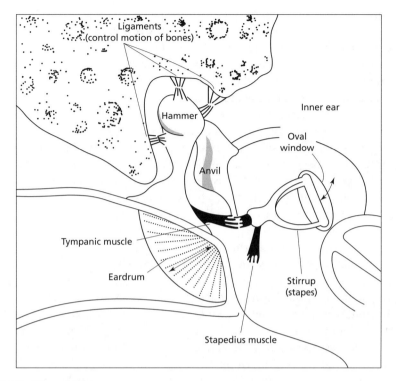

Figure 13.3 The middle ear

opened surgically. Infections and tumors of the sort that can occur on any part of the skin can also occur in the outer ear. Perhaps the most common problem comes from excessive or impacted ear wax, technically called cerumen. This is a substance formed by secretions of two types of glands in the outer two-thirds of the auditory canal. One secretes a sweat-like and the other an oily substance, which together form the wax. If the wax does not drain, or if it becomes impacted (which may occur as a result of attempts to remove the wax with mechanical objects), reduced hearing may occur (Martin, 1981). This condition is easily alleviated by softening the ear wax with suitable emollients, which allows the wax to drain.

Anatomy and function of the middle ear

The middle ear is a small structure. It begins where the outer ear ends, at the tympanic membrane or eardrum, to which the first of three of the smallest bones (ossicles) in the body, is attached. This bone is named the malleus (hammer). The others are the uncus (anvil) and the stapes (stirrups) and the latter is attached to the interface between middle and inner ears, the oval window. This is illustrated in figure 13.3. Note the presence of two muscles, the tympanic and the stapedius, and that the tympanic membrane is much larger than the oval window; actually, it is about 30 times larger. The importance of this difference in size will be considered below.

The compartment of the middle ear, like the inner ear, is buried in the large temporal bone at the side of the skull. It is filled with air whose pressure is normally that of the atmosphere surrounding the person. What makes it possible to equalize the air pressure inside the compartment buried so deep in the bone is a passageway to the throat called the Eustachian tube, which opens whenever swallowing occurs. Most persons are familiar with the way it functions. When going up in an elevator, an uncomfortable sense of pressure in the ears is experienced which is relieved by swallowing. Since air pressure is lower at higher elevations, as one goes up the pressure of the air trapped inside the middle ear increasingly exceeds air pressure, and the middle ear begins to bulge, which produces an unpleasant sensation. Swallowing allows air to pass in or out of the middle ear, equalizing the pressure and relieving discomfort.

Sound waves coming through the air set the tympanic membrane to vibrating and the chain of middle ear bones mechanically transmits these vibrations to the oval window of the inner ear. The middle ear functions to overcome the difference in energy required to set vibrations going in the air versus what it takes to set them going in liquid, which is what fills the inner ear. Although a vibration in liquid moves faster than a vibration in the air, the initiation of the vibration in liquid takes more energy. If there was nothing to compensate for the air–liquid differences in the outer and inner ears, sounds would have to be much louder for them to be heard. The mechanical organization of the middle ear amplifies the sound (like turning up the volume control) so that the vibrations in the inner ear will be nearly as strong as those in the outer ear. This is accomplished, in part, by means of the size difference at the beginning and end of the chain of bones, by the tympanic membrane being 20–30 times larger than the oval window, by the way the bones act as a lever to increase pressure at the end of the chain, and by the structure of the tympanic membrane which buckles in the middle and thus increases pressure to the ossicles (Pickles, 1988; Handel, 1989; Sekuler & Blake, 1994).

The muscles of the middle ear are activated when sounds of 65 dB or more strike the tympanic membrane. They tighten in reflex fashion, restricting and containing the movement of the tympanic membrane and the ossicles, especially when the dB level reaches 90 or higher. To some extent this prevents the middle ear apparatus from breaking down because of the excessive strain that loud noises can induce. For the most part, however, the effect of this muscle activity is to dampen low frequency sounds, thus transmitting a larger proportion of high frequency sounds. One consequence is to facilitate the perception of complex sounds such as those found in speech since many of their distinctive features are conveyed by high frequencies.

Pathology of the middle ear

There are two major types of pathology that can occur in the middle ear. The one that most affects children is infection. The Eustachian tube opens to the throat, an area highly vulnerable to infection, and it is relatively easy for infectious organisms

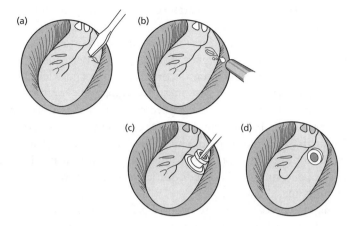

Figure 13.4   Inserting middle ear drainage tubes. (a) Making the incision in the tympanic membrane; (b) aspirating and draining liquid accumulations; (c) inserting a biflanged tube; (d) the tube in position

to make their way up the tube and generate an infection in the middle ear. Such an infection is technically termed otitis media. The infection itself may weaken or destroy the ossicles, their linkages, or the tympanic membrane. Often, the infection will partially or entirely seal off the Eustachian tube and thus prevent pressure equalization from occurring. In addition, the infection may lead to the development of effusions (secretions and byproducts of the infectious process) which fill the middle ear causing it to bulge, produce severe pain, and overall malaise. If this occurs in older children with language, they can communicate about their pain and its location and thus facilitate the initiation of care and treatment. Nonverbal children may suffer excruciatingly for long periods and experience extreme distress before the source of the difficulty is understood.

With the advent of antibiotics, many children who might have become deaf as a result of infection no longer do so. Nonetheless, middle ear infections are difficult to treat and often recur, partially as a result of the misuse of antibiotics and their growing ineffectiveness. If infections recur frequently and the pressure equalization mechanism is nonfunctional, aspects of the child's hearing relevant to speech perception may be temporarily weakened. If this occurs during periods of rapid language acquisition, lags in language development may take place simply because crucial aspects of the language stimulus are not perceived (Nozza, 1988). This may be due to interference with the mobility of the tympanic membrane and the chain of ossicles. In addition, if the disease recurs often, the physical integrity of the structures of the middle ear may be compromised leading to permanent losses. To minimize these consequences physicians often insert small tubes in the tympanic membrane in order to admit air into the middle ear, relieve pressure build-up, and facilitate the drainage of effusions (Bluestone & Klein, 1988). A depiction of this surgery is seen in figure 13.4.

There has been a fair amount of research on the consequences for language development of middle ear infections, some of which has been controversial. From an early perspective held by most, that such infections were just an ordeal that many children had to endure, evidence has emerged indicating that permanent and nontrivial impairment of language function often occurs. Bluestone and Klein (1988, p. 209) summarized the many factors that determine the outcome. Foremost among these is that a developmental process is being affected, one that is driven by biological factors which vary from child to child and by environmental factors that support, enrich, and stimulate language development or hinder and disregard it. Consequently, the timing, intensity, and duration of the infection, whether it produces permanent structural damage, and the social and educational context in which it occurs all contribute to the outcome.

The other major type of pathology occurring in the middle ear is called otosclerosis. This disorder, which mostly affects older people but occasionally shows up as early as mid-childhood, is a result of the growth of spongy bone over the footplate of the stapes as it rests on the oval window of the inner ear. The bony growth immobilizes the interface between bone and membrane and increasingly prevents the conduction of vibration to the inner ear. This can result in significant hearing loss approaching deafness even though the rest of the apparatus for hearing is intact. However, surgical procedures have been developed which can ameliorate this condition by removing the sclerotic tissue and substituting new linkages between tympanic membrane and oval window. Early versions of this kind of surgery were not very successful, but later versions have been reported to correct the condition in 90 percent of the cases (Martin, 1981). The surgeon often conducts the procedure under local anesthetic so that the patient is awake and can signal when improved hearing is experienced.

Differentiating middle ear and inner ear hearing losses

The role of the middle ear is to conduct vibrations in the air to the inner ear. The test for the integrity of the system is to present a sound and ask if is heard. There are many ways to do this, but physicians often strike a tuning fork and hold it a short distance from the ear. They will ask the subject if anything is heard, and if the answer is yes, to report how long the sound persists. When sounds are no longer heard, the tuning fork, without being struck again, is placed on a bony protuberance of the head, e.g. over the bone just behind the ear or on the forehead. The subject may now report hearing the sound again. What is going on?

When the tuning fork presses on bone, the vibrations are transmitted to bone. The inner ear, which is embedded in the bones of the head, begins to vibrate much as it would if the sound were conducted through the ossicles of the middle ear. The process of bringing sound to the nervous system by imposing vibration on the bones of the skull is called bone conduction, whereas bringing sounds in the air to the nervous system via the little bones of the middle ear is called air conduction. (See figure 13.2: also do not get confused by the way the word "bone" is used in this ter-

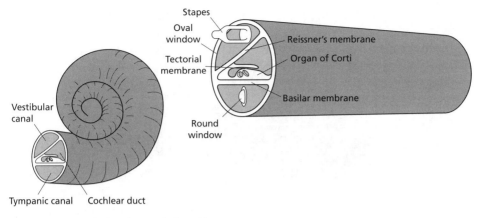

Figure 13.5   Coiled and uncoiled cochlea

minology – bone, in bone conduction, refers to the bones of the skull and not the ossicles of the middle ear.) By studying what many people can detect under each condition, it is possible to establish norms and thereby have a basis for determining differing degrees of abnormality. Normal air conduction indicates that both the middle ear and the inner ear are intact, while abnormal air conduction and normal bone conduction indicate the presence of middle ear impairments. Abnormal bone conduction, of course, indicates inner ear impairments. To complicate matters further, hearing losses due to middle ear abnormalities are often termed conduction losses while those due to inner ear abnormalities are termed nerve losses.

Anatomy and function of the inner ear

The term "inner ear," as seen in figure 13.2, refers both to the semicircular canals, or vestibular system, and to the rounded coil called a cochlea, which means snail. When considering hearing, the terms "inner ear" and "cochlea" are synonymous. The cochlea is the place where the vibrations, whose journey from the outer ear to the oval window has just been reviewed, are transformed into patterns of neural discharge. The next sections review the anatomy of the cochlea and the manner by which the transduction is accomplished.

Anatomy of the cochlea

The cochlea is roughly a two-and-a-half-turn coiled tube. The coiled and schematically uncoiled tube are illustrated in figure 13.5. Note that the tube is grossly divided into three parts by two membranes, one called Reissner's membrane, the other the basilar membrane. Situated on the basilar membrane is a complex structure called the organ of Corti, and prominent just above it is the tectorial membrane, which is attached at one end and sort of "free floating" on the other. These latter structures

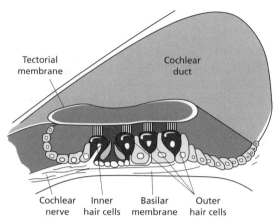

Tectorial membrane

Cochlear duct

Cochlear nerve   Inner hair cells   Basilar membrane   Outer hair cells

Figure 13.6   The organ of Corti

are where transduction takes place (more shortly). The three compartments within the coil are filled with fluid. The compartment into which the oval window vibrates is called the vestibular canal (also called scala vestibuli). It extends the length of the cochlea, ending at the apex where there is a small passageway called the helicotrema, on the other side of which the tympanic canal (also called scala tympani) begins and extends back the entire length of the cochlea. At the end is a structure called the round window. The round window, like the oval window, is an elastic membrane while the rest of the outer structure of the cochlea is inelastic bone.

If a vibration at the oval window pushes some of the liquid forward, it can make the round window bulge outwardly. Thus the fluid in the vestibular and tympanic canals, which is called perilymph, is the same. The middle compartment between the vestibular and tympanic canals, and the one in which the organ of Corti is situated, is called the cochlear duct (also called scala media). It is filled with a liquid called endolymph, and this liquid also flows into the semicircular canals. The fluids serve a number of purposes including providing nutrition. There are no blood vessels in the cochlea. If there were, the sound of pulsing blood would be very distracting.

The length of the stretched-out basilar membrane is about 32 mm (Martin, 1981). Although the size of the cochlear tube narrows some in the inner parts of the coil, the width of the basilar membrane increases gradually from about 0.2 mm at the narrow end beginning at the oval window to 0.35 mm, at the wide end buried deep in the apex at the helicotrema. What changes as the organ of Corti gets larger as it progresses deeper into the coil is the ratio of supporting muscle and ligament to membrane. At the oval window, the basilar membrane is relatively narrow and taut. At the apex, it is relatively broader and less stiff (Handel, 1989).

The organ of Corti

A closer look at the anatomy of the organ of Corti is provided in a cross-sectional schematic drawing in figure 13.6. It consists of about 12,000 outer hair cells lined up in three to five rows and about 3,500 inner hair cells lined up in one row placed roughly in the middle of, and extending the length of, the basilar membrane as it winds through the cochlea.

The main bodies of the hair cells, including their nuclei, are embedded in sup-porting cells resting on the basilar membrane. Protruding into the fluid of the cochlear duct from the top of each hair cell are cilia, little flexible hairs, that bend in response to any motion of the fluid. At the base are synapses with the eighth cranial nerve, the auditory nerve, which will convey the information to the cortex. Each inner hair cell may synapse with as many as 20 auditory nerve fibers while many outer hair cells converge on a single auditory nerve fiber. Over 90 percent of auditory nerve fibers receive their input from the inner hair cells while the more numerous outer hair cells enervate the small remainder. The cilia of outer hair cells appear embedded in the over-arching tectorial membrane while the ends of the inner hair cells float free in the fluid of the cochlear duct.

How does transduction take place in the cochlea?

The vibration of the ossicles of the middle ear will cause the oval window to vibrate, which will set the perilymph in the vestibular and tympanic canals into wave-like motion. This in turn will induce motion in the basilar, tectorial, and Reissner's mem-branes, all of which are flexible, and consequently, in the endolymph of the cochlear duct. These motions will cause the cilia to bend. Bending cilia of the inner hair cells is where most sound transduction takes place since these motions of the cilia induce changes in the rate of firing of the cells. What then is the role of the outer hair cells? Recall that the tectorial membrane is anchored at one end but sort of floats free at the other. The term "sort-of" is used because the tops of the outer hair cells appear to be embedded in the free floating end of the tectorial membrane. Information avail-able suggests that the outer cells function primarily to amplify some of the frequen-cies; those, it turns out, that are related to speech. They do so by contracting and extending, inducing the tectorial membrane into greater vibratory activity somewhat like what occurs when shaking out a blanket after a day at the beach. Thus, the outer hair cells serve an auxiliary function albeit an important one. Destruction of the outer hair cells leads to a sharp decrease in sensitivity to sounds.

The wave of mechanical energy coursing through the ducts of the cochlea will have a maximal impact on a particular place on the basilar membrane depending on its frequency. The basilar membrane is something like a xylophone with a gradual downward progression of sensitivities from about to 20,000 to 20 Hz. The base, the area adjacent to the oval window, is sensitive to the highest frequencies, while the apex, in the center of the cochlear coil, is sensitive to the lowest (see figure 13.7). To be more specific, a wave of a particular frequency will induce a maximal reaction at one particular place on the basilar membrane and less to either side. Sensitivity will fall off sharply at higher frequencies and much less sharply at lower frequencies. The brain will receive a pattern of responses from the cochlea and will have to extract which particular frequency is predominant. This concept was originally worked out by George von Bekesy (1960), for which he was awarded the Nobel prize in 1961.

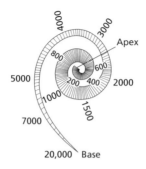

Figure 13.7   Transduction of frequencies in the cochlea

The sensitivity of particular places to specific frequencies does not hold through-out the range. At the lowest detectable frequencies, those between 20 and 1,000 Hz, there is no particular place of maximal displacement on the basilar membrane. A dif-ferent mode of transduction makes possible the detection of these frequencies – the firing of the organ of Corti and the auditory nerve in direct synchrony with the fre-quency of the stimulating tone. Nerves can fire at rates up to about 1,000 Hz and thus can fire at the same frequency as the stimulation. Thus there appear to be two modes of frequency detection: a direct response of the inner cells for frequencies up to 1,000 Hz, and a place on the basilar membrane that is selectively displaced by the traveling wave that detects frequencies between 1,000 and 20,000 Hz.

The full story about how the intensity of stimulation (subjectively, loudness) is coded is not known. It is likely that part of the explanation involves the vigor of the induced fluid motion which in turn will cause the basilar membrane and the cilia in the organ of Corti to bend less or more. The higher the intensity of the sound, the greater the amplitude of displacement of the cilia and, hence, of the number of elec-trical signals transmitted to the auditory nerve. Sensitivity at the point of maximal reaction on the basilar membrane will vary as a function of loudness, the selectivity of the response decreasing as tones get very loud (Pickles, 1988). The overall outcome is that sound is decomposed into its component frequencies with particu-lar hair cells and subsequent nerve fibers responding maximally at specific frequen-cies (thus they are said to be tuned to such a frequency), and the whole ensemble varying in the amplitude of reaction as a function of the intensity of the stimulus. An illustration of the tuning characteristics of a number of auditory nerve fibers (note relative responsiveness of each single fiber to lower frequencies and non-responsiveness to higher frequencies) is found in figure 13.8.

Pathways of the auditory system to the cortex

The auditory nerve, consisting of about 50,000 individual fibers, leaves the cochlea and heads toward the cortex. About 95 percent of these fibers connect to the 3,500 inner hair cells, so each inner hair cell is linked to many auditory nerve fibers. The

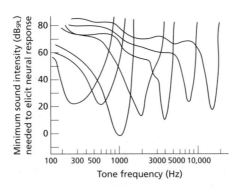

Figure 13.8   Frequency tuning curves for different auditory nerve fibers

pathway to the primary auditory area on the cortex, Heschl's gyrus on the upper surface of the temporal lobe, is complex and involves a number of relay stations. This is quite different from the anatomy of the visual system which goes directly from retina to thalamus to cortex. In the auditory system the relays include the cochlear nucleus, the superior olivary complex, the trapezoid body, the nucleus of the lateral lemniscus, the inferior colliculus in the roof of the midbrain, and the medial geniculate nucleus of the thalamus. Figures 13.9 and 13.10 show this complexity. The operations of these pathways and relay stations have been yielding their secrets to recent research, and several merit presentation here.

Seventy percent of the pathways cross over to the other side while the rest project ipsilaterally. The neat arrangement in the visual system whereby information coming from one side of space ends up in the contralateral hemisphere is not present in the auditory system. In the visual system, location in space is conveyed directly via the spatial organization of receptors in the retina, but the cochlea registers only frequency and intensity and not location. Localization of sound depends on the fact that stimulation coming from one side of space will arrive at one ear a moment sooner and with greater intensity than it will at the other. The place where the comparison is made is in the olivary nuclei, whose own firing rates will vary with whether inputs from each side arrive simultaneously or at slightly different times. Similarly, there are other but similar structures that respond to differences in intensity. Given such a system of analysis, the greatest difficulty in localizing sound occurs when it is coming from directly in front or back of the person. This is because under those conditions the sounds arrive at each ear simultaneously though, as previously noted, the shape of the ear helps make the distinction.

Another general feature of note (Handel, 1989, pp. 521–2) is that there are at least two kinds of pathways going to cortex. One is a direct, tonotopically organized pathway (where adjacent cell groups respond to adjacent frequencies, as in the basilar membrane) that go from cochlea to Heschl's gyrus in the temporal cortex (see figure 3.7). Such pathways are consistent with pure tone perception, the identification and discrimination of particular frequencies. As noted earlier, there are also many pathways in which cells at the lower level connect to more cells at a higher level and the

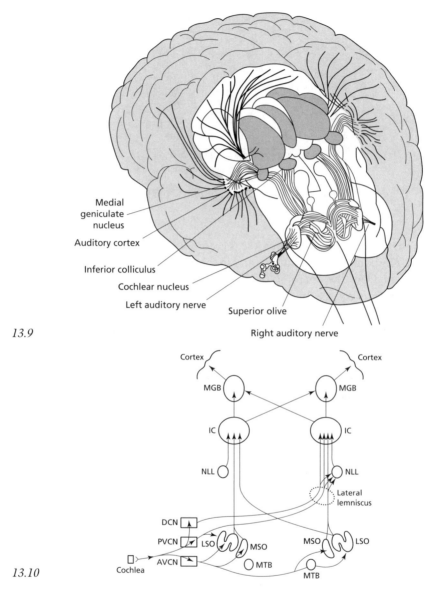

13.9

13.10

Figure 13.9   A view of the auditory pathways from cochlea to cortex
Figure 13.10   Diagram of auditory pathways. IC, inferior colliculus; MGB, medial geniculate body; NLL, nucleus of the lateral lemniscus; AVCN, anteroventral cochlear nucleus; PVCN, posteroventral cochlear nucleus; DCN, dorsal cochlear nucleus; MSO, medial nucleus superior olive; LSO, lateral nucleus superior olive; MTB, medial nucleus trapezoid body

number of transmitting fibers increases. This implies that elaborate processing of a relatively small number of initial reactions is going on. Such a structure can detect features that are dynamic (having to do with change) in that different kinds of cells respond to differences in onset (as noted with regard to localization), offset, and frequency and amplitude modulation. As noted previously, the latter would require cells which react when either the frequency or the intensity of stimulation changes, especially if the change is very rapid. Such cells are particularly numerous in the cortex. The characteristics of these auditory pathways are consistent with capabilities such as the perception of speech, which is processed near, but not in, Heschl's gyrus. Thus, there is an anatomic basis for a disassociation between hearing pure tones and hearing speech. The idea for such a distinction has been expressed by the phrase "speech is special" (Liberman, 1982).

A diagnostic procedure called the brainstem auditory evoked potential is used to assess the integrity of the pathways from receptor to brain and will be described next, first for evoked potentials generally and then for this particular procedure. The measurement of an evoked potential uses the technology of the EEG. What is of interest is not the tonic activity present in the brain at rest, or overall changes in the brain's response to some challenge such as reading or problem solving. Instead, interest is in the brain's response to a specific stimulus repeated several times at precisely defined time intervals. For example, if a light is briefly flashed at the rate of 10 Hz, the EEG will show spikes ten times a second coincident with the light flashes, particularly over the occipital lobes. If a sound stimulus were presented, it would appear most conspicuously over the temporal lobes. The potential (a sudden change in voltage) is said to be "evoked" or "driven" by the stimulus. For some stimuli, the potential recurring in the EEG is easy to observe. For other stimuli, the evoked potential is obscured by other activity present. However, the potential, if there, can be revealed by time-locked averaging. This means averaging the EEG waveforms that occur at an electrode site over a series of stimulus presentations. When this is done over many trials, the potentials not related to the evoking stimulus will average out to zero while those related to the evoking stimulus will emerge more and more clearly.

The stimulus for the brainstem auditory evoked potential is a click, a sharp noise containing all frequencies, which may be presented 1,000–2,000 times at the rate of 4 Hz in order to reveal the evoked potential which is illustrated in figure 13.11. This waveform emerges in the first 10 msec following each click and is thought to reflect the integrity of the relay stations between cochlea and brain. Pathology is indicated by degradation of the waveforms or by increases in the amount of time it takes for a particular part of the curve to appear.

Before further consideration is given to anatomy or pathology of the language system, the discussion turns to the nature of language itself. Some of the ideas and concepts of the field of study called linguistics, and one of its subdivisions, psycholinguistics, are briefly presented.

The Nature of Language and Speech

Dimensions of language behavior

Linguists distinguish at least five components or dimensions of language (Kess, 1992; Finegan, 1994; Blumstein, 1995). They are described in the next paragraphs. Each is an extensive topic in its own right that has merited book-length treatment. Four

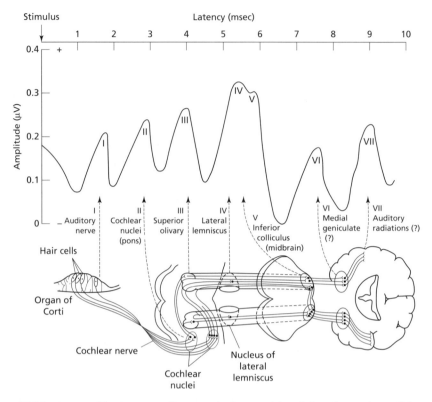

Figure 13.11 A normal brainstem auditory evoked potential and the relay stations of the auditory pathway whose integrity they reflect

of the components – phonemics, semantics, syntactics, and pragmatics – constitute a hierarchy; that is, the more advanced dimensions depend on the integrity of the more basic dimensions and understanding pathology at any level must consider whether any pathology is present in the levels below.

Phonemics – the code of the sounds of a language

This dimension refers to the sounds produced in speech that must be registered by the ear and processed by the brain for spoken language to be understood. A specific language makes use of a finite number of sounds from among all those that the speaking apparatus may produce. A single one of those sounds is called a phoneme. There is a rough correspondence between the term phoneme and the terms vowel and consonant, which refer to two types of phonemes. However, the definition of phoneme includes reference to highly detailed distinctions between similar utterances which occur as a result of the sound's position in a sequence of utterances and the particular phonemes which happen to precede or follow it. Such distinctions are generally not made regarding vowels and consonants.

Children are born with the capacity to detect all known human speech sounds, but they will normally develop sensitivity only to those which they hear. Responsiveness to sounds not used or heard will deteriorate or atrophy. Thus it is that native speakers of many oriental languages cannot differentiate the R's and L's of English if they learned English after adolescence. In general, it is almost impossible to learn to speak a foreign language without an accent after the onset of adolescence because the person loses the ability to discriminate the sounds. There will be more information about the nature of the phonemic code below.

Semantics – the words of a language and their meanings

Language-capable individuals develop a lexicon, a store of words with their associated meanings on which they can draw as needed to express themselves and which enable them to comprehend what others say. English lexicons contain two kinds of words: content words – generally nouns, verbs, adjectives, and adverbs, and function words – articles, prepositions, and other generally small words which along with other devices of language such as prefixes, suffixes, and designations of singularity or plurality, are needed to organize any particular expression. Semantics is concerned with content words and their meanings. Function words, although part of the lexicon, are somewhat independent (selectively impairable) and are an aspect of syntax, which will be considered below.

Generally, the process of finding words is effortless and fairly automatic. It is possible however to have a word in one's lexicon but experience difficulty in its retrieval. This is common when learning new words, but it can also occur with familiar terms. Most people have had a "tip of the tongue" experience, in which they are aware that they know a word but cannot find it. As will be elaborated later, this phenomenon suggests that the learning and storage of words, which produces the lexicon, which is also a part of semantic memory (the lexicon plus storage of factual knowledge such as that Rome is the capital of Italy) is somewhat independent of the retrieval processes which access those words. It should also be noted that semantic memory is independent of motor or procedural memory (how to ride a bike) or episodic memory, memory for events (what happened at your last birthday party). Independence here refers to evidence that one or more of these domains of stored information derived from our experiences may be impaired without affecting the others very much.

The content word lexicon is a kind of handy dictionary we carry around in our heads. Unlike the dictionary, which is organized according to the order of the alphabet, the lexicon is organized in terms of the way word meanings relate to each other. This may be because of a shared conceptual relationship, for example, dog, cat, hamster, goldfish, and parrot may be stored together because they can all be pets. Conceptual categories are not fixed and in another context dog, cat, and hamster, but not the others, might go together because the person was thinking scientifically about the category of mammals. Other types of relationship are part–whole (e.g. house–room); synonymy (e.g. aid–help–assist); antonymy (e.g. top–bottom, or big–small); and converseness (e.g. doctor–patient, or child–parent).

There are several sources of evidence for the idea that the content-word lexicon is organized according to meaningful relationships. One is derived from the analysis of reading and speech errors in certain pathological conditions. A child may read, for example, the letters c–a–t as "dog" and make many such errors. Since there is no overlap in the letters and sounds of each word, there is no obvious basis for the confusion other than their conceptual linkage as "pets." It is as though the child located the semantic field (a group of related words) on the basis of the letter cues but then retrieved the wrong instance from within the field.

Another source of information comes from a research procedure called lexical priming. There are a number of variants on this technique, but a prototype would be one in which a person has to decide whether a group of letters presented on a screen constitute a real word. To make such a decision, one has to access the meaning conveyed by the letters. If there is no meaning, the letters are not a word. This procedure is called a lexical decision task. Subjects may be asked to signify their decision by pressing a lever whenever the letters make up a word and to do nothing when the letters are nonwords. The lever is arranged in such a way that reaction time, from presentation of letters to response, can be measured. Now suppose persons are presented with two words in fairly quick succession and they are asked to make a lexical decision only to the second. Suppose further that they are shown both words and nonwords as second words and that some of the pairs of real words are conceptually related and some are not. If the reaction times to conceptually related and conceptually unrelated pairs are compared, the former will be faster and it can be said that the first word primed access to the second. Why? The interpretation is that a group of letters automatically elicits its meaning as it is read by the subject, and this occurs to the first word even though the subject does not have to respond to it. The first word thus accesses its semantic field. If the second word is conceptually related, the search for its meaning is faster than that of an unrelated word because it is stored in closer proximity.

Syntactics – the grammar of a language, the rules by
which words are strung together to constitute sentences

This refers to the remarkable facility which places words into a sequence with all the necessary ingredients required by a particular language. Consider the following simple sentence: "Jane bought shoes." In English, "Bought shoes Jane" is not uttered, and deciding the correct order is not pondered but emerges automatically and effortlessly. Now consider the following sentence. "Jane bought the expensive shoes she saw in the store window using the money she had saved for three months by skipping lunch." In communicating a richer brew of information, much more is conveyed about Jane and her shoes, and function words such as "the" and words ending in "ing" are used. Furthermore, several different correct word orders could be used. Linguists, observing such regularities in all languages, have suggested that languages possess a deep structure, with transformational rules that permit some ways of using the words and prohibit others, and that these rules generate the grammar of a language. Much effort in the field of linguistics is devoted to discovering, formulating, and comparing the nature of the deep structures and transformational rules in different languages.

What is important to note here is the complexity of the process and the idea that this capability is inherited in such a way that it can be learned fairly quickly despite its incredible complexity. Noam Chomsky (1981), one of the pioneers in the study of syntax, has also pointed out that what is learned is a system; with mastery, individuals may utter sentences that they have never heard before but which will be perfectly understood by others who have also never heard that particular sentence before. While learning the language, they will also make errors because they follow rules where the language, for one historical reason or another, makes use of exceptions. Thus a child might say "I eated my lunch," following a rule about past tense that does not happen to apply.

As indicated, function words are aspects of syntax. They tend to be short and one might think easily mastered in comparison to most content words. It may therefore come as a surprise when a child has selective difficulty accurately speaking or reading such words. When this occurs, it is often a sign that there is some kind of impairment in the mechanisms mediating syntax.

Pragmatics – the way meanings are conveyed by the structures
and conventions of language utterance and the purpose
and manner of utilizing language

The first of these aspects of pragmatics concerns the principles by which the same information can be communicated in various ways. It concerns such technical aspects of utterances as their definiteness or vagueness, how word order may change meaning and alter emphasis, and how passive phrasing can convey differing meanings (Finegan, 1994).

The second meaning of pragmatics refers to the goals of language use. These generally are some form of social communication with some purpose, even if the purpose is just to be with people and feel accepted. Consider a cliché such as 'Have a nice day.' This might be uttered to almost any stranger and generally signifies one's good will and intention to be pleasant. This perfectly constructed, commonly used sentence would not be appropriate if conveyed to the mourners at a funeral. A person who said such a sentence would be using the sentence inappropriately and might give offense. Who might do so? Individuals with language problems who have been taught to speak in a parrot-like manner and by rote, those who have trouble sensing the nature of social situations (about which there will be more in a later chapter), and those who might be intending to inflict harm.

Language is so rich in its possibilities that the pragmatic intent must be sensed for the communication to be understood. A single well-formed sentence may have entirely different meanings in different contexts. Thus, for example, the sentence 'It's raining again' may be a comment on the weather or a sarcastic reference to the behavior of an individual who is prone to tears. Those who hear this utterance will generally have no difficulty understanding its highly diverse meanings if the context is clear. Failure to comprehend is generally a consequence of limitations or deficit in the pragmatic aspects of language.

Prosody – the music or intonation patterns of spoken language

Ordinarily, language is not spoken in a flat monotone. Each language and dialect has its own rhythmic and intonation patterns, and these features can be used to convey both linguistic meaning (linguistic prosody) and emotional information (affective prosody). Linguistic prosody refers to conventions within the culture about how meaning can be changed with differing intonation patterns. Consider the sentence "You are going out tonight." If there is no particular emphasis, the sentence might be a reply to a question about the schedule for the evening. If there is emphasis on the first word, you, it could be conveying coercion or demand to someone who is loath to go out. If the sentence is expressed with rising intonation, it could, depending on context, convey a simple question, a challenge to the idea the person will be allowed to go out, or a highly sarcastic, emotionally negative reaction to the person's plans. The last example includes strong elements of affective prosody. It is probable that the earliest understanding of language meanings derives from intonation rather than from the purely semantic meanings of the words.

Development of language

With some familiarity of the components of language, the normal sequence of language development will be briefly reviewed. The following overview is indebted to the chapter on language acquisition in Finegan (1994).

Prerequisites

Children must possess a symbolization facility, i.e. a fundamental capability that allows them to code events and experiences by some means such as a pattern of sound or touch or images with varied forms. Then, implicitly or explicitly, they must be able to equate one kind of stimulation for another, that such and such may stand for something else. Secondly, they must be able to use tools to accomplish goals because such is the nature of language. They must have some sort of recognition that utterances may get them what they want, much like the chimp may learn that a heavy rock can be useful in cracking nuts. There are rare forms of mental retardation in which such basic skills are not present.

Stage 1: babbling

From about six months of age, children begin to emit sounds, typically reduplicated syllables of the na-na-na-na type. These mouthings are universal and do not depend on having listeners present or on being able to hear. However, if the child cannot hear, this behavior will drop out after some time. Otherwise, the child may begin to use some of these babbles as protowords, precursors of words, e.g. ma-ma-ma-ma may generally signify that the child wants something. Furthermore, by about nine months of age, the sounds being babbled will take on the intonation patterns of the language community in which the child lives, and their sensitivity to phonemes not in their language diminishes and even disappears (Jusczyk, 1995).

Stage 2: one-word communications

About the first birthday, children begin to acquire and utter single-word communications. These words generally have a very simple structure; refer to familiar objects, people, actions, and events; may be used in a variety of ways; and have different meanings in different contexts. Thus ma-ma may refer to a person, her clothes, actions, or even her absence.

Stage 3: two-word communications

After acquiring a vocabulary of about 50 words by about the last third of the second year (mostly nouns referring to familiar objects and expressions referring to familiar activities), children begin to combine words to convey more specific meanings. Thus one can hear combinations such as "me hungry," "more milk" or "book mine."

Stage 4: single-clause communications

During the six months following the second birthday, word knowledge increases rapidly and increasingly more complex utterances appear that reflect the acquisition of syntax. Although many of the intricate rules and exceptions of the language have yet to be mastered, basic rules of word order (i.e. subject predicate, object) are followed, though gaps may occur. For example, "me put it back," "that book Joe's."

Stage 5: multiple-clause communications

By around three years, utterances combining clauses can be heard and the complexity of such clauses will progress with increasing age and experience. Words such as "because" and "if," which allow for the expression of subordinate clauses, enter the vocabulary. About this time, children can express negation with more than a simple "No!," offering sentences like "I don't know" or "That not go in there" and can formulate questions with more than voice intonation.

Easily demarked boundaries for further stages of development are not discernible, but the sequence of acquisition of the particular forms used by a language will mostly be the same for most normal speakers. Thus, children will acquire the regular rules for making plurals before they utilize the articles "the," "and," and "a" appropriately. Vocabulary growth is explosive. By age six, when most children begin formal education, they will generally have fully mastered all the phonemes used in their language and have a vocabulary of about 8,000 words, not counting different forms of the same word. This means that basic word acquisition is progressing at the rate of 13–21 words per day.

Nature and nurture in language development

The description of language development just completed may be interpreted to reflect the direct unfolding of genetically encoded programs. Precisely such a position is taken in a book by Pinker (1994), whose title includes the phrase "The language instinct." Instinct is a term used to designate genetically determined behavior patterns. Pinker, following the ideas pioneered by Chomsky, emphasizes the syntax component of language and argues essentially that the underlying wherewithall for syntactic organization found in adult language is transmitted whole by genetic means and guides and supports language development. A similar theoretical position regarding genetically determined unfolding, it was noted in chapter 11, previously dominated thinking about motor development. As in that area of study, there are alternate views about the nature of language development.

Such views are vigorously propounded by Tomasello (1995) in a review of Pinker's book titled straightforwardly "Language is not an instinct." Tomasello challenges the use of the term instinct, appropriate say for the weaving of a spider's web, to describe the diverse forms that the world's languages take, or to describe behaviors that require the experience of a language community and do not develop on their own. He points out that much of the Chomsky–Pinker view is based on a strongly held *ápriori* theoretical position about the nature of syntax and grammar, and that proponents of this view have paid little attention to the increasingly rich data now available about the nature of language development. The alternate approach is that language development occurs in the context of cognitive and social development; that phonemics, semantics, and pragmatics are every bit as important as syntax; and that language learning experience will influence the quantity and quality of language skill.

The research of Hart and Risley (1995) is pertinent in this regard. Attempting to foster increased readiness for school in four-year-old children, they noted that their target subjects, who came from impoverished environments, increased their rate of vocabulary acquisition, but no matter what interventions were attempted, they fell increasingly behind the rate of improvement that occurred in more advantaged children. They concluded that, by the age of four, a trajectory of language development had been set which was very difficult to modify. They set out to find what the language environments of comparable children were like from the time before overt language begins. To do so, they enlisted 42 families from diverse socioeconomic levels and visited them for an hour once a month for $2\frac{1}{2}$ years. An observer recorded, as unobtrusively as possible, the language stimulation received and the language production of a target child, beginning at the age of ten months. The essence of the results is contained in figure 13.12, the first graph showing a simple count of the words addressed to the child and the second, the cumulative vocabulary displayed by the child. These findings indicate a strong relationship between stimulation and vocabulary development, and disconfirm the notion that language is simply propelled

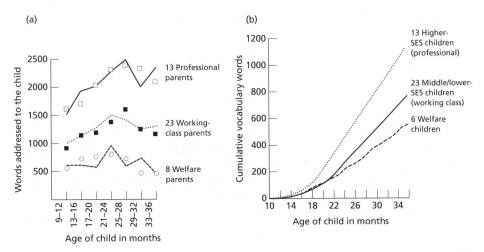

Figure 13.12(a) Average number of words addressed per hour to children from three different social backgrounds

Figure 13.12(b) Cumulated average number of vocabulary words expressed by children from three different social groups

by some genetic mechanism set at the moment of conception. The trajectories of development diverge as early as 16 months and are clearly different by 24 months. At three years they are widely separated and diverging so that the differences between groups are increasing. Further consideration of the nature–nurture issue and the critical time for the organization of trajectories of development will be found in the chapter on mental retardation.

Relationship of comprehension to expression

Through the course of language acquisition, comprehension of speech will precede expression. Children will understand communications directed at them, and much of what they overhear as well, before they can express themselves at the same level of sophistication to others. Furthermore, they appear to know the correct mode of expression before they can utter such expressions successfully. Thus, the legendary example of the child who pronounced the word "fish" as "fis." When an adult, trying to communicate with the child referred to her fish as "fis," the child rejected the communication, saying "No, my fis." When, finally, the adult said "Your fish," the child assented, saying "Yes, my fis."

As language expression improves, the relationship between comprehension and expression changes. It has already been noted that babbling shifts toward those sounds used by the language community of the child. This, of course, precedes meaningful comprehension, but it points to a close tie between receptive and expressive processes in language. In the adult, there is further support for such linkage (Nygaard & Pisoni, 1995). One such class of evidence is that it has been impossible to prevent the appearance of electrical activity in the muscles of the throat and voice box, of the sort that would appear when subjects do speak, when they are instructed to comprehend but not speak. This implies that components of talking to oneself are an ordinary accompaniment to comprehension. More compelling is the evidence that, when making decisions about differences in phonemes, frontal (Broca's area) activation occurs as well as Wernicke area activation, and that direct electrical stimulation of frontal areas can interfere with such decisions as much as stimulation of temporo-parietal areas (Blumstein, 1995). Also, Ojemann (1983) found that stimulating brain areas that would disrupt speech and mouth movements also disrupted comprehension of speech.

To better understand these complexities, and why speech is so special, the discussion turns back to phonemes and the ways in which they are perceived. To do so requires some consideration of the speech apparatus and the production of different phonemes, and then, what can be learned from examining the sound stream conveying language.

The vocal apparatus and the production of speech sounds

Sound production is an activity of an apparatus also devoted primarily to breathing, to chewing, and to swallowing food. The sounds we are able to make are limited by the ways in which the airways from the nose and mouth to the lung are constructed, the shape of the mouth, the position of the teeth and tongue, the muscles of the throat and tongue, and by a special organ lodged in the throat, the larynx, or the voice box. Figure 13.13a is a schematic overview of this apparatus, figure 13.13b is a view of the larynx from above, and figure 13.13c shows one cycle of larynx vibrations.

In the material that follows, readers will do well to check what is being described by making the relevant oral movements and experiencing the sounds that occur for themselves. To begin, consider the larynx which receives air coming from the lungs via the trachea. The larynx is essentially a pair of flexible muscles called vocal folds or vocal cords attached to cartilage. Pressure of air coming from the lungs can force the vocal folds apart through an opening called the glottis, and the tension under which the muscles are held can lead them to close. These events recurring many times a second will generate a vibration and produce sounds. The rate of glottis opening and closing, which will vary with the tension under which the muscles are held, will produce differing pitches. If you place your fingers lightly over your Adam's apple on the throat and pronounce the sound zzzz as in "zip," you should feel the vibration. If you now sing the sound zzzz at different pitches, you will feel your Adam's apple move as pitch changes. Now if you pronounce the sound ssss as in "miss," you will note that the vibrations in the Adam's apple are gone. This is the basis of the distinction between two classes of phonemes, the voiced and the voiceless. If there is vibration, then the phoneme is voiced.

Other features of phonemes depend on the rest of the apparatus and how it is used in making sounds. Go back to ssss and zzzz and note that the positions of the mouth and tongue are identical, the two sounds differ only in voicing. Now con-

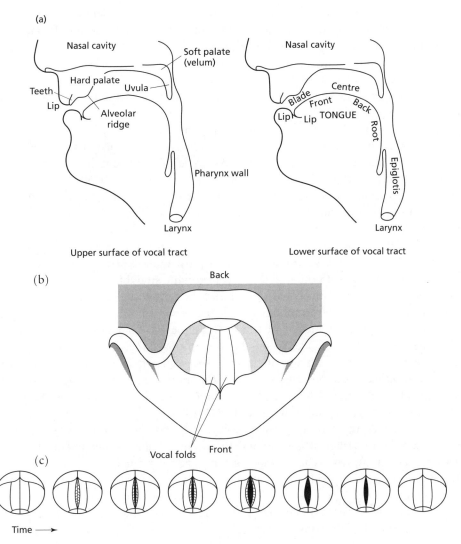

Figure 13.13(a)   The vocal tract
Figure 13.13(b)   The larynx and the vocal folds seen from above
Figure 13.13(c)   One cycle in the vibration of the vocal folds

sider the sounds ffff, as in "five," and vvvv as in "victor." These latter two sounds also differ only in voicing, but the position of the mouth is different from that used to make the ssss or zzzz sounds. The lips are folded in a special way over the teeth for ffff and vvvv so that for these it is said that the place of articulation is labio-dental (lips–teeth). For ssss and zzzz the place of articulation is alveolar, a slightly prominent ridge on the upper surface of the mouth just behind the teeth (see figure 13.13a). The other dimension that differentiates the production of phonemes is the manner of articulation. All of the sounds considered so far are fricatives, sounds made by passing a continuous stream of air through the vocal apparatus.

There are many combinations of the three variables that determine the sound qualities of phonemes, voicing, place, and manner of articulation, but only one other class of phonemes will be presented here, those that share the manner-of-articulation property of stopping the air flow completely and then releasing the air in a small burst. These are called stops. These phonemes are selected for special consideration because they illustrate the extremes of what the brain must discriminate in order to decipher the flow of speech sounds.

There are six major stop consonants in English, "b," "p," "d," "t," "g," and "k." They all share the same manner of articulation but differ in place of articulation and voicing. For those stop consonants that are voiced, voicing begins immediately as the air is released or within 20 msec. If the voicing is delayed by 40–60 msec or longer, then these consonants are termed voiceless. The six consonants can be grouped in pairs as a function of their place of articulation (see figure 13.13a). "B" (as in bed) and "p" (as in pod) are bilabials involving both lips, "d" (as in dig) and "t" (as in time) are dentals with the tongue tip on the upper teeth, and "g" (as in gift) and "k" (as in kin) are velar. Velar refers to the soft palate in the back of the roof of the mouth, an area you will note if you run your tongue straight back from your teeth, and observe first the relatively hard palate and then the softer tissues back further. If you will sound each letter as though you were starting to sound out each word, you will note voicing in the first of each pair and either no voicing or delayed voicing with the second. The remarkable thing about all this is that the difference between these pairs of consonants is the duration of the silence before voicing begins. This duration is called voice onset time. There is more to be presented about stop consonants, but that requires some explanation about the physical nature of the sounds emitted when speaking and how these sounds are studied.

First, however, the contrast between consonants and vowels. All vowels in English are voiced. The vocal tract is open and the sound is fairly steady and unchanging. Differences among vowels are a result of the position and height of the tongue and the position of the lips (Handel, 1989). Compared to consonants, the duration of vowels is quite long. Thus, for vowels, the brain does not have the challenge of detecting and identifying very rapidly changing sounds or the duration of the silence. The situation is different for consonants.

The nature of the speech signal

Technology – the sound spectrogram

The development of rapid computers and sensitive tape recorders has made possible the invention of a technique which has both increased understanding of the speech signal and posed problems that are not yet fully resolved. The technique is called a sound spectrogram (Liberman, 1995) and what it does is to represent visually the frequencies of sound emitted as a person speaks. Two examples, uttering different sentences, are presented in figure 13.14.

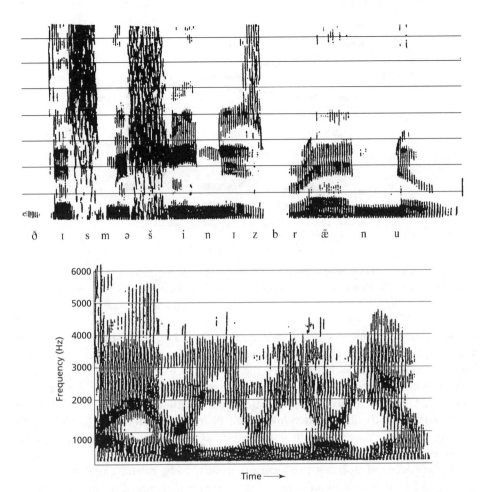

ð ɪ s m ə š i n ɪ z b r æ̃ n u

Figure 13.14 Sound spectrograms of sentences. *Top*: "This machine is brand new."
Bottom: "I owe you a yo-yo."

There are several features to note. First, the sounds of speech are obviously and
visibly complex with many frequencies being uttered simultaneously. Second, amidst
the complexity of the illustration, one can discern a series of bands, representing clusters of frequencies progressing from left to right. These bands turn out to be important and they were given the special name of formants. One can discern three or four
such formants in different spectrograms and they are labelled with consecutive
numbers from the bottom up. Thus the band of lowest frequencies is called the first
formant, the next highest the second formant, and so forth.

That the formants are indicative of the crucial parts of the speech signal was
confirmed when calculations about the width of the formants and the way they
changed over time during utterances were taken as specifications for synthesizing

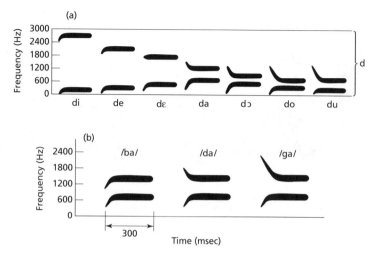

Figure 13.15(a)   Schematized sound spectrograms of one consonant and several vowels
Figure 13.15(b)   Schematized sound spectrograms of three consonants and one vowel

sounds. That is, engineers could regulate sound frequency generators to produce the sounds specified by the bands of the spectrogram. When these sounds were played back to human listeners, they reported the words that had been uttered to create the original sound spectrogram. Thus the spectrogram contained the crucial information about what had been uttered. Such procedures became part of the technology for synthesizing speech. The reader may recall hearing monotone declarations while walking through airports or train stations. One could comprehend the message but the voice sounded eerily inhuman. Such were the consequences (currently, considerably improved) of isolating the formants from the rest of the sound stream. This technique was also used in an effort to get a better understanding of the details of the nature of the language signal and some of those findings will be considered next.

Vowels and consonants on the spectrogram

A schematized spectrogram of utterances of a stop consonant and a vowel is found in figures 13.15a and 13.15b. In 13.15a there are a series of vowels with one consonant, and in 13.15b a series of consonants with one vowel. First note that only two formants are required for each of these speech sounds. Second, the shorter, frequency-changing, leftmost part of each individual figure represents the sounds of consonants. Third, the longer, so-called steady, state represents the vowels. Notice in figure 13.15a that differences among vowels are largely due to the distance of the steady state portion of the second formant from the first formant and that as one progresses from the high-pitched "di" to the low pitched "du," the top formant decreases in frequency and the two formants come closer and closer together. It is the relationships between the formants, not their absolute frequency levels, that are

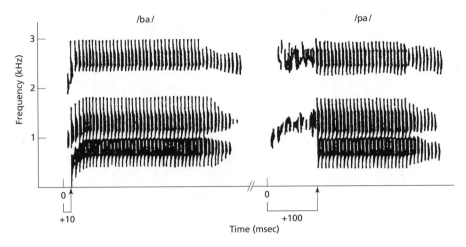

Figure 13.16   Spectrograms of syllables with different voice-onset times

perceived. This helps explain why it is just as easy discriminating vowels uttered by a high pitched soprano as by a low pitched bass.

The discrimination of consonants is in some ways a more complex matter. Notice in figure 13.15b that the only difference between three stop consonants which vary in their place of articulation, but are followed by an identical vowel, is at the beginning of the second formant, since the first formants have the same shape. Thus, in the course of speech, these important and very different consonants must be differentiated on the basis of rapid changes in one small part of the range of sounds being emitted. Careful study of the spectrograms of stop consonants also revealed that the system most discriminate not only rapidly changing sounds but also differing durations of silence. This and the special manner in which it is accomplished are considered next.

Voice onset time in stop consonants and categorical perception

Figure 13.16 enlarges the scale of the sound spectrogram and permits a closer look at the details of the difference between a voiced and a voiceless consonant. Note that in uttering the syllable "pa" it takes 100 msec to voicing onset and only 10 msec or less for "ba." This difference in time cannot be changed by voluntary intention. That is, if you were asked to produce voicing at 50 msec, the task is impossible to perform. However, since stop consonants can be synthesized on the computer, it is possible to program any voice onset time. This has been done in a large number of studies, and the question is what is perceived, which syllable, if either, is heard by the listener when the voice onset time is 20 msec, 30 msec, 40 msec, and so forth?

An idealized answer to this question is found in the graph shown in figure 13.17. The abscissa indicates a continuum and the reader might just imagine it to indicate

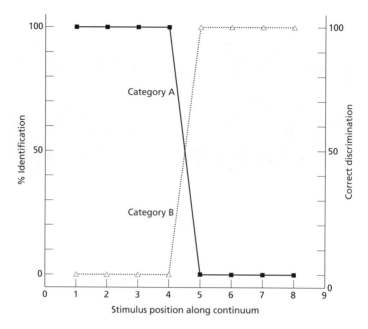

Figure 13.17 An idealized depiction of categorical perception for two stimuli varying on a continuum

voice onset time ranging from 10 to 80 msec. The terms Category A and Category B can be thought to refer to the hearing of either the voiced stop consonant "ba" or the unvoiced (actually delayed voicing) "pa." Examine the line marked by small triangles. Whenever the listener is presented with stimuli with voice onset times of less than 40 msec, they will never report hearing "ba," but when presented with stimuli of voice onset times greater than 50 msec they will always identify the signal as "pa." The converse is found in the line marked by squares. The boundary creates two zones called categories. From viewing this graph one can decide that there is a boundary between 40 and 50 msec. What this means is that any two stimuli that straddle the boundary can be consistently discriminated (will be given different labels, "ba" or "pa") while those within the boundary, even if they differ by an amount greater than the difference that straddles the boundary, will be perceived as the same. In this hypothetical example, only 10 msec separates "ba" from "pa" at the 40–50 msec range. However, if presented with stimuli with voice onset times of 50 and 80 msec, where there is a 30 msec difference, the listener would nonetheless report hearing "pa" for both. Stimuli that fall between the boundary limits will sometimes be called "pa" and sometimes "ba."

It is for this reason that the term categorical is used. A range of stimuli are perceived as occurring in one category, then there is a boundary, and stimuli beyond the boundary are perceived as being in another category. Discrimination of stimuli is possible if they straddle the boundary and not if they are within categories. One fascinating aspect of this phenomenon is that we are apparently born with the capacity to make these distinctions in this manner. The story of how this was determined is one of the major accomplishments of developmental psychology in the last several decades and full details can be found in a number of sources (Eimas, Miller, & Jusczyk, 1987; Jusczyk, 1995).

Briefly, the original authors (Eimas et al., 1971) made use of the phenomenon of habituation in order to study infants as young as one month old. Habituation was indexed by rate of sucking. Earlier it had been discovered that infants enjoyed sucking and could be encouraged to suck at a high rate if they were rewarded for sucking by presenting them with the sound of a speech syllable such as the syllable "ba" produced with a voice onset time in the center of its category. The more the infant sucked the more the speech syllable was played. But even infants get tired of the same thing over and over again, and they habituate (decrease their responding) to repeated stimulation. When a predetermined level of habituation was reached, the study continued under one of three conditions. Some of the infants continued to hear the same stimulus every time they sucked. A second group heard a "pa," a stimulus across the categorical boundary. The third group heard another "ba" – a stimulus with a different voice onset time than the first but one that was still within the "ba" categorical boundary.

The question was would the second or the third group behave like the first or would they differ. The behavior would reveal whether the infants who had no speech, and really did not yet babble, would respond to the sound as something novel, in which case their rate of sucking would go up, or as the same old thing, in which case it would respond like the first group who were hearing the same old thing. The results were that the first group continued to show evidence of habituation as did the third. Only the second group hearing "pa" increased their rate of sucking. The data were interpreted to mean that only the second group perceived the changes and that the way they perceived the changes was similar to the manner found in adults – categorically.

This work was verified many times by others and was applied to the study of many other phonemic types. One overall conclusion confirmed the idea that children are born with the ability to perceive the phonemes of any language, and that these capabilities atrophy if these phonemes are not heard. Furthermore, where category boundaries exist (not all language is categorical), they may initially be wider or in a somewhat different location than is found in adults. Thus through the course of development, category boundaries are narrowed and tuned to the sound patterns of a language and there are even circumstances where new boundaries are developed. In these findings one gets a clearer picture of the kind of contribution made by genetic endowment, the role of experience, and the intricate ways nature and nurture interact.

Summary of information about the speech code and its perception

Research into the nature of the speech code has been productive. Much is known about the relatively slow aspects of speech (mostly vowels) and its rapidly changing aspects (mostly consonants). Speech is produced by various combinations of voicing, place, and manner of articulation in the mouth and throat, and its accurate decoding depends on the registry of rapidly changing sounds, brief episodes of silence, and the sequences in which they occur. Some crucial aspects of the speech code are categorical in nature, which must require an intricate set of neural processors that would permit the necessary timing to occur. Given this special quality of language, much of early language learning consists of learning how to hear and differentiate its sound codes. Despite all that is known, crucial questions about the perception of the speech code remain unresolved. As presented by Nygaard and Pisoni (1995), these questions include how segmented units are extracted from a continuous, overlapping stream of sound, and how specific units are so easily perceived when their physical characteristics vary considerably and depend on what other sounds precede or succeed them. Progress has also been made in understanding the impairments that occur when language does not develop normally or when disease alters previously acquired language capabilities. These topics will be considered below.

The components of language and the adult brain

There is considerable evidence that language in the adult brain is modularized, i.e. that the different aspects of language just described are regulated by different parts of the brain (Blumstein, 1995). The dimensions of analysis are front (motor areas) vs back (sensory areas), and right hemisphere vs left. An overly simple formulation which will be amended shortly is that the left hemisphere is specialized for language, that the frontal areas anterior to the representation of the throat and mouth on the motor strip regulate language expression, and an area adjacent to Heschl's gyrus (see figure 3.7) in the temporal lobe and extending up and around the end of the lateral sulcus (the one that is the upper boundary of the temporal lobe) in the angular gyrus is responsible for language comprehension. The frontal area is also known as Broca's area, named for the neurologist who first described a type of language impairment acquired in adulthood, often after a stroke, in which language is understood but cannot be expressed. This condition is variously termed motor, expressive, nonfluent, or Broca's aphasia. The temporal–angular gyrus area is also known as Wernicke's area, named for the neurologist who described a kind of aphasia in which language is not understood or spoken meaningfully, although fluent speech sounds may be uttered. This condition is variously termed receptive, sensory, fluent, or Wernicke's aphasia. Figure 13.18 displays these language-related areas and the band of white matter fibers that connects them, the arcuate fasciculus. Lesions that cut this band of fibers prevent communication between front and back and produce a disorder called conduction aphasia whose hallmark symptom is that the patient has difficulty repeating utterances that have been heard. Finally, if all of these areas, and subcortical areas as well are seriously impaired, an individual will suffer from global aphasia, the most devastating language impairment where neither comprehension, expression, nor repetition is possible.

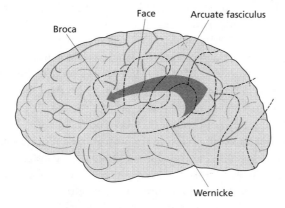

Figure 13.18   Major areas of the brain involved in language

Some restrictions, amendments, and extensions

The statements made above are based largely on data obtained by correlating behavioral changes with anatomical changes in brain-injured adults. Furthermore, they are restricted to right-handed males who come from right-handed families. In women, and when there are differences between the individual and the immediate family in handedness, there are modifications in the degree to which the statements hold. Keeping such limitations in mind, available evidence suggests that the perception of phonemes occurs equally in both the left and right hemispheres, though there is also evidence of selective contributions by each hemisphere (Molfese, Buhrke, & Wang, 1985). Both hemispheres can comprehend words but the left is vastly superior in this regard, particularly when it comes to abstract words and concepts (Zaidel, 1985). The content words of the lexicon are stored in the back of the brain, especially the left hemisphere. The right hemisphere has almost no syntactic capability, and syntactic organization and function words appear to be the province of Broca's rather than Wernicke's area. By contrast, only the left hemisphere controls the motor apparatus for language expression. Language, as it is spoken and experienced, is intertwined with emotion, and the prosodaic and emotional aspects of language are under greater control by the right hemisphere than the left.

Thus, "dominance" of the left hemisphere for language appears to occur primarily in the control of the speech-motor apparatus, in the production and comprehension of the syntactic aspects of language, and in abstract, logical thought. Even in the right-handed and right-familied male, there is considerable involvement of the right hemisphere. Evidence obtained with newer imaging techniques which non-invasively allows for a much finer-grained analysis of how the brain functions, has confirmed and extended these findings (e.g. Binder et al., 1994). As a general rule, the main extensions are that brain activation occurs over more widespread areas in the left hemisphere and also extends significantly into the right hemisphere than was originally thought, and secondly, there is much variation in the locale and pattern of activation across individuals. Furthermore, prior evidence that the brains of the two sexes activate in different ways when performing language tasks has been verified by these new techniques (Shaywitz et al., 1995). Male brains tend to be more modularized (more delimited areas are activated for particular tasks) than female brains. In addition, it is also clear that brains vary considerably in the details of their structure and in the way they function, even though they may perform with the same proficiency.

Finally, there seems to be much less in the way of fixed modularity during the early stages of language development. Indeed, the brain as a whole, and particularly the right hemisphere, is involved in very early language perception (Molfese & Molfese, 1986). Damage which occurs to brain areas after modularity is developed and stabilized, roughly at about the onset of puberty, leads to language impairments that are resistant to rehabilitation. Receptive impairments are much harder to ameliorate than expressive deficits. On the other hand, damage which occurs very early, during the first two or three years of life, even to the extent of removing an entire hemicortex, may not be an obstacle to nearly normal language development, but the outcome is better if the left hemisphere is the one that is spared (Dennis & Whitaker, 1976). Further consideration of the pathology of language development is the topic of the next section of this chapter.

Pathology of Language Development – Developmental Dysphasia

Research on developmental language handicaps is fairly recent and has been facilitated by devising measurement techniques which can separate receptive from expressive disorders. This is accomplished by using tests of reception and comprehension which are not dependent on utterance; for example, inquiring about comprehension by means of a yes–no or multiple-choice format or by using pictures. Such tests contrast with methods in which responses must be formulated into spoken words or sentences. In addition, the assessment of developmental language difficulties must differentiate weaknesses in the mastery of a specific language, for example, standard English, from impairment in language capability. Brain function is not impaired if a child is poor in standard English, for example, but speaks in a dialect, such as Cockney or Black English, whose rules of expression are different from standard English. Such individuals have simply learned a somewhat different language and are not neuropsychologically impaired no matter how disadvantaged they may be from the social perspective of those who speak the dominant language (Labov, 1972).

As data about language development became available, early ideas about what was wrong emphasized hierarchically high language impairments such as those of pragmatics, syntax, or semantics or higher cognitive functions such as conceptual ability (see Tallal, 1980, for review). Much of that perspective has changed in the light of the work of Tallal and others, which will be reviewed next.

Auditory successiveness and developmental dysphasia

Tallal hypothesized that children with abnormal language development are impaired in their abilities to perceive the correct order of rapidly changing sound sequences. Such sequences can be very important in language, for example, in words such as "nest" and "nets" where the difference in meaning lies in the order of the sounds. To evaluate this hypothesis, she devised a procedure called the Repetition Test, which made use of a response box which consisted of two slightly movable panels, one above the other. Each was wired in such a way that slight pressure would close a switch. Subjects could press either the upper or lower panel and their decision and their reaction time would be recorded and measured. To evaluate the perception of auditory successiveness, subjects were presented with a series of 75 msec tones at two frequencies and taught to depress the bottom panel when they heard the lower tone and the top panel when they heard the higher tone. They were then taught to report the order of two tones by pressing the appropriate panels in sequence. The tone pairs were either identical or different and were presented in all possible orders at an interstimulus interval (the time between the conclusion of the first stimulus and the initiation of the second) of 428 msec (almost half a second). Once subjects were trained, they were tested for their ability to track successiveness at shorter and shorter interstimulus intervals. The shortest interval at which they could perform accurately was determined. Also assessed was the ability to discriminate two different tones at short intervals. The response box was turned on its side and subjects were trained to press the left panel when the stimuli were different and the right when they were the same. The detection of difference is simpler than the detection of stimulus order.

Tallal and colleagues (Tallal, 1980) then compared dysphasic children with language delays defined by well-known tests of language development, with age-matched children whose level of non-verbal competence was similar. The results were that the children differed in their perception of these auditory stimuli, both in discrimination and successiveness, when they were presented rapidly but not when they were presented at longer intervals. Children with normal language development could perform these tasks at interstimulus intervals as short as 8 msec while the language-impaired subjects could not perform the task unless the interval was at least 305 msec. By arranging similar tests with visual stimuli, they found that the impairment was limited to the auditory modality. In later research (Tallal et al., 1981), this conclusion was modified as visual temporal processing impairments were found in language-impaired children although they were of lesser magnitude than those found in the auditory modality and tended to disappear as the children got to be older than eight years.

Tallal suggested that the short durations at which the dysphasic children differed from those with normal language were comparable to the timing features of many consonants. Thus, there was evidence that the handicap in developmental language impairment was at the level of phoneme registration, and more particularly in the ability to sequence and discriminate rapidly changing sounds. Such findings were consistent with contemporary research describing the physical nature of phonemes, thereby specifying what was required of the nervous system in order to perceive language (Liberman, 1995).

Tallal's work has progressed in two directions. She and her colleagues have taken advantage of the development of sophisticated imaging procedures such as magnetic resonance imaging (MRI) that permit noninvasive detailed images of brain structures. They have obtained such images from samples of their language-impaired subjects and from normal controls (Tallal, Sainburg, & Jernigan, 1991). When the images were read clinically, no differences in the number of abnormalities were found. However, quantitative measures of structural differences in the volume of various regions of the brain, including Wernicke's area, were different in the two groups. It is of interest that not only the left but also the right side of this brain region was smaller in the dysphasic children. The quantitative differences were initially interpreted to be a possible cause of language dysfunction, and thought in many cases to have been determined genetically.

A second direction has been to train dysphasic children to identify sequences of short interval sounds accurately (Merzenich et al., 1996; Tallal et al., 1996). The children were asked to identify and discriminate sequences of language and language-like stimuli in the context of highly motivating games and exercises. The innovative aspect of the training was to vary the crucial rapid transitions whose tracking was thought to be impaired. As the children mastered the detection of changes at those speeds they could manage, they were challenged with faster and faster changes. In this gradual manner, with four weeks of intensive training, the dysphasic children were able to improve their performance the equivalent of two or more years of language experience and came to perform like the controls. The children were tested before and after training with Tallal's Repetition Test as well as with a number of standard measures of language proficiency, and demonstrated comparable gains which were maintained for at least six weeks after the training period.

Noting the rapidity with which the children improved, the authors expressed doubt that the smaller brain volumes found previously indicated genetically determined deficits in language capabilities. Rather, they speculated that brain growth in certain regions had been arrested because the children were not processing language well. What, then, might account for the language lag? At present their speculations are not very clear, but developmental processes appear to be crucial. That is, some factors, largely unknown (although middle ear infection may be a likely candidate in some) may make it hard to learn or may set a pattern of learning in which phonetics are not processed accurately even though the "molecular and cellular elements of the learning machinery of their brains" are not defective (Merzenich et al., 1996, p. 80).

Tallal and colleagues' work on auditory successiveness and its relationship to developmental dysphasia concurs nicely with the evidence of the special character of the phonemic code found in the work of Liberman and his colleagues. Thus, language problems, both those that appear spontaneously in development and those acquired as a result of some pathological process, very often involve phonemic impairments. This does not mean that all language impairments have phonemic difficulties at their root. Impairments may occur at hierarchically higher dimensions of language in semantics, syntactics, and pragmatics and in higher cognitive functions, but studies which rule out phonemic deficits before implicating such functions are not readily found. Much research is needed to clarify our knowledge in this area. Meanwhile, a cautionary note: in the three years since Tallal et al.'s and Merzenich et al.'s (1996) exciting research reports appeared, their treatment has been made available to the general public through the offices of speech pathologists and other professionals on a fee-for-service basis, but, as far as can be ascertained, no further research reports have appeared. Readers will want to check the current literature if they are interested in this method of treatment.

Receptive and expressive dysphasia

It should be clear by now that having a language (in the most common and simplest sense of the word; exceptions will be discussed below) means being able to hear it. By hearing, reference is made not only to transducing the sound frequencies but to segregating different features in the sound stream, registering the sequences and the duration of the silences, and being able to remember what has been heard. Thus receptive language capabilities are crucial, and much language learning consists of tuning the ear to hear the language. The importance of reception does not mean that expression is immune to impairment. A child can display various kinds of articulatory difficulties which interfere with the production of understandable expression and reduce the richness of what one can say. There are two major classes of such disorders. In one, the problem is in the musculature and other structures which produce speech sounds. This type of disturbance is called a dysarthria. In the other, the problem is not in the apparatus itself but in the brain mechanisms which regulate the apparatus. This type of disturbance is called an expressive dysphasia. Since, as has been noted, later development of comprehension is facilitated by the ability to speak, expressive difficulties may lead to some relative weakness in understanding.

Further evidence for the special nature of the receptive process in language comes from the study of a remarkable disorder of language called the Landau–Kleffner syndrome. A description of this disorder will close the discussion of developmental language disorders.

Landau–Kleffner syndrome, also known as acquired epileptiform aphasia

In Landau–Kleffner syndrome (Landau & Kleffner, 1957; Rapin et al., 1977; Roget et al., 1993; Stefanatos et al., 1998), children who have developed normally for roughly three to seven years cease to progress in language development and then begin to lose their receptive and, later, their expressive language skills. The order sometimes is reversed and the disorder may progress to global aphasia. Although unable to process auditory language, the children continue to hear a large range of sounds including noises, bells, music, and the like. (Further definition of nonlanguage "pure tone hearing" can be found both earlier and later in this chapter.) The deterioration of language often co-occurs with the appearance of ictal activity, hence the newer designation of acquired epileptiform aphasia. This includes changes in the EEG, particularly over the temporal lobes during sleep, and the onset of overt seizures in 70 percent of the cases. Many of the children show continuous 3–4/sec spike and wave activity during slow wave sleep (e.g. Rintahaka, Chugani, & Sankar, 1995). The frequency, type of seizure, and EEG findings are poorly correlated with changes in language. Furthermore, seizures are often brought under control with standard anticonvulsant medications, but such control does not influence language capability or the course of the illness. This gives rise to the hypothesis that both the seizures and the aphasia are consequences of some unknown pathological process, e.g. possibly of the immune system (Lagae et al., 1998): the seizures themselves are not responsible for the aphasia (Stefanatos et al., 1998). Additional behavior symptoms often accompany the deterioration in language, most commonly attentional, oppositional, or withdrawal symptoms. Less common but more frequent in children whose dysphasia begins early, are psychotic and autistic like symptoms (see chapter 15).

Although the disorder is quite rare, it is of great interest because it clearly demonstrates that the processes making possible receptive language go beyond those required for pure tone hearing. Furthermore, the presence of seizures, no matter how poorly correlated with language changes, suggests that the mechanism underlying the disorder is a type of dyscontrol, and thus reversible, rather than a type of subtractive deficit, i.e. loss of the processors. This idea is supported when it is learned that there is rarely any evidence of a structural lesion despite study with various techniques, even extending to biopsy (a procedure in which a small amount of tissue is extracted and examined microscopically (Cole et al., 1988)). There is evidence of inadequate blood flow to the left temporoparietal area but no explanation as to why. Yet further verification comes with evidence that the condition is sometimes reversible. Some children who have endured total loss of language may fully recover. This may occur spontaneously and may be helped by continuing efforts at speech therapy (Stefanatos et al., 1998). It may also occur in response to two kinds of medical intervention: treatment with steroids (Marescaux et al., 1990) or surgery which involves making parallel cuts in temporal cortex (Neville et al., 1995), an intervention among a class of surgical strategies designed to curtail the spread of excessive excitability.

Stefanatos, Green, and Ratcliff (1989) devised a procedure which may be particularly useful in the study and diagnosis of developmental dysphasia, including the Landau–Kleffner syndrome. The procedure is an evoked potential with a special stimulus whose detection was thought to depend on the same mechanisms that decode speech, even though it sounds subjectively like a wavering tone (Kay, 1976). The stimulus was constructed by causing a tone of 1,000 Hz to fluctuate sinusoidally from peak to trough, changing its peak gradually ±4 Hz every ¼ sec. The modulation rate was either 10, 20, or 40 Hz. In children with normal language, an evoked potential appeared (if averaged over 400 ¼-sec epochs) which followed the envelope of sound produced by the frequency modulation. No such evoked potential appeared in children with receptive dysphasia or Landau–Kleffner syndrome. What did appear was a flat wave which also occurred in all subjects when hearing unmodulated tones.

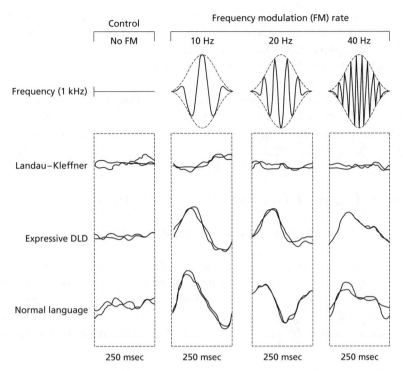

Figure 13.19 Evoked potentials to frequency-modulated tones in subjects with Landau–Kleffner syndrome, expressive language delays, and normal language. The stimuli consisted of a continuous 1-kHz pure tone carrier frequency modulated at rates of 10, 20, and 40 Hz. The depth of modulation was 4 Hz and occurred four times per second. Evoked potentials are time-locked to the envelope imposed by the modulation depth. The two responses depicted for each condition come from left and right hemispheres

This procedure is not easy to understand if one is unfamiliar with these concepts, but examination of figure 13.19 (Stefanatos, 1993), which presents the data for Landau–Kleffner, expressive dysphasia, and normal-language subjects may aid in grasping the nature of the methods and of the results obtained. Note that expressive dysphasics are like normals in terms of receptive skills and have an evoked response comparable to that of the normal children. The Landau–Kleffner children showed no evoked potentials to the frequency modulated tones and responded much like they would to ordinary sounds. Another interesting finding was that there was essentially no difference between the evoked potentials in each hemisphere, which is consistent with other data about the bilateral reception of phonemes. Finally, and most important, if language improved, the evoked potential returned. Thus, Stefanatos and colleagues have provided a promising measurement procedure for assessing the integrity of the speech-detecting mechanism of the brain.

Independent replication of these findings has not appeared despite the passage of several years. On the other hand, Duffy, one of the pioneers of quantitative EEG, has begun to use Stefananatos' procedure, and on his web page, reports favorably as to its validity only with preliminary data. (It would certainly be of interest to know how Tallal and Merzenich's language-impaired subjects performed on Stefanatos' evoked potentials both before and after training.)

This chapter next turns to the study of hearing loss, both mild and severe, and the lessons learned from experience in educating those who have sustained such impairments. There shall be further evidence of the nature of the plasticity of the brain and the interaction of experience and tissue over time in producing behavioral outcomes.

Deafness, Impaired Hearing and its Consequences

Definitions of deafness and hearing impairment – audiometry

Given the complexity of the auditory system and the special processing required for the detection and comprehension of language, it may come as no surprise that the definition of hearing loss and of deafness is also a matter of considerable complexity. The diagnosis of hearing loss generally occurs by means of an audiometric (which means measurement of hearing) examination. A central feature of this evaluation is an audiogram.

The audiogram

A standard hearing test is composed of several parts (Martin, 1981), only some of which will be presented here. Generally, the subject is seated in a sound-attenuated cubicle so that ambient noise can be controlled. Air conduction thresholds are determined by presenting tones at different frequencies. The amplitude at each frequency is varied to determine the loudness at which the tone can be detected. Most often, six or seven specific frequencies are tested, covering the range utilized for language and somewhat beyond. Loudness is measured in dB of loss; i.e. 0 indicates no loss or normal hearing, and increasing positive numbers indicate greater hearing loss. A negative number indicates hypersensitivity to a particular frequency. Each ear is tested separately and, by convention, the results for the right ear are represented in circles and the left in x's. A normal audiogram of pure tone hearing is presented in figure 13.20. According to one system of classification, losses up to 15 dB are not considered significant. Borderline impairment would be 15–25 dB, mild between 26 and 40 dB, moderate, 41–55 dB, moderate to severe losses between 56 and 70 dB, severe losses 71–90 dB and profound losses those greater than 90 dB (Bernero & Rothwell, 1986). Legally, deafness is often defined as a loss of 80 dB or greater.

Since transduction of sound at particular frequencies is determined by hair cells in particular regions of the basilar membrane, it is possible for hearing at certain frequencies to be quite impaired while nearby frequencies are intact or less impaired. To deal with this complexity, the definition of deafness may refer to an 80 dB loss or more for the average of three frequencies (500; 1,000; and 2,000 Hz) which are com-

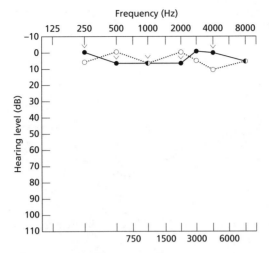

Figure 13.20 A normal pure tone audiogram

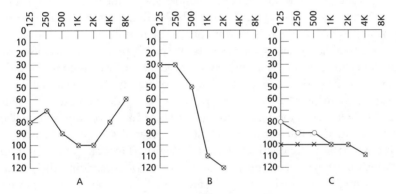

Figure 13.21 Three audiograms each averaging 95 dB of loss in the speech range

monly found in speech. Figure 13.21 shows three different audiograms where the average for the speech range is 95 dB of loss (Meadow, 1980). Each of these individuals will be severely impaired in hearing but in different ways. Thus, even in the range of loss considered as deafness, residual hearing exists, and the strengths and weaknesses at particular frequencies make a difference.

Another aspect of the standard audiogram is illustrated in figure 13.22. Here one can see a banana-shaped figure superimposed on the audiogram within which are indicated at which frequencies and what dB level the various components of speech can be detected. Later, there will be a discussion of technical devices that aid hearing. If the decibel loss level can be raised above the "banana" by means of such devices, audiologists would anticipate that the subject would be able to learn to perceive the phonemes below. Thus audiometric findings would provide the language teacher with targets that could be attained with reasonable effort.

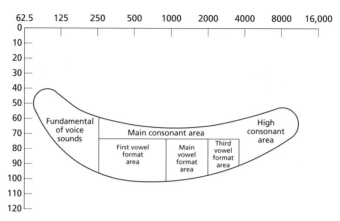

Figure 13.22 The audiogram "banana" – dB levels at different frequencies required to detect different features of language

Other parts of the audiometric exam almost always include the determination of bone conduction thresholds to contrast with air conduction findings, and thus help specify whether the problem is in the cochlea or middle ear. In addition, word or sentence discrimination and other aspects of speech perception are also evaluated. The subject is presented with a single word or groups of words containing the range of phonemes and is asked to repeat the words or signify their meaning. The level of amplification at which an adequate response is made is noted. A child with Landau–Kleffner syndrome might do well at all of the pure tone frequencies in air and bone conduction but fail to repeat all but a few of the spoken words.

Such examinations are conducted by audiologists. The data are useful in the diagnosis of hearing impairment and provide the basis for prescribing the technical and educational means to ameliorate the condition. Several points are relevant. First, hearing is complex and it is probably inappropriate to summarize the condition of any individual with a single number or index. Rather, a pattern of scores is required to assess the complexities of the system adequately. Second, very few individuals have absolutely no hearing. Most functionally deaf individuals have some residual hearing in at least some frequencies. Third, there are many varieties of hearing impairment, and impairment of sensitivity in the speech range may produce different consequences than impairments outside that range.

Technological amelioration of hearing impairment

There are two basic techniques for aiding hearing: amplification and cochlear implants. The development of this latter technology has been controversial, but it has significantly influenced methods of education and habilitation.

Amplification of sound is the oldest means of aiding the hard-of-hearing. Such techniques increase the intensity of the sound impinging on the tympanic membrane

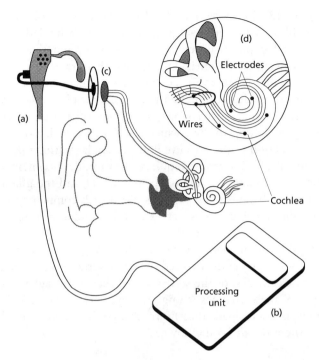

Figure 13.23   The components of a cochlear implant: (a) tiny microphone worn behind ear picks up sounds, which are transmitted to processing unit; (b) processing unit, carried in a pocket, selects and codes the sounds most useful for understanding speech and sends them back to transmitter; (c) transmitter sends signal across skin to receiver implanted underneath skin behind the ear; (d) receiver forwards signal along wires inserted in ear and to an array of individually programmable electrodes implanted along the cochlea, where they stimulate hearing nerve fibers with signals varying in loudness and pitch. Nerves relay the signals to the brain, which interprets them as sound

and stimulate residual hearing capabilities. The technology began with horn-shaped instruments in which the narrow apex of a cone-shaped device is placed in the ear and the wider base faces outwardly and collects sound waves which summate and intensify as they move inward. With the development of electronics and its increasing miniaturization, sensitive microphones and louder amplification was made possible in smaller instruments. More recently, computerized technology has permitted tuning the amplification to specific frequencies and thus customizing the aid to the particular pattern of deficits of the hearing-impaired person.

Cochlear implants are a much more recent development. They are employed when the hearing loss is due to severe impairment or destruction of the hair cell transduction mechanism in the cochlea but where the acoustic nerve, which originates in the cochlea and carries auditory signals to the brain, is functional. The technique was originally designed to deal with acquired deafness in adults, but more recently has been used with children, including those who have never heard normally. In current versions (see figure 13.23), more than 20 electrodes may be implanted at different points in the cochlea. A tiny microphone, worn in or behind the ear, transduces sounds into electrical impulses which are sent to a computerized processing unit which shapes and organizes the signal. The signal is then transmitted to an implanted receiver which sends the signals to the cochlea. This signal conveys information, but the information is not readily comprehensible to the recipient, not any more than a newborn child understands what sounds, speech or otherwise, might mean. The meaning of the signal getting to the cochlea has to be learned, a process which normally occurs over a period of three to five years. A similar learning period is required with cochlear implants. Such learning requires intensive, developmentally progressive stimulation, the involvement and support of the family, and the guidance of audiologically sophisticated therapists and teachers. With such complexity, the technology and associated educational effort is very expensive and not available to all who need it.

The technology of the implant has been progressing at an extraordinary rate in each of the component processes involved, whether surgical technique, the type and positioning of the electrodes, or the software that shapes the signal. Research evaluating the efficacy of these changes is ongoing and very active (Uziel et al., 1995). Accordingly, one may anticipate that more changes will appear in the immediate future, and that the costs will come down.

Development and education of the deaf

If a case still needs to be made that tissue (or constitutional factors) and experience interact in producing psychological outcomes, the study of the development of the hearing-impaired and of deaf persons leaves no room for doubt. Some of the factors that interact include the cause and timing of the hearing impairment, the family and circumstances into which the child is born, and the timing and type of the child's education. Consideration of what is known about some of these variables follows.

Former patterns of "typical" education for the deaf

(Note: What follows was typical through the fifth or sixth decade of the twentieth century and may still occur.) Most deaf children were born to hearing parents. Severe hearing impairment would occur because of genetic anomalies or gestational insult such as rubella during the first trimester. After birth, some infants lost their hearing early as a result of infection, e.g. meningitis or scarlet fever. It was unlikely that a definitive diagnosis of deafness would be made much sooner than their first birthday. Children born to hearing parents who were made deaf early on would have no means of direct communication other than gesture through the preschool years. When the children reached school age, enrollment into a school or special class for the deaf occurred. In such schools, a persistent effort was made to teach lip reading and speaking (with or without the amplification of powerful hearing aids). This approach was called the oral method, and schools using the method discouraged or actively forbade the use of any other means of communication. (Note: the term oral method emphasized speech output. To the extent that hearing aids were used and the children were trained to listen, the similar-sounding term aural method was used. Sometimes the terms were combined as the oral–aural method.)

The children had much difficulty talking, enunciated with limited discriminability and no prosody, and often failed altogether. They lived in a communication vacuum. Things would change, earlier if at residential schools and later if in special classes at a day school, when they would come in contact with older deaf children. The older children would teach the younger ones how to communicate in sign language, often over the active opposition of teachers and family. At this point, the children would psychologically enter the community of the deaf and no longer be alone. They would leave their hearing families and enter this community physically and independently as soon as they were old enough (Furth, 1973; Meadow, 1980; Neisser, 1983).

Modifications in the pattern of typical education and consequences for development

Suppose children become deaf between the ages of 4 and 6 and at the age of $6\frac{1}{2}$ were entered into the same type of school described above. In such cases, the long-term outcome was likely to be much more favorable. Readers who recall the phenomenon of amblyopia from chapter 12 should have no difficulty understanding why. The children who became deaf after they learned a language also developed the phonemic feature-detector mechanisms in their brains. They could grasp more readily what the teacher was getting at when attempting to help them form sounds and lip read, and they were better able to discern some pattern of information when the muted signal coming from their auditory system was amplified.

Before the advent of antibiotics and vaccines for rubella, children with acquired deafness constituted a far greater percentage of deaf people than is true today. Their ability to benefit from oral training may have misled many into believing that this educational approach should work with all deaf children. Thus, it is possible that antibiotics have made the oral method obsolete because, currently, relatively few persons become deaf after learning language.

A different scenario occurs to those born deaf whose parents are deaf. Such children learn to communicate by means of sign language and enter the deaf community naturally. These children will not be burdened by the lack of a communication system. A variant on this situation occurs when a hearing child is born to deaf parents. Such children grow up with two languages, sign language and their broader community's tongue, but they are very different from their parents and thus have the challenge of being more on their own in constructing their identity. A vivid description of these circumstances can be found in Preston (1994).

Yet another scenario modified the typical curriculum with its exclusive reliance on the oral method. For a long time, oralists (as those who support the exclusive use of the oral method are termed) assumed that the use of sign language would interfere with the development of speech because the children would prefer signing to the hard work of learning to talk (Meadow, 1980, p. 143). With evidence that any form of adequate communication facilitates the learning of other forms of communication (e.g. Vernon & Koh, 1971; Meadow, 1966), a synthesis of methods termed total communication was developed. This educational approach made communication by any means the prime goal. Thus sign language was introduced early on and combined with the oral method. A teacher presenting subjects such as science, history, or literature might both speak and sign at the same time. Total communication is probably the most common approach to the education of the deaf today and is associated with some evidence of improved outcomes. However, both Meadow (1980) and Neisser (1983) suggest that its implementation often leaves much to be desired. Teachers frequently concentrate on speech itself rather than on social communication or information transmission.

Finally, there was a scenario which was based on the assumption that even the most profoundly impaired had some residual hearing and that such hearing could be used to prevent the atrophy of the feature detectors. To do so depended entirely on early diagnosis, a goal not easily accomplished (Kenworthy, 1987; Diefendorf, 1988; Downs & Gerkin, 1988). There were, however, observations and assessment techniques that could be used with young infants and which could alert parents and professionals to hearing impairment. Foremost were observations that the children's eyes and head did not turn to sound or show a startle response to sudden loud noises. Other assessment procedures (Martin, 1981) made use of the evoked response, the EEG procedures described earlier in this chapter. Once severe hearing loss was verified, children, even in the first months of life, were fitted with the most powerful hearing aids available. They were then subjected to a program of auditory and verbal stimulation and vocalization practice which was graded to follow the sequence of normal development (Pollack, 1985; Moeller, Osberger, & Morford, 1987; Ling, 1989). This program was called auditory–verbal therapy and capitalized on the special capabilities of preschool children to learn language. The technique was time-consuming and expensive, and requiring periodic lessons with a trained teacher–therapist, support and active teaching from family members, and special preschool and kindergarten environments.

The results of this early intervention, particularly if begun early in the first year, were often remarkable. By the ninth or tenth year, children could speak clearly, free of the limited intelligibility that was the fate of almost all born-deaf children educated in the oral method (Canadian Broadcasting Corp., 1991). Such children did not need to sign or to join the community of the deaf, even though their hearing remained severely impaired. They were mainstreamed into regular classes from the beginning, whereas mainstreaming for those who sign is a controversial issue.

Many proponents of the auditory–verbal method have warmly embraced the use of cochlear implants in preschool hearing-impaired children. Auditory–verbal techniques of early education and graded language stimulation appear to be well suited to take advantage of the sound sensations the implants make possible. Often, early-implanted children may require no further special training by the time they are old enough for first grade. Examination of the pure tone audiometry of such children suggests that this is no surprise since their thresholds after implanting and training may be in the 20–30 dB range (above the "banana" in figure 13.21), which ordinarily allows the learning of language.

Deafness, identity, and self-esteem

Many people in the deaf community have endured long periods of social isolation and stigmatization because of their lack of hearing. Historically, the deaf were considered intrinsically stupid and were often reviled or ostracized. Later, when education for the deaf became an accepted standard, teachers, parents, and others went to great lengths to keep their deaf children from signing even at the expense of being able to communicate. Given the difficult circumstances of their development, many deaf individuals have come to take great pride in their hard-earned accomplishments. Rather than think that their society and mode of communication is an approximation of what the hearing community has, they have asserted the validity and value of how they live and communicate. Many have also come to think that reluctance to expose deaf children to sign language is a form of prejudice against the deaf and a sign of unwillingness to accept their being different.

In some, this pride has become militant, much as it has in many groups who have fought against assumptive prejudices and sought recognition and acceptance for themselves as they are. Some deaf adults have expressed the preference that their children be born deaf, much like devout practitioners of a religion might wish their children to become members of their own faith. Programs such as the auditory–verbal approach, which have as their goal the integration of the deaf into the hearing community, have been opposed. In the more extreme arguments coming from this position, cochlear implants have been described as a form of genocide (destroying the deaf community and its culture) and as experimentation on deaf children in a manner akin to Nazi medical experiments on holocaust victims (Balkany, 1995). A related factor is economic. All techniques attempting to educate the deaf so that they can fully enter the community of the hearing require resources of money and personnel which are not available to many. Thus a number of philosophical, economic, and political issues appear in controversies about how best to educate the deaf, and decisions are influenced by many factors other than scientific evidence about efficacy. This may actually be true about many applications of science, but such issues are very conspicuous in deaf education.

Summary of some of the factors that determine language outcome in the deaf and severely hearing-impaired

The five education-outcome scenarios described above represent discernlible combinations of factors that influence outcome in those whose hearing is compromised early in life. A summary of the relevant issues would consider the specific variables that contribute to each of those constellations. Such variables would include:

(1)   the magnitude of the hearing loss at specific frequencies and the residual hearing that remains;

(2)   the age at the time of loss and prior level of language development;

(3)   the age when remediation is initiated;

(4)   the details of the remediation program and its manner of implementation;

(5)   the resources, support, and involvement of the family and the school the child attends;

(6)   the presence of handicaps other than deafness;

(7)   the general competency of the child;

(8)   the philosophical and political stance of the family regarding deafness.

Given such complexity, it is no wonder that much controversy remains about how best to educate the severely hearing-impaired. From the perspective of our general knowledge about brain functions, it is clear that outcome is not determined solely by the nature of the handicap but is heavily influenced by the environment and the way it has stimulated, supported, and taught the individual.

What is the nature of the verbal language that the hard-of-hearing acquire?

Suppose a deaf person has learned to speak well, with good intonation, fluency, and intelligibility. Is such a remarkable achievement identical to the speech of a normally hearing person? In one sense, pragmatically and functionally, the answer is yes. In another sense, however, the answer is no. There is strong evidence, obtained mostly in the 1970s, that the speech and linguistic information processing of the deaf is different from that of the hearing. Several experiments about this issue will be sampled and then their implications will be considered together.

One example comes from the work of Conrad (1972), who studied the errors deaf and hearing children made in a short-term memory task in order to determine whether these two groups remembered in the same way. In earlier work, it had been established that normally hearing individuals remember words by their sounds. That is, if given a list of words to remember, whether the words are presented acoustically (by hearing speech) or visually (by reading print), one stores the memory of words as sound patterns.

The question is whether the deaf store words that way or whether they remember words by the way they look when spelled or by some other means such as the movement pattern used when they are signed. Devising a method to approach this question, Conrad reasoned as follows. Some letters sound the same (rhyme) when named, and he selected six that do: B, C, D, P, T, and V. Because they sound the same, if you are trying to remember different letters by the way they sound, then you are likely to get them mixed up because their similarity makes them acoustically confusable. By contrast, one can select another group of letters, K, N, V, X, Y, Z, which are all made up of straight lines. If, having stored them acoustically, you are trying to remember letters from this group, there will not be much similarity in the way the names of the letters sound because they are all different. However, if you remember them by the way they look, then errors may occur because they share the similarity of straight lines and are visually confusable. Thus errors would be more likely to occur with the group of letters that were more confusable in the modality being used to remember them.

Conrad (1972) sought to find out whether deaf children who could read the letters were remembering them like hearing children did or in a different manner. He showed a group of letters from each of the two letter groups described above for 1 sec and then tested memory by having subjects write down what had been displayed. Deaf and hearing children made an equivalent number of errors overall, but the hearing children made about twice as many errors on the acoustically confusable as on the visually confusable letters while the deaf made two and half times as many errors on the visually confusable than on the acoustically confusable letters. The error pattern suggested that the deaf were not remembering the letters like the hearing children, but were storing visual images of the letters rather than the sounds of their names.

Another approach to the question of how the deaf code or process verbal information can be found in the work of Allen. In one study (Allen, 1971), she examined efficiency of learning rather than errors. The technique used was one called paired-associate learning. Subjects were visually presented lists of eight word pairs, a pair at a time, and asked to memorize which word went with which. After a study trial of the list, they received a test trial in which they had to provide the second word after being presented with the first. The number of test trials to reach the criterion of eight completely correct pairs was the measure of learning; the lower the score, the faster the learning. To determine in which kind of processing the subjects were engaging, two kinds of lists were constructed. One consisted of word pairs that rhymed but were spelled differently, such as SIGN–LINE. The other was made up of word pairs spelled similarly but which did not rhyme, such as CAVE–HAVE. It was expected that normally hearing children would benefit from the rhyming word pairs since that made each pair more distinctive. Of course you have to hear to experience a rhyme, and it was not known how the hearing-impaired would react to the visually presented rhyming words. The results indicated that deaf children took much longer to learn the rhyming lists than the normally hearing, suggesting that their mode of learning and encoding the information was different from that of the hearing. Allen also studied groups of children with lesser degrees of impairment than deafness and found that they too showed the same pattern as the deaf on this task.

Yet a different approach was taken by O'Connor and Hermelin (1973). They found a way to examine mode of information processing quite directly. In their method, subjects were presented with three small windows lined up horizontally from left to right. A letter would appear for a half-second or so and then disappear. A sequence of three letters would appear, one for each window, but the order in which the windows displayed letters varied randomly. Thus, on a particular trial, a letter might first appear in the central window, then in the right window and finally in the left. After each sequence of three letters, subjects wrote down the letters they remembered. The task was so simple that almost no errors were made, but the authors examined the sequence in which the numbers were remembered. Normally hearing subjects remembered the letters temporally, that is, in the order in which they had been presented irrespective of their spatial location. By contrast, the deaf subjects remembered the letters in a fixed spatial order no matter in what temporal sequence they had been displayed. It will be recalled that language for the hearing is an intrinsically sequential task, that is, the nature of the information is obscure unless a sequence of events can be tracked. If you hear the sounds designated by the letters AB, you do not know whether what is to follow is STRACT or SURD or YSMAL or SOLUTE and these sounds do not mean anything unless the AB is recalled. The deaf who learn a language used by the normally hearing are not able to do this. They circumvent their impairment by finding a way to code and store the information in a different way, often visually.

Conclusion about language processes in the deaf and hard of hearing

It was noted earlier that ordinary language depends on the processing of rapidly changing sound patterns. The study of ordinary language processes in the deaf shows that some individuals can find a way to deal with such information, but that they do so in a way different from hearing individuals. That a deaf or hard-of-hearing person finds a way to use the visual or somatosensory system to code language information may not be surprising, but the evidence that the coding is not some abstract representation of meaning but is of a specific, alternate, sensory-modal character, is important in understanding the neuropsychology of ordinary language. It suggests, for example, that translation from auditory coding to visual coding is not likely to be complete, and that only an imprecise correspondence will exist between sign language and spoken language when one translates from one to the other. For simple types of communication, such imprecision may be of no significance. But the differences may loom large if what is being communicated is complex or occurs under time pressure and stress.

Allen's work, in particular, has provided evidence that it does not take much hearing loss for the brain to come to use and perhaps rely on non-auditory information in the processing of speech. This writer, who has suffered considerable hearing loss in late middle age and uses hearing aids, has noted that perception of speech is much clearer when looking at the person speaking. I am not aware of ever having deliberately attempted lip reading. The brain can apparently readily integrate comparable information in more than one sensory modality but the impact of such modifications on overall language quality and cognitive skill is not known, particularly when such modifications take place early in the course of development.

Part IV

Disorders Involving Several Modalities

14

Academic and Social Learning Disabilities

In this and the next three chapters several conditions are considered in which impairments of a single modality are not predominant across all cases. Rather, cases with similar symptoms may turn out to have different mechanisms of impairment. Prior chapters will be drawn on to help understand these complex conditions. These chapters will be about academic and social learning disabilities, autism and childhood psychoses, brain injury, and mental retardation.

This chapter concerns learning disabilities. Until the 1990s, this term referred primarily to difficulties in academic achievement. However, work that had been going on for some time about a different class of learning problems – the learning of social skills – came to be increasingly recognized. Both types of impairment will be reviewed here.

A neuropsychological orientation should immediately suggest to the reader that academic disabilities are going to involve hierarchically high neurological mechanisms that make possible language, reasoning, and memory. Social disabilities, by contrast, are impairments which affect the skills that make possible complex human social interactions. Hence, social disabilities teach us about the neural mechanisms that make possible social connectedness. Given that the foundations of social attachment begin in infancy long before language is functional, and involve strong emotional components, the mechanisms involved are likely to be found throughout the hierarchical range.

Academic Learning Disabilities

General definitions

It is perhaps best to acknowledge immediately that there are no scientifically validated definitions of academic learning disabilities. Legislation has been passed which provides such definitions, and many individual and collective authorities have agreed upon particular definitions, but we are still at the point of trying to sort out mechanisms of impairment from symptoms, and about this there is no consensus. Often there is not even any concern about this issue. In current actual practice, the diagnosis is based on failure to make satisfactory progress in the mastery of one or more of the basic academic skills – reading, writing, spelling, or arithmetic, in the absence of any obvious explanation for the failure. Obvious explanations that must be ruled out include a sensory impairment such as losses in vision and hearing, a condition of severe cognitive impairment, e.g. mental retardation (which will be considered in greater detail in the last chapter), or environmental factors, such as poverty or social–emotional conflict with parents, peers, or teachers. Poverty might keep a child away from instruction, while social–emotional conflicts can distract attention from learning or lead to failure as a form of rebellion. If the concept of learning disabilities is to be at all useful, it must mean something more than poor grades or failure in specific academic activity. To qualify as a learning disability, there must be evidence that the failure is primarily associated with some form of impairment or limitation in the information processing mechanisms that make possible the particular skill. For example, failures in learning to read associated with family conflict are serious problems that require attention, but these are secondary reactions and not learning disabilities. Overall, then, the identification of a learning disability requires the exclusion of many other possible causes of failure.

Two other aspects of learning disabilities must be kept in mind. First, these are developmental disorders which must appear at the developmentally appropriate time. So, for a diagnosis of an academic learning disability to be meaningful, evidence for the impairment must appear during the time the skill is developed, generally in the primary grades or, to the extent that the precursors of early academic skills are understood, before. From this perspective, a learning disability cannot begin in adolescence or later. Children beyond the primary grades who experience learning difficulties may have one or another problem, but it is not a developmental learning disability unless there is evidence that an impairment has been present all along.

For example, a child who does not read up to grade level but who has not had the reading problem diagnosed will have difficulty with the curriculum which increasingly depends on reading. Such a child may finally fail in the sixth grade and only then receive diagnostic attention. This does not mean that the learning disability began in the sixth grade. Sadly, many persons reach adulthood who have never had their disabilities evaluated or have not been helped to circumvent them. The needs of these individuals are increasingly being recognized (Johnson & Blalock, 1987). Of course, a disease or injury may occur that destroys previously developed skills. Such a condition is termed acquired; for example, acquired reading disability in a fifth-grader which follows a head injury.

A second major characteristic found in academic disabilities is specificity. Specificity indicates that the impairment is selective rather than general in nature. That is, the children do well in some areas so expectations are created that they should do as well in related areas. Thus, one child may read well but have great difficulty with arithmetic, while another may show the reverse pattern. If a child has mediocre accomplishments in all academic areas and tests of competence are consistent with those accomplishments, the diagnosis would not be that of learning disability but that of slow learner or, depending on the degree to which they have fallen behind, mental retardation. However, as will be discussed below, "specificity" itself is a subject of controversy.

In the next section, each of the major academic learning disabilities will be examined in turn. To the list of four basic academic skills which must be learned for competent adjustment in a literate culture, i.e. reading, writing, spelling, and arithmetic, each of which may be selectively disabled, conceptual skill is added because it is a prerequisite for education beyond the primary grades. Reading, which is basic to academic accomplishment, has been given the greatest research attention and will be given the most space here.

Reading disability

The nature of the reading process

In the usual course of events, reading is based on language; that is, the child acquires a language and can speak quite fluently before learning to read. There are exceptions to this truism which will be considered in the chapter on psychosis. Ordinary reading requires deciphering visually detected strings of symbols which in English are called letters and in some analytic systems are called by a general term, orthography. Historically, language and speech developed in prehistory, while writing was invented about 5,000 years ago (Jaynes, 1976, p. 68) – a time which coincides (obviously) with the beginning of formal history. Writing preserves a record of events far longer and more veridically than is possible with transmission via story telling from one generation to the next.

Types of orthography.   Different kinds of orthography are found in different cultures. In some, such as Chinese, a unit of orthography, a written character, represents an object, an idea, or an event (Gibson & Levin, 1975, p. 158). There may be 50,000 such characters in Chinese, although 90 percent of text utilizes only about 1,000 of them. Nevertheless, this is a vastly greater number of symbols than the 26 letters of English. The characters in Chinese writing are termed ideographs or logographs. By contrast, the system of writing used in English and most of the languages in the world is alphabetic, in which the symbols, singly or in combination, stand more or less for one of the component sounds, or phonemes, of the language. As noted, such a system generally requires a relatively small number of characters and permits them to be combined in many different ways to represent many different combinations of sounds. These two different kinds of representation will make different demands on the brain: the ideographic draws more on visual–spatial and simultaneous information processing skills, while the alphabetic relies on successive and purely verbal skills. Ease of learning to read will depend on the type of orthography and the integrity of the brain systems required for successful processing of that type.

Symbolization capability.   Ordinary reading of any language requires that the successive sounds of spoken language be mapped onto visually displayed symbols. To learn to read therefore requires that a person have the cognitive wherewithal to symbolize, to be mentally capable of letting a sign stand for something else, a capability previously noted as a prerequisite for language itself. In ideographic languages, the symbolization may be pretty simple in the case of nouns where, for example, a grouping of lines looking something like a tree represents a tree. The symbolization may be rather complex when verbs and abstract concepts are represented. Gibson and Levin (1975) give the example that, in Chinese, the concept of "peace" is made up of the symbols for "a woman" positioned under the symbol for a "roof." Obviously, such combinations may not necessarily convey only one particular meaning, but shared meanings within a culture come to occur by convention. That is, a roof over a woman may not convey the concept of peace to every human being, but within the culture, the symbol, often schematized and stylized from its origins, comes to stand for the concept of peace. An educated person must master a great many ideographs.

Reading, sensory modality and type of information processing. Reading any written script requires cross-modal translation. That is, the reader must be able to translate back and forth from orthography, which is processed visually, to the sounds uttered by the spoken voice, and back again. For ordinary reading, the direction is from visual–spatial forms, either ideographs or letters, to sound, and from sound to the meanings that have been attached to those sounds. After reading is mastered, there is evidence that the process may be short-circuited so that the reader may go directly from visual pattern to meaning, at least for some types of words, generally simpler ones. When reading Braille, the direction is from tactual–spatial to sound to meaning. Spoken words progress over time. Read words progress over space and time. Any of these processes may not develop adequately or may break down. From this point on, only such processes relevant to alphabetic writing systems will be considered.

Mastering orthography. The first challenge in learning to read is to learn the alphabet – letter recognition. This means learning the names of the letters, which in turn requires the skill of instantly differentiating their critical features. In English, there are some fairly difficult discriminations that must be made. Consider the letters C, G, O, Q, and U. To the experienced reader, each configuration is quite distinct. To the novice, there is considerable similarity between these forms which differ only slightly in some detail. Novices become experts by engaging in perceptual learning, during which the distinctive features become increasingly salient. The components of this process were studied in important experiments which are summarized in the first chapters of Gibson and Levin (1975). They include increasing specificity in responding to the critical and invariant aspects of the stimulus (i.e. that which makes a "G" a "G" in different typefaces), optimization of attention to focus on these critical features, disregarding of nondiscriminative characteristics, and increasing economy of information pickup. The latter refers, for example, to how many times one has to look separately at each of two letters before deciding whether they are the same or different. A four-year-old might require five to seven glances whereas an eight-year-old might accomplish this in a glance.

The most difficult, distinctive cues in the English alphabet are those based on rotation and reversal. The small print letter pairs, "p" and "q," and "b" and "d," differ primarily in their orientation. Orientation matters greatly in many other ways, for example, in differentiating "m" and "w," and in correctly orienting the bottom feature of letters such as "J" and "L" (Gibson, Gibson, Pick, & Osser, 1962; Willows & Terepocki, 1993; Corballis & Beale, 1993). Scholars have speculated that the reason orientation discriminations are the most difficult to learn is that the challenge is unique to reading and does not occur in any other aspect of experience. That is, animals and people will respond appropriately to stimulation coming from the right or left but there is nothing distinctive about the difference. Nowhere else is left facing or right facing particularly important in its own right, requiring deliberate knowledge of left and right.

From a neuropsychological perspective what we know about the visual system must be relevant (see chapter 12). The mastery of orthography must draw on the resources of the parvocellular system for resolving fine spatial detail, and on the orientation slabs to specify direction. The two eyes must work in tandem and not interfere with each other. Since the image of small configurations at close distances will differ in the two eyes, the eyes should not be vying for dominance. Established dominance patterns should make possible consistent selection of one image over the other. The geon system should be functioning to facilitate discrimination of letter shapes. Finally, since the learning involved is both new and largely visual–spatial in nature, the right hemisphere should be more involved than the left, and any limitation of its integrity might compromise normal achievement (Bakker, 1990).

From orthography to words: word recognition. With the learning of orthography, the next challenge is learning the correspondences between the letters and the word-sounds they represent, or as scholars like to put it, grapheme-to-phoneme translation rules. Some languages, e.g. Italian and Spanish, are almost entirely phonetic, which means that specific graphemes always stand for specific phonemes, a situation which simplifies the task of learning to read, since only one set of rules must be mastered. English is a language in which large segments follow general rules, but there are a number of different rules and these rules have many exceptions, which makes it a difficult language to learn to read. In what follows, the many exceptions and complexities of English orthography will first be ignored and then will be considered later.

Suppose an initial set of words to be read by children just beginning to learn to read are chosen on the basis of their phonetic regularity, which is mostly what actually occurs in many first-grade classes. What then is the challenge to the child in accomplishing this task? Ample research in recent decades (e.g. Snowling, 1980; Liberman & Shankweiler, 1985; Perfetti et al., 1987; Maclean, Bryant, & Bradley, 1987; Mann, Tobin, & Wilson, 1987; Vellutino & Scanlon, 1987; Lundberg, Frost, & Petersen, 1988) has shown that, in speaking, children treat words holistically; that is, the sequence in the sound stream is treated as a unit and not as a series of sequential components. Thus, for example, the term for a furry animal with whiskers who meows is a unitary "cat." Children generally do not spontaneously recognize that "cat" is made up of phonemes beginning with a "k" sound, followed by a soft "a," and ending in a "t." Worse, sometimes children in first grade are found that think that "once upon a time" is one word. Thus, children may not hear words as separate entities, nor do they segregate the sequence of sounds that make them up. Technically it can be said that children do not parse (segregate, subdivide) the sound stream. Of course, in conversation there is no such need. If, however, reading is the goal, the graphemes are intrinsically separated into letters and words and must be mapped to components of the sound stream. This process is readily accomplished if the sound stream can be segmented into its phonemes.

At this point the discussion must consider a dispute in elementary reading education. From the paragraph above it might seem that the way to teach reading is to teach the children to parse the sound stream so that when they encounter new words they can break the sound sequence down and sound it out. This used to be the primary mode of teaching reading, and often goes by the name of the phonic approach. The children learn to sound out the words and, with practice, the segmented, awkward stream of phonemes maps onto the preexisting language repertoire and a sight vocabulary develops. Sight words can be deciphered in their entirety at a glance and read fluently with little effort. But what about the many exceptions in English? Well, as these words are encountered, the child will mispronounce them and have to learn that they are indeed exceptions. Some words, e.g. "the," can only be taught by sight.

The opposing school, often called the whole word approach, is concerned about this sort of educational disillusionment in which a rule is taught that often does not apply, and seeks to avoid it by avoiding phonic analysis. Instead, words are taught as whole words from the beginning. Thus, the reading approach coincides with the way the child speaks, and the word "cat" is presented as a global configuration of letters. Much teaching is devoted to developing a sight vocabulary and often involves practice with flash cards. Phonic drills are considered burdensome, boring, and, to the child, meaningless. Instead, there is an early emphasis on the pleasures of reading and the joys of self-expression in writing, with little concern about accuracy or correct spelling.

Research on the relative outcomes of these two methods indicates that for many children, particularly those who are bright and who come from homes where reading is emphasized and reinforced, no measurable differences are observed. This is probably because the children may develop their own parsing skills even though these have not been taught explicitly. However, when risk factors are present, the whole word method, particularly if carried out so that parsing is actively discouraged or even punished, may lead to disaster. Many children taught in this manner move into adulthood with very poor reading skills. Research has shown that preschool activities, e.g. rhyming games, that draw attention to the components of speech are associated with greater early success in learning to read.

Although the evidence is very clear that parsing skills aid reading and do not hamper its development, there is merit in both approaches. The key appears to be in the mode of execution rather than in the underlying theory. Phonic drills can be tedious and turn children off of the reading process, or they can be game-like and fun and increase interest in reading. Certainly, promoting the pleasures of reading and communication is desirable. It appears, however, that not infrequently the approach to the controversy is doctrinaire and based on philosophical notions regarding human existence and society and not just about how to teach reading successfully. Under such circumstances, reading accomplishment may be less than what it might be otherwise. When a more pragmatic approach is taken, and results are examined in the light of evidence, it is abundantly clear that inoculation against reading failure is fostered by phonic skills.

From single-word recognition to fluent reading. To read fluently requires that one go beyond reading one word at a time. Instead, one must move along the printed line, register the visual information, decode the word sounds symbolized by the orthography, and access the meaning of what is being communicated. As noted before, with greater reading proficiency, many individuals may be able to go directly from orthography to meaning without accessing phonology for many words. Two major classes of variables appear to be related to advanced skills in reading: eye movements and prior verbal skill.

Eye movements in reading have been the subject of much research and much is known about their characteristics (Pollatsek, 1993). First, when any static display such as a page of print is viewed, the eyes do not move continuously. Rather, they fixate a particular group of letters constituting two to four words (depending on word length) for 200–400 msec and then jump quickly to another group of letters, a process taking 10–40 msec, depending on the distance of the jump. The rapid eye movement, as noted previously in chapter 12, is called a saccade. During saccades, the person is functionally blind. This means that extraction of information occurs during fixations and not during saccades. It will also be recalled from chapter 12 that the parvocellular system capable of extracting the high frequency information found in the distinctive features of letters originates mostly in the fovea and macula and that these structures register only about 5 degrees of visual angle at a time.

In reading, of course, eye movements do not occur in every possible direction but are constrained by the organization of the text. In English, this means moving from left to right, except at the end of a line when large leftward saccades, known as return sweeps, occur to permit fixation at the beginning of the next line. Short leftward saccades, often termed regressions, occur while reading and this back-going probably is a kind of checking, or reprocessing. More and longer regressions occur while learning to read or when reading difficult material, but even normal readers reading fairly easy material have short regressions in about 10 percent of their saccades. Regressions can thus constitute an index of reading fluency.

In looking at a static display such as a painting in a museum, viewers have the leisure of maintaining fixations for whatever duration they wish. In reading, however, there is time pressure intrinsic to the reading process. If the rate of processing successive words does not approximate the rate at which successive words in speech are processed, it will be very difficult to extract the meaning of a sentence, especially long sentences. If many regressions occur, or if fixations are very long, the words and their meanings at the beginning may be forgotten by the time the end is reached. There is thus a short-term memory component in successful reading.

As scanning and decoding skills become proficient, reading skill comes increasingly to reflect the overall level of verbal proficiency. Reading thus becomes a tool for accessing words, information, and ideas, and is no longer a challenge in its own right. Somewhere in the course of this development, generally by the third or fourth grade, the reading process begins to contribute to verbal proficiency. Reading and written materials become one of the means to intellectual growth, expanding vocabulary and the range of knowledge to which the child is exposed. As with other skills, practice increases facility.

Learning to read fluently then is a process that generally takes two to four years and involves starting with complex speech and language skills, attaining instantaneous visual identification of the orthography, developing skill in parsing the language sound stream; building up a repertoire of grapheme to phoneme translation rules; acquiring a sight vocabulary especially for exceptions to translation rules; and learning a set of automatized, efficient, eye scanning movements. The early stages of learning to read have an emphasis on mastery of visual perceptual skills and, it has been argued, depend predominantly on the activity of the right hemisphere, while the later stages have an emphasis on verbal skill and depend predominantly on left hemisphere activity (Bakker, 1990). With this background, the discussion turns to some of what is known about what is impaired in reading disability.

The definition of reading disability in practice

Although some children learn to read before the first grade, generally age six, most children in the United States are exposed to formal reading instruction and are expected to learn to read during the course of that year and the next. By the third grade the children should be fairly proficient and most certainly so by the fourth, because the curriculum increasingly draws on reading skills to present new materials to be learned. It is possible to measure by means of group and individual tests whether children are ahead, keeping up with, or behind their peers in reading attainment. However, as with any developmental process, it is difficult to specify a particular point in the sequence where a significant lag or a deficit can be said to be present. Unless the limitations are very gross, most teachers and educational psychologists are loath to identify a child as having a problem during their first year of instruction, particularly since the curriculum may permit catch-up in the second year. If reading achievement lags significantly by the end of the second year, however, there is an urgency to get to the bottom of the matter because there is less opportunity to catch up in the third and certainly the fourth grades, and the entire educational career of the child is in jeopardy.

Consequently, most reading-disabled children are not identified until the beginning of the third grade or even beyond, when they are lagging two or more years behind in reading achievement. Incidentally, it used to be thought that boys far outnumbered girls in the incidence of reading disability. This was based on the number of boys and girls referred for remedial services. Shaywitz, Shaywitz, Fletcher, and Escobar (1990) evaluated reading competence in whole classrooms and found that the incidence of impairment did not differ very much by sex. Girls had often been overlooked for remedial services.

By some definitions a two-year lag in reading achievement, providing there is no other evidence of intellectual incompetence (about which there is more to discuss below), may qualify as a reading disability. In some settings the condition may be termed dyslexia. This combination of the prefix "dys," often encountered before and referring to impairment, and the root "lex" which refers to reading, may convey the sense of having identified a selective disorder with a known mechanism of impairment. Such is not the case and considerable further study, as shall be evident in the next sections, is needed to determine the mechanisms of impairment. When, then, should term "dyslexia" be employed as opposed to such general terms such as "reading disability"?

Despite the impressive sound of the Latin term, dyslexia, in present usage and with current knowledge, is essentially synonymous with impaired reading and describes a symptom without specifying what precisely has gone wrong. There is a distinction that does have some importance; namely, the difference between developmental and acquired dyslexia. The meanings of these terms were previously discussed.

As suggested above, the term reading disability generally has been reserved for those with selective impairments. Evidence of selectiveness was provided by at least average range scores on intelligence tests to contrast with impaired reading skills. This practice was based on the assumption that intelligence can be measured and that available tests could accurately assess it, assumptions that are controversial. Siegel (1989) suggested that available measures of intelligence are irrelevant to the definition of reading disabilities, both because the presence of a disability affects intelligence measures (children who cannot read do not learn the answers to many questions asked on intelligence tests), and because many children with low intelligence test scores read competently. She views reading as a modular skill which is relatively independent of other cognitive skills, one which should be defined solely in terms of its own characteristics. This position was strongly supported by a series of studies which indicated that children with selective reading impairments were no different in any measurable aspect of reading from children with comparable reading difficulties that were not selective (Fletcher & Morris, 1986; Lyon & Chhabra, 1996). Furthermore, available evidence indicates that both groups of impaired readers are helped equally by the same remedial techniques (Taylor, 1989). Consequently, according to these data, reading disabilities, despite their variability, do not vary with the cognitive context in which they occur.

This position is strongly disputed (see issue of the *Journal of Learning Disabilities* edited by Wong, 1989). Given this state of affairs, there is little controversy about the label of reading disability when a poor reader scores on tests of intelligence in the superior or average range (yes), or in the severely retarded range (no), but much dispute when scores occur throughout the rest of the range. The resolution of such controversies depends on knowing why a particular child has not learned to read.

Mechanisms of impairment have been sought in research and a number have been suggested. These will be discussed in the next sections.

Neuropsychological analysis of reading disability – language-related impairments

Phonemic and semantic impairments

A major advance in understanding reading deficits has occurred over the past two or three decades. The finding has been that children who are behind in reading achievement suffer from language impairments (e.g. Vellutino & Scanlon, 1987; Liberman, 1983; Perfetti et al., 1987; Snowling, 1987). When language impairments are examined further, they appear to fall into two classes. One class of poor readers are those with language difficulties of the sort described in the previous chapter. It might strike the reader that something is amiss in a classification scheme when "dyslexia" is at the same level as "developmental dysphasia" given that reading depends on language. Put another way, one would surely expect language-impaired children to be poor readers and that the diagnostic term for their disorder would refer to their primary impairment and not solely to one of its consequences. Dyslexia in these children would then be categorized as secondary to language impairment. However, reading impairments may often be a more salient symptom and the diagnostic system is based on symptoms, so it may be a long while before such changes occur.

How does it come about that the children's language handicaps elude detection until reading instruction is initiated? Apparently, most aspects of family life and social play in the world of many children may not require very complex language skills. These children may lag in the early acquisition of words, but they do acquire a basic vocabulary of oft-repeated and familiar words which may serve them adequately until the time comes to meet the higher standards of the school and of the challenge of learning to read. It is only then that the existing deficit blocks the way to accomplishment.

The types of language deficit found in poor readers have ranged through the phonemic, semantic, and syntactic dimensions of language, but they predominate in the phonemic and to some extent in the semantic. That is, these children are most often impaired in the most fundamental aspect of the speech code, the registry of the rapidly changing, phonemic sound stream (Metsala, 1997). Additional frequent findings are slowness in verbal access and naming (Denckla & Rudel, 1976; Wolf, Bally, & Morris, 1986; Murphy, Pollatsek, & Well, 1988; Wolf & Obregon, 1992) and in verbal memory (reviewed in Snowling, 1987, pp. 18–26). Verbal access is often measured by the speed with which children name a series of repeated drawings of familiar objects whose names have been rehearsed before testing. Katz, Curtis, and Tallal (1992) have provided evidence suggesting that this slowness of naming is not confined to language and speech but is associated with general motoric slowing. (There shall be more about motor impairment in reading disability later in this chapter.) Verbal memory refers to measures ranging from memory for heard sentences to recall of stories. Problems with verbal memory may well be a function of the limited and incomplete processing that occurs during impaired reading or listening. That is, if there is little comprehension of what is read or heard, not much will be remembered. There are also studies which have found evidence in poor readers of deficits in syntax or the more complex aspects of semantics (Lovett, 1992). It appears that impairments of these hierarchically more complex functions may occur, but their incidence is much less than the incidence of phonemic deficits. Snowling (1987) provides a detailed review of research which analyzes the way in which poor readers differ from good readers. The upshot of many studies is that, with auditory–verbal processing impairments present, the children must rely on other coding systems to access meaning. The other systems are often ways of analyzing and storing the information visually. That is, instead of accessing the lexicon and the meanings of words via a sound code (for example, going from the letters C A T, to the sound of the word, to the varied meanings and associations one has to the furry animal that likes to catch mice), language-impaired poor readers attempt to use visual symbols to access meaning (that is, they would go from the letters C A T, to an image of the letters, to an image of a cat and various images of what cats are like and do). This example is oversimplified and an exaggeration, but it appears that this frequently found type of poor reader operates much like a hearing-impaired child (see chapter 13) who utilizes visual processing skills to deal with language stimuli. Considerable proficiency can be achieved this way although the process appears to be more laborious and slower in development and may never reach the level of fluency that is possible for language-normal individuals.

Parsing

The second class of language deficit falls in the domain of parsing. Of course the children with serious language deficits just discussed will also have difficulty parsing, but there are many children with no discernible language inadequacies who nonetheless either happened not to learn parsing before reading instruction was initiated or who were directed away from parsing by the whole word instruction method. If no auditory language deficits are present, and there are no other barriers to learning, training in parsing is accomplished fairly easily and very large improvement in reading skill is observed (Perfetti et al., 1987; Lundberg, Frost, & Petersen, 1988; Maclean, Bryant, & Bradley, 1987).

Neuropsychological analysis of reading disability – visual–perceptual impairments

Some history

The study of reading impairments (Venezky, 1993) began in earnest at the end of the 19th and the early part of the 20th century, a time when universal literacy came to be the standard expectation in Western societies. In Britain, physicians such as

Hinshelwood, Kerr, and Morgan described cases of both developmental and acquired dyslexia with the primary symptom of word blindness, that is they could see but they were "blind" to the meanings of groups of letters. In the United States, Orton, the director of a county medical clinic in Iowa, described impaired readers as suffering from strephosymbolia (twisted signs) which focussed on particular kinds of errors that poor readers are prone to make, confusing p's and q's and b's and d's, and reading many words backwards (for example, confusing "was" for "saw"). This terminology emphasized limitations in the visual–perceptual aspects of reading, a plausible perspective given that reading requires the addition of visual processing to language processing. This perspective dominated the field until the middle of the second half of the twentieth century when a number of authors, Vellutino and Stanovich in the forefront (Willows and Terepocki, 1993), provided evidence that good and poor readers had equivalent visual–perceptual skills. What evidence there was for differences in the two groups was interpreted either as trivial or artifactual. It was trivial in the sense that it was equally present in good and poor readers. For example, perceptual reversals commonly occur in good readers while they are learning to read but disappear as reading is mastered. Thus, reversals were dismissed as a hallmark of reading disability. The artifactual interpretation argued that visual–perceptual difficulties were a consequence of not learning to read, rather than its cause. That is, it was speculated that learning to read fostered the skills measured on perceptual learning tests.

As a result of these arguments and the massive evidence found for language impairments reviewed earlier, there was a shift in the way reading disabilities were viewed. Rather than emphasizing visual–perceptual difficulties, the predominant interpretation, especially in the United States, emphasized language problems exclusively. However, there were several lines of evidence that suggested that visual–perceptual processes may be impaired in some proportion of people with reading disability, though probably not the majority of cases. This evidence was reviewed in a book edited by Willows, Kruk, and Corcos and published in 1993. From this book and other sources, several findings will be considered.

Evidence of visual spatial impairment persists

One approach to studying reading disabilities is to compare subjects on commonly used measures of (a) overall skill in reading; (b) component functions of reading such as oral comprehension or mastery of grapheme to phoneme correspondence rules as demonstrated by the ability to read nonsense words; (c) accomplishment in academic subjects other than reading (especially arithmetic, spelling, and motor skills); and (d) measures of intellectual capability and its components. The goal of such work is to ascertain whether lags in overall reading are associated with one or more patterns of impairment in the other measures. Such work may be termed subtyping research and may make use of a variety of sophisticated statistical classification procedures.

Watson and Willows (1993) reviewed more than a dozen such studies published between 1977 and 1991 and concluded that (p. 304) "a subgroup manifesting deficits in some aspects of visual perception, visual memory, or visual–spatial–motor skills, has repeatedly emerged both in clinical and statistical classification research." It should be noted that, in this work, the language impairment hypothesis is always amply confirmed in that a majority of the reading-impaired subjects demonstrate primarily those deficits. Those with evidence of primary visual–perceptual limitations number about 20 percent of the impaired readers studied. This, of course, is not an insubstantial number.

The significance of the visual symptoms such as reversals has been reconsidered. Although acknowledged to be common early in the course of learning to read, reversals that persist are not trivial. Corballis and Beal (1993) discuss the issue from the perspective of limitations in hemispheric asymmetry and the perception of left–right spatial differences. Willows and Terepocki (1993) review most of the research and clinical evidence for persistent difficulties with form recognition, with specific emphasis on left–right directional confusion. They argue strongly that these conditions do interfere with reading and merit further research. They counter the position which states that such difficulties are derived from poor linguistic capabilities by pointing out that many with these symptoms will write the directionally confusable letters in capitals (even in the middle of words) to circumvent the visual confusion present in the lower-case letters. Such children clearly know which sound they wish to represent, they just get confused about its grapheme if it involves directionality. Also, such children may spell poorly (about which more later) but do so with phonetic accuracy, indicating that purely linguistic functions are not malfunctioning.

Hemispheric difference and reading

As noted, a number of approaches to analyzing reading impairment give major emphasis to differences between the hemispheres. Bakker (1990), for example, has proposed a theory of reading development and impairment in which right hemisphere functions are viewed as dominant in the early stages of reading and left in later stages. He hypothesizes that the early stages of reading require mastery of the identification of letter forms, learning the linkage between specific graphemes and specific phonemes, and the development of a basic sight vocabulary. These skills are believed to be mediated largely by the right hemisphere. (He does not consider that many of these children come to reading instruction with preexisting language limitations and left hemisphere impairments.) As these elementary skills of reading become increasingly automatic and fluent, control shifts to the verbal functions of the left hemisphere, and reading skill is increasingly determined by the level of language skill.

Different kinds of reading errors are believed to occur depending on the stage of learning and the locus of pathology. In the early stages, reading, generally, is halting and slow, if accurate, and errors are often corrected. This according to Bakker is because attention is devoted to extracting information from orthography which has not yet been mastered. In one type of pathology, mastery does not occur, the slowness may persist, and the shift to fluent reading may not take place. Halting, slow reading suggests problems with the perception of letter forms and right hemisphere impairments. Another type of pathology occurs when beginning readers attempt to read fluently before perceptual skills are mastered. They jump into a fluent, verbally oriented, reading style prematurely and make substantive errors – omissions, additions, and gross misreadings – while they speed through the text, often guessing at words. These individuals are viewed as suffering from the premature use of a left hemisphere response style. (Bakker does not link this group of children to those taught to sight-read by the whole word method, but this seems to be a possibility.) Finally, there are children who progress normally through the early stages of reading but lack the language skills to shift to fluent, rapid reading. These children are thought to suffer from impairments of left hemisphere function. (They may correspond to the large language-impaired group of reading-disabled children described above, although Bakker does not discuss whether parsing and segmentation problems are an issue. They may also correspond to a group with visual problems, to be described shortly.)

Bakker's approach has received some verification, particularly with regard to right hemisphere impairments, and he has had some success with treatment methods generated on the basis of his hypothesis, namely, the stimulation and activation of the hemisphere that is thought to be malfunctioning. An important merit of this work is that it draws attention to different stages and different impairments of the reading process. He acknowledges that only about 60 percent of the reading-disabled children he has studied have been classified by his methods, leaving 40 percent that are not. There has been little effort to follow-up on this work by others. One recent independent study has not verified his treatment methods (Dryer, Beal, & Lambert, 1999).

Reading rate and accuracy: relation to hemispheres

A somewhat similar, perhaps simpler approach to classifying reading disability comes from Lovett (1992). Impairments are grouped according to speed and accuracy. "Accuracy-disabled" readers are poor at basic orthographic decoding and have not mastered the earliest stages of learning to read. They often give evidence of underlying language problems. 'Rate-disabled' readers have problems with more advanced aspects of reading, especially fluency and speed. They give evidence of problems in visual decoding and of visual naming. If Lovett's scheme is sketched in a two-by-two table, with slow and fast rates going horizontally and low and high accuracy going vertically, the resulting four cells show strong parallels to Bakker's proposals. (a) The cell with fast rates and high accuracy would contain normal readers. (b) The cell with slow rates and high accuracy would contain those who master first stage orthography but could not shift to fluent reading. (c) The cell with fast rates and poor accuracy contains those who prematurely shifted to fast reading before orthography was mastered and perhaps those who were taught by the whole word method. (d) The cell with slow rates and poor accuracy would represent the most impaired reading group, those still in the stage of mastering orthography. Whereas Bakker attributes early stage orthographic difficulties to right hemisphere impairments, Lovett finds evidence that these children suffer from language problems, presumably mediated by the left hemisphere. Also rate-impaired children are viewed by Bakker as having left hemisphere language impairments, but Lovett finds evidence of visual function deficits in them. Yet other views about reading impairment, to be reviewed next, may help resolve these differences.

Unstable eye dominance

Another approach that emphasizes visual factors in reading disability is that of Stein (1993), who studied the eye dominance of impaired readers. He reports (p. 331) the following kinds of complaints from some poor readers: "The letters go all blurry," "T's and d's sort of get the wrong way round," "The letters move over each other," "Things go double and drift away from each other." Such subjective experience could occur if the separate images from each eye were in competition with each other in the manner which would occur if there was unstable eye dominance. Utilizing methods for testing eye dominance described in chapter 12, he found, in one study, that 63 percent of impaired readers but only 1 percent of normal readers showed unstable eye dominance. This was measured by simply repeating the test several times and noting whether the same eye was dominant each time.

Since this disorder involves the coordination of the two eyes, reading might improve if the eyes did not have to coordinate; that is, if one eye were occluded so that it could not interfere while the other did the reading. Stein reviews studies in which reading-disabled children improved significantly over a control group when given six months of monocular reading experience. Perhaps even more interesting, he reports research attempting to understand causation; that is, does learning to read cause consistent eye dominance or does inconsistent eye dominance cause reading impairment? He compared eye dominance in older dyslexics and reading-age matched younger normal readers, and found greater eye dominance stability in the younger normal readers. Such data support the idea that binocular stability fosters better reading and not that better reading fosters eye dominance stability.

Magnocellular–parvocellular factors

Another approach to the study of visual impairments in reading comes from research conducted by Lovegrove, Williams, Breitmeyer and others on the relationship between magnocellular and parvocellular activity while reading (Lehmkuhle, 1993, is an especially fine summary). The theoretical basis of this work can be found in Breitmeyer and Ganz (1976), who suggested that transient and sustained channels had separate roles in fluent reading. (Note that this is a theory that applies to late stages of learning to read.) Sustained (later termed parvocellular) activity, sensitive to high frequency spatial information, is responsible for decoding orthography during the 200–400 msec fixation as the eyes pause during a scan of a line of print. Transient (later termed magnocellular) activity, sensitive to high frequency temporal information, is responsible for targeting and regulating the saccade which follows. Normally, magnocellular activity inhibits parvocellular activity. Inadequate magnocellular inhibition would muddle processing by allowing information from one or more saccades to overlap and combine into a kind of visual noise. Restating the idea another way, they suggested that a saccade would normally stimulate the

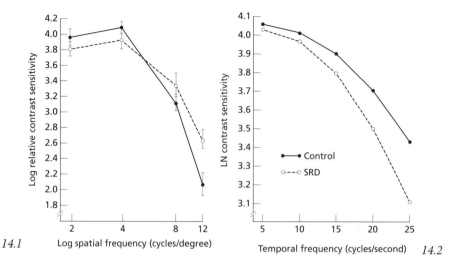

Figure 14.1   Spatial contrast sensitivity functions for selectively reading-impaired and normal readers (dashed line = reading-impaired; solid line = normal)

Figure 14.2   Temporal contrast sensitivity functions for selectively reading-disabled (SRD) and normal readers (control)

magnocellular system to inhibit prior parvocellular activity and thus clear the screen, so to speak, for parvocellular processing of the next chunk of information. If magnocellular inhibition did not erase what was in the previous saccade, the two images would either blend, so that the letters earlier in the line would be mixed up with those later in the line, or the earlier images would totally suppress the later ones. Under such conditions, reading could not be fluent but would be halting and word by word. Reading single words would be much better than reading text.

Perhaps the foremost behavioral researcher in this area is Lovegrove, who studied reading-disabled children examining visual persistence, the continuation of imagery beyond the duration of a stimulus, contrast sensitivity, and evoked potentials. For a review of the history of this work see Lovegrove, Martin, and Slaghuis (1986) and Lovegrove and Williams (1993). For present purposes, perhaps the easiest aspects of Lovegrove's work to understand are his findings on contrast sensitivity. (At this point, it might be useful to review contrast sensitivity in chapter 12.) Studying carefully selected poor readers, two or more years behind in reading, and comparing them with matched normal readers, Lovegrove and colleagues found the disabled readers in five separate samples to have lower sensitivity to low spatial frequencies and equal or even greater sensitivity to high spatial frequencies (Lovegrove & Williams, 1993). Figure 14.1 is an example of their contrast sensitivity findings. Here, small but significant differences are observed such that the impaired readers are less sensitive at low frequencies and more sensitive at high spatial frequencies. The inference drawn from the data was that the disabled readers had impaired magnocellular systems and normal parvocellular systems. That some of the disabled readers showed superior sensitivity in the high spatial frequency range suggests the possibility of attempts at compensation.

Further evidence of transient weaknesses in poor readers can be seen in figure 14.2 where the magnocellular system is assessed directly by studying sensitivity to flicker. It will be noted that, throughout the range of values, the reading-disabled subjects were less sensitive than the normal controls. Thus the disabled readers were not impaired in the parvocellular mechanisms which detect form. This likely explains why they showed no impairments on the tasks used in earlier research or in single word reading despite their impairments in magnocellular functions. Magnocellular function impairments would affect only fluent reading.

Anomalous visual function in dyslexia

Another line of related research was that of Geiger and Lettvin (1987). They studied letter identification under circumstances in which subjects were asked to look directly at a point in space and a single letter then appeared there, and one or more letters also appeared to the side for some milliseconds. Over trials the letters to the side appeared at varying degrees of eccentricity. Normal readers identified the letter in the center of vision quite well and their accuracy at identifying the other letters dropped off quite sharply as they appeared more and more to the side. This is a well-established finding and is consistent with the idea that foveal vision, where the subject is looking directly, would make use of sustained channels and be proficient at identifying letters while peripheral vision, with a preponderance of transient channels, is not. What was new was that they also found that dyslexic adults who were still poor readers were much better able to identify letters in the periphery than the normals, and that dyslexics who had learned to read fairly well were intermediate in that capability.

These finding were confirmed in other studies and have led to research on an unusual technique to help dyslexic individuals learn to read (Geiger, Lettvin, & Fahle, 1994), the details of which are beyond the scope of this book. Lovegrove and Williams (1993, p. 320) interpret these findings as further evidence of transient system deficits in dyslexia. Normally magnocellular activity in the periphery would be a very powerful inhibitor of any kind of sustained activity needed to decode the letters. That dyslexic subjects do more decoding in the periphery than normals is interpreted as another consequence of impairment in the transient system.

Anatomical evidence of magnocellular impairment

Further confirmation of Lovegrove's hypothesis came with the publication of findings which directly investigated the integrity of magnocellular and parvocellular channels in the brains of disabled readers and controls who had come to autopsy. Livingstone et al. (1991) examined cell size and organization in these channels in the lateral geniculate and found the magnocellular channels to have smaller cells and their placement in layers to be more disorganized in disabled readers than in controls. No differences in the tissues of parvocellular channels were found between reading skill groups.

It should be noted that the assumption that, normally, saccadic activity inhibits parvocellular activity (thereby preventing overlap of successive fixations) has been challenged. Review of six independent studies assessing this assumption (Skottan & Parke, 1999) found that magnocellular rather than parvocellular activity was suppressed during saccades. The argument is that such a mechanism suppresses awareness of movement and maintains the subjective sense of a steady line of print. These findings have not as yet been studied in the reading-impaired, and of course they do not make the extensive data available on magnocellular weaknesses in reading-disabled persons disappear. How such challenges will be resolved, if they can be, will make an interesting story to follow.

Can the language and visual impairment hypotheses be reconciled?

In the research literature on reading disability, evidence is often cited that 70–100 percent of the impaired subjects, chosen solely on the basis of their symptoms, have the particular deficit that is being studied. Only very rarely have measurements relevant to differing deficits been obtained in the same subjects, so there is little knowledge available about whether, for example, both language and visual impairments are simultaneously present. It is conceivable that selection procedures have somehow segregated different kinds of impairment into the samples studied by researchers investigating differing hypotheses.

There have been exceptions. Tallal and Stark (1982) sought to study reading-impaired children with normal language. They selected a sample of children who were at least a year behind in reading but who, in language skills, were within nine months of their chronological age level and compared them with a group of children who were at age level in both reading and language. Actually, the impaired subjects, on average, were two to three years (significantly) behind in reading but they were also six months behind (though insignificantly) in language. They were not different from the normal group in a wide variety of cognitive skills and specifically in their level of phonic skills. They did have greater difficulty on tests of scanning, segmentation, memory, and concept generalization. That is, these children with normal phonic skills and poor reading gave some evidence of impairment in visual processes when they had to scan rapidly and when they had to remember and process material they had encountered sequentially.

Slaghuis, Lovegrove and Davidson (1993) measured an early stage of visual processing, the duration of visible persistence to gratings of differing frequency. It will be recalled that this is a measure of the time a visual image continues after the physical stimulus has been terminated, and that it reflects transient channel inhibitory activity; the longer the persistence the less the transient inhibition. The results for groups of 35 normal readers and 35 dyslexics (about three years behind in reading achievement) are presented in figure 14.3, where it is seen that the two groups are quite different. A measure taken from the slopes of those lines for each individual subject correlated significantly with measures of reading. The authors also evaluated the presence of language problems by assessing grapheme to phoneme translation skills by means of a test of nonword reading, and found there to be no

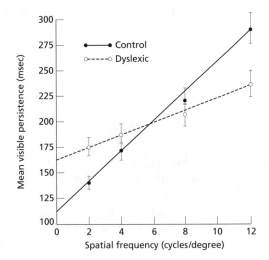

Figure 14.3 Mean duration of visual persistence as a function of spatial frequency (Slaghuis, Lovegrove, & Davidson, 1993)

overlap between the two groups, the dyslexics being severely impaired. Thus, the authors conclude that dyslexics have concurrent language and visual perceptual impairments.

A possible explanation as to why impairments may often be present in both auditory and visual processes in reading disability can be found in the same article that reported magnocellular, but not parvocellular, anatomic abnormalities in autopsied dyslexics (Livingstone et al., 1991). These authors pointed out that fast and slow systems paralleling the distinction between magnocellular and parvocellular exist throughout the nervous system and that there is evidence that antibodies, substances created in the body to fight invasive infections, that selectively stain magnocellular visual channels also stain fast channels in the somatosensory, motor, and other areas of the brain. Thus, there exists a possible mechanism for selective impairment of fast channels in many different modules of the brain. It could turn out that this aspect of the organization of the nervous system provides a better basis for classifying pathology than sensory modality or language versus visual–spatial functions. It would be in the fast channels, not sensory modality *per se*, where the real culprit in reading disability could be found. Certainly, language modules involve fast activity, but so far, fast and slow channels in the auditory system have not been elaborated.

Such an hypothesis would account for the presence of both visual and auditory impairments in the same subjects, and also be consistent with the observations, first mentioned in the previous chapter, and corroborated in many research studies, that reading-impaired children are often motorically awkward. This hypothesis does not necessarily require dismissing modality-specific hypotheses altogether, because any pathology which might cause fast channel impairments in one modality might not necessarily equally affect all such activity in the brain, but could have a greater impact in some places than others. Since some forms of dyslexia have definite genetic components, it is also possible that what is transmitted does not necessarily have to affect all fast channels but can produce structural or other kinds of weakness in just one part of a system.

Summary considerations about reading disabilities

Overall, then, there is considerable evidence for a number of different mechanisms of impairment in reading disability, and differing impairments during early and late stages of learning to read. Clearly, language impairments, including naming difficulties and some aspects of memory storage, will make reading problematic at any stage. Although the details of current hypotheses about how the impairment comes about may not be accurate, it seems that fast-acting, most likely magnocellular, impairments, sometimes primarily in the visual system, sometimes in the auditory–language system, and sometimes in both will prove to be significant, particularly in the development of fluency. The work of Merzenich et al. (1996), discussed in the chapter on language, suggests that appropriate training may increase the functional speed of fast-acting channels in the auditory–language system.

Creative ways may be found to do the same in other modalities. Inconsistent binocular dominance might have some impact on early stages of learning but more certainly would interfere with fluent reading. The source of reversals and other difficulties in learning the graphemic code might be found in impairments of right hemisphere functions and/or in parvocellular channels, but there does not appear to be any evidence for this hypothesis as yet. Clearly, much more needs to be learned about individual differences in reading disability and about the brain mechanisms that are impaired. In this regard, we need to understand how some children learn to compensate for and circumvent the impairments they have, and manage to develop an adequate repertoire of academic skills.

The reader should be aware that reading impairments may be secondary to other conditions. This was made vivid to the writer early in his experience when he was referred a ten-year-old who could not read and also could not control his temper. My initial assumption was that the reading impairment was a disability that led to frustration which in turn contributed to his aggressive behavior. Test results however indicated no clear-cut impairments. The aggressive behavior was a serious problem. He would periodically tear his home apart and beat up his siblings and friends. He was also known to perform unprovoked aggressive acts such as throwing rocks at girls in the school playground while in sight of the principal. For these acts he was often punished. At home, upon receipt of a report of such activity or upon observing it, his father would take him to his room and whip him with a belt. Since these family rituals had been going on for a long time with no effect, I suggested that other forms of punishment might be considered. This recommendation was not accepted until one day, perhaps out of weariness, the father delayed entering his son's room.

He then overheard the boy praying that he be punished soon! The father then told the boy that he would not be whipped, and this initiated a series of changes in their relationship. The boy learned to read with the help of a tutor over the following summer. During the course of working with the family, I learned that the father, uncomfortable with his own socioeconomic status, had vowed that his son, unlike himself, would go to college. He set about teaching the boy to read when the child was four, and was so intent on success that he spanked him whenever he made a mistake.

This case illustrates a general principle that poor teaching methods and familial issues may negatively influence learning to read. Children in the first and second grades, the crucial times during which the foundations of early reading skills are mastered, may well be distracted from the academic task at hand if their parents are going through a messy divorce. Some children find that their parents can agree only about their children's education so somehow having a problem in school may bring the parents together, something that would not happen if the child progressed academically. Sometimes neuropsychological problems in domains other than those that are directly involved in reading may be the source of difficulty. For example, it was mentioned in chapter 8 that certain rare forms of epilepsy occur only while reading. Picard et al. (1998) found 50 percent of children with severe receptive language problems and no history of seizures to show normal waking EEGs and abnormal paroxysmal (ictal) activity during sleep. Since language and behavior in such children improves with anticonvulsant medication, subictal activity may be a more common mechanism of impairment in reading and language problems than was previously apparent. On the other hand, in a better-understood condition, children with serious problems in attention (chapter 10) may fail to learn to read simply because they do not slow down long enough to learn. The upshot of these considerations is that an evaluation of a particular reading problem must cast a wider net than just the adequacy of the language and visual skills on which reading rests, and the possibility that reading difficulties are secondary to some other condition needs to be entertained because it may lead to more rational and explicit interventions.

Spelling impairments

Spelling is closely related to reading and there are many similarities in the problems that appear in each. Once the child begins to spell, the errors made provide clues as to the mechanism of impairment in reading. This was pointed out in the influential work of Elena Boder (1973), who classified the different kinds of spelling errors into three groups: dysphonetic, dyseidetic, and combined. Dysphonetic refers to spellings where it is impossible to retrieve the word meant to be spelled. Thus, she provides examples of spelling "rough" as "ride," "uncle" as "vlnt," "was" as "wet." Such writers are not registering the speech code accurately and/or have not mastered grapheme-to-phoneme translation rules. The dyseidetic group also spell poorly but it is possible to determine the word being spelled. The problem is in memorizing the "look" of the word or the specific sequence of rule-breaking letters. If the language had no exceptions to a set of grapheme-to-phoneme translation rules, these individuals might have no problems spelling. Thus, Boder gives examples of this kind of error including "litil" for "little," "lisin" for "listen," and "bissnis" for "business." Individuals with combined spelling impairments are generally grossly impaired in language skill and show evidence of both types of errors.

Occasionally, one observes a different kind of spelling error in which there is no similarity between the intended word and what is spelled. Suppose the context requires the word "dog" but what is written is "cat." It appears that the writer has accessed the general neighborhood of the appropriate word within the lexicon (pets) but has selected the wrong specific word. Such problems in word retrieval reflect difficulties at the semantic level. Yet another problem sometimes appears in which the little "function" words, like "the," "of," "because," are selectively omitted, misspelled, or misused. Such occurrences are evidence of problems with syntax. Overall, problems in spelling reflect the problems seen in language and reading. When they occur often they constitute particularly vivid evidence of language disability.

Writing impairments

There are at least two meanings associated with the term "writing impairments." One has to do with the mechanical aspects of writing and boils down, first, to whether the individual's writing progresses toward fluency (the kinetic melodies Luria described), and whether the script is easily legible and attractive. Good handwriting was a virtue in years past and the educational system used to devote considerable energy to assuring that children learned to make their letters well. In the present age of typewriters, computers, and word processors, less attention is given to such matters so that handwriting has probably deteriorated considerably over the years irrespective of any kind of neuropsychological impairment. There are, however, individuals who have neuropsychological impairments in fine motor functions, or whose disinhibited tonic reflexes get in the way of writing skills, and under these conditions, practice is more burdened and progress slower. If disinhibited tonic reflexes are present, some reflex inhibiting postures might be helpful.

The other meaning of "writing impairment" has to do with skills in translating verbal ideas into writing. This presupposes integrity in verbal skills and the mechanical aspects of writing and impairment only in the integration of the two. In the literature on the consequences of adult brain damage, there are dramatic examples of adults who have lost the ability to write while supposedly retaining their other skills, but such examples do not occur developmentally. The issue is complicated because learning to write facilitates learning to read and vice-versa, and the assessment of the separate component skills is not possible with great precision. For the most part, impairments of writing when verbal skills and the mechanics of writing are intact, appears to be a matter of inadequate learning and practice.

Arithmetic impairments

There have been a number of different approaches to the study of impairments in the learning of arithmetic (e.g., see Fleischner & Garnett, 1987; and Morrison & Siegel, 1991, for reviews). The general conclusion is that the problem is complex and has received insufficient research attention. Part of the problem is that there is some consensus that arithmetic is often poorly taught so that sorting out which subjects do badly because of inadequate instruction and which because of some kind of cognitive limitation is difficult. Another problem has to do with the complexity of the cognitive demands required to progress in arithmetic. Obviously, arithmetic draws on verbal, mnemonic, and conceptual skills and it appears that those with these limitations will have arithmetic difficulties commensurate with their impairment. This would lead to the expectation that arithmetic achievement in such children should be at about the level of their reading and verbal skills. More interesting are children who are average or better in reading and spelling but impaired in arithmetic. When tests of academic achievement that separately evaluate reading, spelling, and arithmetic are administered to large groups of school children (Fletcher, 1985; Rourke, 1989, 1991; Rourke & Del Dotto, 1994; Siegel & Linder, 1984) the existence of these two contexts for arithmetic impairment is verified. It is the latter group that constitutes the selectively disabled in math.

Further examination of these children selectively impaired in arithmetic found them to display bilateral tactile–perceptual, psychomotor, and visual–perceptual impairments as well. They were quite normal in phonological and many higher verbal skills, particularly rote skills, but they showed weakness in higher conceptual abilities and comprehension. (Note: what is meant by conceptual abilities will be discussed further in two different contexts in this chapter and again in the final chapter of the book.) Since the overall nature of the children's limitations extended beyond arithmetic alone, and because their relatively better verbal and reading skills most often enabled them to progress through school, Rourke (1989, 1995), in particular, has described this condition as a nonverbal learning disability. Further study indicated that their social skills and consequent social adjustment were often a disaster. More consideration of this condition will be found in the last part of this chapter.

Rourke has also gone on to suggest that the neuropathology underlying this disorder is primarily in the white matter, the bands of axon fibers interconnecting modules near and far, of the right hemisphere. This is an hypothesis which argues that the disorder is fundamentally one of nonverbal information processing, and that it is a disorder of modular integration, not of the integrity of the modules themselves.

In the neurology literature an acquired, late-appearing adult condition, the Gerstmann syndrome, is described in which three other symptoms accompany acalculia (calculation, or arithmetic impairment). These are left–right confusion (confusion about spatial orientation, using the body as a frame of reference, and letter orientation as seen in children with perceptual reading deficits); dysgraphia (poor writing mechanics); and finger agnosia (difficulty identifying which finger has been touched). An argument has persisted about whether the syndrome exists in children – that is, whether these four symptoms can be found to cluster together. There are some studies that support this idea and others which do not (Spreen, Risser, & Edgell, 1995, p. 490). In actuality, the tactual–perceptual (finger agnosia) and psychomotor (dysgraphia) impairments found in selectively math-disabled (dyscalculic) children are similar to the findings in a longitudinal study of the preschool precursors of later difficulties in learning to read (Satz et al., 1978). They found that measures of the ability to identify which finger had been touched (finger agnosia) predicted later reading impairment. To make matters even more complicated, the Gerstmann syndrome in adults is a disorder associated with left parietal lesions, while the hypothesized impairment in developmental nonverbal learning disabilities is in the right hemisphere. However, this evidence may not be contradictory if the principle holds that early learning involves the right hemisphere but later switches to the left.

The important lesson derived from the study of the deficits associated with impairment in arithmetic, whether conforming precisely to the Gerstmann syndrome or not, is that mathematical skill, even at the level of elementary arithmetic, involves a strong spatial component. This spatial component is a major attribute of visual information processing but also, as noted in the study of the blind, an attribute of motor and somatosensory functioning. Observation of the way mathematics is taught and learned directly reveals the crucial role that a grasp of spatial relations plays. First, basic quantitative concepts such as more or less and numerosity, and operations such as counting, formalize what is apparent in space. A teacher may help a child to grasp the symbolic meaning of numbers by taking two small rods of equal length and demonstrating that, laid end to end, they constitute a length equal to double their individual sizes. The understanding will be facilitated by the integrity of spatial perceptual skill although it could be accomplished by rote verbal memorization that $1 + 1 = 2$. Secondly, as arithmetic instruction progresses, there are many routines and concepts that depend on spatial position, i.e. that the meaning of any number in a series of digits depends on its position – units, tens, hundreds, etc. – or that when multiplying by two or more digits, the products are arrayed one digit to the left for each succeeding digit multiplied. An individual with an insecure sense of spatial relationships lacks the basis for the ready absorption of such ideas or memorization of such routines.

Conceptual impairments

This type of learning disability is not much discussed in the literature, but there are good reasons to affirm its existence. Whether the condition should be termed a learning disability or something else is subject to debate. The symptoms that signal its existence are easily described. A child enters school at the expected time and does well in the first two or even three years. Beginning in the third or fourth year, grades begin to slip and, despite hard work and even remedial instruction, academic achievement is below average. Sometimes a grade may be repeated, but most often, progress through school occurs without failure. In high school, a college preparatory course will be very difficult and frustrating, but a vocational curriculum may be accomplished with some success, at least in some areas.

What may explain this developmental trajectory is a handicap in conceptual thinking. The handicap is one of being able to understand and deal with abstractions. The level of skill available permits successful achievement when dealing with the concrete, the immediately perceptible, and with rote learning. The curriculum in the first two or three years of school which constructs the building blocks for later cognitive development, learning the letters and the grapheme-to-phoneme translation rules of reading, learning vocabulary, and learning basic number concepts, are absorbed largely by rote memory with frequent repetition and rehearsal. In the third and fourth grades, however, the school curriculum begins to expand to deal with more abstract ideas and symbols. In doing so, it relies on the maturation of capabilities for abstract thought which tend to show a spurt in development beginning about the age of seven or eight and which will continue into late adolescence (Bruner, 1968; Piaget, 1960). At this point, rote memory is not enough. The child must begin to organize ideas and be able to go beyond the perceivable to what might be possible. Ideas about social relations and the experience of others, concepts such as democracy or beauty, means of symbolic communication such as poetry or fiction, or scientific concepts such as gravity or the cell, all enter the curriculum and are difficult to grasp if abstract thinking capabilities are limited.

The neuropsychology of higher cognitive functions is just now being studied intensively. Ways of thinking about the brain and intelligence will be considered in the last chapter of this book. For the present discussion it will suffice to point out that some children lack the resources for much abstract thought. These persons can live and function independently and generally require no special care. However, they do not readily absorb higher education. In a society which emphasizes higher education, they may be subject to achievement pressure and stress which can do harm to their self-esteem, and, in turn, impact on their potential accomplishments and overall adjustment.

A final note about research methods and findings on academic learning disabilities

A few researchers have studied learning-disabled children longitudinally and have had the opportunity to examine the consistency with which they maintained their diagnosis over time. Silver et al. (1999) reviewed three such studies before reporting on their own work of this type. Taking into account what has been presented in this chapter, it is possible to create a framework within which to examine the findings in those studies. First, it would not be surprising if younger children with a diagnosis lost the diagnosis when studied later, if they were successfully treated. This might also occur in children who were late bloomers. Second, it can be anticipated that some children would receive the diagnosis somewhat later after escaping it at an earlier age, if their disabilities were limited to higher level functions. Third, one would mostly anticipate that there would be little switching among the different types of learning disability, reading, spelling, arithmetic, etc., although combinations of deficits are likely to appear. Fourth, in a longitudinally studied group, one would not expect new disabilities to appear beyond the fourth or fifth grade. Silver et al. found in one study that 50 percent of children diagnosed at age seven retained the diagnosis two years later, whereas of those diagnosed at age 11, 36 percent were not previously diagnosed. In another study, only 28 percent of first-graders retained the same diagnosis two years later and less than half the children with a diagnosis in the third grade kept it in the fifth. In a third study, which followed children 15 years after their elementary school experience, the proportion of the sample diagnosed solely with reading disabilities moved from 6 to 10 percent and those diagnosed solely with arithmetic disability moved from 3 to 16 percent, 15 years later. In Silver et al.'s (1999) study, only about one-third of the children with an arithmetic learning disability diagnosis retained that diagnosis 19 months later. This group included both children who had and who had not been treated. The experience of the large group that lost the diagnosis was not described. Depending on the exact criteria used for diagnosis, some children added disabilities and others changed diagnoses. In all studies, a group of children had persistent and continuing diagnoses, and these tended to be those with the most severe disabilities, but they often accounted for only 50 percent or less of the children studied.

Data such as these are disquieting. With rare exceptions, what factors might account for the changes have not been studied. There may be very plausible explanations that will emerge once the issue is addressed, but another possibility is that what is being measured primarily are normally distributed, variably determined symptoms and not dysfunctional brain mechanisms (Shaywitz et al., 1992). If so, present-day assessment procedures generate only shadows of neuropsychological reality, and we have a long way to go to arrive at more reliable and useful classifications. One possible culprit is the reliance placed on intelligence tests to provide a standard against which school achievement is assessed. Swanson and Alexander (1997) found that poor readers with average intelligence, the standard for normal functioning, are nonetheless deficient on many component cognitive processes, both general skills and specific skills, e.g. phonemic deficits. That weaknesses in the more general processes were a better predictor of reading disability suggests that these children lacked the resources to find a way to compensate for whatever specific weaknesses they might have possessed. In neuropsychology, such general capabilities are usually attributed to frontal lobe functions, which have been discussed here before and will be considered again. This section therefore concludes with the idea that a more complete picture of the nature of academic learning disabilities will be attained when measurement procedures more closely reflect neuropsychological reality, and will include measurement and analysis of the myriad ways the organism copes with whatever problem it must face.

Social Learning Disabilities

Beginning in the 1980s and accelerating into the 1990s, three or more independent lines of research and clinical activity have concerned themselves with maladept social behavior. One approach stemming from a social-learning perspective (Nowicki & Duke, 1992, 1994; Duke, Nowicki, & Martin, 1996) has emerged from research on the characteristics of normal social behavior, the expression of emotion, and the understanding of emotion expressed by others. A second line of work, already introduced, has a distinct neuropsychological perspective (Rourke, 1989; Rourke & Del Dotto, 1994) and emerged from noting characteristics associated with selective learning impairments in arithmetic when reading was relatively normal. The last approach occurred in psychiatry where individuals with serious maladjustment in social behavior were found who had good verbal skills but who nonetheless used those skills in peculiar ways. Each of these approaches will next be considered in more detail.

Social learning disabilities – dyssemia

This work on disabilities is an outgrowth of work on normal social behavior, and the perspective of its authors, Nowicki and Duke, is on the phenomenon of impaired social behavior. Although they probably have a bias that the impairments they describe are a consequence of distorted learning circumstances, they are systematically neutral about etiology and are open to evidence regarding constitutional determinants. They have done much work on the diagnosis and remediation of the condition, although public dissemination of their results in the form of scientific papers has been limited. Publication of their work has accelerated in the latter half of the 1990s.

In a popular book for parents and professionals dealing with children who have recurrently experienced social rejection, Nowicki and Duke (1992) coined the term dyssemia, as both a synonym for social learning disabilities and as a means of specifying the problem. The reader already knows that the prefix "dys" refers to difficulty or impairment. The rest of the term refers to the Greek root for the term signs or signals. The authors suggest that most social behavior is mediated not by spoken language but by a nonverbal language communicated through posture, proximity, gesture, facial expression, and intonation (prosody). They suggest that children who do not master this language of signs make frequent social errors, and that this is the source of their frequent rejection. Since these are individuals who seek social relationships, the resulting failures contribute to poor self-esteem, depression, and many other possible forms of pathology, depending on the means that are found to cope with the situation. The core of appropriate remediation is to teach appropriate social skills.

In order to treat a condition objectively, it is necessary to have appropriate diagnostic tools to determine precisely what has gone wrong. Duke and Nowicki found the available diagnostic tools in this area to be very limited, and have done a great deal of work to create more valid and appropriate instruments. The results are the DANVA, the Diagnostic Analysis of Nonverbal Accuracy scale (Nowicki & Duke, 1994), used to evaluate skills directly, and the Emory Dyssemia Index (Love, Nowicki, & Duke, 1995) which queries informants about skills. The items on these tests indicate their conceptualization of the important dimensions of social skill. They include the discrimination of four core emotions – happiness, sadness, anger, and fear. Four media – facial expressions, body postures, gestures, and prosody are examined for receptive accuracy. Three expressive modes of the four emotions are evaluated via facial expressions, body posture, and prosody.

Nowicki and Duke's 1994 report is that of work in progress. Much more had been done with receptive than with expressive skills. It is of interest that one of their most predictive and hence valid tests was that of phonology. In this procedure, subjects heard tape recordings of someone speaking. Such stimuli are intrinsically temporal and successive in nature, and their meaning derives from the sequence of sounds. The other receptive skills were assessed using still photographs, stimuli which are simultaneous in nature and not successive as are videotapes or films. It is likely that further development of more valid assessment procedures will require use of more stimuli which move and change over time as the phonological stimuli do, presenting the kinds of challenges people are faced with in actual social situations.

In addition to doing much research on diagnosis, they have also proposed techniques of amelioration. In a book written with Elisabeth Martin (Duke, Nowicki, & Martin, 1996), they separately discuss paralanguage (intonation, emphasis, speed); facial expressions (eye contact, mimicry, the specifics of emotional expression); space and touch (interpersonal distance, degrees of privacy); gestures and postures (both resting and active); the timing of responses; and what they call objectics, the use of current, culturally defined materials such as dress or hair styles to signal status, lifestyle, values, and social attitudes. The presentation of each of these aspects of nonverbal social communication is accompanied by a manual of exercises, games, and activities designed to increase awareness of the range of possible responses and to provide practice in effective social behavior. For example, charade games are suggested for both expressing and identifying emotion; charts and figurines are used to find comfortable interpersonal distances for conversations with the mailman, school principal, a sibling, or best friend.

Nonverbal learning disabilities – the white matter hypothesis

Some of the findings that initiated the work on nonverbal learning disabilities summarized in Rourke (1995) were described earlier. From a large set of data consisting of the results of neuropsychological and academic achievement tests obtained from children referred for learning problems, it was noted that there was a subgroup whose reading recognition (ability to read single words accurately) was relatively normal but who were impaired in arithmetic. These children were noted to have a series of impairments in visual and touch perception and in psychomotor functions. These deficits involve those avenues of information processing most used when very young children are first learning about the world, what Piaget called the sensory-motor stage, when the world of objects and settings is explored directly by vision and touch, by manipulation, and by exploratory locomotion.

Further study indicated that some of these children were delayed in language development but that once they had been in school a year or two, they had solid phonic skills, good single word reading, and excellent rote verbal learning. As school progressed, they turned out to have weaknesses in concept formation, displaying difficulty learning science and other subjects that depended on logical reasoning and complex concepts. Furthermore, they had particular difficulty with new ideas and materials, and when challenged to master new skills, adapted only slowly to change. Finally, these children also were found to be socially inept, with impaired social perception and judgment and impaired interaction skills, and to be susceptible as they got older to excessive anxiety and depression. Because these children often matriculate through school and learn to read (even though their comprehension lags), Rourke, as previously noted, termed this syndrome nonverbal learning disability.

Although the syndrome has a range of perceptual, cognitive, and motor features, the most salient are the social disabilities. Rourke and colleagues' position is that the whole constellation is a neuropsychological condition, and that the perceptual, cognitive, and motor deficits are constitutional in origin and the source of the social deficits. This is a fairly radical position since the bias of most psychologists appears to be that social problems are generally a consequence of social experiences.

If one thinks about it, there is something very plausible about linking social skills and nonverbal functions. Much social information is transmitted via body posture, intonation, and gesture, and not infrequently is inconsistent with what is being said. Such information is subtle, occurs rapidly, and may convey a particular meaning by a particular sequence of such signs. Individuals without handicaps may walk into a room and immediately sense the tenor of the activity in progress – whether tension or hostility or amicability mark ongoing interactions. Such sensing occurs rapidly and is generally not formulated verbally, but is available to guide the choice of behaviors adaptively. People who do not pick up those cues may quickly make social blunders as they rely on purely verbal formulations to interpret ongoing interactions.

Where then are the lesions or the dysfunctional circuits that would produce a nonverbal learning disability? The original and persisting answer was that the impairment is in the right hemisphere. This was based on a variety of evidence found in the data obtained from the tests the children received. For example, when each hand is separately required to fit forms to a formboard while blindfolded, a test of tactual perception, deficiencies were found in the left when compared to the right hand in these children. Since the left hand is controlled by the right hemisphere, the inference was that the deficiency is in the right hemisphere. More generally, verbal functions, thought to be mediated by the left hemisphere, were relatively intact but visual–spatial skills, generally thought to be mediated by the right hemisphere, were impaired.

Rourke (1995) has gone further in theorizing about the brain dysfunction underlying nonverbal learning disabilities. Drawing on the work of Goldberg and Costa (1981), previously considered in chapter 5, who reviewed evidence suggesting that the right hemisphere is particularly important in dealing with novel information, Rourke has suggested that what makes possible new learning and the rich development of concepts requires the linking of information coming from different sense modalities. This capacity is termed intermodal integration, a function for which the right hemisphere is particularly specialized. Thus as the child with a normal brain cumulates experience, what is retained and stored as a repertoire of understandings, strategies, and concepts is not limited to some strictly verbal formulation but is a rich brew of verbal and nonverbal, visual, tactual, olfactory, somatosensory, and movement information. When we "know" something, what we know is much more than we can say, and involves feelings and a variety of implicit knowledge. A nonverbal learning disability child might be able to label the experience and retain certain relevant words, but the richness of the experience and hence the possibilities inherent in a range of types of information are not present. This, it is suggested, is the source of the mechanical, rigid, by-the-book quality of behavior and thought in this disorder. Since there is no evidence that sensory functions, *per se*, are deficient, what is missing is the linkage between the neural centers mediating the different types of sensory input. This gives rise to Rourke's major hypothesis, that the impairment in intermodal integration is due to dysfunction in the white matter, the pathways that link the different parts of the brain.

There are three types of major pathways in the brain. Commissural fibers connect the left and right hemispheres. The largest commissure is the corpus callosum (see figure 3.8). Others are the anterior and posterior commissures and connections of the left and right deep midline structures – for example, the thalamus. Association fibers connect cortical sites within a hemisphere. There are two subclasses: relatively short fibers that connect nearby areas of brain, and long fibers, sometimes known as fasciculi, that connect the different lobes within a hemisphere. Examples are the parietal and inferotemporal pathways going from the occipital to the frontal lobe discussed in the chapter on vision. Finally, there are projection fibers, fibers which connect subcortical areas to cortex. For example, there are elaborate interconnections between the thalamus, basal ganglia, and the frontal lobes. These pathways also include those responsible for the upward transmission of sensory signals to the brain and the downward motor commands to the muscles.

Rourke and colleagues have hypothesized that white matter impairment is responsible for many different kind of behavior pathology whose specific form depends on which of the white matter groups are dysfunctional, when in the sequence of development the impairment originated, and whether the impairing process is progressive or not. The reader is referred to Rourke's (1995) book for detailed consideration of these issues. For present purposes, it is enough to note that he postulates that, to produce a nonverbal learning disability, some degree of normal functioning of white matter in the left hemisphere (both long and short association fibers and probably projection fibers as well) is needed to organize the basic language system. Once organized, the system might function in some degree on the basis of short association fibers alone. However, the necessary precondition for the syndrome is that right hemisphere white matter and the commissural fibers linking right and left hemispheres fail to make the rich connections that permit intermodal integration (Rourke, 1995, pp. 20–4).

Techniques for the study of the integrity of these connections in the human child are not readily found. What is available includes the same visualizing procedures currently used to evaluate other aspects of brain function, such as magnetic resonance imaging, which yields detailed, but not microscopic, images of brain structures in three dimensions (Fuerst & Rourke, 1995). There is also a technique of quantitative

EEG data analysis, called coherence analysis, which essentially computes the extent to which activity at one EEG electrode site corresponds to the activity at another. Coherence can be calculated between any two electrode sites, whether nearby, at a distance, in the same or different hemispheres, just so long as the EEG was recorded simultaneously at each site. It can be calculated from data obtained during resting states or in an activated state while performing various cognitive tasks. The assumption is that high levels of correspondence (coherence) are evidence that two sites are interconnected. Since correspondence is never perfect, the specification of normal levels of coherence depends on the availability of normative information for subjects of that age and sex who were tested under comparable conditions. Either too much or too little coherence may be an index of pathology.

In pioneering and laborious work, Thatcher (Thatcher, Walker, & Giudice, 1987; Thatcher, 1992; Thatcher, 1994) studied over 500 individuals between the ages of two months and adulthood, and found that postnatal cerebral maturation is marked by increasing interconnectedness between the different parts of the brain. These linkages take place over time, often in spurts of two to four years' duration rather than gradually, and are characterized by a progressive anterior to posterior gradient, i.e. connections generally progress from the front to the back of the brain. Even more interesting, Thatcher found the pattern of development to be different in the left and right hemispheres. In the left, development consists of the integration of differentiated subsystems, the separate modules coming increasingly to coordinate their functioning. By contrast, in the right hemisphere, more integrated or perhaps more primitive, less differentiated systems become increasingly differentiated with time. For further details the reader may consult Thatcher's fascinating papers. It remains to future work to determine to what extent Thatcher's data coincide with the hypotheses of Goldberg and Costa (1981), adopted by Rourke, but one may anticipate that this technique will contribute to an evaluation of the white matter hypothesis as an explanation of the nonverbal learning disability syndrome.

Thatcher has applied his work to evaluating a number of conditions and productive applications have been found in cases of mild head trauma, circumstances in which shearing of fine axon filaments is postulated to be a major mechanism of the diverse symptoms that appear (Thatcher et al., 1989; Johnstone & Thatcher, 1991). This provides preliminary supporting evidence that coherence analysis is useful in evaluating the interconnectedness of the brain. However, there is a great deal of evidence in developmental disorders (Freides, 1974) that failures of crossmodal (e.g. visual to auditory) function are associated with impairments in at least one of the modalities involved and little or no evidence, so far, that a deficit of crossmodal functions occurs without such modal impairments. (See, however, Rose et al., 1999, for an exception to this statement.) It remains to be seen whether coherence analysis or any other measure will permit the objective determination of whether deficits in developmental disorders are due to modular dysfunction, to deficient white matter connections between the modules, or perhaps to some combination of both. Perhaps adequate short-range coherence in areas known to contain important information processing modules will provide an index of the integrity of the modules themselves, while the coherence of long-range connections will provide a test of the white matter hypothesis.

Asperger's syndrome

In 1944, in the midst of World War II, a Viennese child psychiatrist, Hans Asperger, published a paper in a German-language medical journal titled in translation "Autistic psychopathy" in childhood (Asperger, 1944). In it, he describes a developmental syndrome with marked resemblances to both social learning and nonverbal learning disabilities. Specifically, Asperger noted impairments in social behavior; a lack of interest in the feelings of others; social isolation in children who were, however, reactive to the existence of other people; impaired nonverbal communication; motor clumsiness; relatively normal language skills by the time of entering school, even if there might have been delays along the way; and a tendency to become selectively and obsessively interested in esoteric subjects. Not much was known about Asperger's observations in the English-speaking world until his ideas were introduced by Lorna Wing in a paper published in 1981. There then followed a gradual development of interest in Asperger's syndrome, first in England and then in the United States.

As it happened, the year before Asperger's paper first appeared, Leo Kanner, an American child psychiatrist, published a paper titled Autistic disturbances of affective states (Kanner, 1943). Kanner's paper initiated the intensive study of autistic disorders in childhood in the English-speaking world, a topic that will be considered in some detail in the next chapter. As Asperger's syndrome began to receive attention, a controversy arose as to whether the two syndromes should be considered as separate or identical disorders, or possibly whether they should be considered as different points on a continuum of pathology. Both disorders certainly involve impaired social skills and both authors used the term 'autism' in the titles of their papers. The evidence for these alternative hypotheses was reviewed in a book edited by Uta Frith (1991) (which also contains Asperger's original paper in English translation) and will be considered in the next chapter.

Here it can be noted that both authors were psychiatrists operating within a mode of scholarship in which detailed case histories are taken and patients are carefully observed clinically. From this myriad of evidence, certain threads that seem to form a pattern are selected and described as a syndrome. These creative insights of classification are then subject to refinements in specifying both inclusionary and exclusionary criteria and in determining whether the syndromes do or do not share other characteristics. The characteristics studied are symptoms. As more knowledge is accumulated, hypotheses about mechanisms of impairment can be tested. Most of the research regarding the similarity of Kanner's and Asperger's syndromes has had to do with the overlap of symptoms and has led to mixed conclusions, partly because different authors use broader or narrower symptomatic criteria for the diagnosis of either syndrome (Wing, 1991).

As noted above, Asperger's syndrome appears to be a severe form of social learning disability, one that has come to psychiatric attention. If this is the case, then those diagnosed with Asperger's syndrome should show socially expressive and receptive deficits and right hemisphere, white matter deficits. Research making such comparisons is in its infancy at the time of this writing but a paper by Klin et al. (1995) provides strong supporting evidence for the position taken here. These researchers established stringent criteria for diagnostic assignment in each syndrome and independently specified a neuropsychological profile that was or was not consistent with Asperger's syndrome. They then ascertained the relationship between the diagnostic classification and the neuropsychological data. The relationship which emerged was very strong, with the Asperger cases showing the neuropsychological profile expected of nonverbal learning disabilities while the Kanner cases did not. The results of this study, as well as the explicit inclusion of verbal skill as a required symptom in Asperger's syndrome, provides the basis for the inclusion of this condition in this section. The main implication of this conclusion is that treatments appropriate to social learning disabilities should be most helpful in cases diagnosed as Asperger's syndrome.

Summary considerations about social learning disabilities

The evidence to this point leads this writer to the tentative hypothesis that all three conditions are part of the same family of disorders. A particular question of interest is the extent to which this family of disorders is determined by environmental–experiential factors or by constitutional limitations. One might think of social skills as coming about via incidental learning rather than explicit teaching, and being dependent simply on having intact equipment (right hemisphere and multimodal integrative skills) that registers the relevant information. Thus, it is evident that where to stand when talking with a stranger, how to intone a sarcastic sentence, when and how to wave your hands while talking, or how to ascertain that you are covertly being humiliated by others is generally not part of any formal curriculum. On the other hand, it is also evident that manners and forms of politeness, and standards for raising one's voice, and all of the behaviors mentioned in the prior sentence, can be taught and often are taught explicitly even though there may be no formal curriculum. What is taught, deliberately or incidentally, varies with the idiosyncrasies and resources of the family, school, friends, and social institutions to which the child is exposed.

Social skills are certainly a very complex set of behaviors influenced by many factors. What if a common correlate of social learning disability, motor awkwardness, were singled out as being most important? Surely that is determined by the constitutional state of the organism? Not necessarily so! In the absence of systematic evidence, the writer cannot disregard many observations made of parents who actively overprotect their children and prevent motor learning in the early stages of life. One set of parents were so concerned about germs that they never allowed anyone other than themselves to pick up the child, and they kept any such activity of their own to an absolute minimum. With a history of this sort, it would be as difficult to argue that any motor awkwardness that appeared later was due to purely constitutional limitations as it would be to argue that a child who never heard music was constitutionally incapable of carrying a tune.

At present, what can be done is to examine the range of verbal and especially nonverbal skills in those who display problems of social learning. Finding co-occurring arithmetic, visual–spatial, somatosensory, and motor weaknesses would bolster the assumption of right hemisphere impairment. Such data should be augmented with a careful history that would aim at understanding the training circumstances experienced in the course of development. A formulation which followed from such an evaluation should permit the design of intervention strategies and predict the speed with which its goals might be reached. I would guess that Rourke's singular emphasis on neuropsychological deficits and disregard of social learning circumstances will fail to account for some proportion of those with social learning disability symptoms just as I would guess that many cases studied by Nowicki and Duke, and those given the diagnosis of Aspberger's syndrome, will prove to have neuropsychological deficits. Theoretically, coherence analysis may provide the means for resolving the question, although it too may be as much determined by experience as by genetic makeup (see chapter 17). Its promise, however, has yet to be tested.

15

Childhood Psychoses

This chapter concerns a group of the most severe behavioral disturbances that can beset a child. They present in a variable and often inconsistent manner and severely challenge the nurturing skills of parents, caretakers, and teachers. We are far from having a detailed understanding of these conditions but much progress has been made over the years. The goal of the chapter is to convey some of the most important aspects of what is known. In what follows, the meaning of the term psychosis and the way it is used here will be reviewed. Then, a number of specific conditions will be described, with major emphasis on autism, primarily because it has received the most research attention.

What is Meant and Implied by the Term "Psychosis"?

The term "psychosis"

When a person or a set of behaviors is described as psychotic, a general term is being used which attempts to convey a sense being maladaptively helpless, out of control, unable to communicate meaningfully, and, perhaps, strange, odd, weird, mad, or crazy. The latter adjectives are often uttered pejoratively and such use influences the acceptability of the term psychosis for some who find it offensive. However, in professional usage, it is a simply a blanket term referring to a group of symptoms with no implicit assumptions about causation, duration, or treatment. When such are known, they become modifiers of the term; for example, acute toxic psychosis refers to a short-duration, severe disturbance of behavior which follows exposure to a poison.

One way of thinking about psychoses is that they are severe disorders of self-regulation with either excessive or insufficient activity present. When overactivity is present one may observe disorganization, agitation, or lack of control. When underactivity is present withdrawal or catatonia may be seen. Catatonia refers to a kind of physical immobility. Powerful emotion is almost always thought to be present, being either expressed overtly by those with excessive activity or barely contained by those with low activity. Disturbances of language, thinking, and communication are also frequently present. Given the presence of behavior that fits some of these descriptions, there are several issues about these behaviors and their meaning which will be considered next.

When do the psychotic behaviors begin?

The disturbances of some individuals are apparent at or shortly after birth, either at the time or retrospectively. That is, sometimes it is clear that something is remiss in a newborn child; for example, excessive continuous activity or crying, or the reverse – failure to ever cry, failure to adapt to a schedule, nonresponsiveness or stiffening to touch or cuddling, or very poor total body motor tone may be noted. These characteristics may signal the presence of a temperamentally difficult child (chapter 4) or may turn out to be the forerunner of the symptoms of psychosis. Sometimes such characteristics may have been present, but their significance was not appreciated until the later course of development produced more salient symptoms that could not be overlooked. Happily, sometimes they prove to be nothing much more than transient ripples in the course of development.

    Since psychoses may begin at any point in the course of development, maturity, or senescence, they can be differentiated as geriatric, adult, or childhood onset psychoses. However, lumping all the phases of childhood together may miss important differences that occur during the stages of early development differentiated in psychological theory (Bruner, 1968; Piaget, 1960). A possible scheme based on such stages might separate onset at birth and say the first month or two of life; onset in the remainder of the first year; and then onset from ages one to three, four to eight, and eight to puberty. Following puberty, early and late adolescence onset might be separated, the dividing point being about the age of 15 or 16. Such a classification is not commonly used but may prove important in understanding the behavioral differences that appear when onset occurs at different stages of childhood.

What is the duration of the psychosis?

When symptoms first appear, they are considered acute. If symptoms persist the condition becomes chronic. Sometimes, they might disappear and then recur or wax and wane. If observations are made shortly after symptom onset, it is impossible to know whether the acute symptoms will become chronic. As time goes by, however, there is increasing information about the chronicity of the condition. Some acute psychoses never recur. Other initial episodes that appear acute prove with time to be either a recurrent or a chronic condition. The magnitude of the symptoms during an acute episode does not predict the course of the disorder. The writer recalls a room left in a shambles after attempting psychological testing of an out-of-control eight-year-old girl, two days after her admission to a children's psychiatric ward. About three weeks later, she came to say goodbye just prior to discharge, and was sociable, sensible, and appropriately and confidently in control of her behavior. She had been admitted after witnessing her mother's murder while sitting next to her on a couch. This case example leads to the next issue.

*What roles do constitutional and environmental factors play in
psychotic behavior?*

The fields of abnormal psychology and psychiatry have had ongoing controversies
about this issue throughout the 20th century. Many have argued for the primacy
of one alternative over the other. It is the experience of many observers that
some individuals respond psychotically to trauma or acute stress and get better as the
stress wears off, as was the case of the girl just described. Others will remain
psychotic. By contrast, yet others, subjected to the same stress, will not react
psychotically at all. To deal with this complexity, the stress – diathesis hypothesis
(Rosenthal, 1970) has been proposed and has been adopted by many scholars.
Diathesis refers to a vulnerability of some kind that leaves the individual susceptible
to psychotic reactions. Generally, diatheses are thought to be constitutional neuropsychological characteristics, either genetically determined or acquired as a result
of injury or pathology, that are the source of the vulnerability. Constitutional diatheses may also be the result of stressful experience which can alter the structure of the
brain and nervous system (Sapolsky, 1996). The environment is generally the source
of stress. Thus, stress may play two roles in the stress–diathesis formula, stress at the
time of onset as the source of the first term, and chronic stress, often long ago, as a
contributor to the diathesis part of the formula. To make matters more complicated,
the functioning (as distinct from the structure) of the nervous system is influenced
by learning, which in turn is based on environmental experience and may also
constitute a diathesis.

Thus the stress–diathesis hypothesis provides a complex means of integrating
ideas about the role of constitution and environment in psychosis. It sets the stage
for searching for ways of specifying each type of variable. One research strategy
attempting to specify genetic diatheses is to seek characteristics in psychotic individuals that are present in excess in nonpsychotic family members of individuals
with psychoses. Experientially induced diatheses are studied by examining the size
and integrity of brain structures in individuals who have experienced different
amounts of stress. The stress part of the stress–diathesis formula may be studied by
examining individuals shortly after known events that are stressful such as combat or
trauma.

Often, there is no apparent acute stress and sometimes, no evidence of any stress
whatsoever. The tendency then is to attribute the disturbed behavior entirely to dia-
thetic factors. The diathesis may be obscure, but often it can be fairly obvious. A case
in point was actually the first example of child psychosis ever observed by the author.
The five-year-old girl was hospitalized for such behaviors as spending hours licking
the cracks in the linoleum floor. She was also nonresponsive socially and very limited
verbally. The staff of psychiatrists and psychologists of a large medical center would
come to witness this marvel of pathological behavior over a period of several weeks
until the nursing staff put an end to the psychotic behavior by simply not allowing
it to occur. The explanation for what was going on rests partly on the next issue to
be considered.

What is the role of mental retardation or cognitive incompetence in psychotic behaviors?

A large proportion (often 50–75 percent or more) of children who receive diagnoses of psychosis are also found to be mentally retarded. Retardation will be considered in more detail in the last chapter of this book but, for present purposes, retardation or mental incompetence can be taken to refer to the failure to develop adequate verbal, visual–spatial, and conceptual abilities, all of which have been discussed in earlier chapters. Often, the presence of retardation is treated as a comorbid condition, one independent of psychosis, much like a cut on the finger would be unrelated to having the 'flu. Such may or may not be the case with psychosis and retardation. The child described in the previous paragraph, who was also retarded, fits the pattern of non-independence. The mother, a lonely, isolated individual, abandoned by her spouse and of somewhat limited competence herself, was utterly devoted and attached to her daughter, who provided the only regular source of human contact and emotional gratification available to her. The mother totally indulged the child and could not bear to frustrate her in any manner. If normal children require a good deal of guidance and boundary setting, retarded children need even more and adapt best under highly structured conditions. It was thus that a child who lacked cognitive resources actually controlled the structure of events determining her rearing. When the nurses simply interfered and redirected her psychotic behavior, the "psychosis" quickly disappeared leaving just the mental retardation. Thus, in this case, mental retardation and psychosis were not simply comorbid. The mental retardation was a diathesis while a lack of structure and inadequate parenting was the stress. This broadens the notion of stress by requiring consideration of the particular needs of the individual.

Another case in the author's experience is perhaps even more pertinent, because this five-year-old child, on weekdays, was psychotic from about 6 in the evening until 7 in the morning and all weekend as well, and mentally retarded, but not psychotic the rest of the time. On a diagnostic visit to the child's home on a Saturday, everything was in disarray with pots and pans, papers, and magazines strewn randomly through all areas observed. In addition, there was evidence of feces smeared on the wall which had been partially cleaned. As I sat down on a stained couch, a scissors, thrown by the designated patient, flew by my ear and landed in the wall behind me. The father's first words to me were to apologize for his son's behavior, an apology that also conveyed the idea "see what we're up against." The father then removed the scissors from the wall and placed it within easy reach of the child. I kept an eye on the scissors through the remainder of the visit.

An interview with the parents yielded the following information. When the mother learned of her pregnancy, she did not want to bear the child. She proceeded with a number of folklore-guided attempts to induce an abortion, all of which failed. She then carried the child to term, and when she first saw him after his birth, was stricken by guilt because she felt herself to blame for what appeared to be a somewhat abnormal-appearing face. Subsequently, this child could do anything he pleased, and

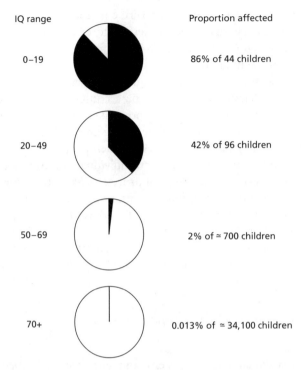

IQ range

Proportion affected

0–19

86% of 44 children

20–49

42% of 96 children

50–69

2% of ≈ 700 children

70+

0.013% of ≈ 34,100 children

Figure 15.1 Proportion of children with social impairment at different levels of impaired intelligence

was never structured, limited, or disciplined. As he grew, his behavior increasingly became a problem which she dealt with by going to work and hiring a kindly, if uneducated, woman as a household maid and daytime caretaker of the child. The maid informed me that when she was home alone with the child, his behavior changed completely and was easily controlled, although he appeared somewhat immature and not too bright. The maid arrived at the home at 7 a.m. and left at 6 p.m.

Two cases do not constitute systematic data and, given the data presented, the diagnosis of psychosis may be disputed, but much of the research on childhood psychosis is based on samples of cases in which retarded children are included, but an evaluation of the family environment is not made. The incidence of these unstructured-environment psychoses in retarded children is not known. In the two cases described, psychotic symptoms were ameliorated with easily implemented changes in the environment. Continued toleration of their behavior might have led to a less easily changed condition.

The other side of the coin is that whatever does damage to the brain that produces mental retardation may also directly, not secondarily, predispose the child to psychosis. Wing and Gould (1979) studied the relationship between social impairment, one of the common symptoms of psychosis, and the degree of retardation. Frith (1989, p. 58) graphed their data and it can be seen in figure 15.1. It will be noted that the incidence of social impairment goes up sharply as intelligence decreases. It is very unlikely that most of these children are similar to the case examples just presented. The upper three graphs in the figure are all in the retarded range and it is clear that all mentally retarded individuals are not psychotic. Nonetheless, it is also clear that, with more profound cognitive impairment, psychotic symptoms are more likely to be diagnosed. This may be a consequence of a relatively simple principle: less competent individuals are more likely to be overwhelmed by the demands of life and the less likely to cope adequately. What are small stresses for competent individuals may be huge stresses for such people.

On the other hand, that which makes an individual enduringly psychotic might be an independent, comorbid, pathological process as likely to occur in the retarded as in the nonretarded. This conception of pathology, which is the one most commonly found in the scientific literature on childhood psychosis, is quite different from the view that psychotic symptoms are secondary to retardation. Future research may provide support for both, either or neither view. That both hypotheses may be true would be verified if some cases followed one model while others fit the alternative.

Further consideration of the role of the environment in psychotic behavior

It is somewhat unfashionable to discuss environmental factors in the etiology of psychotic behavior. The reasons for this are many, but younger readers may not be aware that the assumption of environmental determination only recently dominated the field of mental health, and, sadly, that in cases of childhood psychosis, this concept was a powerful iatrogenic force. This occurred because parents and particularly mothers were blamed for their child's psychosis. Professionals, observing childhood psychosis, concluded (generally without a shred of evidence) that the children must have been reared in an abusive and destructive manner which provoked the severely disturbed symptoms they displayed. Overt abuse was not required. "Ice-box mother" was a frequently used, pejorative and totally assumptive label that was applied to mothers of psychotic children. One of the leaders of this approach was Bruno Bettleheim, who, for example, wrote (1967, p. 63) "all psychotic children suffer from the experience of having been subject to extreme conditions of living and that the severity of their disturbances is directly related to how early in life these conditions arose, for how long they obtained, and how severe was their impact on the child." By "extreme conditions of living," Bettleheim meant the wish for the child's death.

Parents who consulted professionals, many of whom operated from this perspective, often were told that there was nothing that could be done for the child unless the parent was treated intensively. Often it was recommended that the child be institutionalized pending the outcome, two or more years later, of the parents' treatment. A particularly poignant description of the problems parents faced in trying to find help for their child during the middle decades of the century can be found in Kysar (1968) and is echoed in many popular books describing what it is like to deal with

professionals while rearing a psychotic child. Subsequently, the general view of childhood psychosis has changed and, as we enter the twenty-first century, the consensus
is that severe constitutional diatheses are present in all childhood psychoses. Currently, consideration of environmental variables has been slim in the scientific literature. On the other hand, very helpful treatment techniques, developed within the
framework of behavioral science, emerged over this time period. This merits some
further discussion.

The role of behavior modification

At a time when parents were being blamed by professionals for their children's psychotic condition, a number of researchers and clinicians operating within a framework created by B. F. Skinner, called behavior modification, began to work at
changing psychotic behaviors. The underlying theory was relatively simple: behavior
was under the control of reinforcers or rewards and this was as true of pathological
behavior as it was of normal behavior. Hence treatment consisted of changing the
environment to specifically reward desirable behavior and to not reward (or to
punish) undesirable behavior. With this simple foundation rooted in decades of
research on learning, researchers working within this framework have built a complex
and sophisticated edifice of behavioral theory which is beyond the scope of this book.
What is appropriate here is the understanding that behavior modifiers courageously
undertook to change just about any kind of behavior, and that they often succeeded
to the degree that, over the years, their procedures have been incorporated into just
about every educational and intervention procedure devised to aid psychotic children, as well as those with mental retardation. Such techniques often called for
parents to change their behavior, but there was no component of blame or any
assumption that the parents had caused the disturbance in the first place. Thus, over
the period of 30–40 years since mid-century, there has been a large shift away from
the assumption that the environment produced by parental behavior caused psychosis
and a strong shift toward utilizing behavioral techniques.

If one asks what the natural history of any child with psychosis may be, the answer
today is inevitably indeterminate unless the history of behavior intervention methods
in the home, school, and clinic is also known. The methodology has grown in sophistication, complexity, and intensity and has penetrated in varying degrees into most
every type of intervention. It ranges from discrete individualized trial procedures in
which the attentional command "look at me" is followed by a request for a particular response which, if correct, is followed by a reward, often something tangible like
a piece of candy, but also by praise or a hug (Lovaas, Calouri, & Jada, 1989), through
subtle techniques of incidental learning in a group classroom or at home where a
casual observer might not notice that behavior modification was being implemented
(McGee, Krantz, & McClannahan, 1985; McGee et al., 1992). The technique has
been used to promote just about every aspect of behavior, including attention, language, self-control, and social behavior. It has been applied to very young children
and to adults. It has been administered with great intensity, including deliberate

efforts lasting for two to three years at a rate of 30 or more hours a week and in a more casual manner with perhaps daily sessions lasting an hour or two. From a neuropsychological perspective, behavior modification can be thought of as providing an environmental structure to a nervous system that lacks the wherewithal to structure its own experience, a task most brains can accomplish with ordinary child rearing. Lewis (1996, p. 234) has pointed out that studies on the efficacy of medications have not controlled for variations in behavioral programming that are now parts of the experience of many children with autism.

In reports of autistic individuals about their own experience, it is noteworthy that credit for progress is given to intrusive efforts of the part of caretakers, especially parents, to change their poorly controlled behavior. Formal enrollment in schools or therapeutic programs are not what is crucial: it is the substance of the intrusion. Behavior modification may be implemented by intuitive, sensitive, committed, and wise parents or teachers whether they call it behavior modification or not. The observer trying to understand particular individuals at some stage of their life needs to know what kinds of formal and informal training occurred during their development.

Summary and extensions about the nature of psychosis.   Manifestations of psychoses will vary with the age of onset and level of development of the child, in part because these factors will influence the resources available to such children to cope with both the stresses they experience and the diatheses they have. When the stress–diathesis model was presented, mention was not made that the consequences of stress depend on how the stress is coped with or that the development of coping techniques requires the experience of stress and practice in coping. Nonetheless these complexities exist. Diatheses can be present but psychosis may never occur because the course of development has fostered adequate coping. What it takes to cope adequately with psychotic diatheses is not particularly obvious or readily appreciated.

Mental retardation restricts the range of potential coping techniques and so leaves the child particularly vulnerable to stress. However, making a determination of mental retardation is not always possible. All children at birth, for the sake of argument at least, are retarded. They cannot talk, think, plan, or move in a controlled and adaptive fashion. Most have the potential to develop cognitive and motor skills, while some do not, but at the very beginning we do not know how to assess potential capabilities, although various signs may suggest risk of impairment. The same is true for somewhat older autistic children. There is a study on autism that shall loom large when presented below, in which two- and three-year-old children were treated in a very special way, as a result of which some became normal and some did not. For all of those who became normal, levels of intelligence rose into the normal range, while those who failed to attain normality remained in the retarded range where all had begun. From this we learn that, among psychotic children who are found to be retarded, some, but not all, have the potential for normal competence, even though we do not know how to tell in advance who they are. Finally, intellectual limitations may be a diathesis only in some cases of psychosis. An independent pathological process, affecting individuals at any level of intelligence, may be the culprit.

With this background, the discussion turns to consideration of specific syndromes of childhood psychosis. The greatest attention will be given to autism, since the largest literature is available on this syndrome. In the course of the presentation, it will be necessary to consider the similarities and differences between autism and Asperger's syndrome. Afterward, a number of other childhood psychoses will also be described.

Early Childhood Autism

In 1943 Leo Kanner, an American child psychiatrist, published a paper entitled "Autistic disturbances of affective contact" which is generally credited with opening the modern era in the study of a particular syndrome of child psychosis – autism, sometimes called Kanner's syndrome. In his paper Kanner described eight boys and three girls who, despite diverse symptoms, shared a number of features which he argued merited consideration as a syndrome. This paper is of historical interest and has been examined closely by many writers (e.g. Rimland, 1964; Frith, 1989; Wing, 1991). Rather than reviewing the history of how Kanner's original designation of symptoms has evolved to the present day, the discussion will begin with current depictions of the disorder.

The symptoms of autism

Various diagnostic schemes for autism exist which have changed their criteria as research proceeds. The most conspicuous and generally agreed upon symptoms are described next. The reader will note that, since they do not necessarily constitute a coherent picture of the disorder, some major alteration of classification may occur in the future. Such issues will be considered as the chapter progresses.

Impairments of social behavior

The core symptom that gave the disorder its name, autism, is an impairment of the active components of social connectedness. An observer has the sense that the person with autism is indifferent to the reactions of other human beings, family as well as strangers, children as well as adults. Normal babies smile in response to a moving human face, show special interest in other people, and early on come to share attention (that is, get interested in what other people are interested in). This is not only a reactive process but a process that children soon come to initiate, and one in which they generally take great pleasure. By contrast, autistic children take an inordinate interest in inanimate objects. They may spend endless hours in ritualistic behaviors, for example, building and dismantling towers of blocks or watching spinning toys. The meaning of these behaviors is not obvious, but, of course, inanimate objects do not change their characteristics and affordances like people do. When interacting with adults, which must be done to gratify their needs, they are described as treating people like objects, moving the others' hands toward the refrigerator, for example, in order to get food, where the hand is not so much a part of a person as a tool to accomplish a concrete task. It is said that autistic children avoid eye contact with others, and that if they do look at other people, it is more like they are looking through them than at them. It has also been observed that many children with autism intently examine events of interest visually out of the corner of their eyes rather than with direct foveal gaze.

Language deficits

Another primary symptom of autism is impairment of language. The course of language development, if it occurs at all, is delayed and aberrant. Final outcomes in adulthood range from global aphasia or total inability to speak, through a very limited repertoire of speech skills with a grossly limited range of output, up to an intact repertoire of phonetic, semantic, and syntactic skills, but with pragmatic deficits which may be subtle. There are rare instances in which speech and language is essentially normal. For example, Temple Grandin (1995), who considers herself still autistic, commands language skills adequate for writing books, giving lectures, and granting interviews. It is generally agreed that the ultimate level of adjustment and ability to function independently depends on attained verbal skill. The small percent that develop some language skill and, usually, considerable nonverbal skill, are often diagnosed as having high-level autism.

Frith (1989), Wing (1991), Tager-Flusberg (1989) and others provide detailed descriptions of the highest levels of language attained by individuals with autism. What they portray is a condition that is very similar to social learning disability and Asperger's syndrome. Indeed, the question has been raised as to whether Asperger's syndrome and high-level autism are really the same disorder. That the issue arises at all is surprising in that the modal individual with autism avoids social interactions, has poor verbal skills, and, as will be discussed further, often has good visual–spatial and motor skills, while those with Asperger's syndrome have good verbal skills, seek social interactions although they are poor at attaining and holding them, and are often awkward visual–spatially and motorically. However, some have very definite mixtures of these symptoms, others go through the early years of development with a symptom picture that is very definitely autistic, and then, in middle childhood and adulthood, display a very well defined Asperger's syndrome (the reverse sequence does not appear to have been reported), and both groups may display similar kinds of very disturbed behavior if they are observed under circumstances of high stress. This state of affairs suggests that the understanding of these disorders is still limited, and that further search for mechanisms of impairment is warranted.

Theory of mind deficits

Beginning with a research report (Baron-Cohen, Leslie, & Frith, 1985), Baron-Cohen (1995) has been in the forefront of a number of researchers who have argued that a primary deficit in high-functioning autism is the lack of a theory of mind. What is meant by a theory of mind is a mental capability which can attribute mindfulness to others, i.e. assumes that the behavior of others is a product of the others' minds and their thoughts, feelings, and motives. It may help clarify what is meant by theory of mind by describing one of the tests used to evaluate its presence. Consider the following problem. Suppose John and Suzy each have a marble and each have a closed container. Suzy puts her marble in her container and goes out of the room. While Suzy is gone, John takes her marble and puts it into his container. The question then posed is where will Suzy look for her marble when she returns. A person with a theory of mind will respond that Suzy will look where she left the marble. Individuals who do not appreciate the way other minds work indicate that Suzy will look first in John's box because, having been told the story, they know that it is there. Many children with autism fail this test while many retarded children pass it. Thus, it has been argued, theory of mind, at least to some extent, does not depend on cognitive normality.

A serious lag or failure to develop a theory of mind is devastating to social relationships because the behavior of others cannot be predicted, and deception, teasing, and various kinds of pretend play do not occur and are not understood. Although absence of theory of mind does not preclude the ability to detect direct emotional expressions such as happiness, sadness, or anger, cognitively based reactions such as surprise are not comprehended. That is, one has to realize that someone else's mind is anticipating something other than what occurred in order to comprehend surprise. Altogether, not possessing a theory of mind means that the child does not understand that other people know, believe, anticipate, intend, think, pretend, hope, or fantasize. This deficit thus directly accounts for other commonly reported symptoms of autism such as a lack of imaginative and pretend play and a lack of empathy toward others.

A child is not born with a theory of mind, but it develops through the course of early childhood and is operative as early as the age of three or four, about the time children enter into reciprocal social relationships. Further development produces increasing sophistication about how thoughts and beliefs may guide behavior or generate deceptive practices. Baron-Cohen (1995, chapter 4) has proposed that a number of factors contribute to the development of a theory of mind. These hypotheses deal with how the brain detects intentionality or purposefullness, and the social and perceptual experiences that foster such operations.

Theory of mind is the subject of active research. The topic is not without controversy, particularly since a number of individuals with autism pass tests measuring this skill, although when they succeed it is almost always at a relatively older age. A comprehensive picture of the field at the beginning of the 1990s can be obtained by consulting the volume edited by Baron-Cohen, Tager-Flusberg, and Cohen (1993). A recent study (Peterson & Siegal, 1999) verified Baron-Cohen's and others expectations in finding children with autism to be inferior in theory of mind to three groups of children; (1) deaf children with oral language (made possible by very early intervention); (2) deaf signers coming from families with at least one deaf, signing parent;

and (3) normally hearing children. Expectations were disconfirmed however in that non-autistic, signing deaf children born to normally hearing families (who experienced no fluent discourse until after they entered school and learned to sign) were as impaired as the autistic children. Such data link the development of theory of mind to early opportunities to engage in discourse, and suggest that impairments in autism may be a secondary rather than a primary symptom.

In Kanner's original paper, and especially in his later discussions of the disorder, the need for an unchanging environment was emphasized as a primary symptom and many authorities still so consider it. The children had great difficulties adjusting to changes in routine or even to trivial changes such as moving the furniture around. They would become very upset upon perceiving such changes, often insisting that everything stay the same. This symptom is commonly seen in individuals whose information processing capabilities are compromised, particularly if the left hemisphere is involved, likely in autism in view of the language deficits present. Quite simply, when it is hard to understand what is going on, composure and control are easier to maintain if the world stays the same. Kurt Goldstein (1939), a pioneer in human neuropsychology, described something very similar in soldiers who sustained injuries to the left hemisphere, especially the frontal lobes. He termed this kind of panic in the face of change and the need for rigid routines, a catastrophe reaction.

Hyperarousal and/or hypersensitivity

The symptoms described so far are mostly cognitive and social, not the most disturbing symptoms common in autism. The most disturbing symptoms are overt behaviors that are disruptive to social interaction and elicit the aversion of others. They include high-intensity rocking, head-banging, unpredictable and often seemingly random acts of aggression, and self-mutilation. Less intense hand-flapping and other persistent motor mannerisms are common, as are unpredictable hypersensitivity and hyperreactivity to sensory stimulation. Thus the sound of a vacuum cleaner may elicit a major aversive reaction including covering the ears, closing the eyes, screaming, and flight. Dawson and Lewy (1989, p. 56), in a review of the literature on arousal in children with autism, conclude that research supports the idea that many autistic individuals respond to stimuli aversively and have chronically high levels of arousal. This means that levels of intensity of many stimuli that most people find tolerable or which might not even be noticed may be experienced as noxious or punishing. Punishing experiences are naturally associated with an increase in arousal and tendencies toward flight or avoidance. The types of stimulation that have these consequences are most often auditory and somatosensory. Temple Grandin (1995), a person with autism previously mentioned, who has written extensively about her own experience, writes: "I wanted to experience the good feeling of being hugged, but it was just too overwhelming. . . . Being touched triggered flight; it flipped my circuit breaker. I was overloaded and would have to escape, often by jerking away suddenly" (p. 62).

Different types of behavior are associated with hypersensitivities. Some appear to be direct aversive reactions to external stimulation, for example, screaming, running away, or plugging the ears with fingers. Behaviors such as withdrawal and avoidance appear to be coping reactions. Behavior such as intense rocking or self-mutilation may be both avoidant and ways of maintaining some modicum of self-control over high levels of arousal, the children doing to themselves in preference to experiencing an unpredictable and subjectively overwhelming provocation. There is some tendency for hyperarousal to decline with age, at which time cognitive and social behavior is more amenable to study. Meanwhile the presence of hyperarousal during the early formative years may be the key factor in the disorder. If so, the social and cognitive symptoms already described would be secondary consequences of grossly unregulated mechanisms of excitability and inhibition in the brain. Hyperarousal present when crucial learning must occur will interfere with such learning. Chronic hyperarousal will interfere with developmental processes.

Hyperarousal and hypersensitivity imply inadequate inhibition and a type of disorder that most certainly includes and may be limited to dyscontrol (see discussion at the end of chapter 4). If ways were found to introduce inhibition into the system, and relative stability followed, cognitive capabilities that were previously arrested by the throes of hyperarousal would now be free to develop. If the potentiality for cognitive skill were not there, the overall condition would still improve but normality would not be attained. There are a number of observations of seemingly unrelated facts that may provide clues about these kinds of relationships.

Seizures. There is a strong association between autism and epilepsy, which in some sense is the biological epitome of hyperarousal and inadequate inhibition. A large proportion of children diagnosed with autism will have frank (observable, motor) seizures at some time in their life, most frequently beginning either in infancy or adolescence. The earliest estimates (Knobloch & Pasamanick, 1975) were as high as 75 percent while present estimates tend to be between 14 and 42 percent, all of which are significantly higher than the general population rate which is 0.5 percent (Coleman & Gillberg, 1985, p. 45). Most authors tend to view these findings as evidence that this is an additional, independent, comorbid condition. Coleman and Gillberg (1985, p. 46) believe that the link between these two disorders may be rather specific, but this possibility – that the seizures and the episodic, disruptive, hyperaroused aspects of autistic behavior have a common basis – has generally not been accepted. From the perspective of this book, there are at least two ways in which this linkage may occur. One is that ictal dyscontrol present in autism may occur in motorically "silent" areas found in sensory, association, and frontal areas of the brain. The second is that disorganized ictal activity, as in the earlier stages of kindling, may take place at levels below the threshold for appearance at the scalp EEG or in overt motoric seizures but may nonetheless disrupt cognition, self-regulation, and emotional control (see chapter 10). There are segments of a chain of evidence, important in their own right, that support this link between seizure activity and autism.

1. Vitamin B6 and magnesium. The Autism Research Institute (4182 Adams Avenue, San Diego, CA 92116), in its publication *Autism Research Review Inter-*

national periodically disseminates the results of surveys of large numbers of self-selected parents of children with autism regarding what interventions have been helpful. Consistently (e.g., 1994), just under 50 percent of respondents report that high doses of vitamin B6 and magnesium help improve focal attention and responsiveness to language in children diagnosed with autism. This treatment began empirically as an attempt to explore the effects of megavitamins on a variety of conditions (Pauling, 1968) but B6 and magnesium emerged as being selectively important for autism and became the subject of a number of research studies. Reviews of clinical experience and research (Rimland, 1987; Pfeiffer et al., 1995) conclude that B6–magnesium may be a promising adjunct in the treatment of autism, although flaws in methodology require that more work be done to specify the details of their efficacy.

The literature concerning the efficacy of B6 and magnesium in autism reports this relationship empirically, as a fortuitous finding with no theoretical basis. However, it is known that B6 is involved in the formation of GABA, the major inhibitory neurotransmitter (Gualtieri, Golden, & Fahs, 1983). Also known but generally not linked to autism is that B6 can be a perfect, curative, anticonvulsant for a type of infantile seizure known as B6-dependent seizures (Coker, 1992; Aicardi, 1994). (B6-dependent seizures is a strange diagnostic term in which a disorder is defined by its cure.) Coker suggested that B6-curable seizures may also occur beyond the neonatal period, and Aicardi (1994, p. 239) recommends a trial of B6 for all infantile seizures because, when it works, the treatment is completely effective and is entirely free of side effects. It is possible that the efficacy of B6 in autism is that it fosters or mobilizes inhibitory and anticonvulsant mechanisms in the neuron. This interpretation is bolstered by evidence that inadequate B6 in the diet is associated, in normal children, with an increase in temperamental irritability (McCullough et al., 1990), a sign of disinhibition.

2. Landau–Kleffner syndrome. This condition was discussed in chapter 13 because it involves the selective loss of receptive and later expressive language capabilities while preserving pure tone hearing. The syndrome also includes seizures although the relationship between the seizure activity and the language disorder is not clear. What was not mentioned before is that many children with Landau–Kleffner also develop autistic symptoms. If the child recovers language, the autism will also disappear. It is not known whether autistic symptoms are a secondary reaction to the communication impairment or are a direct reflection of ictal hyperarousal, but again a link between seizures and autism is suggested.

3. Frontal lobe seizures. Two major objections to linking autism directly with ictus are: (a) that there is no consensus that anticonvulsants are of use in autism (though see below) and (b) that there is no pattern of EEG activity characteristic of autism. Gedye (1991, 1992), however, pointed out that many of the symptoms of autism also appear in seizures with foci in the frontal lobes, and that frontal lobe seizures often do not produce scalp EEG findings, even though depth electrodes implanted in brain tissue sometimes reveal that seizures are actually occurring. That there are no associations between EEG findings and autistic symptoms thus may be a consequence of the limitations of scalp EEG.

4. Seizures and autism – comorbid conditions or common source? Despite the notion that anticonvulsants are irrelevant to autism, the Autism Research Institute (1994) surveys of treatment effectiveness indicate anticonvulsants to be mostly helpful. In a review of pharmacological treatment of autism (Holm & Varley, 1989), the authors have remarkably little to report about the use of anticonvulsants even in children with frank seizures. If epilepsy were just a comorbid condition, effective treatment of the seizures should leave the symptoms of autism untouched. Stores, Zaiwalla, & Bergel (1991) also report on misdiagnosis associated with frontal lobe seizures. However, they report that in their own clinical experience there were several children presenting with autism, severe developmental delays, and explosive behavior who had raised no clinical suspicion of a seizure disorder. When seizure activity was detected, apparently by means of an EEG, and anticonvulsants initiated, not only were seizures controlled, but the behavior and the amenability to education, i.e. the autism, also improved. Coleman and Gillberg (1985, pp. 46–8) review several published case studies that come to similar conclusions. Later, Gillberg et al. (1996) reported on two boys with intractable epilepsy, rage attacks, and autism who were found to have specific seizure foci. After the foci were removed surgically, they both became seizure-free. The autistic symptoms of both boys initially improved dramatically. Several years later, one of the boys had maintained his gains and continued to improve while the other regressed considerably but was still doing better than he had before surgery.

In another review (Gualtieri, Evans, & Patterson, 1987), caution about the side effects of anticonvulsant medications was emphasized, and those who administer such drugs were urged to increase their expertise in this area. It is possible that the paucity of information and investigation in this area is because the physicians who treat autism tend to be psychiatrists, but those who treat epilepsy are neurologists. Psychiatrists may not be highly experienced epileptologists but may often be responsible for treating their seizing autistic patients. Both the neurologist and the psychiatrist treating epilepsy are likely to think that they are treating a comorbid condition. The idea that ictal activity may directly influence many aspects of behavior, including thought, social skills, memory, and emotional control, is not commonly held.

Opioid blockers. Evidence consistent with the hyperarousal hypothesis also comes from attempts to treat those children with autism who are self-mutilators. The harm that these children can do themselves can be life-threatening, and control of these behaviors may be difficult to attain. Deutsch (1986) suggested that the children may be harming themselves in part because they are producing high levels of opioids, natural substances produced by the brain in states of high arousal that block pain receptors and hence eliminate the necessity to avoid pain. Opiates have provided an explanation for such phenomena as the absence of pain following serious injury if it occurs at times of high excitement or stress, and the runner's high, which is a feeling of euphoria that comes after a lengthy expenditure of energy and effort. The proposal was that, if the opiate mechanism could be blocked, the self-mutilators would feel pain and stop injuring themselves. The drug naltrexone hydrochloride blocks opioids from inhibiting pain and has been found in many studies to be effective in reducing self-injurious behavior, but has also proved ineffective in some instances (Bouvard et al., 1995). Effects may vary with age and with specific neurochemical levels.

Auditory Integration Training or Modulated Auditory Stimulation.   Auditory Integration Training is a procedure devised by the French otolaryngologist, Guy Berard, for treating hypersensitivities to sound and a number of other conditions. (Rimland & Edelson (1994) describe the origins of this procedure and provide further references.) In this procedure, the subject listens to music through earphones for durations of half an hour twice a day for ten days. The music is altered or modulated by an electronic device that may be set to filter out certain frequencies altogether, and which otherwise randomly removes and then reinstates frequencies and intensities at different levels of the auditory spectrum. The result of these manipulations is to produce recognizable but somewhat fuzzy-sounding music. Since no specific retraining takes place, and the meaning of the term "integration" in this context is obscure, a descriptive name for the procedure will be used here, Modulated Auditory Stimulation (MAS).

By all standards, this treatment is unusual, its rationale obscure, and its mechanism of action unknown. It was applied to autism because hypersensitivity to sounds is a commonly reported symptom. The sound frequencies which are hypersensitive on audiometric exam are filtered out during the stimulation, and it was thought that, at the very least, this particular symptom might be diminished. A popular book by the mother of a child with autism and auditory hypersensitivities who was treated with MAS (Stehli, 1991) brought the procedure to widespread public attention. Following treatment, the child was not only rid of auditory hypersensitivities but her overall condition dramatically improved and was considered to be normal. The discussion here is based on the results of two studies that have made use of the procedure with autistic children (Rimland & Edelson, 1994, 1995). One of the studies included a control procedure in which children heard music that was not modulated. Those that heard modulated sound for 10 hours improved on measures of aberrant behavior, attention, and auditory sensitivity while the control children showed no improvement. Note that the nature of the improvement was an increase in control and in focal attention. Although dramatic cures were not seen, the improvement persisted for at least nine months. Contrary to expectation, the procedure benefited low-functioning children the most, and its effectiveness did not depend on there being evidence of auditory hypersensitivity prior to the intervention.

Research on this technique is in its infancy. One recent paper that casts doubt on its efficacy found both modulated stimulation and a control condition of just listening to music through earphones to be equally helpful (Bettison, 1996). That listening *per se* may influence autism in any degree provides support for further research in this general area, but the utility of this line of inquiry remains to be seen.

Summary note about the symptoms of autism

If the symptoms described above occur, and there is no evidence that they have emerged secondary to some other condition, then autism is thought to exist in relatively pure form. Among the primary symptoms, impairments of social behavior are present in all persons diagnosed with autism. Furthermore the history must indicate that these impairments had been present at least from early childhood if not from birth. With regard to the other primary symptoms, there is the possibility that there may be separate subgroups. Studies of language and theory of mind in children with autism, of necessity confine themselves to high-functioning individuals. Mention is generally not made about the level of arousal and/or the presence of symptoms associated with high arousal in those subjects, whether at the time of study or in their past. As noted previously, the possibility exists that both cognitive and language impairments may occur, not because of some inherent limitation in those capabilities, but because hyperarousal has disrupted the realization of potentialities that were present. The reader may infer that what now appears to be "pure" autism may, with further research, turn out to be symptoms secondary to one or more types of pathology that have yet to be understood. Already there are substantial data supporting the idea that autism may occur secondary to other conditions, and these will be considered next.

Autism secondary to other disorders

In this section, conditions with evidence that symptoms of autism occur secondary to some other disorder will be presented. In this context, the term secondary means that, if the primary disorder can be treated or circumvented successfully, the symptoms of autism improve or disappear. Even here there is a caveat. If the condition persists for a long time before it is successfully overcome, normal development will not have taken place. Time and effort will be required to get things back on track and this may never be fully attainable. For example, if autism accompanied by global aphasia were present from birth through the eighth or ninth year and then the primary condition were cured, permanent limitations in language functioning would still be likely. A weaker sense of the term secondary is when autism occurs in a larger than expected proportion of the cases of the primary disorder yet not every case of the primary disorder shows symptoms of autism. A comprehensive overview of these conditions can be found in Baker and Pangborn (1996).

Circumventing primary language problems in autism

Earlier in this chapter, language difficulties were described as one of the primary symptoms of autism. In the early stages of research on autism, the idea was proposed that language impairment was at the heart of the disorder with the possible implication that if a means of social communication were found, the autism would disappear. This idea was largely abandoned in the face of evidence that children with severe developmental language problems do not necessarily develop autistic social symptoms, and that some individuals with autism do attain language but do not thereby lose their autistic social behavior. Evidence of theory of mind limitations is generally invoked to account for the residual social deficit. By contrast, there is a literature which takes the view that if the auditory–verbal channel is blocked or disrupted, alternate means of communication, especially those that use the visual channel, may resolve the social problem. Readers may recall the study of O'Connor and Hermelin (1973), discussed at the end of chapter 13, in which deaf and hearing subjects were compared as to whether they remembered information in temporal or spatial order, and it was found that deaf subjects utilized a spatial strategy. In the same paper, results for children with autism were entirely comparable to those found in the deaf. With such evidence, it is plausible to examine what would happen to autistic symptoms if the children were given an alternate means of communication such as sign language.

Actually, individuals with autism sometimes provide evidence of alternate developmental pathways to language and literacy than the usual one based on hearing. It has been observed that some autistic children learn to communicate first by means of writing. There is a film, for example, which shows an otherwise uncommunicative boy with autism laboriously writing out the title of a television show. Having watched the show regularly, he apparently was able to make some connection between the printed letters and their meaning, although he did not say the words. The film suggested that writing, a visual and motor task, then became the medium through which more language was learned.

Such observations and research pointing to auditory processing impairments (not auditory sensitivity) and visual strengths in autistic individuals led to intervention research on the efficacy of sign language. An early review (Konstantareas, Oxman, & Webster, 1978) found the results to be promising in that there was increased communication and decreased psychotic symptoms. Sometimes vocal speech increased as well. It should be noted that this work was carried on largely in the hope that speech would be enabled. Subjects were not given a full program of sign language training but were taught a type of signing that preserved the syntax of spoken speech. The syntax more natural to the language used by the blind was not taught, and speech was ever-present as well, possibly interfering with the processing of signs. Although there are anecdotal reports of some children doing so well that they left their autism behind, the available systematic evidence was of improvement, but not cure.

A later review (Jordan, 1993), which reflects increased understanding of language as rooted in social interaction (p. 249) and of theory of mind limitations in autism, found that children with autism show the same kind of social deviances in sign language that are apparent in speech. The communication skills that developed via signs were relatively nonsocial and directed at achieving some immediate end rather than shared communication with others. Since the work reported utilized the modified sign language described earlier and accompanied signs with speech, there is still no systematic evidence available on the consequences of sign training such as might be provided to a deaf child by a signing deaf parent. At this point, the available evidence is simply that signing is helpful in building some forms of communication and decreasing some of the hyperaroused behaviors often found in autism.

Temple Grandin (1995) titled her book *Thinking in pictures and other reports from my life with autism*, and devotes considerable effort to explaining to the verbally normal reader how her thinking is different from theirs. Specifically, she could not think or remember or represent an idea without forming a visual image that represented the issue and its components. She consequently had great difficulty with abstract ideas and the description of emotion, although in many instances she has found ways to visualize such nonconcrete entities. She also recognized that people who think in words find it very hard to understand those who do not. I believe that academic and scholarly approaches to autism still have great difficulty appreciating her message. Empathic study of the blind and the deaf makes it easier to appreciate the notion that, when a specific channel of information processing is not available or disrupted, the person will attempt to use other available channels to deal with that information. This appreciation in turn depends on the recognition that input modalities are not equivalent ways of getting information into the nervous system, but that each has special attributes and adeptnesses (Freides, 1974). This is one reason why, in this book, vision and audition, blindness and deafness were considered before dealing with childhood psychosis.

Gut problems and their effect on the brain

The autism–tetanus hypothesis.   This section begins with an account of an hypothesis proposed by Ellen Bolte (1998) to account for some unknown percent of cases with autism. Her proposal has the merit of specifying a mechanism of pathology with features that account for fluctuation and variability of symptoms, hyperexcitability, palliation by inhibitory neurotransmitter enhancers and anticonvulsants, potential onset at any age with disruption of development in the young, occurrence at any level of capability, and involvement of the cerebellum (the significance of which will be presented later). Although research on this hypothesis has begun, no direct evidence has been offered in its support. Bolte's argument, however, is closely reasoned and each component is based on prior scientific evidence, mostly animal research. Furthermore, there is related research evidence available, which will be reviewed below, which provides indirect support for her line of reasoning.

Like many novel hypotheses, its main feature is counterintuitive. It attributes autism in youngsters to the tetanus bacillus although, with one possible exception, no link of this sort has been noted previously. Parents have reported that autistic symptom onset has followed shortly after a DPT (diphtheria, pertussis – also known as whooping cough – tetanus) vaccination. The tetanus bacillus can be found everywhere, is anaerobic (does not require oxygen), and lives off of organic matter. A typical case of tetanus occurs following infection of an open wound. The bacillus produces a toxin which binds to peripheral nerves and is transported back to the ventral roots of the spinal cord (chapter 3, figure 3.4) where it blocks the release of inhibitory neurotransmitters from synaptic vesicles. Synaptic vesicles, it will be recalled (chapter 2 and figure 2.2) are the tiny compartments at the nerve terminal that contain packets of neurotransmitter substance whose release makes possible synaptic transmission. Tetanus neurotoxin blocks this release, and hence blocks inhibition, which, in turn, leads to excessive excitation. Under these conditions, muscles cannot be properly regulated and become overactive, producing spasms. This virulent form of tetanus often leads to death, and is preceded by hours and days of painful spasms of the trunk and of muscle groups all over the body. Tetanus spasms have not been described in the scientific literature on autism, but some parents have reported seizure-like spasms at the time of onset.

In autism, a different route of pathogenesis (pathology production) for the tetanus neurotoxin is suggested by Bolte. The research literature on humans and animals indicates that the guts of healthy individuals are free of the presence of either the tetanus bacterium or the spores by means of which it reproduces. The normal flora and the digestive enzymes in the gut destroy any vagrant bacteria or spores which happen to be ingested or get there some other way. However, if the environment of the gut is compromised, which occurs when an individual, especially a baby, is treated with oral antibiotics, conditions become much more favorable for the tetanus bacteria to thrive. Although the toxins produced in the gut are mostly decomposed rather quickly, and are not known to do harm to the gut, the bacteria, and especially the spores, may continue to survive. If conditions are right, the colony of residual organisms will then produce more toxin. Toxin produced in the gut does not go to the spinal cord, where the familiar symptoms of tetanus are produced. Instead, the hypothesis suggests, the toxin invades the vagus nerve (figure 3.6) which enervates the gut and proceeds upward to the solitary nucleus in the upper portion of the medulla. This nucleus has connections with cells in the cerebellum and with many other areas of brain including the thalamus. The toxin may mediate cerebellar cell death directly or indirectly, but will also exert a more complex effect. Tetanus toxin, even if weakened by the defenses of the gut, can increase the rate of destruction of a delicate membrane present in the synapse which is needed for normal neurotransmission. In this circumstance, the cell does not die, but membrane destruction rate is increased. These membranes can be, and are, regenerated, but meanwhile, neural regulation is out of balance. There is inadequate inhibition and excess excitation disrupting thought, plans, and emotional control.

Here then is a mechanism which accounts for hyperarousal, but, more significantly, for fluctuating hyperarousal. As conditions in the gut fluctuate, neuroinhibitory membranes are dismantled at rates which vary from normal to excessively high, and behavior improves or deteriorates accordingly. If, as suggested below, autism, and childhood and adult schizophrenia, may share similar mechanisms of impairment, the tetanus hypothesis, or something like it, may explain the dyscontrol present in these conditions. There already exists some suggestive evidence of tetanus involvement in some cases of adult-onset schizophrenia (De Beaurepaire et al., 1994). Tetanus can invade the body at any time in life but, if it does, its consequences for the nervous system would depend on the organism's stage of development and the integrity of its nervous system at the time of invasion. Of course tetanus-toxin-autism may occur only in a small proportion cases. But, as shall be evident in the next sections of this chapter, considerable data exist indicating an association between autism and disorders of gut.

One other point: biological research on childhood autism and psychosis has suffered because there is no adequate animal model of the pathology. Bolte's hypothesis suggests that antibiotic compromise of gut flora and the introduction of some organism such as tetanus might provide a suitable model that could increase understanding of these conditions substantially.

Measles immunization. Wakefield et al. (1998) reported on 12 children who developed severe gut symptoms and behavioral disorders after immunization with measles, mumps, and rubella vaccine. Further work seeking to understand this linkage is under way. Although different from Bolte's hypothesis, there are similarities in the way gut symptoms and behavioral disorganization are linked. Varied reports of huge increases in the incidence of autism and related disorders (e.g. Rimland, 1999a) have also been linked to the possibility that something goes awry in the immunization process. A major candidate for the source of the trouble is the weakening of the natural ecology of the gut by oral antibiotics frequently administered in the treatment of middle ear infections. A critique of Wakefield's conclusions (Fombonne, 1999) has pointed out very strongly that the link between vaccines, gut, and psychosis has by no means been firmly established. He notes, for example, that there is no evidence that measles epidemics or inflammatory bowel diseases are associated with an increase in autism. But such evidence may be irrelevant since it does not specify the developmental status of the child or the special circumstances, e.g. oral antibiotic treatment, that might make the child vulnerable. It should be interesting to see how the further evidence about Wakefield's observations emerges.

Celiac disease and sensitivity to gluten and casein. Celiac disease (Coleman, Landgrebe, & Landgrebe, 1976a; Shaw, 1998) is a rare, genetically determined disorder due to the absence of enzymes needed to digest a portion of the gluten molecule. Glutens are commonly found in many foods, especially grains, but the troublesome portion is particularly rich in wheat, rye, oats, and barley. In celiac disease, improperly digested gluten-containing foods are poorly absorbed, especially in the jejunum portion of the small intestine. As a result, many villi, the small projections in the gut lining whose function is to absorb nutrients, are destroyed and/or malfunction, and the ecology of the gut, which is teeming with microorganisms, is disrupted. Absorption of other food substances, particularly fats, is also disrupted, and the patient, though ingesting adequate amounts of food, becomes malnourished. The symptoms of celiac disease include nausea and vomiting, excessive flatulence and abdominal bloating, diarrhea and/or constipation, poor stool formation, and bleeding. Such symptoms appear as soon as glutens are consumed. Inadequate digestion also produces byproducts which are poisonous to neurons, and these appear to be the causes of autism. Avoidance of gluten ingestion, a difficult but not impossible task, results in relief of both gut and behavioral symptoms.

Studying a group of 72 randomly chosen autistic children, five were found to have gut symptoms consistent with celiac disease (Coleman, Landgrebe, & Landgrebe, 1976a). At the time of this study, definitive tests of celiac disease did not exist, but confidence in the findings was strong because improvement in behavior occurred after switching to a gluten-free diet. Later, when the newer more definitive tests were used (Coleman and Gillberg, 1985, p. 161; Pavone et al., 1997) celiac disease was not confirmed. Accordingly, the linkage between celiac disease and autism was perplexing, and Coleman and Gillberg (1985) concluded that knowledge in this area was inadequate. Later, Shaw (1998, pp. 125–6) pointed out that there is evidence that a subgroup of adults with schizophrenia suffer celiac disease symptoms (e.g. Dohan, 1983) and he reiterated the clinical observation that autistic children with such symptoms improve on a gluten-free diet.

Shaw reconciled these inconsistent observations by suggesting that most psychotic persons with celiac symptoms do not suffer from the genetic and severe form of celiac disease and thus fail the definitive tests for the disorder. They do however suffer from sensitivity to gluten and, unlike genetic celiacs, are also sensitive to casein, a major component of cow's milk. Shaw believes that the difficulty with both casein and gluten is that they are incompletely digested because of an enzyme deficiency. The resulting fragments are peptides which are absorbed in blood and circulate to brain where they activate opiate receptors. It is via this route that the brain is set into states of high hyperarousal in these cases. If this mechanism of pathology is treated, for example, with a diet containing no gluten or casein, autism spontaneously improves. Reichelt et al. (1997) followed children with autism and high peptide levels from seven countries for four years and found those who stayed with a casein- and gluten-free diet progressed developmentally while those who stopped the diet regressed.

Secretin.   Early in the process of digestion, food in the stomach is broken down by acid. As the food passes into the small intestine, the pancreas secretes enzymes that further digest the food but these enzymes do not function normally in an acid medium. To neutralize the acid, the pancreas secretes bicarbonate if prompted by the release of a hormone called secretin. Secretin comes from cells in the small intestine which react to the presence of acid. The possible relevance of secretin to autism emerged when a child with autism and a number of gut problems was given an intensive digestive system evaluation. This included a recently developed test of pancreatic function in which secretin is administered and the production of bicarbonate is monitored (Shaw, 1998, p. 132). The child produced much bicarbonate, but more importantly, showed a dramatic improvement both in gut symptoms and behavior. Subsequently, the positive effects of administering secretin have been verified in some cases and not in others. In some with a positive response, the effect has been enduring; in others, transient (Rimland, 1999b). The assumption was that secretin had some direct or indirect effect on brain. Other research on secretin has provided evidence of its presence in brain, where it may function in a number of ways including service as a neurotransmitter (e.g. Charlton et al., 1983; Karelson, Laasik, & Sillard,

1995). A fuller explanation regarding the role of secretin in mechanisms regulating behavior and the boundaries of its efficacy as a form of treatment should emerge in the early years of the twenty-first century.

Candida albicans.   *Candida albicans* is a very common yeast that is primarily known as the culprit in two conditions: a mostly annoying, rather common and not very serious vaginal infection, and a condition known as thrush, which produces a white, cheese-like coating of the mouth and tongue in infants (Rimland, 1988). Normally, some candida is found in the gut, but under certain conditions overgrowth occurs. The defenses that keep candida in check in the gut include a range of bacteria and other microrganisms which reside there (the flora of the gut) which aid digestion and the absorption of food and fight off invading infectious agents. Any condition which disrupts the flora, such as gluten and casein sensitivity or prolonged treatment with oral antibiotics, leaves the gut susceptible to candida overgrowth. Proliferation of candida or other yeasts, for whatever reason, leads to the production of toxins which compromise the immune system and also attack the brain (Shaw, 1998, pp. 31–62). Cases of successful treatment of yeast overgrowth in autistic children and concomitant improvement in symptoms have been reported. The treatment strategy attacks the yeasts with antifungal drugs, restores normal flora to the gut by administering helpful bacteria such as are found in acidophilus and cultured milk products such as yogurt, and makes changes in the diet and lifestyle to minimize the opportunities for yeast infestations. Coleman and Gillberg (1985, p. 138) point out that systematic research evidence about candida infestations in autism is lacking. However, the surveys of treatment efficacy in the Autism Research Review consistently find antifungal agents, which are unlikely to have been used unless there was evidence of a yeast infection, to have been distinctly helpful.

Purine autism

In June of 1974, 69 children with autism were taken by their families to a convention of an association devoted to aiding autistic children, and were each subjected to close to an hour of medical testing (Coleman, Landgrebe, & Landgrebe, 1976b). Twenty-two percent of those self-selected children were found to have elevated levels of uric acid in their urine. Such abnormalities are found for a variety of reasons, and subsequent study has attributed the abnormality to errors in the biosynthesis of the purines, a class of organic compounds that are essential components of all living cells. Three different enzyme abnormalities have been found to be associated with autistic symptoms. Coleman and Gillberg (1985, pp. 150–8) present more information about the biochemistry of the disorder and also review one report which describes how symptoms improved on a low purine diet. Such a diet is highly restrictive both as to range of foods and amounts, and is very difficult to implement.

Allergies and autoimmune disorders of the nervous system

In chapter 10, mention was made of the possible linkage between allergies and attentional disorders, and references were cited suggesting that the nervous system could be directly subject to autoimmune reactions. In the anecdotal lore about autism, there are stories of mothers who were convinced that their autistic children were suffering from allergic reactions who then took heroic steps to locate and remove the allergens from the child or remove the child from the allergens and thus successfully treat the autism. There is also a scientific literature on the subject, beyond the scope of this book (Coleman and Gillberg, 1985, p. 107; Yuwiler & Freedman, 1987, p. 270; Shaw, 1998, pp. 95–123), which implicates an immune response to receptors for the neurotransmitter serotonin, to a basic protein component of myelin, the fatty nerve sheath, and a number of other, often surprising, targets.

Summary note about autism as a secondary symptom

There has been an explosion of hypotheses about biological mechanisms that are associated with brain dysfunction and autism. There is much work to be done to know how to identify the particular individuals who suffer from a particular mechanism of impairment. But who knows? In the next two decades the diagnosis of autism may disappear, to be replaced by explicit specifications of particular biological and/or social conditions, the autism remaining only as a symptom cluster that initiates the diagnostic process. This would parallel what now takes place when one suffers from a cough, and the diagnostic process must choose between bacterial or viral sinus infection, tuberculosis, cancer, emphysema, or any number of other conditions before embarking on intervention.

Genetic flaws and autism

There are a large number of conditions producing symptoms of abnormal behavior and mental retardation which are now known to be associated with genetic flaws, errors in the genetic makeup of the individual that were determined at the moment of conception. Some of these conditions will be described in greater detail in the last chapter of this book, which will deal with mental retardation. Here it is noted that a much higher than expected incidence of autism is often diagnosed in fragile-X syndrome, tuberous sclerosis (Coleman & Gillberg, 1985, chapter 13) and phenylketonuria (p. 144). Why autism occurs in some cases with these genetic conditions and not in others is a question to which no clear answers have yet been found. Since these genetic conditions generally lead to severe retardation, a significant diathesis for psychosis is present in these children. In addition, unknown environmental–experiential factors may play a role. Also a particular genetic condition may vary in its consequences and somewhat different areas of the brain may be compromised, so autism may appear only when areas crucial for autism (see next section of this chapter) are affected. Coleman and Gillberg point out that, in the case of tuberous sclerosis, autistic symptoms may appear long before there is evidence of the tubers, the tumor-like abnormalities that grow in the skin and nervous system, so such an explanation may not be valid in this instance. On the other hand, disruption of nervous system control does not necessarily require abnormalities so large in mass that they can be easily noted.

Brain abnormalities in autism

In recent years, studies of the biological basis of autism have multiplied. They make use of new imaging procedures which can reveal the size and integrity of the structures of the living brain in considerable detail and older techniques such as the EEG which can illuminate the way it functions. The latter, if quantified, can allow comparison of measures in particular areas or regions of the brain and of the coherence present between different regions. Some of the newer techniques can evaluate rate of metabolism and neurotransmitter utilization in specific areas while behavior and active information processing are actually taking place. Reviews of this burgeoning literature have appeared (e.g. Coleman & Gillberg, 1985; Schopler & Mesibov, 1987; Minshew, 1992; and volume 26, no. 2, the April 1996 issue of the *Journal of Autism and Developmental Disorders*, which contains a series of brief reports on the status of many areas of research in autism). Current knowledge may be summarized as follows. Autism appears to be a disorder of hierarchically high (see chapter 5) brain mechanisms, those that are multimodal and require the integration of information from different sources. Despite the evidence that autism is frequently associated with mental retardation, it is not a disorder of basic mechanisms of information processing (Minshew, 1996).

According to Minshew (1996) three kinds of neuropathological findings have been consistently verified in autism: an increase in brain weight, decreased dendritic tree development (interconnectivity) in the limbic system, and decreased Purkinje cells in the cerebellum. Minshew points out that the first two may appear paradoxical in that one implies too much brain and the other too little. Such conditions are not paradoxical, however, if an injury-to-a-stable-system view of brain damage is replaced by a concept of brain maldevelopment in a growing, changing organ where overgrowth and pruning regularly occur and are subject to error. Localization of pathology in the limbic system puts the problem squarely in a place where emotion, old information, new information, intentions, and plans coincide, and is easy to assimilate to familiar knowledge about brain function. The role of the cerebellum, however, challenges our understanding of brain function because, as previously noted, it has been associated primarily with the integration of motor activity. Although some autistic children show various motor mannerisms or motor overexcitement, many other autistic children are motorically agile and show no signs of classically defined cerebellar deficit such as is seen in ataxic cerebral palsy (see chapter 11). Available evidence coming from high-functioning autistic individuals is that their impairment is at the

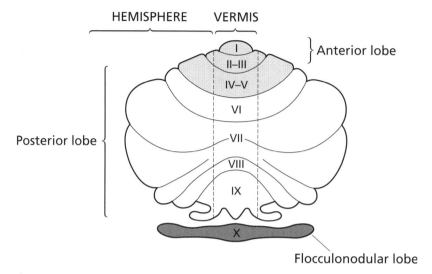

Figure 15.2 Schematic design of the fissures and lobules of the cerebellum. Note that the vermis is a region in the center

highest levels of cognitive function (theory of mind), not motor function. What has happened however is that recent work has brought to light a considerably broadened view of the functions of the cerebellum. Some of that literature will be briefly reviewed next.

Cerebellar limitations in autism

Courchesne and colleagues (1989, 1994), noting prior autopsy reports of cell loss in the cerebellum in persons with autism, began to study the integrity of this part of the brain as well as the rest of the brain as revealed in the images provided by magnetic resonance imaging (MRI). This is a constantly developing technique that produces highly detailed images of the living brain. It allows quantitative estimates of the area of any cross-section or the three-dimensional volume of any substructure. Three types of abnormalities were found in subjects with high-functioning autism, who were free of other conditions such as mental retardation, epilepsy, and fragile-X syndrome. The first was a 15 percent reduction in size or hypoplasia, of the cerebellar vermis, particularly lobules VI and VII. (These structures will be described shortly.) The second group had the same cerebellar abnormality as the first but also showed evidence of loss of parietal lobe tissue. The third, smaller, group had an abnormal 15 percent increase in size or hyperplasia, of the same lobules of the cerebellar vermis.

The generally accepted understanding of the functions of the cerebellum (as an integrator of complex motor movements) and the newer conceptualization as an inte-

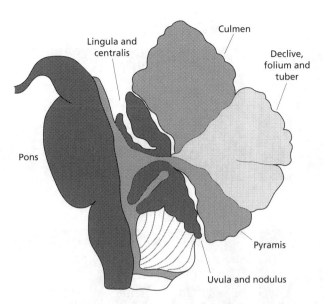

Figure 15.3 A sketch of a side view of the cerebellar vermis (the lobules are named rather than numbered)

grator of all aspects of information processing) was presented in chapter 11 and should be reviewed before proceeding further. Straddling the midline in the cerebellum is an area called the vermis. Figure 15.2 (similar to figure 11.9 which should also be reexamined) shows a schematic view of the structure of the cerebellum and it consists of a series of numbered layers, called lobules, the midpart of which is vermis. The lobules are grouped in three lobes called the anterior, posterior, and flocculonodular lobes on the basis of the presence of deep fissures; these areas are also different functionally. The phylogenetically oldest lobe at the bottom is also called the vestibulocerebellum, and is linked to vestibular nuclei in the medulla. Thus, this part of the cerebellum is concerned with position in space while moving, and with body equilibrium. The anterior lobe is also called the spinocerebellum, because it receives its inputs from the spinal cord. It is concerned with limb movement. The phylogenetically newest layer is the posterior lobe, which includes lobules VI and VII and is also called the cerebrocerebellum. It receives its inputs from nuclei in the pons that relay information from the cerebral cortex. Its outputs, via nuclei deep in the cerebellum, go back to thalamus and thus can modulate cortical activity. All output of the cerebellum is via special large cells called Purkinje cells which are entirely inhibitory and utilize GABA as a neurotransmitter. It will be recalled that Purkinje cell loss was one of the recurrent findings in autism.

A representation of a side view of the cerebellum cut through the vermis can be seen in figure 15.3. A different set of labels are employed here but the white areas labeled Declive, Folium, and Tuber are comparable to lobules VI and VII. A direct appreciation of these differences can be seen in figure 15.4, which shows the brain

NORMAL

AUTISTIC

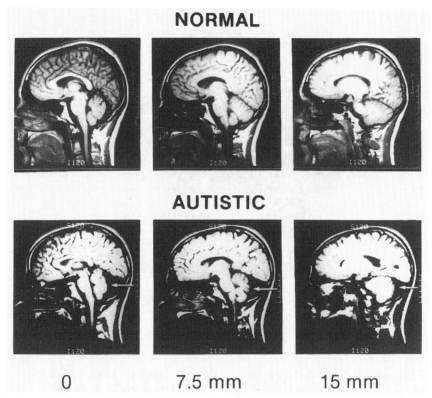

0	7.5 mm	15 mm

Figure 15.4 Magnetic resonance images of brains from a normal person and one with autism. The first image is at midline, the second and third are 7.5 and 15 mm to the left. Note that maximal differences are at midline, and major differences are not seen elsewhere

in profile at midline and compares MRI scans in a person with autism and a normal individual. Apparent also in these images is that there are no major differences anywhere else in the brain.

Courchesne et al. (1994) found evidence in just about all of their autistic subjects of either hypoplasia or hyperplasia of vermal lobules VI and VII. He points out (Courchesne, 1989) that these abnormalities are different from those found in known types of cerebellar disease. Furthermore, if such selective pathology is present from birth, it must be due to something going awry at the time that cells migrate during gestation to form this newest part of the cerebellum. It turns out that this occurs in the middle of the first trimester, a time when many women may not even be sure they are pregnant. The cause of these pathological developments is not known.

Finding anatomical evidence of differences between those with autism and those without is an important achievement, but the researchers wanted to determine what the precise behavioral consequences of this aberrant anatomy might be. Theorizing that the cerebellum is involved in the deployment of attention, they examined the problem in a number of different ways. A major finding was that subjects with autism had difficulty shifting their attention if the task demanded rapid shifts. At a more leisurely pace, the autistics functioned just like normals. To verify that it was cerebellar dysfunction that was the source of the difficulty, the same tests were also administered to individuals who had sustained extensive cerebellar lesions as a result of cancer or other pathological conditions. These subjects also displayed impairments in rapid attentional shifting, supporting the idea that the cerebellum is involved.

Those with acquired cerebellar lesions were comparable to individuals with autism in their inability to shift attention rapidly, and they generally had other symptoms of cerebellar impairment such as ataxia, but they were not particularly autistic. If cerebellar lesions are so crucial to autism, how come the acquired lesion group did not become autistic? Courchesne et al. (1994, pp. 128–32) suggested that the answer lay in the different consequences of early- and late-acquired deficits. In those with autism, the cerebellar limitation present early on made quick shifts of attention impossible. In turn, such limitations would interfere, they speculated, with the development of joint attention. The latter, it will be recalled, is believed to be the foundation of social awareness and social behavior. For those with later-acquired lesions, joint attention will have already been established, so that the impact of the consequent deficit on social behavior would be relatively small.

Broader implications of the cerebellar deficit hypothesis

The evidence of cerebellar dysplasia in autism offers the possibility of providing at least a partial explanation as to why autism appears in so many contexts, and possibly why a number of treatments that may increase inhibitory neurotransmitter functions are helpful. If the very young child has not yet had the time to establish basic social skills and theory of mind, any pathology that limits, cuts off, or inhibits cerebellar function might make the child vulnerable to autism. If mental retardation is present, but autism is not, it would be expected that cerebellar functions, at least of the crucial vermis areas, are intact. In this view, cerebellar dysfunction alone, without mental retardation, would foster high-level autism. Since what the cerebellum does in performing its integrative function makes heavy use of inhibitory neurotransmitters, anything that enhanced such functions might mitigate some of the consequences of cerebellar impairment. Put another way, vitamin B6 and magnesium may be effective in aiding attentional behavior in some autistics because it contributes to the production of neurotransmitters in heavy use by the cerebellum. These hypotheses require verification. For example, we do not know whether the children who respond to B6 are high-level subjects who have cerebellar dysplasia or whether the reverse is true, that it is the nonresponders who have dysplasia, or for that matter whether there is any relation between cerebellar dysplasia and B6 responsiveness.

From the beginning of active research on autism, this disorder has been considered different from late adolescent- and adult-onset schizophrenia. However there is a small but growing literature on cerebellar involvement in schizophrenia, some of which goes back a good many years (Taylor, 1991). In this literature, there are even largely disregarded reports of vermal dysplasia in chronic schizophrenia (Heath et al., 1982) and sophisticated current studies of cerebellar circuitry dysfunction (Andreasen et al., 1996). It seems likely that, as mechanisms of impairment underlying the disorganization present in various forms of psychosis are better understood, our current classifications of these conditions may change considerably. There will be more about this below where childhood schizophrenia is reviewed.

Treatment effectiveness in autism

From what you have already read, it is obvious that autism is a diverse condition, sometimes apparently a primary disorder, sometimes apparently a disorder secondary to other conditions. Although the goal of scientific research is to understand the mechanism of impairment and then find a treatment that remediates the impairment, this sequence does not occur often. Professionals of all sorts, and non-professionals as well, try to help change the disturbed behavior. Physicians are likely to try different medications, a psychologist may attempt psychotherapy or some form of behavior therapy, a speech pathologist will try speech training, and so forth. Out of these efforts, a general lore develops about what works and what does not. Surveys such as those obtained by the Autism Research Institute about effective interventions also add to the information available. Such findings have been mentioned repeatedly through the course of the chapter and lead to the somewhat paradoxical circumstance that the results of treatment have helped clarify the nature of the condition. Thus, in children with autism and candida, if effective treatment of the candida overgrowth leads to a cure of the autism, it verifies the idea that, in this instance, autism is a secondary consequence of the condition. It would then be of interest to determine whether candida is simply a nonspecific stressor coming at a time of developmental vulnerability or whether the candida does something specific to the nervous system, something which also occurs in other cases of autism where candida is not a problem.

Schreibman (1996) pointed out that, although there is a great deal of progress in specifying the biological substrate of autism, there has been even greater progress in finding effective intervention procedures at the level of environmental structuring, education, and behavior modification. Whereas most children with autism, prior to the 1960s, faced institutionalization by the time they reached adolescence, far fewer have had this outcome in the 1990s. Earlier, parents with special strengths might have been able to facilitate their children's progress (e.g. Gajzago & Prior, 1974, or Sullivan et al., 1992), but they were mostly alone and reliant on their own ingenuity. At the time of this writing, there are many resources to draw on, and many professionals who devote their careers to applying the wisdom gained from intervention experience. In many communities, the wisdom has permeated the public schools which are charged with educating all children including those with autism. Many have developed programs for educating children with autism and, depending on the assets the child may possess, for making possible adaptation to independent living (see Berkell, 1992 or Schopler & Mesibov, 1995, for examples). Schreibman points out (1996, p. 249): "We no longer speak in terms of degree of change in individual behaviors. Rather, we can now speak in terms of the overall improvement in the quality of the individual's life."

The most dramatic claims of improvement have come from a long-term, intensive treatment study conducted by Lovaas and colleagues (Lovaas, 1987; McEachin, Smith, & Lovaas, 1993). This study has been alluded to earlier but is now presented in some detail. It began in 1970 and follow-up of the children, now fully grown, is still under way. Participants all had received independent and later confirmed diagnoses of autism, were less than four years old, and had an intelligence quotient greater than 36. This score is in the range of moderate mental retardation, and indicates a low level of responsiveness. Over time, 38 subjects were recruited for the study and half were given intensive treatment and the other half were given standard treatment, the latter consisting of state-of-the-art-at-the-time involvement in education and up to ten hours a week of behavior modification. Yet another 21 children were followed by another agency. The intensive-treatment group received more than 40 hours of individual one-on-one treatment (Lovaas et al., 1980; Lovaas & Leaf, 1981) for two or more years, 50 weeks per year, after which the children were enrolled in a school appropriate to their level of functioning. Parent education was also an important part of the program. The staffing demands of the intensive-treatment group and the timing of the initial referral to the research program determined assignment to group. If a team of therapists were available when eligible referrals appeared, they were assigned to the intensive-treatment group. Otherwise they were placed in the standard-treatment group.

Follow-up at about the age of seven indicated that nine of the 19 children given intensive treatment were performing normally in school, had intelligence in the average range (having gained an average of 30 IQ points), and were indistinguishable emotionally and cognitively from normal children. The other intensively treated children at follow-up were mostly mildly retarded and in special classes for the language-delayed; a few were profoundly retarded and in classes for retarded and autistic individuals. Of the 40 children who either received standard treatment or were followed by the external agency, only 2 percent attained normality and the remainder were divided approximately equally in classes for the mildly and severely retarded. The gains obtained by the intensively treated children were sustained in all but one when they were reexamined at a mean age of 13, whereas one child, who at age seven follow-up did not qualify for the best outcome group, later was found to be in regular classes in junior college. Thus at the 13-year follow-up, there were again nine of 19 "cures." The term "cure" was not used in the cited research reports but that appears to be the message.

Since autism has been thought to be a chronic and essentially incurable condition, this is an extraordinary claim, and it has received close scrutiny and criticism (Bear et al., 1993). Readers just beginning their study of psychology need to be aware that some of the controversy has to do with theoretical biases, which makes it difficult for those with a neuropsychological or cognitive perspective to accept the accomplishments of those with a behavioral orientation, and vice-versa. Even so, the study has earned the respect of all students in the field: just about everyone agrees that it merits replication, and several such studies are under way. Assuming that the findings can be replicated, there are many implications, perhaps the most important of which is that the pathological processes producing these massive symptoms, in at least a portion of those who obtain the diagnosis, are reversible and hence reflect some forms of disorganization or dyscontrol rather than deficit. Lovaas and colleagues, in reporting their accomplishments, emphasize changes in intelligence and the normality of the intelligence in the best-outcome group, even though there was no relationship between intelligence at entry and ultimate outcome. It thus appears that the poor-outcome subjects in the intensively treated group may have had irreversible deficits in intellectual function in addition to whatever it was that caused their autism. It would be of interest to know whether any of the autistic symptoms of this poor-outcome group improved even if their intelligence did not normalize. Published reports do not contain this information but a personal communication (Lovaas, May 1997) suggested that autistic symptoms had improved.

Lovaas and colleagues cannot be held responsible for my report of this conversation, but it suggested to me a number of ideas about autism and its treatment. First, Lovaas reported that although it was impossible to predict who would improve to normality based on presenting symptoms and test scores, rate of progress in treatment (the details of which await further reports from the researchers) during the first four months was predictive of ultimate outcome. In other words, early rate of learning predicted level of outcome. Second, Lovaas reported that, since all subjects could hear, there was a heavy emphasis in the program on training ordinary speech. Much later in their experience, and too late to change the research protocol, the researchers observed that some of the children who made little progress in learning to speak appeared to have communication capabilities via the visual channel. Again, we await the details of these findings but it is theoretically possible that greater gains might have been accomplished in some subjects if the initial efforts at language training had been devoted to signing. Third, much that has been learned in recent years about pathological syndromes was not available to the researchers when they began. Thus, although the diagnosis of autism was reliable within the knowledge available at the time, it is not known how many children really had Landau–Kleffner, or fragile-X syndrome (a genetic condition that most likely appeared among Kanner's original cases), or any of the other now much better understood conditions. No measurements were taken to determine the level of theory of mind, although such measures will be obtained on later follow-up, nor was it known whether any of the children did benefit or might have benefited from taking B6 and magnesium. Finally, Lovaas also suggested that some cases of poor outcome appeared to be influenced by family pathology and dissension, which made it difficult to provide the highly structured and consistent environment required for treatment.

One report that has appeared in print (Smith, Klevstrand, & Lovaas, 1995) is about Rett syndrome cases. This condition will be discussed below but it occurs in girls and appears by 18 months, possibly after a short period of normal development. The original symptoms look very much like autism but, instead of improving or remaining static, deterioration in mental and physical functions occurs. It emerged that two of the children in Lovaas' standard treatment group really had Rett syndrome. Another case of Rett syndrome was found in an intensive-treatment group that is part of a Norwegian replication of the Lovaas work that is still under way. The authors review the outcome of these three cases and find that behavioral treatment had no efficacy for them. Such findings raise the possibility that as yet unknown conditions may also explain why some or all of the nine or ten children who received intensive treatment were not "cured."

From these data, it is plausible to conclude that children presenting with autistic symptoms comprise two groups. One consists of those who are suffering from profound, so far irreversible, deficiencies, of which some are static and some are in continuing decline. These individuals also may suffer from various kind of dysregulation and dyscontrol which may be reversible. The second group consists of those whose deficiencies are consequences of massive but reversible impairments of regulation and control. Treatments which help to bring about better neural regulation and control may be curative, and one of those treatments is behavior modification. This should come as no surprise. If behavioral techniques can aid in controlling epilepsy (see chapter 8), they should be helpful in the treatment of other dyscontrol conditions. The right pharmacology or special nutrition may also do the same job, perhaps more efficiently. This is yet another challenge for future research.

Summary notes about autism

Autism is a type of childhood psychosis that appears early in life. It occurs in many contexts, often accompanied by mental retardation. In its purest forms, where mental retardation is not present, it is marked by limitations in some of the perceptual–cognitive–emotional mechanisms that make possible reciprocal social interactions and by serious impairments or lags in the development of theory of mind. Most frequently the disorder is accompanied, at least in some of the early stages of development, by behaviors that are hyperaroused, including various kinds of self-stimulation, aggression, and/or panic-like reactions. Some forms of autism, or at least the hyperaroused symptoms of autism, may be curable: when autism is secondary to some other, treatable, pathology, or when the primary disorder is treated with intensive, early, behavioral intervention. There are a number of likely sites for brain neuropathology that may be the source of the problem, particularly the limbic system, but promising recent work has suggested that the evolutionary more recent parts of the cerebellum also play a crucial role.

Other Childhood Psychotic Conditions

In this section childhood psychotic conditions other than autism will be described. In all instances except the last, there is often a normal period of development which precedes the onset of psychosis.

Rett syndrome

The first description of this syndrome is in a German-language paper written by an Austrian physician named Andreas Rett (Perry, 1991; Clarke, 1995) which was published in 1966. His initial observations were of two girls sitting in his waiting room with comparable hand-wringing mannerisms. These observations were confirmed by others, at first sporadically, but by the late 1980s, with considerable frequency, so that at the time this is written, there is fair consensus about the syndrome's defining characteristics. It occurs almost only in girls, although some believe that it has also been seen in boys. Symptoms become apparent following a nearly normal-appearing course of development both prenatally and for the first six to 18 months of life. With careful study evidence can be found that, even during this phase, development is less than normal. Somewhere between five months and four years of age, head growth, as measured by circumference, decelerates, psychomotor development deteriorates, and gait, as walking is learned, is wide-based and ataxic. In addition, language as it appears is severely impaired in both expressive and receptive characteristics, and the marker symptom of stereotyped hand movements that Rett first noticed, appears. Other commonly occurring symptoms include breathing dysfunctions, EEG abnormalities with or without overt seizures, severe curvature of the spine, muscle wasting, and/or spasticity. The children become severely retarded and many are impaired motorically and must use a wheelchair. For those who survive into adulthood, the deteriorating pattern of symptoms stabilizes and the symptoms may actually improve somewhat, especially with treatment. During the early stages of the condition, the child often receives a diagnosis of autism.

There is evidence that the syndrome is a genetic disorder, but the details are far from worked out. Various treatments have been applied to ameliorate the symptoms but have not been successful in preventing deterioration. As noted, Smith, Klevstrand, and Lovaas (1995) report treatment failure even with intensive behavior modification. No specific biological marker for this degenerative disorder has yet been found so the mechanism of impairment is unknown, although it is known that Rett children do not have any other known degenerative diseases. On the other hand, this disorder also has its spectrum of variants, and it is not known whether they will turn out to have the same biological causation or several different ones. These variants include cases that never show regression but develop the full syndrome by showing clear signs before six months of age, and others who do not show the full syndrome until considerably later in life.

Later childhood-onset psychoses

Childhood schizophrenia

In the early phases of research on autism, it was thought that autism was different from both childhood- and adult-onset schizophrenia, if for no other reason than that the developmental course of each was different (Rimland, 1964). Autism was thought to be a disorder essentially present when development begins, whereas schizophrenia was a disorder that came later and involved regression. Regression is a term which means a going back or unravelling of development, so regression must be preceded by a period of normal development. In adult-onset schizophrenia, the most frequent age of onset is in late adolescence or young adulthood. Childhood-onset schizophrenia was a downward extension of adult schizophrenia, the regression occurring in middle to late childhood, say between the ages of six and 12 (Coleman & Gillberg, 1996) or 14 (Asarnow, 1994), supposedly after a period of normal development.

Childhood schizophrenia shares major characteristics with the adult form which tends to occur with a predominance of one of two diverse symptom clusters, although some individuals have both (Walker, 1987). Positive symptoms include hallucinations (perception in the absence of stimulation), delusions (false beliefs), especially those of the well-organized paranoid (suspicious) variety, bizarre behavior including agitation, violence toward self and others, and active abnormalities of thought including irrelevance of associations and violation of the conventions that make possible social communication. An example of the latter might be a response to the question "How old are you?" with "I like moon pies." There is evidence that these symptoms are associated with disturbances of the neurotransmitter dopamine. Negative symptoms include blunted affect, inability to experience pleasure, limited speech, lack of motivation or drive, and poor attention to anything. Negative symptoms are associated with enlarged ventricles in the brain, a sign commonly taken to indicate atrophy. Also, there is greater evidence of genetic transmission (Dworkin et al., 1987).

Positive symptoms commonly occur in reactive schizophrenia, where breakdown of function is fairly sudden, the prior history appears normal, and the symptoms are florid and dramatic. Often the individual is described as suddenly going berserk. Some of these cases spontaneously improve or respond quickly to treatment, and the individual may never again suffer a similar reaction. Other cases with similar onset go on to have recurrent psychotic episodes. Still others never improve and remain in a psychotic, if, over time, less florid, state for the rest of their lives. Negative symptoms commonly appear in process schizophrenia, where the prior history indicates serious difficulty in adaptation; the symptoms suggest peculiarity, idiosyncrasy, and social isolation; and major decline in function is not noted. The individual is described as marginal or poorly adjusted beforehand and almost never becomes normal. Some remain permanently psychotic and others fluctuate between marginal adjustment and more active psychosis. In their nonpsychotic state they may be termed schizoid, or, more recently, schizotypal (the diagnosis is schizotypy). The alert reader will note that process schizophrenics, who make up the majority of those with schizophrenic diagnoses, fit a pattern which does not clearly indicate regression. Apparently, at some point, they do something or encounter someone to earn their diagnosis, but their premorbid and morbid states do not appear to be vastly different.

Returning to childhood schizophrenia, the evidence is that negative symptoms and insidious onset predominate (Asarnow, 1994). These children frequently show abnormalities and delays in early language, motor functions, social responsiveness, peer relationships, and scholastic achievement. Many also show signs of conduct and oppositional disorder, and of depression. They also show symptoms of thought disorder, hallucinations, and delusions (Russell, 1992), even though these are generally considered positive symptoms. Not all manifestations of delusions and hallucinations are the same. The better organized and more systematic ones are indeed considered positive symptoms, but the less well organized, inconsistent forms are considered negative symptoms. It is the latter type that would accompany delays in language and social responsiveness. It is beyond the scope of this book to consider the intricacies of psychiatric diagnosis, but, for many schools of psychiatric thought, delusions and hallucinations are considered to be the hallmark of schizophrenia. This is true despite evidence that they occur in other disorders (Russell, 1992) and even in normal individuals (Jaynes, 1976).

There is evidence that childhood schizophrenia may have continuity with autism and may not be a separate disorder. A follow-up study, some 42 years later, of childhood schizophrenics whose age at onset was from six to 14 years (Eggers & Bunk, 1997), found that sudden onset had not occurred frequently in those less than 12 years old. Only 25 percent of all the patients reviewed in middle age had improved significantly and, of these, none came from the larger group with gradual onset. This evidence disconfirms the notion that childhood schizophrenia is a regressive disorder. Clearly, most of those who obtained a diagnosis of childhood schizophrenia had long-standing handicaps of a cognitive, emotional, and social nature. The other side of the assertion that autism and childhood schizophrenia are different disorders has been weakened by the broadened age criteria for autism. Children are now called autistic even if symptoms first appear as late as three or four years of age after some period of normal development. Russell (1992, p. 31), reviewing the work of Kolvin, notes that the early-onset group, generally diagnosed autistic, will show predominant symptoms of "gaze avoidance, abnormal preoccupations, stereotypy, poor supervised play, disinterest in people, echolalia, and overactivity." The late-onset group who will be diagnosed schizophrenic will show predominant symptoms of "hallucinations, disorder of thought content, and blunting and incongruity of affect."

One view of the latter observations is that the real difference between autism and childhood schizophrenia may be in the developmental level of the child at the time the pathological process is initiated or exceeds a certain threshold, and the extent to which that process shapes subsequent development. In addition, the type of pathological mechanism, and perhaps the way the environment responds to the child's behavior, may be important. There are data supporting this view. Russell (1992, p. 50) reviews studies which find older children with a diagnosis of childhood schizophrenia who clearly met the criteria for autism when they were less than 30 months old. Cantor (1988) makes similar observations. Furthermore, as noted above, the major structural anomaly found in autistic patients, dysplasia of the cerebellar vermis, was earlier found in a large percentage of hospitalized, chronic adult schizophrenics (Heath et al., 1982). That finding had previously received very little systematic attention because it did not seem to account for the symptoms of psychosis. It was not, however, an ephemeral discovery since cerebellar dysfunction in adult schizophrenia has been confirmed with more recent imaging procedures (e.g. Andreasen et al., 1996). To complete the argument, it needs to be determined whether childhood schizophrenics have cerebellar dysplasias, but I have not yet been able to locate relevant evidence.

There may come a point when something like specific cerebellar dysplasias at a particular stage of development or some toxic mechanism responsible for such dysplasias may become the basis of diagnostic classification. Diagnoses then will reflect etiology and be much more prescriptive as to treatment than are current, descriptive diagnoses. An example of the continuing emphasis on descriptive segregation is presented next.

Multiple Complex Developmental Disorder

It has been noted that the symptoms of childhood psychosis are diverse to begin with and change over the course of development. Such diversity has led to the proposal of many diagnostic classifications. One such effort, Multiple Complex Developmental Disorder (Towbin et al., 1993) is briefly presented as an example of where trying to bring order among apparent symptoms can get when the only basis used for classification is a description of the symptoms themselves.

The authors sensitively note that a subgroup of psychotic children have a range of symptoms so large that it covers every domain of social, cognitive, sensory, and motor behavior. These children are subject to periods of intense anxiety and episodes of gross disorganization. More importantly, the level of functioning can fluctuate radically within the same child, sometimes over a period of minutes or hours, sometimes over a period of days or weeks. The levels can range from age-appropriate mature behavior to severely regressed, primitive behavior expected of a much younger, very disturbed, child.

Thirty hospitalized children with such characteristics were compared with comparable numbers of hospitalized children with a diagnosis of dysthymia, a mood disorder, or conduct disorder. In comparison to these nonpsychotic diagnoses, the multiple complex developmental disorder children were found to have earlier symptom onset, more severe impairments, poorer peer relations, be more refractory to treatment, and come from families with higher rates of serious pathology. The authors suggested that it would be useful to segregate this group diagnostically, but the only evidence offered is the magnitude of variability in behavioral regulation found in these particular patients. That all psychosis is marked by poor regulation, and that these patients may just be the extreme of a continuum, is not considered. No apparent criterion permits one to evaluate why this particular way of grouping patients is superior or inferior to a myriad of other possibilities.

Pervasive Developmental Disorder

As noted, the diagnosis of psychosis is based on finding specified clusters of symptoms. Since variability in psychotic behaviors is extreme, especially in children, there are many cases where it is clear that much is wrong, but the designated symptoms for a particular diagnosis are not present. To deal with such fairly common occurrences, a general category is used such as Atypical Child, or Childhood Psychosis;

Not Otherwise Specified, or, more recently, Pervasive Developmental Disorder. Despite their don't-know-what-else-to-do quality, such categories may actually be closer to the real status of our knowledge as long as symptoms are the basis of classification and the evidence that autistic youngsters may later become Asperger's syndromes (see chapter 14) or adult schizophrenics stares us in the face. As information about the nature of the diatheses, the stresses, and the mechanisms of the pathology emerge over the course of development, one can imagine, I repeat, a rather different diagnostic system from the one now in use.

16

Acquired Brain Damage

As the reader knows, this book is about the functioning of the brain in relation to the development of behavior. Often, malfunctioning occurs in the course of development without any evidence that the brain has been injured in an explicit way. Such malfunctions, for the most part, have been attributed to genetic variations, experiential factors, or to unknown or idiopathic "impairments." In this chapter, some conditions of known injury to the brain will be reviewed. The term "acquired" in the chapter title is intended to convey the idea that a known, explicit, injurious event occurred at a particular time in development.

Given the emphasis on explicit injurious events, one might expect to find explicit consequences in behavior, e.g. that given injury A, consequence X follows and given injury B, consequence Y follows. However, the situation appears to be far more complex. To deal with this complexity, explicit injurious events are viewed as diathesis producers or, in terms commonly used in the infancy literature, creators of conditions of risk. Their impact on behavior will depend, to be sure, on the nature, locale, extent, and level of development at the time of the injury and on its further course, but also on the way coping with its consequences occurs. Coping, it turns out, depends on many factors that have little to do with the injury itself. This idea will be elaborated as the chapter proceeds.

Brain injury may be diffuse or localized (focal), and may occur in gray matter, white matter, or both. Small focal lesions in gray matter may occur in an area of nonspecific processing and have minimal consequences for behavior and development, or may destroy a particular modular processor and generate a very specific deficiency in some aspect of behavior. Focal lesions in white matter may disrupt the integration of the specific modules necessary for the execution of a particular behavior even though the modules themselves have not been injured, while diffuse lesions may interfere broadly with complex classes of behavior. Please note that the term "interfere" may designate a change in the probability that a behavior or a type of control will occur, not its absolute abolition. For example, stable, effortless deployment of attention to what might be required could shift, after injury, to occasional success. White matter lesions, whether localized or diffuse, will also have differing consequences if they occur in long or short or in intrahemispheric or interhemispheric pathways (Fletcher, 1994).

Gray and white matter lesions are not completely independent. The destruction of a gray matter neuron will lead to the degeneration of its axons buried in white matter. Similarly, a white matter lesion which cuts off or interferes with the functioning of a neural axon may lead to a range of effects on the upstream neuron from which the axon originated and on the downstream neurons with which it will synapse.

One of the issues to be considered is whether the consequences of injurious events in the immature brain differ from those in the mature. On the one hand, immature organisms are vulnerable. They have not yet had the opportunity to build up either biological or psychological coping mechanisms, so the consequences of any particular injurious event may be more devastating than if it occurred later in development. On the other hand, the rate of learning of the immature is faster than that of the mature, and more resources have not yet been committed to specific functions, so that the reallocation needed for compensation may be easier. These characteristics add up to greater plasticity, a term designating the wherewithal of brain cells to serve functions other than those they most commonly perform.

Background: Some General Issues in Studying Brain Damage and Development

To obtain information about outcomes of gestational and infantile events, questions must be posed about the course of development. There are two basic kinds of research designs that provide answers to those questions. In a longitudinal study, individual subjects are followed over time and studied at least twice and often repeatedly. In a cross-sectional study, groups of individuals of different ages are evaluated and compared after being tested once at approximately the same time. Suppose we wish to know the consequences at ages five and 14 of birth at very low weight (1,000–1,500 g). In a longitudinal study, the children would be identified and studied at birth or in infancy and then restudied first at age five and then at age 14. In a cross-sectional study, five- and 14-year-olds with a history of very low birth weight would be sought for study and then compared. Both kinds of study would also be likely to examine subjects with normal birth weights or some other condition for contrast.

Cross-sectional research is accomplished over a relatively short time span and hence is more likely to be completed. As a rule, longitudinal studies provide more definitive answers about development, but both types of study are vulnerable to error. For example, a cross-sectional study in 1998 might show 14-year-olds with a history of low birth weight to be doing relatively worse than their five-year-old counterparts and the data might be interpreted to mean that the five-year-olds are fated to do relatively less well later. However, in 1998 the 14-year-olds were born in 1984 while the five-year-olds were born in 1993, and perinatal and infantile care and stimulation might have changed favorably between those years, giving an advantage to the younger children. Thus, instead of the adolescent "deterioration" that might be inferred from the cross-sectional data, the 14-year-olds might have been at a disadvantage all along. If the children had been studied longitudinally this interpretive error would not have been made.

Correspondingly, results of a longitudinal study might be interpreted erroneously if it is assumed that whatever developmental trajectory is found was inevitable. Changes in obstetric, neonatal, and child-care practices might accelerate later patterns of development. A longitudinal study might well obtain valid data, given the conditions that apply when it was initiated, but those results may be quite different if the study were initiated a decade or more later and conditions had changed. If it is accepted that psychobiological functions are organized as open systems (see chapter 4), definitive understanding of developmental trajectories may require the comparative study of longitudinal research conducted at different times.

What injurious events are being considered?

A great many injurious events are correlated: this means that they are associated or that they go together. Thus, poverty is associated with poor nutrition and health care, infant prematurity, anoxia, intraventricular hemorrhage, and hydrocephalus. If the goal is to understand the effects of any of these variables, cases must be found that have only the specific condition being examined. Selection criteria for subjects must not only specify that they have experienced the pathological condition under scrutiny (positive criteria), but that they also have not experienced any of the other conditions that commonly co-occur (negative criteria). It is relatively easy to find children with multiple gestational and perinatal complications; it is quite difficult to find "pure" cases.

Which consequences are being examined?

In doing follow-up studies, there are a range of targets of interest. When the condition may lead to death in infancy or before, survival may be the only issue examined. The early stages of medical research on new procedures to ameliorate conditions that may cause death are often satisfied to establish lowered mortality rates. Subsequently, there is interest in the incidence of obvious types of impairment such as epilepsy, cerebral palsy, blindness, deafness, psychosis, and gross mental retardation. After that, studies may be directed to less obvious but nonetheless burdensome behavioral conditions such as hyperactivity and learning disabilities or emotional disorders. Finally, research may be done to examine subtleties of individual differences within the normal range, e.g. temperament; particular cognitive, motor, or social skills; or variations in overall intellect. At times, researchers even seek to evaluate overall success in life and turn to variables such as income levels, job satisfaction, marital success, or happiness. This type of research was cited in chapter 10, when the long-term effects of attention deficit disorder were considered.

When in the course of a person's life will the evaluation take place?

Longitudinal research over the lifespan is time-consuming, laborious, and very difficult to accomplish. Many researchers settle for an examination of shorter spans. Thus, children might be examined in the third year when there is a spurt in language and social development, just before they start formal schooling in the sixth year, during

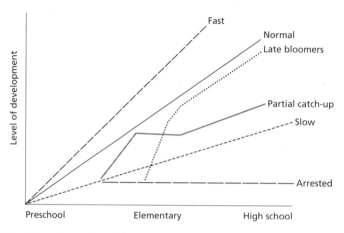

Figure 16.1 Possible trajectories of development

their eighth or ninth year when important cognitive changes take place, or in late adolescence when they are at the brink of adulthood. Any such information can be useful if the limitations of any particular study are kept in mind. Children at risk may follow several different courses of development. Figure 16.1 presents one attempt to summarize some of the theoretical possibilities. Thus there are those who through the course of development simply lag consistently, others who show early arrested development, and some who lose previous gains. More perplexing are children who might lag in infancy and early childhood, catch up in the primary school grades, and then lag again as adolescence approaches. In the latter case, a single follow-up might infer a totally normal trajectory if measurements were taken in the early school years, but arrive at different conclusions if assessed at other points in development.

The issues of vulnerability and plasticity, and the complexities of obtaining knowledge about the development of open systems, should be kept in mind as the chapter progresses through reviews of several of the most common types of insult to the brain. The next sections of the chapter will consider circumstances of risk sustained during gestation, the perinatal period, and early infancy. Later sections will deal with risk-creating events that commonly occur later in life.

Injurious Events Occurring During Gestation, the Perinatal Period, and Early Infancy

Background: definition of normal gestation and prematurity

Full-term gestation, as defined by the World Health Organization, has a duration between 37 and 42 weeks, and the baby is expected to weigh 2,500 g (5 pounds, 8 ounces) or more at birth. Of the two aspects, weight is easier to measure objec-

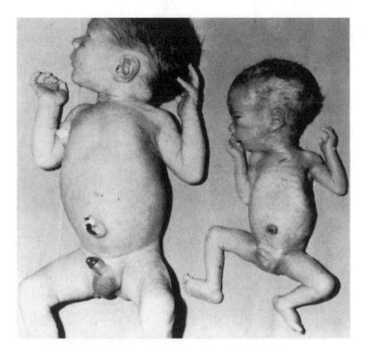

Figure 16.2 Twins, one with intrauterine growth retardation

tively. Because of this, early studies of the consequences of prematurity often defined gestational age by weight. Since gestation begins with conception and since, under ordinary circumstances, that moment is not known, precise evaluation of gestational age is not possible. The most available objective referent is the time of the mother's last menstrual period, and that has an error of measurement ±2 or more weeks (Korner, 1997). In studies in which the time of conception was estimated (see Spreen, Risser, & Edgell, 1995, chapter 7), it was found that some children with low birth weights (below 2,500 g) had normal gestational durations. Labels of low birth weight and intrauterine growth retardation have been used to classify these infants. A vivid example of such growth retardation can be seen in the twins pictured in figure 16.2, one of whom lost out in the competition for nutrients. It later came to be recognized that a fetus at any stage of gestation might lag in weight gain. A diagram from Lubchenko (1976) and Spreen, Risser & Edgell (1995) – see figure 16.3 – summarizes the range of possible variations. Babies may be born at term, pre-term or post-term. They may be small, appropriate, or large for gestational age. Being large for gestational age probably is not a problem until the time of delivery, unless the extra-rapid growth is due to factors such as the overproduction of insulin, the hormone that regulates the metabolism of blood sugar (Alistair & Sunshine, 1997). Low birth weight, as noted, is less than 2,500 g. Very low birth weight is below 1,500 g and extremely low birth weight is below 1,000 g.

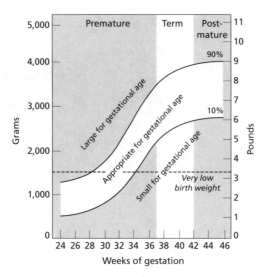

Figure 16.3 Newborn weight chart by gestational age

Low birth weight is associated with a number of factors including chromosomal and genetic abnormalities, fetal infection and toxicity, and impaired delivery of nutrients to the fetus (Alistair & Sunshine, 1997). The latter factor, in turn, may be due to maternal illness, especially problems with blood circulation, maternal malnutrition, maternal toxicity from substance abuse or environmental poisons, or disorders of the placenta (the cord which attaches the child to the mother). An example of what an infant with placental insufficiency looks like can be seen in figure 16.4. Shorter durations of gestation and diminished growth are associated with particular injurious events. Teratology is the study of conditions that harm the fetus and its potential for development. A teratogen is an external agent that induces such harm. Dietrich and Bellinger (1994) quote Wilson as indicating that harm can manifest itself as death, malformation, growth retardation, or functional deficit. These outcomes represent landmarks on a continuum of reproductive casualty. It had been thought that the placenta was a formidable barrier protecting the fetus from noxious agents, but this has been disconfirmed in many ways by later knowledge. Since neonatologists (physicians specializing in the care of newborns) have found ways to help infants-at-risk to survive, there is an increase of individuals with impairments (Dorman & Katzir, 1994, chapter 4). Some specific teratogens and injurious conditions will be considered next.

Some injurious events and conditions that occur during gestation and birth

Anoxia

Anoxia means lack of oxygen and implies asphyxiation. The most common type of deprivation is less extreme, and is termed hypoxia. Often the former term is used

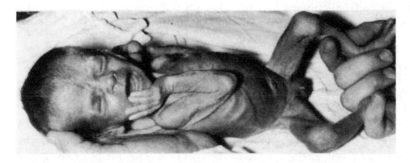

Figure 16.4 Infant appearance after placental insufficiency

when the latter is more appropriate. Oxygen is required for basic metabolism and is conveyed to the cells via the blood stream. If the blood supply is inadequate for some reason, the cells will not receive enough oxygen even if there is adequate oxygen in the blood. Tissues inadequately supplied with nutrients and oxygen will begin to die, a condition termed ischemia. If the blood supply is curtailed by a blockage within the blood vessel, an infarct is said to occur. At birth, the child must shift from reliance on the mother's blood supply via the placenta, to independent oxygenation of its own blood, and hypoxic–ischemic encephalopathy (brain damage) is the most common complication of the perinatal period.

The most frequent specific causes of fetal hypoxia are of maternal, placental, or fetal origin (Holbrook et al., 1997; Spreen, Risser, & Edgell, 1995). Maternal problems include uterine anomalies, both low and high blood pressure, and anything else that may occur to interfere with adequate nutrition and oxygen in maternal blood flow. The placenta may be the source of the problem if it has an inadequate blood vessel network or if it becomes compressed. Mechanical compression can occur if the umbilical cord precedes the child during birth, if it becomes tied in knots, or if it gets wrapped around some part of the child. Fetal origin of hypoxia most often is due to anomalous development of the heart or failure to initiate respiration. Hypoxia occurring during gestation may be a cause of low birth weight. It is much harder to diagnose and treat hypoxia if it occurs during gestation rather than at birth or afterward.

Premature infants are particularly vulnerable to hypoxic episodes because their lungs lack a substance called surfactant which coats lung tissue and facilitates the absorption of oxygen. The resulting condition, known descriptively as respiratory distress syndrome and mechanistically as hyaline membrane disease, leads to asphyxiation. This was a major cause of death until the 1980s when a way was found to provide the child with surfactant harvested from animals, or from the fluids in the uterus of women undergoing cesarian section (Mullett, 1989; Ghai, Jain, & Vidyasagar, 1989). Not only is insufficient oxygen a problem but excessive oxygen can also lead to difficulties. Before the process of respiration was better understood, physicians eager to assist a child in respiratory distress often administered excessive concentrations of oxygen, which resulted in hyperoxia and chronic lung disease as well as a condition called retrolental fibroplasia in which the retina is destroyed and blindness results. Such sensitivity to oxygen is not present in the full-term baby and is an example of the relative vulnerability of the immature.

Hemorrhage

If there is a break in a blood vessel and blood spills into the tissues, hemorrhage occurs. Such breaks are rare in the full-term infant and, when they occur, are most often associated with trauma that might follow the use of mechanical devices to push or pull the head of the fetus in aiding delivery. The locus of such hemorrhages is likely to be subdural, at the surface of the cortex and beneath its covering protective membranes (Shankaran, 1997). Hemorrhage is more frequent in the premature infant, especially when under hypoxic stress. The area of greatest vulnerability for the premature is in the tissues of the lining of the ventricles, the ependyma, and in the adjacent layers, the subependymal germinal matrix. These germinal layers contain cells that are going to migrate to other sites in the process of completing the construction of the brain. The germinal matrix has a delicate and temporary blood supply which is particularly vulnerable to disruption. (In the full-term fetus these layers and their blood supply are no longer present.) The hemorrhage may occur in the ventricles (intraventricular), in the germinal tissues, in the choroid plexi (see figure 3.8 for these structures inside the ventricles which are the major source of cerebrospinal fluid) or in the mass of brain, the parenchyma (Enzmann, 1997). Hemorrhage in the parenchyma will produce specific effects which will depend on its exact site and magnitude, but hemorrhage in and around the ventricles may have general and far-reaching effects because it can produce hydrocephalus, the subject of the next section.

Hydrocephalus

Types of hydrocephalus.   It was noted in chapter 3, when describing the anatomy of the brain, that the liquid-filled ventricles can become enlarged (hydrocephalus – literally, water-on-the-brain) if too much cerebrospinal fluid is produced, if its circulation is blocked, or if its reabsorption is inadequate. One type is consequently termed noncommunicating or obstructive hydrocephalus due to a stenosis (narrowing) or occlusion (blocking) of ventricular circulation, for example, of the aqueduct of Sylvius between the third and fourth ventricles. In the other type, communicating hydrocephalus, circulation within the ventricles occurs, but the reabsorption of the cerebrospinal fluid in the subarachnoid spaces under the dura around the brain is inadequate for the amount of fluid produced (Gaskill & Marlin, 1993; Lemire, 1997).

Chronic hydrocephalus that begins during gestation can lead to an enlarged head at birth. Hydrocephalus during early infancy results in a rapid enlargement of the head because the bones of the skull have not yet fused, and the soft tissues allow for expansion (see figure 16.5). The pressure created by the excess fluid in the ventricles compresses the parenchyma and stretches the white matter. The depth of a normal

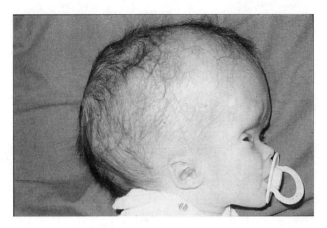

Figure 16.5 The enlarged head of a child with hydrocephalus

cerebral mantle (the outer layer of the cortex) at five months is generally close to 5 cm. If, as a result of compression, the depth is only 2.0 cm, later compromise of mental functions was found to be inevitable while if the depth was 2.8 cm, mental capability was no different from that found in those with thicker mantles. Since such measures of depth are inevitably associated with some error, 3.5 cm has become a conservative criterion for normal mantle depth (Rekate, 1994). If the mantle remains compressed at five months, something must be done to relieve the pressure or normal brain development will be disrupted.

In the past, children with hydrocephalus often died or, if they survived, were left with an ungainly, enlarged head and many psychological handicaps such as cerebral palsy, learning disabilities, attention problems, mental retardation, and epilepsy. The development of a neurosurgical procedure which allowed the shunting of excessive cerebrospinal fluid to an area of the body where it could be reabsorbed has made possible both the survival of life and preservation of cognitive functions. There are three components to a shunt. One is a tube that penetrates the high-pressured ventricular system. The second is a valve that regulates the flow of cerebrospinal fluid so that the ventricles do not suddenly empty and collapse. The valve also ensures that there is only one direction of flow – away from the ventricles. The third component is the tubing that takes the fluid to some site where it will be reabsorbed. There are several alternative placements of these components, but one of the most commonly used arrangements is illustrated in figure 16.6. The shunt is often placed in the right hemisphere, the distal component where the fluid is reabsorbed is in the peritoneal cavity, and the valve is under the skin in the neck (Rekate, 1994).

Although the ventricular shunt is a marvelous development it is not without its problems, some of which may further compromise brain function. Shunts may malfunction because they become obstructed, they may move out of position because the child grows or for other reasons, or they may become the sites of infection (see

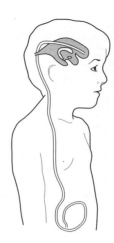

Figure 16.6 Typical placement of a shunt used to treat hydrocephalus

next section). Whatever the reason, replacement and revision of the shunt then become necessary, and further neurosurgical intervention must occur (Marlin & Gaskill, 1994). It is nearly inevitable that shunts will require periodic revision. Thus shunted children are at continuing risk of further diathesis induction and the stresses associated with brain surgery. If hydrocephalus can be controlled without a shunt, the child will be that much better off. If hydrocephalus follows hemorrhage, such stratagems as lumbar puncture to remove cerebrospinal fluid, or the administration of diuretics (drugs that increase the removal of liquid via the kidneys) may be used until the hemorrhage resolves. Shunting would still be available as a last resort if such measures failed.

Consequences of hydrocephalus. A study which identified the deleterious consequences of shunting in preterm infants has been reported by Fletcher et al. (1997). They compared three samples of preterm children with birth weights between 900 and 1,750 g. In the first sample there was no hydrocephalus, in the second and third there was hemorrhage and hydrocephalus at or shortly after birth: the second group did not require shunting (arrested hydrocephalus), but the third group did. All three groups were compared with a group of full-term children, and all four groups were comparable in age, sex, race, and socioeconomic status. The children on average were 8.5 years old on follow-up. Before reporting the results, it should be noted that exclusionary criteria included any children who at follow-up had a history of retardation, psychosis, uncontrolled seizure disorder, head trauma, tumors, child abuse, neurological anomalies, severe cerebral palsy, retrolental fibroplasia, or severe bronchopulmonary dysplasia, where cysts were found in x-rays of the lungs. Any findings are thus not secondary to any of these sequelae of very low birth weight.

There were no abnormalities in the magnetic resonance brain images of term children and the premature group without hydrocephalus, but both the arrested and the shunted group had many abnormal findings, mostly related to ventricular enlargement. The neurological exam on follow-up was normal in the full-term and the non-hydrocephalic children, but there were some abnormalities in the arrested group and somewhat more in the shunted group, mostly spasticity (cerebral palsy). Finally, behavioral evaluation indicated that the shunted group was distinctly impaired in comparison to the other three groups. Whereas the shunted group was in the borderline range, particularly in nonverbal as compared to verbal skills, the others were essentially in the average range on most measures. Borderline is a term that will be explained more fully in the next chapter but characterizes impaired mental capability just short of mental retardation. Those with arrested hydrocephalus lagged behind those with no hydrocephalus in attentional and academic skills and the non-hydrocephalic preterm children lagged behind the full-term normals in motor development, although these differences were relatively minor in comparison to the lags shown by the shunted children. The authors speculate that the damage done originally by the hydrocephalus was the source of the significant deficits observed in the shunted group, but they also report that all subjects had required at least one shunt revision and most between two and five. Clearly, the shunted children had a different set of life experiences than the others.

Infections

The brain is susceptible to infection by many organisms, including bacteria, viruses, fungi, and protozoa, and such infections are often teratogenic. An infection of the brain tissue is called an encephalitis and an infection of the meninges, the tough protective membranes that cover the brain, is called a meningitis. Often both are present and this condition is termed a meningoencephalitis. The fetus may become infected as a consequence of chronic or acute infection in the mother, either during gestation through the placenta, or during passage through the birth canal. After birth, the child can get infected from any source, but may be specially vulnerable to infections from the mother that can be conveyed via breast milk. Infection during gestation is likely to have very severe consequences, and the earlier it occurs the more severe it is likely to be. This is because, early on, organ-formation can be disrupted, and because the earlier the infection the longer time it has to fester. Infections incurred during birth are, of course, infections of a completed organism if the fetus is at full term and may have less severe consequences. If the fetus is premature, it will be more vulnerable. In the next section, the most common infections will be reviewed briefly. Information is derived from Adams and Victor (1993), Gaskill and Marlin (1993), Gordon (1993), Cheek (1994), Spreen, Risser, & Edgell (1995), Prober & Arvin (1997), and Maldonado (1997).

Rubella.   Rubella, a familiar childhood disease also known as German measles in the United States, is an acute viral infection which can be transmitted via the placenta from an infected mother to the fetus. If the mother gets the disease during the first trimester, especially the first eight weeks, devastating effects on the fetus are very likely to occur, including cataracts and blindness, auditory problems, and mental retardation. Infection of the mother late in the pregnancy is not likely to affect the child adversely. Because of these special conditions, it is important that women not get rubella during the early stages of their pregnancy. Immunity may be provided by having had the disease previously or via vaccination before pregnancy.

Cytomegalovirus.   Cytomegalovirus is a less well known pathogenic (disease-causing) virus, only first discovered in 1956. It is the most common cause of neonatal brain damage due to infection. The virus is widespread (a type of herpes virus) and may be present in many adults who show no symptoms and therefore do not know that they are at risk to themselves or others. The virus can be passed from pregnant mother to fetus via the placenta, especially during the first two trimesters but, even then, the child may appear normal at birth. If infection has occurred during gestation, however, a series of pathological developments may emerge by the age of two years, which include encephalitis, hydrocephalus, seizures, mental retardation, and microcephaly (small head).

Toxoplasmosis.   Toxoplasmosis is the second most common infection that occurs during gestation. It is due to a protozoan organism that gets into the mother's body via the consumption of undercooked meat and into the fetus via the placenta. Infection during the first two trimesters is likely to have more devastating effects than later onset. Common symptoms are similar to those found in cytomegalovirus infections. This general pattern of intrauterine infection and symptom presentation is also found in congenital syphilis, a disease caused by a microorganism called the spirochete, which has mostly been eradicated since the discovery of antibiotics, but still shows up from time to time. Symptoms begin to appear two weeks after birth and later.

Herpes simplex.   Herpes simplex is an omnipresent virus that is usually warded off by the immune system. It can produce a chronic genital infection which may be asymptomatic or one where symptoms wax and wane. In adults, a variant of the virus rarely may find its way into the nervous system, where it is likely to produce an encephalitis with devastating consequences to the brain. If a pregnant mother has a genital infection, whether symptomatic or not, she may readily transmit the infection during the birth process and, more rarely, during gestation. The likelihood that a herpes simplex infection will invade the nervous system and the brain is much greater in infants and young children than in adults. If the brain is involved, the mortality rate is very high and survivors are usually very impaired.

Pediatric acquired immunodeficiency syndrome (AIDS).   This is a result of infection with the human immunodeficiency virus (HIV). The HIV virus gradually disables the immune system, the body's defense against infection. The body is then suscep-tible to many opportunistic infections which ordinarily are almost never observed in the immunologically competent. At that point the person is said to have AIDS. The length of time from HIV infection to AIDS varies considerably and, in some cases,

AIDS never appears. Infants get HIV from infected mothers via the placenta during gestation, from encounters with maternal blood during vaginal delivery (the incidence is less with cesarean section), and from breast milk, whether from an infected mother or wet nurse. Although children with HIV infections may appear normal at birth, over 80 percent will develop symptoms within the first two years of life. Some of these children will follow a very rapid downhill course, and most will die in the first year, while others will have a much slower pattern of symptom appearance and a life that will extend at least to the school-age years. A significant proportion, perhaps one-fourth, will give evidence of direct invasion of the nervous system while all will show nonspecific consequences of being chronically ill.

Meningitis.   This is an infection, as noted above, of the protective membranes of the brain. The symptoms of the disorder in infants may include irritability, drowsiness, fever, vomiting, convulsions, and bulging fontanels (the soft spots on the baby's scalp where the cranial bones have not yet fused). As the child gets older, neck rigidity may appear. There are a large number of organisms which produce somewhat different consequences, the details of which are beyond the scope of this book. What should be understood, however, is that rather different consequences generally ensue depending on whether the source of infection is bacterial or viral. If the infection is viral, the child may be quite sick but will only rarely die, and residual deficits are either limited or nonexistent. On the other hand, bacterial infections are generally life-threatening, and if the child survives, residual deficits are likely to be severe. Choice of treatment depends on accurate identification of the infectious organism and this generally is accomplished by examining a sample of cerebrospinal fluid obtained via lumbar puncture, a needle inserted into the spinal column.

Maternal substance abuse

Substance abuse refers to the ingestion of agents which influence the nervous system in a manner that is subjectively pleasurable in some way. (Note: Unless otherwise referenced, material in this section is indebted to the excellent review by Halamek, 1997.) These agents often produce conditions of dependency such that the individual must ingest escalating amounts or suffer distressing symptoms of withdrawal. Substance abuse varies in frequency and amount consumed. There are those who indulge in a fairly regular pattern (e.g. smoking a pack of cigarettes a day) and there are bingers (e.g. weekend alcoholic drunkenness). When ingestion occurs during pregnancy, the intoxicating substances cross the placenta and then must be detoxified by fetal enzyme systems. The fetus' capabilities in this regard are likely to be suboptimal. Consequently, the metabolism and decomposition of the intoxicating compounds may be slowed and incomplete, leaving residues within the fetus for longer periods than the same processes might take in the mother. Ingestion may occur at a time when the woman does not know that she is pregnant, and thus teratogens may be present during the earliest stages of gestation when organ formation is occurring.

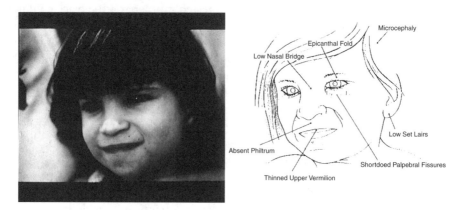

Figure 16.7 Photograph of a child with fetal alcohol syndrome, and a diagram of physical features

Drug-abusing mothers may give birth to intoxicated infants who will then have all the major adjustments of their first days of life burdened by withdrawal symptoms. After birth, substances of abuse in the mother may be ingested by the child via breast milk.

Alcohol. Perhaps the most common substance subject to abuse is ethanol, the intoxicating ingredient in alcoholic beverages. There is a higher incidence of fetal death in women who consume as little as two ounces of alcohol per week (Coles, 1992). If the child is born alive, a range of effects have been found to occur in the fetus which are a consequence of the amount and timing of alcohol consumed through the pregnancy and factors in the fetus that may resist those effects. With heavy alcohol consumption, there is an increased likelihood that the child will have fetal alcohol syndrome, a condition which includes altered physical structures, growth retardation, and central nervous system impairments.

Altered appearance is marked by a series of interrelated midline facial abnormalities including short palpebral fissures (the horizontal opening between the eyelids), a diminished philtrum (a flattening or disappearance of the shallow groove in the upper lip under the nose), a thin upper lip, and a flattening of the jaw (see figure 16.7). Visible characteristics of underlying bone structure and skin are accompanied by a range of abnormalities in the nervous and cardiovascular systems. Common brain findings include sensory abnormalities, decreased size of the cerebellar vermis lobules I–V (Sowell et al., 1996: note the lobules affected are different from those implicated in autism), decreased size of the basal ganglia (Mattson, et al., 1996) and agenesis (failure of development) of the corpus callosum (Don & Rourke, 1995). Some normalization in facial appearance occurs with growth, but the underlying abnormalities persist and are easily measured (see Coles, 1992, for review). Newborns with fetal alcohol syndrome tend to be small for gestational age and show growth retardation thereafter, especially in head circumference and height, though often not in weight. A high proportion show evidence of serious behavior limitations throughout life, and it is thought that this may be the largest identifiable nongenetic cause of mental retardation affecting 0.01–0.05 percent of live births (Coles, 1992).

Children with less than the full complement of fetal alcohol syndrome symptoms are said to have fetal alcohol effects or alcohol-related birth defects. Streissguth et al. (1994) have amassed evidence that even when fetal alcohol syndrome is not present, rates of alcohol consumption during pregnancy are associated with grade-school deficits in attention, memory, perceptual-motor skills, and rate of learning.

The effects of the same amount and rate of alcohol consumption on the fetus, or for that matter the adult, vary from individual to individual, which suggests that the genetic makeup of the person plays a role. This was confirmed in a study by Streissguth and Dehaene (1993), who compared identical (same genes in each child) and fraternal twins (50 percent difference in genes) born to severely alcoholic mothers. They found that five out of five identical pairs had the same diagnoses, whereas only seven out of 11 fraternal pairs did. In the latter case, of the four pairs with differing diagnoses, two pairs differed because one twin had fetal alcohol syndrome while the other had fetal alcohol effects. In the other two pairs, one child had a diagnosis of fetal alcohol effects while the other had no discernible evidence of any teratogenic effect of alcohol.

Tobacco. Tobacco generally is consumed by directly inhaling smoke while it burns, but it can also enter the body via inhalation of air polluted by other smokers. The smoke contains many substances, some of which induce cancer and other diseases, including nicotine and related compounds that are addictive. Given the widespread dissemination of knowledge about these pathology-inducing characteristics of tobacco, one might think that this is no longer a public health problem, but many people continue to embark on smoking careers. If a pregnant female is exposed to tobacco smoke, many of its compounds will reach the fetus via the placenta. After birth, the baby can be exposed to such compounds via breast milk or the inhalation of smoke-polluted air. The main, repeatedly confirmed, teratogenic effect of tobacco is low birth weight (Streissguth et al., 1994). This appears due to interference with the blood supplied through the placenta. A related consequence after birth in infants who have stored tobacco byproducts in their tissues may be sudden infant death syndrome, where the child unpredictably ceases to breathe. Autopsies of such children yield evidence consistent with hypoxic changes. A less direct, but nonetheless significant, effect of tobacco is an increased incidence of placenta previa, a condition in which the placenta is positioned over the opening to the birth canal. When labor starts, the placenta may rip, producing hemorrhage which can place both mother and child at risk for death and for a range of negative consequences if they survive.

It should be noted that the outlook for children with mothers who smoke heavily during pregnancy is not as bad as it is for those whose mothers drink heavily. Initial growth retardation associated with smoking does not persist as it does when it is associated with fetal alcohol syndrome. Also, documented intellectual and cognitive limitations are relatively minor. However, research data on the effects of tobacco and other substances to be considered next are much sparser than are available for alcohol (Coles & Platzman, 1993), and much is still unknown.

Marijuana.   Marijuana, the dried leaves, seeds, and stems of the *Cannabis sativa* plant, is probably the most abused illicit drug in the United States. Ingestion of the plant, either by smoking or swallowing it, leads, in the adult, to a state of euphoria and relaxation that interferes with directed thinking and objective learning and problem solving. Students intoxicated with marijuana, though generally not conspicuously different from when sober, do not learn very much and display short-term memory deficits. They can repeat information to which they have just been exposed, but they do not retain much. "Potheads", a euphemism for those who ingest regularly and frequently, do not do as well in school as they otherwise might. The teratogenic consequences of marijuana use, as far as is presently known, are relatively small. Infants of heavy users tend to be somewhat less than average in birth weight, and have been found to show somewhat poorer verbal and memory skills at four years of age. Such findings at the time of this writing are not well established.

Cocaine.   Cocaine, or a variant called "crack", is a derivative of the leaves of the cocoa plant. It provides the user with a rush of intense excitement by blocking the reuptake of excitatory neurotransmitters and a feeling of euphoria by blocking the reuptake of dopamine (see chapters 2 and 4), thus leaving more than usual amounts in the synaptic cleft. It is an addictive drug whose withdrawal produces a series of highly distressing subjective experiences and an intense craving for more of the drug that can last for months or even years. Although research is still relatively limited, the best-known teratogenic effects of cocaine occur by constricting the blood supply to the fetus. Specific local effects may also occur as a result of a spasmodic response of placental blood vessels to sudden, intense intoxication, and a variety of physical anomalies may appear in the baby. Cocaine is also associated with a number of complications, e.g. premature labor, precipitous delivery, and rupture of the uterus, which place the fetus at risk. Fetal and neonatal brains are also at risk for excessive blood pressure, stroke, and hemorrhage, and, after the birth, difficulties breathing and sleeping. If a child born to a cocaine user manages to avoid these secondary complications, there is some evidence of lags for the first two or three years, although there currently is little or no evidence of long-term negative effects on later brain development or other aspects of growth.

Heroin.   Heroin and other opioids are drugs which are derived from, or are synthesized to emulate, compounds found in the poppy plant. The term narcotic is used to describe this group of substances. Narcotics inhibit pain (i.e. they are analgesics), induce relaxation and sleep, and are highly addictive with repeated use. Like endorphins – naturally occurring, pain-inhibiting compounds found in the brain which are produced when individuals experience a natural "high" (see material about treating self-injurious behavior with opioid blockers in chapter 15) – concentrated opioids such as heroin produce an intense euphoric high. Unlike naturally occurring endorphins, the sedation that follows heroin use can lead to low blood pressure, failure to breathe, and death. Newborns of addicted mothers may have large amounts of drugs in their tissues and are at risk for withdrawal reactions during their first days of life, which may compromise circulation and produce brain ischemia. Residual opioids and further ingestion via breast milk may also lead to respiratory failure, especially during sleep. Although there are further complications requiring the attention of the obstetrician and the neonatologist, there are few known subsequent teratogenic consequences of this class of drugs.

Stimulants.   Stimulants are drugs such as amphetamine ("speed") which have alerting and sleep-resisting properties, and which, when ingested in concentrated form, produce high levels of sustained excitement. This is followed by a "crash" involving much sleep, increased food consumption, and heightened negative mood. Frequent use in the adult may be followed by the appearance of a range of chronic symptoms including anxiety, agitation, paranoia, seizures, and movement disorders. Although there is currently no evidence of teratogenic structural consequences in the fetus, there is risk of brain-damaging changes in blood pressure, premature delivery, and hemorrhage. Again, infants of addictive mothers will have to metabolize the drugs that have found their way into their tissues, and symptoms such as tremors, feeding difficulties, and irritability may occur which are due either to direct expressions of toxicity or to withdrawal.

The Interaction of Environmental and Constitutional Factors

In this chapter on brain damage, emphasis has been given so far to describing brain-injuring variables, and there is more to come. This can be misleading if it fosters the impression that most brain injuries have inevitable consequences. To be sure, a brain infection or anoxia can lead to death or leave the victim in a state of gross and irreversible impairment. But many brain-injuring events have outcomes that depend significantly on how the environment reacts. This statement is not just based on wishful thinking but is verified repeatedly by solid research. An example of such evidence at the interface of child development and neuropsychology is reviewed next in some detail.

Landry et al. (1997) examined the relationship between parenting behaviors observed in the first year of life and rates of change in development between six and 40 months in three groups of children. Two of the groups were both of low birth weight (<1,600 g) and short gestation age (<36 weeks), but 73 were medically high-risk and 114 were low-risk. High-risk children had suffered from one or more severe medical complications known to be associated with abnormal or delayed development. These included bronchopulmonary dysplasia (a condition that compromises breathing, puts the infant at risk for anoxia, and requires supplements of oxygen for a month or more), severe intraventricular hemorrhage, and periventricular leukomalacia (a pathological softening of the white matter in the region around the ventricles). Low-risk children had suffered from one or more less severe conditions such as transient respiratory distress or mild forms of intraventricular hemorrhage. The risk groups were compared with a group of full-term infants with a normal history of pregnancy and birth. Excluded from the study (negative selection criteria) were children with sensory impairments, structural brain abnormalities, short bowel syndrome, meningitis, encephalitis, syphilis, or HIV infection. Also excluded were children whose mothers abused alcohol or drugs or were under 16 at the time of the child's birth.

Maternal behaviors and infant cognitive and social skills were assessed in four home visits at six, 12, 24, and 40 months. Landry and co-workers distinguished between two kinds of social skills developing in the young children: those that were responsive to the mother's initiations and those that were initiated by the child. In the former case the structure of what is taking place is provided by the mother, while in the latter case the child provides the structure. Initiative at an early age appears to be a precursor of later executive skills and is likely to be compromised in high-risk children. Maternal behaviors of interest included their warmth, positive affect, attention-directing skills, directive and restrictive behaviors, and their ability to maintain their child's focus of involvement in tasks that have been initiated.

Maternal behaviors during the first year were analyzed to determine their influence on the trajectory of cognitive and social development in the child across the first 40 months of life. The bottom line was that parental behaviors that were sensitive to the child's initiative and were neither highly controlling nor overly restrictive had a positive effect on later cognitive–language and social development. Restrictive maternal behaviors led to slower rates of initiating, and maternal skill in maintaining behaviors (helping the child to persist in attention) led to greater increases in initiating behaviors. These effects were present in all groups of children but were strongest in the high-risk group. The implication of these findings specifies a greater role for caretakers in influencing the course of development in children at risk than is the case for children who are not. It is reminiscent of the importance of environmental structure in influencing the course of development in children with early manifestations of severe psychosis, and specifies ways in which caretaker interventions can mitigate constitutional vulnerabilities. One caution in considering the evidence is that the research is confined to the earlier stages of development and provides no information about longer-term consequences. It does however provide detailed information about a crucial period in development which sets the trajectory for future achievements.

Environmental teratogens

Most environmental teratogens are byproducts of human activity. A great many such products are incidental to the manufacture of materials such as plastics, fertilizers, insecticides, or herbicides. Some of the oldest and best-known teratogens are heavy metals which have been fashioned into objects and tools that have come in contact with drinking water or food, or whose manufacture creates dust particles that are inhaled. Two such substances will be reviewed briefly here.

Lead

Lead is one of the first metals used by man. Notation of its pathologic consequences goes back to ancient history when metallurgical workers were found to suffer from uncontrollable movements, pallor, and intestinal symptoms. Lead's effects on brain function have even been implicated as the insidious agent that robbed the Roman empire of much of its mental resources and thus led to its fall, given that lead was used to line the aqueducts bringing water to cities, and lead vessels were used to prepare and cook food and drink (Tesman & Hills, 1994). Popular lore (Bellinger & Needleman, 1994) recognized that maternal lead poisoning would affect the fetus more than it would affect the mother. The lead concentrates in the fetus and has the effect of cleansing the lead from the mother's body. Pregnancy, consequently, would treat the mother's lead poisoning.

At present, lead generally does not get into the body via contamination of food or water. Not long ago, a major source of air contamination was lead compounds that were added to gasoline to eliminate engine knocking, and which were then emitted in the exhaust. These practices have largely been banned in Western countries, as has the use of solder containing lead to seal food containers such as cans. Currently, the most widespread source of lead is airborne dust particles found near industries that smelt lead or manufacture products made with lead. The other continuing source of contamination for young children is in chips of old flaking paints whose pigments or other components included lead. Such paint chips are often attractive to toddlers who are inclined to chew and swallow them. Obviously, children with access to flaking paint are likely to come from impoverished circumstances and to not have careful supervision.

The study of the relationship between lead and behavior is fraught with many problems. First, the lead burden with which the child is born must be determined. This can be accomplished only if planned measurements are taken at the time of birth. Then there is the problem of monitoring both chronic exposure, such as might occur if living near a smelter, and acute poisoning, which would occur if a toddler has access to peeling paint. Finally, there is the issue of determining what aspects of behavior at each stage of the life span are affected by the range of lead levels. Poisoning, in varying degrees at different ages, may have different effects on different behaviors.

Determination of just how much lead is in the body is difficult. Various techniques for assaying levels in the blood are available, but blood levels reflect only recent exposure to lead, especially in children, and not the chronic burden which they bear. Since lead gravitates to places where calcium is deposited in the body (Bellinger & Needleman, 1994), lead levels in cast-off baby teeth and in bone scans have provided relatively good data about chronic burdens. However, these measures are not frequently used because of practicality and expense. The units of measurement in blood samples are micrograms per decaliter ($\mu g/dL$). It was not until the 1960s that lead was even considered to be a public health problem; at that time a level of $40\,\mu g/dL$ or even higher was thought to be a threshold for pathological effects (Tesman & Hills, 1994). Since that time, the idea of a particular threshold has not been supported since different behaviors have different thresholds. Pathological effects have emerged when blood levels are even as low as $10\,\mu g/dL$ or less. Bellinger, Stiles, and Needleman (1992) reported small but significant differences in cognitive measures at the age of 10 in children who at the age of two years had mean lead elevations of only $6.5\,\mu g/dL$. Their subjects came from upper middle class families, had received favorable environmental care and education, and their blood levels at age 10 were only an average of $2.9\,\mu g/dL$, yet they lagged behind peers who at age two had not had elevated lead levels.

Exactly how lead produces toxic effects is not fully known, possibly because potential causal mechanisms are legion (Bellinger and Needleman, 1994). At high doses, lead is known to affect the permeability of blood vessels in a manner which can lead to malnutrition, hemorrhage, and all that can follow from those conditions. At low levels, it appears to interfere with the timing and sequence of developmental events, with the operation of calcium (to which it is structurally similar) regulated signalling processes at the cellular level, and with the formation of synapses, the mechanisms that interconnect the cells of the brain and are the basis for information processing.

Methyl mercury

This is a compound containing mercury that is organically active and is readily absorbed into animal tissue. Most of the mercury in the environment is in the form of phenyl mercury which is biologically inactive. However, microorganisms may transform phenyl mercury to methyl mercury. Awareness of the neurotoxic and teratogenic qualities of methyl mercury emerged after two disasters, one in Japan in the 1950s and the other in Iraq in the 1970s. In the former case, inhabitants of the fishing village of Minamata became acutely ill after consuming fish and shellfish from a bay in which a mercury catalyst used in manufacturing had been dumped (Weiss, 1994). The characteristics of the bay were favorable for the methylation of the non-organic mercury. In the latter case, wheat seed was distributed to farmers after the seed had been directly treated with a methyl mercury fungicide. Although cautioned not to use the grain for food, a shortage of flour from a previous drought induced many families to grind the wheat seed into flour which was then baked into bread and later consumed. The illnesses that appeared in both contexts included sensory symptoms in all modalities, motor disturbances of gait, tremor, dysarthria, and weakness, headaches, rashes, and mental disturbances. Many individuals died, and those that did not suffered symptoms over a period of many years.

From both Japan and Iraq, evidence emerged that methyl mercury was a teratogen that was particularly toxic to the developing brain. The incidence of cerebral palsy and mental retardation in children born during the period of poisoning, and for some time afterward, rose to ten times the expected rate. Interestingly, there was no direct relationship between the degree of illness in the mothers and the magnitude of the pathology in their offspring. A relatively healthy-appearing mother, with few or no symptoms, might give birth to a very handicapped child. This appeared to be a consequence of variations in the way the placental apparatus and the fetus "attracted" mercury compounds. Often, the fetus showed greater concentrations of mercury than was found in the mother. Autopsies of children who died revealed widespread damage all over the brain. The pattern of disturbances was consistent with interference with the cell migration that occurred during brain growth.

Research has turned from studying the effects of acute poisoning where levels of methyl mercury (in hair, which is a reliable source of information about current and recent ingestion) can go as high as 1,000 ppm (parts per million) to the consequences of low levels in the range of 50 ppm or less. Current food and drug regulations in the United States specify 1 ppm of methyl mercury in fish as safe. Fish is the main source of mercury in the diet. However, commercially available fish in parts of the United States and the rest of the world may exceed 3 ppm or more and, as noted, mercury may concentrate in fetal tissue. Are there discernible effects at such levels? Weiss (1994) publishes a graph which shows the proportion of children who do not walk by 18 months, a measure of motor development, as a function of the mercury levels in the hair of their mothers at the time of the children's birth. The incidence begins to rise above zero percent abnormality when mercury concentrations are as low as 10 ppm, rise to about 20 percent when there are 150 ppm, and to over 50 percent when the concentration is 400 ppm. Note that mothers with high mercury concentrations in their hair have some children who are normal by this criterion. This does not mean that these same children would be normal if other areas of function were tested, or if a more stringent criterion of normality were used. The data suggest that this teratogen takes its toll of the resources present at birth, even when only a little is present.

Circumstances of labor and delivery

Birth is laborious, not only for the mother but also for the fetus. The stresses inflicted on the fetus as it progresses through the birth canal are substantial and place the child at risk for permanent impairments. A very large number of independent and interrelated factors are operative at the time of birth, and they have been studied extensively. Perhaps the richest source of information comes from the National Collaborative Perinatal Project which took place between 1958 and 1974 at 14 university hospitals. Extensive data were obtained on 58,806 women and their offspring, of whom 45,142 had complete records, beginning with the first obstetric exam. Particularly detailed records were kept of the birth process and the medical interventions that occurred, and this was followed by assessments of the children every day while they remained in the hospital, including a neurological exam at two days of age. Subsequently, each child was followed for eight years and received evaluations of psychological status at eight months, four and seven years of age, neurological exams at one and seven years, and hearing, speech, and language exams at three and eight years. Many publications have emerged which report on the relationships observed. The book published by Friedman and Neff (1986) summarized information about the effect of labor and delivery. The report classifies the variables reviewed into four groups: labor progression (variations in the stages of labor), adjunctive drugs, intrinsic factors (such as mother's pelvic size), and delivery factors (such as the position at which the fetus presents at birth). Given the complex interactions of the many variables involved, the authors performed complex statistical analyses on the data in an effort to ascertain the specific influence of single factors.

Here consideration will be given to only a few of these variables, but their comprehension requires some familiarity with the various ways in which the fetus can position itself at birth (Oxorn, 1986; Berkow, 1992). The process begins with a latent phase of the first stage of labor. Contractions of the uterus begin at irregular intervals, the cervix (the opening of the uterus) begins to soften and dilate, and the fetus begins to move toward the lower portion of the uterus. The latent stage may last eight or more hours if this is the mother's first child (a nullipara) and about five hours if she has given birth before (a multipara), and is followed by an active phase which lasts five hours (on average) in nulliparas and two hours in multiparas. This phase and the first stage of labor are completed when the cervix has dilated from 2 cm to 10 cm, and the baby is in a position to emerge. It is directly followed by the second stage of labor which lasts until the baby is born, perhaps an hour in nulliparas and 15 min in multiparas. By this time contractions are strong, and come at regular, and at increasingly rapid, intervals.

Some part of the child's body appears first, and this is called the presentation. The most frequent presentation, and the one with the least complications, is a vertex (topmost) presentation, where the child's head shows first (see figure 16.8). Other presentations may be the face, an arm or a leg, or the buttocks (a breech presentation) (see figure 16.9). Presentations other than vertex, for which the organism is not well adapted, place stress on the skull and its contents, and often result in stretching and tearing of brain tissues and hemorrhage. Knowledge that the child is positioned for a presentation other than vertex may lead the attending physician to deliver the child by cesarian section, a surgical procedure that opens the uterus by cutting into it, which avoids the complications of a stressful labor, but subjects the mother and child to its own set of possible complications. The obstetrician also has a number of tools that can be used to facilitate the delivery. One of these is a group of instruments called forceps, which are essentially large clamps that can be used to pull, push, or rotate the fetus as needed (see figure 16.10).

Friedman and Neff (1986, p. 278) found that vaginally delivered babies with breech presentations did poorly early in life, and that children born to multiparas continued to show deleterious effects in speech, language, and measured intelligence through the seventh year. Nullipara babies did better, apparently because first-borns had been considered to be at greater risk and thus were more likely to have been delivered by planned cesarian, whereas multipara babies were erroneously thought to be at less risk and were delivered vaginally. Use of forceps was also associated with

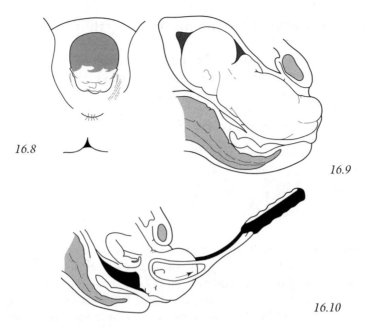

Figure 16.8 Vertex presentation
Figure 16.9 Breech presentation
Figure 16.10 Use of forceps

persistent negative outcomes under some circumstances and a favorable outcome under others. Further explication would require obstetric information that is beyond the scope of this book. Finally, deciding on a cesarian procedure when a vaginal delivery was well advanced but going badly was also associated with deleterious consequences in the child over the range of time studied.

Before going on to review injurious events occurring in childhood after birth, it should be noted that all the conditions described in this chapter are associated with increased adverse developmental outcomes. What this means in detail is that an increased percentage of children will display one or more pathological conditions. In any particular condition and any particular study, the percentage of adverse outcomes may vary from less than 5 percent to more than 80 or 90 percent. Thus, for example, severe pathology appears in a very high proportion of children whose mothers had rubella in the first two months of their pregnancy, but even then, 10–20 percent appear to escape such a fate. Similarly, severe anoxia, toxoplasmosis, and cytomegalovirus infections are all associated with high percentage of severe pathology. These conditions produce diatheses which are somewhat ameliorable, but the overall outcome is generally disappointing. By contrast, there is a definite risk with breech delivery, but only 25 percent show lifelong consequences (Friedman & Neff, 1986, table 29.2), and the magnitude of the consequences is generally relatively small.

Some Injurious Events Occurring After Birth

Once the perinatal period is passed, the child is vulnerable to the range of injurious events that are threats throughout life. The difference is that, for the subsequent 12–16 years, varying degrees of immaturity are present. Understanding both the increased vulnerability and resiliency of the immature brain to injurious events is an important component in the overall challenge of understanding brain–behavior relations.

Brain tumors

Types of tumors

The term tumor means a swelling. In common use, the word refers to tissue growths that do not belong where they occur. (Information about tumors and their consequences, unless otherwise cited, comes from Adams & Victor, 1993; Morris et al., 2000; Ris & Noll, 1994; Spreen, Risser, & Edgell, 1995.) Some tumors are disseminated, which means that the abnormal cells do not clump together in one place but spread over a wide area. In the tumors to be discussed here, the abnormal cells do clump together to form a space-occupying lesion. Of these, some show unregulated, rapid growth, may move to other tissues, and are malignant. Others grow slowly, may reach a specific size, and then remain stable. Some solid tumors develop a cystic structure which means they have a central cavity containing liquid or semisolid materials.

An ideal way to study the psychological consequences of brain tumors would be, first, collect data about the individual before the tumor starts to grow so as to provide a baseline; second, collect data at the time of tumor diagnosis but before treatment, to evaluate the direct and the indirect consequences of tumor presence; third, collect data during the course of every successive phase of treatment; and finally, evaluate the subject one or more times after treatment to determine the long-range consequences of the tumor and its treatment. Such comprehensive data collections have never occurred. Most of our knowledge is retrospective and derived from observations made after diagnosis, usually after treatment was completed. Even when data are obtained before treatment, it is difficult to sort out which results are due to the tumor alone and which to the secondary consequences of the tumor, e.g. hydrocephalus. When data are obtained after treatment, it is impossible to specify exactly which deficits, if any, are attributable to the tumor, which to the treatment, and which to developmental variables such as the child not attending school for up to a year or more. As a result, indirect methods to estimate the contribution of each relevant variable have been used, and such results must be viewed with caution.

Tumors vary in rate of growth, age at which symptoms appear, size, location, and type of cell that has gone awry, all of which will affect their influence on behavior. The most common types are astrocytomas, which are proliferations of a certain type of glial cell that may occur anywhere in the brain but are relatively frequent during childhood in the cerebellum; medulloblastomas, which also commonly originate in the cerebellum; craniopharyngiomas, located at or near the bone structure in which the pituitary gland is found in the front undersurface of the brain below the optic chiasm; ependymomas, which grow out of the cells that line the ventricles, most frequently the fourth; choroid plexus papillomas which develop in the structures within the ventricles that produce cerebrospinal fluid and generally invade the ventricles; and meningiomas which arise from the meninges and are generally separate from brain but can compress its tissue. Not infrequently, the effects seen in behavior and the symptoms presented are due to the pressure exerted on other areas of the brain by a structure that usurps limited space. These effects include hydrocephalus, seizures, nausea, diplopia, headache, and motor coordination symptoms.

Treatment of tumors

Brain tumors are often life-threatening and, not too long ago, almost inevitably led to death. Long-term survival rates for many tumors are still low, yet progress in devising treatments has led to increasingly longer survival rates. Survival, unfortunately, does not always mean return to normality. The techniques commonly utilized to treat tumors – surgery to remove as much of the tumor as possible, one or more courses of chemotherapy, and either focal or whole brain radiation to destroy remaining malignant cells – affect not only the tumor but also normal tissue. The ratio of doing harm to the tumor versus doing harm to normal tissue varies. Thus, surgically removing a benign meningioma located over the top of the cortex generally inflicts trivial damage to the healthy parts of the brain, but that might not be true if the tumor's location was over the lower parts of the brain and it had grown into any number of nooks and crannies of the skull. Accessing a craniopharyngioma or an optic chiasm astrocytoma requires cutting into and through areas of brain containing many pathways and neural processors, many of which regulate sensory and endocrine functions. It follows that successful surgery, which allows the person to live, may leave that person with visual defects, a lifelong requirement to take replacement hormones, obesity, and cognitive and emotional changes (Cohen & Duffner, 1994). Many tumors originating in childhood seem to occur in the cerebellum, and it is common for there to be residual motor-integration problems as a result of both the tumor itself and of the treatment. The reader will recall from the work on children with autism that attentional and cognitive dysfunctions are also likely consequences of cerebellar impairment.

Radiation can be administered selectively to a part of the brain or to the whole brain. The latter is done in an effort to prevent stray tumor cells from seeding new tumors after treatment is completed. It can be beamed at the brain in graded doses with powerful electronic equipment or brought to the tissues by surgically implanting radioactive pellets. Awareness of the negative effects of radiation came from experience with cases of leukemia, a malignant cancer of blood cells which before the advent of radiation therapy generally had survival durations of only four months after diagnosis. Utilizing radiation and chemotherapy led to remission and survival in a large percentage of cases. Radiation also was used, usually in high doses, in the treatment of malignant tumors, and was particularly effective in cases of medulloblastoma (Punt, 1995). Negative consequences of radiation in both clinical groups is similar. Although in the short term there may be few negative effects, declines in cognitive function and development over the long term are apparent, particularly in children treated before the age of three and especially in females (Waber et al., 1990; Moore, Ater, & Copeland, 1992; Roman & Sperduto, 1995; Dennis et al., 1996). The data imply that radiation interferes with mechanisms of remembering and learning but does not greatly affect knowledge and skills that are already learned. Estimates of cognitive decline from levels that would have been attained range from 10 to 30 IQ points. Of course, for a child who has much to learn, such consequences are not trivial. Since there is evidence that radiation is particularly adverse to myelin, the mechanism that interferes with learning may be the disruption of the interconnectivity of the brain rather than its processors. Along these lines, Rourke (1995) has argued that radiation is one source of white-matter disease.

Chemotherapy involves the injection of one or more chemical agents that are destructive to tumor cells. These agents are also destructive to normal cells but, unlike radiation, their effects do not appear to be delayed and prolonged (Krauseneck & Müller, 1995). The agents do whatever damage they do, less to normal cells than to tumor cells, and then the normal cells apparently recover. Various treatment protocols (which are always being modified) involve readministration of the agents at varying time intervals, or in various combinations. Moore, Ater, and Copeland (1992) found that, six years after diagnosis, survival rates for those treated with radiation or chemotherapy were comparable, but those treated only with chemotherapy functioned mostly in the average range, while those treated with radiation were mostly impaired. However, significant visual–spatial impairments were associated with chemotherapy so it is not totally benign.

Few data have been available about the pretreatment psychological status of tumor patients. Brookshire et al. (1990) asked about the magnitude of impairment that could be attributed directly to the effects of the tumor in order to sort those effects out from those consequent to treatment. They assessed the neuropsychological characteristics of children with a variety of brain tumors after diagnosis but prior to treatment, and found most of them to be within the normal range. Of course, with no pretumor data, they could not be sure that at least some declines had not already occurred. They did find that some tumors were associated with specific, relative deficits. Frontal location was associated with executive function deficit (discussed in chapter 9), cerebellar involvement with visual–motor and fine motor function impairments, and midline tumors and hydrocephalus with declines in a wide range of functions including measured intelligence. Given that most of the children were functioning in the average range despite their tumors, it is evident that the declines found after treatment, especially radiation, may be far greater than that due to the tumor. Improvements in current modes of treatment can be expected, but it appears that, as long as the existing approach persists, serious side effects with deleterious consequences will persist. When enough is learned about the nature of tumor formation, and how these essentially foreign bodies come to be supported rather than cast out, then new and selective ways of attacking the tumor will be devised that will spare healthy tissue. Recent reports describe a technique for tumor eradication by deprivation of its blood supply, a procedure still in the experimental stage at this writing, and this is one such possibility.

Meanwhile, Morris et al. (2000) point out the role of what many studies of the consequences of brain tumors have neglected to consider – the quality of support the child receives. Support includes emotional support, quality of parenting, and appropriateness of educational intervention. This means that, given the same tumor and the same medical treatment, the state of the child some years later will vary as a function of the way caretaking events have occurred. Some quantitative evidence was provided in a study by Carlson-Green, Morris, and Krawiecki (1995) evaluating tumor patients on average four years after diagnosis. In this sample, adaptive behavior and behavior problems at follow-up were not predicted by either tumor characteristics or treatment variables, but were associated with family characteristics such as socioeconomic status. Intellectual functioning at follow-up was related to characteristics of the tumor and the treatment, but so also were family qualities.

Sturge–Weber syndrome and hemispherectomies

Reasons for hemispherectomy

Hemispherectomy is a surgical procedure in which the entire cortex, much of the white matter, often the basal ganglia and other structures, are removed, essentially doing away with a hemisphere. This, obviously, is a radical treatment that is used only under extraordinary circumstances. For example, hemispherectomy may be performed when contralateral spasticity is apparent at birth or during the first year and then intensifies, and seizures that originate unilaterally increase in frequency and cannot be controlled. In addition, as the children get older, severe behavioral disorders appear marked by impulsivity, disinhibition, and outbursts of violence (Goodman, 1986). If such neurological and behavioral symptoms occur in the presence of a deep red–purple discoloration of the skin around the eye, which may extend in all directions on the side opposite the spasticity, a Sturge–Weber syndrome is diagnosed. The underlying pathology of the Sturge–Weber syndrome is a proliferation of interconnecting blood vessels in the meninges of one hemisphere near the nerve enervating the face and eye which, paradoxically, deprives that hemisphere of an adequate supply of blood. This then leads to abnormal calcification of tissue (Adams & Victor, 1993, p. 1034; Spreen, Risser, & Edgell, 1995). Resort to hemispherectomy also occurs for conditions with other etiologies which produce similar symptoms and an inexorable downhill course.

Hemispherectomy outcome

A hemispherectomy will inevitably leave the patient with a permanent homonymous hemianopia (see figure 12.16) and with at least some degree of residual hemiplegia. However, and this is the reason the operation is performed, it will most often either completely eliminate or considerably reduce the number of seizures, arrest the progress of the hemiplegia, and facilitate improved behavioral control (Verity et al., 1982; Goodman, 1986). Furthermore, with time, motor functions will improve. It is of great interest that some previously absent motor functions may appear almost immediately following the surgery. For example, Verity et al. report that most of their patients moved previously paralyzed limbs spontaneously within hours of the operation, and a three-year-old who had never walked did so six months after the operation.

Diaschisis

That patients cannot voluntarily move their paralyzed limbs before surgery, but can shortly after the brain tissue controlling that limb is removed, challenges the notion that the contralateral hemisphere controls limb movements. There are at least two sets of factors that must be considered to make sense of these puzzling facts. The first is to recall the hierarchy of muscle control mechanisms (chapter 11). Hemispherectomy would destroy corticospinal and rubrospinal control systems. However, the ventromedial system, which does not originate in cortex, would be spared, since its sources of enervation are bilateral. Thus, there is a mechanism for crude motor control on the side opposite the hemispherectomy. Recall that all individuals who have endured hemispherectomy are left with a permanent, residual hemiplegia. This means that limb movement contralateral to the hemisphere removed will never be fully normal. Nevertheless, it appears that the young brain can learn how to maximize the potentials of the crude system of controls. If, then, there is an explanation for some movement control, the question remains as to why such crude movements were not apparent prior to the surgery. To explain this requires consideration of the second set of factors, namely, the remote effects of the malfunctioning cortex (known to be malfunctioning because of hemiplegia and seizures). The idea is that pathology in part of the system not only has its own direct effects but may also interfere with the functions of normal areas with which it is interconnected. This type of interference is termed diaschisis (Glassman & Smith, 1988). In the present instance it appears that diaschitic consequences of the involved hemisphere suppressed the normal functioning of the ipsilateral ventromedial system. When the core pathology is surgically removed, the interference with other areas is also removed, so residual normal function quickly reappears. This is one of those instances where less is more.

Plasticity or hemispheric differentiation?

Given the improvements that often occur, and neglecting consideration of variations in surgical technique (e.g. whether to reattach the dura to the skull or to position it over the cut half of the brain – Goodman, 1986), a question arises as to what mental function may be like and what effects hemispheric specialization may have if half the brain is removed. In adults, removal of a hemisphere has devastating immediate consequences. If the left is removed, most of the deficits are in the verbal domain; if the right is removed, the impairments are in visual–spatial functions. Of particular interest is the question of what happens to verbal and visual–spatial functions when they must develop in a single hemisphere, and does it matter if the hemisphere happens to be the right or the left? If the surgery occurs during the first year or two of life, before language is solidly established, it is possible to address the question as to the degree to which the hemispheres are predifferentiated early on for the functions that they will assume later.

What can be learned about hemispheric differentiation
from hemispherectomy?

The data available to answer this question are mostly in the form of detailed study and follow-up of individual cases (Dennis & Kohn, 1975; Dennis & Whitaker, 1976; Dennis, 1980; Dennis, Lovett, & Wiegel-Crump, 1981). If findings over the span of development are examined, it is apparent that many of the children are severely compromised intellectually. The sources of the incompetence vary. One factor is how old the person is at the time of surgery. The later the surgery (particularly after the age of seven or eight) the more likely will there be inadequacy. Another factor is the amount of damage sustained before surgery. Resort to surgery often follows several bouts of status epilepticus, each episode of which may take a toll on the individual's brain resources. Finally, the mental resources of the to-be-hemispherectomized individual may not have had normal potential to begin with. However, hemispherectomy is not necessarily a barrier to either normal (Dennis & Whitaker, 1976) or even superior (Smith & Sugar, 1975) competence, and incompetence in a hemispherectomized individual should not necessarily be attributed to the surgery. The later papers of Dennis and colleagues focussed intensively on three individuals whose pathology was evident at birth and who had surgery before the age of five months. Postsurgically, they were essentially seizure-free and had similar general competencies in the lower part of the average range on measures of verbal and nonverbal skills regardless of which hemisphere had been removed. Their language skills, especially syntactic functions, were assessed intensively, and the findings are straightforward. Although superficially similar in competence, those who had to develop language solely with a left brain were at an advantage over their right-brain counterparts in mastering subtle and sophisticated aspects of syntax usage and comprehension.

How should the evidence be interpreted regarding the degree to which the hemispheres are intrinsically differentiated? Dennis' evidence, and that of many others, suggests remarkable plasticity in that the children whose left hemispheres were removed attained verbal intelligence scores in the normal range. That they were not equal in every respect to those whose right hemisphere was removed suggests that there is a predifferentiated advantage for the left hemisphere in regard to language. However, Dennis' sample was very small, the children were followed only till they were about aged nine, and their adult outcome is not known. When the effects of early unilateral lesions such as tumors are examined for evidence regarding this question (i.e. will a lesion on the left selectively diminish the development of verbal skills?), the evidence increasingly appears to support plasticity (Vargha-Khadem, Isaacs, & Muter, 1994). On the other hand, age at follow-up and the difficulty of the assessment procedure used to evaluate the children are factors which may yield evidence in support of predifferentiation. For example, no differences in the consequences of right or left hemisphere damage (supporting plasticity) may be evident on general measures of competence such as intelligence tests, but may emerge with more specific and challenging types of assessment.

A sophisticated study further illustrates some of this complexity. Caplan et al. (1993) evaluated the development of joint attention in children who had undergone hemispherectomy. Joint attention, it will be recalled, is a landmark for early cognitive development. Because of the motor and spatial aspects of the measurement procedures for joint attention, it was anticipated that the children with an intact right hemisphere would do better than those with a remaining left hemisphere. Data about the rate of change of metabolic activity in each hemisphere were available which had contributed to the decision about going ahead with the surgery. Higher rates of change were indications of better functioning. It was found that levels of joint attention were strongly related to rates of change of presurgical metabolism in the frontal lobe of the nonremoved side, but the results did not depend on which particular side had been removed (evidence for plasticity). On the other hand, laterality played some role in that activity in the right mesial temporal lobe, but not the left, was associated with the level of joint attention (evidence for predifferentiation).

This study, though very sharply focussed on a particular set of behavioral competencies over a short span of follow-up, nonetheless found the same sort of limited predifferentiation that emerges from other kinds of data. The bottom line appears to be that subtle predifferentiation effects can be found, but plasticity effects are very strong in the very young brain.

Traumatic Brain Injury

Who gets injured?

Traumatic brain injury is a very serious public health problem that receives relatively little attention in comparison to that given to other causes of incapacitation and death. For example, more children die from brain injuries than from leukemia, yet the funded support for efforts at prevention, treatment, and research are far less. Although there are controversies about the details (Goldstein & Levin, 1990), there is good consensus (a) that brain injury is most common in adolescents and young adults and in the elderly; (b) that except for the elderly, the incidence for males exceeds that of females; (c) that the most common causes of injury for the youngest and the oldest are falls; and (d) that brain injuries are most frequent in males between the ages of 15 and 25; these occur as a result of sports accidents, assault, and especially motor vehicle accidents (Naugle, 1990). Figures 16.11 and 16.12 are samples of the sort of evidence that substantiates these generalizations.

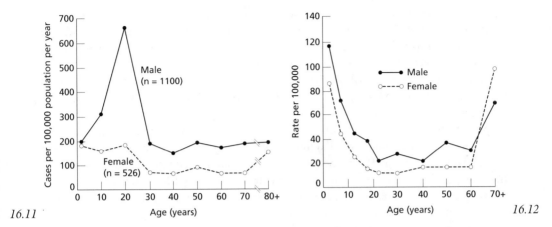

Figure 16.11 Incidence of head injuries as a function of age and sex
Figure 16.12 Incidence of head injuries due to falls

What happens physically when the brain gets injured?

Types of injury

When the head is subjected to intense external force, the brain may be injured. Such a process may occur in many ways. If the head is relatively stable and struck by a blunt object, e.g. a brick, the force of the blow will be imparted to the skull and, in turn, will be transmitted to the underlying brain tissue. If the external force fractures the bones of the skull, an open head injury is said to occur. The bone may just be cracked but remain in place (a hairline fracture) or large pieces or fragments of bone may be pushed into the meninges or beyond into the parenchyma, a condition called a depressed skull fracture. If the skull is not fractured, and the force of the blow is strong enough, a closed head injury may occur. The remainder of this presentation will focus primarily on closed head injury.

Before going into the nature of the damage, consider some other ways in which the head can be subjected to intense external force. Tall persons stooping in an area where there is a low ceiling may forget where the ceiling is and raise their heads quickly. Persons on a ladder may lose their balance and fall to the floor, striking their heads. Driver and passengers, waiting in their car for a traffic signal, may be hit from behind by another car such that the head is suddenly propelled forward as far is it can go and then back (whiplash). If the force is great enough, and the individuals are unrestrained by seat belts, the head may continue to move forward with the body behind it until it strikes the windshield. Finally, persons may be in an automobile moving at considerable speed, when another auto, coming in the opposite direction, crashes head-on. In all of these instances, forces are present to rapidly accelerate the movement of the head in some direction. There are also barriers that suddenly decelerate that movement. Some of these "barriers" (as in a whiplash injury) are in the structure of the head or between the head and the neck so that the head can only bend forward or back, or rotate to the left or right. Other barriers are in the structures of the external world (the ceiling, the windshield). The consequences of such circumstances can be described as acceleration–deceleration injuries (Rizzo & Tranel, 1996).

To understand the pathology that occurs in acceleration–deceleration closed head injury requires consideration of at least four more factors. First, when the head is accelerated, it is likely to move not only in the direction of the force impinging on it, pure translational acceleration, but also in a rotational direction, pure angular acceleration, with an increased likelihood of twisting the brain mass that may shear neural filaments (Pang, 1985). Second, the scalp, skull, meninges, blood vessels, and the white and gray matter of the parenchyma are not of uniform density and mass. Consequently, the impact of accelerative forces on the different parts of the brain will not be uniform and some parts will move faster than others. As a result, stretching and tearing will occur, particularly at the boundaries of the different types of tissue. This is something like what occurs if a raw egg is shaken vigorously and the delicate membranes that separate the denser yoke from the white are torn so that the egg is scrambled inside the intact shell. Third, the mesial and ventral surfaces of the temporal and frontal lobes lodge in bony structures with edges that provide a further opportunity for tearing as the tissues are thrust forward and back over these edges. (See figure 16.13 for the most common sites of damage following closed head injury.) Finally, the place in the brain that absorbs the initial brunt of the force of deceleration is directly under the point of impact on the scalp. Since the brain mass is then accelerated in the opposite direction within the cranium, the next major impact within the cranium will be directly opposite the original point of impact. One may thus find that, for example, following a forehead's encounter with a windshield, conspicuous frontal lobe damage will occur, but there may also be conspicuous injury at directly opposite occipital regions. This combination of damages is called coup–contrecoup injury. Note that the first two of the four factors provide a basis for understanding why the damage that occurs in closed head injury is widespread or diffuse, while the latter two suggest ways in which localized or focal damage may occur. The general rule in closed head injury is that there may be some conspicuous localized findings, but diffuse damage is almost always inevitable.

By contrast, localized damage is the rule if the injury is caused by a missile or bullet. These injuries, called penetrating wounds, involve the skull (often in two places, entrance and exit), the meninges, and the parenchyma that lies in the path of the bullet. The damage, however, depends on the specifics of the trajectory, and there is relatively little in the way of diffuse or remote damage.

What does the person experience after force is imparted to the head?

Concussion

There are a range of possibilities when sudden force is imparted to the head. Many such experiences are trivial – one may bump one's head and not even have a sore spot

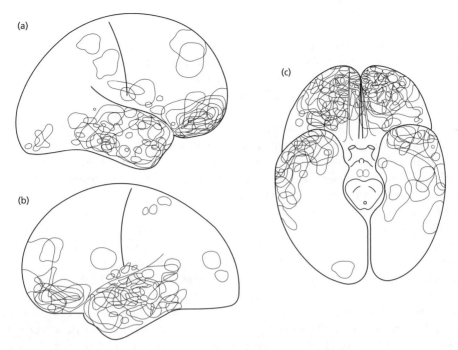

Figure 16.13 The markings indicate common sites of brain damage following closed-head injury

at the point of impact to remind one of the experience. With more force, the intensity of the experience may be more vivid and the reverberations of longer duration. The place of impact may remain tender for a period of time. One may be momentarily dazed and have unusual sensory experiences such as seeing stars, hearing ringing in the ears, or being momentarily blinded or deafened. Although scary, such experiences are mostly followed by no sequelae of any significance. Sometimes, however, blows to the head are followed by experiences such as disorientation, dizziness, neck pain, headache, and loss or clouding of memory for events both before and after the impact. When such symptoms, whose duration may range from minutes to days to weeks, are present, a concussion is said to have occurred. The term concussion is a commonly used word whose precise meaning is hard to pin down because it refers to both subjective and objective events. If the symptoms extend to include unconsciousness or coma, there is general consensus that a concussion has taken place, although it is also generally agreed that a person can have a concussion, even a serious brain-injuring concussion, without losing consciousness. In that case, however, there is likely to be some controversy as to whether a concussion actually took place. Theoretically, such a concussion may occur if the direction of the shock produced by the impact does not progress to the brain stem (Levin, 1993; Ommaya, 1996).

Coma

One can become unconscious in many ways, including following temporary failure of blood pressure regulation which deprives the brain of an adequate blood supply and results in fainting, poisoning, and asphyxia (Kelly, 1991), but concern here is with post-traumatic coma. This may be defined as a usually reversible, traumatic paralysis of nervous function lasting from seconds through hours, days or longer (Adams & Victor, 1993, p. 752). A comatose person cannot stand because supportive postural reflexes are abolished, cannot initiate movement or speech, and is nonresponsive to stimulation. Teasdale and Jennett (1974) developed the now widely used Glasgow Coma Scale, which permits individuals with a range of training, including police officers and emergency ambulance personnel, to rate three subscales of wakefulness uniformly; these are assessments of the stimulation required to elicit eye opening, voluntary motor behavior, and speech. The three subscales combine to a range of scores from 3 to 15; a score of 8 or less is indicative of a comatose condition. The Glasgow Coma Scale may be rated repeatedly and the sequence of scores provides a crude but effective and predictive index of the status of the brain.

Entry into trauma-induced coma is frequently instantaneous upon impact, will last for a variable time period (see below) and then be followed by emergence from coma if death does not occur. However, in a fair percentage of individuals, a syndrome described by Ommaya (1996) as "patients who talk and die or deteriorate" depicts a different sequence of reactions in which the individual immediately following impact is no more than temporarily dazed or very briefly unconscious and so is soon talking but then moves into a severe, life-threatening comatose state, hours or even a day or two later. The explanation for such a sequence will be found below under the heading of early sequelae of brain injury.

A common scenario is that a comatose person is found at the scene of an accident. Within 15 minutes, when the ambulance arrives, the victim has begun to respond but is dazed, confused, and cannot recall what happened. By the time the patient is brought to the hospital, he or she may be able to respond to all elements of the Glasgow Coma Scale adequately and attain a score of 15, but cannot recall the scene of the accident or the arrival of the ambulance, nor, after arriving at the emergency room, that the nurse who greeted him/her there and then departed is the same person who 15 minutes later is cleaning and bandaging some minor cuts. Thus, in the sequence of recovery from coma, consciousness may clear and the person will not be dazed or look confused, but memory may remain impaired.

Amnesia

Post-traumatic amnesia, or PTA, refers to memory losses following trauma. There are two aspects to PTA: retrograde and anterograde amnesia. These terms divide the continuity of memory as a function of the moment of concussion, retrograde referring to recall of events before concussion (what was going on prior to the accident) and anterograde referring to the recall of events subsequent to concussion. Initial retrograde amnesia may extend for some time back from the moment of concussion and then, as recovery takes place, shrink to minutes or even seconds before the accident. Anterograde amnesia, which refers to failure to store and retrieve memories of ongoing events subsequent to concussion, begins to resolve with fragmentary recollections that get increasingly detailed. PTA is said to have resolved when ordinary short- and long-term memory resumes, i.e. when anterograde amnesia disappears and retrograde amnesia is minimal. This does not mean that memories of the trauma or from the period of active anterograde amnesia will be recovered. The duration of PTA is a useful index of the injury done to the brain and a predictor of its recovery (Levin, 1993).

When coma is prolonged

With severe trauma, coma may have longer durations than the common scenario described above. It can last for hours, days, or even months. Recovery from prolonged coma follows the same pattern found with emergence from brief coma, but the duration of each step is longer, and often fraught with problems of management and control. In particular, the early stages of emergence from coma which, when coma is brief, may be marked only by transitory confusion and disorientation, can take place over a period of weeks or even months when coma is prolonged. During this stage of recovery, behavior is marked by varying modes of disinhibition such as agitation, impulsivity, low frustration tolerance, and aggressiveness. These characteristics are determined by the physiology of recovering brain functions in that recovery of excitatory processes precedes the recovery of inhibition. Not only are the patients difficult to manage, but they also often cannot remember what they have done. Recovery of memory, and with it of learning, is slow and arduous, and during this period requires the care of a variety of professional skills. These include knowledge of how to organize and implement a structured supportive environment as well as how to provide learning experiences commensurate with the diminished capabilities of the brain-injured person. Individuals recovering from prolonged coma do best in intensive-care facilities dedicated to this condition.

What is the nature of the primary injury at a cellular level?

Recall that the brain is composed of clusters of neurons (ganglia), the gray matter, and interconnecting nerve fibers covered with myelin, termed white matter. Nerve fibers are made up of groups of axons with their myelin headed more or less in the same direction. Some are in very large groups (fasciculi), some in smaller groups. The arrangement is similar to a major trunk line whose components peel off, first in smaller and smaller groups and finally, at the level of the single axon, to head toward their synaptic targets. An axon will synapse with at least one and generally with many more neurons. A slice of brain tissue will reveal cross-sections through all of these levels, and if viewed with amplification that is strong enough (usually an electron microscope is required), may reveal the infinitesimally small filament of the single axon. With this kind of structure, the tissues most vulnerable to injury will be these individual axonal microfilaments. Depending on the force of the impact and the direction of rotation, diffuse axonal injury at the level of the filaments will be the most likely to occur first. The axon's outer membranes may be bruised, stretched, or twisted, and the axon may be partially or totally severed. With more intense forces, increasingly more axons and larger and larger fasciculi will be affected so that one can envision a continuum of axonal damage (Ommaya, 1996; Bigler, 1997).

Axonal injury does not necessarily kill the cell body of the neuron from which it emerged upstream from the site of damage, though over time it might. Often, the injured axon may be repaired or the severed axon may be replaced by other axons which make new connections. However, immediately after injury, undamaged neurons downstream from the site of injury will be deprived of normal input from damaged axons. As a result, the damage done to particular neurons is compounded by its effects on other neurons. Normal downstream neurons may reorganize successfully, but this takes time, often months or even years. Thus, some of the pathological consequences of an injurious event are maximal immediately while others are delayed. These will be considered next.

Early sequalae of brain injury

Infection

Infection is an ever-present threat with penetrating wounds, all other kinds of skull fracture, and when shunts or other devices are placed in the brain for some therapeutic purpose. The infection may directly destroy brain tissue and may lead to the formation of abscesses (Landesman & Cooper, 1993). Such infections generally progress considerably beyond the entry site of the pathological organisms and produce much-more-than-local damage. The treatment of brain infections is a medical challenge whose discussion is beyond the scope of this book. It should be understood, however, that a relatively benign head injury may have a very poor outcome if infection is not treated early and successfully.

Hemorrhage

Hemorrhage may occur as a result of trauma. The system that supplies blood to the brain parallels the structural organization of axons with large trunk lines branching into smaller and smaller ones. Large arteries give way to smaller ones, then to capillaries (the level at which the blood does its work), and then to first small and then larger and larger veins. The capillary beds and the small arteries and veins are nearly as fragile as the axonal filaments and are also susceptible to shearing stress. If a blood vessel is ruptured, the magnitude of the hemorrhage will vary with the size of the blood vessel. A capillary hemorrhage may produce only a very small area of abnormality whose consequence will depend on its location and size, and may often be trivial if it is a singular, localized event. (In some older adults, many such small trivial events can add up and produce dire consequences.) A rupture of a large blood vessel will pour blood into the crowded space within the skull at a rate proportional to the size of the vessel, and brain structures are subjected to increased pressure. The ventricles are constricted and the small spaces between the gyri and sulci of the cortex are occluded. The pressure squeezes normal blood vessels, and remote parts of the brain become ischemic because they do not receive an adequate blood supply. After concussion, medical personnel watch for signs of hemorrhage since unconsciousness and death can follow. If hemorrhage occurs, steps to reduce the pressure are required. In the most common procedure, the neurosurgeon penetrates the skull and meninges as soon as possible to drain the pool of blood and reduce the pressure. If not done promptly, and the subject survives, the long-term consequence will be widespread cell loss, thinning of brain structures, and widening of the sulci and ventricles.

Edema and other post-traumatic complications

The brain does not have to bleed for there to be an increase in intracranial pressure. Injury leads to edema, a swelling of the tissues, which again leads to elevated intracranial pressure. Research in recent years has clarified some of the specific events that contribute to the production of edema. Two such mechanisms will be mentioned here. One is excitatory amino acid release. Immediately following trauma, injured nerve tissues spontaneously release massive amounts of excitatory neurotransmitters into extracellular space, the milieu of the neuron. Such release is excitotoxic, i.e. it is excessively and poisonously excitatory and alters the careful homeostatic balance of ions necessary for normal neurotransmission. It also leads to swelling of neurons and glia and to cell death (Zauner & Bullock, 1996; Bigler, 1997). A second mechanism found in experimentally injured animals, and confirmed in humans who have endured brain injuries, is termed secondary axotomy (Povlishock & Christman, 1996). The fascinating aspect of this mechanism is that it has a time course of hours following the moment of injury, and it does not depend on shearing. Rather, a process is described wherein a perturbation at some point along the axon leads to a disruption of axoplasmic transport downstream from that point. There follows, over the course of several hours, a process in which the materials being transported down the axon jam up at that point and create a balloon-like swelling in the axon. Somewhere between six and 12 hours later there is a severing of the axon, leaving a retraction ball that is visible with high-powered amplification techniques. The distal end of the axon subsequently degenerates while the upstream nerve cell may or may not survive. Finally, although the injured brain requires more energy, cerebral blood flow, which transports nutrients to the tissues, is reduced (Hovda, 1998), jeopardizing healthy as well as damaged cells.

At this point the meaning of Ommaya's somewhat cryptic phrase, "patients who talk and die or deteriorate" should be clear. Following trauma, events such as hemorrhage and excitatory amino acid release and secondary axotomy associated with edema may take hours to fully evolve. During this period, the victim may be lucid and be able to talk but if these post-traumatic pathological processes are under way, and are not treated, the patient may lapse into unconsciousness later and be at risk of dying. The toll incurred by post-traumatic reactions within the brain may often be greater than the damage inflicted by trauma.

Seizures

Seizures which occur for the first time following brain trauma are classified as early or late (Jennett, 1990). Early seizures occur within the first week following injury and are attributed to the many post-traumatic changes taking place in the brain. They occur in 5 percent or less of head traumas and do not necessarily signal the onset of a persisting epileptic disorder, although early seizures are a risk factor for later seizures. There is a greater likelihood of early seizures in children than in adults, and the younger the child the more likely that seizures and status epilepticus will occur (Shapiro & Smith, 1993). If only one seizure occurs, physicians may rely on treatments instituted to deal with brain injury complications to prevent further seizures. If more seizures occur, anticonvulsant medications are generally administered. Late epilepsy emerges months to years after trauma and is generally persistent and chronic in nature, although often responsive to anticonvulsant medications. This means that, with medication, the seizures are reduced in number but that the individual cannot be weaned from medication and must live with the side effects. Late seizures are most likely to occur in individuals who had depressed skull fractures and/or intracranial bleeding. Presumably, many late post-traumatic seizures are a result of the creation of scar tissue which then becomes a seizure focus.

Treatment of brain injury complications

Given that, in many instances, more enduring damage can occur from the secondary reactions of the brain to injury than from the injury itself, and that some of these reactions take considerable time to occur, the possibility of their arrest looms large in the care of the head-injured. The need to prevent or arrest infection is obvious and the treatment of hemorrhage has been mentioned. Available treatments for edema are not entirely satisfactory. They include surgical procedures such as shunting to remove cerebral spinal fluid, use of diuretic agents, physically cooling the head, sedative and antiepileptic medications which slow down neural metabolism, and steroids which are often used to reduce swelling just about anywhere in the body (Shapiro & Smith, 1993; Wilberger, 1993). It is likely that these treatments will be supplanted with new interventions as knowledge accumulates about what is actually taking place at a cellular level in the aftermath of injury.

Meanwhile, there is a promising line of research (Stein, Roof, & Fulop, 1998) which draws on evidence that females generally recover better from stroke and brain trauma than do males. Experiments with brain-damaged animals, which manipulated levels of female sex hormones, found that progesterone, the predominant hormone in the latter phase of the menstrual cycle, rather than estrogen, dominant in the early phase, had the beneficial effect of reducing edema and facilitating recovery. This evidence coincided with data indicating that more enduring recovery occurred in women if they experienced trauma (for example. mastectomy for breast cancer) during the latter phase of their cycles. Subsequent experiments on male animals showed that progesterone had the same beneficial effects for them. Stein et al. (1998) suggest that progesterone reduces edema and facilitates recovery via a number of mechanisms including the inhibition of excitatory amino acid release.

Pragmatic classification of brain injuries

Scaling severity

Brain injury is often classified into three categories on the basis of severity – mild, moderate, and severe – although the detailed criteria for inclusion into each category vary across clinical centers and research studies (Dacey, Vollmer, & Dikmen, 1993; Asarnow et al., 1995). One commonly held set of criteria for mild brain injury specify an admission-to-hospital Glasgow Coma Scale of no less than 13, coma durations no more than 20 minutes, and hospitalization not exceeding two days, which rules out the development of post-traumatic hemorrhage or significant swelling (Levin et al., 1987). Generally speaking there is no, or only very brief, anterograde amnesia and very limited, if any, retrograde amnesia. A further current criterion is that, if brain imaging is done, no significant lesions are revealed. The general notion is that the individual did sustain a blow on the head, and had experienced some postconcussive symptoms. At the severe end of the mild range, symptoms such as headaches, disrupted attention, agitation, emotional control, sleep disturbances, and difficulty in concentration, organization, and sequencing behavior occur for a period of time.

Severe head injury is often defined as a Glasgow Coma Scale of 8 or less with coma lasting from six to 24 hours or more, and post-traumatic amnesia of greater than 24 hours, though sometimes the criterion is up to a week. If imaging is done, there is clear evidence of lesions of recent origin. There may also be evidence of edema and hemorrhage. Having described the extremes of the scale, the reader might guess that moderate injury will lie somewhere in between. It does, and since the criteria for classification vary across studies, there are instances in which the middle group will be more like the mild group, others where it will be more like the severe group, and yet others where it is in between.

Outcome as a function of severity

As a general rule, the outcome of mild head injury is benign (Asarnow et al., 1995), although it may take six months or more (generally less in children) before all vestiges of postconcussive symptoms are gone. The big problem for most individuals is being tolerant of the changes they experience while the injury resolves and the symptoms disappear. It helps to receive accurate information about the nature of the condition and supportive counseling during the period when the symptoms are at their height so that reactive, deleterious behaviors (e.g. turning to drink when despairing about the loss of mental skill) are avoided. It should be noted that there are a few persons with a sequence of events generally consistent with mild brain injury who will, nonetheless, show major, enduring consequences. These exceptions have been termed "occult" (Levin et al., 1987). However, better resolution of imaging procedures has made these cases less mysterious. Although the patients did escape the behaviorally evident landmarks of severe injury (e.g. coma) they actually did sustain shearing lesions of the cortex. The main point is that, although there is an association between symptoms immediately following injury and long-term outcome, the association is not perfect. What is crucial is the actual damage done. As noted earlier, the brain can be severely injured even though no coma occurs. Conversely, it is possible, though rare, for a severely comatose brain to not be severely damaged. This might occur if the concussive wave got to the brainstem without creating much havoc en route.

There is a particular type of mild head injury that is likely to recur, in which the head is often struck or is used to strike, as in boxing, American football, soccer, and rugby (Barth et al., 1989). Research on the consequences of the concussions experienced with some frequency in these activities has found that repeated injury takes a toll of the cognitive and motor functions of the athlete. In sports such as boxing, blows to the neck may stun the vessels supplying blood to the brain and lead to a diminished supply, while direct blows to the back of the head may impact the cerebellum and brainstem directly and cause immediate or delayed localized ischemia. The overall conclusion of this work is that participation in these kinds of sport entails considerable risk of at least mild reduction of mental competence.

Persons surviving severe brain injury are likely to suffer from permanently incapacitating deficiencies (Vollmer, 1993). The process of recovery is long, and it is generally agreed that it takes at least 18 months before the bulk of recovery will occur, although small further gains may appear subsequently. It used to be thought that whatever recovery was possible would occur spontaneously in a manner that was determined by the magnitude of the injury and the particular brain's inherent ability to recover, whatever it might be. There is good evidence now that intensive and comprehensive efforts at rehabilitation make a significant and cost-effective difference (Cope, 1995). As a general rule, it will cost less to care for brain-injured persons over the lifespan, whatever the level of impairment, if they experience intensive rehabilitation during the period following the injury.

That rehabilitation leads to cost-effective improvement does not mean that patients return to their pre-injury level. Depending on the details of the injury, the immediate post-injury course, the promptness and efficacy of treatments received for edema and hemorrhage, and the quality of rehabilitative efforts, the person may still be left with a range of handicaps in the areas of sensory processing or motor control, attention, language and memory, emotional regulation, and executive function. From the perspective of what it takes to adapt successfully as a social human being, the ability to do productive work and to maintain a range of social relationships, deficits in executive (Stuss, 1987) and related attentional functions (Dennis et al., 1995) play a large role. Given the likelihood that severe and even moderate injury is likely to be associated with lesions of the frontal and temporal lobes, the prognosis for successful social adaptation is guarded, and it is not surprising that there is a high incidence of psychiatric disorder following severe brain injury (Grant & Alves, 1987; Lishman, 1998).

The complications of insurance and compensation

The assessment of head injury is complicated by the social and legal circumstances associated with injury. Injuries, especially those due to assault and automobile accidents, are often the responsibility of someone other than the victim, and hence are subject to litigation seeking compensation. Once the prospect of monetary reward comes into play, a series of variables, in addition to the specifics of the injury and the circumstances of rehabilitation, become operative. These include the adversarial nature of the legal system and the individual behavior of lawyers within the system, the policies and interests of insurance companies, the patient's needs and hopes for monetary compensation, the patient's moral values, and the patient's susceptibility to suggestion. The interaction of these factors may produce reasonable and satisfactory outcomes, with legitimate and fair compensation for injury sustained or unwarranted outcomes on either side of the opposition. Patients may be led to not work at their rehabilitation, and develop unnecessary invalidism through outright malingering or reactions to subtle suggestion, in their hope of obtaining large monetary settlements which they sometimes get. Conversely, seriously handicapped individuals have been denied fair monetary settlements because many of their symptoms are cognitive and emotional in nature and may not be substantiated by the diagnostic procedures commonly accepted by the courts as revealing the presence of injury. There is a large literature on this subject (e.g. Kolpan, 1990; Faust, Ziskin, & Hiers, 1991).

The nature of the evidence verifying brain injury

The problem of verifying brain injury merits some further discussion. As recently as the middle of the 20th century, the only objective imaging procedure available to ascertain the presence of brain injury was the x-ray. X-rays may reveal fractures, large hemorrhages, and the size of the ventricles, but lack the resolution to pick up the shearing injuries and small hemorrhages common to closed head injury. Many individuals who had sustained such injuries could obtain no compensation because there was no way to verify a brain injury objectively unless they were willing to undergo an autopsy or at least a brain biopsy. The developing field of clinical neuropsychology filled this gap, in part, with studies of the relationship between different kinds of brain injury and detailed analyses of the patient's competencies (Benton, 1989). The neuropsychologist could then contribute to the diagnosis of brain injury, and this work was considered by the courts in assessing injury. Although behavior is, in some sense, the ultimate test of brain integrity, less than optimal performance is under the control of the patient and, if money is at stake, there may be ample motivation for it to occur. The detection of malingering or less than optimal functioning has been the subject of considerable research (Faust, Ziskin, & Hiers, 1991, p. 409) but has not yielded fully satisfactory results. Although some behavioral assessment procedures can generate evidence that patients are doing less than their best, there is no procedure that assures that they are doing their best. Judges and juries have to deal with the pattern emerging from a variety of evidence in order to arrive at what is, ultimately, a fallible judgment.

However, with the development of imaging procedures of increasing resolution, more individuals who had been suspected of exaggerating and prolonging their injury have been found to have documentable lesions. Such improvements do not mean that we can be sure that there was no injury when imaging data are not confirmatory. Even greater resolution and quantitative methods of analysis are needed. Beyond that, non-invasive methods of studying altered function at a neuronal level would also be helpful, given that brain injury may alter function without altering structure. Such refinements are the subjects of current research.

Differences between Injuries Incurred in the Child and Adult

The Kennard principle

The presentation, to this point, has not been specific about the consequences of brain injury in children, especially young children. This topic will be the focus of this last section of the chapter. A framework for considering this issue is provided by what has been termed the Kennard principle (Spreen, Risser, & Edgell, 1995). Kennard was an experimental scientist who worked with animals between 1930 and 1960, exploring the consequences of brain lesions inflicted at different ages (Finger & Almli, 1988). She began her career participating in pioneer studies mapping the motor cortex in mature animals and made observations which are now common knowledge, e.g. that lesions made in the left motor cortex would produce flaccid paralysis and hemiplegia on the right, lesions of the premotor cortex would affect but not devastate motoric skill, but that lesions farther forward in the frontal association cortex had no immediately observable effects. When, in later studies, she removed both motor and premotor areas of an infant brain, she was surprised to observe that, within 24 hours of surgery, the animal was walking about with hardly any sign of deficit and later appeared entirely normal. The evidence was replicated and extended in many subsequent studies and she was credited with the general principle that the immature brain is much more capable of recovery from insult than is the mature brain.

As data on closed head injury have accumulated, the Kennard principle has been challenged and Kennard herself has been impugned. Finger and Almli (1988) review her work in detail. In contrast to other writers' presentations of her work, they credit her with acknowledging that she was not the first to make such observations, and that she spelled out the limitations of the infant-sparing effect. Kennard reported that it was not universal or absolute, and that late-appearing deficits may appear even if the immediate effects of damage were negligible. Finger and Almli's review of the sophistication and the modesty of Kennard's work supports the credit she receives when her name is invoked in association of the principle of infantile sparing. The oversimplifications that have been made in her name, which subsequently brought disrepute to the principle, have not been deserved. The Kennard principle, properly understood, is a useful reminder of the importance of developmental processes in behavior. Some of the difficulty associated with the principle is the tendency to make broad generalizations about brain injury without taking into account the specific nature and magnitude of the insult and the extent to which healthy tissue remains. Hemispherectomy, where validity of the Kennard principle is fairly obvious, is not the same as severe closed head injury. Consider the differences. In hemispherectomy, abnormal tissue is removed leaving healthy tissue, albeit that the commissures have no place to go and will atrophy. In closed head injury, existing axodendritic connections are disrupted and lesions are likely to occur in both temporal and frontal lobes. Although there are processes within the brain that will clean up much of the debris, a substantial amount of abnormal tissue is likely to remain and function disruptively. Growth and development will be burdened by the continuing influence of such chronic disruption.

Inflicted injuries

Given that head injuries produce different kinds of damage compared with surgical lesions, it has emerged that there are different types of head injury when those sustained by young children are considered. Babies and preschool-aged children are small and can be picked up by adults and older children. They can be shaken vigorously, during the course of which their head, whether deliberately intended or not, may strike a solid surface. Abusive injuries caused in this manner produce different consequences from those due to the other common causes of head injury in childhood, e.g. falls and automobile accidents (Shapiro & Smith, 1993; Ewing-Cobbs, Dubaime, & Fletcher, 1995). They are far more likely to present with retinal and subdural hemorrhages, multiple, bilateral skull fractures, and coexisting bodily injuries. Most of the noninflicted injuries of the very young involve direct translational forces and focal injury rather than the rotational forces that produce shearing and diffuse injury. Even in automobile injuries, babies act more like singular missiles hitting a target directly than a hinged-at-the-neck twistable mass with a limited range of movement. Whereas young children show considerable resilience to noninflicted injuries, those who sustain inflicted injuries often do not survive or are left with major impairments.

Outcome of brain injury in children

There is a large literature on the consequences of brain injury in children but it is not possible to state these consequences in a simplistic fashion. In this last section of this chapter, many of the variables known to influence outcome will be reviewed again. The last variable to be discussed will be age, which will provide an opportunity to examine the range of applicability of the Kennard principle.

Variables affecting outcome of brain injury (Fletcher et al., 1995)

(A)   Pre-injury status of the injured.
(B)   The nature of the injurious event.
    1.   Closed versus open head injury.
    2.   Penetrating versus acceleration–deceleration versus inflicted.
(C)   Observable behavioral characteristics at the time of injury and a week thereafter.
    1.   Duration of coma, if any.
    2.   Duration of PTA, if any.
    3.   Continuity of recovery or presence of setbacks.
    4.   Occurrence, timing, and type of seizures.
(D)   Evidence of pathology from imaging and other medical procedures shortly after injury.
    1.   Focal lesions.
    2.   Edema.
    3.   Hemorrhage.
    4.   Infection.
(E)   Nature and timing of the pharmacological or surgical treatment received for edema, hemorrhage, infection, seizures, or skull fractures.
(F)   Availability of emotional and financial support and other family and social variables (Taylor et al., 1995; Yeates et al., 1997).
(G)   Quality of rehabilitation effort (Ylvisaker, 1985; Rosenthal et al., 1990; Ensher & Clark, 1994; Michaud, 1995; Bigler, Clark, & Farmer, 1997).
(H)   Length of time since injury.
(I)   What is being measured to assess recovery.
    1.   Neurological status.
    2.   Evidence of brain status from imaging, EEG, and other diagnostic procedures.
    3.   Skills in so-called activities of daily living, dressing, hygiene, feeding, etc.
    4.   Academic standing for those of school age.
    5.   Basic academic skills in reading, writing, math, and conceptual thinking.
    6.   General measures of mental competence such as intelligence.
    7.   General indices of adaptation, like marriage, employment, income, satisfaction with life.
    8.   Diagnoses of emotional disorder and psychopathology.
    9.   Neuropsychological assessment of specific components of cognitive skills; including attention (Dennis et al., 1995), fine motor skill, visual

spatial memory, language and discourse skills (Chapman, 1995), and frontal lobe skills.

10. Age at the time of injury.

Commentary on the outline

The above outline can serve as a partial summary and review of material presented in this chapter. However, a few variables were introduced for the first time and some additional comment is warranted.

Pre-injury status (A) bears on the question of whether pathological characteristics seen after brain injury can be attributed to that particular injury. For example, a group of head-injured children who show signs of attention disorder in comparison to a group of non-head-injured can claim to have suffered this consequence from the head injury. This claim may be valid only if they did not have the attention disorder prior to the injury, especially since attention-disordered children are more vulnerable to having head injuries. Comparably, it is important to know whether they had a prior head injury since brain-injured individuals are at higher risk than others for subsequent injury (Annegers et al., 1980). It would be wise for any researchers to know about these variables when selecting their subjects.

Family and social variables (F), noted earlier for their significance in recovery from brain tumors, have come to receive increasing attention as evidence has emerged indicating their impact on recovery from brain injury. To the extent that studies disregard these variables and the nature of the rehabilitative effort (G), one's view of brain damage is static and fixed – largely that recovery occurs in areas not destroyed by the damage. In fact, Yeates et al. (1997) have found that, with regard to many aspects of recovery, high-functioning families buffer the effects of head injury while low-functioning families burden recovery. The impact of such evidence is to shift from waiting to see what happens following brain injury to searching for the best ways to augment the buffering and decrease the burden. This may well require working with families and their manner of interaction which developed prior to the injury of one of its members.

Neuropsychological components of cognitive competence (I.9) includes the example of discourse skills, not mentioned heretofore in this volume. The evaluation of outcome may depend on which particular outcome is being measured. Chapman (1995) notes that results of tests of language skill including vocabulary and syntax showed good recovery following closed head injury, yet actual language interactions, such as in conversation and story telling, appeared to be quite impoverished. When discourse skills of persons with closed head injury were assessed directly using techniques borrowed from linguistics, the realities of the consequences of brain injury became apparent. The injured had recovered the ability to define single words or recognize their meanings and differentiate erroneous from correct syntactic formulations, but they had difficulty following the ebb and flow of a conversation, of making utterances of any complexity, and of telling a coherent story. The history of research about the consequences of brain injury has many similar parallels. For example, when the criteria used to evaluate recovery were standard tests of intelligence (I.6), many patients were said to have recovered because they attained average or better scores on those tests. Casual observation suggested, however, that they were appallingly deficient on such cognitive functions as planning, organization, self-monitoring, and other frontal lobe functions. With specific tests of those functions, more of their deficits became apparent (Duncan et al., 1996).

What are the effects of age at the time of injury?

There is no research available at this time whose design is comprehensive enough to do justice to the outline above, so any conclusions about the effects of age at injury must be tentative. A paper by Taylor and Alden (1997), which reviews research that reflects the state of the art as of 1996, provides the basis for what is to follow.

It appears that the Kennard principle has been verified, as noted above, in the case of hemispherectomy for intractable seizures and in isolated instances with a variety of conditions, but does not hold at all when systematic studies of closed head injury are reviewed. Research going back to the 1950s, though not entirely consistent, finds that children are affected more adversely than adults, and younger children more adversely than older children. Most of the data refer to the effects of moderate to severe injury since mild injury is generally reported to have no discernible consequences. However, Gronwall, Wrightson, and McGinn (1997), in a series of studies in Auckland, New Zealand, find that children with mild injuries in the pre-school years lag in the acquisition of academic skills one or more years later. These findings are consistent with an hypothesis that the injury uses up resources which will not be available for developments yet to come. Thus, youngsters may recover to the level of development attained at the time of their injury but lag in their subsequent development. Similarly, Ewing-Cobbs et al. (1997) compared children two years post-injury who at the time of injury were either four to 41 months or 42–72 months and found that age at injury did not affect the magnitude of the consequences. They did find that those with severe injuries showed significant losses, on average measuring more than a standard deviation, in all areas tested, especially in motor functions. Those with mild to moderate injuries for the most part were in the average range, but showed decreased verbal functions, precisely the skills that are central to academic achievement. The children improved significantly over the first six months following injury but then ceased to progress. Anderson et al. (1997), following their somewhat older sample of children 12 months post-injury, obtained similar results and also found persisting effects on memory.

These recent studies are fairly short-term follow-ups. Klonoff, Clark, and Klonoff (1993) located and reported on 159 of 231 survivors of closed head injury, 23 years later. Their average age at the time of injury was a little under eight. About 90 percent had sustained mild head injuries, the rest severe. At follow-up, about 30 percent reported subjective sequelae associated with the injury. These included problems with learning, memory, and concentration; emotional disorders; and complaints such as headaches, back pain, and seizures. Those who reported subjective complaints were more likely to have failed grades in school, to be unemployed, and to have strained relationships with family members. Those with intellectual and emotional sequelae had lower intelligence test scores shortly after injury and presented other signs of early and continuing deficit as well. The good news from this study of mostly mildly injured individuals is that many had neither objective indices of dysfunction nor subjective complaints. The bad news is that, even 23 years later, some still showed the effects of their injury.

Overall, follow-up research findings indicate the likelihood of fairly severe, multi-function, negative effects with severe injury in childhood, roughly the same magnitude of effect found in adults. With mild injuries there is evidence of interference with language functions in children which do not occur in adults whose language skills are well mastered. There is thus evidence of a type of vulnerability in the course of development that is not present later. Perhaps it is no surprise that what is most affected are skills highest in the evolutionary hierarchy.

17

Mental Retardation

Although the details may vary, definitions of mental retardation include some notion referring to level of mental capability. The measurement of mental capability is the subject of a more-than-a-century-old field of inquiry called psychometrics, a term which means mental measurement. The first part of this chapter will review this field and its methods, concepts, and data. This will be followed by a description of several types of retardation. The last part of this chapter will focus on the neuropsychology of cognitive impairment, an area of research that is in its infancy even though it has long been assumed that most types of mental retardation have constitutional causes.

Before going further, note the following on terminology. The commonly used term for conditions of sub-par mental functioning is "mental retardation." It is the term that is currently used in the diagnostic manual of the American Psychiatric Association (1994) and in many other contexts. The term suggests a slow, lagging rate of mental development, but this is an assumption that may be valid in only some of the conditions to be reviewed in this chapter. It contrasts with another term, often used previously. Although "mental deficiency" is just descriptive, and makes no assumption as to the nature of the impairment, it is not favored currently, apparently because it is thought to be stigmatizing, demeaning, and makes unwarranted assumptions about ultimate accomplishments. The term "amentia," which is still used in neurology and psychiatry, means "without mental capability" and is absolute and extreme and does not allow for degrees of impairment (there is no word "dysmentia" in common parlance). There is also a term "dementia" which refers to conditions of declining mental competence which occur after the attainment of higher levels of function.

Psychometrics

Origins of psychometrics

Psychometrics began in the last half of the nineteenth century in England following the publication of Darwin's theory of evolution, with its emphasis of survival of the fittest. Darwin asserted that inherited intelligence differentiated humans from other primates, and among humans predicted success and survival. His young cousin, Francis Galton, initiated early systematic research into individual differences in competence. He selected his measures from procedures used to study individual differences in the laboratory. They included sensitivity in vision, hearing, and somatosensory functions, and of speed of reaction time to signals to move, the movement generally being a depression or release of some kind of lever or telegraph key with a finger. This work was taken up in the United States and other parts of world but showed little relation to academic success and was considered a failure. The work occurred during the infancy not only of psychometry but of psychology in general. With hindsight, its failure was due primarily to methodological flaws which were probably inevitable at the time. The substance of the idea of assessing sensitivity and speed of reaction time has had a continuing, and by no means unproductive, history and will be considered further below. (Sources for this review of history include Jenkins & Paterson, 1961; Carroll, 1982; Brody, 1992; Herrnstein & Murray, 1994.)

Useful assessment procedures came from another source. Alfred Binet, in France, had judged the approach taken in England to be elegant and precise but trivial in focus. The French Ministry of Education, which had begun providing public education for all, needed to identify those children who could not benefit from regular classes. Binet reasoned that tests suitable to such purposes should sample the kinds of skills utilized by children in school. Accordingly, he and his colleagues devised test items that evaluated complex skills such as language comprehension, reasoning, and memory for both verbal and visuospatial information. For example, one kind of item, called picture vocabulary, asked for the name of an object or animal which was displayed on an illustration.

Binet had to find a scale of measurement (the equivalent of inches in length, or pounds of weight) that would permit comparisons. He chose a scaling method propounded by a man named Damaye (Brody, 1992, p. 7) which led to the concept of mental age. This concept rested on data obtained by presenting possible items to large groups of children of different ages and ascertaining which items were passed at each age level. An ideal item had a percent curve of passing in which almost all of the children at a certain age failed, about 50 percent who were a year older passed, and nearly 100 percent passed who were two years older. Using such cross-sectional data, and going through several revisions during the first decade of the twentieth century, he sought and found groups of items which were characteristic of each age of the elementary-school years. Children who answered the questions appropriate for their own age and below would earn mental age scores at, or close to, their age level and would be deemed average or normal. Those who correctly answered questions appropriate for older children would have mental ages higher than their chronological age and were considered advanced. Those who could not answer the questions appropriate for their own age level were thought to be behind, and, if they were far enough behind, to be impaired.

In 1912, a German psychologist named Wilhelm Stern proposed that if the mental age score obtained by testing was divided by the child's chronological age, the resulting number, an intelligence quotient (or IQ) would be generated which would permit comparison of competencies across ages. If the quotient was multiplied by 100, average or normal intelligence becomes 100. The dispersion of scores around this average (the standard deviation) was about 16. Thus more than 99 percent of the population was included in a scale which ranged from 53 to 147.

Scores obtained with Binet's method were found to predict academic success, and the method was soon adopted all over the world. Coming first, Binet-type procedures became a standard by which other procedures were judged. New tests of intelligence proposed by others had to have high correlations with Binet-type tests in order to be considered valid. During the first part of the 20th century, there was a rapid proliferation of test construction for use in many settings other than elementary schools. Tests came to be used for selection rather than for determining the basis for remediation (Brown et al., 1992). They were used in determining assignments in the military, in selecting individuals for admission to higher education, and for admission to training programs for different kinds of jobs. In order to implement massive testing programs, the procedures devised by Binet, which required an individual examiner for each subject and one to two hours' time, were changed to paper-and-pencil procedures which could be administered to large groups of people at once. A technology was developed so that the tests could be scored by machine. Tests such as the Scholastic Aptitude Test (SAT), which began to be used in the 1920s, became a familiar experience to large segments of the population. Throughout, however, an individual examination with a procedure like that of Binet was the gold standard for determining mental retardation.

Note several aspects of the history presented so far. First, Binet's method was not based on any theory of mental function but a reasonable response to a perceived social need. At any point in time, science may not have solutions for social needs although it can provide the means to test the efficacy of any proposed remedy. Second, Binet was primarily interested in identifying the low end of the competency spectrum. His methods were not primarily designed to examine the full range of competency. Third, Binet did not set out to measure intelligence, whatever that may mean. A science of cognition did not exist, and he did not propose even a vague theory regarding mental age. His goal was entirely practical and pragmatic: the selection of those who would or would not benefit from schooling and the determination of what means might help those in difficulty. Fourth, the root of his measurement procedures was a comparison of individual function against a group norm. No independent meter stick or kilogram scale existed or was invented. What was devised was norm-referenced testing.

This accomplishment, however, occurred just as people were exposed to more and more formal education and when communication technologies were developing which provided access to information beyond the confines of the schoolroom. It is now known that the norms of norm-referenced testing are a moving target. Over the past century, as tests have been renormed, or as the same tests have been used to evaluate large populations, it has been found that average children of average parents must know more (technically, answer more and harder questions accurately) in order to attain the same place on the scale of measurement as their parents. Roughly, the magnitude of this change has been about 15 IQ points every 20 years (Flynn, 1987, p. 184).

Later developments; "g" and "s" and the Wechsler scales

The British and Americans adopted Binet's approach, developed statistical methods to study mental competence, and initiated theories attempting to account for the data that emerged. The foremost authority in Great Britain was Charles Spearman, who noted that people who did well on any test of mental competence tended to do well on any other. Stated another way, performances on various kinds of tests evaluating mental skill consistently show positive correlations (i.e., if you do well on one test, you are likely to do well on another). If there were no common underlying skill, the argument goes, there should be no correlations or as many negative correlations as positive, and this simply does not occur. These facts have been verified countless times and require consideration by any theory of intellectual function.

Simple correlational data have been supplanted by complex statistical procedures, which Spearman helped develop, called factor analysis. This method of analysis is purported to reveal the underlying structure of the correlations obtained when a large group of different kinds of tests are administered. The statistical procedure generates a relatively small number of factors on which each of the tests originally given has a "loading." Factors are defined by the kind of the tests which load high on it, and the loading may be considered a kind of correlation between a specific test and a factor. If this seems somewhat circular, it is; but the circularity is mitigated considerably if independent studies arrive at the same factor solution.

Factors emerge from the computational analysis in a sequence, the first of which has highest overall loading; the second, the next highest loading, and so forth. The first factor often has high loadings from a variety of tests while the remaining factors have high loadings from relatively homogeneous groups of tests. For Spearman, and those who have followed his lead, such data are part of the evidential basis for the theoretical concept of "g," or general intelligence. The assumption is that the high loadings of diverse tests on the first factor point to an underlying general ability that is a component of all competencies and which determines where in the range of human talent the person can be ranked.

Spearman elaborated what he meant by "g" by characterizing it as "the ability to educe relations and correlates." The language employed is obscure and was never operationalized, e.g. specified in enough detail so that one would know exactly how to go about measuring it. This is not surprising given the state of cognitive science at the time, but clearly Spearman was groping for a definition about skill in problem solving, in seeing relations in the face of superficially diverse appearances, and in comprehending similarities in the face of apparent differences. There were two further assumptions about "g." One was that measures of intelligence such as Binet invented were the best, though not perfect, measures of "g." The other was that "g" is largely, if not entirely, inherited; "g" is not the only component of human intelligence according to Spearman. The rest is made up of special abilities or talents called "s" which are reflected in the relatively homogeneous factors which emerge after the first factor, and in the varied talents that humans display such as mathematics, music, athletics, etc. Because he postulated both "g" and "s," his theory is sometimes described as a two-factor theory.

Spearman's work occurred during the first third of the 20th century. Subsequently, a modification of the nature of "g" was proposed by R. B. Cattell (1971) and later elaborated by Horn (1978), which looms large in the thinking of many. This idea is that "g" is composed of two subcomponents, fluid ("g_f") and crystallized ("g_c") intelligence. Fluid abilities refer to capacities to acquire knowledge while crystallized abilities refer to knowledge that is already acquired. "g_c" is more resistant to aging and injury than "g_f"; that is, once we acquire knowledge, it tends to endure, but our ability to learn new things decreases with age and injury. Tests of verbal knowledge and problem solving are thought to measure crystallized intelligence while nonverbal, visual–spatial problems are thought to measure fluid intelligence. Cattell and Horn have gone on to elaborate different subdivisions of the two basic types of "g," which to some observers (Jensen, 1998) takes them away from the essence of "g" and closer to Spearman's opponents. There is, however, fair agreement that the critical, heritable component of "g" is the fluid and not the crystallized component.

The major opposition to Spearman's two-factor theory was led by an American psychometric researcher named Thurstone. There was little or no disagreement about the existence of "s"; the dispute was about the existence of "g." Thurstone believed that "g" was essentially a superfluous concept; that instead, there were a relatively few discrete capabilities which he called primary mental abilities. For Thurstone and followers, the challenge for mental measurement was to determine where each person stood with regard to each of the primary abilities, while Spearman and followers sought primarily to evaluate "g" and, after Cattell's contribution ("g_f"), a concept thought of as capability or potential for learning. It should be noted that all these leaders were well aware that they were dealing with hypothetical constructs, useful ideas, and that their measurement procedures were, at best, an approximation regarding what was a kind of abstract essence. Put another way, researchers, no matter what theory they preferred, were well aware that any particular measure of intellect could not assess capability directly. Instead, they knew that what was being measured was the product of some combination of capability, experience, motivation, opportunity, and a host of other variables. If readers know something about genetics, another way of understanding the point is by stating that intelligence tests, whatever their margin for error, were only able to measure phenotypes, the actual realization of the inherited design, not genotypes, the design inherent in one's genetic makeup.

There will be more to consider about this history but one more, important, landmark began just before World War II. Recall Binet's age scale construction procedures and the percent curve of passing. It was possible to find test items that differentiated children at each of the pre-school and early school years and to extend this procedure somewhat to older children, but what items would differentiate 18- and 20-year-olds or 30- and 40-year-olds? There was a strong need to have a gold standard of intellectual assessment for adults and Binet-type procedures simply did not work, although ways of using age scales were contrived. It had even been argued that mental development ceased somewhere around the middle of adolescence simply because items which differentiated ages could no longer be found.

Answers came from many sources but the victor in the competition was the work of David Wechsler, an American psychologist who produced the first widely accepted, individually administered, test of adult intelligence. Earlier, Wechsler had worked with Spearman in London while serving in the army during World War I and had extensive experience with the tests devised to help classify personnel for the military (Edwards, 1974, p. 6). Taking a lead from others who had preceded him, Wechsler understood that the basic operation in intelligence testing was the comparison of an individual against a suitable norm and that there was no need to produce age scales. The work of test construction was in finding good tests and in providing adequate norms, year by year in childhood and at longer intervals thereafter. Adequate norms meant approximating census figures for the population at large in the normative sample for all variables that might be pertinent to intelligence: age, years of education, socioeconomic class, etc. Although the closeness by which population norms were approximated in the normative samples for the first editions of Wechsler's test left much to be desired, subsequent editions have come closer and closer to the ideal.

Wechsler's conception of intelligence was broader than Spearman's two-factor theory because Wechsler thought intelligence encompassed more than cognitive ability. He assumed it involved the personality as a whole and was equally determined by emotion and motivation. Nonetheless, within the cognitive domain, he largely agreed with Spearman. Whereas Binet-type scales mixed up different types of test items (e.g. memory, judgment, reasoning, math) and did not provide separate indices for the different types, Wechsler chose ten to twelve different types of tests, presented many items of increasing difficulty for each, and provided norms for each (Frank, 1983). In addition, the results of the various tests were combined into an overall index of competence which he called a Full Scale IQ, even though his was not an age scale and no quotients with age in the denominator were computed. He chose many procedures from tests developed by the military, largely on the basis of his judgment about the results of prior research. However, he did a curious thing for even a partial advocate of "g." He chose his tests in such a way that about half had a large verbal component (e.g. definitions of words, range of information, memory for strings of heard digits) and their combination yielded an index he called a Verbal IQ. The other half was largely nonverbal in nature (detecting gaps in drawings of objects, animals or scenes, reconstructing designs with tiles containing their components, jigsaw-like puzzles requiring assembly) and their combination yielded an index he called Performance IQ.

The verbal and performance distinction had been the subject of a controversy regarding the best way to test intelligence. Tests of verbal skills came first (remember, intelligence tests had to do with school skills) but the recruitment of soldiers for World War I revealed many American-born citizens to be illiterate. Furthermore, through the first third of the century, the US was a nation of immigrants, many of whom had limited competence in English. Illiteracy, however, was not the same as incompetence. Nonverbal or performance tests provided the means to evaluate the competence of illiterates. Wechsler's resolution of the controversy was to include both, and weigh each type more or less equally. His first test was for adults, but soon, using the same basic format and the same kinds of subtests, there were versions normed for children. All have gone through several revised editions, each time with better norming but with little change in format or type of test.

To summarize, Wechsler tests are composed of ten (in various versions, one or two more) subtests (each of which generates an index of competence) grouped into a verbal scale and a performance scale for which IQ scores are calculated. There is also a Full Scale IQ which combines the results of the verbal and performance scale and is considered to be an excellent measure of "g." Note that the verbal and performance IQs of most individuals are near each other so Full Scale IQs can be plausible. But there are also persons, neither illiterates nor immigrants, who may attain high verbal IQs and low performance IQs or the reverse, whose Full Scale IQs are duly reported and interpreted to reflect their general level of capability when the number is totally meaningless.

Approaches to Mental Retardation

In the chapter on brain damage it was noted that there are many conditions, including severe anoxia; infections such as rubella, cytomegalovirus, and toxoplasmosis; and fetal alcohol syndrome which are associated with mental deficiency. There are also many different kinds of genetic errors which often produce children who are markedly aberrant in appearance and who are mentally deficient. These conditions will be discussed later in the chapter. To start, the discussion will focus on a type of child whose birth was normal and was not preceded by maternal infection, substance abuse, or any known insult to the brain, and where the child's appearance has no stigma. Generally, the first signs which might portend retardation will be lags in attaining the early milestones of development, such as independent head-holding, sitting alone, or walking. After the first year, aspects of language and social development will also be delayed. In many instances, these "signs" may signify nothing more than a somewhat unique pattern of development because catch-up will occur. However, if these lags are not isolated, but are present in most domains of development, and catch-up has not occurred by the time of kindergarten, someone – parents and other family members, teachers, or medical personnel – may suggest that a formal psychological evaluation be done. An intelligence test such as has been described above will then be administered. In addition, parents or caretakers will be interviewed about the child's social adaptation, which will emphasize practical self-help skills e.g. dressing, tying shoes, personal hygiene, and social skills in relating to others. If the results of the two procedures are reasonably consistent and low, a diagnosis of mental retardation will be made.

It is likely that the child described above will be considered to have familial mental retardation. In order to explain this diagnosis, and the thinking that lies behind it,

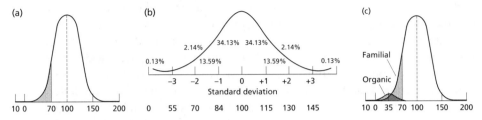

Figure 17.1 Normal or bell-shaped curves. The shaded portion of (a) indicates the frequency of expected mental retardation; (b) also shows the corresponding values of IQ, standard deviation and percent of the population under each portion of a normal curve. Curve 17.1(b) has a wider dispersion than figure 17.1(a). Figure 17.1(c) displays the excess frequency of mentally deficient individuals beyond what is expected from the normal distribution

some familiarity with population genetic theory and with statistical concepts and ideas is required, and they will be reviewed next.

The Polygenic Determination of Intelligence and the Normal, or Bell-shaped Curve

It will be recalled that Binet was successful in finding a method to predict school achievement when he used questions that tapped complex skills, whereas researchers who preceded him failed when they tried to use assessments of highly specific selective skills. Now if one speculates as to the genetic determination of intellectual functions, it is highly likely that a great many genes must be involved because of the complexity of the processes being measured. This would imply that there are so many genes involved in determining intelligence that, if a relatively small number of genes were deficient in some way, it might not matter very much if the rest were all normal. (It shall be apparent in a later part of the chapter that for certain genes this statement is not true.) In any event, practically all scientists who have given the matter any thought agree that intelligence has a very large number of determinants, and insofar as one's genetic makeup is part of those determinants, the number of genes must be very large. Stated another way, intelligence is polygenic (many genes).

When some outcome has a large number of determinants, statisticians agree that the normal curve (also called the bell-shaped curve) provides a good approximation of what the outcomes may be. An illustration of the normal curve can be found in figure 17.1a. The ordinate, which is not shown, should be read as "frequency," and refers to the number of persons who score at each level of what is being measured, in this case IQ. The abscissa presents all the possible scores on an intelligence test. Low scores are on the left and they get larger as one moves to the right. The bell curve is a particular distribution of scores and can be read to mean that the frequency of outcomes will be greatest in the middle of the range of all possible outcomes while both superior and inferior outcomes will be much rarer. The peak of the bell curve is at the value of the average, or the mean, of all the scores represented. At the bottom of figure 17.1a, below the peak of the curve, the number 100 appears, the number which designates average intelligence. A measurement may have a wide or a narrow range of dispersion or variation. Figure 17.1b is also a normal curve but has a wider range of variation than figure 17.1a. There is more information on the latter graph. The standard deviations are shown with positive digits to the right and negative digits to the left along with the corresponding IQ scores on Wechsler's tests. The percentage of the population under each portion of the curve is also shown.

It is possible to compare the scores obtained on different measures by taking into account the degree of dispersion or the standard deviation. If one calculates how far any particular score is from the mean, keeping track of the sign (+for above the mean, −for below) and divides that number by the standard deviation, the result will represent how many standard deviations above or below the mean that score may be. Such a score, called a standard score, is what IQ scores are. Because the original distribution of IQ scores obtained by Terman, the scholar who adopted and extended Binet's procedures in America, approximated a normal curve, and had standard deviations across the various years of about 16 and a mean of about 100, the Wechsler scales' mean scores were set equivalent to 100 and their standard deviation was set to 15 (a somewhat rounder and easier number to track than 16). Note two further features of figure 17.1b. Six standard deviations, from 3 below to 3 above the mean, includes 99.72 percent of the entire population. An IQ of 70, which is 2 standard deviations below the mean, is generally accepted as a cutoff score for mental deficiency.

When data from measures of intelligence are obtained from large populations, the resulting frequency distributions (tables or graphs of the number of people at each different score) have approximated a bell-shaped curve except in one aspect (Zigler & Hodapp, 1986). The low end of the curve has had an excessively high number of subjects, and instead of tapering to infinity has produced an unseemly bump in the distribution (figure 17.1c). The explanation for this departure from normality in the distribution of measured intelligence has been that the intellectually deficient population is made up of two groups. One is assumed to be determined by the same factors that influence those who fell in rest of the normal curve but just ended up at the low end. The other is a group called "organic," where some known factor has disrupted the developmental process. This "organic" group can be subdivided into three groups. The first is made up of individuals who have lived in highly deprived environments and have received inadequate stimulation. The second consists of those who have had their intelligence destroyed early on by pathological processes. The third is composed of those whose chromosomes and genes, as determined at the moment of conception, contained inherent flaws which led to mental deficiency. From a neuropsychological perspective, these groups are very different, but they have often been mixed indiscriminately in research on mental deficiency where individuals have been classified solely on the basis of their level of intelligence. This practice is now changing (Hodapp & Zigler, 1997). Each of the four groups will be considered separately next.

Familial mental retardation

Familial mental retardation is said to occur when a child tests low on intelligence and there is no evidence of either brain-destroying events such as anoxia or infection, or of gene–chromosome aberrations. The latter criterion is somewhat problematic in that there is no assured way of knowing that the gene–chromosome complement is normal, since new abnormalities are being discovered all the time. If the child's appearance is not dysmorphic (structurally distorted), chances are increased that such abnormalities are not present but, in truth, the physical features of children with fetal alcohol syndrome, discussed previously, or of fragile-X syndrome, to be presented below, which can now be identified with fair consistency, were not previously noted, and those children were often grouped with the familials. The classification of familial mental retardation is more assured if the child's parents score in the low end of the intelligence distribution, whether they are low enough to meet the criteria for retardation or not. One problem here is that there are also children in this group who Zigler and Hodapp (1986) call polygenic isolates, intellectually deficient offspring of parents with normal or even superior intelligence. The idea is that, on rare occasions, bright parents beget a child whose intellect, by chance, is compromised. If the genes that determine mental competence are thought of as so many dice, then in their case, a lot of 1's showed up. In the population this rare occurrence will be offset by its opposite, when intellectually compromised parents conceive a bright child.

This mode of explanation comes from the field of behavior genetics which examines genetic influences on behavior in populations, not individuals (Willerman, 1979; Thompson, 1997; Jensen, 1998). Genetic influence has been studied by comparing the behavioral similarities of identical twins, who possess the same genes, with individuals of varying degrees of kinship. Also studied is the influence of different kinds of environments; for example, when identical twins are adopted by differing families. Within this framework, studies have been conducted on the relationship between parental and offspring intelligence. The general finding is that the expected IQ of children is midway between that of their parents. Complicating this finding is regression to the mean, which refers to a tendency for offspring to have talents that are closer to the average for the population. Thus, children whose parents' IQs are on the low side will tend to be brighter than their parents, and the reverse is true for children of parents with higher IQs.

All this is based on the assumption of random mating; that it is as likely for any male to have children with one female as with any other, but this assumption is generally not true. Humans engage in assortative mating, which means that people from similar circumstances are far more likely to mate than persons from dissimilar circumstances. Thus, individuals of low intelligence are much more likely to mate with each other than with much brighter individuals, and the familial retarded group will be composed mostly of the offspring of low-intelligence parents and of a few polygenic isolates.

Persons with familial mental retardation generally fall in the mild retardation category. That is, they generally score on IQ tests in the top end of the retarded range, between 50–55 and 70. They constitute the largest portion of the retarded population. IQ scores between 35–40 and 50–55 are termed moderately retarded, and those between 20–25 and 35–40 as severely retarded (American Psychiatric Association, 1994). Another classification system refers roughly to the same ranges of competence in more functionally descriptive terms. These are the educable mentally retarded, individuals who can learn to read and write, and perhaps attain a level equivalent to a 4th to 6th grade education, but who require a far longer time to reach that level, and who, when mature, may be employed and attain quasi- or full independence; the trainable mentally retarded, who can learn self-help skills such as those required for personal hygiene and dressing, some language and elementary social amenities, and who when mature will require care and supervision; and the untrainable, who will essentially require nursing care all their lives. These classifications have been applied to the retarded population irrespective of etiology; as noted, the familial group generally can be found at the top of the range. Those who have suffered competency-destroying and genetic conditions tend to be found in the lower portions of the range, but of course there is a continuum of disability, and some show up in the mild range. Familial mental retardation and mild mental retardation are not synonymous.

In a theory of familial retardation, one consistent with random, throw-of-the-dice genetic determination of retardation, the central emphasis is on lag. The essence of lag is that the sequence of developmental steps is the same, but that the pace is slower than that found in typical children. In addition, retarded children will not attain the complexity and sophistication that normal children will. Opposing lag theory is defect theory, which postulates that some flaw or abnormality is interfering with the attainment of normal competence. This theory admits the possibility of nongenetic determination of cases that appear to be familial, although the etiology may also be of random genetic origin. Incidentally, the term, retardation, clearly fits a condition of lagging development but may not be appropriate if a defect is present.

Evidence testing lag versus defect theories comes from research conducted with mental age (MA) controlled designs. (Note that Binet's MA concept has had a continuing life in mental retardation research.) When this design is followed, retarded children at a specified level of competence are compared with normal children of the same MA (who will inevitably be much younger than the retarded children) and with normal children of the same chronological age (CA) on some behavior or cognitive function. The normal children of the same CA will exceed the scores obtained by the retarded children, thus verifying that the retarded children are behind. The logic of lag theory is that the retarded children should function at the same level as the much younger children with the same MA. If they do, then lag theory is supported; if they do worse, lag theory is disconfirmed.

The evidence for lag theory, as reviewed by Zigler and Hodapp (1986) and others, is sometimes confirmatory, sometimes not. One of the reasons for this may be that the retarded groups that have been studied may not have been composed solely of familials since, as noted, more specific conditions are being discovered all the time. For example, there is no way of knowing how many children with fragile-X syndrome, to be discussed below, were considered familials before the genetic basis of that disorder was known.

Whatever the detailed merits of the familial hypothesis may be, and there will be further consideration of this question below, the conceptualization of developmental lag and the increasing influence of behavior modification, mentioned in chapter 15, has had an enormous influence on the care and education of those with mental retardation. From the mid-twentieth century back for hundreds of years, retarded persons were commonly treated, for the most part, as a group apart, to be segregated as much as possible from the mainstream of society. Even when educational leaders and humanists sought to stimulate and train retarded children so as to maximally realize their potential, they built residential schools or training centers which were remote from the centers of population (Zigler & Hodapp, 1986). Common professional advice given to parents of retarded children was to have them institutionalized as soon as possible. Often the advice was to sever all relations with the child so that the child would experience no conflict of loyalty, and the parents would not be burdened with an impossible task. Furthermore, retarded individuals were often portrayed in the media and in political debate as violent, immoral, and dangerous to society, and as a potential source of corruption. By contrast, with the developmental perspective (Clarke & Clarke, 1985) and behavior modification (Kiernan, 1985), the retarded child was seen as existing within the range of human variability and as being capable of learning.

Today, all but the most impaired persons with retardation live with their families when young, and are educated at schools in their community. In the United States and many other Western countries, there are opportunities for early detection and early intervention with remedial programs beginning long before the child reaches school age. Large, state-run residential institutions for the retarded have largely been closed. Education is often geared toward preparing the child to be independent when grown, with an emphasis on learning job, social, and practical skills (Whelan, 1985). Clarke and Clarke (1985) point out that, even before these institutional changes had occurred, mildly retarded persons often found ways to become independent, finding work and sometimes establishing families of their own after their school days were over. Such findings were verified in a study (Ross et al., 1985) that followed the lives of persons diagnosed as mentally retarded in the late 1920s who were enrolled in special-education classes in San Francisco. Successful outcome in these mildly retarded persons was related to the level of support provided by their families, education opportunity, job opportunity as determined by economic conditions, and whether they married a supportive spouse. Much of the change in educational programs has been designed to foster independence as much as possible early on, and to avoid repeated frustration and failure. In this regard, there is increased emphasis on evaluating adaptive skills and in utilizing those data in assessment, diagnosis, and educational planning, and to give a somewhat less central role to traditional IQ measures. Accompanying these trends is research on family coping skills (Stoneman, 1997) and in finding ways to assist families. Self-help groups make an important, often the most important, contribution. There are also new efforts to find ways to teach the intellectually compromised

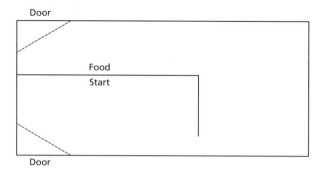

Figure 17.2   Floor plan of the experiment by Thompson and Heron (1954) with dogs

to improve their mental capabilities in fundamental ways, and these are reviewed later in the chapter.

Mental retardation due to environmental deprivation

Before beginning this section, it is worthwhile to note again that there are no means available to assess capability or intellectual potential, no matter how the results may be termed. We assess skill manifested at the time of the examination and infer capability. In this section, evidence will be reviewed about the impact of three broadly construed sets of environmental variables on measured intelligence. It is understood that, although much of the available data refers to changes in persons in the middle range of normal intelligence, an adverse effect of the environment may move a child already adversely affected for other reasons from the lower range of normal intelligence into the retarded range. If the circumstances are particularly adverse, an even greater drop may occur and middle-range or even high-level children may function at a retarded level. The three sets of environmental conditions are prolonged sensory and psychosocial deprivation, psychosocial disadvantage, and acute and chronic malnutrition.

Prolonged sensory and psychosocial deprivation

In 1954, Thompson and Heron described a series of experiments in which adult dogs reared as pets were compared with dogs reared in laboratory cages – the latter a very deprived psychosocial environment. All the experiments had similar results, but only one will be presented here. Figure 17.2 illustrates the setting of the experiment. A hungry dog is brought in on a leash and placed at the start position. Immediately in front, and also to the right, there is a barrier made up of wire mesh that is too high for the dog to jump over but does not block vision or smell. An assistant brings in a piece of meat, and places it directly in front of the dog, but on the other side of the barrier, and leaves the room. As soon as it is clear that the dog sees the food, the leash is removed and a stopwatch is started, which is stopped when the dog reaches the food. Over five trials the cage-reared dogs required an average of 72.1 seconds to get to the food while the pet-reared dogs required an average of only 29.4 seconds. The cage-reared dogs kept trying to access the food directly through the mesh and took much longer before turning their backs to it in order to move around the barrier. In some sense their behavior was "stupid." If, in a variant of the experiment, they were detained in front of the meat for more than 25 seconds and then released, the cage-reared dogs could not find their way around the barrier at all, and then their behavior became very stupid. The experiment demonstrated that some aspects of intelligent behavior were influenced by the richness of the animal's early experience.

It should come then as no surprise to learn that when children who have been reared under grossly deprived circumstances are evaluated on intelligence tests, they are found to lag. Much of the early evidence in support of this conclusion was reviewed by Hunt (1961). Data on humans came from research on children reared in orphanages in which they were provided with adequate nutrition and medical care but little of the kind of stimulation an infant or young child might receive from a parent or an involved caretaker. If the children are tested while still living under such conditions, there is little doubt that their scores are depressed and can extend far into the retarded range. Skuse (1984) reviewed published case studies of nine children, two pairs of which were twins, who had been grossly deprived and abused, and then, when discovered, were removed to far more favorable circumstances. These children presented with a characteristic picture of motor retardation, absent or rudimentary language, retarded perceptuomotor skills, very limited emotional expression, and social withdrawal. Altogether, these features added up to a diagnosis of profound retardation and autism. With time and care, a number of the children improved to apparent normality and they displayed a very rapid rate of improvement once conditions changed. For those who did not, there was generally evidence of biological compromise and/or of severe nutritional deprivation as well. When improvement occurred, the main agent of change was judged to be the quality of the care the children received once they were removed from the depriving environment.

Evidence has begun to emerge about a recent social experiment with an apparently tragic outcome. As a result of the population-increasing policies of Nicolae Ceausescu, citizens of Romania, between 1970 and 1990, were encouraged to have large families, even if they lacked resources to care for the children, because they would be welcomed in state-run orphanages. Although the orphanages provided mostly adequate nutrition and medical care, they increasingly lacked the resources to provide adequate stimulation and individual attention. Initial evidence (Kaler & Freeman, 1994; Carlson & Earls, 1997) suggest serious cognitive and social retardation, and neuroendocrine changes in the stress response system. Some of these children have been adopted by families in other countries and reports in the media indicate that many show problems in cognitive functions and socialization and that their brains, as viewed by scanning techniques, are aberrant.

Clarke (1985) reviewed the impact of environmental deprivation. One question that arises is whether a continuum of deprivation has a continuum of effects or whether there is a threshold of environmental adequacy which, if attained, will support normal development. She noted a paper by Jensen (1977) the foremost proponent of "g" and a researcher on intelligence not known for his emphasis on environmental factors, which deals with a repeated finding in the literature in which children coming from deprived environments peak early, about the age of five or six, and then decline in IQ at about the rate of 1.4 points a year. This evidence suggests that the decline must reflect environmental factors since endowment does not change and there is evidence that children from adequate environments do not decline. Furthermore, these findings suggest a continuum of effect. If so, some children scoring in the deficient range might have done better under more favorable circumstances. This takes the discussion to the effects of less than extreme deprivation.

Mental retardation due to psychosocial disadvantage

Before considering psychosocial disadvantage directly, a caveat of sorts is needed which draws attention to the perspective of the observer. Some children may lack the skills measured by intelligence tests not because they lack the resources to learn those skills but because they are learning different skills that are not assessed by the tests. Such a situation, when it occurs, takes place when observers evaluate the intellects of individuals in unfamiliar societies; in recent immigrants from other cultures; in castes within some societies that are precluded from access to mainstream socialization and education; or in groups who deliberately isolate themselves for religious or ideological reasons from mainstream influences. In order to deal with such variations, so-called culture-free tests were devised. How well they perform this function is a matter of debate, but it would behoove anyone trying to ascertain the intelligence of a person from such a "different" background to go beyond standard testing in arriving at a decision.

There are perhaps two main groups of people who are described as socially disadvantaged in the United States. One lives in the midst of, or near, those who are more advantaged, for the most part share the same culture and the same aspirations, and nonetheless participate in a culture apart, the culture of poverty. Much has been written about families caught up in a chronic cycle of poverty. The offspring of such families are often at the low end of a continuum of intelligence. One view is that their poverty status is largely determined by limited competence and that this is due primarily to their genetic makeup (Herrnstein & Murray, 1994; Jensen, 1998). Another view points to what amounts to a conspiracy of deprivation. For example, Kozol (1992) presents much hard data on how public school systems do not distribute their resources equally to middle-class and poor neighborhood schools, and moving descriptions of how innovative educational modifications pioneered by creative educators are often, somehow, sabotaged. The polarities of this argument will be discussed further at the end of this chapter.

The second group of socially disadvantaged may not exist any more, but a half-century ago they still did. These are small, rural, impoverished communities that have been physically isolated from mainstream societies and have not shared mainstream culture very much. Such societies have disappeared largely because electricity is now available just about everywhere, and with it comes radio, television, and other means of communication that override isolation-creating barriers. Mountains seem to have been conducive to the creation of such communities, and in the United States they could be found in the Appalachians, and in Canada, in the Cape Breton Highlands of northern Nova Scotia. Edgerton (1979), discussing the work of Gazaway, describes a particular community in the Appalachians in which most individuals are illiterate, cannot tell time or do elementary calculations, nutrition is poor, disease is endemic, sanitary facilities are non-existent, family structure is very diffuse, and incest and inbreeding common. The children are described as being appallingly limited in problem-solving skills, certainly at a verbal level but also at a practical level. Searching for evidence of intelligence within the context of the culture in that specific setting, about the only thing that could be reported was a certain "wiliness" or cleverness in dealing with the welfare authorities.

If intelligence can be lowered by psychosocial disadvantage, then one might imagine that it could be improved by intervention programs designed to ameliorate the disadvantage. It has turned out that this is not easy to accomplish. The evidence is reviewed in many places (cf. Odom & Kaiser, 1997; Jensen, 1998), and some success has been achieved. There are several hard-won lessons coming from this experience. One is that intervention must begin early and be longitudinally continuous. The positive influences of two years in an enriched nursery school program mostly disappear if the child returns to conditions of poverty. Another is that programs that work solely with the child and do not enlist parental support are likely not to accomplish very much. A related third lesson is that, to be successful, intervention must teach those responsible for raising the children – parents, teachers, and caretakers – how to behave in a manner that fosters cognitive development. Again, there will be more about this at the end of the chapter. Jensen (1998, p. 344) judges the Abecedarian Early Intervention Project (Ramey, 1994), which began in infancy and continued to adolescence, to be among the most successful, and credits it with improving IQ a third of a standard deviation or about 5 points.

Malnutrition and mental competence

Nutrition is a highly complex subject. For present purposes, requirements can be simplified into a small number of categories; these are carbohydrates, fats, proteins, and other. "Other" is important because it includes vitamins, minerals, and other substances critical to nutritional well-being. Carbohydrates and fats (lipids) are both sources of energy. Lipids are also specially important because they constitute much of the cell wall of neurons and myelin and are a solvent for a number of vitamins. (Recall that a high lipid diet has been found to be effective in arresting some forms of intractable seizures in juveniles.) Proteins and minerals are construction materials for body tissue. Vitamins and minerals are both catalysts and major functional components of the biochemistry and physiology of life.

As a general rule, short bouts (days) of malnutrition and starvation, if not recurrent, are of little significance for biological normality. There are mechanisms within the body that deal adequately with such stress without major detriment to any major organ system. Chronic malnutrition is another matter. When generalized, prolonged, and severe it can lead to death. Short of that, protein–energy malnutrition can occur (Berkow, 1992, p. 956). There are two major subtypes. One is kwashiorkor, which generally appears between the first and third years and is primarily a consequence of deficiencies in protein intake when there is adequate carbohydrate intake. The children become apathetic, sleepy and nonreactive to stimulation but also tearful and irritable and, as a result of edema, show a characteristic bloating of their bellies. They also have sparse, depigmented hair. The other is marasmus which typically occurs during the first year of life and is sometimes termed failure to thrive. This is primarily a disorder of insufficient sources of energy, carbohydrates, and fats, and is marked by failure to grow, apathy, and irritability. Malnutrition can also be much more selective. Failure to obtain adequate amounts of vitamin C will produce a condition known as scurvy, marked by lassitude, weakness, irritability, weight loss, joint and muscle pains, and a tendency to hemorrhage. Failure to obtain adequate amounts of the mineral iodine, especially during gestation, affects thyroid function and can cause a type of severe mental deficiency called cretinism (Berkow, 1992, p. 976). Lower levels (by six to eight IQ points) of intellectual function in those born prematurely may be due to inadequate triiodothyronine, a component of thyroid hormone, although the reasons for the deficiency are not known (Lucas, Morley, & Fewtrell, 1996). Growing up poor in a severely iodine-deficient area of India, compared to growing up poor in a mildly deficient area, exacts a significant toll on rate of learning and achievement motivation (Tiwari et al., 1996).

Research regarding the effects of malnutrition on cognitive function has been reviewed extensively (cf. Edgerton, 1979; Clarke, 1985; Brody, 1992; Spreen, Risser, & Edgell, 1995; Eysenck & Schoenthaler, 1997; Jensen, 1998). Studies have ranged from those which inferred poorer chronic nutrition by examining children coming from poor families to studies, years later, of the consequence of having had kwashiorkor or marasmus. Not surprisingly, these studies never find any advantage associated with malnutrition but often find serious compromise of cognitive function and lowered IQs. Sometimes no disadvantage is found, and one oft-cited study of this sort is the evaluation, years later, of Dutch military draftees who were born in the midst of an intense famine in the Netherlands at the end of World War II. The results of these soldiers' intelligence test scores were compared with scores of soldiers born before and after the famine, and no difference in intelligence was found (Stein et al., 1972). Herrnstein and Murray (1994, p. 391) point out that the famine was only three months in duration, which may not have been long enough to produce significant effects. That some studies find no effects of malnutrition, and that some that do, that some may have flaws in their design or limitations in their generalizability, does not mean that it should be concluded that the impact of hunger and malnutrition on cognition is trivial. This section will conclude with a description of two well-designed nutrition studies which perhaps go beyond the state of affairs where psychological science sets about to prove what everybody already knows.

In the first of these studies, Lucas et al. (1992) examined, at the age 7.5–8, a group of 300 (of an original 313) children who were born weighing under 1,850 grams. This study evaluated the effects on later cognitive status of breast milk versus baby formula during infancy in premature children. The decision to breastfeed was the mother's. Since there is a tendency for more educated women and those from higher socioeconomic circumstances to choose breastfeeding, there was a possibility that any advantage attained by the breastfed infants might have been due to socioeconomic level and all the many benefits that come with greater advantage, so the researchers went to considerable trouble to determine whether factors other than type of milk during infancy could account for the findings. Note that the study was concerned with variables in two very different domains: nutrition in infancy and IQ scores during the early years of schooling. The authors found about a ten-point advantage for the breastfed children which, when other factors were taken into account, reduced to about eight points or about one-half standard deviation. The increase was found in both verbal and nonverbal intelligence.

In a subanalysis, the results for children whose mothers wanted to nurse their babies, but found that they could not, were examined. Such a group constitutes a kind of control for mothering inclinations. If their children turned out to be like the breastfed children, that would be evidence that it was not so much the nutrition but the caregiving attitude that made the difference; but if they were like the formula-fed children, the nutrition itself would be implicated as the active agent. It turned out that the children whose mothers intended to but could not breast feed had IQs like the formula-fed children, so there was further support that nutrition was the factor that made the difference. The authors cautioned that the positive effects of breastfeeding on intellect were less in full-term babies. A later study, however, did find a 5–6 IQ point advantage if the full-terms were breastfed for more than 12 weeks (Greene et al., 1995).

The second study was truly an experiment since the researchers could control who got the active agent and have it assigned to subjects randomly. Its premise is even more daring than the Lucas et al. study described above, because it inquired as to whether vitamin–mineral supplements given over a period of only 13 weeks might influence IQ scores in 8th and 10th grade California adolescents who were not known to be nutritionally deficient or otherwise compromised. Schoenthaler et al. (1991) randomly assigned 615 participants to one of four conditions: a placebo control condition and three vitamin–mineral supplement conditions that differed in the amount of supplement. One group was provided with the government-determined recommended daily allowance, another was at 50 percent of that, and the third was at 200 percent. Pills were administered in the school with double doses on Friday and Monday to make up for weekend gaps, and neither the teacher or the child had any idea as to which group they were in. Participating students were administered Wechsler-type intelligence tests before and after the 13 weeks. On Verbal IQ, all four groups showed just the expected gain that would occur as a result of the practice effect that comes from repeating the tests, especially at so short an interval. On Performance IQ, however, the group getting the supplements at 100 percent gained 3.7 points more than the other groups, a significant finding.

In a subset of students, blood studies were done to determine pre- and post-nutritional levels. It was understood that many subjects probably had no deficiency and that these participants were diluting the effect of those who needed the extra nutrition. It was found that, among those who were malnourished, the 100 percent supplement group increased their IQs over controls by 8.1 points and the 200 percent group by 5.1 points and that these gains were not significantly different. This represents an improvement in IQ of about 1/3 to 1/2 standard deviation in three months. Interestingly, the types of test that were responsive to nutritional supplements were the same types that Flynn (1987) found to increase by a standard deviation every 20 years. These are also the type of test that Cattell (1971) suggested measured fluid intelligence.

If the middle ranges of IQ in non-malnourished adolescents can be improved by as much as 3 or 4 points in 13 weeks with vitamin–mineral pills, then either the measuring instrument is flawed or a powerful intervention has been demonstrated. This raises a serious question as to what proportion of children diagnosed as mentally retarded have lacked such components of fully adequate nutrition and what might have happened had they had that benefit. In truth, whatever the flaws of intelligence tests may be, there are many studies which indicate that improving IQ is not easily accomplished. Thus, in a field where interventions are hard to come by, and tend to be expensive, there may be some relatively simple, inexpensive things that can be done that are readily available.

Mental deficiency associated with chromosomal and genetic flaws

During the second half of the twentieth century, over 500 different conditions have been discovered in which genetic flaws are associated with mental deficiency. As recalled from the discussion in chapter 4, one's genetic makeup or genotype is determined at the time of conception and should be thought of as a construction plan. In familial mental deficiency, genetic transmission is thought to be normal even if the product or phenotype is not. Recall that when any aspect of behavior is measured, what is being assessed is the phenotype. In the conditions to be discussed next, errors have occurred in the way in which the egg, the sperm, or both have been constructed or in the way they have come together at the moment of conception. There are two kinds of errors. In genetic errors, one or only a few of the specific genes that determine individual characteristics, such as skin pigment or a particular enzyme, are missing or aberrant. It is estimated that there are between 50,000 and 100,000 human genes, and many different ones contribute to the nervous system structures that make behavior possible. Genes are arranged on strands of material called chromosomes which normally occur in 23 pairs in humans, and their formation and organization is also subject to error. Chromosomal errors will inevitably involve large numbers of genes and hence many traits. In the next two sections of this chapter these two types of genetic disorder will be discussed, and examples of each type of mental retardation will be presented.

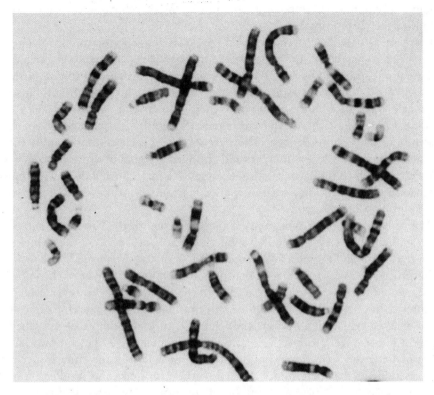

Figure 17.3   The appearance of chromosomes when viewed through a microscope

Chromosomal disorders

Background information.   In the nineteenth century, after improved technology of the microscope permitted increased magnification, strands of material were observed in the nucleus of cells which stained brightly when dyes were applied. The term chromosome, which means colored body, was given to these structures (Gardner & Sutherland, 1996). It was understood that these strands of materials had some important role in heredity, but its full import was not made clear until a technique for examining them became available in 1956. Shortly thereafter, Lejeune discovered the extra chromosome in Down syndrome (to be discussed below), and with that finding, and much other research, the story of the structure and function of chromosomes has emerged. An illustration of how human chromosomes appear under the microscope can be seen in figure 17.3. This material is taken from lymphocytes, an easily accessible blood cell, but cells from other tissues, skin, bone marrow, or amniotic fluid can be used. Cells chosen for study are undergoing division, a process called mitosis, splitting in two, the only time the chromosomes line up and are readily distinguishable. Notice that the strands are banded. These bands can be seen when the material is stained. The pattern of banding helps to identify each chromosome.

Banding techniques are improving, permitting more refined specification of the regions of the chromosome.

There are actually 46 chromosomes in the illustration and they are made up of 23 pairs. In 22 pairs, called autosomes, each member of a pair is of comparable size, configuration, and band pattern. The other pair, called sex chromosomes, varies as a function of the sex of a person, females having two comparable X chromosomes, while males have an X chromosome from their mothers and a much smaller Y chromosome from their fathers. The chromosome material is separated so as not to overlap, and then photographed. The photograph of each chromosome is cut out and matched up with its counterpart and arranged roughly in order of size, as seen in figure 17.4 which displays the chromosomes of a male. Such a display permits the designation of the individual's karyotype, i.e. a summary of the number and nature of the chromosomes present.

One of each pair of chromosomes comes from one of the parents of the person being studied. The way this comes about is a result of a process called meiosis in which the sperm and the ovum (together called gametes) are formed. The first stage of this process in males is similar to that of mitosis in that each pair of chromosomes duplicates and separates into identical cells. In the second stage, however, each of the daughter cells splits so that only half the chromosomes, one from each pair, separates into individual cells which become the sperm. Thus each primordial cell scheduled to produce sperm will produce four sperm – two containing X the chromosome and two containing the Y chromosome. As a result, it is which of the father's sperm that fertilizes the egg that determines the sex of the offspring. The production of the ovum is similar to that of the sperm, but at each of the two stages of cell division, only one cell survives to go on and become an egg. The other genetic material forms cells called polar bodies which are discarded. Figure 17.5 shows the process of meiosis for one pair of chromosomes. The reader must imagine this process going on simultaneously for 23 pairs (Willerman, 1979, p. 51; Evans & Hamerton, 1985, p. 214; Gardner & Sutherland, 1996, p. 21).

There are two major types of chromosomal errors: additions or subtractions of entire chromosomes called aneuploidy, and abnormalities in parts of the chromosome structure called partial aneuploidy (Evans & Hamerton, 1985). Both types of abnormality are generally initiated when something goes wrong during the process of meiosis and gamete formation. In aneuploidy, there may be one or more extra chromosomes, or one of a chromosome pair may be missing in the nucleus of the fertilized egg. This may occur for autosomal pairs or for the sex chromosome pair, and may be due to a failure of the chromosomal pair to split into two daughter cells during meiosis. The other type of error may occur because of breakage of the chromosome strand in which some material is lost, relocates to another chromosome, or reattaches to the chromosome from which it broke off. Most such chromosomal abnormalities are lethal and are responsible for a large proportion of spontaneous abortions. However, some do survive and they generally display both physiognomic and mental abnormalities. Rarely, for reasons largely unknown, the chromosomes will not be identical in every cell. This condition is known as a mosaic, and when the mixture includes normal cells, the symptoms may be less severe.

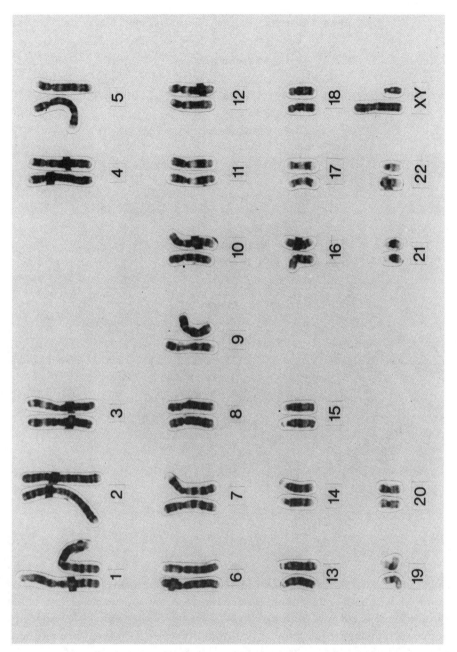

Figure 17.4 Chromosomes arranged in formal karyotype

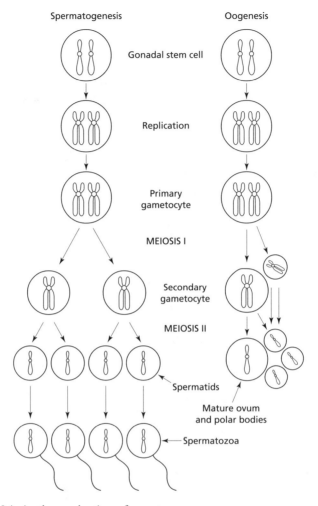

Figure 17.5 Meiosis: the production of gametes

When cytogeneticists, those who study the cellular mechanisms of inheritance, communicate with each other, they use descriptive codes and nomenclature about the chromosomal makeup of an organism (Gardner & Sutherland, 1996, Appendix B). In one such code, the full number of chromosomes is given first, then a comma and a designation of the sex chromosomes. Thus a normal male is a 46,XY and a normal female 46,XX. A condition called Turner syndrome, in which there is only one X chromosome, is 45,X or 45,X0. Further complications are noted by adding a comma followed by descriptive notation. For example, Down syndrome is a condition in which an extra chromosome 21 is present (trisomy) making for a total of 47 chromosomes. This is designated for a male as 47,XY,+21. A small proportion of Down syndrome cases are mosaics and have a mixture of cells with normal and abnormal chromosome composition. A female with this condition would be designated as 47,XX,+21/46,XX. If one of the pair of chromosome 21 was missing in a male, it would be coded as 45,XY,–21.

When breaks and translocations occur, the locations on the chromosome need to specified. To understand the way this is done requires more consideration of the structure of the chromosome and its bands. There are two obvious features of each chromosome that provide references for mapping its structure. The first is that each has a constricted area called a centromere. The center of the centromere is taken as a point of origin for delineating adjacent areas. The second is that the centromere divides the chromosome unevenly into long and short arms. The short arm is designated "p" (petit, French for small) and the long arm "q" (simply the next letter of the alphabet). Figure 17.6 shows a fairly detailed banding of chromosomes 13–22 and X and Y. Note the centromeres and areas p and q on each chromosome. Also note that there are numbers increasing in each direction from the centromere. The first digit may range from 1 to 4 depending on the size of the chromosome (chromosome 1 is the longest) and designates regions of the chromosome at increasing distance from the centromere in both directions. The second, which may range from 1 to 8, designates a band within a region. There follows a dot and then up to two more digits which designate sub-bands within bands. The number plus "p" or "q" specifies location, and a variety of abbreviations specify abnormality. Thus 46,XX,del(18)(q12) specifies a deletion on the long arm of chromosome 18 beginning in the first region, second band. As methods of banding become more refined, increasing specification of locus becomes possible. A full description can be found in ISCN (1995).

Down syndrome – autosomal trisomy. "Trisomy is the most commonly identified chromosome abnormality in humans, occurring in at least 4% of all clinically recognized pregnancies" (Hassold, Sherman, & Hunt, 1995, p. 1). Most trisomies spontaneously abort, and when miscarriages occur, there is evidence of trisomy at least 25 percent of the time. The most common viable manifestation of trisomy occurs when there is an extra chromosome 21, which constitutes the chromosomal pathology of 94 percent of the individuals with Down syndrome, a condition first clearly described by Langdon Down in 1866. Other individuals with this syndrome will have structural realignments or a mosaic condition involving chromosome 21. The discussion here will concern only trisomy 21 conditions where about 95 percent receive the extra chromosome from their mothers and 5 percent from their fathers (Wisnieweski, Kida, & Brown, 1996). In mothers, the error most often occurs in the first stage of meiosis, and its incidence is associated with maternal age, rising from 1/1,000 at age 30 to 1/80 at age 40, to 1/18 at age 45 (Evans & Hamerton, 1985). Down syndrome children have a characteristic appearance that is generally easily recognized, sometimes even at birth. Figure 17.7 presents photographs of the same female aged 4 and 16 months.

Commonly seen features include a relatively small, short head, short stature, flat nasal bridge, epicanthic folds (a vertical fold of skin extending from each side of the nose toward and over the corner of each eye), Brushfield spots (crescent-shaped white

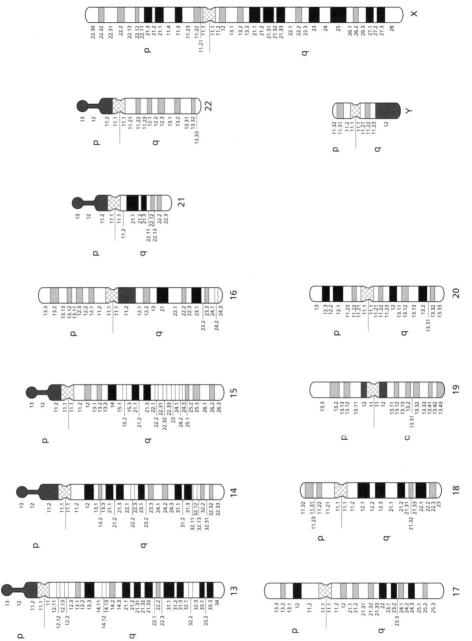

Figure 17.6 Illustration of banding and regional naming of chromosomes 13–22 and X and Y

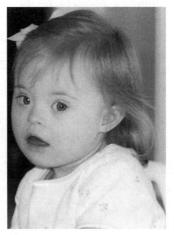

a *b*

Figure 17.7 Down syndrome girl aged 4 months and 16 months

spots in the periphery of the iris), a fissured tongue, small fingers, palms with a single transverse crease, and wide-spaced first and second toes. Internally, there are often cardiovascular anomalies, small intestine malformations, and susceptibility to infections and leukemia, a cancer of the blood. Down syndrome individuals age early, and by age 40 the majority show the same neuropathological signs found in the brains of individuals with Alzheimer's disease, a disorder of early senility that occurs in normal individuals (Evans & Hamerton, 1985). Actual decline in mental function usually appears later than the neuropathological signs.

There have been and continue to be immense changes in the treatment and care of persons with Down syndrome. In 1929, life expectancy was only nine years, a figure which increased only to 12 years by 1947. By 1970 life expectancy was over 50 years, and in the 1990s it is not uncommon for persons to live into the seventh or even the eighth decade (Carr, 1994; Rasore-Quartino & Cominetti, 1995). These changes can be attributed to medical advances in the treatment of infection and in corrective surgery, but also to changes in social attitudes about the eligibility of all individuals for such services. Paralleling changes in the medical domain have been changes in child rearing and education. Whereas most Down syndrome children were previously institutionalized, the vast majority are now reared at home. Previously, there was a commonly held assumption that there was no point in educating persons with a short lifespan or with different learning skills, while the current attitude is that all are entitled to treatment and to stimulation that will help them maximize their potential. Children with Down syndrome living at home are enrolled early in preschool intensive stimulation programs that work on motor functions, language, and early concept formation (Lauras et al., 1995). These changes did not come about as a result of some mysterious enlightenment that transformed attitudes in legislatures and school boards. Most changes occurred as a result of untiring struggle and lobbying on the part of families and some professionals to gain access to care and stimulation for their children, and the subsequent demonstration of the cost-effectiveness of such procedures.

It is difficult to know how to present information about the mental capabilities and limitations of persons with Down syndrome because the consequences of all these changes, with more to come, are not yet known. The trend in psychological changes, although less dramatic than that of the lifespan, has also been one of improvement. What will be presented consequently must be understood to be prefaced with some phrase such as "on the basis of current practice and knowledge."

Relatively few studies have been done on prenatal brain development in Down syndrome, but the evidence available indicates that differences from typical children are relatively subtle and not apparent until the second half of fetal development. Differences include decreased neural and synaptic densities in occipital, frontal, and temporal areas (Wisniewski, Kida, & Brown, 1996). The structure of the neurons appears to be normal. More evidence is available postnatally. Larger differences are found, including lower overall brain weight and size, narrowed superior temporal gyrus, smaller cerebellum, smaller brainstem, lower density of neurons in the hypothalamus and consequent reduction in hormone secretion, and delays in myelination. Not every person with Down syndrome has every abnormality. Percentages range from 25 percent for myelination delays, to 33 percent for temporal gyrus size inferiority, to 80 percent for lower brain weight (Nadel, 1996; Wisniewski, Kida, & Brown, 1996). As mentioned, the brains of Down syndrome individuals, beginning in the second decade of life, often show the pathologic signs characteristic of Alzheimer's disease. These are deposits of materials called plaques and neurofibrillary tangles, which are what they sound like – clumps of disorganized neural fibers. Incidentally, although about 3 percent of Alzheimer patients have abnormalities on chromosome 21, most do not, and there are apparently many ways in which the dementing pathology comes about (St George-Hyslop, 1995). Overall, the picture is one of maximal brain integrity at birth and a downhill course from there, but since the brain is still immature, the deterioration is complicated by growth and development. This pattern is generally taken to indicate the playing out of a faulty design plan that is determined by the extra chromosome. Another possibility is that the altered design is producing products toxic to normal brain function, and that these are taking their toll of the brain's potential. The latter view leads to a search for treatments of those toxicities. The variability of outcomes is likely to be a consequence of the many genes on chromosome 21 and the different roles they may play in individual cases. In addition many factors other than the added chromosome may be operative.

Further evidence along these lines comes from analyses of intellectual competence through the course of development. Down syndrome infants often show the same rates of learning as typical infants. Very soon thereafter, serious lags, both quantitative and qualitative, appear in development. First, a variety of auditory problems, often associated with middle ear infections, to which children with Down syndrome are particularly susceptible, are often present. When children who have avoided infections and have normal pure tone acuities are studied, auditory processing problems still occur. Visual–spatial processing skills of shape and form are relatively normal in these children (Pueschel & Sustrova, 1996), while those specifying location are more compromised. EEG coherence is frequently abnormal, especially in the posterior left hemisphere (Nadel, 1996). Down syndrome children lag particularly in muscle tone and fine motor functions, and in both receptive and expressive aspects of language. On average, Down syndrome individuals have IQs in the 40s (with a high degree of variability) and ultimately attain the cognitive level of normal six- to eight-year olds (Wishart, 1996), but language skills often lag behind their levels of measured intellectual competence. More detailed analyses of the rate and conditions of language development (Fowler, 1995) suggest an overall lag in even the earliest stages of semantic acquisition, but the sequence of emergence of these skills follows the pattern seen in typical children. Syntactic skills are especially slow to emerge and ultimately show very limited development.

Earlier data indicated that Down syndrome children actually decline in intelligence as they grow older, peaking perhaps by the age of five or six. The reasons for the decline are not clear but include the possibility that limitations in language and communication skills interfere with or even preclude progress in many other areas of cognitive development. Other hypotheses have emerged from the work of Wishart (1995, 1996), who found that children with Down syndrome tend to develop very passive attitudes about learning, to be avoidant when faced with cognitive challenges, and to be inconsistent in applying what they have already learned well. Thus, if tested on the same questions on two occasions close in time, they not only will pass items the second time that they missed first, they will also fail items they previously passed. This may occur to anyone, but may represent 30 percent or more of the behaviors of Down syndrome persons. What is not clear from Wishart's work is whether these defects in persistence and strategy are response biases, options that may be utilized or not as the person wishes, or whether these tendencies are based on constraints imposed by their cognitive impairments. There will be more about this at the end of the chapter.

By contrast, what is known about Down syndrome is not only about impairments and declines. Rondal (1996), for example, presented a case of a trisomy 21 with a nonverbal IQ of 60 and an overall cognitive status that was moderately advanced compared to most Down syndrome cases. Nonetheless, this person demonstrated nearly normal syntax, a capability in which most trisomy 21s lag seriously. Recent evidence indicates that intellectual declines may be halted and even somewhat reversed in adulthood (Carr, 1994). Evidence of a different sort, the appearance on television of individuals with Down syndrome who have graduated from college(!) raises questions both about the accuracy of some chromosome assays and about the inevitability of mental deficiency. These latter "data" are hardly scientific in nature, but Rondal's plea that such exceptions be studied intensively makes great sense.

Available evidence indicates that, in trisomy 21, a flawed genotype is associated with a highly variable phenotype. This variability was not apparent a century ago but has emerged with changes in social attitudes, medical knowledge, and practice (Rogers & Coleman, 1992), educational approach (Dunst, 1990) and consequent increased longevity. The design errors in trisomy 21 are under direct study with techniques that are beyond the scope of this book. However, it is now possible to relate many of the physiognomic and metabolic characteristics of Down syndrome to flaws at specific sites which are found most often on the long arm (q) of the chromosome. Furthermore, gene mapping has offered insight into genetic mechanisms of disorders such as senile dementia, leukemia, and heart disease in persons who are not trisomic (Epstein, 1991, 1993). As work progresses, trisomy 21 has come to be viewed as a condition in which the extra chromosome leads to metabolic overactivity which, in turn, has pathological effects. Known examples include the amyloid precursor protein gene, the overproduction of which is associated with the formation of senile plaques, and the gene for the production of an enzyme called superoxide dismutase, which may play a role in premature aging and decreased function of the immune system. There are, of course, many more genes on chromosome 21 and a great many more on all the other chromosomes. How they are expressed jointly to determine the phenotypic symptom picture in any individual is the subject of ongoing, intensive research.

Meanwhile, with as complicated a set of determinants as an aneuploid condition and with evidence that outcomes can be improved, parents have to sort through competing claims regarding the efficacy of various interventions. Parents want to rely on medical personnel for direction and guidance in these matters but they may still encounter residues of pessimism and even rejection from physicians, or they may perceive realistic advice in that way. In addition, the fact that many initiatives for improvements in treatment often came from parents rather than professionals reduces their willingness to follow their physician's advice automatically. The widespread and near-instantaneous dissemination of all kinds of information, both sound and faulty, via television and the internet, has exposed the public both to sources of knowledge and to exploitation. Today, the parents of a newborn child with Down syndrome may see a television program on which a young person, purportedly with the same syndrome, recently graduated from college. Parents can quickly communicate with hundreds of other parents all over the world and consult with varying degrees of sophistication scholarly papers about their child's condition. Naturally, they are going to be interested in any procedure, nostrum, or treatment that may proffer hope of improving their child's condition, and they are very likely to pay close attention to the experience of other parents. They will be exposed to ideas which range from the harmful to the nonsensical to the promising. For an example of current informational turmoil, the reader might explore links to the words "Down syndrome" on the web. For contrast, read the statement written by Mary Coleman (1997), a pediatric neurologist and researcher, about the efficacy and dangers of multivitamin, multimineral therapy.

In a personal communication (May 1999), Mary Coleman wrote the following sensible statement about how to maximize the potential of Down syndrome children:

> What we do know at this time about creating a high achieving Down syndrome child is three things: (1) find an infant without thyroid, cardiac and the other major problems often seen in Down syndrome; (2) have a highly motivated mom with time to spend every day really stimulating that child, particularly in the first 18 months of life; and (3) have the child checked annually by the Preventive Medicine Checklist so that any physical problems that interfere with brain function (such as thyroid, cardiac, vitamin A deficiency, etc.) are caught early and treated before they can hurt the brain.

Disorders associated with specific genes

Fragile-X syndrome.   The X in fragile-X syndrome refers to the X chromosome and hence might be thought to belong among the chromosomal disorders. Indeed, the disorder was first given its name when an apparent flaw on the X chromosome was identified on the karyotype. This was first noted in some mentally retarded persons by Lubs in 1969 as a kind of thinning in the terminal portion of the long arm of the X chromosome (Lubs, 1969); hence the label "fragile" (Evans & Hamerton, 1985; Dykens, Hodapp, & Leckman, 1994). It was difficult to reproduce these observations until it was determined that only certain of the media used in preparing the cells for karyotyping consistently revealed the fragility. With reliable identification of fragility, it became evident that fragility *per se* was not crucial, since fragile sites are not unusual and not necessarily harmful. What was needed was a closer look than was possible with karyotyping – and the development of molecular genetics and DNA testing (to be discussed below) provided answers. Such techniques revealed the nature of the flaw to be an abnormal gene. Here is an instance in which one of perhaps 100,000 genes leads to severe mental retardation but its persisting name, fragile-X syndrome, is something of a misnomer.

The discovery of the fragile-X syndrome specified a biologically determined type of mental deficiency second only to Down syndrome in frequency, and provided an explanation for a long-known but previously unexplained fact, that the incidence of retardation among males is higher (1/4,000 males; 1/10,000 females; Gardner & Sutherland, 1996, p. 209). Identification of persons with fragile-X syndrome removed many individuals from the familial-retarded classification because those affected are not strikingly dysmorphic. View the individual in figure 17.8, who has fragile-X, and decide if there is something distinctive about his appearance. It is partially for this reason, and because fragile-X is inherited, that these persons were thought to be familially mentally retarded. They may still be so considered if the appropriate diagnostic procedures are not performed.

There are, however, physical clues (now that it is known what to look for) that increase the likelihood of identifying the syndrome before molecular diagnostic procedures are performed (Hagerman, 1996). These include a large head circumference, prominent ears, a high forehead, and a relatively long and narrow face. Such features are present in fully involved (to be explained later) females as well as males, but often become conspicuous only in adulthood and are not discernible in childhood. On the other hand, a long-known and frequent physical characteristic of the fragile-X condition present in males is large testicles, technically called machroorchidism. An increased incidence of other physical conditions and ailments is also found. These include strabismus (crossed eyes), otitis media (middle ear infections), sinusitis (infections of the sinuses), flat feet, double jointedness, knock knees, heart abnormalities, high blood pressure, autism, hyperactivity, aggressiveness, and seizures (Hagerman, 1996). Of course these symptoms are common in many contexts where there is no mental retardation or evidence of fragile-X. In order to grasp the complexity of the fragile-X condition, the nature of the genetic abnormality requires explanation.

a   b

Figure 17.8   Male with fragile-X syndrome as a boy and at 22 years of age

Chromosomes are made of DNA (deoxyribonucleic acid) which, in turn, is made of nucleotides, complex molecules consisting of a sugar and phosphate group and a nucleic acid. Nucleotides are structured as a double helix, a twisted ladder or spiral staircase-like structure with sugars and phosphates forming the sides and base elements forming the steps. Base elements occur in pairs: adenine (A) and thymine (T) or guanine (G) and cytosine (C) (Watson, 1968; Dykens, Hodapp & Leckman, 1994). Within pairs, the position or order varies. Figure 17.9 is a schematic drawing which envisions this complex structure. Genes, the plan for the structure of the organism, are embedded in the sequence and relative position of the base pairs. As one progresses along a chromosome there are active regions and inactive regions. The active regions are the genes, and the inactive regions separate them. A particular gene is an ensemble of sequential base pairs that contains the plan for a particular segment of the organism's ultimate structure, the molecules that will make up an enzyme, an amino acid, or a protein. The unit of coding is three sequential base pairs. The order of these triplets contains the information for the body's construction and repair of the stuff of which it is composed. The genome is the total ensemble of genes on all the chromosomes. The entire human genome is not known at this time, but is under intensive study.

The gene for fragile-X has been located and named the FMR-1 (fragile mental retardation, first discovered) gene. It is located at a site, Xq27.3, which would be

Figure 17.9 A model of DNA showing its double helix, twisted ladder structure with the adenine (A)–thymine (T) base pair or the guanine (G)–cytosine (C) base pair

down on the long arm of the X chromosome. At this site, a particular CGG triplet (i.e. CG, GC, GC) normally recurs somewhere between six and 54 times, the greatest frequency being around 30 repeats (Brown, 1996; Dykens, Hodapp, & Leckman, 1994). If a mutation occurs, it may repeat more often and, if it does, different consequences occur. With repetitions in the range of 54–200, an intermediate alteration called a premutation occurs. When repeats exceed 200 (and can extend upwards to 1,000), an alteration termed full mutation occurs, which is associated with severe mental retardation. Determination that a full FMR-1 mutation is present by DNA testing provides the only definitive basis for diagnosing fragile-X syndrome.

The FMR-1 gene controls the production of a protein, but overactivity associated with the excessive number of repeats (the threshold being about 200) leads to a process called methylation, which shuts down or drastically reduces gene activity and protein production. The protein was given the name FMRP (fragile-X-mental-retardation-protein), thus naming a normal protein for the pathology that occurs in its absence (Brown, 1996; Dykens, Hodapp, & Leckman, 1994; Hagerman, 1996), again exemplifying how the study of pathology facilitates knowledge of normal function. The function of this protein has been difficult to determine, and as of this writing is the subject of intensive research. Some approaches suggest that it may play a crucial role in making possible synaptic plasticity, both the creation of new synapses and their subsequent pruning, the mechanism by which the brain learns from experience and masters skills (Weiler et al., 1997). Work is also under way in animal models to determine if the condition can be treated by finding a way to replace the missing protein or to correct the genic flaw (Rattazzi & Ioannou, 1996).

The way in which the genetic flaw (excessive CGG repeats) expresses itself phenotypically is complicated. Not only are there permutations and full mutations with the varying number of repeats and varying degrees of methylation, but the source of the repetition (either from father or mother) and the number of generations from the origins of the mutation determine the degree of expression of the flaw. Mosaicism is common and further contributes to variability. Females are often spared the more extreme effects of the affected X chromosome because they have a second X chromosome which is unlikely to be flawed. However, these chromosomes compete with each other for control of what they express, and one (which may be the flawed one) may partially or totally inactivate the other, thus further contributing to phenotypic variability. The relation between the two X chromosomes can be measured as the ratio of normal X chromosome activity to total X chromosome activity and is termed an X activation ratio. In summary, with fragile-X, severe deficits occur often in males, although there are some with a full mutation and normal behavior, while females with excessive repeats will more often show no symptoms or only mild abnormalities, but severe involvement may occasionally occur. The tracking and measurement of these complexities is not easily accomplished and burdens the study of the relationship between the genome and behavior.

The psychological and behavioral characteristics associated with this complex set of genetic determinants is under intensive study by a number of research groups. A comprehensive review (Bennetto & Pennington, 1996) indicates the following is known so far. The typical fragile-X male has an IQ in the moderately to severely retarded range, but there is considerable variability, and some with the full mutation are spared retardation. Factors contributing to variability include age: deterioration has been found in longitudinal as well as cross-sectional studies, as have decreases in the proportion of gray matter to whole brain with increased age (Dykens, Hodapp, & Leckman, 1994); mosaicism (the higher the proportion of normal cells the less the deficit); and the degree of methylation and amount of FMRP produced, since even a small amount of protein is associated with improved functioning. In some individuals with the full mutation, methylation does not occur and IQs are normal. Why this is the case is not known.

Studies examining the nature of the cognitive deficits found in males with fragile-X which attempt to sort out which characteristics are common to all forms of mental deficiency and which are unique to fragile-X are just beginning to appear. Bennetto and Pennington's (1996) review finds a wide range of impaired characteristics covering just about every domain to some degree, including language, short-term auditory memory, spatial and visual motor skills, arithmetic, and executive functions. Findings distinctive for fragile-X include impairments in the rate and prosody of speech. Such people often speak rapidly and dysrhythmically, producing a kind of "cluttering" of the sound stream, and also tend to be repetitive or perseverative. Prosody is jocular, or litany-like, or harsh. Executive control problems in motor programming and sequencing are prominent, and pragmatic use of language is limited.

It is difficult to detect specific deficits when the overall level of competence is low. In females, the overall level of competence is higher and the effects of the abnormal gene are more variable, so it is possible to detect more specific consequences. Recent studies have begun to examine such variables as the number of repeats, the percent methylation and the degree of X-activation. IQ in females with a fully mutated X chromosome tends to fall in the low average range (80–90) with a wide range of variation extending, in one study, from 23 percent who were mentally retarded (<70), 33 percent in the borderline range (70–84) and 45 percent with IQs greater than 85. In that study, reviewed by Bennetto and Pennington (1996, p. 230), half of those in the normal range had learning disabilities. In other work, it was confirmed that the impairments seen were due to the X chromosome abnormality and were not familial in nature since mutation-free sisters of involved subjects had IQs entirely in the normal range. IQ scores have also been found to be negatively related to the number of repeats and positively related to the X activation ratio. Women with the permutation do not appear to be affected cognitively, and have IQs in the average range, while women with the full mutation do not appear to suffer the longitudinal IQ decline seen in males. More detailed analyses of the nature of the cognitive deficits in full mutation fragile-X originally emphasized selective spatial and short-term memory impairments, but with adequate controls most of these problems appear to be common to various forms of retardation. There is evidence that the prime sources of impairment are executive function deficits, which loom increasingly large in understanding retardation. Further consideration of executive function and dysfunction is found later in this chapter.

So far, there are no specific treatments for fragile-X syndrome. A variety of nonspecific symptomatically oriented, pharmacologic, behavioral, and language approaches are used which have not reversed the developmental course of the disorder. If the hypothesis about FMRP mediation of synapse formation is verified, then this resistance to modification will be understood because the mechanism impaired may be the mechanism of learning. If that is the case, further progress will depend on better understanding of the protein and its dynamics which is, as noted, an area of active current research.

Phenylketonuria (PKU). PKU is an example of a group of genetic disorders in which a missing gene or a small group of genes leads to an error of metabolism which in turn may destroy brain functions and produce mental deficiency. In the case of PKU, a group of enzymes needed to transform phenylalanine – an amino acid common in many protein foods – into tyrosine, the precursor of the neurotransmitter dopamine, is missing. The enzymes are missing because of an autosomal recessive trait on chromosome 12. A recessive trait means that the child must inherit the flaw from both parents for it to be expressed in the phenotype. (Information about PKU is based on reviews by Stern, 1985; Spreen, Risser, & Edgell, 1995; Diamond et al., 1997.) Phenylalanine is an essential amino acid needed by the brain, but the metabolic error leads to an excess of up to ten times or more of phenylalanine and an insufficiency of tyrosine circulating in body fluids. Under these conditions, phenylalanine is secreted in the urine in the form of phenylpyruvic acid, a substance with a characteristic odor. The disorder was first described by Følling in 1934 after a mother of two retarded children noted the characteristic odor and brought it to his attention. Excessive byproducts of phenylalanine metabolism in the urine are the basis of a test administered to newborns to screen for the presence of PKU.

PKU babies are born with normal brains. Untreated, they progressively deteriorate, showing decreased attention and responsiveness to the environment, seizures, tremors, spasticity, and severe mental retardation. In 1954, Bickel, Gerrard, and Hickmans reported that dietary restriction of foods containing phenylalanine prevented mental deterioration. This finding has been repeatedly confirmed although a small (<3 percent) subgroup of PKU children was later discovered to have a malignant form of the disorder (a particular enzyme in a family of enzymes) that does not respond to dietary intervention. Newborns are now screened for PKU right after birth and, if found to be affected, they are placed on diets with low phenylalanine. It may take several weeks for this to occur during which phenylalanine levels may soar. Two controversial issues have since been raised. One related to the amount of phenylalanine that could be consumed without detriment, since some amount was absolutely needed. The other issue involved the number of years before the diet could be given up since the more mature brain could tolerate excess phenylalanine. There is considerable pressure to return to an ordinary diet since appropriate foods are often not tasty. Authorities have differed as to when it might be safe for affected persons to resume ordinary diets so recommendations have been as early as five years of age and as late as late adolescence.

Research on the consequences of the phenylalanine-free diet have some inconsistencies but it is generally found that, as indicated, mental retardation is avoided. However, the children do not attain the IQ levels of their siblings. Some studies found PKU-treated individuals to have IQs in the borderline (70–80) range, and others in the lower part of the normal range (80–90) when unaffected members of the family were average or higher. At the least, affected children have IQs 4–6 points lower than their siblings. Furthermore, in many cases, termination of the diet before the age of eight was associated with a subsequent drop of 5–9 IQ points. Other factors that contribute to outcome are the degree to which parents and child adhered to the diet and the age at which the diet began. In addition to lowered IQ, PKU-treated individuals appear to have a high incidence of a variety of personal–social problems including irritability, restlessness, hyperactivity, temper outbursts and tantrums, and impaired executive functions and social relations.

A major step in clarifying the nature of the impairment found in diet-treated PKU persons occurred with the publication of a monograph by Diamond et al. (1997). They noted that the diet did not normalize phenylalanine levels, but rather moved them in a normal direction. The diet had generally been considered satisfactory if blood plasma levels of phenylalanine were maintained below 10–12 mg/100 ml, which is five to six times normal, but were not allowed to fall below 2 mg/100 ml. Diamond and colleagues reasoned that, in diet-treated PKU persons, circulating phenylalanine levels would be increased relative to the level of tyrosine. For much of the brain, such altered ratios were of no importance. But tyrosine is the precursor of dopamine, and there are places in the brain requiring much dopamine that are exquisitely sensitive to its availability. When the supply is not adequate, function deteriorates. These places include the dorsolateral prefrontal cortex, some of the major pathways feeding into it, and the retina and those parts of its structure that control contrast sensitivity (see chapter 12). On the basis of this analysis, Diamond and Herzberg (1996) earlier had found lowered contrast sensitivity across all spatial frequencies (thus implicating both parvo and magnocellular systems) in diet-treated PKU subjects, even though there had previously been no suspicion of visual impairments in this condition. Using the same reasoning in the later study cited above, Diamond and coworkers expected to find selective behavior deficits in a number of the executive functions processed and regulated by the dorsolateral prefrontal cortex.

Diamond and colleagues' study focussed on two aspects of executive function – working memory and inhibitory control – particularly when both were required for problem solution. Working memory refers to tasks in which the problem depends on the retention of information that is no longer present. An example of a simple task of this type is remembering, after a delay, where one has observed that an object has been hidden. A more complex example would be the nonmatching to sample procedure in which an object is presented and then removed from view. Subsequently two objects are presented, one of which was the one just seen, and the subject has to chose the novel object in order to gain a reward. The working memory component in this type of task is remembering both the sample and the rule. Inhibitory control refers to capabilities required in tasks in which the correct solution is not a previously learned or a well-established response but is a novel, unpracticed, or incongruent response. Thus, in a task devised by Luria, the Russian neuropsychologist whose ideas were discussed in chapter 6, a child is first asked to tap once when the examiner taps once and to tap twice when the examiner does. This is generally very easy for most individuals past the age of three or four. Then, however, the rules are reversed. The subject is asked to tap once after the examiner taps twice, and twice after the examiner taps once. Now the strong tendency to imitate and repeat must be inhibited and a less likely response must be selected. Finally the task might be to tap once after the examiner taps twice but to not tap at all after the examiner taps once. Now the strong tendency to do something must be inhibited. Notice also that working memory is involved because the examiner's behavior must be remembered in order to make the correct decision. Since Diamond et al. predicted a selective impairment in executive functions, for contrast they also examined a variety of tasks presumed not to be executive functions.

Diamond et al. (1997) longitudinally studied 37 children in three age groups, 6–12 months, 15–30 months, and 3½–7 years old, all of whom were treated early and continuously for PKU. They were compared with three groups of normal children; siblings of the affected children; a control group matched over many characteristics such as gender, gestational age, birth weight, birth order, child-care arrangements, family religion, education, and occupational status, both tested longitudinally like the PKU children; and a large randomly sampled normal group covering the age range of the study, each of whom was tested once. In addition, another comparison group consisted of children with mild hyperphenylalaninemia. This is a milder version of PKU caused by a minimally functional, rather than a nonfunctional, gene. If these children eat a normal diet, they develop plasma levels of phenylalanine comparable to those of PKU children on a dietary regimen. They differ from PKU children because they never have highly elevated levels of phenylalanine, as most PKU children do during the first weeks of life before their diets are begun, and their tyrosine levels are not significantly depressed.

The results of the study were straightforward. Recall that diets that kept phenylalanine levels below 10–12 mg/ml had been considered to be adequate. Diamond et al. found that the PKU diet-treated children and those with hyperphenylalaninemia fell into two groups, those with levels above 6 mg/ml and those below. PKU children with phenylalanine levels above 6 mg/ml, and not those below, uniformly across ages showed impairments of dorsolateral prefrontal cortex functions involving working memory and inhibitory control. The impairments were selective: other functions tested were not deficient. The level of deficit fluctuated with plasma levels obtained at the time of testing, not those obtained previously or some average over a long period of time. This indicates that the underlying structures of the prefrontal lobes were not irreversibly damaged, and that those whose executive functions were not up to par might still improve with further dietary changes. Prefrontal cortex deficits were not seen in the children with hyperphenylalaninemia, even those with higher levels of circulating phenylalanine, a finding also confirmed by Weglage et al. (1997). These individuals have normal or near-normal levels of tyrosine and hence dopamine; thus, the crucial factor is not the phenylalanine level *per se*, but its effects on the availability of dopamine.

The picture that emerges from Diamond et al.'s findings and that of other studies is that circulating levels of phenylalanine should be kept below 6 mg/ml in PKU children before the age of 10 (Burgard et al., 1997). After age ten, reversion to an ordinary diet is feasible. In one study (Griffiths et al., 1998), high loads of phenylalanine were added to the diet of previously treated, 10–16-year-old PKU subjects for three months. As expected, circulating phenylalanine was raised to very high levels but led to no impairment of cognitive functions. On the whole, the results of this research present a fairly optimistic outlook for the cognitive status of persons who not too long ago were doomed to a life of severe mental retardation.

Although cognitive status can be normalized, high circulating levels of phenylalanine are a source of other problems. Lenke and Levy (1980) reported that women with PKU who were spared retardation by dietary treatment as children, and then resumed a normal diet so that they had high circulating levels of phenylalanine, regularly gave birth to children who had microcephaly, low birth weight, heart defects, and severe retardation. Less severe effects were also found in hyperphenylalaninemic mothers who had high levels of phenylalanine all of their lives (Levy et al., 1996). High levels of circulating phenylalanine are a dose-related teratogen (Levy & Ghavami, 1996) – the more the circulating phenylalanine the higher the frequency of abnormal offspring. Returning to a low phenylalanine diet, preferably before conception or soon afterward, and an otherwise adequate diet is associated with a much-improved reproductive outcome (Michals et al., 1996). It is also possible that direct supplements of tyrosine may be helpful (Rohr, Lobbregt, & Levy, 1998).

Williams syndrome.   Williams syndrome was first described in 1961 with emphasis on the cardiac symptoms which appear in about three-quarters of the cases. It has since been learned that this is a rare, genetic disorder due to a deletion on the long arm of chromosome 7 which includes at least four genes and most likely more.

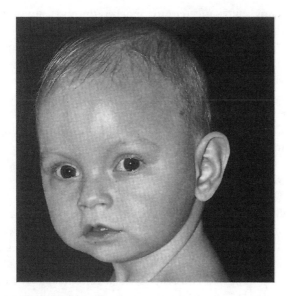

Figure 17.10 A child with Williams syndrome

One, called ELN, has little activity in brain but is responsible for the cardiac symptoms and some of the facial features of the syndrome because of its regulation of elastin, components of blood vessels and other organs that give them elasticity. Another, called LIMK1, is strongly expressed in brain and is apparently responsible for some of the visuospatial cognitive characteristics found in the syndrome. Other genes in this region whose functions, as yet, are unclear have been identified, and more may be found (Lenhoff et al., 1997; Mervis et al., 1999). Apparent features common in the syndrome include short stature, a broad brow, wide mouth, full lips, malocclusion of the jaw, prominent ear lobes, a long neck, and what has been called an elfin appearance. They often have a hoarse voice and their hair grays prematurely. Figure 17.10 presents a child with Williams syndrome. (Note: unless otherwise cited, the material on Williams syndrome is based on Bellugi, Wang, & Jernigan, 1994; Lenhoff et al., 1997; Mervis, 1999; Mervis et al., 1999.)

The mix of psychological and social characteristics present in Williams syndrome is of extraordinary interest because it challenges some of the ways brain function is understood. There are four main psychological features of the syndrome: mental retardation, relative language and musical skill, grossly impaired spatial cognition, and high sociability. Each is discussed in turn.

Although there is considerable variability, persons with Williams syndrome, on average, are mentally retarded. Some may attain IQ scores in the lower part of the normal range but most are in the mild to moderate range with scores averaging about 60. These scores are consistent with limitations in their ability to function independently as adults, hold jobs, manage their finances, and the like. For the most part, persons with Williams syndrome require supervision and care and do not live independently (Davies, Howlin, & Udwin, 1997). Furthermore, like other mentally retarded persons, they show many deficits in the domain of concept formation, arithmetic, and reading, and in these respects perform similarly to, for example, persons with Down syndrome who are functioning at the same overall level.

In most persons with mental deficiency, language limitations are generally among those that are the most conspicuous. By contrast, adolescent and adult individuals with Williams syndrome are loquacious and facile with spoken language. They tell stories, and they tell them inventively. They are also musical and can often sing and perform on instruments and remember what they have learned. Component skills contributing to language fluency have been evaluated. Phonemic skills appear to be entirely intact. Most utterances are semantically complex, and it has even been remarked that Williams persons use a rich and unusual vocabulary. However, in one study by Mervis and colleagues with 127 subjects, only 4 percent had scores greater than average on a standard test of word knowledge, and 96 percent were below average. On the other hand, on simple measures of word fluency (for example, coming up with the names of animals) those with Williams syndrome performed similar to normal subjects. Persons with Williams syndrome have also been observed to use complex grammar far exceeding the syntactical complexities which mentally retarded individuals generally display. Nonetheless, on a standard test of receptive grammar, in the study by Mervis et al., the average score was only at the 4th percentile of the norm. Other limitations in syntactic skills have been found by Karmiloff-Smith et al. (1998). Close study of language pragmatics has not yet been done, but it appears that a fair proportion of the utterances made by persons with Williams syndrome, while making sense to others, may nonetheless have a strong quality of talk for its own sake. That is, conversation may be used primarily in an effort to maintain social contact, rather than as a means of communication. Finally, the timing of language development is slower than in normals, suggesting the possibility that its organization and structure may function in some unique way.

In contrast to their language skills, visual–spatial skills are grossly impaired. When asked to draw, to represent, to find their way around, and to remember how they did it, persons with Williams syndrome have a terrible time. On a standard test of spatial skills which involved pattern matching, 88 percent of the Williams syndrome subjects scored in the 1st percentile. On tests developed to evaluate the integrity of "northerly route" parietal visual functions (moving a card into slots positioned at different angles and sensitivity to motion), children and adolescents with Williams syndrome were impaired even though they showed less or no impairment on tests of static angle matching, a ventral route visual function (Atkinson et al., 1997).

It has also been suggested that spatial impairments are due to an inability to attend to the global aspects of what they see and that, instead, children with Williams syndrome focus most frequently on local details and miss the big picture. Certainly, many of their reproductions have such characteristics. Examples of the kind of data produced by children with Williams syndrome who are asked to copy a large D (global aspects – the big picture) made up of small y's (local aspects – the detail) is found in figure 17.11, and illustrate this point. The contrasting response of a

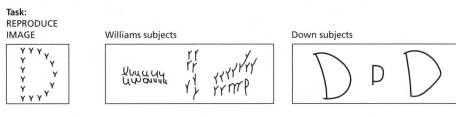

Figure 17.11   An example of a person with Williams syndrome having difficulty reproducing the global aspects of a stimulus while successfully reproducing its local aspects. In contrast, a person with Down syndrome reproduces the global aspects but omits the local aspects

subject with Down syndrome to the same task, who reproduces the global configuration but misses the detail, is adjacent. Nonretarded individuals tend to reproduce both the local and the global aspects of the stimulus. However, Mervis and her group utilized a special test to determine whether persons with Williams syndrome were indeed insensitive to the global aspects of a stimulus, and found that they were not. She argued that an explanation for their behavior may be that their weakness is in segmenting their perceptions, breaking them up into workable parts. When administered a procedure in which segmentation was facilitated, considerable improvement occurred. The explanation for the spatial deficits seen in Williams syndrome is far from settled, but it should be noted that segmenting skills, dividing a whole into workable component parts, is generally considered to be an aspect of executive functioning.

The remaining salient feature of Williams syndrome persons is their sociability. They have a knack for approaching strangers and initiating social contact. This begins in childhood and is expressed despite cautionary warnings by their parents, relatives, and teachers about the dangers of being utterly trusting of strangers. Despite their engaging and overly friendly social manner, their actual social relationships as adults are often impoverished. Furthermore, they are described as vulnerable to high levels of anxiety and distractibility (Davies, Udwin, & Howlin, 1998). This is not surprising. Their verbal skills would lead others to expect more from them than their capabilities might permit, and such circumstances often leads to much anxiety.

It is noteworthy that two skills that ordinarily accompany spatial skills, and hence would be expected to be deficient in Williams syndrome, are not impaired. One is skill in facial recognition and sensitivity to emotional cues; the other is prosody and musical talent. Despite their inability to represent a pattern or configuration on a diagram or read a map, Williams people read faces and emotions well, and remember what they see. Their modes of expression are animated and dramatic and amply express emotion just as they are sensitive to such expressions in others. In some respects, it appears that the genetic flaw simulates a right hemisphere injury to a normal brain, but the exceptions noted indicate that something different is occurring.

Both autopsy and imaging studies find no evidence of selective right hemisphere pathology. Karmiloff-Smith (1997), using Williams syndrome as an example, has pointed out that when brains are different from the very outset, which is true of only some genetic disorders, equivalent behavioral functions may have different underlying mechanisms of operation. When that occurs, understanding of function based on the normal brain may not apply.

Mervis and colleagues made an interesting observation that bears on the dissociations found in Williams syndrome. Recall that all of the facts cited about typical performance in this condition were associated with high levels of variability. These data indicating contrasting strengths and weakness in Williams syndrome were intercorrelated and then corrected for the age of the subjects (because age alone can produce spuriously high correlations). The results indicated that all the important measures were significantly intercorrelated, including measures of verbal strength and spatial weakness. Thus although subjects would have a relatively high verbal score and a low spatial score, their standing in the range of verbal scores would predict where they would appear in the range of spatial scores. Such correlations imply that some underlying factor is affecting all functions. Mervis et al. interpreted this factor to be "g" (general ability), which is thought to be crucially deficient in mental retardation. It is also noteworthy that there is recurrent evidence of executive function impairment. The relationship between executive function and "g" is discussed below.

As noted, the structure of the brains of persons with Williams syndrome has begun to be examined. Beyond the absence of right hemisphere dysplasia, the following has been noted. Overall, the brains are somewhat microcephalic, but the volume of the frontal lobes, the limbic portions of the temporal lobes, and the cerebellum approximate normal values. The vermal areas of the cerebellum, the same areas that are dysplastic in autism, may even be enlarged. On the other hand, there are abnormal clusterings of neurons in the visual areas of the occipital lobe. These anatomical findings appear to be consistent with the behavioral strengths and weaknesses that occur in the syndrome, although further investigation of the functioning of the apparently normal-sized frontal lobes is needed. These anatomical findings again bring into focus the significance of the cerebellum in functions other than motor integration. Several authors have speculated that the requirements of the language system for rapid sequential selection of words may be mediated by a heretofore not understood function of the cerebellum. Now that Williams syndrome can be readily identified, study of the characteristics of affected individuals should increase understanding of the role of the cerebellum in language function.

Meanwhile, it has been suggested (Lenhoff et al., 1997) that the condition may be more familiar than the scientific literature suggests. Folktales from many cultures describe "little people" – pixies, elves, trolls, and other fairies who may be modeled after short-stature individuals with a characteristic elfin appearance who sing and tell stories and are goodhearted and kind, yet different from other humans. These special creatures may have been incorporated into folklore as a way of accounting for the persons who actually looked and behaved this way, and appeared every now and then in a community's life, but had what is now known as Williams syndrome.

Mental Retardation and Psychosis

The relationship between psychosis and mental retardation was addressed at the beginning of chapter 15 on childhood psychosis, and might well be reviewed before reading further. It will be recalled that a stress-diathesis model was described, and it was suggested that mental retardation may be a diathesis for psychotic behavior. It will also be recalled that the term "psychosis" covers a range of behaviors that often imply poor control, disorganization, disruption of routines and social interactions, and unpredictability. Retarded persons generally have poor understanding, poor communication skills, motoric clumsiness or worse, and diminished inhibitory capabilities. They have difficulty explaining themselves or describing their experiences. They may not be able to communicate understandably about symptoms such as malaise or pain, or be able to specify time of onset, locale, or quality of their experience, all of which may be crucial to an accurate diagnosis. Instead, they may shriek, withdraw, become aggressive or self-injurious, or engage in any number of behaviors that will be considered disturbed (Schroeder et al., 1997). It is then easy to simply think of the disturbed behaviors as just another manifestation of the mental deficiency or as a comorbid disorder. Formally, this may lead to adding some form of psychosis to the already-existing diagnosis of mental retardation and letting it go at that. Progress in understanding the relationship between brain functions and behavior has been made and there is a scattered literature which points out plausible explanations for many symptoms often termed psychotic. Such understandings can lead to rational and effective treatments.

Lishman (1998), a psychiatrist, has brought this literature together in a very comprehensive work whose subtitle is *The psychological consequences of cerebral disorder*. The book is organized by disorders and describes possible symptoms in each context which can lead to psychiatric diagnoses. Often these symptoms require treatments quite different from those commonly used in psychiatry. Another important work of this sort focusses on developmental disabilities and is organized in terms of symptoms (Gedye, 1998). This is in the form of a manual useful to caretakers and professionals with seven chapters, each dealing with a class of symptoms: aggression, self-injury, screaming, sleep disturbances, eating disturbances, dementia, and falls. Within each chapter specific classes of symptoms are described in detail using both inclusive and exclusive criteria. Diagnostic conditions in which the symptoms are most likely to appear are specified in detail. Methods of collecting relevant information via observation and medical testing are suggested along with a description of possible biochemical and anatomical involvement.

Described another way, Gedye and Lishman have provided a catalog of ways in which mechanisms of impairment that may underlie a particular disturbed behavior may be specified, and thus provide a basis for a rational approach to treatment. For Gedye, for example, aggression is not just a symptom manifested by a proportion of mentally retarded individuals but may be a reaction to pain associated with a hidden illness or physical condition; a response when compulsive behaviors are disrupted; a consequence of a frontal or temporal lobe ictal condition; a toxic reaction to drugs;

a manifestation of delirium, hallucinations, or altered state of consciousness; a flash-back reaction to remembered prior assault; a learned behavior from watching others; or a premeditated assault responsive to some interpersonal or emotional provocation. These similar behaviors require different interventions, and appropriate interventions would probably preclude the need for restraints, whether physical or pharmacologic, or comorbid diagnoses.

What is the Core of Intelligence?

This final section of the chapter reviews what is meant by the term intelligence in the light of neuropsychological data generally, and frontal lobe, executive functions specifically. The discussion pertains to data about the range of variation of intelligence within populations, to population differences in intelligence, and to data about familial (throw of the dice) mental retardation.

Merits and weaknesses of "g"

If one asks: what is the essence of what is impaired in mental retardation, scholars working in the tradition of Spearman have a ready answer – "g." Jensen, perhaps the foremost researcher working in that tradition, devoted an entire book (1998) detailing the evidence in favor of the existence of "g" and discussing the ramifications and consequences of having more or less "g." In that book, evidence is mustered that "g" is largely inherited. There is not much controversy about genetic contributions to "g" within populations, although the specific magnitude of the influence may be in some dispute, but there is controversy about whether genetic differences determine IQ differences across populations, particularly different racial groups. Jensen has devoted the bulk of a lengthy professional career to researching these issues, has published much research, and has a strong reputation as an objective, empirical scientist. (However, for contrasting evaluations by two people who disagree with him, see Flynn, 1999, and Hirsch, 1975, 1997.) Jensen is not alone. There are a large number of scholars who share his position (cf. Gottfredson, 1997).

The tradition of scholarship in which most of this work has occurred is a combination of psychometrics and behavior genetics. Psychometrics was described at the beginning of the chapter and stems from the work of Spearman and Binet, and generates methods of mental measurement. Behavior genetics makes use of identical twins reared together, whose genetic makeup and environment is the same, and studies their characteristics in comparison to persons with a range of familial relationships and environmental circumstances; for example, comparing identical twins reared together and those reared apart, or identical twins, fraternal twins, and other siblings. Some studies examine differences in nationality, race, or socioeconomic status, or some combination of these characteristics. Individual differences in cognitive ability comprise a topic that has played an important role in clinical and educational psychology, but has been relatively neglected in other areas of psychological research. Recently, however, much greater interest in these differences has been shown in the areas of cognitive neuroscience and developmental psychology. Such influences will be apparent in what follows.

Supporting evidence for "g"

The role of information-processing speed – chronometric research

Psychometricians and some cognitive researchers have been interested in the question of the relationship between information-processing speed and intelligence, and have examined the question using techniques which Posner (1978), a cognitive psychologist, has called mental chronometry (referring to the time it takes to perform mental operations). These are procedures in which reaction time is measured in tasks with varying informational complexity. The general rule is that all tasks are easy to do (Jensen calls them elementary cognitive tasks), so the only issue is the speed with which they are accomplished.

The simplest task is called simple reaction time. A person is asked to depress a push button when a signal, either a tone or a light, is perceived. The reaction time is the duration between stimulus onset and the depression of the push button and generally takes 200–300 msec. Such a measure provides an index of the overall integrity of both the receptive and the motor system and the coordination of the two, but makes minimal cognitive demands. The task is made more difficult and is called a "go–no-go" procedure if one of two signals is presented on each trial and the subject is asked to respond only to one. Correct responses now take 300–500 msec. If the response time in the simple procedure is subtracted from the response time in the "go–no-go" procedure, a measure of how long it takes to make the decision is obtained. The task can be made more complex by presenting one start button and an array of illuminable push buttons, as few as two and as many as can be engineered in the space available, and reaction time is known to get longer as a function of the number of alternatives. An eight-choice apparatus, with a start button at the bottom center and eight possible push buttons arrayed nearby, one or more of which may be illuminated as targets, is illustrated in figure 17.12a. This apparatus can be used to provide a more difficult task, the odd-man-out task. Here, three lights are illuminated simultaneously, two close together and one apart. The task is to depress the push button of the more isolated light. Figure 17.12b illustrates yet another choice reaction time apparatus which can be used to assess a range of informational complexities from the simplest (e.g. was the color red? were there two flashes?) to the far more complex (e.g. were the two words synonyms? were all the numbers prime numbers?).

Jensen (1998) reviewed a body of such research, some from his own laboratory. His conclusions and those of earlier reviews such as that of Brody (1992), Cooper and Regan (1982) and Campione, Brown, and Ferrara (1982) are fairly consistent and extremely interesting. Chronometric measures (mental speed) correlate significantly with both complex psychometric measures of "g" such as IQ (which is thought

(a)   (b)

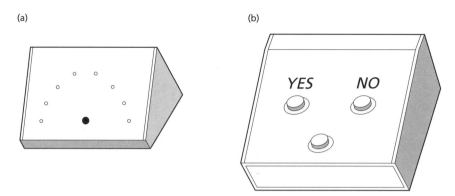

Figure 17.12(a)   An eight-choice reaction-time apparatus
Figure 17.12(b)   A choice reaction-time apparatus

to reflect crystallized "g") and a relatively brief measure of "g" (thought to reflect fluid "g") called Raven's Progressive Matrices. The correlations are higher for fluid than crystallized "g" and are negative because the shorter the response time, the higher the measure of "g." The level of correlation increases as the level of complexity goes up, or as results from different kinds of elementary cognitive tasks are combined. Although chronometric procedures do require close attention, they do not require much thought or problem-solving ability and are very different from the kinds of tasks found in mental competency tests. Consequently, Jensen argues that speed is an important component of "g," giving experimental verification to the popular notion that the less competent are slower.

The speed with which another kind of processing occurs, actually one more fundamental than reaction time, has also been shown to relate highly to "g." This is simply the minimum duration required for the perception of a stimulus. Jensen calls it stimulus identification time. Such durations are measured by masking procedures (Breitmeyer, 1984). A stimulus is presented and then followed at varying short intervals by another stimulus, the mask, which, if the interval is short enough, will prevent the perception of the original stimulus. In vision, for example, the stimulus might be a hollow square with one side missing and the mask might be a complete, identically sized and positioned square. The task is to identify whether the north, south, east, or west side of the square is missing. The perception is either clear and obvious or the subject must guess, in which case accuracy will occur on 25 percent of trials by chance. Any significant increase above 25 percent indicates that perception is taking place. The shortest time interval between stimulus and mask at which accurate perception is occurring (the masking threshold) provides a measure which correlates significantly with "g." Subjects can take as much time as they wish in arriving at a decision, so reaction time is not measured, just the stimulus duration required to enable accurate identification of the stimulus.

Jensen also reports that the very highest correlations come with measures of reaction time variability. Again, the correlations are negative, the less variable the higher the "g." In each type of measurement described above, the measure of competence is an index of speed. Variation of individual trials is essentially a measure of consistency. Jensen acknowledges that measures of variability are not measures of competence because he believes speed to be the crucial index of competence, and consistency is independent of speed. That is, one may be fast or slow, consistently or inconsistently. His interpretation (Jensen, 1998, p. 226) of these reliable and robust results is less assured than most of the data he presents. This important finding suggests that something more than speed, the attentional resources to respond consistently to the task, an aspect of executive functions, may be operative. A summary of the empirical evidence is that speed of perception, speed of information processing, and, particularly, the consistency of response speed, are all related to "g." The body of data involved is substantial and the results have a remarkable coherence.

Group differences in "g"

Chapter 11 in Jensen's (1998) book is devoted to data about population differences in "g." He is intensely interested in evidence about differences in mental competence among racial and ethnic groups. He believes that the evidence supports the conclusion that such differences exist, and that they can be attributed to genetic differences. He acknowledges that such conclusions do not apply to particular individuals since the range of variation within populations exceeds their differences. He also believes that available data are a basis for population planning and social policy.

Jensen's favorite tool for determining whether group differences exist is based on what he calls the Spearman Hypothesis. This hypothesis states that differences in "g" between groups that are different in "g" are greater when measured with tests which measure "g" better. Evaluation of the hypothesis require several steps. Tests must be selected some of which are known to be good measures of fluid "g." The test battery must be administered to large representative samples of each group to be compared. When the test results are analyzed separately for each group, the structure or dimensions of the factors being measured for each group should be very similar, thus verifying that the tests chosen are measuring the same psychological characteristics in each group. It will then emerge that some tests are very good tests of "g," and others much less so. The degree to which a test measures "g" is called its "g loading." If the score differences of the two groups being compared show a relationship with the "g loadings" found in each of the tests, the Spearman Hypothesis is verified.

Jensen presents study after study in which the Spearman Hypothesis is strongly verified when comparing Black and White samples. From these and other analyses, he concludes that there is strong evidence of inherited population differences in "g." He was not able to verify the Spearman Hypothesis when comparing Chinese-American and White American samples (Jensen, 1998, p. 399). Nonetheless, he finds Chinese orientals to be highest in "g," Caucasians of European descent next, then Blacks of African descent lowest. The reader will need to consult Jensen's writing to appreciate the magnitude of the research data presented and the precision of his thought. If the implications he draws from the data are disputed, the data themselves demand consideration and some alternate explanation.

Disconfirming evidence regarding "g"

It was noted that Jensen found established measures of "g" to be more highly correlated with indices of variability than with measures of speed. This is a disquieting finding since it is speed of information processing that is considered to be a central component of "g." The finding is by no means a death blow to "g" theory, with its formidable array of supporting data, but it raises the possibility that something is missing in the "g" account of mental competence. Consistency may mean that a certain kind of executive function capability exists which makes possible the maintenance of a relatively invariant level of attention to the boring tasks that make up chronometric procedures. This idea adds a separate component to the singular emphasis on "g," additions which Jensen (who prefers parsimony) finds undesirable. When one thinks of it, Spearman and Jensen have taken what everyone acknowledges must be a product of many genes, and find that it is expressed in a singular entity – from this angle, an unlikely possibility.

Another perhaps not very important disconfirmation of "g" theory is the nonverification of the Spearman Hypothesis when comparing Chinese and White samples. More data are being obtained and the hypothesis may yet be confirmed. Evidence that IQ can be raised, at least in some degree, by environmental factors such as nutrition and extra intellectual stimulation, and lowered by toxins such as heavy metals, are reported and acknowledged by Jensen. Such evidence chips away at his emphasis on the genetic determination of competence but does not much affect his main interpretations of the available data.

For some of the leading researchers on "g," belief in the genetic determination of population differences gave rise to the fear that the gene pool for cognitive excellence would be degraded if interbreeding occurred. The line of reasoning was that, since those with excellent capabilities bred at a slower rate than those who had less "g," it could be anticipated that the overall level of talent would decline. This prediction has been disconfirmed every time it has been tested, an outcome consistent with what is known about the variability and dispersion of the human genome (Cavalli-Sforza, Menozzi, & Piazza, 1996). Nonetheless, this line of thought, not the facts, has been cited in support of various eugenic movements designed to preserve the purity of race. A number of important psychometricians, especially R. B. Cattell (who developed the concept of fluid and crystallized intelligence) have taken public positions somewhere on this continuum of thought regarding racial interbreeding (Cattell, 1979). Between 1920 and 1940, intelligence test results were used to justify discriminatory practices against groups of people who scored low on intelligence tests largely on the implicit assumption that the genotype had been measured (Kamin, 1974; Fischer et al., 1996; Hirsch, 1997, among others). After the horrors of World War II, those voices were muted for several decades. More recently, echoes of that kind of thinking have been resuscitated. Although people with a range of darker skin hues generally are attributed some version of genetic inferiority, they are not alone. Conviction that Binet-derived intelligence tests provide a measure a genotypic capability leads to the fear that those who measure lower, if allowed to interbreed, can only bring things down. See, for example, Cyril Burt's (1958) discussion of the dangers posed to the English gene pool by educational policies of the post-World War II British government that admitted more and more less-advantaged (Caucasian) English persons to higher schooling, and thus provided them with increased opportunity to mate with the elite.

An arguably fatal flaw to "g" theory comes from the data, mentioned near the beginning of this chapter, reviewed by Flynn (1987, 1999) that has come to be called the Flynn effect. This finding is that the level of measures of fluid intelligence has risen significantly over the past 80 years all over the world and among all racial groups at the rate of about 15 IQ points every 20 years. To date, the phenomenon has been verified and it appears to be robust, but no one has an adequate explanation for it. It is clear however that the effect is due to environmental factors since the gene pool could not possibly have changed that much in so short a period of time, and since all racial groups have shown comparable effects. The Flynn effect challenges acceptance of IQ testing, since it is clear that measurement standards are changing all the time, and questions genetic interpretations of the origin of "g," since those with supposedly less "g" have gained more in IQ over 20 years than the amount they were behind. The reader is referred to a recent paper (Flynn, 1999) for more detail about the implication of the Flynn effect for evidence of group differences in intelligence.

It is a truism in science that the disconfirmation of a theory does not lead to the theory's demise until a better theory comes along to replace it. No such theory now exists. But I would argue that answers are likely to come from cognitive neuroscience, and this book will end with a sketch of such possibilities.

Before addressing a possible "new look," a comment about the social and historical context in which the "g" idea emerged seems worthy of mention. I believe there is a scholar who merits citation for this idea, but his or her identity has escaped my memory. The idea is that both the concept of "g" and related notions about superiority are derived from, and embedded in, the experience of a people living on an island off the coast of Europe who dominated the world for centuries. Reference, of course, is being made to the historical epoch of the British Empire, in the midst of which Darwin proposed evolutionary theory with its corollary of the survival of the fittest, and Spearman theorized about "g." Both of course were English and, during those times, the English could easily justify the notion that they came from superior stock, since little England controlled the seas and colonized much of the land mass of the world. The "g" concept may also have a related, implicit origin. In British imperialist society, there was a curious (to an American, at least) devaluation, or better, lessor valuation of the highly trained specialist in science, engineering, or medicine, in comparison to a talented generalist (whence cometh the precursors of "g," I speculate). It was the generalist who could serve a variety of roles, actually almost any role, in the administration of a far-flung empire.

Alternatives and/or additions to "g"

In what follows, a chain of evidence will be outlined about the importance of the frontal lobes and executive functions for intelligence. It then becomes important to understand when and how environmental factors influence the development of executive functions.

How do persons with retardation learn?

If one sets a group of persons with mental retardation to engage in a learning task, repeatedly confirmed findings are that they either show no learning whatsoever or their learning is slower than that of a comparison group of typical persons. Learning can be measured by the rate at which a response that is not present at the beginning of a task later occurs consistently as a result of the training experience. In real life, there is a point at which one does not know how to ride a bike. After many trials and perhaps a period on training wheels and a fall or two, one can get on the bike and ride away and, it is said, one has learned. In the laboratory, for example, circumstances can be arranged so that a person can see two shallow opaque dishes covered by easily removable cards, one with a circle, the other with a triangle, drawn on top. A token or some reward such as a piece of candy may be found in one of the dishes. In a discrimination learning experiment, one of the symbols will designate where the reward will be found, and that is what the subjects have to learn – that a particular symbol will point the way to the reward. Reaching for one of the dishes constitutes a trial. Circle and triangle are randomly shifted between the two dishes across trials. If blocks of ten trials are plotted, then learning is said to have occurred if the percent of correct responses rises significantly above chance (which is 50 percent since there are two alternatives). In a simple case such as this, 100 percent correct responses will often occur.

Figure 17.13 depicts the slower rate of learning accomplished by persons with retardation in comparison to normals. The data are plotted by averaging percent correct for each block of ten trials for groups of subjects, and the slower rate of learning of the retarded group is clearly apparent. Such findings are however misleading because they distort what actually occurs in individual subjects. Zeaman and House (1963) examined data from individual retarded subjects and noted a pattern that suggested an interpretation different from slow learning. Specifically, they noted that those with retardation did not have a slower rate of learning; rather, they stayed at chance levels before they started learning far longer than did the comparison group. When they began to show learning, the rate of improvement approximated that of normals. This can be seen in figure 17.14 where the data are plotted as backward learning curves, i.e. calculating percent correct on all trials prior to those trials on which they attained 90–100 percent correct. (It should be noted that some of their subjects never learned although those data are not shown.) Zeaman and House reasoned that the backward learning curves indicated not a learning problem, *per se*, but a problem in determining what to learn. They suggested that retardates took a long

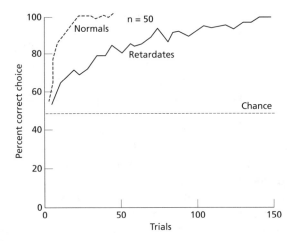

Figure 17.13   Discrimination learning in groups of normals and persons with retardation

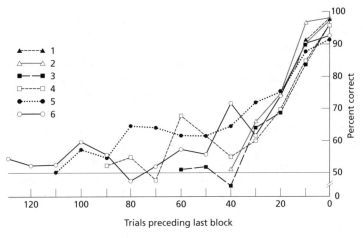

Figure 17.14   Backward discrimination learning curves of retardates indicate the rate of learning is rapid; figuring out what to learn is slow

time to figure out the pertinent aspects of the complex situation they were in, but that once they figured out what was crucial, their learning was quite rapid.

Figuring out what is pertinent to learn is an aspect of what cognitive scientists call metacognition (Flavell, 1976). Metacognition refers to a variety of skills that make possible successful learning and problem solving, and includes knowledge of one's own mental processes, awareness of success or failure in problem solving, knowing when to rehearse and to double check, and how to orchestrate one's resources to pick the best available strategy to deal with whatever problem is at hand. It involves the ability to select, deploy, and maintain attention to relevant cues, to keep these cues in mind as long as they remain relevant, and to search for other cues if previously relevant cues turn out to be no longer relevant. It is clear that the terms "metacognition" and "executive functions" overlap substantially if they are not synonymous. The reader will recall that cage-reared dogs in the Thompson and Heron (1954) experiment described earlier in the chapter were considerably delayed in figuring out a path to obtain the meat they could see. That experiment suggested that metacognitive strategies are influenced by experience as well as by constitutional factors.

Ann Brown, and others in cognitive psychology, examined metacognitive processes in mild to moderately retarded persons and found them seriously impaired. Subsequently, efforts were made to study how to teach metacognitive strategies, in this instance how to go about memorizing, and it was found that functioning improved. Disappointingly, the strategies learned by persons with retardation did not generalize or transfer spontaneously to contexts different from the one in which they had been trained. This work, and much more, is reviewed in Campione, Brown, and Ferrara (1982). Brown then embarked on a program of research that focussed on how to optimize the circumstances in which metacognitive strategies can be learned, transferred, and applied. Brown and Campione (1984) and Brown et al. (1992) report about that work and present a view about cognitive skill (or intelligence), its cultivation, and assessment, which is quite different from the psychometric approach which underlies intelligence testing.

Brown's approach was heavily influenced by the work of a Russian educational psychologist, Vygotsky, and there is space here to present only some its features. The learning child is viewed as an active agent rather than as a passive recipient of knowledge. Teaching is not the transmission of knowledge to the unlearned but a process of setting conditions under which learning occurs and providing guidance regarding strategies of learning when needed. Learning is viewed as an active social interaction and the instructor is not reluctant at the beginning to provide answers the novice may lack, but at every stage the teacher turns the tables and elicits teaching of what has been learned and problem solving from the novice and thereby fosters initiative and the seeking of solutions rather than the passive repetition of answers. Such skills flower regularly only in the context of a warm supportive relationship.

Brown and colleagues report success in turning around the academic careers of many poor learners. It is fair to say that their greatest success has occurred with children who have come from socioeconomic circumstances adverse to learning, with some unknown proportion of those who might have been or were headed toward some level of psychometric retardation, rather than to those with neuropsychological deficits or severe retardation. On the other hand, in their focus on metacognitive skills and transfer, their work has targeted those places where intelligence falters, and it remains to be seen whether the lessons learned can foster cognitive development hindered by genetic flaws and/or brain damage, particularly if interventions can be introduced early in life.

The tentative answer to the question about learning in persons with retardation is that their learning is burdened by limitations in metacognitive strategies and executive functions. From other literature, it is known that there may be frequent evidence of serious problems in sensory-perceptual processing, motor functions and memory, but these limitations can be compensated for by intact executive functions. If there are profound deficits in executive functions, however, the most that can be done is to structure the environment maximally and keep things as simple as possible. The other implication of the work of Brown and others is that executive functions are susceptible to environmental influence both positively and negatively, that is, both formal and informal education can foster or stifle their development.

What has been learned about the development of executive functions?

The frontal lobes, along with the cerebellum, are the last of the major brain structures to be studied regarding their role in behavior and cognition. Basic research is beginning to sort out different aspects of frontal lobe function (e.g. Stuss & Benson, 1986; Levin, Eisenberg, & Benton, 1991; Stuss, 1992) and the determinants of their course of development. It is known that myelination in the frontal lobes extends into adulthood and it is one of the places in the brain where changes occur in cycles which culminate in sloughing (Yakovlev & Lecours, 1967; Barbas & Pandya, 1991; Diamond, 1991). These very large areas of human brain have the longest span of development and thus may be most susceptible to environmental influence.

It is generally accepted that executive functions mediated by the prefrontal lobes normally emerge clearly and measurably in early and middle adolescence, more or less at the same time that myelination of the frontal lobes is completed. In adolescence and beyond, after executive functions have developed, what changes when prefrontal damage occurs is deterioration of the range of skills described above when describing metacognitive and executive functions.

Much has yet to be learned about how executive functions manifest themselves through the course of development. In attention deficit disorder and other conditions, the inference that executive functions were faulty was made for children with years to go before reaching adolescence, so precursors and early manifestations of these functions must be present. Recall that Barkley (1997) propounded a theory about two kinds of attention, one structured by the environment and the other structured from within, and that it was the latter type of attention that was impaired in ADHD. Structuring attention from within is an aspect of executive functions. A similar kind of a analysis was at the basis of Landry's work described in the previous chapter. Landry et al. (1997) reported outcomes for children at risk over the first 40 months of life following premature birth and subsequent brain damage. Favorable cognitive and social outcomes were associated with parenting styles that were sensitive to and helped maintain the child's initiatives during the course of episodes of joint attention. Recall that initiating behaviors provide the child with experience in structuring situations from within, while being responsive to the caretaker's initiations provides no such experience. Landry hypothesized that initiating skills are precursors of executive functions. Gelman et al. (1998) studied the way mothers interacted with normal children younger than three, and found evidence that the children's abilities to make use of categories, a precursor of abstract thinking and a component of executive functions, varied with the caretaker's way of presenting categorical information.

Thus, research and cognitive development theory have begun to trace environmental influences on the development of executive functions prior to adolescence. Doing such research is immensely difficult, involving the maintenance of relationships with many families over a long period of time, taking repeated measures, and analyzing masses of data. It has taken most of the 20th century to devise the techniques that go into such efforts and the results are new, so that psychometricians have not had access to such data. Furthermore, the stage of development that has been studied, between six months and three or four years, had previously received very little attention. The new evidence indicates that this is a crucial period, environmental contributions are important, and that developmental trajectories are well in place by the age of three. This does not mean that the final path the trajectory will take is absolutely fixed, but it does mean that something substantial is under way, and that, once under way, the likelihood that its course will continue as projected is greater than that it will change. Recall also that Hart and Risley (1995) found that the trajectory for vocabulary development was set by the age of three as a function of the environmental factor of the number of words spoken to the child. Clearly something is being shaped before the age of three that will be fully manifest a long time later. A recent book (Bruer, 1999) that criticizes excessive emphasis on the importance of stimulation during this early stage of development presents an alternate viewpoint but gives no consideration to the kinds of stimulation that foster executive functions.

It is not empirically known whether or how population groups who differ in intelligence differ in the way their members foster initiative in two- or three-year-olds. Blacks, who as a group score about 15 points lower in IQ than Whites in the United States, live in a culture with a legacy of prior slavery, segregation, and legal discrimination. Older Black children and adults showing much initiative, as compared with passive compliance, were in danger of severe punishment and even death, so it would not be too surprising if caretakers found ways of dampening initiative in their youngsters in order to foster survival. It is not known to what extent such practices, if any, continue to this day. Schooler (1976), in a paper entitled *Serfdom's legacy*, describes data which indicate that ethnic groups with a recent history of serfdom show intellectual inflexibility and lack of self-direction. Is this in any way the negative side of the self-initiated attention described by Barkley (1997) or the initiative fostering behavior described by Landry et al. (1997)? A discomfirmable hypothesis is that early ways of discouraging initiative may still be part of child-rearing practices in the Black community. Perhaps research now under way, or future research, will provide an answer.

What might the contribution of neuropsychology be to the understanding of measured intelligence, executive functions, and mental retardation?

Psychometric methods, at their best, assess an individual's level of cognitive function, but do not specify what types of brain dysfunction may be present that underlie a specific level of performance. Neuropsychological methods are used to determine specific sources of impairment, but their application to the study of mental retardation has only recently begun (Pulsifer, 1996). Experience with neuropsychological evaluations of adults with acquired brain damage of the frontal lobes and subsequent deterioration in cognitive functioning has revealed a major limitation of intelligence tests. Standard intelligence tests do not reveal changes in executive functions (Lezak, 1988). Following prefrontal injury, previously successful lawyers who no longer can organize and present their cases, or great cooks who no longer produce decent meals, or skillful mothers who no longer can manage their children, continue to score on intelligence tests much like they did before their injury. Neuropsychologists are thus aware that the executive function component of intelligence is not measured by intelligence tests. Instead they have turned to a number of "frontal lobe tests" which, though useful to some extent, do not do justice to the complexity of these functions. The search for better frontal lobe assessment procedures is an active theme in the neuropsychological literature. Duncan et al. (1996) have suggested a psychometrician's interpretation of the relationship between standard intelligence testing and executive functions; standard tests of intelligence primarily evaluate crystallized intelligence and do not assess fluid intelligence, and it is fluid intelligence that decreases in frontal lobe dysfunction.

After about a century of scientific research on intelligence, the field is in considerable turmoil. Several alternate approaches to evaluating intelligence have appeared (e.g. Kaufman & Kaufman, 1983; Gardner, 1983; Sternberg, 1988; Goleman, 1995) which attempt to meet the various criticisms of traditional tests. Some of these efforts have been somewhat influenced by cognitive neuroscience but it is too early to gauge their impact. One test battery, the Differential Ability Scales (Elliott, 1990), has dropped the term intelligence and simply evaluates cognitive skills in several domains, and thus gets away from the implicit assumption that, in some way, "potential" is being evaluated.

The work of Thatcher on EEG coherence (first described here in chapter 14 in the discussion of the white-matter hypothesis in social learning disability: Thatcher, Walker, & Giudice, 1987; Thatcher, 1992, 1994), which indicated that brain development is driven and organized by the frontal lobes may provide an important clue regarding the way the brain orchestrates cognitive and intellectual development. It suggests that frontal executive functions, rather than emerging as a consequence of developments occurring elsewhere – for example, in language or visuospatial functions – actually organize and drive development in specific modules of the brain.

Research findings on the genetics of brain coherence (van Baal, de Geus, & Boomsma, 1998) offer some possible new insights on how this comes about. They also provide new information about the relationship between hereditary and environmental factors in intellectual development. Coherence differences in the EEGs of identical and fraternal five-year-old twins were studied, and estimates of heritability and environmental influence were calculated. The results indicated that the influence of heredity was greatest for long-distance coherence measures, those between back-of-the-brain sensory areas and frontal areas, whereas the environment played a greater role in the coherences of all adjacent short-distance areas, i.e., of specific modules. Note that the important role of the environment and the lesser role of heredity occurs not only in coherences for modules in sensory areas at the back of the brain but also in frontal areas. These findings are tentative because they have yet to be confirmed by other studies, and data must be collected at other stages of development where the relationship patterns may be different. However, making the assumption that the findings can be repeated, and are applicable to children aged five and somewhat younger, their implications might be as follows.

The finding that the local modules of the frontal lobes (those mediating executive functions) are more under the influence of the environment and experience than of heredity implies a window of opportunity during the course of development in which the environment plays a larger role, in some sense, than heredity. The special importance of these findings is that the modules being influenced by the environment include the ones that will organize and drive the course of development. Now obviously, the influence of heredity is not trivial since the creation of the local modules as well as the integration of distant modules are under hereditary control. Recall that "g," which is strongly heritable, is most reliably measured when it is based on summations of diverse functions. "g," therefore, may be some kind of index of the integration achieved over separate modular information processing skills. It will take detailed longitudinal study of the genetics of coherence to map out how the interplay of these factors leads to cognitive outcomes. Such studies may help to clarify why heritability estimates of cognitive functions vary at different stages of development (McCartney, Harris, & Bernieri, 1990; Plomin et al., 1994; Devlin, Daniels, & Roeder, 1997).

Meanwhile there is evidence in other domains that the trajectory of module development, as has been noted, is well established by the age of three, and that this trajectory is strongly influenced by the type of stimulation received from the environment. Three is about the time the child ceases to be maximally dependent and begins a more independent social life. It seems plausible that the behavior of the caretakers who structure the youngster's early experience may contribute significantly to the kind of executive functions the child may develop. It also means that if the relevant knowledge were available, this might be the time period in which intervention could be effective. At present, however, we know little about these matters. The study of how early experiences shape and promulgate the origins of executive functions has barely begun.

To summarize, it is hypothesized that the way the brain puts together and integrates various aspects of experience is largely determined by heredity. That which drives the trajectory of development and ultimately determines cognitive outcomes are local modules in the frontal lobes that control metacognitive and executive functions and are strongly influenced by experience in a way which is not yet well understood. "g" reflects accomplished heredity-determined integrations between modules, but what is being integrated is heavily influenced by experience. Since this is all taking place at stages of life when the child is still very immature and very dependent, behaviors of caretakers who structure those experiences loom large and may be responsible for some of the correlation of the IQ found between parents and children.

What then is intelligence according to this view? A neuropsychological answer could be that it is the sum total of all the realized information processing skills inherent in the human genome. Every potentiality is important in its own right, but some are vastly more important than others. Consider first the perceptual and feature-detecting systems of the back of the brain. A color-blind individual is less competent than one with color vision, but the difference is fairly trivial. A totally blind person would be seriously compromised in certain very important capabilities, yet this would not preclude intelligent behavior. Helen Keller's life (Lash, 1980) is evidence that even blindness and deafness are not necessarily a barrier to competence although, with such limitations, greater effort and specially skilled instruction are required. Now consider the front of the brain and consider motor skills first. Although retardation often accompanies cerebral palsy, it is not inevitable, and many cerebral palsied individuals demonstrate much intelligence despite severe motor dysfunction. However, when the executive functions of the premotor cortex are considered, failings are consistently associated with mental deficiency while adequacy of at least some executive functions may preclude mental deficiency no matter what deficits may be present in other modules. In this sense, frontal lobe executive function modules are vastly more important than other brain modules. The qualifier, "may preclude," is used because it may be very hard to mobilize remaining perceptual modules when those that permit easy communication are impaired. All deaf persons were thought to be retarded until creative people found ways to communicate with them, and it is unlikely that Helen Keller would have been thought to be intelligent if her teacher, Anne Sullivan, had not found the means to communicate with her. Executive functions are a crucial part of what is deficient in familial mental retardation, Down and Williams syndromes, and PKU, and are not deficient in persons who are not retarded even though they may have severe sensory and/or motor handicaps.

Adult intelligence is a moving target. Today, an average seven- or eight-year-old child can tell you about the solar system and the earth's revolution about the sun, an understanding that required the genius of Copernicus centuries ago. Each succeeding generation builds on the knowledge of prior generations and the amount of such knowledge and the complexity of life is such that it becomes extremely unlikely that one can keep up on all fronts. The twig gets bent in a certain direction because of some combination of talent, opportunity, and circumstance, and a trajectory of development gets established which inevitably benefits some potentialities at the expense of others. The modules of the prefrontal lobes regulate those developments. They themselves are subject to hereditary influence and to environmental input as well. Obtaining data that shed light on these relationships, especially how things get started in the first three years of life, will provide the basis for a theory of intelligence adequate to establish social policy in the twenty-first century. Not enough is known to do so rationally now, but we may know enough about where to look for better answers than we have so far.

Postscript

It is November 1999. The media inform us daily of progress in neuroscience which is unravelling the secrets of the brain. There are reports that we may not be limited to the complement of neurons with which we were born and that new neurons may develop in the course of life. There are periodic reports of progress in completing the map of the human genome. Public health authorities are concerned about long-term consequences for the nervous system of vaccinations in some individuals. New neurotransmitters and neuromodulators are discovered frequently. Little by little, but at faster and faster rates, the complexity of the interactions of billions of neurons is coming to be understood.

While there is unquestioned progress in our comprehension of the genetic and biological characteristics of the brain, there are also breakthroughs in understanding the role of the environment and human relationships in shaping the vast capacities for learning and executive function. The evidence is that the brain continues to display learning capabilities almost until the very end of life, but the more intriguing evidence is that the trajectories of development, especially of executive functions, are set early, before the third year, at which time the future genius, ordinary citizen, and functionally impaired individual are not very different. This does not mean that trajectories cannot be modified, but it does mean that it is easier to get things right from the beginning than it is to modify things later. The intricacies of the interaction between genetic factors and experience during this period have yet to be studied, but it seems likely that our ways of thinking about genetic influence will shift from that of genetic determination to that of genetic interaction.

For the reader who has just been initiated into this field by reading this book, what looms ahead is continued updating and revision of what is known. Sorry about that, but that is the way it is. But readers should be in a different place than they were when they began. What may have seemed incomprehensible before may now be approachable, whether it be the depths of despair in depressed persons, the distractibility of an 8- or a 28-year-old, or the disorganization of a psychotic child or adult. Test yourself. Return to the first chapter and see if the behavior of the teacher makes more sense now than it did when you first read it.

Glossary

(With the assistance of Faith Israel-Simmons and Kyle Simmons)

Abduction Moving a limb away from the central axis of the body.

Acalculia A calculation or arithmetic impairment.

Acceleration–deceleration injuries Injuries to the brain caused by sudden acceleration or deceleration of the brain inside the skull.

Accommodation Changes in the shape of the eye's lens and thus its focus, as a results of changes in ciliary muscle tension.

Acetylcholine A neurotransmitter that is the excitatory agent for muscle contraction at the neuromuscular junction and serves as a neuromodulator or neurohormone in the brain, regulating aspects of sleep, pain perception, and long-term memory.

Acquired A disability that begins after a disease or injury rather than being present from birth.

Acquired epileptiform aphasia (Landau–Kleffner syndrome) Deterioration of language, sometimes reversible, that may co-occur with the appearance of ictal activity; generally in preschool-aged children.

Activation In epilepsy, procedures used to lower the thresholds or existing ictal activity so that ictal pathology can be observed and documented: in motor function, the initiation of action.

Acute Short term and not persistent.

Adaptation: light and dark Tuning light receptors to that appropriate for light conditions: also refers to a characteristic of the visual system in which persistent stimulation of any aspect of the visual field over a period of time, whether a particular location, color, orientation, or shape, temporarily decreases the system's sensitivity to that feature.

Adduction Moving a limb toward the central axis of the body.

Affective Pertaining to feelings, emotions, and especially, mood.

Affective prosody A language's rhythmic and intonation patterns that convey emotional information.

Afferent Any neuronal pathway projecting toward the brain: within the neuron, dendrites project toward the nucleus and are afferent.

Affordance Information conveying the possibilities for action such as the "kickability" of small round objects or the "fillability" of cups.

Agenesis Non-development of organs or tissues.

Agnosia The loss of knowing and understanding what is perceived.

Agonist A substance that increases the activity of a given neurotransmitter.

Air conduction The process of bringing sounds in the air to the nervous system via the auditory canal and middle ear.

Akinetic A type of cerebral palsy associated with stiffness and insufficient movement.

Alcohol-related birth defects See Fetal alcohol effects.

Allocentric space Space with objective external coordinates such as are found on maps.

Alpha (α)   A brain wave with the frequency generally defined at eight to 12 cycles per second.

Alpha motor neurons   Efferent neurons which originate in the spinal cord and activate muscles.

Alveolar   Refers to a slightly prominent ridge on the upper surface of the mouth just behind the teeth. The place of articulation for phonemes such as "sss" and "zzz."

Ambient   Refers to the other stimulation present in the background of focal activity.

Amblyopia   Atrophy of vision stemming from disuse that can extend to blindness.

Amentia   A word still used occasionally in the fields of neurology and psychiatry, which means "without mental capability."

Amplitude   The intensity of energy transmission represented by the height of the wave form. In sound, amplitude determines the loudness; in light, brightness.

Amygdaloid complex   An almond-shaped complex of nuclei near the hippocampus in the medial part of the temporal lobe that plays an important role in emotion and the emotional modulation of memory.

Amyloid precursor protein   A biochemical substance, the overproduction of which is associated with the formation of senile plaques in the brain.

Anabolism   Creation and storage of body energy reserves.

Anaclitic   Means "leaning on" and refers to the utter dependency of an infant on others. Babies severely deprived of stimulation, care, and affection during early infancy develop anaclitic depression characterized by dull, listless, and unresponsive behavior.

Analgesics   Substances that inhibit pain.

Analog information   Observable information that parallels and provides an index of information that is not readily observable; for example, the visible expansion of mercury can be employed as an analog of the temperature.

Aneuploidy   An error of chromosome formation in which entire chromosomes are either missing or excessively present.

Angular acceleration   Acceleration of the brain in a rotational direction which may cause a shearing of neural filaments.

Anhedonia   An inability to experience pleasure.

Annulospiral endings   Sensory nerves that originate on muscle spindles and have receptors that are sensitive to stretch.

Anoxia   Insufficient or no oxygen.

Anterograde   Failure to store and/or retrieve memories of experience subsequent to a pathological event such as concussion. As recovery takes place, lost memories return.

Apgar index   A rating from 1 to 10 which quantifies the general health of a newborn that is based largely on the color and reactivity of the infant.

Aphasia   Acquired impairment of language.

Apnea   Refers to lack of oxygen: persons with sleep apnea repeatedly stop breathing for 10–45 seconds during sleep and wake enough to resume breathing before returning to sleep.

Apperceptive visual agnosia   Impairment in identifying the same object from different perspectives.

Apraxia   Loss of ability to organize and perform effective actions and action sequences while muscle function remains intact.

Arcuate fasciculus   The band of white matter fibers that connects Wernicke's area to Broca's area.

Area V1   Another term for the primary visual area located in the occipital cortex.

Arousal   A shift from idling to activity, from relative synchrony to relative desynchrony.

Association areas   See Tertiary receptive and motor areas.

Association fibers   Fibers that interconnect cortical sites within a hemisphere; short fibers connect adjacent areas, and long fibers, known as fasciculi, connect distant nuclei.

Assortative mating   Individuals within a population do not mate randomly, but rather are more likely to mate with persons from similar circumstances.

Astigmatism   Visual blurring due to unevenness in the surface of the cornea.

Astrocytoma   A tumor caused by a proliferation of a certain type of glial cell that may occur anywhere in the brain, but is relatively frequent during childhood in the cerebellum.

Asymmetric tonic neck reflex   If the head is turned to a side, the limbs on the nasal side will extend and those of the occipital side will flex.

Ataxia   Occurs when the components of movement are present, but coordination is impaired, e.g. walking like a toddler or the Frankenstein monster.

Athetosis   Uncontrollable slow movements.

Attention   A range of psychological processes that select, process, and stay with relevant information and exclude distractions until adaptive behavior sequences are completed.

Attention deficit disorder (ADD)   A childhood disorder that is characterized by inattention, impulsivity, and excessive motor activity.

Atypical child   One of the terms used to describe severe disorders of behavior in children that do not meet criteria for more specific diagnoses.

Audiogram   Report of tests which detect the audibility of pure tones at different frequencies and amplitudes.

Auditory canal   A short irregular tube from the pinna to the tympanic membrane.

Auditory nerve   The eighth cranial nerve that transmits auditory and vestibular information to the cortex.

Auditory–verbal therapy   An educational program for those with severely compromised hearing using the most powerful hearing aids available and training involving auditory and verbal stimulation and vocalization practice which is graded to follow the sequence of normal development.

Aura   A sensory experience that precedes a seizure. The aura can provide valuable information about the location of the focus of the seizure.

Aural method   An approach to teaching deaf children that emphasizes the use of hearing aids and training children to listen.

Autism   A disorder beginning in early childhood characterized by impairments of social responsiveness, language, and arousal regulation.

Autoimmune reaction   The body attacks its own tissues as though they were a foreign invader.

Autosomes   The 22 pairs of chromosomes other than the pair of sex chromosomes, each pair of which is comparable in size, configuration, and band pattern.

Axon   A narrow, liquid-filled, tube extending from a neuron cell body that often divides at the end where there are small swellings called terminal buttons which transmit information to other neurons, muscles, and glands.

Axoplasmic transport   Streams within the body of an axon that flow simultaneously toward and away from the cell body, and which carry materials for the maintenance of the cell membrane and for neurotransmission.

B6-dependent seizure   A type of infantile seizure that can be cured with the administration of vitamin B6.

Backward learning curves   A plot of learning curves that display the percent correct of trials prior to those trials on which the subject attained 90–100 percent correct.

Ballistic movements   Rapid movements such as throwing a ball that are controlled by feed-forward mechanisms.

Basal ganglia   A collection of nuclei, including the caudate, globus pallidus, putamen, and amygdaloid complex near the center of the brain involving attention, and motor functioning.

Beta (β)   A brain wave with the frequency generally defined at 14–21 cycles per second.

Binocular rivalry   The competition between two eyes that precedes fusion into one image.

Binocular vision   Single visual images combined from information obtained by two eyes.

Biofeedback   Refers to a class of procedures wherein information about processes which ordinarily produce no sensation and hence convey no information, such as EEG, blood pressure, or skin conductance are transformed so that the subject can obtain information about their relative state.

Bipolar   Cycling between mania and depression.

Bitemporal hemianopia   Blindness in the temporal half of the retina in each eye which occurs when the optic chiasm is cut.

Blindisms   A class of movements occurring in the blind which includes self-stimulation, such as rocking and pressing on the eyeballs and nearby bone structures to the point that the eye sockets can become abnormally depressed or sunken.

Body image   A personal representation of one's own body and its parts which changes with growth but may take a long time to update after amputation and may be subject to emotional distortion.

Body space   A psychological representation or image that enables you to differentiate places on your body and to know where it is being stimulated.

Bone conduction   The process of bringing sound to the nervous system by imposing vibration on the bones of the skull.

Bradykinesia   A marked slowness of movement.

Brainstem auditory evoked potential   The brain's EEG response to sounds during the first 10 msec after onset which requires averaging the wave forms that emerge following repeated stimulation. Provides information about the integrity of the pathway from cochlea to cortex.

Brazelton scale   A rating scale which generates a developmental quotient more detailed than the Apgar index used by medical personnel to quantify the general health of a newborn.

Breech presentation   When an infant's buttocks are the first part to appear during birth.

Broca's aphasia   A type of language impairment acquired in adulthood, often after a stroke, in which language is understood but cannot be expressed.

Broca's area   An area of the left premotor frontal lobe implicated in the motor organization of speech.

Bronchopulmonary dysplasia   Lung disorders in infants, resulting in compromised breathing that can put an infant at risk for anoxia.

Candida albicans   A common yeast that has been implicated as a possible cause of autistic symptoms when it proliferates in infants because body defenses have been compromised.

Catabolism   Expenditure of body energy.

Cataplexy   A sudden loss of muscle tone.

Cataracts   Cloudy opacities of varying degrees of severity in the lens of the eyes that obscure the passage of light.

Catastrophe reaction   Panic in the face of change in persons with a need to keep the environment constant, usually because of compromised information processing.

Catatonia   Physical underactivity or immobility that may accompany psychosis.

Catecholamines   The family of neuromodulators which includes noradrenaline and dopamine.

Categorical   When a range of stimulation up to a boundary leads to the same output, so that variations within boundaries cannot, but stimuli on either side of the boundary can, be discriminated.

Cauda equina   Final cluster of nerves emerging at the bottom of the thoracic spinal cord.

Caudate   A relatively long looping structure in the basal ganglia involved in voluntary muscle control that reaches up from the amygdaloid complex to the interior of the brain.

Cell body   The enlarged section of a neuron where the nucleus and other structures necessary for cell metabolism are located.

Central sleep apnea   Apnea due to absence of automatic respiratory effort.

Centrencephalic   Refers to a hypothetical abnormal focus deep in the brainstem that sets off a seizure process that appears everywhere in the cortex simultaneously.

Centromere   A constricted area on each chromosome that divides it unevenly into short and long arms, which is used as a reference for mapping a chromosome's regions.

Cerebellum   A relatively large structure under the cerebral cortex behind the medulla and pons which is involved in motor integration, and sequencing, attention, and learning.

Cerebral cortex   The outer, visible part of the mantle which surrounds the brain that is composed primarily of gray matter and is involved in higher cognitive functions.

Cerebrocerebellum   Also known as the posterior lobe of the cerebellum, this structure receives inputs from nuclei in the pons that relay information from the cerebral cortex. The outputs of this structure project to the thalamus, and thus can modulate cortical activity.

Cerumen   The technical term for ear wax.

Cervical   The region of the neck.

Channels   In the visual system, the entire range of visible spatial frequencies is divided up into five or more overlapping ranges each of which is processed relatively independently, i.e. in separate channels.

Childhood psychosis; not otherwise specified   One of the terms used to describe severe disorders of behavior in children that do not meet criteria for more specific diagnoses.

Chorea Uncontrolled fast movements.

Choreoathetoid Refers to a combination of fast and slow excessive movement.

Choroid membrane The dark membrane immediately behind the retina toward which the visual sensors point.

Choroid plexus papilloma A type of tumor that develops within the structures in the ventricles that produce cerebrospinal fluid.

Chromosomal errors Errors in the organization or structure of chromosomes which affect large numbers of genes and many traits.

Chromosome Strands of DNA material on which genes are arranged which in humans occur in 23 pairs.

Chronic Persistent over a long period of time, sometimes over the lifespan.

Cilia Flexible hairs.

Ciliary muscle A muscle of the eye that by tensing or relaxing flattens the lens or allows it to bulge and thus controls its shape.

Cingulate gyrus A broad horizontally running gyrus on the medial surface of the cortex above the corpus callosum which has been implicated in attentional and executive functioning and is closely linked to the limbic system.

Closed head injury When an external force impacts on the skull with enough energy to cause damage to the brain without fracturing the skull.

Closed systems A nonliving mechanical or electronic system which is not self-replenishing.

Cochlea Synonym for "inner ear," snail-shaped organ where sound transduction takes place.

Cochlear duct The middle compartment of the cochlea between the vestibular and tympanic canals in which the organ of Corti is situated.

Cochlear implant An electronic device in which electrodes are implanted in the cochlea which convey electrical impulses from a microphone which stimulates the origins of the auditory nerve. Subjects have to learn how to hear the significance of the resulting sound experience.

Coherence An EEG analysis that computes the extent to which activity at one EEG electrode site corresponds to the activity at another.

Collector cells Cells in the retina which include bipolar, horizontal, and amacrine cells. They receive information from transducer cells (rods and cones) and transmit to ganglion cells whose axons make up the optic nerve.

Coma A significant, long-lasting loss of consciousness due to trauma or some pathological process.

Combined spelling errors Misspellings that are both dysphonetic and dyseidetic.

Commissures Bands of neurons between the left and right hemispheres, the largest of which is the corpus callosum, that make possible inter-hemispheric communication and selective inhibition between the two sides.

Commissurotomy An operation in which the bands of tissue connecting the two hemispheres of the brain are cut.

Communicating hydrocephalus Hydrocephalus that results from inadequate reabsorption of cerebrospinal fluid in the subarachnoid spaces under the dura.

Comorbid Multiple, concurrent disorders occurring in the same individual.

Compulsions Repeated uncontrollable action patterns.

Conceptual skill Cognitive skills including abstraction, categorization, symbol manipulation, and reasoning that facilitate higher learning.

Concrete operations The ability to think logically on the basis of concrete premises and to organize thought on the basis of categories which, according to Piaget, develop between the ages of six and eight.

Concussion A condition characterized by disorientation, neck pain, headache, and loss or clouding of memory and consciousness that may last anywhere from minutes to days or weeks following a blow to the head.

Conduct disturbance (CD) A childhood disorder in which the child is easily provoked to aggression, violates the rights and privileges of others, and may be seen as disobedient by adults.

Conduction aphasia A disorder that is caused by a lesion that cuts the arcuate fasciculus and prevents communication between Wernicke's and Broca's areas. The main symptom is difficulty repeating heard utterances.

Cones A type of visual transducer cell that reacts to color and high-frequency spatial and low-frequency temporal information.

Congenital syphilis An intrauterine infection of the fetus caused by a spirochete whose symptoms appear two or more weeks after birth and are similar to those of toxoplasmosis and cytomegalovirus.

Conjunctive eye movements The eyes moving together in tandem; the two types are slow following utilizing negative feedback, and ballistic, using feed-forward mechanisms.

Constitutional A term which refers in a general way to the physical characteristics of the body, particularly to body's architecture and physical structure.

Constructional praxis Skills needed to deal with tasks which require the active organization of structures in space for which old solutions are not available.

Content words In English, nouns, verbs, adjectives, and adverbs.

Continence The ability to regulate excretion as desired.

Continuous performance task (CPT) A commonly used test of attention requiring sustained vigilance and response inhibition.

Contractures The muscles stiffen and permanently resist stretching, immobilizing the joints in maladaptive postures which can occur following prolonged spasticity.

Contralateral Opposite (contra) side (lateral).

Contrast In regard to the visibility of a grating, the amplitude of the wave form which reflects the blackness of the blacks and the whiteness of the whites.

Contrast sensitivity function A graph that displays contrast thresholds for a range of visual—spatial frequencies.

Contusion A technical term for a sore or a cut in tissue.

Cornea The outer transparent layer of the eye.

Corollary discharge A signal that informs the brain that activity was initiated from within which differentiates active from passive movement.

Corpus callosum A massive band of fibers that crosses the longitudinal fissure and connects corresponding points of the cortex in the two hemispheres.

Correlation The degree to which two measures are associated, co-vary, or go along together.

Cortical blindness Blindness due to disruption of visual processing in the occipital cortex; distinguished from blindness caused by impairments of the eye or optic nerve.

Corticotropin-releasing factor (CRF) A secretion of the hypothalamus which regulates a range of physiological responses activated under conditions of stress.

Cortisol A hormone that promotes catabolic activity and is part of the stress response. It is almost totally absent early in sleep and reappears some two to three hours before awakening.

Coup–contrecoup A type of closed head injury in which the brain impacts with one side of the skull (coup) and then bounces back to impact with the skull on the opposite side (contrecoup).

Covert attention The deployment of attention by mental activity without necessarily engaging in receptor orienting activity.

Craniopharyngioma A type of tumor that is found at or near the bone structure in which the pituitary gland is located in the front undersurface of the brain below the optic chiasm.

Cretinism A type of mental deficiency caused by an early failure to obtain adequate amounts of iodine, especially during gestation.

Cross-sectional Research designs in which groups of individuals of different ages are evaluated and compared after being tested once at approximately the same time.

Cycles per second The same meaning as frequency and synonymous with Hertz (Hz).

Cystic structure A tumor with a central cavity that may contain liquid or semisolid materials.

Cytogeneticists Scientists who study the cellular mechanisms of inheritance.

Cytomegalovirus A widespread type of herpes virus which can be passed to a fetus via the placenta, especially during the first two trimesters.

Decibel (dB) A unit for measuring sound intensity that is based on the ratio of the energy present in a particular sound to the minimal intensity audible to the ear.

Decussation Crossing over such as occurs to the cortical motor pathways in the medulla which enables the left side of the brain to control muscles on the right side of the body.

Deep structure   Implicit rules that organize and regulate language production.

Deficit   An impairment of functioning due to the subtraction of realized or potential capabilities; implies that cells and tissues which should be present and functioning have been destroyed or rendered nonfunctional.

Delta (Δ)   Brain waves whose frequencies are between one and three cycles per second. Normally delta waves occur when a person is asleep.

Delusions   False beliefs.

Dementia   Sharply declining mental competence occurring after the attainment of higher levels of functioning.

Demyelinating diseases   Diseases, e.g. multiple sclerosis, which destroy or impair myelin.

Dendrites   From the Greek word "dendron," which means tree, dendrites are the extensions of a neuron that receive information from other neurons.

Deoxyribonucleic acid (DNA)   A complex molecule made up of four nucleotides (adenine, guanine, cytosine, and thymine) constructed in the shape of a double helix in which genes are coded.

Depolarization   The process of losing an electrical charge. When neurons fire, the membrane surrounding the axon allows positively charged potassium ions to enter the cell, causing a rapid decrease in polarization. Depolarization continues in a wave down the length of the axon, and initiates synaptic transmission.

Depressed skull fracture   When an external force (e.g. a brick) fractures the bones of the skull and fragments of the skull are depressed into the underlying meninges or beyond into the parenchyma.

Depression   An affective disorder in which a person feels blue, low, sad, and unhappy.

Desynchrony   Low-amplitude brain wave forms generated when component units are active at their own pace; energy from individual units cancels rather than cumulates with that of other units.

Developmental aphasia   Failure to develop normal language functions.

Diaschisis   The idea that pathology in part of the system not only has its own direct effects, but may also interfere with the functions of normal areas with which it is interconnected, however remotely.

Diatheses   Vulnerabilities which make one more susceptible to the effects of stress.

Diencephalon   The area of the fetal brain lying between the telencephalon and mesencephalon which develops into the thalamus and hypothalamus.

Difficult child   A child characterized by irregularity in biological functions, negative withdrawal responses to new stimuli, non-adaptability or slow adaptability to change and intense mood expressions which are frequently negative.

Diffuse axonal injury   Depending on the force of impact and the direction of rotation of the brain during a traumatic event, neural filaments (i.e. the outer membranes of axons) may be bruised, stretched, twisted, or sheared apart.

Digits   In anatomy, fingers and toes.

Diplegia   Bilateral spasticity of the upper or lower limbs.

Diplopia   Double vision.

Disassociation   A neuropsychological concept indicating that two or more functions are independent and are mediated by separate neural circuits such that, if one is impaired or destroyed, the other may continue to function.

Disengage   Refers to the release of attention from wherever it might have been focussed so that it may be deployed elsewhere.

Disinhibition   Diminished or absent inhibition; a loss of control.

Disorganization   A condition that disrupts the functioning of the nervous system, but may stop spontaneously or may be arrested by treatment, leaving the organism intact and without impairment.

Disseminated tumors   Tumors whose cells do not clump together, but rather spread over a wide area.

Distal space   The space beyond one's reach.

Dopamine   A neuromodulator whose major source is in the substantia nigra which is found in the brainstem, basal ganglia, limbic system, and the prefrontal cortex, which has been implicated in such functions as sustained attention and maintenance of set controlled from within, emotional regulation, and initiation and regulation of movement.

Dorsal   Toward the top; for most vertebrates toward the spinal cord.

Dorsiflexion   Bend back: describes movements of neck or wrist.

Dorsolateral prefrontal cortex   Areas in the upper half and side of the prefrontal cortex; implicated in working memory.

Down syndrome   A condition caused by the presence of an extra chromosome 21 that is characterized by dysmorphic physical features, mental retardation, and the development of plaques and neurofibrillary tangles in middle adulthood.

Dynamic   When used in regard to the auditory system; having to do with detecting change.

Dys   Greek prefix referring to impairment but not total loss of function.

Dysarthria   A disorder of expressive language ability due to impairment of the musculature and other structures which produce speech sounds.

Dyscontrol   A general term for conditions that disrupt behavior but may stop spontaneously or may be arrested by treatment, leaving the organism intact.

Dyseidetic spelling errors   Misspellings which when decoded permit the retrieval of the word meant to be spelled because phonetic structure is preserved.

Dysgnosia   The partial loss of skill in knowing and understanding while sensation and perception are intact.

Dysgraphia   Poor writing mechanics.

Dyskinesias   Flawed, impaired, or uncontrolled movements.

Dyslexia   A selective lag in reading skill synonymous with reading disability.

Dysmorphic   Structurally distorted.

Dysphonetic spelling errors   Misspellings which, when decoded phonetically, do not allow retrieval of the word meant to be spelled.

Dyspraxia   The impairment of a person's ability to organize and perform effective actions and action sequences while muscle function is intact.

Dyssemia   Impairment in the comprehension of symbols, nonverbal social cues such as facial expressions, body posture, and voice prosody.

Dysthymia   Persistent mildly depressed mood.

Eardrum   See Tympanic membrane.

Easy child   A child characterized by regularity, positive approach responses to new stimuli, high adaptability to change, and mild or moderate mood intensity which is preponderantly positive.

Edema   A swelling of tissue which in the brain can lead to increased intracranial pressure.

Educable mentally retarded   Retarded persons who can learn to read and write who ultimately attain about a fifth-grade level of education and who, when mature, may be employed and attain partial or full independence.

Efferent   A neuronal pathway projecting away from the brain toward other neurons, muscles, or glands: within the neuron, axons are efferent.

Ego-alien   Behavior that is not consistent with the person's self-image.

Egocentric space   Space where the self is the reference point.

Electroconvulsive therapy (ECT)   The technique of applying an electric current to the scalp so as to elicit a major convulsive seizure.

Electrode   A device, usually a small piece of metal, that conducts electricity; a transducer for EEG.

Electroencephalograph (EEG)   The assessment tool that represents voltage differences emerging from the brain between a site on the scalp and some neutral reference.

Electromyography (EMG)   Measurement of the electrical output caused by muscle activity.

Emmetropia   The technical term for normal focus vision.

Encephalitis   An infection of brain tissue.

Encephalopathy   A general term for brain pathology.

Endogenous   Not associated with environmental provocation but initiated autonomously.

Endogenous stimulation   In studying attention, information about the location of a stimulus provided by a symbol that must be interpreted by the brain. Contrast with exogenous stimulation.

Endolymph   The liquid in the cochlear duct and semicircular canals.

Endorphins Naturally occurring, pain-inhibiting compounds found in the brain.

Enhance In relation to covert attention, refers to an enhancement of attention to a target that has been detected.

Enuresis When a child past the ages of three to five cannot inhibit urination in sleep and/or respond to urinary urgency by rousing from sleep and going to the toilet.

Enzyme A biochemical catalyst. The postsynaptic membrane releases enzymes which cleave and deactivate the molecules of neurotransmitters.

Ependyma The tissue that lines the cerebral ventricle. Ependyma is particularly susceptible to hemorrhaging in premature infants in hypoxic stress.

Ependymomas A type of tumor that grows out of the cells that line the cerebral ventricles, most often the fourth ventricle.

Epileptogenic Seizure-producing.

Episodic memory Memory for events and episodes (such as remembering what occurred on your last birthday).

Equilibrium reflexes Reflexes that return the body to a stable position when it is off balance.

Ethanol Ethyl alcohol, the intoxicating ingredient in alcoholic drinks.

Eustachian tube A tube between the middle ear and the throat.

Excessive daytime sleepiness A major symptom of narcolepsy. See Multiple sleep latency test.

Excitatory Postsynaptic potentials that are depolarizing and increase the likelihood of a neuron firing.

Excitatory amino acid release Immediately following brain trauma, injured nerve tissues spontaneously release massive amounts of excitatory neurotransmitter into extracellular space. This is excitotoxic and leads to swelling of neurons and glia and often to cell death.

Excitotoxic Excessively and poisonously excitatory, overwhelming negative feedback mechanism that maintains a balance of ions necessary for normal neurotransmission.

Executive functions Mental operations that include working memory, planning, sequencing, and error evaluation; thought to be functions of the frontal lobe.

Exogenous psychopathology Psychopathology associated with environmental stress.

Exogenous stimulation In studies of attention, information about the location of a stimulus coming directly from that stimulus. Contrast with endogenous stimulation.

Expressive dysphasia An impairment of language due to malfunction of brain mechanisms which regulate the apparatus that creates speech sounds. See Broca's aphasia.

Extension Straightening or stretching a joint.

Extrafusal fibers Muscle fibers that do the work of contraction.

Extraocular muscles Three pairs of muscles that control the movement of the eye.

Extrapyramidal system A phylogenetically older area of the brain that helps regulate movement, whose main components are the basal ganglia.

Factor analysis A method of statistical analysis that seeks to reveal the underlying structure of correlations obtained from different kinds of tests.

Failure to thrive See Marasmus.

Familial mental retardation Mental retardation in a person with behavioral evidence of low intelligence and no evidence of genetic or other organic abnormality, whose parents are of low intelligence.

Feed-forward mechanisms Mechanisms that anticipate, predict, and preset levels of reaction for ballistic movements where there is no time for negative feedback to operate, e.g. throwing.

Fetal alcohol effects A condition that is less than the full complement of fetal alcohol syndrome symptoms.

Fetal alcohol syndrome (FAS) Altered physical structures, growth retardation, and central nervous system impairments in the fetus whose mother engages in heavy alcohol consumption during pregnancy.

Fine motor Movement systems capable of rapid and precise control, such as hand and finger movements; eye movements; and movements of the vocal cords, throat, tongue, and mouth that emit speech sounds.

Finger agnosia Difficulty identifying which finger was touched when eyes are closed.

Fissures Deep canyons in the cortex.

Fixations Pausing of eye movement scanning for 200–400 msec while reading to decode small groups of words.

Flexion Bending a joint.

Flicker Refers to reversals of dark and light parts of a grating. At high frequencies the grating disappears and the area which it occupies appears uniform in color.

Flynn effect The finding that actual performance (as opposed to relative performance) on measures of fluid intelligence has risen significantly over the past 80 years all over the world and among all racial groups at a rate of approximately 15 IQ points every 30 years.

Focal Refers to that which is in focus, e.g. what stimulation is activating behavior at a specific time, as compared to what stimulation is also present at that time. See Ambient.

Focus Site in the brain where seizures may originate (plural = foci).

Forceps Large clamps that an obstetrician may use to pull, push, or rotate a fetus as needed during birth.

Forebrain The front portion of the fetal brain whose later development includes the cortex, thalamus, and hypothalamus.

Formants The bands in a sound spectrogram that represent clusters of frequencies emitted over time.

Fornix A structure in the limbic system whose columns rise up from the mammillary bodies and then arch backward and around until they merge with the hippocampus.

Fovea The center of the eye where most of the cones are located; covers one degree of visual angle.

Fragile-X-mental-retardation-protein (FMRP) The protein produced in excess by the FMR-1 gene.

Frequency The number of cycles per second. In sound, frequency determines the pitch; in light, the color.

Frequency distributions A table or graph describing the number of individuals attaining each of a range of scores.

Frontal lobe The area of the cortex that lies in front of the central sulcus, involved with motor and executive functions.

Full mutation In fragile-X syndrome, the repetition of a specific DNA sequence, the CGG triplet (CG, GC, GC) in excess of 200.

Function words In English articles, prepositions, and other generally small words which are needed to organize any particular expression.

Fundamental frequency The strongest sound frequency emanating from a source that determines its perceived pitch.

g loading The degree to which a test measures "g." A theoretical term proposed by Spearman which refers to general intellectual ability thought to be present in all types of competencies.

Gametes A term for either a sperm or an ovum.

Gamma motor neurons Small-diameter nerve fibers that control the tone-setting intrafusal muscles.

Gamma-aminobutyric acid (GABA) An amino acid that is the main inhibitory neurotransmitter.

Ganglia Clumps of neural cell body processors which lie outside the spinal cord (singular; ganglion).

Genes Biochemical codes made of DNA which singly and in combination control the timing and construction of the structure of the body.

Genetic errors A condition in which one or only a few specific genes are missing or aberrant.

Genome The total ensemble of genes on all the chromosomes.

Genotype An individual's genetic makeup which can be thought of as an individual's construction plan.

Geons The elementary components of three-dimensional shapes that are extracted by the visual system when recognizing an object (construct proposed by Biederman).

Gerstmann syndrome An acquired syndrome with symptoms of acalculia, left–right confusion, dysgraphia, and finger agnosia.

Gestation The development of a fetus in the uterus between conception and birth.

Glia Types of cells that hold neurons together and support their functioning.

Global aphasia Serious impairments in all areas of the language function.

Globus pallidus   Part of the basal ganglia; the globus pallidus and the putamen form the lenticular nucleus.

Glottis   A small opening located at the end of the vocal cords.

Glutamate   An amino acid that serves as an excitatory neurotransmitter.

Gnosis   Refers to overall facility in knowing and understanding.

Golgi tendon organ   A sensor embedded in the tendon which attaches muscle to bone which fires at a rate proportional to the intensity of muscle contraction and hence gives information about magnitude of work being done by the muscle.

Goodness-of-fit model   Adjustment problems resulting from a mismatch between the temperament of the parents and that of the child.

Grand mal   French for "big sick"; same as a tonic–clonic seizure: seizure process includes loss of consciousness and most muscle control.

Grapheme-to-phoneme translation rules   Regularities in the correspondences between alphabetic letters and the word-sounds they represent.

Grasp reflex   When any object comes into contact with an infant's open palm, it elicits a simultaneous flexion of all fingers.

Grasping space   The area surrounding the individual that is reachable by movement of the limbs.

Grating   A physical representation of some spatial frequency displaying gradual changes from dark to light and back.

Gross motor   Refers to activity of the entire body; e.g. rolling over, sitting, standing, and locomotion.

Growth hormone   A hormone that promotes growth and anabolic activity secreted from the pituitary gland maximally during the first bout of Stage 4 sleep in normal children and adults.

Gyri   The bulging parts of the convolutions of the cortex; singular, gyrus.

Habituation   The attenuation of orienting reactions to novel events when they become familiar or prove to be benign: the tendency for behavioral reactions to diminish to non-noxious repetitious stimulation.

Hallucinations   Perceptions in the absence of objective external stimulation.

Handicap dynamics   The psychological consequences of having a handicap to those who have them or to those who associate with or treat persons who have them.

Helicotrema   The small passage-way in the cochlea that connects the vestibular canal to the tympanic canal.

Hemianopia   Blindness in half of the visual field.

Hemiplegia   Unilateral spasticity.

Hemispherectomy   A surgical procedure in which the entire cortex, much of the white matter, often the basal ganglia, and other structures are removed, essentially doing away with a hemisphere.

Hemispheres   The halves of the brain that are separated by the longitudinal fissure.

Hemorrhage   A rupture in a blood vessel that results in blood spilling into the surrounding tissue.

Herpes simplex   An omnipresent virus, usually warded off by the immune system, which in adults can produce a chronic genital infection. It may occasionally find its way into the central nervous system resulting in a devastating encephalitis. In infants, the possibility of invading the nervous system is much greater, often resulting in significant impairment or death.

Hierarchy   Refers to the complexity and evolutionary stage at which a behavior or function emerged. For example, language is hierarchically high and habituation is hierarchically low.

High-level autism   Persons with autism who develop relatively high levels of language skill.

Hindbrain   The rear portion of the fetal brain whose later development includes the pons and the medulla.

Hippocampus   A part of the limbic system that is buried in the temporal lobes and which plays an important part in the encoding and retrieval of memories.

Histologic   A term referring to cell form and organization (noun, histology).

Homonymous   Refers to the same half (either left or right) of the visual field in each eye.

Homunculus   Means "little person." The homunculus describes the representation of different body parts along the precentral gyrus, the size devoted to a specific body part reflecting the complexity of motor control of which it is capable.

Human immunodeficiency virus (HIV) A virus that gradually disables the body's immune system, thus leaving it susceptible to other viruses and infections that would normally pose no threat.

Huntington's chorea A debilitating disorder in which a genetic flaw present from birth exerts itself 35–40 years later by causing the depletion of a crucial neurotransmitter resulting in mental and physical deterioration soon followed by death.

Hyaline membrane disease A condition that may occur in premature infants, which can result in hypoxia and asphyxiation because of an insufficient surfactant in the lungs that facilitates the absorption of oxygen.

Hydrocephalus A condition resulting from the obstruction of the circulation, production, or reabsorption of cerebrospinal fluid within the ventricular system, which results in the excessive accumulation of fluid, increased interventricular pressure, and enlargement of the cerebral ventricles at the cost of adjacent brain structures.

Hypercolumn A grouping of cortical cell columns each preferentially sensitive to specific visual features impinging on a particular point on the retina of one eye.

Hyperopia Farsightedness, occurs because light from nearby objects is focussed behind the retina.

Hyperphenylalaninemia A mild version of PKU caused by a minimally functional gene in which highly elevated levels of phenylalanine do not occur and tyrosine levels are not significantly depressed.

Hyperplasia A term denoting an increase in tissue or organ size due to excessive/abnormal development.

Hyperpolarize The mechanism of neural inhibition in which a neurotransmitter causes positive ions to flow out of the cell so that polarization is increased, making it more difficult to fire.

Hyperventilation Intense, voluntary, rapid breathing which may activate some types of seizures, especially absence.

Hypoplasia A term denoting a reduction in tissue or organ size due to insufficient/abnormal development.

Hypothalamus A collection of nuclei deep in the brain that are involved in the regulation of a number of vegetative functions such as feeding and drinking and the expression of emotion.

Hypothetical constructs Useful theoretical ideas that do not necessarily have a physical manifestation in nature.

Hypoxia Inadequate oxygen.

Hypsarrhythmia The EEG pattern associated with infantile spasms or West's syndrome which contain high-voltage spikes all over the brain.

Ictus A seizure state: a state of neural dyscontrol (adjective, ictal).

Ideographs Quasi-pictorial systems of representing a language visually; written Chinese is ideographic.

Idiopathic Pathology without known cause.

Impulsivity The failure to inhibit behavior in accord with social conditions. For example, speaking out of turn.

Inattention Failure to maintain attention where attention can be expected.

Indoleamines A type of monoamine neuromodulator, the prime example of which is serotonin.

Infarct Ischemia due to a blockage within a blood vessel.

Inferior prefrontal cortex The area at the bottom and side of the prefrontal cortex which has connections to the limbic system and plays a role in linking motives and emotions to organized behaviors.

Inhibitory Postsynaptic potentials that are hyperpolarizing and decrease the likelihood of a neuron firing. Refers to neural mechanisms that stop or curtail neural activity.

Inner hair cells The main transducers in the organ of Corti that change sound waves into nerve impulses.

Insula An area of cortex the lies within and behind the lateral sulcus. Just inside the insula lies the lenticular nucleus of the basal ganglia.

Intelligence quotient (IQ) Mental age divided by chronological age. Although the term continues to be used, IQ scores are no longer based on calculated quotients.

Intention   Preparation for action.

Interictal   Seizure-related behavior that occurs between seizures.

Intermodal integration   The ability to detect constancies across sense modalities, for example the letter "s" and the sound of "s."

Internalization of speech   Self-directed cueing and speech, a component of executive functioning.

Interneurons   Neurons with short axons that connect to other neurons in the spinal cord; part of the processing mechanisms in the spinal cord.

Interstimulus interval   The time between the conclusion of one stimulus and the initiation of a second.

Intractable   Refers to recurrent seizures, resistant to any treatment.

Intrafusal fibers   Muscle fibers that stretch when the extrafusal fibers stretch and are involved in setting the tone and readiness for action of the muscle.

Intrauterine growth retardation   Synonymous with low birth weight at full-term gestation.

Ionotropic   Postsynaptic receptors which receive direct transmission.

Ions   Charged particles. Ions are atoms which have either more or less electrons than protons, and so have either a positive or negative charge. Changes in the ratio of sodium (Na^-) and potassium (K^+) ions within the axon are critical for the depolarization necessary for an action potential to take place.

Ipsilateral   Same (ipsi) side (lateral).

Iris   The colored circular muscle band that opens and closes to admit more or less light into the eye.

Iron deficiency anemia   A non-life-threatening condition caused by an inadequate intake of iron in children six to 24 months of age that is associated with fearfulness, irritability, and fussiness.

Ischemia   Blocked blood supply depriving tissues of nutrients and oxygen.

Jacksonian march   A type of seizure that begins at a particular place in the brain and then captures other areas.

Jacksonian seizure   Uncontrollable movements or muscle twitches caused by a focal seizure.

Joie de vivre   A French phrase meaning "joy of life."

Joint attention   Shared attention directed at specific external objects or events between a child and caretaker.

K complexes   Singular high-amplitude waves in the sleep EEG that vaguely resemble a written "K" which occurs during Stage 2 sleep.

Karyotype   A pictorial summary of the number and nature of the chromosomes present in a tissue sample.

Ketosis   The process during starvation in which the body digests its own fat as a source of energy.

Kinaesthetic   Refers to sensors in the muscles and tendons which provide information about the movements of joints.

Kindling   In the epilepsy literature, kindling refers to the cumulative effects of below-threshold doses of epileptogenic agents.

Kinetic   A type of cerebral palsy associated with writhing and excessive movement.

Kinetic melody   Well-organized complex movements found in skills such as typing, sewing, or dancing. A term coined by Luria describing the functions of the premotor cortex.

Kwashiorkor   A type of protein–energy malnutrition which generally appears during the first and third years and is primarily a consequence of deficiencies in protein intake when there is adequate carbohydrate intake.

Labio-dental   The place of articulation for a sound that is produced by the lips and teeth, as in "fff" or "vvv."

Labor: latent phase of first stage   The earliest stage of labor in which contractions of the uterus begin at irregular intervals, the cervix begins to soften and widen, and the fetus begins to move toward the uterus.

Labor: first stage   The events of childbirth that occur prior to the cervix dilating to 10 cm, and when the baby is positioned to emerge.

Labor: second stage   The final stage of labor, lasting anywhere from 15 minutes to one hour, characterized by strong and regular contractions which occur at increasingly rapid intervals until the child emerges.

Landau–Kleffner syndrome See Acquired epileptiform aphasia.

Larynx The voice box including the vocal cords and the glottis.

Lateral corticospinal tract A tract of neurons in the lateral funiculus that originate in the cortex, and that synapses directly onto motor neurons controlling the digits.

Lateral geniculate A nucleus of the thalamus that relays information from the eyes to the primary visual cortex in the occipital lobe.

Laterodorsal tegmental nucleus (LDT) One of the two sites that initiates REM sleep. It can be found in the upper part of the front end of the pons and a little behind and below the pedunculopontine nucleus.

L-dopa A precursor of dopamine used in treating Parkinson disease.

Learning disability Difficulty in mastering the basic academic skills of reading, arithmetic, and writing, or the conceptual skills needed to understand many academic subjects because of some limitation in component information processing skills.

Left–right confusion Confusion about spatial orientation (left and right), and letter orientation.

Lens The part of the eye that bends and focusses admitted light onto the retina.

Lenticular nucleus A part of the basal ganglia comprising the globus pallidus and the putamen.

Leukemia A malignant cancer of blood cells which before the advent of radiation therapy generally had survival durations of only four months after diagnosis.

Lexical decision task A procedure used to study mental functions in which the subject must decide whether a group of letters make up a real word. Accuracy and reaction time are measured.

Lexicon A store of words with their associated meanings needed for expression and comprehension of language.

Limbic system A collection of nuclei (including the fornix, hippocampus, mammillary bodies, and amygdaloid complex) and pathways that are located in or near the underside of the brain, which are involved in memory and emotional functioning.

Linguistic prosody A language's rhythmic and intonation pattern that conveys linguistic meaning, e.g. asking a question.

Lipids Fats; lipids are important because they constitute much of the cell wall of neurons and myelin and are a solvent for a number of vitamins.

Lobules Layered regions of brain tissue. The ten cerebellar lobules are grouped into three lobes called the anterior, posterior, and flocculonodular lobes.

Locus ceruleus A structure in the brain just under the upper part of the cerebellum that is a rich source of the neuromodulater noradrenaline.

Logographs See Ideographs.

Longitudinal studies Research designs in which individual subjects are followed over time and studied at least twice and often repeatedly.

Low birth weight Infants born weighing less than 2,500 grams.

Lower motor neurons Neurons in the spinal cord which exit via the ventral root and enervate muscle.

Lumbar The region of the lower back.

Lumbar puncture A procedure in which a needle is inserted into the spinal cord and a sample of cerebrospinal fluid is collected for analysis.

Machroorchidism Large testicles, a frequent physical characteristic occurring in fragile-X syndrome.

Macula The area of the eye that surrounds the fovea, containing mostly cones and some rods, which covers five degrees of visual angle.

Magnetic resonance imaging (MRI) A non-invasive scan of the brain that produces detailed images of brain structures which makes use of the magnetic properties of tissues.

Magnocellular Those visual channels made up of larger cells, that are sensitive to low-frequency spatial information and high-frequency temporal information.

Magnocellular nucleus Located in the upper lateral portion of the medulla, the source of motor neuron inhibition of the spinal cord which produces REM sleep paralysis.

Mammillary bodies Rounded limbic structures at the end of the fornix in the limbic system.

Mania An affective disorder in which a person's mood is euphoric, activity level and subjective confidence is high, and judgment is impaired.

Manner of articulation Differences in the production of phonemes by how the sound is produced, e.g. fricatives such as "sss" made by passing a continuous stream of air through the vocal apparatus or stop consonants such as "b" or "t" which are created by stopping the air flow completely and then releasing the air in a small burst.

Marasmus A type of malnutrition, generally in the first year of life (sometimes referred to as failure to thrive) due to insufficient sources of carbohydrates and fats, and marked by failure to grow, apathy, and irritability.

Masking procedures A procedure used in vision research in which a stimulus is presented and then followed at varying short intervals by another stimulus – the mask – which, if the interval is short enough, will prevent the perception of the original stimulus.

Mass action A view that emphasizes the functioning of the entire brain working as a whole, rather than its modular aspects in which specific types of information processing occur in specific structures.

Medial Toward or in the middle.

Medial geniculate A nucleus of the thalamus that relays information from the cochlea to the primary auditory cortex in the temporal lobes.

Medial prefrontal cortex Areas on the undersurface of the frontal lobes which are an extension of the inferior and orbital prefrontal cortices.

Medulla Located just above the spinal cord, contains nuclei which control tonic reflexes and a major part of the reticular formation.

Medulloblastoma A type of tumor which commonly originates in the cerebellum in childhood.

Meiosis The process by which gametes are formed such that each carries only half the chromosomes, one from each of the 23 pairs, found in humans.

Melatonin A substance secreted in the brain which plays a role in sleep and responds to day–night cycles.

Meningiomas Tumors which arise from the meninges and are generally separate from the brain but can compress its tissue.

Meningitis An infection of the meninges, the tough protective membranes that surround the brain.

Meningoencephalitis An infection of brain tissue and the surrounding meninges.

Mental age In intelligence testing, denotes the level of mental functioning of an average individual of a particular age.

Mental chronometry The measurement of the time it takes to perform mental tasks, e.g. the time it takes to press a button after the onset of a signal.

Metabolism The regulation of the storage and consumption of energy.

Metabotropic Postsynaptic receptors which require amplification via cyclic AMP and thus operate more slowly then ionotropic receptors.

Metacognition A variety of skills that make possible successful learning and problem solving, and includes knowledge of one's own mental processes, awareness of success or failure in problem solving, knowing when to rehearse and double check, and how to orchestrate one's resources to pick the best available strategy to deal with whatever problem is at hand.

Microcephaly "Small head," a condition associated with mental retardation in which the brain is compacted.

Midbrain During gestation the midbrain is the location where there is a major bend in the developing brain which divides it into front and rear portions. Later, the tectum and tegmentum are differentiated.

Milieu Refers to the environment: used as a general term to refer to adjacent structures and to the fluids which bathe and nurture neurons.

Minisaccades Tiny eye movements, invisible to the naked eye, that occur continuously.

Mitosis The process of cell division for all cells other than gametes.

Mixed sleep apnea Apnea combining the features of both central and obstructive sleep apnea.

Modulation　Refers to changing the frequency or amplitude of a sound.

Modules　Areas of the brain that are each responsible for relatively specific functions or types of information processing.

Monoamines　A family of neuromodulators that are separated into two subgroups: the catecholamines (e.g. noradrenaline, dopamine), and the indoleamines (e.g. serotonin).

Monotherapy　The use of a single drug to treat a condition.

Mosaic　A condition that occurs when the chromosome complement differs from cell to cell.

Motor accessory system　Regions in the brain known to contribute to motor control and integration, which include the supplementary motor area, the premotor and prefrontal cortices, and the cerebellum.

Motor or procedural memory　The memory of how to do something, such as how to ride a bike.

Motor units　A bundle of muscle fibers that function together in the control of muscle groups. Neural control of muscle is via the unit and not the fiber.

Multimodal　Involving many sensory modalities.

Multipara　A woman carrying her second or subsequent child.

Multiple sclerosis　A demyelinating disorder.

Multiple sleep latency test　A test used to help diagnose narcolepsy in which a patient is asked to sleep at two-hour intervals during the day while the EEG is recorded. Rapid onset of sleep and short REM latencies under these conditions support the diagnosis of narcolepsy.

Myelin sheath　A layer of oligodendroglia wrapped around an axon in one-half to two millimeter segments.

Myopia　Nearsightedness; occurs because light from distant objects is focussed in front of the retina.

Narcotic　A term used to describe a group of substances which are derived from, or are synthesized to emulate, compounds found in the poppy plant.

Nasal retina　The vertical half of the eye that is closest to the nose.

Negative criteria　Characteristics that must be absent for a person to be included in a study.

Negative feedback　Information about deviation from a set point used to negate the deviation, thus producing stability in a system.

Negative symptoms　A cluster of schizophrenic symptoms that include blunted affect, the inability to experience pleasure, limited speech, lack of motivation, and poor attention.

Neglect　Deficits of attention to one side of space; typically occurs following lesions of the right hemisphere.

Neonatologists　Physicians specializing in the care of newborns.

Nerve losses　Hearing loss due to abnormalities in the cochlea or the acoustic nerve.

Neurofibrillary tangles　Clumps of disorganized neural fibers in the brain found in disorders producing senility.

Neuromuscular junction　The synaptic junction for a somatic motor neuron and a skeletal muscle unit. The neurotransmitter is acetylcholine.

Neuron　A particular type of cell specialized to transmit information by changing its rate of firing.

Neurotransmitters　Biochemically active substances that are released by a neuron into the synapse, that either excite or inhibit the postsynaptic neuron.

Nodes of Ranvier　Small gaps in the myelin sheath surrounding an axon.

Noise　The context out of which a signal arises.

Noncommunicating hydrocephalus　Also known as obstructive hydrocephalus, this condition occurs because of a stenosis (narrowing) or occlusion (blocking) of ventricular circulation.

Nonmatching to sample　A procedure used to test working memory in which a sample object is presented and then removed from view, after which two objects are presented, one of which is the previously seen object. The subject must select the novel object, a task which requires the recall of both the prior sample and the selection rule.

Nonspecific thalamic nuclei　Nuclei in the thalamus that project to all or many areas of the brain.

Nonverbal learning disability　Learning impairment characterized by relatively normal verbal and reading skills but weaknesses in arithmetic, somatosensory, psychomotor, visual–perceptual, and social abilities.

Noradrenaline A neuromodulator whose major source is in the locus ceruleus which is implicated in such functions as short-term, phasic reactivity to novel stimuli and the orienting response, wakefulness, alertness, and attention to the external world.

Norm-referenced testing An assessment in which an individual's score is compared to the scores obtained by a large representative sample of persons.

NREM Non-REM. All other stages of sleep besides REM.

Nucleus A structure located within the cell body of a neuron which contains its chromosomes.

Nullipara A woman pregnant with her first child.

Nystagmus Visible, tremor-like oscillations of the eye, generally a sign of abnormality if spontaneous. Occurs normally after rotation.

Objectics Culturally defined lifestyle and status signals such as dress or hairstyle whose comprehension is impaired in dyssemia.

Obsessions Repeated, uncontrollable thoughts.

Obstructive sleep apnea Apnea due to closing off the air pathway during sleep, which is often marked by loud snoring.

Occipital lobe The area of cortex that extends from the rearmost portion of the brain to the preoccipital notch where it meets the temporal lobe, and up to the parieto-occipital sulcus where it meets the parietal lobe; involved with visual functions.

Occlusion A blocking of a passageway.

Oculomotor Refers to control of eye movement.

Olfactory nerves The nerves of smell that project from the nose to the brain.

Oligodendroglia Special glial cells that wrap themselves around axons to form the myelin sheath.

Open head injury When an external force (e.g. a brick) tears the tissues of the scalp and fractures the bones of the skull.

Open systems A living system which is engaged in a constant interchange of information, energy, and matter with its environment.

Opioids Natural substances produced by the brain in states of high arousal that block pain receptors.

Oppositional defiant disorder (ODD) A childhood disorder that is a more severe form of conduct disturbance and is marked by persistent opposition to authority.

Optic chiasm The visible structure on the undersurface of the brain where the projections from the left and right nasal retina cross over into the contralateral hemisphere.

Optic radiations Pathways between lateral geniculate and occipital lobe conveying visual information.

Optical flow Changes in visual input that an observer sees when moving in space. Flow refers to the sense that, while moving, the world looks like it is passing to each side.

Optical placing reflex A relatively fixed visual focus 10–12 inches from an infant's eyes, about the distance between the mother's face and the child's eyes while the baby is nursing.

Oral method An approach to teaching deaf children that emphasized lip reading and speaking (with or without the amplification of powerful hearing aids), while discouraging the use of other means of communication (such as sign language).

Oral–aural method A combination of the oral and aural methods of training hearing-impaired children to listen, lip read, and speak.

Orbital prefrontal cortex The rounded poles at the front of the brain and adjacent areas.

Organ of Corti The structures within the cochlea that transduce a sound into neural firing codes via the bending of cilia.

Organic A term which refers in a general way to the physical characteristics of the body.

Orientation The reaction, both internal and overt, to novel events, which includes receptor-orienting activity, autonomic arousal, exploratory activity, and increased readiness for activity; also, in vision, refers to the angle of a plane or line with reference to the vertical.

Orthography The way in which a language is represented visually; in English it is the alphabet.

Oscillation The variation in a system around a set point.

Ossicles A group of three small bones: the malleus (hammer), uncus (anvil), and the stapes (stirrups) that are attached to the tympanic membrane at one end and the oval window at the other.

Otitis media An infection of the middle ear.

Otosclerosis A middle ear disorder, seen mostly in older adults, which is due to the growth of spongy bone over the footplate of the stapes as it rests on the oval window of the middle ear.

Outer hair cells Supplementary transducers in the organ of Corti.

Oval window A band of elastic tissue between the middle ear and the inner ear.

Overactivity Body movement greater than required for accomplishing task demands.

Palpebral fissures The horizontal openings between the eyelids.

Paranoia A condition marked by false beliefs of persecution, often coupled with feelings of grandiosity.

Parasympathetic nervous system The part of the autonomic nervous system that controls anabolic functioning.

Parenchyma The mass of brain tissue.

Parietal lobe The area of the cortex that lies immediately behind the central sulcus; involved with somatosensory functions.

Parieto-occipital sulcus The sulcus that separates the occipital and parietal lobes.

Parse In reading, to segregate or subdivide the phonemes of each word.

Parvocellular Those visual channels made up of smaller cells that are sensitive to high-frequency spatial information and low-frequency temporal information.

Pathogenesis Pathology production; the way pathology develops.

Pathogenic Pathology inducing.

Pediatric acquired immunodeficiency syndrome (AIDS) A condition that results from infection by the human immunodeficiency virus (HIV) which is often passed from mother to fetus during gestation via the placenta, or during birth, or via nursing.

Pedunculopontine nucleus (PPT) One of the sites in the brain that initiates REM sleep. It can be found in the upper part of the front end of the pons and is somewhat to the front and above the laterodorsal tegmental nucleus.

Penetrating wounds Injuries to the brain caused by a missile or bullet whose damage is limited largely to the trajectory of the penetrating object.

Percent curve of passing The percentage of individuals at a certain age that answer a given question correctly. The ideal curve of passing for selection of an item in constructing mental tests is when almost all children at a certain age fail an item, about 50 percent who are a year older pass, and nearly 100 percent of children who are two years older respond correctly.

Periaqueductal gray matter A collection of neurons in the tegmentum that surround the tube that connects the third and fourth ventricles and whose cell bodies are involved in species-specific motor programs, such as mating behavior.

Perilymph The fluid in both the vestibular and tympanic canals of the cochlea.

Periphery The retina other than the fovea and macula: mostly made up of rods.

Periventricular leukomalacia A pathological softening of the white matter in the regions around the ventricles.

Pervasive developmental disorder One of the terms used to describe severe disorders of behavior in children that do not meet criteria for more specific diagnoses.

Petit mal French for "little sick," also called an absence seizure: a seizure marked by sudden disruption of consciousness for short periods without loss of postural control. Information processing is "clouded" but not totally disrupted.

Phantom limbs A condition experienced by individuals who, after enduring amputations, later experience sensations in the locations where the appendage normally would have been; provides evidence for the existence of a body image.

Pharmacology The study of drugs and their effects.

Phase Sinusoids of identical frequency and amplitude that ascend and descend together are in phase. When such sinusoids are out of phase, one lags behind the other by some constant amount.

Phase lag The duration from the onset of detecting a deviation from a set point to the return of the system to the set point.

Phasic Refers to a specific, time-limited, response of biological systems. Contrasts with "tonic."

Phenotype The actual structural and behavioral manifestation of the genotype.

Phenylpyruvic ketonuria (PKU) A genetic disorder in which the genes producing the enzymes needed to transform phenylalanine to tyrosine are missing. The resulting excess phenylalanine can produce mental retardation.

Philtrum The shallow groove in the upper lip under the nose.

Phobias Irrational fears.

Phoneme A single speech sound. There is a rough correspondence to vowels and consonants.

Phonics An approach to reading in which written words are broken down and sounded out into a sequence of constituent phonemes.

Photic driving Flashing a light at increasing frequencies into the eyes of the subject, to determine if seizures or ictal activity can be detected.

Photopic vision The way the visual system operates in light bright enough for colors to be seen.

Pinna Technical term for the outer, visible ear.

Pituitary gland A gland at the base of the brain which secretes hormones that circulate widely in brain and body, which affect many functions including growth, skin pigment, menstrual cycle, and adrenal output.

Pixel The smallest unit that can emit or reflect light, such as on a television screen.

Place of articulation The place in the mouth where a sound is produced as a distinct phoneme.

Placenta The cord which attaches a fetus to its mother, through which nutrition is obtained.

Placenta previa A condition in which the placenta is positioned over the opening to the birth canal and thus may rip when labor starts, producing hemorrhage which can be dangerous to both mother and child.

Plaques Abnormal deposits in the brain found in disorders producing senility.

Plasticity The neural wherewithal of the brain to function and recover function after injury.

Polarized The state of having an electrical charge. When an axon is at rest, the area inside its membrane is polarized with a −70 millivolt charge in comparison to the outside milieu.

Polygenic Means "many genes" and implies that a singular function such as intelligence is determined by many genes.

Polygenic isolates Intellectually impaired offspring of parents with normal or even superior intelligence, who have no other evidence of organic compromise.

Polygraph A machine that represents physiologic changes such as brain waves on steadily moving paper. The pen's deflections are an analog of the voltage at an electrode site.

Polysomnography The polygraphic study of changes in EEG and other variables such as eye movements that occur in sleep.

Polytherapy The administration of multiple drugs for the same condition.

Pons A prominent bulging structure containing nuclei that control many vegetative functions including sleep.

Positive criteria Characteristics that must be present for a person to be included in a study.

Positive feedback Information about deviation from a set point that is used to further increase the deviation. Positive feedback is inherently unstable and can lead to a runaway.

Positive supporting reaction A reflex that occurs in newborns when the soles of their feet are bounced on a surface. The infant will stiffen and thrust its legs forward in an alternating fashion that is similar to walking.

Positive symptoms A cluster of schizophrenic symptoms that include hallucinations; delusions; paranoia; agitation; and bizarre, irrelevant associations.

Postconcussion The time after a head injury.

Postictal amnesia and confusion A state of confusion and difficulty remembering which occurs after many types of seizure that may be used as evidence that a seizure has occurred.

Postrotatory nystagmus A normal response of the eyes after rotation is abruptly stopped. See Nystagmus.

Postsynaptic membrane The membrane across from the terminal button at the synapse which contains neurotransmitter receptor sites.

Post-traumatic amnesia (PTA) Memory loss, either retrograde (events before the trauma) or anterograde (events after the trauma), or both, following brain trauma.

Post-traumatic stress disorder A disorder that develops immediately subsequent to or even years after a traumatic experience and is characterized by profound sleep disturbances, anxiety attacks, flashbacks, and recurrent experiences of guilt and shame.

Praxis A term denoting the overall facility, especially higher-level capability, for organizing and performing actions and action sequences.

Prefrontal cortex The tertiary processing area in front of the premotor cortex that is critical for working memory, executive functions, emotional inhibition, and behavioral organization.

Premotor cortex The secondary area in front of the motor strip including Broca's area which elaborates and organizes motor habits and kinetic melodies.

Premutation In fragile-X syndrome, intermediate alteration in the structure of a chromosome caused by excessive (54–200) repetitions of a specific DNA sequence, the CGG triplet (CG, GC, GC).

Preoccipital notch An indentation at the bottom of the occipital lobe that demarks its edge.

Preoptic-anterior hypothalamus (POAH) The region in the brain where the cells that activate delta sleep are located, which is at the base of the forebrain in front of the optic chiasm and near the front part of the hypothalamus.

Presbyopia Farsightedness found in older adults that is a result of decreased accommodative ability.

Presentation The part of an infant's body that appears first during child birth.

Presynaptic vesicles Containers inside the terminal button of a neuron which are filled with neurotransmitters.

Primary receptive and motor areas Areas in the cortex that are responsible for elementary modality-specific processing such as flashes of light, pure tones, or muscle contractions.

Primary visual area The place in the brain (area 17) where the optic radiations end in the occipital lobe.

Process schizophrenia Schizophrenia, in which the prior history indicates chronic difficulty in adaptation and the symptoms suggest peculiarity, idiosyncrasy, and social isolation.

Project Regarding the nervous system, projections refer to pathways from one area of the body or brain to another area of the brain.

Projection fibers Fibers within the gray matter that connect the subcortical areas to the cortex.

Pronation Move toward the belly or underside.

Prone On the undersurface of the body: lying on the belly.

Prosopagnosia A type of agnosia in which a face can be recognized as a face, and the sex of the face can often be discriminated, but the identification of the face is gone.

Pseudoseizures Seizure-like behavior in which there is no biological evidence of ictal activity; generally psychosocial determinants are found.

Psychometrics The measurement of mental ability.

Psychomotor agitation Excessive motor activity such as restlessness, pacing, or hand rubbing.

Psychomotor retardation Generally, the slowing of motor activity.

Psychomotor seizures A seizure involving complex behavior that may appear purposeful.

Psychophysiology The study of changes in physiological functions such as heart rate or skin conductance in relation to psychological events.

Psychotic A general term which attempts to convey a sense of being maladaptively helpless, out of control, unable to communicate meaningfully, and, perhaps, strange, odd, weird, mad, or crazy. In professional terms, the word is a blanket term for a group of generally incapacitating symptoms with no implicit assumptions about causation, duration, or treatment.

Psychotropic Mind-influencing drugs that selectively modulate synaptic processes, for example slowing or speeding reuptake, or blocking postsynaptic receptor sites.

Pure tone The sound produced by a single frequency.

Putamen Part of the basal ganglia, the putamen and the globus pallidus form the lenticular nucleus.

Pyramidal system A network of effector nerves that regulate voluntary movement which originates on the motor strip at the precentral gyrus.

Quadriplegia Spasticity of all four limbs.

Raphe nuclei A string of nuclei which occur near the midline of the pons, which are an important source of serotonin.

Reaction time The time between the onset of a stimulus and the designated response.

Reactive Associated with environmental stress.

Reactive schizophrenia Schizophrenia in which breakdown of functioning is fairly sudden, after an apparently normal prior history, and which is characterized by florid and dramatic, positive symptomology.

Receptive dysphasia Impairment in language comprehension.

Receptor orienting activity Behaviors that move the sensory organs to maximize the information they receive, e.g. turning the eyes toward an object.

Red nucleus A collection of neurons in the tegmentum that is the source of the rubrospinal tract, which brings motor information from the cortex to the cerebellum and spinal cord.

Reflex inhibiting posture A component of treatment for cerebral palsy in which an individual is placed in positions which are the reverse of those provoked by disinhibited tonic reflexes so as to inhibit those movements and permit the excitation of normal to near-normal, developmentally sequenced, phasic movements and their accompanying sensations.

Reflexes Genetically determined organizations of muscle tone and phasic movement elicited by particular sensory stimuli.

Regression A term which suggests a going back or unraveling of development. By definition, regression must be preceded by development. In reading, eye movements which go back to reread a section of text.

Regression to the mean The statistical tendency for offspring to have talents that are closer to the average for the population than their parents might have been.

REM "Rapid eye movement" sleep. A sleep state which recurs through the night beginning $1\frac{1}{2}$ hours after sleep onset characterized by desynchronized EEG, rapid eye movements, and motor immobility.

REM latency The time between sleep onset and REM onset.

Remission Periods of spontaneous improvement by a patient suffering from a physical or psychological disorder.

Renshaw cells Interneurons in the spinal gray matter that inhibit the stretch reflexes of antagonistic muscle groups opposing the intended action. Renshaw cells make possible "higher" brain influence over "lower" reflex mechanisms.

Respiratory distress syndrome See Hyaline membrane disease.

Reticular formation A fairly large area of net-like (reticulum) gray matter in the dorsal portion of the medulla which has connections to virtually every part of the nervous system and is involved in arousal and alertness.

Reticulospinal tract A tract of neurons in the ventromedial funiculus that originates in the reticular formation and activates and regulates arousal to all forms of sensory stimulation.

Reticulum Net-like in appearance.

Retina The transducer of light into nerve cell activity which is located at the back of the eye.

Retraction ball A balloon-like swelling along an axon at the point of secondary axotomy. See Secondary axotomy.

Retrograde amnesia Loss of recall for events occurring just before a concussion and backward in time which shrinks to minutes or even seconds before the accident as recovery takes place.

Retrolental fibroplasia A condition in premature infants in which the retina is destroyed by excessive oxygen.

Return sweeps During reading, large saccades of the eyes occurring after coming to the end of a line, which move the eyes to the beginning of the next line.

Reuptake The process in which the terminal button reabsorbs the neurotransmitter it has just released.

Rewards Substances or events that are limbic-arousing and non-habituating. When paired with behaviors, rewards increase the likelihood that a behavior will reoccur.

Righting reactions A group of automatically evoked, patterned reactions stimulated by displacement of the head from an upright position in space.

Rods A type of transducer cell found maximally in the retinal periphery which reacts to shades of light and dark, low-frequency spatial and high-frequency temporal information.

Rooting A reflex that occurs when an infants' cheek is touched, and the head turns toward the source of stimulation. This reaction facilitates the location of the nipple and enables feeding.

Round window An elastic membrane at the end of the cochlea.

Rubella A viral infection, also known as German measles, which can be transmitted via the placenta to a fetus, which can result in cataracts, blindness, auditory problems, and mental retardation if it occurs in the first trimester.

Rubrospinal tract A tract of neurons in the lateral funiculus that originates in the cortex, synapses in the red nucleus of the midbrain and then with neurons in the spinal gray matter which control the movements of the shoulders, arms, and hands.

Runaway When a system is in a cycle of positive feedback so that it moves inexorably toward instability or shutdown.

Saccade A movement of the eyes.

Saccule Along with the utricle, a circular structure in the vestibular system of the inner ear that is lined with hair cells suspended in fluid, which register changes in the movement of the fluid as the head moves.

Sacrum The small fused bones at the end of the spinal column in the lower back (adjective, sacral).

Schizoid See Schizotypy.

Schizotypy Refers to a condition in which some of the characteristics of schizophrenia are present but not to the extent of an active psychosis.

Schwann cells Cells responsible for producing the myelin sheath of neurons outside the brain.

Scotomas Blind spots in the visual field.

Scotopic vision Vision in dim light mediated by the rods.

Scurvy A condition caused by inadequate intake of vitamin C that is marked by lassitude, weakness, irritability, weight loss, joint and muscle pains, and a tendency to hemorrhage.

Seasonal affective disorder (SAD) A depressive syndrome that occurs seasonally, most often in the Fall and Winter when the hours of daylight are minimal, which responds to increased exposure to light.

Secondary axotomy Several hours following brain injury, a series of events may take place in which a perturbation at some point along an axon leads to a disruption of axoplasmic transport. Materials being transported downstream then begin to jam up at that point, creating a balloon-like swelling in the axon which ultimately results in a severing of the axon and the development of a retraction ball at the point of disruption.

Secondary receptive and motor areas Areas of the cortex elaborating modality-specific information into percepts or simple action patterns.

Secretin A hormone produced by cells in the small intestine which reacts to the presence of acid, prompting the pancreas to release bicarbonate, which then neutralizes stomach acid in the small intestine. There is some evidence that secretin may also function in the brain as a neurotransmitter.

Seizure threshold The concept that seizure activity varies in quantity and that some specified level is needed for an overt seizure to occur.

Self-regulated pacemakers Special groups of cells which transmit information to other neurons but appear to initiate much of their activity on their own with relatively little direct influence from other neural inputs.

Self-regulation of affect/arousal Modulation of the expression of emotion, generally to facilitate social adaptation.

Semantic field In the context of memory, a group of conceptually or experientially related words.

Semantic memory   Memory for facts and information (such as word meanings, historical facts, or scientific information).

Semantic priming   A procedure using the lexical decision task in which the relatedness of word meaning is evaluated by noting changes in reaction time to words preceded by related words as compared to unrelated words.

Sensitization   Similar to habituation but opposite in effect, sensitization involves an increase in response with repeated exposure. Occurs particularly to stimuli that are noxious.

Sensors   Neurons in sense organs which transform physical stimulation such as a light or sound into patterns of neural firing.

Sensory and motor processors   Networks of neurons which elaborate and modulate information to enable intricate control.

Sensory-motor rhythm (SMR)   A 12–14 Hz brain wave observed during active inhibition: also found in sleep spindles, which may reflect motor inhibition when falling sleep.

Serotonin   A neuromodulator whose major source is the raphe nuclei in the pons. Serotonin is associated with feelings of quiet alertness and well-being; many drugs used to treat depression function by increasing available serotonin at the synapse.

Sex chromosomes   A pair of chromosomes that vary as a function of a person's sex; females having two X chromosomes, while males have an X chromosome from their mother and a Y chromosome from their father.

Shock therapy   See Electroconvulsive therapy (ECT).

Sight vocabulary   The ability to decipher a word without sounding it out.

Sighting dominant eye   The eye which wins out in binocular rivalry.

Signal   A stimulus/event that communicates meaning.

Simian   Means "ape-like"; in the context of reflexes in infants, it means a primitive grasp reflex.

Simultaneous processing   The ability to integrate diverse information from many points in space into some sort of unitary whole, making use of imagery (not necessarily visual), and producing relatively instantaneous understandings and conceptualizations about events and experiences.

Sine waves   Curves indicating continuous, gradual, symmetric changes. Waves vary in frequency and amplitude.

Sinusoids   See Sine waves.

Skin conductance   A measure of the ease (or impedance) with which an electric current may be passed between two electrodes placed on the skin, generally on the hand. Increased activity of the sweat glands decreases resistance and facilitates current flow. Because sweat gland activity is associated with increased activity of the sympathetic nervous system, skin conductance provides a measure of sympathetic arousal.

Sleep architecture   The quantitative description of different aspects of a person's sleep pattern through the night.

Sleep paralysis   An inability to move while partially awake or upon awakening.

Sleep spindles   12 to 14 cycles per second wave forms in the sleep EEG during Stage 2, that last about a half-second, and taper at each end giving the appearance of a spindle.

Slow writhing movements   A movement, controlled by negative feedback, with a slow, imprecise trajectory.

Slow-to-warm-up child   A child with a combination of negative responses of mild intensity to new stimuli with slow adaptability after repeated contact, mild intensity of reactions, whether positive or negative, and mild irregularity of biological function. If given the opportunity to reexperience new situations over time and without pressure, such a child gradually comes to show quiet and positive interest and involvement.

Solitary nucleus   A group of neurons in the medulla that is a target of the vagus nerve which, in turn, has connections with the cerebellum, thalamus, and many other areas of the brain.

Somatosensory   Sensory information from body sensors such as touch, pressure, pain, heat, proprioception, and kinaesthesis.

Somnambulism   Also known as sleep walking, occurs in Stage 4 NREM sleep.

Sound spectrogram   A technique that visually represents the frequencies of sound emitted in speech.

Spasticity   Limb rigidity stemming from excessive muscle tone.

Spatial frequency   The rate per unit of space (visual angle) at which contrast regularly changes from maximum to minimum. Low frequencies change over relatively long distances while high frequencies change repeatedly over short distances: expressed as cycles per degree of visual angle.

Spatial information   The organization of features such as the shapes of objects in a perceived space.

Spatial summation   The more synapses of the same type near a particular location on the postsynaptic cell, the more likely they will cumulate in their effect.

Spearman hypothesis   A hypothesis which states that differences in "g" between groups that are different in "g" are greater when measured by tests that have higher "g" loadings.

Special abilities or talents   A construct proposed by Spearman to designate specific cognitive abilities such as mathematics, music, or athletic ability.

Specific thalamic nuclei   Nuclei in the thalamus that process information from individual sensory modalities and then send that information to modality-specific areas of the cortex for further processing.

Specificity   Refers to selective rather than global impairments.

Spikes   Sudden, massive, synchronous discharge of neurons which are displayed in the EEG as a wave form with a sharp peak.

Spina bifida   A malformation of gestation due to the failure of the primordial neural tube to close completely.

Spinal cord   The primary conduit for transmitting information from body to brain and from brain to muscles, glands, and organs throughout the body; also contains processors which provide local forms of regulation.

Spinal nuclei   Clumps of cells which serve as processors within the spinal cord.

Spinocerebellum   Also known as the anterior lobe of the cerebellum, this structure receives inputs from the spinal cord and is concerned with limb movement.

Square wave   Wave forms that have sharp edges rather than the gradual changes found in sign waves.

Standard deviation   A measure of the degree of variability or dispersion of a group of scores around their average value.

Status epilepticus   Occurs when tonic–clonic seizures persist beyond a few minutes.

Stenosis   A narrowing of a passageway, as in stenosis-induced noncommunicating hydrocephalus.

Stigmata   Observable signs of difference and abnormality. Singular: Stigma.

Stimulus identification time   The minimum duration required for the perception of a stimulus.

Strabismus   The technical term for "crossed-eyes," due to imbalanced muscle control.

Strephosymbolia   Means "twisted signs," and refers to directional confusion regarding the structure of certain letters such as p's and q's, and the order of letters in a word, such as reading "was" as "saw."

Stress response   The nervous system's reaction to trauma and to the anticipation of trauma which involves preparation for flight or fight.

Stretch reflex   An automatic tendency of stretched muscles to contract. This tendency is regulated in the spinal cord.

Striate cortex   Another term for the primary visual area in the occipital lobe.

Sturge–Weber syndrome   A condition marked by contralateral spasticity at birth; uncontrollable unilateral seizures; severe behavioral disturbances including impulsivity, disinhibition, and outbursts of violence; and deep red–purple discoloration of the skin around the eye contralateral to the spasticity. The disorder is caused by a proliferation of interconnecting blood vessels in the meninges of one hemisphere near the nerve enervating the face and eye which, paradoxically, deprives that hemisphere of an adequate blood supply.

Subependymal germinal matrix   The layers of cells adjacent to the ependyma whose blood supply is particularly susceptible to hemorrhaging in premature infants.

Subictal states   Partial-seizure-like symptoms in individuals who have never experienced an overt seizure. These may include moments of inexplicable confusion, or peculiar and unrealistic sensory or emotional experiences.

Substantia nigra Literally means "black substance," a collection of neurons in the tegmentum beneath the superior colliculi that are rich in the neurotransmitter dopamine and which have projections to the basal ganglia.

Successive processing Step-by-step sequential processing of information involving language, logic, and reasoning from premises.

Successiveness The detection of the order in which different stimuli are presented, crucial for the phomenic aspects of language.

Sudden infant death syndrome (SIDS) Asphixa in the first year of life, possibly due to ineffectual rousing mechanisms when oxygen deprived.

Sulci Grooves that result from the infolding of the cortex that takes place during development; singular, sulcus.

Superior colliculus An area located on the tectum which is the target of some fibers coming from the retina; known to be involved in the control of eye movements.

Superoxide dismutase A biochemical substance which may play a role in premature aging and decreased functioning of the immune system.

Supination Move toward the back or topside.

Supine On the upper surface of the body: lying on the back.

Surfactant A substance which coats the lung tissue of infants and facilitates the absorption of oxygen into the blood supply.

Sustained channels Another term used to refer to the parvocellular channels.

Symmetric tonic neck reflex Upper limbs extend and lower limbs flex if the neck is dorsiflexed, and upper limbs flex and the lower limbs extend if the neck is ventroflexed.

Sympathetic nervous system The part of the autonomic nervous system that controls catabolic functioning.

Synapse The space or cleft surrounding the terminal button of the axon, the gap across which a neurotransmitter must travel to find a postsynaptic receptor site.

Synchrony Simultaneous activity in a large number of cells generally produces large-amplitude EEG waves because energy from individual units summate.

Synoptophore A stereoscope used in studying eye dominance with a device that enables divergence or convergence of the stimuli presented to each eye so that binocular fusion can be studied.

Systems theory A collection of principles that aid in understanding how systems containing many components function in a stable way or produce change.

Tectorial membrane A membrane that is part of the organ of Corti in the cochlea.

Tectospinal tract A tract of neurons in the ventromedial funiculus that originates in the superior colliculus, controls automatic orienting movements of the eyes to visual stimuli, and contributes to attention.

Tectum Means "roof." The tectum is the dorsal surface of the midbrain just above the fourth ventricle, the location of the superior and inferior colliculi.

Tegmentum Means "floor." The tegmentum is the ventral portion of the midbrain and the site of several important nuclei including the periaqueductal gray matter, the red nucleus, and the substantia nigra.

Telemetry Continuous recording of psychophysiological activity at a distance using miniaturized radio transmitter equipment which permits the subject to move freely.

Telencephalon The frontmost area of the fetal brain which eventually bends back and produces the cerebral cortex.

Temperaments Constitutionally determined, enduring characteristics such as activity level or fearfulness, which can be observed over the lifespan and which influence reactions to the environment.

Temporal information Information that is dependent on a succession of events over time, such as a melody or speech.

Temporal lobe The area of the cortex that lies below the lateral sulcus, which is involved with auditory functions.

Temporal retina The vertical half of the retina that is closest to the temples.

Temporal summation The higher the rate at which synapses of the same type fire the more likely will postsynaptic firing occur.

Teratogen A substance in the environment that harms a developing fetus.

Teratology The systematic study of abnormalities of gestation caused by exogenous substances that interfere with normal fetal development.

Tertiary receptive and motor areas Association areas of the cortex responsible for integrating multimodal information.

Thalamus An egg-shaped group of nuclei straddling the third ventricle above and behind the hypothalamus which serves as a relay station for modality-specific information en route to primary cortical processing areas and other functions as well.

Theory of mind The ability to attribute mindfulness to others, i.e. understand that the behavior of others is a product of their minds and thoughts, feelings, and motives.

Theta (θ) Brain waves whose frequencies are between four and seven cycles per second.

Thoracic The region of the chest.

Threshold The level at which excitation must exceed inhibition for subsequent activation to occur.

Thrush A yeast (*Candida albicans*) infection which produces a white, cheese-like coating of the mouth and tongue in infants.

Tic Uncontrollable relatively brief motor or phonic acts such as a grunt or flicker of the eyelids or a jerk of the shoulder. More complex behavior may also occur.

Timbre A characteristic tonal quality, e.g. a piano and a violin, though producing the same pitch, will each have a unique sound.

Time-locked averaging Averaging the EEG wave form that occurs at an electrode site over a series of stimulus presentations, beginning each calculation at stimulus onset or some constant interval before.

Tonic A term which refers to a state of readiness for activity in a system; also refers to the context out of which phasic reactions occur in biological systems.

Tonic labyrinthine prone reflex Total flexion when the body is pronated.

Tonic labyrinthine supine reflex Total extension when the body is supinated.

Tonic reflexes Patterns of organization for mechanisms regulating muscle tone. Different patterns emerge early in the course of development.

Tonic–clonic A type of seizure in which the body alternates between general stiffening and jerking movements.

Tonotopic organization Auditory processing neurons organized such that adjacent cell groups respond to adjacent frequencies.

Topographic organization Regional spatial proximity such that the sensors for adjacent areas of muscle, skin, or vision project to adjacent areas in the brain.

Total communication An educational approach for hearing-impaired children which emphasizes communication by any means as the prime goal; e.g. combining sign language and the oral method.

Toxoplasmosis An infection caused by a protozoan that enters the mother via the consumption of undercooked meat, and the fetus, via the placenta, which can cause encephalitis, hydrocephalus, seizures, mental retardation, and microcephaly.

Trainable mentally retarded Retarded persons who can learn self-help skills such as those required for personal hygiene and dressing, some language and elementary social amenities, and who, when mature, require care and supervision.

Transducers A term for any instrument that transforms one form of physical energy into another, e.g. rods and cones which transform light into neural firing patterns.

Transformational rules The rules of a language's grammar that determine acceptable combinations of words and word sequences.

Transient channels Another term referring to magnocellular channels.

Translational acceleration When an object moves in the direction of the force impinging on it.

Trauma A time-limited, intense experience of stimulation which is beyond the range of intensities ordinarily experienced. The nature of the trauma may be entirely physical, as in the case of a burn; purely psychological, as when one experiences a profoundly humiliating social experience; or, most commonly, some combination of the two, as when one is mugged or raped or in an automobile accident.

Tremors An involuntary rhythmic movement of a body part.

Trimester A three-month period.

Tuberous sclerosis A genetic disorder characterized by tumor-like abnormalities that grow in the skin and nervous system.

Tumor Literally means a swelling; more commonly, the term refers to tissue growths that do not belong where they occur.

Tympanic canal Part of the inner ear that extends back the entire length of the cochlea, ending at the round window.

Tympanic membrane The eardrum; a band of elastic tissue at the border of the auditory canal and the middle ear.

Unimodal Involving a single sensory modality.

Unipolar Depression or mania with no cycling between conditions.

Untrainable mentally retarded Mentally retarded individuals who essentially require nursing care all of their lives.

Upper motor neurons Neurons in the brain which are involved in muscle control.

Utricle See saccule.

Vegetative symptoms Symptoms associated with endogenous depression, such as decreased appetite and energy, constipation, sleep disturbances and, especially, early-morning waking.

Ventral Towards the belly.

Ventral corticospinal tract Part of the ventromedial system that transmits information from the brain to the spine regarding movement of the trunk.

Ventral posterior lateral nucleus A nucleus of the thalamus that relays information from areas of the body to the precentral gyrus in the cortex.

Ventricles Cavities within the brain in which cerebrospinal fluid circulates.

Ventroflexion Move down: describes movements of neck or wrist.

Verbal access The ability to draw on the meaning of a word as needed in discourse and reading.

Vergences When both eyes move inwardly (convergence) toward the nose or outwardly (divergence) toward the ears.

Vermis A recently evolved region of tissue at the midline of the cerebellum.

Vertebrates Animals with spinal cords.

Vertex presentation When an infant's head is the first part to appear during birth, the most frequent and least complicated presentation.

Vestibular canal Also called the scala vestibuli. A fluid-filled canal that extends the length of the entire cochlea, at the beginning of which the oval window vibrates.

Vestibulocerebellum Also called the flocculonodular lobe of the cerebellum; this structure is linked to the vestibular nuclei in the medulla and is concerned with the body's position in space while moving and with body equilibrium.

Vestibulospinal tract A tract of neurons in the ventromedial funiculus that originates in the vestibular system and provides information about the position of the body with regard to gravity.

Visual angle The size of the image on the retina, measured in degrees of arc.

Visual associative agnosia A type of agnosia in which the person has difficulty integrating the different components of what is seen into a holistic, meaningful perception.

Visual module A pair of hypercolumns registering various aspects of information about the same point in space for both eyes.

Vitreous humor The jelly-like liquid which fills the eyeball.

Vocal cords Flexible muscles of the larynx that are attached to cartilage that, when forced apart by air, may produce sound.

Vocal folds See Vocal cords.

Voice-onset time The duration of silence before voicing of a stop consonant begins.

Voiced In the context of language, a phoneme that has a distinct vibration, the z in "zip" in comparison to the s in "miss."

Voiceless In the context of language, a phoneme that does not produce a vibration, the d in "did" in comparison to the b in "bird."

White noise A large range of frequencies generated simultaneously and continuously over a period of time, producing a sound that is generally experienced as a complex hiss.

Whole word An approach to reading that teaches recognition of words in their entirety and emphasizes the development of sight vocabulary.

Word blindness An inability to decipher the sounds and meaning of a group of letters even though vision is normal.

Working memory The ability to hold in mind various pieces of information so as to be able to perform certain cognitive tasks; a component of executive functions. Also see Nonmatching to sample.

X activation ratio The ratio of normal X chromosome activity to total X chromosome activity.

References

Abikoff, H. (1991). Cognitive training in ADHD children: less to it than meets the eye. *Journal of Learning Disabilities, 24,* 205–209.

Adamec, R. E. (1990). Does kindling model anything clinically relevant? *Biological Psychiatry, 27,* 249–279.

Adams, R. D., & Victor, M. (1993). *Principles of neurology,* 5th ed. New York: McGraw-Hill.

Adrian, E. D., & Matthews, B. H. C. (1934). The Berger rhythm: potential changes from the occipital lobes in man. *Brain, 57,* 355–385.

Aicardi, J. (1994). *Epilepsy in children,* 2d ed. New York: Raven Press.

Akiskal, H. S. (1997). Overview of chronic depressions and their clinical management. In H. S. Akisakal & G. B. Cassano (eds.) *Dysthymia and the spectrum of chronic depressions.* New York: Guilford Press.

Akisakal, H. S., & Cassano, G. B. (eds.) (1997). *Dysthymia and the spectrum of chronic depressions.* New York: Guilford Press.

Alexander, G. E., Crutcher, M. D., & DeLong, M. R. (1990). Basal ganglia–thalmocortical circuits: parallel substrates for motor, oculomotor, "prefrontal" and "limbic" functions. In H. B. M. Uylings, C. G. Van Eden, J. P. C. DeBruin, M. A. Corner, & M. G. P. Feenstra (eds.), *Progress in Brain Research, 85,* 119–146.

Alistair, G. S. P., & Sunshine, P. (1997). Intrauterine growth retardation. In D. K. Stevenson & P. Sunshine (eds.), *Fetal and neonatal brain injury.* Oxford: Oxford University Press.

Allen, D. V. (1971). Modality of similarity and hearing ability. *Psychonomic Science, 24,* 69–71.

American Psychiatric Association (1994). *Diagnostic and statistical manual of mental disorders,* 4th ed. Washington, DC: American Psychiatric Association.

American Psychiatric Association task force on laboratory tests in psychiatry (1987). The dexamethasone suppression test: An overview of its current status in psychiatry. *American Journal of Psychiatry, 144,* 1253–1262.

Anch, A. M., Browman, C. P., Mitler, M. M., & Walsh, J. K. (1988). *Sleep: A scientific perspective.* Englewood Cliffs, NJ: Prentice Hall.

Andermann, F., & Robb, J. P. (1972). Absence status: a reappraisal following review of thirty eight patients. *Epilepsia, 13,* 177–187.

Anders, T. F., Sadeh, A., & Appareddy, V. (1995). Normal sleep in neonates and children. In R. Ferber & M. Kryger (eds.), *Principles and practice of sleep medicine in the child.* Philadelphia: W. B. Saunders.

Anderson, N., & Wallis, W. E. (1986). Activation of epileptiform activity by mental arithmetic. *Archives of Neurology, 43,* 624–626.

Anderson, V. A., Morse, S. A., Klug, G., Catroppa, C., Haritou, F., Rosenfeld, J., & Pentland, L. (1997). Predicting recovery from head injury in young children: A prospective analysis. *Journal of the International Neuropsychological Society, 3,* 568–580.

Andreasen, N. C., O'Leary, D. S., Cizadlo, T., Arndt, S., Rezai, K., Ponto, L. L. B., Watkins, G. L., & Hichwa, R. D. (1996). Schizophrenia and cognitive dysmetria: A positron-emission tomography study of dysfunctional prefrontal–thalamic–cerebellar circuitry. *Proceedings of the National Academy of Sciences, 93,* 9985–9990.

Angold, A. (1988). Childhood and adolescent depression II: Research in clinical populations. *British Journal of Psychiatry, 153,* 476–492.

Annegers, J. F., Grabow, J. D., Kurland, L. T., & Laws, E. R. (1980). The incidence, causes, and secular trends of head trauma in Olmsted County, Minnesota. *Neurology, 30,* 912–919.

Antonuccio, D. O., Danton, W. G., & DeNelsky, G. Y. (1995). Psychotherapy versus medication for depression: Challenging the conventional wisdom with data. *Professional Psychology: Research and Practice, 26,* 574–585.

Antonuccio, D. O., Thomas, M., & Danton, W. G. (1997). A cost-effectiveness analysis of cognitive behavior therapy and fluoxetine (Prozac) in the treatment of depression. *Behavior Therapy, 28,* 187–210.

Antrobus, J. (1983). REM and NREM sleep reports: Comparison of word frequencies by cognitive classes. *Psychophysiology, 20,* 562–568.

Appelbaum, S. A. (1979). *Out in inner space: A psychoanalyst explores the new therapies.* Garden City, NY: Anchor Press/Doubleday.

Arms, S. (1975). *Immaculate deception: A new look at women and childbirth in America.* Boston: Houghton Mifflin.

Asarnow, J. R. (1994). Annotation: Childhood-onset schizophrenia. *Journal of Child Psychology and Psychiatry, 35,* 1345–1371.

Asarnow, R. F., Satz, P., Light, R., Zaucha, K., Lewis, R., & McCleary, C. (1995). The UCLA study of mild closed head injury in children and adolescents. In S. H. Broman & M. E. Michel (eds.), *Traumatic head injury in children.* New York: Oxford University Press.

Aserinsky, E., & Kleitman, N. (1953). Regular occurring periods of eye motility and concomitant phenomena during sleep. *Science, 118,* 273–274.

Askenasy, J. J., Mendelson, L., Keren, O., & Braun, Z. (1990). Juvenile Parkinson's disease and its response to L-dopa therapy. *Journal of Neural Transmission. Parkinson's Disease and Dementia Section, 2,* 23–30.

Asperger, H. (1944). Die "Autistischen Psychopathen" im Kindesalter. *Archiv für Psychiatrie und Nervenkrankheiten, 117,* 76–136.

Asperger, H. (1991). "Autistic psychopathy" in childhood. In U. Frith (ed.), *Autism and Asperger syndrome.* Cambridge: Cambridge University Press.

Atkinson, J., King, J., Braddick, O., Nokes, L., Anker, S., & Braddick, F. (1997). A specific deficit of dorsal stream function in Williams' syndrome. *Neuroreport, 8,* 1919–1922.

Azrin, N. H., & Besalel, V. A. (1979) *A parent's guide to bedwetting control: A step-by-step method.* New York: Simon & Schuster.

Azrin, N. H., & Foxx, R. M. (1971) A rapid method of toilet training the institutionalized retarded. *Journal of Applied Behavior Analysis, 4,* 89–99.

Baddeley, A. D. (1976). *The psychology of memory.* New York: Basic Books.

Baer, L., Rauch, S. L., Ballentine, H. T. Jr, Martuza, R., Cosgrove, R., Cassem, E., Giriunas, I., Manzo, P. A., Dimino, C., & Jenike, M. A. (1995). Cingulotomy for intractable obsessive–compulsive disorder: Prospective long-term follow-up of 18 patients. *Archives of General Psychiatry, 52,* 384–392.

Bakeman, R., & Adamson, L. (1984). Coordinating attention to people and objects in mother–infant and peer–infant interaction. *Child Development, 55,* 1278–1289.

Baker, S. M., & Pangborn, J. (1996). *Clinical assessment options for children with autism and related diorders: A biomedical approach.* San Diego, CA: Autism Research Institute.

Bakker, D. J. (1990). *Neuropsychological treatment of dyslexia.* New York: Oxford University Press.

Balkany, T. (1995). The rescuers. *Advances in Otorhinolaryngology, 50,* 4–8.

Banich, M. T. (1997). *Neuropsychology: The neural bases of mental function.* Boston: Houghton Mifflin.

Barbas, H., & Pandya, D. (1991). Patterns of connections of the prefrontal cortex in the rhesus monkey associated with cortical architecture. In H. S. Levin, H. M. Eisenberg, & A. L. Benton (eds.), *Frontal lobe function and dysfunction.* New York: Oxford University Press.

Barbosa, E., Freeman, J., & Elfert, G. (1984). Ketogenic diets for treatment of childhood epilepsy. In M. Walser (ed.), *Nutritional management: The Johns Hopkins handbook.* Philadelphia: W. B. Saunders.

Barkley, R. A. (1990). *Attention-deficit hyperactivity disorder: A handbook for diagnosis and treatment.* New York: Guilford Press.

Barkley, R. A. (1997). *ADHD and the nature of self-control.* New York: Guilford Press.

Baron-Cohen, S. (1995). *Mindblindness: An essay on autism and theory of mind.* Cambridge, MA: MIT Press.

Baron-Cohen, S., Leslie, A., & Frith, U. (1985). Does the autistic child have a theory of mind? *Cognition, 21,* 37–46.

Baron-Cohen, S., Tager-Flusberg, H., & Cohen, D. J. (1993). *Understanding other minds: Perspectives from autism.* Oxford: Oxford University Press.

Barry, M. J. (1996). Physical therapy interventions for patients with movement disorders due to cerebral palsy. *Journal of Child Neurology, 11* (Suppl. 1), S51–S60.

Barth, J. T., Alves, W. M., Ryan, T. V., Macciocchi, S. N., Rimel, R. W., Jane, J. A., & Nelson, W. E. (1989). Mild head injury in sports: Neuropsychological sequelae and recovery of function. In H. S. Levin, H. M. Eisenberg, & A. L. Benton (eds.), *Mild head injury.* New York: Oxford University Press.

Bassetti, C., & Aldrich, M. S. (1996). Narcolepsy. *Neurologic Clinics, 14,* 545–571.

Bates, J. E., & Wachs, T. D. (eds.) (1994). *Temperament: Individual differences at the interface of biology and behavior.* Washington, DC: American Psychological Association.

Bauer, R. M. (1993). Agnosia. In K. M. Heilman & E. Valenstein (eds.), *Clinical neuropsychology,* 3rd ed. New York: Oxford University Press.

Bear, D. M., & Fedio, P. (1977). Quantitative analysis of interictal behavior in temporal lobe epilepsy. *Archives of Neurology, 34,* 454–467.

Bear, D. M., Foxx, R. M., Kazdin, A. E., Mesibov, G. B., & Mundy, P. (1993). Commentaries on McEachin, Smith, and Lovaas. *American Journal on Mental Retardation, 97,* 373–385.

Beatty, J. (1995). *Principles of behavioral neuroscience.* Madison, WI: Brown & Benchmark.

Beck, A. T. (1967). *Depression: Clinical, experimental and theoretical aspects.* New York: Harper & Row.

Behrman, A. L., Teitelbaum, P., & Cauraugh, J. H. (1998). Verbal instructional sets to normalize the temporal and spatial gait variables in Parkinson's disease. *Journal of Neurology, Neurosurgery, and Psychiatry, 65,* 580–582.

Bellinger, D., Leviton, A., Waternaux, C., Needleman, H., & Rabinowitz, M. (1987). Longitudinal analyses of prenatal lead exposure and early cognitive development. *New England Journal of Medicine, 316,* 1037–1043.

Bellinger, D., & Needleman, H. L. (1994). The neurotoxicity of prenatal exposure to lead: Kinetics, mechanisms, and expressions. In H. L. Needleman & D. Bellinger (eds.), *Prenatal exposure to toxicants: Developmental consequences.* Baltimore: Johns Hopkins University Press.

Bellinger, D. C., Stiles, K. M., & Needleman, H. L. (1992). Low-level lead exposure, intelligence and academic achievement: A long-term follow-up study. *Pediatrics, 90,* 855–861.

Bellugi, U., Wang, P., & Jernigan, T. L. (1994). Williams syndrome: An unusual neuropsychological profile. In S. H. Broman & J. Grafman (eds.), *Atypical cognitive deficits in developmental disorders: Implications for brain function.* Hillsdale, NJ: Lawrence Erlbaum Associates.

Bennetto, L., & Pennington, B. F. (1996). The neuropsychology of fragile X syndrome. In R. J. Hagerman & A. Cronister (eds.), *Fragile X syndrome: Diagnosis, treatment, and research,* 2d ed. Baltimore: Johns Hopkins University Press.

Benton, A. L. (1989). Historical notes on the postconcussion syndrome. In H. S. Levin, H. M. Eisenberg, & A. L. Benton (eds.), *Mild head injury.* New York: Oxford University Press.

Berkell, D. E. (ed.) (1992). *Autism: Identification, education and treatment.* Hillsdale, NJ: Lawrence Erlbaum Associates.

Berkovic, S. F., Andermann, F., Andermann, E., & Gloor, P. (1987). Concepts of absence epilepsies: discrete syndromes or biological continuum? *Neurology, 37,* 993–1000.

Berkow, R. (1992). *The Merck manual of diagnosis and therapy,* 16th ed. Rahway, NJ: Merck Research Laboratories.

Bernero, R. J., & Rothwell, H. (1986). *Relationship of hearing impairment to educational needs.* Springfield, IL: Illinois Department of Public Health and Office of Superintendent of Public Instruction.

Berntson, G. G., & Torello, M. W. (1977). Expression of Magnus tonic neck reflexes in distal muscles of prehension in normal adults. *Physiology & Behavior, 19,* 585–587.

Bettison, S. (1996). The long-term effects of auditory training on children with autism. *Journal of Autism and Developmental Disorders, 26,* 361–374.

Bettleheim, B. (1967). *The empty fortress: Infantile autism and the birth of the self.* New York: Free Press.

Bever, T., & Chiarello, R. (1974). Cerebral dominance in musicians and nonmusicians. *Science, 185,* 137–139.

Bickel, S., Gerrard, J., & Hickmans, E. M. (1954). The influence of phenylalnine intake on the chemistry and behavior of the phenylketonuric child. *Acta Paediatrica, 43,* 64–77.

Biederman, I. (1987). Recognition-by-components: A theory of human image interpretation. *Psychological Review, 94,* 115–147.

Biederman, I. (1995). Visual object recognition. In S. M. Kosslyn & D. N. Osherson (eds.), *An invitation to cognitive science,* vol. 2: *Visual cognition.* Cambridge, MA: MIT Press.

Biederman, I., & Cooper, E. E. (1991a). Priming contour-deleted images. Evidence for intermediate representations in visual object recognition. *Cognitive Psychology, 23,* 393–419.

Biederman, I., & Cooper, E. E. (1991b). Object recognition and laterality: Null effects. *Neuropsychologia, 29,* 685–694.

Biederman, I., Gerhardstein, P. C., Cooper, E. E., & Nelson, C. A. (1997). High level object recognition without an anterior inferior temporal lobe. *Neuropsychologia, 35,* 271–287.

Bigler, E. D. (1990). Neuropathology of traumatic brain injury. In E. D. Bigler (ed.), *Traumatic brain injury: Mechanisms of damage, assessment, intervention, and outcome.* Austin, TX: Pro-ed.

Bigler, E. D. (1997). Brain imaging and behavioral outcome in traumatic brain injury. In E. D. Bigler, E. Clark, & J. E. Farmer (eds.), *Childhood traumatic brain injury.* Austin, TX: Pro-ed.

Bigler, E. D., Clark E., & Farmer, J. E. (eds.) (1997). *Childhood traumatic brain injury.* Austin, TX: Pro-ed.

Binder, J. R., Rao, S. M., Hammeke, T. A., Yetkin, F. Z., Jesmanowicz, A., Bandettini, P. A., Wong, E. C., Estkowski, L. D., Goldstein, M. D.,

Haughton, V. M., & Hyde, J. S. (1994). Functional magnetic resonance imaging of human auditory cortex. *Annals of Neurology, 35,* 662–672.

Bisiach, E., & Luzzatti, C. (1978). Unilateral neglect of representational space. *Cortex, 14,* 129–133.

Blakemore, C., & Campbell, F. W. (1969). On the existence of neurons in the human visual system selectively sensitive to the orientation and size of retinal images. *Journal of Physiology, 203,* 237–260.

Blakemore, C., & Cooper, G. F. (1970). Development of the brain depends on the visual environment. *Nature, 228,* 477–478.

Blatt, S. J., D'Affitti, J. P., & Quinlan, D. M. (1976). Experiences of depression in normal young adults. *Journal of Abnormal Psychology, 85,* 383–389.

Bluestone, C. D., & Klein, J. O. (1988). *Otitis media in infants and children.* Philadelphia: W. B. Saunders.

Blumstein, S. E. (1995). The neurobiology of language. In J. L. Miller & P. D. Eimas (eds.), *Speech, language, and communication.* San Diego, CA: Academic Press.

Bobath, B., & Bobath, K. (1964). The facilitation of normal postural reactions and movements in the treatment of cerebral palsy. *Physiotherapy, 50,* 246.

Bobath, K. (1966). *The motor deficit in patients with cerebral palsy.* London: Heinemann Medical Books.

Boddy, J. (1978). *Brain systems and psychological concepts.* Chichester, England: John Wiley.

Boder, E. (1973). Developmental dyslexia: A diagnostic approach based on three atypical reading–spelling patterns. *Developmental Medicine and Child Neurology, 15,* 663–687.

Bogen, J. E., & Vogel, P. J. (1962). Cerebral commissurotomy in man: Preliminary case report. *Bulletin of the Los Angeles Neurological Society, 27,* 169–172.

Bolte, E. R. (1998). Autism and *Clostridium tetani. Medical Hypotheses, 51,* 133–144.

Boothe, R. G., Dobson, V., & Teller, D. Y. (1985). Postnatal development of vision in human and nonhuman primates. *Annual Review of Neuroscience, 8,* 495–545.

Borland, B. L., & Heckman, H. K. (1976). Hyperactive boys and their brothers: A 25-year follow-up study. *Archives of General Psychiatry, 33,* 669–675.

Bouvard, M. P., Leboyer, M., Launay, J., Recasens, C., Plumet, M., Waller-Perotte, D., Tabuteau, F., Bondoux, D., Dugas, M., Lensing, P., & Panksepp, J. (1995). Low-dose naltrexone effects on plasma chemistries amd clinical symptoms in autism: a double-blind, placebo-controlled study. *Psychiatry Research, 58,* 191–201.

Bracewell, R. N. (1989). The Fourier transform. *Scientific American, 260,* 86–95.

Brackbill, Y. (1971). The role of the cortex in orienting: orienting reflex in an encephalic human infant. *Developmental Psychology, 5,* 195–201.

Bradley, W. (1937). The behavior of children receiving benzedrine. *American Journal of Psychiatry, 94,* 577–585.

Brazier, M. A. B., Cobb, W. A., Fischgold, H., Gastaut, H., Gloor, P., Hess, R., Jasper, H., Loeb, C., Magnus, O., Pampiglione, G., Remond, A., Storm van Leeuwen, W., & Walter, W. G. (1961). Preliminary proposal for an EEG terminology by the Terminology Committee of the International Federation for Electroencephalography and Clinical Neurophysiology. *Electroencephalography and Clinical Neurophysiology, 13,* 646–650.

Breitmeyer, B. (1984). *Visual masking: an integrative report.* Oxford: Oxford University Press.

Breitmeyer, B., & Ganz, L. (1976). Implications of sustained and transient channels for theories of visual pattern masking, saccadic suppression, and information processing. *Psychological Review, 83,* 1-36.

Brody, N. (1992). *Intelligence,* 2nd ed. San Diego, CA: Academic Press.

Brookshire, B., Copeland, D. R., Moore, B. D., & Ater, J. (1990). Pretreatment neuropsychological status and associated factors in children with primary brain tumors. *Neurosurgery, 27,* 887–891.

Brown, A. L., & Campione, J. C. (1984). Three faces of transfer: Implications for early competence, individual differences, and instruction. In M. E. Lamb, A. L. Brown, & B. Rogoff (eds.), *Advances in Developmental Psychology, 3,* 143–193.

Brown, A. L., Campione, J. C., Webber, L. S., & McGilly, K. (1992). Interactive learning environments: A new look at assessment and instruction. In B. R. Gifford & M. C. O'Conner (eds.), *Changing assessments: Alternate views of aptitude, achievement and instruction.* Boston: Kluwer Academic Publishers.

Brown, G. W., Harris, T. O., & Hepworth, C. (1994). Life events and endogenous depression: A puzzle reexamined. *Archives of General Psychiatry, 51,* 525–534.

Brown, S. W., & Fenwick, P. B. C. (1989). Evoked and psychogenic epileptic seizures: II. Inhibition. *Acta Neurologica Scandinavica, 80,* 541–547.

Brown, W. T. (1996). The molecular biology of the fragile X mutation. In R. J. Hagerman & A. Cronister (eds.), *Fragile X syndrome: Diagnosis, treatment, and research,* 2d ed. Baltimore: Johns Hopkins University Press.

Bruce, V., & Green, P. R. (1990). *Visual perception: Physiology, psychology and ecology.* Hillsdale, NJ: Lawrence Erlbaum Associates.

Bruce, V., & Humphreys, G. W. (1994). Recognizing objects and faces. *Visual Cognition, 1,* 141–180.

Bruer, J. T. (1999). *The myth of the first three years: A new understanding of early brain development and lifelong learning.* New York: Free Press.

Brumback, R. A. (1988). Childhood depression and medically treated learning disability. In D. L. Molfese & S. J. Segalowitz (eds.), *Brain lateralization in children: Developmental implications.* New York: Guilford Press.

Bruner, J. (1968). The course of cognitive growth. In N. S. Endler, R. L. Boulter, & H. Osser (eds.), *Contemporary issues in developmental psychology.* New York: Holt, Rinehart & Winston.

Bruun, R. D. (1988). The natural history of Tourette's syndrome. In D. J. Cohen, R. D. Bruun, & J. F. Leckman (eds.), *Tourette's syndrome and tic disorders: Clinical understanding and treatment.* New York: John Wiley.

Burgard, P., Rey, F., Rupp, A., Abadie, V., & Rey, J. (1997). Neuropsychologic functions of early treated patients with phenylketonuria on and off diet: Results of a cross-national and cross-sectional study. *Pediatric Research, 41,* 368–374.

Burt, C. (1958). The inheritance of mental ability. *American Psychologist, 13,* 1–15.

Butters, N., & Delis, D. C. (1995). Clinical assessment of memory disorders in amnesia and dementia. *Annual Review of Psychology, 46,* 493–523.

Calvin, W. H., & Ojemann, G. A. (1994). *Conversations with Neil's brain.* Reading, MA: Addison-Wesley.

Campbell, F. W., & Robson, J. G. (1968). Application of Fourier analysis to the visibility of gratings. *Journal of Physiology, 197,* 551–566.

Campione, J. C., Brown, A. L., & Ferrara, R. A. (1982). Mental retardation and intelligence. In R. J. Sternberg (ed.), *Handbook of human intelligence.* Cambridge: Cambridge University Press.

Canadian Broadcasting Corp. (Producer) (1991). *Children who learned to listen* [film]. (Available from Film-makers Library, Inc., 124 East 40th St, New York, NY 10016.)

Cantor, S. (1988). *Childhood schizophrenia.* New York: Guilford Press.

Cantwell, D. P. (1983). Depression in childhood: Clinical picture and diagnostic criteria. In D. P. Cantwell & G. A. Carlson (eds.), *Affective disorders in childhood and adolescence: An update* (pp. 3–18). New York: SP Medical & Scientific Books.

Cantwell, D. P., & Carlson, G. A. (eds.) (1983). *Affective disorders in childhood and adolescence: An update.* New York: SP Medical & Scientific Books.

Caplan, R., Chugani, H. T., Messa, C., Guthrie, D., Sigman, M., de Traversay, J., & Mundy, P. (1993). Hemispherectomy for intractable seizures: Presurgical cerebral glucose metabolism and post-surgical non-verbal communication. *Developmental Medicine and Child Neurology, 35,* 582–592.

Carlson, G. A., & Cantwell, D. P. (1983). Case studies in prepubertal childhood depression. In D. P. Cantwell & G. A. Carlson (eds.), *Affective disorders in childhood and adolescence: An update* (pp. 39–59). New York: SP Medical & Scientific Books.

Carlson, G. A., & Garber, J. (1986). Developmental issues in the classification of depression in children. In M. Rutter, C. E. Izard, & P. B. Read (eds.), *Depression in young people: Developmental and clinical perspectives.* New York: Guilford Press.

Carlson, M., & Earls, F. (1997). Psychological and neuroendocrinological sequelae of early social deprivation in institutionalized children in Romania. *Annals of the New York Academy of Sciences, 807,* 419–428.

Carlson, N. R. (1998). *Physiology of behavior,* 6th ed. Boston: Allyn & Bacon.

Carlson-Green, B., Morris, R. D., & Krawiecki, N. (1995). Family and illness predictors of outcome in pediatric brain tumors. *Journal of Pediatric Psychology, 20,* 769–784.

Carney, M. W. P., Roth, M., & Garside, R. F. (1965). The diagnosis of depressive syndromes and the prediction of the ECT response. *British Journal of Psychiatry, 111,* 659–674.

Carpenter, L. L., Leckman, J. F., Scahill, L., & McDougle, C. J. (1999). Pharmacological and other somatic approaches to treatment. In J. F. Leckman & D. J. Cohen (eds.), *Tourette's syndrome – tics, obsessions, compulsions: Developmental psychopathology and clinical care.* New York: John Wiley.

Carr, J. (1994). Annotation: Long term outcome for people with Down's syndrome. *Journal of Child Psychology and Psychiatry, 35,* 425–439.

Carroll, J. B. (1982). The measurement of intelligence. In R. J. Sternberg (ed.), *Handbook of human intelligence.* Cambridge: Cambridge University Press.

Carroll, J. L., & Loughlin, G. M. (1995). Obstructive sleep apnea syndrome in infants and children: Clinical features and pathophysiology; diagnosis and management. In R. Ferber & M. Kryger (eds.), *Principles and practice of sleep medicine in the child.* Philadelphia: W. B. Saunders.

Cattell, R. B. (1971). *Abilities: Their structure, growth and action.* Boston: Houghton-Mifflin.

Cattell, R. B. (1979). Ethics and the social sciences: The "beyondist" solution. *Mankind Quarterly, 19,* 298–310.

Cavalli-Sforza, L. L., Menozzi, P., & Piazza, A. (1996). *The history and geography of human genes.* Princeton, NJ: Princeton University Press.

Cermak, S. (1985). Developmental dyspraxia. In E. A. Roy (ed.), *Neuropsychological studies of apraxia and related disorders*. Amsterdam: Elsevier.

Chabot, R. J., Merkin, H., Wood, L. M., Davenport, T. L., & Serfontein, G. (1996). Sensitivity and specificity of QEEG in children with attention deficit or specific developmental learning disorders. *Clinical Encephalography, 27*, 26–34.

Chabot, R. J., & Serfontein, G. (1996). Quantitative electroencephalographic profiles of children with attention deficit disorder. *Biological Psychiatry, 40*, 951–963.

Chapman, S. B. (1995). Discourse as an outcome of pediatric closed head injury. In S. H. Broman & M. E. Michel (eds.), *Traumatic head injury in children*. New York: Oxford University Press.

Charlton, C. G., Miller, R. L., Crawley, J. N., Handelmann, G. E., & O'Donohue, T. L. (1983). Secretin modulation of behavioral and physiological functions in the rat. *Peptides, 4*, 739–742.

Cheek, W. R. (1994). Suppurative central nervous system infections. In W. R. Cheek (ed.), *Pediatric neurosurgery*, 3rd ed. Philadelphia: W. B. Saunders.

Chess, S., & Thomas, A. (1984). *Origins and evolution of behavior disorders from infancy to early adult life*. New York: Brunner/Mazel.

Chess, S., Thomas, A., & Hassibi, M. (1983). Depression in childhood and adolescence: A prospective study of six cases. *Journal of Nervous and Mental Diseases, 171*, 411–420.

Chomsky, N. (1968). *Language and mind*. New York: Harcourt Brace Jovanovich.

Chomsky, N. (1981). *Lectures on government and binding*. Dordrecht: Foris Publications.

Christie, S., Guberman, A., Tansley, B. W., & Couture, M. (1988). Primary reading epilepsy: Investigation of critical seizure-provoking stimuli. *Epilepsia, 29*, 288–293.

Clarke, A. (1985). Polygenic and environmental interactions. In A. M. Clarke, A. D. B. Clarke, & J. M. Berg (eds.), *Mental deficiency: The changing outlook*, 4th ed. London: Methuen.

Clarke, A. (1995). Rett syndrome. *Neuropediatrics, 26*, 693–699.

Clarke, A. M., & Clarke, A. D. B. (1985). Lifespan development and psychosocial intervention. In A. M. Clarke, A. D. B. Clarke, & J. M. Berg (eds.), *Mental deficiency: The changing outlook*, 4th ed. London: Methuen.

Cohen, D. J., Young, J. G., Nathanson, J. A., & Shaywitz, B. A. (1979). Clonidine in Tourette's syndrome. *Lancet, ii*, 551–553.

Cohen, M. E., & Duffner, P. K. (1994). *Brain tumors in children: Principles of diagnosis and treatment*, 2nd ed. New York: Raven Press.

Cohen, N. J., & Douglas, V. I. (1972). Characteristics of the orienting response in hyperactive and normal children. *Psychophysiology, 9*, 238–245.

Cohen, R. A. (1993). *The neuropsychology of attention*. New York: Plenum.

Coker, S. B. (1992). Postneonatal vitamin B6-dependent epilepsy. *Pediatrics, 90*, 221–223.

Cole, A. J., Andermann, F., Taylor, L., Olivier, A., Rasmussen, T., Robitaile, Y., & Spire, J.-P. (1988). The Landau–Kleffner syndrome of acquired epileptic aphasia: Unusual clinical outcome, surgical experience, and absence of encephalitis. *Neurology, 38*, 31–38.

Cole, M., Gay, J., Glick, J. A., & Sharp, D. W. (1971). *The cultural context of learning and thinking*. New York: Basic Books.

Coleman, M. (ed.) (1976). *The autistic syndromes*. Amsterdam: North-Holland.

Coleman, M. (1997). Editorial: Vitamins and Down syndrome. *Down Syndrome Quarterly, 2*, 11–13.

Coleman, M., & Gillberg, C. (1985). *The biology of the autistic syndromes*. New York: Praeger.

Coleman, M., & Gillberg, C. (1996). *The schizophrenias: A biological approach to the schizophrenia spectrum disorders*. New York: Springer.

Coleman, M., Landgrebe, M. A., & Landgrebe, A. R. (1976a). Celiac autism. In M. Coleman (ed.), *The autistic syndromes*. Amsterdam: North-Holland.

Coleman, M., Landgrebe, M. A., & Landgrebe, A. R. (1976b). Purine autism. In M. Coleman (ed.), *The autistic syndromes*. Amsterdam: North-Holland.

Coles, C. D. (1992). Prenatal alcohol exposure and human development. In M. Miller (ed.), *Development of the central nervous system: Effects of alcohol and opiates*. New York: Wiley-Liss.

Coles, C. D., & Platzman, K. A. (1993). Behavioral development in children prenatally exposed to drugs and alcohol. *International Journal of Addictions, 28*, 1393–1433.

Commission on Classification and Terminology of the International League Against Epilepsy (1981). Proposal for revised clinical and electroencephalographic classification of epileptic seizures. *Epilepsia, 22*, 489–501.

Conners, C. K. (1973). Rating scales for use in drug studies with children. *Psychopharmacology Bulletin, 9*, 24–84.

Conners, C. K. (1980). *Food additives and hyperactive children*. New York: Plenum.

Conrad, R. (1972). Short-term memory in the deaf: A test for speech coding. *British Journal of Psychology, 63*, 173–180.

Cooper, J. R., Bloom, F. E., & Roth, R. H. (1996). *The biochemical basis of neuropharmacology*, 7th ed. New York: Oxford University Press.

Cooper, L. A., & Regan, D. T. (1982). Attention, perception, and intelligence. In R. J. Sternberg (ed.), *Handbook of human intelligence*. Cambridge: Cambridge University Press.

Cope, D. N. (1995). The effectiveness of traumatic brain injury rehabilitation: A review. *Brain Injury, 9*, 649–670.

Corballis, M. C., & Beale, I. L. (1993). Orton revisited: Dyslexia, laterality, and left–right confusion. In D. M. Willows, R. S. Kruk, & E. Corcos (eds.), *Visual processes in reading and reading disabilities*. Hillsdale, NJ: Lawrence Erlbaum Associates.

Coren, S., Porac, C., & Ward, L. M. (1979). *Sensation and perception*. New York: Academic Press.

Cornsweet, T. N. (1970). *Visual perception*. New York: Academic Press.

Cottraux, J., & Gérard, D. (1998). Neuroimaging and neuroanatomical issues in obsessive–compulsive disorder: Toward integrative model – perceived impulsivity. In R. P. Swinson, M. M. Antony, S. Rachman, & M. A. Richter (eds.), *Obsessive–compulsive disorder: Theory, research, and treatment*. New York: Guilford Press.

Courchesne, E. (1989). Neuroanatomical systems involved in infantile autism: The implications of cerebellar abnormalities. In G. Dawson (ed.), *Autism: Nature, diagnosis and treatment*. New York: Guilford Press.

Courchesne, E., Townsend, J. P., Akshoomoff, N. A., Yeung-Courchesne, R., Press, G. A., Murakami, J. W., Lincoln, A. J., James, H. E., Saitoh, O., Egaas, B., Haas, R. H., & Schreibman, L. (1994). A new finding: Impairment in shifting attention in autistic and cerebellar patients. In S. H. Broman & J. Grafman (eds.), *Atypical cognitive deficits in developmental disorders: Implications for brain function*. Hillsdale, NJ: Lawrence Erlbaum Associates.

Cowey, A., & Stoerig, P. (1991). The neurobiology of blindsight. *Trends in Neurosciences, 14*, 140–145.

Crandall, P. H., Risinger, M. W., Sutherling, W., Chugani, H., Peacock, W., & Levesque, M. F. (1990). Surgical treatment of the partial epilepsies. In M. Dam & L. Gram (eds.), *Comprehensive epileptology*. New York: Raven Press.

Cratty, B. J. (1971). *Movement and spatial awareness in blind children and youth*. Springfield, IL: C. C. Thomas.

Cutsforth, T. D. (1932). The unreality of words to the blind. *Teachers Forum, 4*, 86–89.

Dacey, R. G., Vollmer, D., & Dikmen, S. S. (1993). Mild head injury. In P. R. Cooper (ed.), *Head injury*, 3rd ed. Baltimore: Williams & Wilkins.

Dahl, J., Brorson, L., & Melin, L. (1992). The effects of a broad-spectrum behavioral medicine treatment program on children with refractory epileptic seizures: An 8-year follow-up. *Epilepsia, 33*, 98–102.

Dahl, J., Melin, L., & Leissner, P. (1988). Effects of intervention on epileptic seizure behavior and paroxysmal activity: A systematic replication of three cases of children with intractable epilepsy. *Epilepsia, 29*, 172–183.

Das, J. P., Kirby, J. R., & Jarman, R. F. (1979). *Simultaneous and successive cognitive processes*. New York: Academic Press.

Davidson, R. J. (1988). EEG measures of cerebral asymmetry: Conceptual and methodological issues. *International Journal of Neuroscience, 39*, 71–89.

Davies, M., Howlin, O., & Udwin, O. (1997). Independence and adaptive behavior in adults with Williams syndrome. *American Journal of Medical Genetics, 70*, 188–195.

Dawson, G., & Lewy, A. (1989). Arousal, attention, and the socioemotional impairments of individuals with autism. In G. Dawson (ed.), *Autism: Nature, diagnosis and treatment.* New York: Guilford Press.

De Beaurepaire, R., Fattal-German, N., Kramartz, P., Gekiere, F., Bizzini, B., Rioux, P., & Borenstein, P. (1994). Etude des réactions immunitaires humorales et cellulaires dans diverses formes de pathologies psychiatriques chroniques. *Encephale, 20,* 57–64.

Dement, W., & Kleitman, N. (1957). Cyclic variations in EEG during sleep and their relation to eye movements, body motility and dreaming. *Electroencephalography and Clinical Neurophysiology, 9,* 673–690.

Denckla, M. B., & Rudel, R. (1976). Rapid "automatized" naming (RAN): dyslexia differentiated from other disabilities. *Neuropsychologia, 14,* 471–479.

Dennis, M. (1980). Capacity and strategy for syntactic comprehension after left or right hemidecortication. *Brain and Language, 10,* 287–317.

Dennis, M., & Kohn, B. (1975). Comprehension of syntax in infantile hemiplegics after cerebral hemidecortication: Left hemisphere superiority. *Brain and Language, 2,* 472–482.

Dennis, M., Lovett, M., & Wiegel-Crump, C. A. (1981). Written language acquisition after left or right hemidecortication in infancy. *Brain and Language, 12,* 54–91.

Dennis, M., Spiegler, B. J., Hetherington, C. R., & Greenberg, M. L. (1996). Neuropsychological sequelae of the treatment of children with medulloblastoma. *Journal of Neuro-Oncology, 29,* 91–101.

Dennis, M., & Whitaker, H. A. (1976). Language acquisition following hemidecortication: Linguistic superiority of the left over the right hemisphere. *Brain and Language, 3,* 404–433.

Dennis, M., & Wiegel-Crump, C. A. (1981). Written language acquisition after left or right hemidecortication in infancy. *Brain and Language, 12,* 54–91.

Dennis, M., Wilkinson, M., Koski, L., & Humphreys, R. P. (1995). Attention deficits in the long term after childhood head injury. In S. H. Broman & M. E. Michel (eds.), *Traumatic head injury in children.* New York: Oxford University Press.

Deutsch, C. H. (1986). Rationale for the administration of opiate antagonists in treating infantile autism. *American Journal of Mental Deficiency, 90,* 631–635.

De Valois, R. L., & De Valois, K. K. (1990). *Spatial vision.* New York: Oxford University Press.

DeVivo, D. C., Malas, K. L., & Leckie, M. P. (1975). Starvation and seizures: Observations of the electroconvulsive threshold and cerebral metabolism of the starved adult rat. *Archives of Neurology, 32,* 755–760.

Devlin, B., Daniels, M., & Roeder, K. (1997). The heritability of IQ. *Nature, 388,* 468–271.

Diamond, A. (1991). Guidelines for the study of brain–behavior relationships during development. In H. S. Levin, H. M. Eisenberg, & A. L. Benton (eds.), *Frontal lobe function and dysfunction.* New York: Oxford University Press.

Diamond, A., & Herzberg, C. (1996). Impaired sensitivity to visual contrast in children treated early and continuously for PKU. *Brain, 119,* 523–538.

Diamond, A., Prevor, M. B., Callender, G., & Druin, D. P. (1997). Prefrontal cortex cognitive deficits in children treated early and continuously for PKU. *Monographs of the Society for Research in Child Development, 62* (4, Serial No. 252).

Diefendorf, A. O. (1988). Pediatric audiology. In N. J. Lass, L. V. McReynolds, J. L. Northern, & D. E. Yoder (eds.), *Handbook of speech–language pathology and audiology.* Toronto: B. C. Decker.

Dietrich, K. N., & Bellinger, D. (1994). The assessment of neurobehavioral development in studies of the effects of prenatal exposure to toxicants. In H. L. Needleman & D. Bellinger (eds.), *Prenatal exposure to toxicants: Developmental consequences.* Baltimore: Johns Hopkins University Press.

Dodrill, C. B., & Batzel, L. W. (1986). Interictal behavioral features of patients with epilepsy. *Epilepsia, 27* (Suppl. 2), S64–S76.

Dohan, F. C. (1983). More on celiac disease as a model for schizophrenia. *Biological Psychiatry, 18,* 561–564.

Dollinger, S. J. (1982). On the varieties of childhood sleep disturbance. *Journal of Clinical Child Psychology, 2,* 107–115.

Don, A., & Rourke, B. P. (1995). Fetal alcohol syndrome. In B. P. Rourke (ed.), *Syndrome of nonverbal learning disabilities.* New York: Guilford Press.

Dorman, C., & Katzir, B. (1994). *Cognitive effects of early brain injury.* Baltimore: Johns Hopkins University Press.

Douglas, V. I. (1972). Stop, look, and listen: The problems of sustained attention and impulse control in hyperactive and normal children. *Canadian Journal of Behavioral Science, 41,* 259–282.

Douglas, V. I. (1984). The psychological processes implicated in ADD. In L. M. Bloomingdale (ed.), *Attention deficit disorder: Diagnostic, cognitive and therapeutic understanding.* New York: Spectrum.

Downs, M. P., & Gerkin, K. (1988). Early identification of hearing loss. In N. J. Lass, L. V. McReynolds, J. L. Northern, & D. E. Yoder (eds.), *Handbook of speech–language pathology and audiology.* Toronto: B. C. Decker.

Dreyfus, J. (1981). *A remarkable medicine has been overlooked.* New York: Dreyfus Medical Foundation.

Dryer, R., Beale, I. L., & Lambert, A. J. (1999). The balance model of dyslexia and remedial training: An evaluative study. *Journal of Learning Disabilities, 32,* 174–186.

Duffy, F. H., Burchfiel, J., & Lombroso, C. T. (1979). Brain electrical activity mapping (BEAM): a method for extending the clinical utility of EEG and evokedpotential data. *Annals of Neurology, 5,* 309–321.

Duffy, F. H., Hughes, J. R., Miranda, F., Bernad, P., & Cook, P. (1994). Status of quantitative EEG (QEEG) in clinical practice, 1994. *Clinical Encephalography, 25,* VI–XXII.

Duke, M. P., Nowicki, S. Jr, & Martin, E. (1996). *Teaching your child the language of social success.* Atlanta, GA: Peachtree.

Dulac, O., & Plouin, P. (1993). Infantile spasms and West syndrome. In E. Wylie (ed.), *The treatment of epilepsy: Principles and practice.* Philadelphia: Lea & Febiger.

Duncan, J., Emslie, H., Williams, P., Johnson, R., & Freer, C. (1996). Intelligence and the frontal lobe: The organization of goal-directed behavior. *Cognitive Psychology, 30,* 257–303.

Dunst, C. J. (1990). Sensorimotor development of infants with Down syndrome. In D. Cicchetti & M. Beeghly (eds.), *Children with Down syndrome: A developmental perspective.* Cambridge: Cambridge University Press.

Dworkin, R. H., Lenzenweger, M. F., Moldin, S. O., & Cornblatt, B. A. (1987). Genetics and the phenomenology of schizophrenia. In P. D. Harvey & E. F. Walker (eds.), *Positive and negative symptoms in psychosis: Description, research, and future directions.* Hillsdale, NJ: Lawrence Erlbaum Associates.

Dykens, E. M., Hodapp, R. M., & Leckman, J. F. (1994). *Behavior and development in fragile X syndrome.* Thousand Oaks, CA: Sage.

Edgerton, R. B. (1979). *Mental retardation.* Cambridge, Mass.: Marvard University Press.

Edwards, A. J. (1974). Introduction. In D. Wechsler (ed.), *Selected papers of David Wechsler.* New York: Academic Press.

Eggers, C., & Bunk, D. (1997). The long-term course of childhood-onset schizophrenia: A 42-year followup. *Schizophrenia Bulletin, 23,* 105–117.

Eimas, P. D., Miller, J., & Jusczyk, P. W. (1987). On infant speech perception and the acquisition of language. In S. Harned (ed.), *Categorical perception: The groundwork of cognition.* Cambridge: Cambridge University Press.

Eimas, P. D., Siqueland, E. R., Jusczyk, P., & Vigorito, J. (1971). Speech perception in infants. *Science, 171,* 303–306.

Eisenberg, L. (1986). When is a case a case? In M. Rutter, C. E. Izard, & P. B. Read (eds.), *Depression in young people: developmental and clinical perspectives.* New York: Guilford Press.

Elliott, C. D. (1990). *Differential ability scales.* San Diego, CA: Harcourt, Brace, Jovanovich.

Elman, J. L., Bates, E. A., Johnson, M. A., Karmiloff-Smith, A., Parisi, D., & Plunkett, K. (1996). *Rethinking innateness: A connectionist perspective on development.* Cambridge, MA: MIT Press.

Ensher, G. L., & Clark, D. A. (1994). *Newborns at risk: Medical care and psychoeducational intervention.* Gaithersburg, MD: Aspen.

Enzmann, D. R. (1997). Imaging of neonatal hypoxic–ischemic cerebral damage. In D. K.

Stevenson & P. Sunshine (eds.), *Fetal and neonatal brain injury*. Oxford: Oxford University Press.

Epstein, C. J. (ed.) (1991). *The morphogenesis of Down syndrome*. New York: Wiley-Liss.

Epstein, C. J. (ed.) (1993). *The phenotypic mapping of Down syndrome and other aneuploid conditions*. New York: Wiley-Liss.

Erickson, M. H. (1954). Indirect hypnotic therapy of a bedwetting couple. *Journal of Clinical and Experimental Hypnosis, 2,* 171–184.

Eriksen, H. R., Ellertsen, B., Grønningsæter, H., Nakken, K. O., Løyning, Y., & Ursin, H. (1994). Physical exercise in women with intractable epilepsy. *Epilepsia, 35,* 1256–1264.

Evans, J. R., & Abarbanel, A. (eds.) (1999). *Introduction to quantitative EEG and neurofeedback*. San Diego: Academic Press.

Evans, J. A., & Hamerton, J. L. (1985). Chromosomal anomalies. In A. M. Clarke, A. D. B. Clarke, & J. M. Berg (eds.), *Mental deficiency: The changing outlook*, 4th ed. London: Methuen.

Everson, C. A. (1997). Sleep deprivation and the immune system. In M. R. Pressman & W. C. Orr (eds.), *Understanding sleep: The evaluation and treatment of sleep disorders*. Washington, DC: American Psychological Association.

Ewing-Cobbs, L., Dubaime, A., & Fletcher, J. M. (1995). Inflicted and noninflicted traumatic brain injury in infants and preschoolers. *Journal of Head Trauma Rehabilitation, 10,* 13–24.

Ewing-Cobbs, L., Fletcher, J. M., Levin, H. S., Francis, D. J., Davidson, K., & Miner, M. E. (1997). Longitudinal neuropsychological outcome in infants and preschoolers with traumatic brain injury. *Journal of the International Neuropsychological Society, 3,* 581–591.

Eysenck, H. J., & Schoenthaler, S. J. (1997). Raising IQ level by vitamins and mineral supplementation. In R. J. Sternberg & E. L. Gigorenko (eds.), *Intelligence, heredity, and environment*. Cambridge: Cambridge University Press.

Fahn, S., & Erenberg, G. (1988). Differential diagnosis of tic phenomena: A neurologic perspective. In D. J. Cohen, R. D. Bruun, & J. F. Leckman (eds.), *Tourette's syndrome and tic disorders: clinical understanding and treatment*. New York: John Wiley.

Faust, D., Ziskin, J., & Hiers, J. B. Jr. (1991). *Brain damage claims: Coping with neuropsychological evidence*. Los Angeles, CA: Law and Psychology Press.

Featherstone, H. (1981). *A difference in the family: Living with a disabled child*. New York: Penguin Books.

Feingold, B. (1975). *Why your child is hyperactive*. New York: Random House.

Feldman, R. G., & Paul, N. G. (1976). Identity of emotional triggers in epilepsy. *Journal of Nervous and Mental Disease, 162,* 345–352.

Feldman, R. G., Ricks, N. L., & Orren, M. H. (1983). Behavioral methods of seizure control. In T. R. Browne & R. G. Feldman (eds.), *Epilepsy: Diagnosis and management*. Boston: Little Brown.

Ferber, R. (1995). Sleeplessness in children. In R. Ferber & M. Kryger (eds.), *Principles and practice of sleep medicine in the child*. Philadelphia: W. B. Saunders.

Ferrendelli, J. A., & Mathews, G. C. (1993). Neuropharmacology of antiepileptic medications: Mechanisms of action. In E. Wylie (ed.), *The treatment of epilepsy: Principles and practice*. Philadelphia: Lea & Febiger.

Ferson, J. (1970). The seizure as a breach of the parent–child contract: Severe discipline problems in children with epilepsy. *Unpublished paper*.

Filloux, F. M. (1996). Neuropathophysiology of movement disorders in cerebral palsy. *Journal of Child Neurology, 11* (Suppl. 1), S5–S12.

Finegan, E. (1994). *Language: its structure and use*, 2nd ed. Fort Worth, TX: Harcourt Brace.

Finger, S., & Almli, C. R. (1988). Margaret Kennaard and her "Principle" in historical perspective. In S. Finger, T. E. Levere, C. R. Almli, & D. G. Stein (eds.), *Brain injury and recovery: Theoretical and controversial issues*. New York: Plenum Press.

Fioretino, M. R. (1963). *Reflex testing methods for evaluating C.N.S. development*. Springfield, IL: C. C. Thomas.

Fischer, C. S., Hout, M., Jankowski, M. S., Lucas, S. R., Swidler, A., & Voss, K. (1996). *Inequality by design: Cracking the bell curve*. Princeton, NJ: Princeton University Press.

Flavell, J. H. (1976). Metacognitive aspects of problem solving. In L. B. Resnick (ed.), *The nature of intelligence.* Hillsdale, NJ: Lawrence Erlbaum Associates.

Fleischner, J. E., & Garnett, K. (1987). Arithmetic disability. In K. A. Kavale, S. R. Forness, & M. Bender (eds.), *Handbook of learning disabilities*, Vol. 1: *Dimensions and diagnosis.* Boston: Little, Brown.

Fletcher, J. M. (1985). Memory for verbal and noverbal stimuli in learning disability subgroups: Analysis of selective reminding. *Journal of Experimental Child Psychology*, 40, 244–259.

Fletcher, J. (1994). Afterword: Behavior–brain relationships in children. In S. H. Broman & J. Grafman (eds.), *Atypical cognitive deficits in developmental disorders: Implications for brain function.* Hillsdale, NJ: Lawrence Erlbaum Associates.

Fletcher, J. M., & Morris, R. (1986). Classification of disabled learners: Beyond exclusionary definitions. In S. J. Ceci (ed.), *Handbook of cognitive, social and neurological aspects of learning disabilities*, Vol. 1. Hillsdale, NJ: Lawrence Erlbaum Associates.

Fletcher, J. M., Ewing-Cobbs, L., Francis, D. J., & Levin, H. S. (1995). Variability in outcomes after traumatic brain injury in children: A developmental perspective. In S. H. Broman & M. E. Michel (eds.), *Traumatic head injury in children.* New York: Oxford University Press.

Fletcher, J. M., Landry, S. H., Bohan, T. P., Davidson, K. C., Brookshire, B. L., Lachar, D., Kramer, L. A., & Francis, D. J. (1997). Effects of intraventricular hemorrhage and hydrocephalus on the long-term neurobehavioral development of preterm very-low-birthweight infants. *Developmental Medicine and Child Neurology*, 39, 596–606.

Flor-Henry, P. (1969). Psychosis and temporal-lobe epilepsy: A controlled investigation. *Epilepsia*, 10, 363–395.

Flor-Henry, P. (1979). On certain aspects of the localization of the cerebral systems regulating and determining emotion. *Biological Psychiatry*, 14, 677–698.

Flynn, J. R. (1987). Massive IQ gains in 14 nations: What IQ tests really measure. *Psychological Bulletin*, 101, 171–191.

Flynn, J. R. (1999). Searching for justice: The discovery of IQ gains over time. *American Psychologist*, 54, 5–20.

Fombonne, E. (1999). Are measles infections or measles immunizations linked to autism? *Journal of Autism and Developmental Disorders*, 29, 349–350.

Foulkes, W. D. (1966). *The psychology of sleep.* New York: Scribners.

Foulkes, W. D. (1982). *Children's dreams: Longitudinal studies.* New York: Wiley.

Foulkes, D., & Schmidt, M. (1983). Temporal sequencing unit composition in dream reports from different stages of sleep. *Sleep*, 6, 265–280.

Fowler, A. E. (1995). Linguistic variability in persons with Down syndrome: Research and implications. In L. Nadel & D. Rosenthal (eds.), *Down syndrome: Living and learning in the community.* New York: Wiley-Liss.

Fraiberg, S. (1977). *Insights from the blind.* New York: Basic Books.

Frank, E., Anderson, B., Reynolds, C. F., Ritenour, A. M., & Kupfer, D. J. (1994). Life events and the research diagnostic criteria endogenous subtype: a confirmation of the distinction using the Bedford College methods. *Archives of General Psychiatry*, 51, 519–524.

Frank, E., Kupfer, D. J., Wagner, E. F., McLachran, A. B., & Cones, C. (1991). Efficacy of interpersonal psychotherapy as a maintenance treatment of recurrent depression: contributing factors. *Archives of General Psychiatry*, 48, 1053–1059.

Frank, G. (1983). *The Wechsler enterprise.* Oxford: Pergamon Press.

Free, M. L., & Oei, T. P. S. (1989). Biological and psychological processes in the treatment and maintenance of depression. *Clinical Psychology Reviews*, 9, 653–688.

Freeman, J. M. (1995). A clinician's look at the developmental neurobiology of epilepsy. In P. A. Schwartzkroin, S. L. Moshé, J. L. Noebels, & J. W. Swann (eds.), *Brain development and epilepsy.* New York: Oxford University Press.

Freeman, J. M., Vining, E. P., Pillas, D. J., Pyzik, P. L., Casey, J. C., & Kelly, L. M. (1998). The efficacy of the ketogenic diet – 1998: A prospective evaluation of intervention in 150 children. *Pediatrics*, 102, 1358–1363.

Freeman, R. D., Mitchell, D. E., & Millodot, M. (1972). A neural effect of partial visual deprivation in humans. *Science, 175,* 1384–1386.

Freides, D. (1974). Human information processing and sensory modality: Cross-modal functions, information complexity, memory, and deficit. *Psychological Bulletin, 81,* 284–310.

Freides, D. (1976). A new diagnostic scheme for disorders of behavior, emotion, and learning based on organism–environment interaction. Part I: Theory; Part II: Clinical implementation and research. *Schizophrenia Bulletin, 2,* 218–248.

Friedman, E. A., & Neff, R. K. (1986). *Labor and delivery: Impact on offspring.* Littleton, MA: PSG.

Frith, C. D., & Done, D. J. (1988). Towards a neuropsychology of schizophrenia. *British Journal of Psychiatry, 153,* 437–443.

Frith, U. (1989). *Autism: Explaining the enigma.* Oxford: Basil Blackwell.

Frith, U. (ed.) (1991). *Autism and Asperger syndrome.* Cambridge: Cambridge University Press.

Frost, R. O., Marten, P., Lahart, C., & Rosenblate, R. (1990). Dimensions of perfectionism. *Cognitive Therapy and Research, 14,* 449–468.

Fuerst, K. B., & Rourke, B. P. (1995). White matter physiology and pathology. In B. Rourke (ed.), *Syndrome of nonverbal learning disabilities.* New York: Guilford Press.

Furth, H. G. (1973). *Deafness and learning.* Belmont, CA: Wadsworth.

Gajzago, C., & Prior, M. (1974). Two cases of "recovery" in Kanner's syndrome. *Archives of General Psychiatry, 31,* 264–268.

Gardner, H. (1983). *Frames of mind: The theory of multiple intelligences.* New York: Basic Books.

Gardner, R. A. (1979). *The objective diagnosis of minimal brain dysfunction.* Cresskill, NJ: Creative Therapeutics.

Gardner, R. J. M., & Sutherland, G. R. (1996). *Chromosome abnormalities and genetic counseling.* New York: Oxford University Press.

Gaskill, S. J., & Marlin, A. E. (1993). *Handbook of pediatric neurology and neurosurgery.* Boston: Little, Brown.

Gedye, A. (1989). Episodic rage and aggression attributed to frontal lobe seizures. *Journal of Mental Deficiency Research, 33,* 369–379.

Gedye, A. (1991). Frontal lobe seizures in autism. *Medical Hypotheses, 14,* 174–182.

Gedye, A. (1992). Anatomy of self-injurious, stereotypic, and aggressive movement: evidence for involuntary explanation. *Journal of Clinical Psychology, 48,* 766–778.

Gedye, A. (1998). *Behavioral diagnostic guide for developmental disabilities.* Vancouver, BC: Diagnostic Books (PO Box 39081 Point Grey, Vancouver, BC V6R 4P1, Canada).

Geiger, G., & Lettvin, J. Y. (1987). Peripheral vision in persons with dyslexia. *New England Journal of Medicine, 316,* 1238–1243.

Geiger, G., Lettvin, J. Y., & Fahle, M. (1994). Dyslexic children learn new visual strategy for reading: a controlled experiment. *Vision Research, 34,* 1223–1233.

Gelman, S. A., Coley, J. D., Rosengren, K. S., Hartman, E., & Pappas, A. (1998). Beyond labeling: The role of maternal input in the acquisition of richly structured categories. *Monographs of the Society for Research in Child Development, 63* (1, Serial No. 253).

Gesell, A., & Ilg, F. L. (1943). *Infant and child in the culture of today.* New York: Harper & Bros.

Ghai, V., Jain, L., & Vidyasagar, D. (1989). Surfactant: Its role in the therapy of respiratory distress syndrome. In M. Rathi (ed.), *Current perinatology.* New York: Springer-Verlag.

Ghez, C. (1991). The cerebellum. In E. R. Kandel, J. H. Schwartz, & T. M. Jessell (eds.), *Principles of neural science.* Norwalk, CN: Appleton & Lange.

Gibson, J. J. (1966). *The senses considered as perceptual systems.* Boston: Houghton Mifflin.

Gibson, E. J., & Levin, H. (1975). *The psychology of reading.* Cambridge, MA: MIT Press.

Gibson, E. J., Gibson, J. J., Pick, A. D., & Osser, H. (1962). A developmental study of the discrimination of letter-like forms. *Journal of Comparative and Physiological Psychology, 55,* 897–906.

Gillberg, C., Uvebrant, P., Carlsson, G., Hedström, A., & Silfvenius, H. (1996). Autism and epilepsy (and tuberous sclerosis?) in two pre-adolescent boys: neuropsychiatric aspects before and after epilepsy surgery. *Journal of Intellectual Disability Research, 40,* 75–81.

Glassman, R. B., & Smith, A. (1988). Neural spare capacity and the concept of diaschisis. In S. Finger, T. E. Levere, C. R. Almli, & D. G. Stein (eds.), *Brain injury and recovery*. New York: Plenum Press.

Gloor, P. (1979). Generalized epilepsy with spike-and-wave discharge: A reinterpretation of its electrographic and clinical manifestations. *Epilepsia, 20*, 571–588.

Gloor, P. (1988). Neurophysiological mechanism of generalized spike-and-wave discharge and its implication for understanding absence seizures. In M. S. Myslobodsky & A. F. Mirsky (eds.), *Elements of petit mal epilepsy*. New York: Peter Lang.

Glotzbach, S. F., Ariagno, R. L., & Harper, R. M. (1995). Sleep and the Sudden Infant Death Syndrome. In R. Ferber & M. Kryger (eds.), *Principles and practice of sleep medicine in the child*. Philadelphia: W. B. Saunders.

Goddard, G. V., McIntyre, D. C., & Leech, C. K. (1969). A permanent change in brain function resulting from daily electrical stimulation. *Experimental Neurology, 25*, 295–330.

Goldberg, E., & Costa, L. (1981). Hemisphere differences in the acquisition and use of descriptive systems. *Brain and Language, 14*, 144–173.

Goldstein, F., & Levin, H. S. (1990). Epidemiology of traumatic brain injury: Incidence, clinical characteristics, and risk factors. In E. D. Bigler (ed.), *Traumatic brain injury: Mechanisms of damage, assessment, intervention, and outcome*. Austin, TX: Pro-ed.

Goldstein, K. (1939). *The organism: A holistic approach to biology derived from pathological data in man*. New York: American Book Press.

Goleman, D. (1995). *Emotional intelligence*. New York: Bantam Books.

Goodman, R. (1986). Hemispherectomy and its alternatives in the treatment of intractable epilepsy in patients with infantile hemiplegia. *Developmental Medicine and Child Neurology, 28*, 251–258.

Gordon, J., & Ghez, C. (1991). Muscle receptors and spinal reflexes: The stretch reflex. In E. R. Kandel, J. H. Schwartz, & T. M. Jessell (eds.), *Principles of neural science*. Norwalk, CN: Appleton & Lange.

Gordon, M., & Mettelman, B. B. (1988). The assessment of attention: I. Standardization and reliability of a behavior based measure. *Journal of Clinical Psychology, 44*, 682–690.

Gordon, N. (1993). *Neurological problems in childhood*. Oxford: Butterworth-Heinemann.

Gotlib, I. H., & Goodman, S. H. (1999). Children of parents with depression. In W. K. Silverman & T. H. Ollendick (eds.), *Developmental issues in the clinical treatment of children and adolescents*. New York: Allyn & Bacon.

Gottfredson, L. S. (ed.) (1997). Intelligence and social policy. *Intelligence, 24*, 1–320.

Graham, F. K. (1973). Habituation and dishabituation of responses innervated by the autonomic nervous system. In H. V. S. Peeke & M. J. Herz (eds.), *Habituation*, vol. 1: *Behavioral studies*. New York: Academic Press.

Graham, P. J. (1989). Practical aspects of dietary management of the hyperkinetic syndrome. In T. Sagvolden & T. Archer (eds.), *Attention deficit disorder. Clinical and basic research*. Hillsdale NJ: Lawrence Erlbaum Associates.

Grandin, T. (1995). *Thinking in pictures and other reports from my life with autism*. New York: Doubleday.

Grant, I., & Alves, W. (1987). Psychiatric and psychosocial disturbances in head injury, In H. S. Levin, J. Grafman, & H. M. Eisenberg (eds.), *Neurobehavioral recovery from head injury*. New York: Oxford University Press.

Graves, R. E., & Jones, B. S. (1992). Conscious visual perceptual awareness vs. non-conscious visual spatial localisation examined with normal subjects using possible analogues of blindsight and neglect. *Cognitive Neuropsychology, 9*, 487–508.

Greene, L. C., Lucas, A., Livingstone, M. B. E., Erasmus, P. S., Harland, G., & Baker, B. A. (1995). Relationship between early diet and subsequent cognitive performance during adolescence. *Biochemical Society Transactions, 23*, 3765.

Greenough, W. T., & Chang, F. L. F. (1988). Plasticity of synaptic structure in the cerebral cortex. In A. Peters & E. G. Jones (eds.), *Cerebral cortex*. New York: Plenum.

Griffiths, P., Ward, N., Harvie, A., & Cockburn, F. (1998). Neuropsychological outcome of experimental manipulation of phenyalanine intake in treated phenyketonuria. *Journal of Inherited Metabolic Disease, 21*, 29–38.

Grisell, J. L., Levin, S., Cohen, B. D., & Rodin, E. A. (1964). Effects of subclinical seizure activity on overt behavior. *Neurology, 14*, 133–135.

Gronwall, D., Wrightson, P., & McGinn, V. (1997). Effect of mild head injury during the preschool years. *Journal of the International Neuropsychological Society, 3*, 592–597.

Grove, W., M., Andreasen, N. C., Young, M., Endicott, J., Keller, M. B., Hirschfield, R. M. A., & Reich, T. (1987). Isolation and characterization of a nuclear depressive syndrome. *Psychological Medicine, 17*, 471–484.

Gualtieri, C. T., Golden, R., & Fahs, J. (1983). New developments in pediatric psychopharmacology. *Developmental and Behavioral Pediatrics, 3*, 202–209.

Gualtieri, T., Evans, R. W., & Patterson, D. R. (1987). The medical treatment of autistic people. In E. Schopler & G. B. Mesibov (eds.), *Neurobiological issues in autism.* New York: Plenum.

Gubbay, S. S. (1975). *The clumsy child.* London: W. B. Saunders.

Hagerman, R. J. (1996). Physical and behavioral phenotype. In R. J. Hagerman & A. Cronister (eds.), *Fragile X syndrome: Diagnosis, treatment, and research*, 2d ed. Baltimore: Johns Hopkins Press.

Halamek, L. P. (1997). Fetal and neonatal injury as a consequence of maternal substance abuse. In D. K. Stevenson & P. Sunshine (eds.), *Fetal and neonatal brain injury.* Oxford: Oxford Universty Press.

Handel, S. (1989). *Listening: An introduction to the perception of auditory events.* Cambridge MA: MIT Press.

Hart, B., & Risley, T. R. (1995). *Meaningful differences in the everyday experience of young American children.* Baltimore: Paul H. Brookes.

Harvey, J. H., & Miller, E. D. (1998). Toward a psychology of loss. *Psychological Science, 9*, 429–434.

Hassold, T., Sherman, S., & Hunt, P. A. (1995). The origin of trisomy in humans. In C. J. Epstein, T. Hassold, I. T. Lott, L. Nadel, & D. Patterson (eds.), *Etiology and pathogenesis of Down syndrome.* New York: Wiley-Liss.

Hastings, J. E., & Barkley, R. A. (1978). A review of psychophysiological research with hyperkinetic children. *Journal of Abnormal Child Psychology, 6*, 413–447.

Hawk, B. A., Schroeder, S. R., Robinson, G., Otto, D., Mushak, P., Kleinbaum, D., & Dawson, G. (1986). Relation of lead and social factors to IQ of low SES children: A partial replication. *American Journal of Mental Deficiency, 91*, 178–183.

Heath, R. G., Franklin, D. E., Walker, C. F., & Keating, Jr., J. W. (1982). Cerebellar vermal atrophy in psychiatric patients. *Biological Psychiatry, 17*, 569–583.

Hebb, D. O. (1949). *The organization of behavior: A neuropsychological theory.* New York: John Wiley.

Heilman, K. M., & Gonzalez-Rothi, L. J. (1993). Apraxia. In K. M. Heilman & E. Valenstein (eds.), *Clinical neuropsychology*, 3rd ed. New York: Oxford University Press.

Heilman, K. M., Watson, R. T., & Valenstein, E. (1993). Neglect and related disorders. In K. M. Heilman & E. Valenstein (eds.), *Clinical neuropsychology*, 3rd ed. New York: Oxford University Press.

Helson, H. (1964). *Adaptation-level theory: An experimental and systematic approach to behavior.* New York: Harper & Row.

Henriques, J. B., & Davidson, R. J. (1991). Left frontal hypoactivation in depression. *Journal of Abnormal Psychology, 100*, 535–545.

Herrnstein, R. J., & Murray, C. (1994). *The bell curve: Intelligence and class structure in American life.* New York: Free Press.

Hewitt, P. I., & Flett, G. L. (1991). Dimensions of perfectionism in unipolar depression. *Journal of Abnormal Psychology, 100*, 98–101.

Hirsch, H. V. B., & Spinelli, D. N. (1971). Modification of the distribution of receptive field orientation in cats by selective visual exposure during development. *Experimental Brain Research, 13*, 509–527.

Hirsch, J. (1975). Jensenism: The bankrupcy of "science" without scholarship. *Educational Theory, 25*, 3–27, 102.

Hirsch, J. (1997). Some history of heredity-vs-environment, genetic inferiority at Harvard(?), and The (incredible) Bell Curve. *Genetica, 99,* 207–224.

Hirshkowitz, M., Moore, C. A., & Minhoto, G. (1997). The basics of sleep. In M. R. Pressman & W. C. Orr (eds.), *Understanding sleep: The evaluation and treatment of sleep disorders.* Washington, DC: American Psychological Association.

Hodapp, R. M., & Zigler, E. (1997). New issues in the developmental approach to mental retardation. In W. E. MacLean, Jr. (ed.), *Ellis' handbook of mental deficiency, psychological theory and research.* Mahwah, NJ: Lawrence Erlbaum Associates.

Hodges, K. K., & Siegel, L. J. (1985). Depression in children and adolescents. In E. E. Beckham & W. R. Leber (eds.), *Handbook of depression: Treatment, assessment, and research.* Homewood, IL: Dorsey Press.

Holbrook, R. H., Gibson, R. N., El-Sayed, Y. Y., & Seidman, D. S. (1997). Fetal responses to asphyxia. In D. K. Stevenson & P. Sunshine (eds.), *Fetal and neonatal brain injury.* Oxford: Oxford Universty Press.

Holm, J. L. (1978). Human ability systems. In P. B. Baltes (ed.), *Life-span development and behavior,* vol. 1. New York: Academic Press.

Holm, V. A., & Varley, C. K. (1989). Pharmacological treatment of autistic children. In G. Dawson (ed.), *Autism: Nature, diagnosis and treatment.* New York: Guilford Press.

Horne, J. (1988). *Why we sleep: The functions of sleep in humans and other mammals.* New York: Oxford University Press.

Hovda, D. A. (1998). The neurobiology of traumatic brain injury: Why is the brain so vulnerable after injury? *Brain Injury Source, 2*(2), 22–25.

Howard, I. P., & Templeton, W. B. (1966). *Human spatial orientation.* London: John Wiley & Sons.

Hubel, D. H. (1988). *Eye, brain, and vision.* New York: Scientific American Library.

Hughes, J. R., Kuhlman, D. T., Fichtner, C. G., & Gruenfeld, M. J. (1990). Brain mapping in a case of multiple personality. *Clinical Encephalography, 21,* 200–209.

Hunt, J. McV. (1961). *Intelligence and experience.* New York: Ronald Press.

ISCN (1995). *An international system for human cytogenetic nomenclature,* ed. F. Mitelman. Basel: S. Karger.

Ivry, R. B., & Keele, S. W. (1989). Timing functions of the cerebellum. *Journal of Cognitive Neuroscience, 1,* 136–152.

Jacobs, G. D. (1999). *Say goodnight to insomnia.* New York: Henry Holt.

Jacobson, E. (1938). *Progressive relaxation,* rev. ed. Chicago: University of Chicago Press.

Jacobson, E. (1957). *You must relax.* New York: McGraw-Hill.

Jacobvitz, D., & Sroufe, L. A. (1987). The early caregiver–child relationship and Attention Deficit Disorder with Hyperactivity in kindergarten: A prospective study. *Child Development, 58,* 1488–1495.

Jacobvitz, D., Sroufe, L. A., Stewart, M., & Leffert, N. (1990). Treatment of attentional and hyperactivity problems in children with sympathomimetic drugs: A comprehensive review. *Journal of the American Academy of Child and Adolescent Psychiatry, 29,* 677–688.

Jan, J. E., Freeman, R. D., & Scott, E. P. (1977). *Visual impairment in children and adolescents.* New York: Grune & Stratton.

Jasper, H. H. (1958). The ten twenty electrode system of the International Federation. *Electroencephalography and Clinical Neurophysiology, 10,* 371–375.

Jaynes, J. (1976). *The origin of consciousness in the breakdown of the bicameral mind.* Boston: Houghton Mifflin.

Jenkins, J. J., & Paterson, D. G. (1961). *Studies in individual differences: The search for intelligence.* New York: Appleton-Century-Crofts.

Jennett, B. (1990). Post-traumatic epilepsy. In M. Rosenthal, E. R. Griffith, M. R. Bond, & J. D. Miller (eds.), *Rehabilitation of the adult and child with traumatic brain injury,* 2nd ed. Philadelphia: F. A. Davis.

Jensen, A. R. (1977). Cumulative deficit in IQ of blacks in the rural south. *Developmental Psychology, 13,* 184–191.

Jensen, A. R. (1998). *The g factor: The science of mental ability.* Westport, CT: Praeger.

John, E. R., Karmel, B. Z., Corning, W. C., Easton, P., Brown, D., Ahn, H., John, M., Harmony, T., Prichep, L., Toro, A., Gerson, I., Bartlett, F., Thatcher, R., Kaye, H., Valdes, P., & Schwartz, E. (1977). Neurometrics. *Science, 196*, 1393–1410.

Johnson, D. R., & Blalock, J. W. (1987). *Adults with learning disabilities: Clinical studies.* Orlando, FL: Grune & Stratton.

Johnstone, J., & Thatcher, R. W. (1991). Quantitative EEG analysis and rehabilitation issues in mild traumatic brain injury. *Journal of Insurance Medicine, 23*, 228–232.

Jonas, A. D. (1965). *Ictal and subictal neurosis.* Springfield, IL: C. C. Thomas.

Jordan, R. (1993). The nature of the linguistic and communication difficulties of children with autism. In D. J. Messer & G. J. Turner (eds.), *Critical influences on child language acquisition and development.* New York: St Martin's Press.

Jusczyk, P. W. (1995). Language acquisition: Speech sounds and the beginning of phonology. In J. L. Miller & P. D. Eimas (eds.), *Speech, language and communication.* San Diego, CA: Academic Press.

Kagan, J. (1994). *Galen's prophecy: Temperament in human nature.* New York: Basic Books.

Kaler, S. R., & Freeman, B. J. (1994). Analysis of environmental deprivation: Cognitive and social development in Romanian orphans. *Journal of Child Psychology and Psychiatry, 35*, 769–781.

Kamin, L. J. (1974). *The science and politics of IQ.* Hillsdale, NJ: Lawrence Erlbaum Associates.

Kandel, E. R., Schwartz, J. H., & Jessell, T. M. (eds.) (1991) *Principles of neural science.* Norwalk, CN: Appleton & Lange.

Kanner, L. (1943). Autistic disturbances of affective contact. *Nervous Child, 2*, 217–250.

Karelson, E., Laasik, J., & Sillard, R. (1995). Regulation of adenylate cyclase by galanin, neuropeptide Y, secretin and vasoactive intestinal polypetide in rat frontal cortex, hippocampus and hypothalamus. *Neuropeptides, 28*, 21–28.

Karmiloff-Smith, A. (1997). Crucial differences between developmental cognitive neuroscience and adult neuropsychology. *Developmental Neuropsychology, 13*, 513–524.

Karmiloff-Smith, A., Tyler, L. K., Voice, K., Sims, K., Udwin, O., Howlin, P., & Davies, M. (1998). Linguistic dissociations in Williams syndrome: evaluating receptive syntax in online and off-line tasks. *Neuropsychologia, 36*, 343–351.

Kasper, S., Rogers, S. L. B., Yancey, A., Skwerer, R. G., Schulz, P. M., & Rosenthal, N. E. (1989). Psychological effects of light therapy in normals. In N. E. Rosenthal & M. C. Blehar (eds.), *Seasonal affective disorders and phototherapy.* New York: Guilford Press.

Kasten, S., Spaulding, I., & Scharf, B. (1980). *Raising the young blind child: A guide for parents and educators.* New York: Human Sciences Press.

Katz, W. F., Curtiss, S., & Tallal, P. (1992). Rapid automatized naming and gesture by normal and language impaired children. *Brain & Language, 43*, 623–641.

Kaufman, A. S., & Kaufman, N. L. (1983). *K-ABC administration and scoring manual.* Circle Pines, MN: Americal Guidance Service.

Kay, R. H. (1976). The hearing of complicated sounds. *Endeavour, 35*, 104–109.

Kelly, D. D. (1991). Disorders of sleep and consciousness. In E. R. Kandel, J. H. Schwartz, & T. M. Jessell (eds.), *Principles of neural science.* Norwalk, CT: Appleton & Lange.

Kenworthy, O. T. (1987). Identification of hearing loss in infancy and early childhood. In J. G. Alpiner & P. A. McCarthy (eds.), *Rehabilitative audiology: Children and adults.* Baltimore: Williams & Wilkins.

Kerr, N. H. (1983). The role of vision in "visual imagery" experiments: evidence from the congenitally blind. *Journal of Experimental Psychology: General, 112*, 265–277.

Kerr, N. H., Foulkes, D., & Schmidt, M. (1982). The structure of laboratory dream reports in blind and sighted subjects. *Journal of Nervous and Mental Disease, 170*, 286–294.

Kess, J. F. (1992). *Psycholinguistics: Psychology, linguistics and the study of natural language.* Amsterdam: John Benjamins.

Kessler, J. W. (1980). History of minimal brain dysfunction. In H. Rie & E. Rie (eds.), *Handbook of minimal brain dysfunctions: A critical view.* New York: Wiley.

Kiernan, C. (1985). Behaviour modification. In A. M. Clarke, A. D. B. Clarke, & J. M. Berg (eds.), *Mental deficiency: The changing outlook*, 4th ed. London: Methuen.

Kiloh, L. G., & Garside, R. F. (1963). The independence of neurotic depression and endogenous depression. *British Journal of Psychiatry*, *109*, 451–463.

King, D. S. (1981). Can allergic exposure provoke psychological symptoms? A double-blind test. *Biological Psychiatry*, *16*, 3–19.

King, R. A., Scahill, L., Findley, D., & Cohen, D. J. (1999). Psychosocial and behavioral treatments. In J. F. Leckman & D. J. Cohen (eds.), *Tourette's syndrome – tics, obsessions, compulsions: Developmental psychopathology and clinical care*. New York: John Wiley.

Klin, A., Volkmar, F. R., Sparrow, S. S., Cicchetti, D. V., & Rourke, B. P. (1995). Validity and neurological characterization of Asperger syndrome: convergence with nonverbal learning disabilities syndrome. *Journal of Child Psychology and Psychiatry*, *36*, 1127–1140.

Klonoff, H., Clark, C., & Klonoff, P. S. (1993). Long-term outcome of head injuries: a 23-year follow-up study of children with head injuries. *Journal of Neurology, Neurosurgery, and Psychiatry*, *56*, 410–415.

Klüver, H., & Bucy, P. C. (1939). Preliminary analysis of the temporal lobes in monkeys. *Archives of Neurology and Psychiatry*, *42*, 979–1000.

Knobloch, H., & Pasamanick, B. (1975). Some etiologic and prognostic factors in early infantile autism and psychosis. *Pediatrics*, *55*, 182–191.

Knowles, W. D., & Lüders, H. O. (1993). Normal neurophysiology: The science of excitable cells. In E. Wiley (ed.), *The treatment of epilepsy: Principles and practice*. Philadelphia: Lea & Febiger.

Kolb, B., & Whishaw, I. Q. (1996). *Fundamentals of human neuropsychology*, 4th ed. New York: W. H. Freeman.

Kolpan, K. I. (1990). Medicolegal aspects of head injury. In M. Rosenthal, E. R. Griffith, M. R. Bond, & J. D. Miller (eds.), *Rehabilitation of the adult and child with traumatic brain injury*, 2nd ed. Philadelphia: F. A. Davis.

Konstantareas, M. M., Oxman, J., & Webster, C. D. (1977). Simultaneous communication with autistic and other severely dysfunctional nonverbal children. *Journal of Communication Disorders*, *10*, 267–282.

Korner, A. F. (1997). The scope and limitations of neurologic and behavioral assessments in the newborn. In D. K. Stevenson & P. Sunshine (eds.), *Fetal and neonatal brain injury*. Oxford: Oxford University Press.

Korner, A. F., & Thoman, E. B. (1972). Relative efficacy of contact and vestibular–proprioceptive stimulation in soothing neonates. *Child Development*, *43*, 443–453.

Kovacs, M. (1989). Affective disorders in children and adolescents. *American Psychologist*, *44*, 209–215.

Kozol, J. (1992). *Savage inequalities: Children in America's schools*. New York: Harper Collins.

Krauseneck, P., & Müller, B. (1995). Chemotherapy of malignant brain tumours. In D. G. T. Thomas & D. I. Graham (eds.), *Malignant brain tumours*. London: Springer-Verlag.

Kripke, D. F., Mullaney, D. J., Savides, T. J., & Gillin, J. C. (1989). Phototherapy for nonseasonal major depressive disorders. In N. E. Rosenthal & M. C. Blehar (eds.), *Seasonal affective disorders and phototherapy*. New York: Guilford Press.

Kuban, K. C. K., & Leviton, A. (1994). Cerebral palsy. *New England Journal of Medicine*, *330*, 188–195.

Kübler-Ross, E. (1969). *On death and dying*. New York: Collier Books.

Kysar, J. E. (1968). The two camps in child psychiatry: A report from a psychiatrist–father of an autistic and retarded child. *American Journal of Psychiatry*, *125*, 103–109.

Labov, W. (ed.) (1972). *Language in the inner city: Studies in the Black English vernacular*. Philadelphia: University of Pennsylvania Press.

Lagae, L. G., Silberstein, J., Gillis, P. L., & Casaer, P. J. (1998). Successful use of intravenous immunoglobulins in Landau–Kleffner syndrome. *Pediatric Neurology*, *18*, 165–168.

Lahey, B. B., & Carlson, C. L. (1991). Validity of the diagnostic category of attention deficit disorder without hyperactivity: A review of the literature. *Journal of Learning Disabilities*, *24*, 110–120.

Lambert, N. M. (1988). Adolescent outcomes for hyperactive children. *American Psychologist, 43,* 786–799.

Landau, W. M., & Kleffner, F. R. (1957). Syndrome of acquired aphasia with convulsive disorder in children. *Neurology, 7,* 523–530.

Landesman, S., & Cooper, P. R. (1993). Infectious complications of head injury. In P. R. Cooper (ed.), *Head injury,* 3rd ed. Baltimore: Williams & Wilkins.

Landry, S. H., Smith, K. E., Miller-Loncar, C. L., & Swank, P. R. (1997). Predicting cognitive-language and social growth curves from early maternal behaviors in children at varying degrees of biological risk. *Developmental Psychology, 33,* 1040–1053.

Landry, S. H., Smith, K. E., Miller-Loncar, C. L., & Swank, P. R. (1998). The relation of change in maternal interactive styles to the developing social competence of full-term and preterm children. *Child Development, 69,* 105–123.

Lantz, D., & Sterman, M. B. (1988). Neuropsychological assessment of subjects with uncontrolled epilepsy: Effects of EEG feedback training. *Epilepsia, 29,* 163–171.

Larson, C. L., Davidson, R. J., Abercrombie, H. C., Ward, R. T., Schaefer, S. M., Jackson, D. C., Holden, J. E., & Perlman, S. B. (1998). Relations between PET-derived measures of thalamic glucose metabolism and EEG alpha power. *Psychophysiology, 35,* 162–169.

Lash, J. P. (1980). *Helen and teacher: the story of Helen Keller and Anne Sullivan Macy.* New York: Delacorte Press.

Laufer, M., & Denhoff, E. (1957). Hyperkinetic syndrome in children. *Journal of Pediatrics, 50,* 463–474.

Lauras, B., Gautheron, V., Minaire, P., & DeFreminville, B. (1995). Early interdisciplinary specialized care of children with Down syndrome. In L. Nadel & D. Rosenthal (eds.), *Down syndrome: Living and learning in the community.* New York: Wiley-Liss.

Leber, W. R., Beckham, E. E., & Danker-Brown, P. (1985). Diagnostic criteria for depression. In E. E. Beckham & W. R. Leber (eds.), *Handbook of depression: Treatment, assessment, and research.* Homewood, IL: Dorsey Press.

Leckman, J. F., & Cohen, D. J. (1999). Evolving models of pathogenesis. In J. F. Leckman & D. J. Cohen (eds.), *Tourette's syndrome – tics, obsessions, compulsions: Developmental psychopathology and clinical care.* New York: John Wiley & Sons.

Leckman, J. F., Walkup, J. T., & Cohen, D. J. (1988). Clonidine treatment of Tourette's syndrome. In D. J. Cohen, R. D. Bruun, & J. F. Leckman (eds.), *Tourette's syndrome and tic disorders: clinical understanding and treatment.* New York: John Wiley & Sons.

Lecours, R. R., & Joannette, Y. (1980). Linguistic and other psychological aspects of paroxysmal aphasia. *Brain and Language, 10,* 1–23.

Lehmkuhle, S. (1993). Neurological basis of visual processes in reading. In D. M. Willows, R. S. Kruk, & E. Corcos (eds.), *Visual processes in reading and reading disabilities* (pp. 77–94). Hillsdale, NJ: Lawrence Erlbaum Associates.

Lemire, R. L. (1997). Congenital malformations of the brain. In D. K. Stevenson & P. Sunshine (eds.), *Fetal and neonatal brain injury.* Oxford: Oxford University Press.

Lenhoff, H. M., Wang, P. P., Greenberg, F., & Bellugi, U. (1997). Williams syndrome and the brain. *Scientific American, 277*(6), 68–73.

Lenke, R. R., & Levy, H. L. (1980). Maternal phenylketonuria and hyperphenylalaninemia – An international study of outcome of treated and untreated pregnancies. *New England Journal of Medicine, 303,* 1202–1208.

Levin, H. S. (1993). Neurobehavioral sequelae of closed head injury. In P. R. Cooper (ed.), *Head injury,* 3rd ed. Baltimore: Williams & Wilkins.

Levin, H. S., Eisenberg, H. M., & Benton, A. L. (eds.) (1991). *Frontal lobe function and dysfunction.* New York: Oxford University Press.

Levin, H. S., Gary, H. E. Jr, High, W. M. Jr, Mattis, S., Ruff, R. M., Eisenberg, H. M., Marshall, L. F., & Tabaddor, K. (1987). Minor head injury and the postconcussion syndrome: Methodological issues in outcome studies. In H. S. Levin, J. Grafman, & H. M. Eisenberg (eds.), *Neurobehavioral recovery from head injury.* New York: Oxford University Press.

Levy, H. L., & Ghavami, M. (1996). Maternal phenylketonuria: A metabolic teratogen. *Teratology, 53,* 176–184.

Levy, H. L., Waisbren, S. E., Lobbregt, D., Allred, E., Leviton, A., Koch, R., Hanley, W. B., Rouse, B., Matalon, R., & delaCruz, F. (1996). Maternal non-phenylketonuric mild hyperphenylalaninemia. *European Journal of Pediatrics*, *155*, Suppl. S20–S25.

Lewis, M. H. (1996). Brief report: Psychopharmacology of autism spectrum disorders. *Journal of Autism and Developmental Disorders*, *26*, 231–235.

Lezak, M. D. (1988). IQ: R. I. P. *Journal of Clinical and Experimental Neuropsychology*, *10*, 351–361.

Liberman, A. M. (1982). On finding that speech is special. *American Psychologist*, *37*, 148–167.

Liberman, A. M. (1995). *Speech: A special code.* Cambridge, MA: Bradford/MIT Press.

Liberman, I. Y. (1983). A language-oriented view of reading and its disabilities. In H. R. Myklebust (ed.), *Progress in learning disabilities.* New York: Grune & Stratton.

Liberman, I. Y., & Shankweiler, D. (1985). Phonology and the problems of learning to read and write. *Remedial and Special Education*, *6*, 8–17.

Lilienfeld, S. O., & Waldman, I. D. (1990). The relation between childhood attention-deficit hyperactivity disorder and adult antisocial behavior reexamined: The problem of heterogeneity. *Clinical Psychology Review*, *10*, 699–725.

Ling, D. (1989). *Foundations of spoken language for hearing-impaired children.* Washington, DC: A. G. Bell Association for the Deaf.

Liotti, M., & Tucker, D. M. (1995). Emotion in asymmetric corticolimbic networks. In R. J. Davidson & K. Hugdahl (eds.), *Brain asymmetry.* Cambridge, MA: MIT Press.

Lishman, W. A. (1998). *Organic psychiatry: The psychological consequences of cerebral disorder*, 3rd ed. Oxford: Blackwell Science.

Livingstone, M., Rosen, G., Drislane, F., & Galaburda, A. (1991). Physiological and anatomical evidence for a magnocellular defect in developmental dyslexia. *Proceedings of the National Academy of Sciences*, *88*, 7943–7947.

Lou, H. C., Henriksen, L., Bruhn, P., Børner, H., & Nielsen, J. B. (1989). Striatal dysfunction in attention deficit and hyperkinetic disorder. *Archives of Neurology*, *46*, 48–52.

Lovaas, O. I. (1966). A program for the establishment of speech in psychotic children. In J. K. Wing (ed.), *Early childhood autism.* Oxford: Pergamon Press.

Lovaas, O. I. (1987). Behavioral treatment and normal educational and intellectual functioning in young autistic children. *Journal of Consulting and Clinical Psychology*, *55*, 3–9.

Lovaas, O. I., Ackerman, A. B., Alexander, D., Firestone, P., Perkins, M., & Young, D. B. (1981). *Teaching developmentally disabled children. The me book.* Baltimore: University Park Press.

Lovaas, I., Calouri, K., & Jada, J. (1989). The nature of behavioral treatment and research with young autistic persons. In C. Gillberg (ed.), *Diagnosis and treatment of autism*, New York: Plenum Press.

Lovaas, O. I., & Leaf, R. L. (1981). *Five video tapes for teaching developmentally disabled children.* Baltimore: University Park Press.

Love, E. B., Nowicki, S. Jr, & Duke, M. P. (1995). The Emory Dyssemia Index: A brief screening instrument for the identification of nonverbal language deficits in elementary school children. *Journal of Psychology*, *128*, 703–705.

Lovegrove, W. J., Martin, F., & Slaghuis, W. (1986). A theoretical and experimental case for a visual deficit in specific reading disability. *Cognitive Neuropsychology*, *3*, 225–267.

Lovegrove, W. J., & Williams, M. C. (1993). Visual temporal processing deficits in specific reading disability. In D. M. Willows, R. S. Kruk, & E. Corcos (eds.), *Visual processes in reading and reading disabilities.* Hillsdale, NJ: Erlbaum.

Lovett, M. W. (1992). Developmental dyslexia. In S. J. Segalowitz & I. Rapin (eds.), *Handbook of neuropsychology*, Vol. 7: *Child neuropsychology.* Amsterdam: Elsevier.

Lowe, T. L., Cohen, D. J., Detlor, J., Kremenitzer, M. W., & Shaywitz, B. A. (1982). Stimulant medications precipitate Tourette's syndrome. *Journal of the American Medical Association*, *247*, 1168–1169.

Lozoff, B., Klein, N. K., Nelson, E. C., McClish, D. K., Manuel, M., & Chacon, M. E. (1998). Behavior of infants with iron-deficiency anemia. *Child Development*, *69*, 24–36.

Lubar, J. F., & Lubar, J. O. (1999). Neurofeedback assessment and treatment for attention deficit/hyperactivity disorders. In J. Evans & A. Abarbanel (eds.), *Introduction to quantitative EEG and neurofeedback*. San Diego, CA: Academic Press.

Lubar, J. F., Swartwood, M. O., Swartwood, J. N., & O'Donnell, P. H. (1995). Evaluation of the effectiveness of EEG neurofeedback training for ADHD in a clinical setting as measured by changes in T.O.V.A. scores, behavioral ratings and WISC-R performance. *Biofeedback and Self-Regulation, 20,* 83–99.

Lubchenko, L. O. (1976). *The high risk infant.* Philadelphia: W. B. Saunders.

Lubs, H. A. (1969). A marker X chromosone. *American Journal of Human Genetics, 21,* 231–244.

Lucas, A., Morley, R., Cole, T. J., Lister, G., & Leeson-Payne, C. (1992). Breast milk and subsequent intelligence quotient in children born preterm. *Lancet, 339,* 261–264.

Lucas, A., Morley, R., & Fewtrell, M. S. (1996). Low triiodothyronine concentration in preterm infants and subsequent intelligence quotient (IQ) at 8-year follow-up. *British Medical Journal, 312,* 1132–1133.

Lundberg, I., Frost, J., & Petersen, O. (1988). Effects of an extensive program for stimulating phonological awareness in preschool children. *Reading Research Quarterly, 23,* 263–284.

Luria, A. R. (1973). *The working brain.* Baltimore: Penguin Books.

Lyon, G. R., & Chhabra, V. (1996). The current state of science and the future of specific reading disability. *Mental Retardation and Developmental Disabilities Research Reviews, 2,* 2–9.

Maclean, M., Bryant, P., & Bradley, L. (1987). Rhymes, nursery rhymes, and reading in early childhood. *Merrill-Palmer Quarterly, 33,* 255–281.

Madanes, C. (1980). Protection, paradox, and pretending. *Family Process, 19,* 73–85.

Maldonado, Y. A. (1997). Perinatal HIV infection. In W. R. Cheek (ed.), *Pediatric neurosurgery,* 3rd ed. Philadelphia: W. B. Saunders.

Mann, C. A., Lubar, J., Zimmerman, A., Miller, C., & Muenchen, R. (1991). Quantitative analysis of EEG in boys with attention-deficit–hyperactivity disorder: Controlled study with clinical implications. *Pediatric Neurology, 8,* 30–36.

Mann, V. A., Tobin, P., & Wilson, R. (1987). Measuring phonological awareness through the invented spellings of kindergarten children. *Merrill-Palmer Quarterly, 33,* 365–391.

March, J. S., & Mulle, K. (1998). *OCD in children and adolescents: A cognitive–behavioral treatment manual.* New York: Guilford Press.

Marescaux, C., Hirsch, E., Finck, S., Maquet, P., Schlumberger, E., Sellal, F., Metz-Lutz, M., Alembik, Y., Salmon, E., & Franck, G. (1990). Landau–Kleffner syndrome: a pharmacologic study of five cases. *Epilepsia, 31,* 768–777.

Marks, I. (1997). Behaviour therapy for obsessive–compulsive disorder: A decade of progress. *Canadian Journal of Psychiatry, 42,* 1021–1027.

Marlin, A. E., & Gaskill, S. J. (1994). Cerebrospinal fluid shunts: Complications and results. In W. R. Cheek (ed.), *Pediatric neurosurgery,* 3rd ed. Philadelphia: W. B. Saunders.

Marshall, P. (1989). Attention deficit disorder and allergy: A neurochemical model of the relation between the illnesses. *Psychological Bulletin, 106,* 434–446.

Martin, F. N. (1981). *Introduction to audiology,* 2nd ed. Englewood Cliffs, NJ: Prentice Hall.

Mattson, S. N., Riley, E. P., Sowell, E. R., Jernigan, T. L., Sobel, D. F., & Jones, K. L. (1996). A decrease in the size of the basal ganglia in children with fetal alcohol syndrome. *Alcoholism: Clinical and Experimental Research, 20,* 1088–1093.

McCartney, K., Harris, M. J., & Bernieri, F. (1990). Growing up and growing apart: A developmental meta-analysis of twin studies. *Psychological Bulletin, 107,* 226–237.

McCullough, A. L., Kirksey, A., Wachs, T. D., McCabe, G. P., Bassily, N. S., Bishry, Z., Galal, O. M., Harrison, G. G., & Jerome, N. W. (1990). Vitamin B-6 status of Egyptian mothers: relation to infant behavior and maternal infant relations. *American Journal of Clinical Nutrition, 51,* 1067–1074.

McEachin, J. J., Smith, T., & Lovaas, O. I. (1993). Long-term outcome for children with autism who received early intensive behavioral treatment. *American Journal of Mental Retardation, 97,* 359–372.

McGee, G. G., Krantz, P. J., & McClannahan, L. E. (1985). The facilitative effects of incidental teaching on preposition use by autistic children. *Journal of Applied Behavior Analysis, 18,* 17–31.

McGee, G. G., Almeida, C., Sulzer-Azaroff, B., & Feldman, R. S. (1992). Promoting reciprocal interaction via peer incidental teaching. *Journal of Applied Behavior Analysis, 25,* 117–126.

McGraw, M. B. (1969). *The neuromuscular maturation of the human infant.* New York: Hafner.

McGuinness, D. (1985). *When children don't learn.* New York: Basic Books.

McGuinness, D., & Pribram, K. (1980). The neuropsychology of attention: Emotional and motivational controls. In M. C. Wittrock (ed.), *The brain and psychology.* New York: Academic Press.

McGuire, P. K., Bench, C. J., Frith, C. D., Marks, I. M., Frackowiak, R. S. J., & Dolan, R. J. (1994). Functional anatomy of obsessive–compulsive phenomena. *British Journal of Psychiatry, 164,* 459–468.

Meadow, K. P. (1966). Early manual communication in relation to the deaf child's intellectual, social, and communicative functioning. *American Annals of the Deaf, 111,* 557–565.

Meadow, K. P. (1980). *Deafness and child development.* Berkeley, CA: University of California Press.

Mega, M. S., & Cummings, J. L. (1994). Frontal–subcortical circuits and neuropsychiatric disorders. *Journal of Neuropsychiatry and Clinical Neurosciences, 6,* 358–370.

Mendels, J., & Cochrane, C. (1968). The nosology of depression: The endogenous–reactive concept. *American Journal of Psychiatry, 124,* May Suppl., 1–11.

Mendlewicz, C. (1985). Genetic research in depressive disorders. In E. E. Beckham & W. R. Leber (eds.), *Handbook of depression: Treatment assessment and research.* Homewood, IL: Dorsey Press.

Mervis, C. B. (1999). The Willimas syndrome cognitive profile: Strengths, weaknesses, and interrelations among auditory short-term memory, language, and visuospatial constructive cognition. In E. Winograd, R. Fivush, & W. Hirst (eds.), *Ecological approaches to cognition: Essays in honor of Ulric Neisser.* Mahwah, NJ: Lawrence Erlbaum Associates.

Mervis, C. B., Morris, C. A., Bertrand, J., & Robinson, B. (1999). Williams syndrome: Findings from an integrated program of research. In H. Tager-Flusberg (ed.), *Neurodevelopmental disorders.* Cambridge, MA: MIT Press.

Merzenich, M. M., Jenkins, W. M., Johnston, P., Schreiner, C., Miller, S. L., & Tallal, P. (1996). Temporal procsssing deficits of language-learning impaired children ameliorated by training. *Science, 271,* 77–81.

Metsala, J. L. (1997). Spoken word recognition in reading disabled children. *Journal of Educational Psychology, 89,* 159–169.

Michals, K., Acosta, P. B., Austin, V., Castiglioni, L., Rohr, F., Wenz, E., & Azen, C. (1996). Nutrition and reproductive outcome in maternal phenylketonuria. *European Journal of Pediatrics, 155,* Suppl. S165–S168.

Michaud, L. J. (1995). Evaluating efficacy of rehabilitation after pediatric tramatic brain injury. In S. H. Broman & M. E. Michel (eds.), *Traumatic head injury in children.* New York: Oxford University Press.

Miller, J. L., & Eimas, P. D. (eds.) (1995). *Speech, language, and communication.* San Diego, CA: Academic Press.

Miller, L. (1994). Psychotherapy of epilepsy: Seizure control and psychosocial adjustment. *Journal of Cognitive Rehabilitation, 12,* 14–30.

Minshew, N. J. (1992). Neurological localization in autism. In E. Schopler & G. B. Mesibov (eds.), *High-functioning individuals with autism.* New York: Plenum Press.

Minshew, N. J. (1996). Brief report: Brain mechanisms in autism: Functional and structural abnormalities. *Journal of Autism and Developmental Disorders, 26,* 205–209.

Mirsky, A. F. (1989). The neuropsychology of attention: Elements of a complex behavior. In E. Perecman (ed.), *Integrating theory and practice in clinical neuropsychology.* Hillsdale, NJ: Lawrence Erlbaum Associates.

Mirsky, A. F., Anthony, B. J., Duncan, C. C., Ahearn, M. B., & Kellam, S. G. (1991). Analysis of the elements of attention: a neuropsychological approach. *Neuropsychology Review, 2,* 109–145.

Mirsky, A. F., & Van Buren, J. M. (1965). On the nature of the "absence" in centrencephalic epilepsy: A study of some behavioral electroencephalographic and autonomic factors. *Electroencephalography and Clinical Neurophysiology, 18,* 334–348.

Mishkin, M., Ungerleider, L. G., & Macko, K. A. (1983). Object vision and spatial vision: Two cortical pathways. *Trends in Neurosciences, 6,* 414–417.

Moeller, M. P., Osberger, M. J., & Morford, J. A. (1987). Speech–language assessment and intervention with preschool hearing impaired children. In J. G. Alpiner & P. A. McCarthy (eds.), *Rehabilitative audiology: Children and adults.* Baltimore: Williams and Wilkins.

Mokros, H. B., Poznanski, E. O., & Merrick, W. A. (1989). Depression and learning disabilities: A test of an hypothesis. *Journal of Learning Disabilities, 22,* 230–233.

Molfese, D. L., Buhrke, R. A., & Wang, S. L. (1985). The right hemisphere and temporal processing of consonant transition durations: Electrophysiological correlates. *Brain and Language, 26,* 49–62.

Molfese, D. L., & Molfese, V. J. (1986). Psychophysical indices of early cognitive processes and their relationship to language. *Child Neuropsychology, 1,* 95–115.

Monroe, R. R. (1970). *Episodic behavioral disorders.* Cambridge, MA: Harvard University Press.

Moore, B. D., Ater, J. L., & Copeland, D. R. (1992). Improved neuropsychological outcome in children with brain tumors diagnosed during infancy and treated without cranial irradiation. *Journal of Child Neurology, 7,* 281–290.

Moore-Ede, M. C., Sulzman, F. M., & Fuller, C. A. (1982). *The clocks that time us.* Cambridge, MA: Harvard University Press.

Morris, R. D., Krawiecki, N. S., Kullgren, K. A., Ingram, S. M., & Kurczynski, B. (2000). Childhood brain tumors. In K. O. Yeates, M. D. Ris, & H. G. Taylor (eds.), *Pediatric neuropsychology: research, theory, and practice.* New York: Guilford Press.

Morrison, D. C. (1985). *Neurobehavioral and perceptual dysfunction in learning disabled children.* Lewiston, NY: C. J. Hogrefe.

Morrison, S. R., & Siegel, L. S. (1991). Arithmetic disability: Theoretical considerations and empirical evidence for this subtype. In L. V. Feagans,

E. J. Short, & L. J. Meltzer (eds.), *Subtypes of learning disabilities.* Hillsdale, NJ: Lawrence Erlbaum Associates.

Mullett, M. D. (1989). Respiratory distress syndrome. In M. Rathi (ed), *Current perinatology.* New York: Springer-Verlag.

Murphy, L. A., Pollatsek, A., & Well, A. D. (1988). Developmental dyslexia and word retrieval deficits. *Brain & Language, 35,* 1–23.

Myslobodsky, M. S. (1988). Petit mal status as a paradigm of the functional anatomy of awareness. In M. S. Myslobodsky & A. F. Mirsky (eds.), *Elements of petit mal epilepsy.* New York: Peter Lang.

Nadeau, K. G. (1995). *A comprehensive guide to attention deficit disorder in adults: Research, diagnosis, and treatment.* New York: Brunner/Mazel.

Nadel, L. (1995). Neural and cognitive development in Down syndrome. In L. Nadel & D. Rosenthal (eds.), *Down syndrome: Living and learning in the community.* New York: Wiley–Liss.

Nadel, L. (1996). Learning, memory and neural function in Down's syndrome. In J. A. Rondal, J. Perera, L. Nadel, & A. Comblain (eds.), *Down's syndrome. Psychological, psychobiological, and socio-educational perspectives.* San Diego, CA: Singular.

Naugle, R. I. (1990). Epidemiology of traumatic brain injury in adults. In E. D. Bigler (ed.), *Traumatic brain injury: Mechanisms of damage, assessment, intervention, and outcome.* Austin, TX; Pro-ed.

Neisser, A. (1983). *The other side of silence: Sign language and the deaf community in America.* New York: Alfred A. Knopf.

Nelson, J. C., & Charney, D. S. (1981). The symptoms of major depressive illness. *American Journal of Psychiatry, 138,* 1–13.

Nemiroff, C. B. (1995). The neurobiology of depression. *Scientific American, 278*(6), 42–49.

Nemiroff, C. B. (1996). The corticotropin-releasing factor (CRF) hypothesis of depression: New findings and new directions. *Molecular Biology, 1,* 336–342.

Neville, B. G. R., Harkness, W., Cross, J. H., Cass, H. C., Marmion Burch, V. C., & Taylor, D. C. (1995). Surgical treatment of epilepsy in the context of autistic-like regression in young children. *Developmental Medicine and Child Neurology, 37,* Suppl. 72.

Novelly, R. A. (1992). The debt of neuropsychology to the epilepsies. *American Psychologist, 47,* 1126–1129.

Nowicki, S. Jr, & Duke, M. P. (1992). *Helping the child who doesn't fit in.* Atlanta, GA: Peachtree.

Nowicki, S. Jr, & Duke, M. P. (1994). Individual differences in the non-verbal communication of affect: The Diagnostic Analysis of Nonverbal Accuracy Scale. *Journal of Nonverbal Behavior, 18,* 9–35.

Nozza, R. J. (1988). Auditory deficit in infants with otitis media with effusion: More than a "mild" hearing loss. In D. J. Lim (ed.), *Recent advances in otitis media.* Toronto: B. C. Decker.

Nygaard, L. C., & Pisoni, D. B. (1995). Speech perception: New directions in research and theory. In J. L. Miller & P. D. Eimas (eds.), *Speech, language and communication.* San Diego, CA: Academic Press.

O'Connor, N., & Hermelin, B. M. (1973). The spatial or temporal organization of short term memory. *Quarterly Journal of Experimental Psychology, 25,* 335–343.

Odom, S. L., & Kaiser, A. P. (1997). Prevention and early intervention during early childhood: Theoretical and empirical bases for practice. In W. E. MacLean, Jr (ed.), *Ellis' handbook of mental deficiency, psychological theory and research.* Mahwah, NJ: Lawrence Erlbaum Associates.

Oettinger, L., Nekonishi, H., & Gill, I. G. (1967). Cerebral dysrhythmia induced by reading (subclinical reading epilepsy). *Developmental Medicine and Child Neurology, 9,* 191–201.

Ojemann, G. (1979). Individual variation in cortical localization of language. *Journal of Neurosurgery, 50,* 164–169.

Ojemann, G. A. (1983). Brain organization for language from the perspective of electrical stimulation mapping. *Behavioral and Brain Sciences, 6,* 189–230.

Ommaya, A. K. (1996). Head injury mechanisms and the concept of preventive management: A review and critical synthesis. In F. A. Bandak, R. H. Eppinger, & A. K. Ommaya (eds.), *Trau-matic brain injury: Bioscience and mechanics.* Larchmont, NY: Mary Ann Liebert.

Ornstein, R. E. (ed.) (1974). *The nature of consciousness.* New York: Viking Press.

Oxorn, H. (1986). *Human labor & birth,* 5th ed. Norwalk, CT: Appleton-Century-Croft.

Pang, D. (1985). Pathophysiologic correlates of neurobehavioral syndromes following closed head injury. In M. Ylvisaker (ed.), *Head injury rehabilitation: Children and adolescents.* San Diego, CA: College-Hill Press.

Pauling, L. (1968). Orthomolecular psychiatry. *Science, 160,* 265–271.

Pavone, L., Fiumara, A., Bottaro, G., Mazzone, D., & Coleman, M. (1997). Autism and celiac disease: Failure to validate the hypothesis that a link might exist. *Biological Psychiatry, 42,* 72–75.

Payton, O. D., Hirt, S., & Newton, R. A. (1977). *Scientific bases for neurophysiologic approaches to therapeutic exercise.* Philadelphia: F. A. Davis.

Penfield, W., & Jasper, H. (1954). *Epilepsy and the functional anatomy of the human brain.* Boston: Little, Brown.

Penry, J. K. (ed.) (1986). *Epilepsy: diagnosis, management, quality of life.* New York: Raven Press.

Perfetti, C. A., Beck, I., Bell, L. C., & Hughes, C. (1987). Phoneme knowledge and learning to read are reciprocal: A longitudinal study of first grade children. *Merrill-Palmer Quarterly, 33,* 283–319.

Perry, A. (1991). Rett syndrome: A comprehensive review of the literature. *American Journal of Mental Retardation, 96,* 275–290.

Peterson, A. L., & Azrin, N. H. (1992). An evaluation of behavioral treatments for Tourette syndrome. *Behavior Research and Therapy, 30,* 167–174.

Peterson, C., & Seligman, M. E. P. (1985). The Learned Helplessness Model of Depression: Current status of theory and research. In E. E. Beckham & W. R. Leber (eds.), *Handbook of depression: Treatment assessment and research.* Homewood, IL: Dorsey Press.

Peterson, C. C., & Siegal, M. (1999). Representing inner worlds: Theory of mind in autistic, deaf, and normal hearing children. *Psychological Science, 10,* 126–129.

Pfeiffer, S. I., Norton, J., Nelson, L., & Shott, J. (1995). Efficacy of vitamin B6 and magnesium in the treatment of autism: A methodology review and summary of outcomes. *Journal of Autism and Developmental Disorders, 25,* 481–493.

Pharoah, P. O. D., & Cooke, R. W. I. (1997). A hypothesis for the aetiology of spastic cerebral palsy – the vanishing twin. *Developmental Medicine and Child Neurology, 39,* 292–296.

Piaget, J. (1960). *Psychology of intelligence.* Patterson, NJ: Littlefield Adams.

Picard, A., Cheliout Heraut, F., Bouskraoui, M., Lemoine, M., Lacert, P., & Delattre, J. (1998). Sleep EEG and developmental dysphasia. *Developmental Medicine and Child Neurology, 40,* 595–599.

Pickles, J. O. (1988). *An introduction to the physiology of hearing,* 2nd ed. London: Academic Press.

Pigott, T. A., & Seay, S. (1998). Biological treatments for obsessive–compulsive disorders. In R. P. Swinson, M. M. Antony, S. Rachman, & M. A. Richter (eds.), *Obsessive–compulsive disorder: Theory, research, and treatment.* New York: Guilford Press.

Pinker, S. (1994). *The language instinct. How the mind creates language.* New York: William Morrow.

Plomin, R., Pederson, N. L., Lichtenstein, P., & McClearn, G. E. (1994). Variability and stability in cognitive abilities are largely genetic later in life. *Behavior Genetics, 24,* 207–215.

Pollack, D. (1985). *Educational audiology for the limited-hearing infant and preschooler,* 2nd ed. Springfield, IL: C. C. Thomas.

Pollatsek, A. (1993). Eye movements in reading. In D. M. Willows, R. S. Kruk, & E. Corcos (eds.), *Visual processes in reading and reading disabilities.* Hillsdale, NJ: Lawrence Erlbaum Associates.

Pollitt, E., Gorman, K. S., Engle, P. L., Martorell, R., & Rivera, J. (1993). Early supplementary feeding and cognition. *Monographs of the Society for Research in Child Development, 58*(7), Serial No. 235.

Pollitt, E., Golub, M., Gorman, K., Grantham-McGregor, S., Levitsky, D., Schürch, B., Strupp, B., & Wachs, T. (1996). A reconceptualiztion of the effects of undernutrition on children's biological, psychosocial, and behavioral development. *Social Policy Report: Society for Research in Child Development, 10,* No 5.

Posner, M. I. (1978). *Chronometric explorations of mind.* New York: Oxford University Press.

Posner, M. I., & Raichle, M. E. (1994). *Images of mind.* New York: Scientific American Library.

Povlishock, J. T., & Christman, C. W. (1996). The pathobiology of traumatically induced axonal injury in animals and humans: A review of current thoughts. In F. A. Bandak, R. H. Eppinger, & A. K. Ommaya (eds.), *Traumatic brain injury: Bioscience and mechanics.* Larchmont, NY: Mary Ann Liebert.

Preston, P. (1994). *Mother father deaf: Living between sound and silence.* Cambridge, MA: Harvard University Press.

Pribram, K. H., & McGuinness, D. (1975). Arousal, activation and the control of attention. *Psychological Review, 82,* 116–149.

Prober, C. G., & Arvin, A. M. (1997). Neurological sequelae of congenital infections. In W. R. Cheek (ed.), *Pediatric neurosurgery,* 3rd ed. Philadelphia: W. B. Saunders.

Pueschel, S. M., & Sustrova, M. (1996). In J. A. Rondal, J. Perera, L. Nadel, & A. Comblain (eds.), *Down's syndrome. Psychological, psychobiological, and socio-educational perspectives.* San Diego, CA: Singular.

Puig-Antich, J. (1983). Neuroendocrine and sleep correlates of prepubertal major depressive disorder: Current status of the evidence. In D. P. Cantwell & G. A. Carlson (eds.), *Affective disorders in childhood and adolescence – An update* (pp. 211–227). New York: SP Medical & Scientific Books.

Puig-Antich, J. (1986). Psychobiological markers: Effect of age and puberty. In M. Rutter, C. E. Izard, & P. B. Read (eds.), *Depression in young people: developmental and clinical perspectives.* New York: Guilford Press.

Pulsifer, M. B. (1996). The neuropsychology of mental retardation. *Journal of the International Neuropsychological Society, 2,* 159–176.

Punt, J. (1995). Management of brain tumors in childhood. In D. G. T. Thomas & D. I. Graham (eds.), *Malignant brain tumors*. London: Springer Verlag.

Ramey, C. T. (1994). Abecedarian Project. In R. J. Sternberg (ed.), *Encyclopedia of human intelligence*, vol. 1. New York: Macmillan.

Rapin, I., Mattis, S., Rowan, A. J., & Golden, G. G. (1977). Verbal auditory agnosia in children. *Developmental Medicine and Child Neurology, 19*, 192–207.

Rapoport, J. L., Buchsbaum, M. S., Zahn, T. P., Weingartner, H., Ludlow, C., & Mikkelsen, E. J. (1978). Dextroamphetamine: Cognitive and behavioral effects in normal prepubertal boys. *Science, 199*, 560–563.

Rasmussen, S., & Eisen, J. L. (1991). Phenomenology of OCD: Clinical subtypes, heterogeneity and coexistence. In J. Zohar, T. Insel, & S. Rasmussen (eds.), *The psychobiology of obsessive–compulsive disorder*. New York: Springer.

Rasore-Quartino, A., & Cominetti, M. (1995). Clinical follow-up of adolescents and adults with Down syndrome. In L. Nadel & D. Rosenthal (eds.), *Down syndrome: Living and learning in the community*. New York: Wiley-Liss.

Rattazzi, M. C., & Ioannou, Y. A. (1996). Molecular approaches to therapy. In R. J. Hagerman & A. Cronister (eds.), *Fragile X syndrome: Diagnosis, treatment, and research*, 2nd ed. Baltimore: Johns Hopkins University Press.

Raz, N. Torres, I. J., Spencer, W. D., White, K., & Acker, J. D. (1992). Age-related regional differences in cerebellar vermis observed in vivo. *Archives of Neurology, 49*, 412–416.

Rechstchaffen, A., Gilliland, M. A., Bergmann, B. M., & Winter, J. B. (1983). Physiological correlates of prolonged sleep deprivation in rats. *Science, 221*, 182–184.

Rechtschaffen, A., & Kales, A. (eds.) (1968). *A manual of standardized terminology, techniques and scoring system for sleep stages of human subjects*. Washington, DC: Public Health Service, U.S. Government Printing Office.

Regan, D. (1982). Visual information channeling in normal and disordered vision. *Psychological Bulletin, 89*, 407–444.

Reichelt, W. H., Knivsberg, A., Nødland, M., Stensrud, M., & Reichelt, K. L. (1997). Urinary peptide levels and patterns in autistic children from seven countries, and the effect of dietary intervention after 4 years. *Developmental Brain Dysfunction, 10*, 44–55.

Reilly, E. L. (1987). Nasopharyngeal, sphenoidal and other electrodes. In E. Niedermyer & F. Lopes da Silva (eds.), *Electroencephalography: Basic principles, clinical application and related fields*. Baltimore–Munich: Urban & Schwarzenberg.

Rekate, H. L. (1994). Treatment of hydrocephalus. In W. R. Cheek (ed.), *Pediatric neurosurgery*, 3rd ed. Philadelphia: W. B. Saunders.

Riddoch, G. (1917). Dissociation of visual perceptions due to occipital injuries, with specific reference to appreciation of movement. *Brain, 40*, 15–47.

Riggio, S., & Harner, R. N. (1995). Repetitive motor activity in frontal lobe epilepsy. In H. H. Jasper, S. Riggio, & P. S. Goldman-Rakic (eds.), *Epilepsy and the functional anatomy of the frontal lobe*. New York: Raven Press.

Rimland, B. (1964). *Infantile autism*. New York: Appleton-Century-Crofts.

Rimland, B. (1987). Megavitamin B6 and magnesium in the treatment of autistic children and adults. In E. Schopler & G. M. Mesibov (eds.), *Neurobiological issues in autism*. New York: Plenum Press.

Rimland, B. (1988). Candida-caused autism. *Autism Research Review International, 2*(2), 3.

Rimland, B. (1999a). Huge increase in autism incidence reported in California; autism cluster investigated in Brick, New Jersey. *Autism Research Review International, 13*(2), 1.

Rimland, B. (1999b). Secretin update: March 1999. *Autism Research Review International, 13*(2), 3.

Rimland, B., & Edelson, S. M. (1994). The effects of auditory integration training on autism. *American Journal of Speech and Language Pathology*, May, 16–24.

Rimland, B., & Edelson, S. M. (1995). Brief report: A pilot study of auditory integration training in autism. *Journal of Autism and Developmental Disorders, 25*, 61–70.

Rintahaka, P. J., Chugani, H. T., & Sankar, R. (1995). Landau–Kleffner syndrome with continuous spike and waves during slow wave sleep. *Journal of Child Neurology, 10*, 127–133.

Ris, D. M., & Noll, R. B. (1994). Long-term neurobehavioral outcome in pediatric brain-tumor patients: Review and methodolgical critique. *Journal of Clinical and Experimental Neuropsychology, 16,* 21–42.

Rizzo, M., & Tranel, D. (1996). Overview of head injury and postconcussive syndrome. In M. Rizzo & D. Tranel (eds.), *Head injury and postconcussive syndrome.* New York: Churchill Livingstone.

Roberts, R. J., Varney, N. R., Hulbert, J. R., Paulsen, J. S., Richardson, E. D., Springer, J. A., Shepherd, J. S., Swan, C. M., Legrand, J. A., Harvey, J. H., & Struchen, M. A. (1990). The neuropathology of everyday life: The frequency of partial seizure symptoms among normals. *Neuropsychology, 4,* 65–85.

Rodin, E. (1987). An assessment of current views on epilepsy. *Epilepsia, 28,* 267–271.

Rogers, P. T., & Coleman, M. (1992). *Medical care in Down syndrome; A preventive medicine approach.* New York: Marcel Dekker.

Roget, J., Genton, P., Bureau, M., & Dravet, C. (1993). Less common epileptic syndromes. In E. Wylie (ed.), *The treatment of epilepsy: Principles and practice.* Philadelphia: Lea & Febiger.

Rohr, F. J., Lobbregt, D., & Levy, H. L. (1998). Tyrosine supplementation in the treatment of maternal phenylketonuria. *American Journal of Clinical Nutrition, 67,* 473–476.

Roman, D. D., & Sperduto, P. W. (1995). Neuropsychological effects of cranial radiation: Current knowledge and future directions. *International Journal of Radiation Oncology, Biology, Physics, 31,* 983–998.

Rondal, J. A. (1996). Oral language in Down's syndrome. In J. A. Rondal, J. Perera, L. Nadel, & A. Comblain (eds.), *Down's syndrome. Psychological, psychobiological, and socio-educational perspectives.* San Diego, CA: Singular.

Rose, S. A., Feldman, J. F., Jankowski, J. J., & Futterweit, L. R. (1999). Visual and auditory temporal processing, cross-modal transfer, and reading. *Journal of Learning Disabilities, 32,* 256–266.

Rosen, G., Mahowald, M. W., & Ferber, R. (1995). Sleepwalking, confusional arousals, and sleep terrors in the child. In R. Ferber & M. Kryger (eds.), *Principles and practice of sleep medicine in the child.* Philadelphia: W. B. Saunders.

Rosenthal, D. (1970). *Genetic theory and abnormal behavior.* New York: McGraw-Hill.

Rosenthal, M., Griffith, E. R., Bond, M. R., & Miller, J. D. (eds.) (1990). *Rehabilitation of the adult and child with traumatic brain injury,* 2nd ed. Philadelphia: F. A. Davis.

Rosenthal, N. E., & Blehar, M. C. (eds.) (1989). *Seasonal affective disorders and phototherapy.* New York: Guilford Press.

Rosenthal, S. H., & Klerman, G. L. (1966). Content and consistency in the endogenous depressive pattern. *British Journal of Psychiatry, 112,* 471–484.

Rosenzwieg, M. R., Bennett, E. L., & Diamond, M. C. (1972). Brain changes in response to experience. *Scientific American, 226,* 257–263.

Ross, D. M., & Ross, S. A. (1982). *Hyperactivity: Current issues, research, and theory,* 2nd ed. New York: Wiley Interscience.

Ross, R. T., Begab, M. J., Dondis, E. H., Giampiccolo, J. S. Jr., & Meyers, C. E. (1985). *Lives of the mentally retarded.* Stanford, CA: Stanford University Press.

Rosvold, H. E., Mirsky, A. F., Sarason, I., Bransome, E. D., & Beck, L. H. (1956). A continuous performance test of brain damage. *Journal of Consulting Psychology, 20,* 343–350.

Roth, M., & Mountjoy, C. Q. (1997). The need for the concept of neurotic depression. In H. S. Akiskal & G. B. Cassano (eds.), *Dysthymia and the spectrum of chronic depressions.* New York: Guilford Press.

Rourke, B. P. (1989). *Nonverbal learning disabilities: The syndrome and the model.* New York: Guilford Press.

Rourke, B. P. (1991). *Neuropsychological validation of learning disability subtypes.* New York: Guilford Press.

Rourke, B. P. (ed.) (1995). *Syndrome of nonverbal learning disabilities.* New York: Guilford Press.

Rourke, B. P., & Del Dotto, J. E. (1994). *Learning disabilities: A neuropsychological perspective.* Thousand Oaks, CA: Sage.

Rowland, L. P. (1991). Diseases of the motor unit. In E. R. Kandel, J. H. Schwartz, & T. M. Jessell (eds.), *Principles of neural science.* Norwalk, CN: Appleton & Lange.

Rumelhart, D. E., & McClelland, J. L. (eds.) (1986). *Parallel distributed processing: Explorations in the microstructure of cognition*, Vol. 1: *Foundations*. Cambridge, MA: MIT Press.

Rush, A. J., & Weissenburger, J. E. (1994). Melancholic symptom features and DSM IV. *American Journal of Psychiatry, 151,* 489–498.

Russell, A. T. (1992). Schizophrenia. In S. R. Hooper, G. W. Hynd, & R. E. Mattison (eds.), *Childhood psychopathology: Diagnostic criteria and clinical assessment.* Hillsdale, NJ: Lawrence Erlbaum Associates.

Russman, B. S., Tilton, A., & Gormley, M. E. (1997). Cerebral palsy: A rational approach to a treatment protocol, and the role of botulinum toxin in treatment. *Nerve & Muscle, 20* (Suppl. 6), S181–S193.

Rutter, M., Izard, C. E., & Read, P. B. (eds.) (1986). *Depression in young people: developmental and clinical perspectives.* New York: Guilford Press.

Rye, D. B. (1997). Contributions of the pedunculopontine region to normal and altered REM sleep. *Sleep, 20,* 757–788.

Sapolsky, R. M. (1996). Why stress is bad for your brain. *Science, 273,* 749–750.

Satterfield, J. H., Cantwell, D. P., Lesser, L. I., & Podosin, R. L. (1972). Physiological studies of the hyperkinetic child: I. *American Journal of Psychiatry, 128,* 102–108.

Satterfield, J. H., Cantwell, D. P., & Satterfield, B. T. (1974). Pathophysiology of the hyperactive child syndrome. *Archives of General Psychiatry, 31,* 839–844.

Satterfield, J. H., & Dawson, M. E. (1971). Electrodermal correlates of hyperactivity in children. *Psychophysiology, 8,* 191–197.

Satterfield, J. H., Satterfield, B. T., & Schell, A. M. (1987). Therapeutic interventions to prevent delinquency in hyperactive boys. *Journal of the American Academy of Child and Adolescent Psychiatry, 26,* 56–64.

Satz, P., Taylor, H. G., Friel, J., & Fletcher, J. (1978). Some developmental and predictive precursors of reading disabilities: A six-year follow-up. In A. L. Benton & D. Pearl (eds.), *Dyslexia: An appraisal of current knowledge.* New York: Oxford University Press.

Savage-Rumbaugh, E. S., Murphy, J., Sevcik, R. A., Brakke, K. E., Williams, S. L., & Rumbaugh, D. M. (1993). Language comprehension in ape and child. *Monographs of the Society for Research in Child Development, 58,* 201–255.

Saxena, S., Brody, A. L., Schwartz, J. M., & Baxter, L. R. (1998). Neuroimaging and frontal–subcortical circuitry in obsessive–compulsive disorder. *British Journal of Psychiatry, 173* (Suppl. 35), 26–37.

Schachar, R. J. (1986). Hyperkinetic syndrome: Historical development of the concept. In E. Taylor (ed.), *The overactive child.* Philadelphia: J. B. Lippincot.

Schachar, R. (1991). Childhood hyperactivity. *Journal of Child Psychology and Psychiatry, 32,* 155–191.

Schachar, R., Rutter, M., & Smith, A. (1981). The characteristics of situationally and pervasively hyperactive children: Implications for syndrome definition. *Journal of Child Psychology and Psychiatry, 22,* 375–392.

Schenck, C. H., & Mahowald, M. W. (1996). REM sleep parasomnias. *Neurologic Clinics, 14,* 697–720.

Scher, M. (1993). Evaluation and treatment of neonatal seizures. In Z. Wylie (ed.), *The treatment of epilepsy.* Philadelphia, PA: Lea and Febiger.

Schmahmann, J. D. (1991). An emerging concept: The cerebellar contribution to higher function. *Archives of Neurology, 48,* 1178–1187.

Schoenthaler, S. J., Amos, S. P., Eysenck, H. J., Peritz, E., & Yudkin, J. (1991). Controlled trial of vitamin–mineral supplementation: Effects on intelligence and performance. *Personality and Individual Differences, 12,* 351–362.

Schooler, C. (1976). Serfdom's legacy: An ethnic continuum. *American Journal of Sociology, 81,* 1265–1286.

Schopler, E., & Mesibov, G. B. (eds.) (1987). *Neurobiological issues in autism.* New York: Plenum Press.

Schopler, E., & Mesibov, G. B. (eds.) (1995). *Learning and cognition in autism.* New York: Plenum Press.

Schore, A. N. (1994). *Affect regulation and the origin of the self: The neurobiology of emotional development*. Hillsdale, NJ: Lawrence Erlbaum Associates.

Schreibman, L. (1996). Brief report: The case for social and behavioral intervention research. *Journal of Autism and Developmental Disorders*, *26*, 247–250.

Schroeder, S. R., Tessel, R. E., Loupe, P. S., & Stodgell, C. J. (1997). Severe behavior problems among people with developmental disabilities. In W. E. MacLean, Jr (ed.), *Ellis' handbook of mental deficiency, psychological theory and research*, 3rd ed. Mahwah, NJ: Lawrence Erlbaum Associates.

Schwartz, J. M. (1996). *Brain lock: Free yourself from obsessive–compulsive behavior*. New York: Harper Collins.

Schwartz, J. M. (1998). Neuroanatomical aspects of cognitive–behavioral therapy response in obsessive–compulsive disorder: An evolving perspective on brain and behavior. *British Journal of Psychiatry*, *173* (Suppl 35), 38–44.

Schwartz, R. H., Eaton, J., Bower, B. D., & Aynsley-Green, A. (1989). Ketogenic diets in the treatment of epilepsy. *Developmental Medicine and Child Neurology*, *31*, 145–151.

Schwartzkroin, P. A. (1993). Basic mechanisms of epileptogenesis. In E. Wylie (ed.), *The treatment of epilepsy: Principles and practice*. Phildalephia, PA: Lea & Febiger.

Schwartzkroin, P. A., & Wyler, A. (1980). Mechanisms underlying epileptiform burst discharge: A hypothesis and synthesis of experimental data. *Annals of Neurology*, *7*, 95–107.

Sekuler, R., & Blake, R. (1994). *Perception*, 3rd ed. New York: McGraw-Hill.

Seligman, M. E. P., & Peterson, C. (1986). A learned helplessness perspective on childhood depression: Theory and research. In M. Rutter, C. E. Izard, & P. B. Read (eds.), *Depression in young people: developmental and clinical perspectives*. New York: Guilford Press.

Semmes, J., Weinstein, S., Ghent, L., & Teuber, H. L. (1960). *Somatosensory changes after penetrating brain wounds in man*. Cambridge MA: Harvard University Press.

Sergeant, J. (1989). Functional deficits in attention deficit disorder? In L. M. Bloomingdale (ed.), *Attention deficit disorder*, Vol. 3: *New research in attention, treatment and psychopharmacology*. Oxford: Pergamon Press.

Shankaran, S. (1997). Hemorrhagic lesions of the central nervous system. In D. K. Stevenson & P. Sunshine (eds.), *Fetal and neonatal brain injury*. Oxford: Oxford Universty Press.

Shapiro, K., & Smith, L. P. (1993). Special considerations for the pediatric age group. In P. R. Cooper (ed.), *Head injury*, 3rd ed. Baltimore: Williams & Wilkins.

Shapiro, S. K., & Garfinkel, B. D. (1986). The occurrence of behavior disorders in children: The interdependence of attention deficit disorder and conduct disorder. *Journal of the American Academy of Child Psychiatry*, *25*, 809–819.

Shaw, W. (1998). *Biological treatments for autism and PDD*. Overland Park, KS: Willima Shaw.

Shaywitz, S. E., Escobar, M. D., Shaywitz, B. A., Fletcher, J. M., & Makuch, R. (1992). Evidence that dyslexia may represent the lower tail of a normal distribution of reading disability. *New England Journal of Medicine*, *326*, 145–150.

Shaywitz, S. E., Shaywitz, B. A., Fletcher, J. M., & Escobar, M. D. (1990). Prevalence of reading disability in boys and girls: Results of the Connecticut Longitudinal Study. *Journal of the American Medical Association*, *264*, 998–1002.

Shaywitz, B. A., Shaywitz, S. E., Pugh, K. R., Constables, R. T., Skudlarski, P., Fulbright, R. K., Bronen, R. A., Fletcher, J. M., Shankweller, D. P., Katz, L., & Gore, J. C. (1995). Sex differences in the functional organization of the brain for language. *Nature*, *373*, 607–609.

Sherrington, C. (1923). *The integrative action of the nervous system*. New Haven, CT: Yale University Press.

Siegel, L. S. (1989). IQ is irrelevant to the definition of learning disabilities. *Journal of Learning Disabilities*, *22*, 469–478, 486.

Siegel, L. S., & Linder, B. (1984). Short-term memory processes in children with reading and arithmetic learning disabilities. *Developmental Psychology*, *20*, 241–244.

Siegel, M., Kurzrok, N., Barr, W. B., & Rowan, A. J. (1992). Game playing epilepsy. *Epilepsia*, *33*, 93–97.

Silberman, E. K., & Weingartner, H. (1986). Hemispheric lateralization of functions related to emotion. *Brain and Cognition*, 5, 322–353.

Silver, C. H., Pennett, H. D.-L., Black, J. L., Fair, G. W., & Balise, R. R. (1999). Stability of arithmetic disability subtypes. *Journal of Learning Disabilities*, 32, 108–119.

Singer, H. S. (1997). Neurobiology of Tourette syndrome. *Neurological Clinics of North America*, 15, 357–379.

Skottun, B. C., & Parke, L. A. (1999). The possible relationship between visual deficits and dyslexia: Examination of a critical assumption. *Journal of Learning Disabilities*, 32, 2–5.

Skuse, D. (1984). Extreme deprivation in early childhood – II. Theoretical issues and a comparative review. *Journal of Child Psychology and Psychiatry*, 25, 543–572.

Skwerer, R. G., Jacobsen, F. M., Duncan, C. M., Kelly, K. A., Sack, D. A., Tamarkin, L., Gaist, P. A., Kasper, S., & Resenthal, N. E. (1989). Neurobiology of seasonal affective disorder and phototherapy. In N. E. Rosenthal & M. C. Blehar (eds.), *Seasonal affective disorders and phototherapy*. New York: Guilford Press.

Slaghuis, W. L., Lovegrove, W. J., & Davidson, J. A. (1993). Visual and language processing deficits are concurrent in dyslexia. *Cortex*, 29, 601–615.

Smith, A., & Sugar, O. (1975). Development of above normal language and intelligence 21 years after hemispherectomy. *Neurology*, 25, 813–818.

Smith, C., & Lapp, L. (1991). Increases in number of REMS and REM density in humans following an intensive learning period. *Sleep*, 14, 325–330.

Smith, T., Klevstrand, M., & Lovaas, O. I. (1995). Behavioral treatment of Rett's disorder: Ineffectiveness in three cases. *American Journal on Mental Retardation*, 100, 317–322.

Snowling, M. J. (1980). The development of grapheme–phoneme correspondence in normal and dyslexic readers. *Journal of Experimental Child Psychology*, 29, 294–305.

Snowling, M. J. (1987). *Dyslexia: a cognitive developmental perspective*. Oxford, UK: Basil Blackwell.

Sokolov, E. N. (1963). *Perception and the conditioned reflex*. New York: MacMillan.

Solomon, P., Kubzansky, P. E., & Leiderman, P. H. (eds.) (1962). *Sensory deprivation*. Cambridge, MA: Harvard University Press.

Sonis, W. A. (1989). Seasonal affective disorder of childhood and adolescence: A review. In N. E. Rosenthal & M. C. Blehar (eds.), *Seasonal affective disorders and phototherapy*. New York: Guilford Press.

Sowell, E. R., Jernigan, T. L., Mattson, S. N., Riley, E. P., Sobel, D. F., & Jones, K. L. (1996). Abnormal development of the cerebellar vermis in children prenatally exposed to alcohol: Size reduction in lobules I–V. *Alcoholism: Clinical and Experimental Research*, 20, 31–34.

Sperry, R. W. (1982). Some effects of disconnecting the cerebral hemispheres. *Science*, 217, 1223–1226.

Spitz, R. (1945). Hospitalism. An enquiry into the genesis of psychiatric conditions in early childhood. *Psychoanalytic Study of the Child*, 1, 53–74.

Spitz, R. (1946). Anaclitic depression. *Psychoanalytic Study of the Child*, 2, 313–342.

Sprague, R. L., & Sleator, E. K. (1977). Methylphenidate in hyperkinetic children: Differences in dose effects on learning and social behavior. *Science*, 198, 1274–1276.

Spreen, O., Risser, A. H., & Edgell, D. (1995). *Developmental neuropsychology*. New York: Oxford University Press.

Springer, S. P., & Deutsch, G. (1985). *Left brain, right brain*. New York: W. H. Freeman.

Stefanatos, G. A. (1993). Frequency modulation analysis in children with Landau–Kleffner syndrome. *Annals of the New York Academy of Sciences*, 682, 412–414.

Stefanatos, G. A., Green, G. G. R., & Ratcliff, G. G. (1989). Neurophysiological evidence of auditory channel anomalies in developmental dysphasia. *Archives of Neurology*, 41, 871–875.

Stefanatos, G. A., Kollros, P., Rabinovitch, H., & Stone, J. J. (1998). Acquired epileptiform aphasia (Landau-Kleffner syndrome): Current concepts and controversies. *Journal of Developmental and Learning Disorders*, 2, 3–50.

Stehli, A. (1991). *The sound of a miracle*. New York: Doubleday.

Stein, D. G., Roof, R. L., & Fulop, Z. L. (1998). Brain damage, sex hormones, and recovery. In

D. T. Stuss, G. Winocur, & I. H. Robertson (eds.), *Cognitive neurorehabilitation: A comprehensive approach.* Cambridge: Cambridge University Press.

Stein, J. F. (1993). Visuospatial perception in disabled readers. In D. M. Willows, R. S. Kruk, & E. Corcos (eds.), *Visual processes in reading and reading disabilities* (pp. 331–346). Hillsdale, NJ: Lawrence Erlbaum Associates.

Stein, Z., Susser, M., Saenger, G., & Marolla, F. (1972). Nutrition and mental performance. *Science, 178,* 708–713.

Steriade, M., Gloor, P., Llinas, R. R., Lopes da Silva, F., & Mesulam, M. M. (1990). Basic mechanisms of cerebral rhythmic activities. *Electroencephalography and Clinical Neurophysiology, 76,* 481–508.

Sterman, M. B. (1986). Epilepsy and its treatment with EEG feedback therapy. *Annals of Behavioral Medicine, 8,* 21–25.

Sterman, M. B., & Friar, L. (1972). Suppression of seizures in an epileptic following sensorimotor EEG feedback training. *Electroencephalography and Clinical Neurophysiology, 33,* 89–95.

Sterman, M. B., Shouse, M. N., & Fairchild, M. D. (1988). Zinc and seizure mechanisms. In J. E. Morley, M. B. Sterman, & J. H. Walsh (eds.), *Nutritional modulation of neuronal function.* San Diego, CA: Academic Press.

Stern, J. (1985). Biochemical aspects. In A. M. Clarke, A. D. B. Clarke, & J. M. Berg (eds.), *Mental deficiency: The changing outlook,* 4th ed. London: Methuen.

Sternberg, R. J. (1988). *The triarchic mind: A new theory of human intelligence.* New York: Viking.

Stevens, J. R. (1988). Psychiatric aspects of epilepsy. *Journal of Clinical Psychiatry, 49* (4 Suppl.), 49–57.

St George-Hyslop, P. (1995). Genetic determinants of Alzheimer disease. In C. J. Epstein, T. Hassold, I. T. Lott, L. Nadel, & D. Patterson (eds.), *Etiology and pathogenesis of Down syndrome.* New York: Wiley-Liss.

Stoneman, Z. (1997). Mental retardation and family adaptation. In W. E. MacLean, Jr (ed.), *Ellis' handbook of mental deficiency, psychological theory and research,* 3rd ed. Mahwah, NJ: Lawrence Erlbaum Associates.

Stores, G., Zaiwalla, Z., & Bergel, N. (1991). Frontal lobe complex partial seizures in children: A form of epilepsy at particular risk of misdiagnosis. *Developmental Medicine and Child Neurology, 33,* 998–1009.

Streissguth, A. P., & Dehaene, P. (1993). Fetal alcohol syndrome in twins of alcoholic mothers: concordance of diagnosis and IQ. *American Journal of Medical Genetics, 47,* 857–861.

Streissguth, A. P., Sampson, P. D., Barr, H. M., Bookstein, F. L., & Olson, H. C. (1994). The effects of prenatal exposure to alcohol and tobacco: Contributions from the Seattle Longitudinal Prospective Study and implications for public policy. In H. L. Needleman & D. Bellinger (eds.), *Prenatal exposure to toxicants: Developmental consequences.* Baltimore: Johns Hopkins University Press.

Strelau, J., & Eysenck, H. J. (eds.) (1987). *Personality dimensions and arousal.* New York: Plenum Press.

Stuss, D. T. (1987). Contribution of frontal lobe injury to cognitive impairment after closed head injury: Methods of assessment and recent findings. In H. S. Levin, J. Grafman, & H. M. Eisenberg (eds.), *Neurobehavioral recovery from head injury.* New York: Oxford University Press.

Stuss, D. T. (1992). Biological and psychological development in executive functions. *Brain and Cognition, 20,* 8–23.

Stuss, D. T., & Benson, D. F. (1986). *The frontal lobes.* New York: Raven Press.

Suffin, S. C., & Emory, W. H. (1995). Neurometric subgroups in attentional and affective disorders and their association with pharmacotherapeutic outcome. *Clinical Encephalography, 26,* 76–83.

Sullivan, R., C., Park, C., Torisky, C. V., Akerly, M. S., Offen, N., & Dewey, M. A. (1992). Parent essays. In E. Schopler & G. B. Mesibov (eds.), *High-functioning individuals with autism.* New York: Plenum Press.

Supa, M., Cotzin, M., & Dallenbach, K. M. (1944). "Facial vision": The perception of obstacles by the blind. *American Journal of Psychology, 57,* 133–183.

Swanson, H. L., & Alexander, J. E. (1997). Cognitive processes as predictors of word recognition and reading comprehension in learning-disabled and skilled readers: Revisiting the specificity hypothesis. *Journal of Educational Psychology, 89,* 128–158.

Swanson, J. M., Cantwell, D., Lerner, M., McBurnett, K., & Hanna, G. (1991). Effects of stimulant medication on learning in children with ADHD. *Journal of Learning Disabilities, 24,* 219–230.

Swets, J. A. (ed.) (1964). *Signal detection and recognition by human observers.* New York: Wiley.

Swink, T. D., Vining, E. P., & Freeman, J. M. (1997). The ketogenic diet: 1997. *Advances in Pediatrics, 44,* 297–329.

Taft, L. T. (1995). Cerebral palsy. *Pediatrics in Review, 16,* 411–418.

Tager-Flusberg, H. (1989). A psycholinguistic perspective on language development in the autistic child. In G. Dawson (ed.), *Autism: nature, diagnosis and treatment.* New York: Guilford Press.

Tallal, P. (1980). Auditory processing disorders in children. In P. J. Levinson & C. Sloan (eds.), *Auditory processing and language: clinical and research perspectives.* New York: Grune & Stratton.

Tallal, P., Miller, S. L., Bedi, G., Byma, G., Wang, X., Nagarajan, S. S., Schreiner, C., Jenkins, W. M., & Merzenich, M. M. (1996). Language comprehension in language-learning impaired children improved with acoustically modified speech. *Science, 271,* 81–84.

Tallal, P., Sainburg, R. L., & Jernigan, T. (1991). The neuropathology of developmental dysphasia: Behavioral, morphological, and physiological evidence for a pervasive temporal processing disorder. *Reading and Writing, 3,* 363–377.

Tallal, P., & Stark, R. E. (1982). Perceptual/motor profiles of reading impaired children with or without concomitant oral language deficits. *Annals of Dyslexia, 32,* 163–176.

Tallal, P., Stark, R., Kallman, C., & Mellits, D. (1981). A reexamination of some nonverbal perceptual abilities of language-impaired and normal children as a function of age and sensory modality. *Journal and Speech and Hearing Research, 24,* 351–357.

Taylor, H. G. (1989). Learning disabilities. In E. J. Mash & L. G. Terdal (eds.), *Behavioral assessment of childhood disorders.* New York: Guilford Press.

Taylor, H. G., & Alden, J. (1997). Age-related differences in outcomes following childhood brain insults: An introduction and overview. *Journal of the International Neuropsychological Society, 3,* 555–567.

Taylor, H. G., Drotar, D., Wade, S., Yeates, K., Stancin, T., & Klein, S. (1995). Recovery from trumatic brain injury in children: The importance of the family. In S. H. Broman & M. E. Michel (eds.), *Traumatic head injury in children.* New York: Oxford University Press.

Taylor, M. A. (1991). The role of the cerebellum in the pathogenesis of schizophrenia. *Neuropsychiatry, Neuropsychology, and Behavioral Neurology, 4,* 251–280.

Teasdale, G., & Jennett, B. (1974). Assessment of coma and impaired consciousness: A practical scale. *Lancet, 2,* 81–84.

Tesman, J. R., & Hills, A. (1994). Developmental effects of lead exposure in children. *Social Policy Report: Society for Research in Child Development, 8,* 1–16.

Thatcher, R. W. (1992). Cyclic cortical reorganization during early childhood. *Brain and Language, 20,* 24–50.

Thatcher, R. W. (1994). Cyclic cortical reorganization: Origins of human cognitive development. In G. Dawson & K. W. Fischer (eds.), *Human behavior and the developing brain* (pp. 232–266). New York: Guilford Press.

Thatcher, R. W., Walker, R. A., Gerson, I., & Geisler, F. H. (1989). EEG discriminant analyses of mild head trauma. *Electroencephalography and Clinical Neurophysiology, 73,* 94–106.

Thatcher, R. W., Walker, R. A., & Giudice, S. (1987). Human cerebral hemispheres develop at different rates and ages. *Science, 236,* 1110–1113.

Thelen, E. (1995). Motor development: A new synthesis. *American Psychologist, 50,* 79–95.

Thomas, A., & Chess, S. (1977). *Temperament and development.* New York: Bruner/Mazel.

Thomas, A., Chess, S., & Birch, H. G. (1968). *Temperament and behavior disorders in children.* New York: New York University Press.

Thompson, L. A. (1997). Behavioral genetics and the classification of mental retardation. In W. E.

MacLean, Jr (ed.), *Ellis' handbook of mental deficiency, psychological theory and research.* Mahwah, NJ: Lawrence Erlbaum Associates.

Thompson, P. J., & Trimble, M. R. (1982). Anticonvulsant drugs and cognitive functions. *Epilepsia, 23,* 531–544.

Thompson, R. F. (1985). *The brain: An introduction to neuroscience.* New York: Freeman.

Thompson, W. R., & Heron, W. (1954). The effects of restricting early experience on the problem-solving capacity of dogs. *Canadian Journal of Psychology, 8,* 17–31.

Tiwari, B. D., Godbole, M. M., Chattopadhyay, N., Mandal, A., & Mithal, A. (1996). Learning disabilities and poor motivation to achieve due to prolonged iodine deficiency. *American Journal of Clinical Nutrition, 63,* 782–786.

Tokizane, T., Murao, M., Ogata, T., & Kondo, T. (1951–52). Electromyography studies on tonic neck, lumbar and labyrinthine reflexes in normal persons. *Japanese Journal of Physiology, 2,* 130–146.

Tomasello, M. (1995). Language is not an instinct. *Cognitive Development, 10,* 131–156.

Tomasello, M., & Farrar, J. (1986). The role of attentional processes in early language development. *Child Development, 57,* 1454–1463.

Touwen, B. C. L., & Prechtl, H. F. R. (1970). *The neurological examination of the child with minor nervous system dysfunction.* London: William Heiemann.

Towbin, K. E., Dykens, E. M., Pearson, G. S., & Cohen, D. J. (1993). Conceptualizing "borderline syndrome of childhood" and "childhood schizophrenia" as developmental disorders. *Journal of the American Academy of Child and Adolescent Psychiatry, 32,* 775–782.

Treiman, L. J., & Treiman, D. M. (1993). Genetic aspects of epilepsy. In E. Wylie (ed.), *The treatment of epilepsy: Principles and practice.* Philadelphia: Lea & Febiger.

Trimble, M. R. (1988). Cognitive hazards of seizure drugs. *Epilepsia, 29* (Suppl. 1), S19–S24.

Uziel, A. S., & Mondain, M. (eds.) (1995). Cochlear implants in children. *Advances in Otorhinolaryngology, 50,* 1–206.

van Baal, G. C. M., de Geus, E. J. C., & Boomsma, D. I. (1998). Genetic influences on EEG coherence in 5-year-old twins. *Behavior Genetics, 28,* 9–19.

van Zomeren, A. H., & Brouwer, W. H. (1994). *Clinical neuropsychology of attention.* New York: Oxford University Press.

Vargha-Khadem, F., Isaacs, E., & Muter, V. (1994). A review of cognitive outcome after unilateral lesions sustained during childhood. *Journal of Child Neurology, 9* (Suppl.), 2S67–2S73.

Vellutino, F. R., & Scanlon, D. M. (1987). Phonological coding, phonological awareness, and reading ability: Evidence from a longitudinal and experimental study. *Merrill-Palmer Quarterly, 33,* 321–363.

Venezky, R. L. (1993) History of interest in the visual component of reading. In D. M. Willows, R. S. Kruk, & E. Corcos (eds.), *Visual processes in reading and reading disabilities.* Hillsdale, NJ: Lawrence Erlbaum Associates.

Verduyn, W., Hilt, J., Roberts, M. A., & Roberts, R. J. (1991). Multiple partial seizure-like symptoms following "minor" closed head injury. *Brain Injury, 6,* 245–260.

Verfaellie, M., Bowers, D., & Heilman, K. M. (1988). Hemispheric asymmetries in mediating intention but not selective attention. *Neuropsychologia, 26,* 521–531.

Verity, C. M., Strauss, E. H., Moyes, P. D., Wada, J. A., Dunn, H. G., & Lapointe, J. S. (1982). Long-term follow-up after cerebral hemispherectomy: Neurophysiologic, radiologic, and psychological findings. *Neurology, 32,* 629–639.

Vernon, M., & Koh, S. D. (1971). Effects of oral preschool compared to early manual communication on the education and communication of deaf children. *American Annals of the Deaf, 116,* 569–574.

Voeller, K. K. S., & Heilman, K. M. (1988). Attention deficit disorder in children: A neglect syndrome? *Neurology, 38,* 806–808.

Vogel, G. W. (1975). A review of REM sleep deprivation. *Archives of General Psychiatry, 32,* 749–761.

Vogel, G. W. (1983). Evidence for REM sleep deprivation as the mechanism of action of antidepressant drugs. *Progress in Neuropsychopharmacology and Biological Psychiatry, 7,* 343–349.

Vogel, G. W., Feng, P., & Kinney, G. G. (2000). Ontogeny of REM sleep in rats: Possible implications for endogenous depression. *Physiology and Behavior, 68*, 453–461.

Vogel, G., Neill, D., Hagler, M., & Kors, D. (1990). A new animal model of endogenous depression: A summary of present findings. *Neuroscience and Behavioral Reviews, 14*, 85–91.

Vogel, G. W., Roth, T., Gillin, J. C., Mendelson, W. B., & Buffenstein, A. (1988). REM sleep and depression. In T. Oniani (ed.), *Neurobiology of sleep–wakefulness cycle*. Tbilisi: Metsniereba.

Vogel, G. W., Vogel, F., McAbee, R. S., & Thurmond, A. J. (1980). Improvement of depression by REM sleep deprivation. *Archives of General Psychiatry, 37*, 247–253.

Vollmer, D. G. (1993). Prognosis and outcome of severe head injury. In P. R. Cooper (ed.), *Head injury*, 3rd ed. Baltimore: Williams & Wilkins.

von Bekesy, G. (1960). *Experiments in hearing*. New York: McGraw-Hill.

von Bertalanffy, L. (1968). *General system theory*. New York: George Braziller.

Waber, D. P., Urion, D. K., Tarbell, N. J., Niemeyer, C., Gelber, R., & Sallan, S. E. (1990). Late effects of central nervous system treatment of acute lymphoblastic leukemia in childhood are sex dependent. *Developmental Medicine and Child Neurology, 32*, 238–248.

Wakefield, A., Murch, S., Anthony, A., Linnell, J., Casson, D., Malik, M., Berelowitz, M., Dhillon, A., Thomson, M., Harvey, P., Valentine, A., Davies, S., & Walker-Smith, J. (1998). Ileal-lymphoid–nodular hyperplasia, non-specific colitis, and pervasive developmental disorder in children. *Lancet, 351*, 637–641.

Walker, E. (1987) Validating and conceptualizing positive and negative symptoms. In P. D. Harvey & E. F. Walker (eds.), *Positive and negative symptoms in psychosis: Description, research, and future directions*. Hillsdale, NJ: Lawrence Erlbaum Associates.

Ware, J. C., & Morin, C. M. (1997). Sleep in depression and anxiety. In M. R. Pressman & W. C. Orr (eds.), *Understanding sleep: The evaluation and treatment of sleep disorders*. Washington, DC: American Psychological Association.

Warren, D. H. (1994). *Blindndess and children: An individual differences approach*. Cambridge: Cambridge University Press.

Watson, C., & Willows, D. M. (1993). Evidence for a visual-processing-deficit subtype among disabled readers. In D. M. Willows, R. S. Kruk, & E. Corcos (eds.), *Visual processes in reading and reading disabilities*. Hillsdale, NJ: Lawrence Erlbaum Associates.

Watson, J. D. (1968). *The double helix*. New York: Atheneum.

Weglage, J., Ullrich, K., Pietsch, M., Fūnders, B., Gūttler, F., & Harms, E. (1997). Intellectual, neurologic, and neuropsychologic outcome in untreated subjects with nonphenylketonuria hyperphenylalaninemia. *Pediatric Research, 2*, 378–384.

Weiler, I. J., Irwin, S. A., Klintsova, A. Y., Spencer, C. M., Brazelton, A. D., Miyashiro, K., Comery, T. A., Patel, B., Eberwine, J., & Greenough, W. T. (1997). Fragile-X mental-retardation protein is translated near synapses in response to neurotransmitter activation. *Proceedings of the National Academy of Sciences of the USA, 94*, 5395–5400.

Weinberg, W. A., & Brumback, R. A. (1990). Primary disorder of vigilance: A novel explanation of inattentiveness, daydreaming, boredom, restlessness, and sleepiness. *Journal of Pediatrics, 116*, 720–725.

Weinberg, W. A., & Brumback, R. A. (1992). The myth of attention deficit–hyperactivity disorder: Symptoms resulting from multiple causes. *Journal of Child Neurology, 7*, 431–445.

Weingartner, H., Cohen, R. M., Murphy, D. L., Martello, J., & Gerdt, C. (1981). Cognitive processes in depression. *Archives of General Psychiatry, 38*, 42–47.

Weiskrantz, L. (1986). *Blindsight: A case study and implications*. Oxford: Oxford University Press.

Weiskrantz, L., Warrington, E. K., Saunders, M. D., & Marshall, J. (1974). Visual capacity in the hemianopic field following a restricted occipital ablation. *Brain, 97*, 709–728.

Weiss, B. (1994). The developmental neurotoxicity of methyl mercury. In H. L. Needleman & D. Bellinger (eds.), *Prenatal exposure to toxicants: Developmental consequences*. Baltimore: Johns Hopkins University Press.

Weiss, G., & Hechtman, L. T. (1993). *Hyperactive children grown up: ADHD in children, adolescents, and adults.* 2nd ed. New York: Guilford Press.

Weiss, J. M. (1991) Stress-induced depression: Critical neurochemical and electrophysiological changes. In J. Madden IV (ed.), *Neurobiology of learning, emotion, and affect.* New York: Raven Press.

Weisz, S. (1938). Studies in equilibrium reaction. *Journal of Nervous and Mental Disease, 88,* 150–162.

Wender, P. H., & Klein, D. F. (1981). *Mind, mood, and medicine.* New York: Meridian.

Whalen, C. K., & Henker, B. (1980). The social ecology of psychostimulant treatment: A model for conceptual and empirical analysis. In C. K. Whalen & B. Henker (eds.), *Hyperactive children: The social ecology of identification and treatment.* New York: Academic Press.

Whelan, E. (1985). The habilitation of adults. In A. M. Clarke, A. D. B. Clarke, & J. M. Berg (eds.), *Mental deficiency: The changing outlook,* 4th ed. London: Methuen.

Whitman, S., & Hermann, B. P. (1986). *Psychopathology in epilepsy: Social dimensions.* New York: Oxford University Press.

Wilberger, J. E. (1993). Emergency care and initial evaluation. In P. R. Cooper (ed.), *Head injury,* 3rd ed. Baltimore: Williams & Wilkins.

Willerman, L. (1979). *The psychology of individual and group differences.* San Francisco: W. H. Freeman.

Williamson, P. D. (1995). Frontal lobe epilepsy: Some clinical characteristics. In H. H. Jasper, S. Riggio, & P. S. Goldman-Rakic (eds.), *Epilepsy and the functional anatomy of the frontal lobe.* New York: Raven Press.

Willows, D. M., Kruk, R. S., & Corcos, E. (eds.) (1993). *Visual processes in reading and reading disabilities.* Hillsdale, NJ: Lawrence Erlbaum Associates.

Willows, D. M., & Terepocki, M. (1993). The relation of reversal errors to reading disabilities. In D. M. Willows, R. S. Kruk, & E. Corcos (eds.), *Visual processes in reading and reading disabilities.* Hillsdale, NJ: Lawrence Erlbaum Associates.

Wing, L. (1981). Asperger's syndrome: a clinical account. *Psychological Medicine, 11,* 115–130.

Wing, L. (1991). The relationship between Asperger's syndrome and Kanner's autism. In U. Frith (ed.), *Autism and Asperger syndrome.* Cambridge: Cambridge University Press.

Wing, L., & Gould, J. (1979). Severe impairments of social interaction and associated abnormalities in children: Epidemiology and classification. *Journal of Autism and Developmental Disorders, 9,* 11–29.

Wishart, J. G. (1995). Cognitive abilities in children with Down syndrome: Developmental instability and motivational deficits. In C. J. Epstein, T. Hassold, I. T. Lott, L. Nadel, & D. Patterson (eds.), *Etiology and pathogenesis of Down syndrome.* New York: Wiley-Liss.

Wishart, J. G. (1996). Learning in young children with Down's syndrome: Developmental trends. In J. A. Rondal, J. Perera, L. Nadel, & A. Comblain (eds.), *Down's syndrome: Psychological, psychobiological, and socio-educational perspectives.* San Diego, CA: Singular.

Wisniewski, K. E., Kida, E., & Brown, W. T. (1996). Consequences of genetic abnormalities in Down's syndrome on brain structure and function. In J. A. Rondal, J. Perera, L. Nadel, & A. Comblain (eds.), *Down's syndrome: Psychological, psychobiological, and socio-educational perspectives.* San Diego, CA: Singular.

Wolf, M., Bally, H., & Morris, R. (1986). Automaticity, retrieval processes, and reading: a longitudinal study in average and impaired readers. *Child Development, 57,* 988–1000.

Wolf, M., & Obregon, M. (1992). Early naming deficits, developmental dyslexia, and a specific deficit hypothesis. *Brain & Language, 42,* 219–247.

Wong, B. Y. L. (1989). Is IQ necessary in the definition of learning disabilities? Introduction to the special series. *Journal of Learning Disabilities, 22,* 468.

Woodruff, M. L. (1974). Subconvulsive epileptiform discharge and behavioral impairment. *Behavioral Biology, 11,* 431–458.

Yakovlev, P. I., & Lecours, A.-R. (1967). The myelogenetic cycles of regional maturation of the brain. In A. Minkowski (ed.), *Regional development of the brain in early life.* Philadelphia: F. A. Davis.

Yeates, K. O., Taylor, H. G., Drotar, D., Wade, S. L., Klein, S., Stancin, T., & Schatschneider, C. (1997). Preinjury family environment as a determinant of recovery from traumatic brain injuries in school age children. *Journal of the International Neuropsychological Society, 3*, 617–630.

Yehuda, R. (1998). Psychoneuroendocrinology of post-traumatic stress disorder. *Psychiatric Clinics of North America, 21*, 359–379.

Ylvisaker, M. (ed.), (1985). *Head injury rehabilitation: Children and adolescents.* San Diego, CA: College-Hill Press.

Yuwiler, A., & Freedman, D. X. (1987). Neurotransmitter research in autism. In E. Schopler & G. B. Mesibov (eds.), *Neurobiological issues in autism.* New York: Plenum Press.

Zaidel, E. (1985). Language in the right hemisphere. In D. F. Benson & E. Zaidel (eds.), *The dual brain.* New York: Guilford Press.

Zametkin, A. J., Nordahl, T. E., Gross, M., King, A. C., Semple, W. E., Rumsey, J., Hamburger, S., & Cohen, R. M. (1990). Cerebral glucose metabolism in adults with hyperactivity of childhood onset. *New England Journal of Medicine, 323*, 1361–1366.

Zauner, A., & Bullock, R. (1996). The role of excitatory amino acids in severe brain trauma: Opportunities for therapy: A review. In F. A. Bandak, R. H. Eppinger, & A. K. Ommaya (eds.), *Traumatic brain injury: Bioscience and mechanics.* Larchmont, NY: Mary Ann Liebert.

Zeaman, D., & House, B. J. (1963). The role of attention in retardate discrimination learning. In N. Ellis (ed.), *Handbook of mental deficiency: Psychological theory and research.* New York: McGraw-Hill.

Zentall, S. S., & Meyer, M. J. (1987). Self-regulation of stimulation for ADD-H children during reading and vigilance task performance. *Journal of Abnormal Child Psychology, 15*, 519–536.

Zigler, E., & Hodapp, R. M. (1986). *Understanding mental retardation.* Cambridge: Cambridge University Press.

Zuroff, D. C., Blatt, S. J., Sanislow, C. A., Bondi, C. M., & Pikonis, P. A. (1999). Vulnerability to depression: Reexamining state dependence and relative stability. *Journal of Abnormal Psychology, 108*, 76–89.

Index

Italicized page numbers indicate the indexing of an illustration.